From Victory to Stalemate

MODERN WAR STUDIES

Theodore A. Wilson
General Editor

Raymond A. Callahan
Jacob W. Kipp
Allan R. Millett
Carol Reardon
Dennis Showalter
David R. Stone
James H. Willbanks
Series Editors

Decisive and Indecisive
Military Operations, Volume 1

From Victory to Stalemate

The Western Front, Summer 1944

C. J. Dick

Foreword by David M. Glantz

University Press of Kansas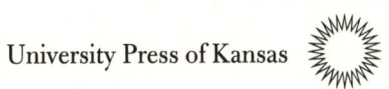

© 2016 by the University Press of Kansas
All rights reserved

Published by the University Press of Kansas (Lawrence, Kansas 66045), which was organized by the Kansas Board of Regents and is operated and funded by Emporia State University, Fort Hays State University, Kansas State University, Pittsburg State University, the University of Kansas, and Wichita State University

Library of Congress Cataloging-in-Publication Data

Names: Dick, Charles, author.
Title: From victory to stalemate : the western front, summer 1944 / C. J. Dick ; foreword by David M. Glantz.
Description: Lawrence, KS : University Press of Kansas, [2016] | Series: Modern war studies. Decisive and indecisive military operations ; volume 1
Includes bibliographical references and index.
Identifiers: LCCN 2016023608
ISBN 9780700622931 (cloth : alk. paper)
ISBN 9780700622948 (ebook)
Subjects: LCSH: World War, 1939–1945—Campaigns—Western Front. | Operational art (Military science)—History—20th century.
Classification: LCC D756 .D528 2016 | DDC 940.54/21—dc23
LC record available at https://lccn.loc.gov/2016023608.

British Library Cataloguing-in-Publication Data is available.

Printed in the United States of America

10 9 8 7 6 5 4 3 2 1

The paper used in this publication is recycled and contains 30 percent postconsumer waste. It is acid free and meets the minimum requirements of the American National Standard for Permanence of Paper for Printed Library Materials Z39.48-1992.

Contents

List of Maps	vii
Foreword by David M. Glantz	ix
Acknowledgments	xi
Abbreviations, Acronyms, and Selected Foreign Words	xiii
Introduction	1
1. Immature Armies	11
Concepts of War Fighting	11
The Challenges of Command	22
The American, British, and Canadian Armies in 1944	43
Conclusions	66
2. The Tipping Point	68
The First Seven Weeks, 6 June–25 July 1944	68
The Land Situation on the Eve of the Breakout	73
Airpower and the Land Campaign	87
Operations behind German Lines	101
Operational-Level Intelligence	105
Conclusions	113
3. July: Breakthrough and Near Breakthrough	115
Operation Cobra	115
Immediate Post-Cobra Operations: 1–6 August	132
Operation Bluecoat	134
Operational Art and Generalship	145

4. August: Incomplete Encirclements — 158

Operations of 12 Army Group: From Cobra to the Falaise Pocket — 158

Operations of 21 Army Group: From Bluecoat to the Falaise Pocket — 167

The Falaise Pocket and the Deep Encirclement — 176

Operational Art and Generalship in August — 184

Conclusions — 216

5. September: Operational Ideas and Developments on the Ground — 219

Rival Concepts of Operations — 219

Allied Intelligence and the German Situation until Mid-September — 236

From Pursuit to Culmination — 241

Back to Stalemate: The Autumn Campaign — 268

6. Logistic Realities — 273

The Logistic System — 273

The System at Work: Growing Problems and Failures — 278

Operational Consequences of Logistic Failure — 289

Logistic Realities and Conclusions — 294

7. Command, Operational Art, and Generalship — 299

Issues of Command — 299

Concepts of Operations, Generalship, and Operational Art — 306

Operational Art and Generalship in September — 315

Conclusions — 359

Postscript — 362

Notes — 367

Selected Bibliography — 423

Index — 433

Maps

2.1. The Projected Progress of Operation Overlord	69
3.1. Normandy on the Eve of Operation Cobra, 24 July	117
3.2. Operation Cobra, 25–31 July	125
3.3. Situation at the End of Operation Cobra, 31 July	131
3.4. Operation Bluecoat, 31 July–6 August	141
4.1. Development of Operations, 1–13 August	162
4.2. Creation of the Falaise Pocket, 1–16 August	163
4.3. Operations Totalize and Tractable, 8–10 and 14–16 August	171
4.4. The Drive to the Seine, 16–25 August	179
5.1. SHAEF Appreciation of Possible Axes to the Rhine	221
5.2. Opposing Operational Concepts: Broad versus Narrow Front	225
5.3. Pursuit to the German Border, 26 August–11 September	231
5.4. Operation Market Garden, 17–26 September	252
5.5. 12 Army Group Operations, 9–19 September	261

Foreword

C. J. Dick's two-volume study is a comparative critique of the differing approaches employed by the Allied powers as they conducted military operations in western and eastern Europe against the Wehrmacht of Hitler's Germany during the summer of 1944. Its uniqueness rests in its comparative nature. Rather than detailing the course of military operations, emphasizing battles and leaders as so many previous books have done, Dick analyzes and compares Allied approaches to conducting war strategically and, more importantly, operationally. As he states in his introduction, "My purpose is to put forward broad arguments about the conduct of war at the operational level—the handling of armies and army groups by both the Western Allies and the Red Army in contemporaneous campaigns." This he accomplishes objectively, sometimes caustically, but always thoroughly, with the "jeweler's eye" of a professional army officer and a skilled student of military history and with the analytical tools of an accomplished military theorist.

Dick's background has uniquely equipped him to do what other military historians have been unable to achieve. His experiences as an airborne and later intelligence officer in the British army, as an accomplished teacher of military history, and as the organizer of countless staff rides to the battlefields of Europe in the service of the British army and NATO's Allied Rapid Reaction Corps provided him with fresh perspectives regarding Allied operations in France during the last two years of the war. Likewise, as a member and then director of the renowned Soviet (later Conflict) Studies Research Centre during and after the Cold War, he possesses keen insights into how and why the Red (Soviet) Army prepared for and conducted war as it did. Accordingly, this two-volume study exploits these experiences in support of its distinctive comparative approach.

Titled *From Victory to Stalemate*, the first volume of this study focuses on why and how the Western Allies—specifically, the United States, Great Britain, and Canada—conducted military operations in France from July through September 1944. Although Dick touches on the difficult task of forming and managing a strategic coalition, his emphasis here is on how the imperatives of coalition warfare affected the nature of subsequent operations or, more specifically, impeded the development of so-called operational art—that is, the ability to perform sequential operational tasks necessary for the timely achievement of strategic aims. Thus, as this volume points out, "victory" in the breakout from Normandy in August 1944 ended with "stalemate" in the fall of 1944.

The chapters in volume 1 unfold chronologically, from the prelude of the dramatic but costly establishment of the Normandy lodgment, through the painstaking fighting in the hedgerows around St. Lô, the euphoric breakout eastward in Operation Cobra, and the frustrated hopes of the dash to Paris, and, ultimately, to the burgeoning stalemate on the approaches to the Rhine in late September. In the end, Dick ponders what all this meant, especially the impact of coalition warfare (as well as national military traditions) on the strategies and operational concepts employed and their positive or deleterious effects on the ability of coalition armies to operate effectively enough to achieve their strategic aims. He understands the truth in this statement: "Tactics makes the steps from which operational leaps are assembled; strategy points out the path." This volume serves as a warning and an exercise in the management of expectations for those countries and their leaders contemplating the conduct of coalition warfare in the future.

David M. Glantz
Carlisle, PA

Acknowledgments

I found writing this book much more difficult than I had expected when I blithely embarked upon the project. There were many times when I stared glumly at my computer, bereft of ideas, or gazed at the little birds industriously building their nests in my garden fence and wished I too could be out in the sun, indeed, anywhere except at my desk. That the project came to fruition is due in significant part to my beloved wife, Heather. She tolerated my spells of irritability or abstraction, demonstrating extraordinary forbearance in the face of periodic neglect. She encouraged me when I seemed despondent and disinclined to work, offering helpful suggestions to make some passages read more mellifluously. But her finest hour came with the proofreading. Her patience, attention to detail, and constructive ideas have combined to make this study more readable and accurate than it would have been if it had been left to me.

The ideas and opinions contained in this work owe much to my reading but more to innumerable discussions over the course of staff rides and battlefield tours, in the wake of lectures, or over a glass of wine or beer. I cannot begin to list all those who, during thirty or so years of study, made a contribution. I can, however, single out for special thanks the five people who read my drafts, made suggestions, and gave me insights. I worked with and came to know each of them when I was with the Soviet (later, Conflict) Studies Research Centre. All are deeply knowledgeable about military history and, critical for my purposes, about the central theme of my study—operational art. Four were soldiers who thought deeply about their profession and spent much of their careers, whether during their military service or after, educating officers in staff colleges and through their writings. In Britain, they are Major Generals Mungo Melvin and John Sutherell. In the United States, they are Colonels David Glantz and Les Grau, both soldiers turned academics. My lone civilian, Professor Jake Kipp, has spent a distinguished career in academe, much of it with David and Les, studying and writing about the same themes. I owe David a double debt. He provided me with indispensable material from his unparalleled collection of Soviet articles and General Staff documents.

Of course, writing a book is but one stage in a journey. It has to be published. I am grateful to Michael Briggs, the editor in chief at the University

Press of Kansas, for his encouragement and advice to expedite this process. My colleague and friend from Soviet Studies days, Anne Aldis, made an invaluable contribution. She edited my work with helpful suggestions about content and structure, an uncanny eye for the details of punctuation and grammar, and proposals for improving infelicitous phrasing. Much more computer literate than I, she organized it into the format required by the publisher and sorted out the endnotes and bibliography. I have Russell Chaluisan to thank for putting his skills as a draughtsman to work to convert my original colored maps with neat but illegible writing into monochrome versions that are easy to read and understand.

My thanks to you all.

Abbreviations, Acronyms, and Selected Foreign Words

ACM	Air Chief Marshal
AEAF	Allied Expeditionary Air Forces
AEF	Allied Expeditionary Forces
AFV	armored fighting vehicle
AGF	Army Ground Forces
AGRA	Army Group, Royal Artillery
ANXF	Allied Naval Expeditionary Forces
APCa	armored personnel carrier
APDS	armor piercing discarding sabot, a type of ammunition
AVM	Air Vice Marshal
AVRE	engineer tank
BAR	Browning automatic rifle
BEF	British Expeditionary Force
BG	battle group
bocage	hedgerow country
CAO	Canadian Army Overseas
CCA	Combat Command A
CCB	Combat Command B
CCR	Combat Command R
CCS	Combined Chiefs of Staff
CIA	Central Intelligence Agency (US)
CIGS	Chief of the Imperial General Staff
C-in-C	commander in chief
COMZ	communications zone
DZ	drop zone
ETO	European theatre of operations
FFI	Forces Françaises de l'Intérieur (French Interior Forces)
flakkampfgruppen	antitank groups
FM	Field Manual
FOO	forward observation officer
FUSAG	First US Army Group
G2	Staff Branch, Intelligence

xiii

G3	Staff Branch, Operations
GHQ	General Headquarters
GOC	General Officer Commanding
GSO	General Staff officer
HE	high explosive
HQ	headquarters
JCS	Joint Chiefs of Staff
KG	*Kampfgruppe* (battle group)
KSLI	King's Shropshire Light Infantry (British)
LD	line of departure
LMG	light machine gun
LST	landing ships tank
LZ	landing zone
MV	medium velocity
NCO	noncommissioned officer
NPAM	Non-Permanent Active Militia (Canadian)
OKW	Oberkommando der Wehrmacht (German High Command)
ORBAT	order of battle
ORS	Operational Research Section
OSS	Office of Strategic Services (US)
PAM	Permanent Active Militia (Canadian)
panzerschreck	manpack 88mm antitank rocket launcher
POL	petrol, oil, and lubricants
RAF	Royal Air Force (British)
RMA	rear maintenance area
SAS	Special Air Service (British)
SF	Special Forces
SHAEF	Supreme Headquarters, Allied Expeditionary Forces
SIGINT	signals intelligence
SMG	submachine gun
SOE	Special Operations Executive
SP	self-propelled
SSV	soft-skinned vehicle
TA	Territorial Army (British)
TAC	Tactical Air Command
TAF	Tactical Air Force
TO&E	table of organization and equipment
TOT	time on target
USAAF	United States Army Air Force
USSTAF	United States Strategic Air Forces in Europe
V	long-range (weapon)
VE	victory in Europe

Introduction

The purpose of this book, which has been divided into two volumes, is to study the practical application of military theory in the most testing of circumstances—fighting the German army in the summer of 1944. It is not, in other words, a straightforward military history, a descriptive account of operations. There are already more than enough narrative histories of the campaign and plenty of studies evoking the horror and pity of war. My purpose is to put forward broad arguments about the conduct of war at the operational level—the handling of armies and army groups by both the Western Allies and the Red Army in contemporaneous campaigns.

The genesis of this work lay in the battlefield tours and staff rides I used to conduct, or contribute to, for the British Army and NATO's Allied Rapid Reaction Corps.[1] These were not military tourism or evocations of past glories but serious didactic exercises aimed at improving the professional education of the participating officers. Not infrequently, at the conclusion of these exercises, senior officers would remark that I had offered interpretations and drawn lessons they had not previously encountered. They also found comparisons between Western and contemporaneous operations on the Russo-German front to be illuminating. Several suggested that I write up these accounts and lessons drawn from them for wider dissemination. This is the origin and primary purpose of my book: through the lens of military history, to broaden Western military officers' perspectives on the conduct of conventional war, together with that of serious scholars of the subject. In fact, I conceive this study as, in essence, a written staff ride of great scope. I follow the same methodology: setting out the operational-strategic context, examining the situation at the start of each operation as perceived by the commanders tasked with its execution, outlining their plans, discussing developments at key points during the evolution of the operation and decisions made in consequence, and evaluating the results and assessing the generalship involved.[2]

This is therefore an analytical study of the choices, compromises, and judgments made by the senior commanders. It is, I hope and believe, exacting but not carping when venturing evaluations. The vast majority of the opinions that follow were informed by discussions that took place on staff rides. Most of them represent consensual views; a few are mine alone. Some of the latter, particularly those involving Generals Montgomery, Bradley, and

Eisenhower, at first surprised, intrigued, or even shocked some British and American officers. That is one of the functions of the staff ride: to stimulate thought, discussion, and argument and to challenge received wisdom. This, in turn, encourages the replacement of stereotypical by original thinking when former students face their own, seemingly intractable problems in future wars.

While the primary audience for this investigation is military, I believe those concerned with shaping government policy can also profit from it. In an age when few policy makers have military experience, especially at senior levels, there is a pervasive superficiality of understanding about what armies can and cannot be expected to accomplish, especially at short notice, in unfamiliar operating environments, and against an imperfectly understood enemy. Similarly, many overestimate what can be provided by military intelligence and underestimate the difficulties, frustrations, and, consequently, the disappointing combat capabilities of coalitions and alliances. These and other problems in contemporary as well as past war fighting are illuminated in the pages that follow; they combine to make war an often unreliable and unpredictable instrument of policy that can lead to unforeseen and unwelcome outcomes. I would be delighted if these volumes, which emphasize the uncertainties of using military force as much as its utility, induced a degree of caution among those charged with deciding on its use.

I believe this is the first comparative analysis of synchronous campaigns in the west and the east during World War II to be published. That in itself enhances its educational value. My staff ride participants found the Soviets' different approach to operational problems not only interesting but also, in some cases, potentially applicable to their own, albeit very different, armies. Examples include concepts such as the forward detachment and the meeting engagement and the approach required to succeed therein.[3] In adopting my methodology, I made every effort to avoid the accusation of comparing apples and oranges. To this end, I carefully selected the operations studied, and I point out the differences as well as the similarities between the western and eastern fronts. My study is largely confined to the high summer of 1944, when both the Western Allies and the Soviets possessed the strategic initiative and disposed of forces capable of mounting strategic offensives against the same, weakening foe. Within that period, I concentrate principally on those operations characterized largely by maneuver, for it is in the conduct of operational maneuver that creative generalship is revealed; attritional methods, however unavoidable on occasion, are its antithesis.

The study has been divided into two volumes; the first and more detailed, as it is aimed primarily at a Western readership, deals with American, British, and Canadian operations in France and the Low Countries. Its title, *From Victory to Stalemate*, reflects the great, though flawed, achievement in Normandy that severely but not fatally damaged a German army group, and the Allies' subsequent failure to convert operational into strategically decisive success. (One might argue that, whatever the inflated hopes or expectations at the time, the Allies could not have delivered a coup de grâce to the Nazi regime that summer. But I contend that, before culminating for logistic reasons, they could have inflicted more damage on the enemy and seized major bridgeheads over the Rhine to launch the final campaign from a favorable line of departure.) Volume 2 deals with the contemporaneous major Soviet offensives. Called *From Defeat to Victory*, it briefly recounts, as essential background, how the Red Army clawed back from the catastrophes of 1941–1942 and survived through 1943, the year of contested strategic initiative. It then concentrates on three successive strategic offensive operations from late June to September 1944 that effectively annihilated three different army groups. Each ended with the Soviets advantageously placed—for example, with bridgeheads over major rivers—to resume the offensive when the effects of operational exhaustion had been overcome. The penultimate chapter of volume 2 looks at the interaction of the western and eastern fronts, compares and contrasts the conduct of operations in the west and the east, and draws conclusions about the different ways the Allied and Soviet militaries approached the problems of campaigning against a formidable enemy. The short, concluding chapter offers some reflections about recent and contemporary American and British approaches to the difficulties of waging war.

My aim is analytical. For that reason, the summaries of operations are restricted in length, giving only enough information to provide a basis for argument and assessment. Accordingly, they are dry but, I hope, for the most part, mercifully short; some, however, are not as short as I would have liked, as there is often a great deal of devil in the detail. Just as chronicling events is a minor part of this work, so too is deconstruction of strategic decisions and, even more so, analysis of tactical methods and their results. Both aspects of military activity necessarily figure to an extent, but only insofar as they bear on my main area of concern—operational art and generalship, the conduct of operations at theatre, army group, and army levels. In order to pass judgment on the soundness or otherwise of commanders' decisions and actions, it is necessary to establish criteria by which all are evaluated. Therefore, I establish a conceptual basis for discussion in chapter 1 of volume 1. The theory of the realms and concerns of strategy, operational art, and tactics and the interaction among them are outlined, along with commonly accepted principles of war and the attributes of senior commanders generally considered prerequisites for success. However, it is not always possible for armies to provide that which is theoretically desirable. Brief résumés of the education, training, and careers of the seven top Allied field commanders in the west in the summer of 1944 show how varied was their preparation for the challenges they faced in Normandy and beyond. Moreover, the armies they led were products of historically derived concepts and practices—all armies are prisoners of their own experience—not all of which proved well suited to the campaigns they would have to fight. These too are briefly described, for all judgments on generalship must take into account the capabilities and limitations of the instruments the generals commanded.

My purpose in the rest of volume 1 is to cast light on the practice of operational art by American, British, and Canadian generals in the European theatre of operations (ETO) in the critical summer campaign of 1944.[4] This project runs into an immediate conceptual obstacle. Although operational art was a concept born in the Red Army of the 1920s and was (after vicissitudes) entrenched there by 1944, it was unfamiliar in Anglo-American thinking until about forty years later.[5] It would be unreasonable to criticize generals for not doing what they had not been taught. They did, however, subscribe to the principles of war discussed in chapter 1. These principles had been set out in the British *Field Service Regulations* of 1935 and parts of Military Training Pamphlet No. 23 (*Operations*) of 1942 and the American *Field Manual 100-5* of 1941 and 1944. They formed the basis of the doctrine that Allied generals had been taught and presumably were expected to implement in 1944. Indeed, this doctrine could more accurately be described as principles of operational art, being devoid of political content and concerned purely with the business of how to fight, including at a higher formation level. Admittedly, for the historical reasons outlined in chapter 1, these principles had been developed with far less rigor and detail than was the case in the Red Army (the evolution of the latter's concepts is outlined in volume 2). The Allies had also had four years to observe—and, in the British case, had been at the receiving end of—the Wehrmacht's methods on the offensive. These methods, like the Soviets', were based on an understanding of the operational level of war. Finally, the British and, to a lesser extent, the Americans had their own experience of waging contemporary, mechanized warfare. However, as chapter 1 describes, the Allies faced an uphill task that was far greater than simply modernizing their military theory and moving past small-wars thinking or the linear, attritional methods of the First World War. They had to grow their small armies into large ones, with all the attendant difficulties of finding, educating, and training a vastly expanded officer corps, including at senior levels. As chapters 3 to 7 of volume 1 make clear, the learning curves of the Allied generals were varied. It took some time before most ceased to rely on superior combat power to grind the enemy down and began to exploit their superior potential for operational maneuver; one or two generals largely failed to make the transition.

This study of the northwest European campaign of 1944 is limited to only a short period within it. I do not dwell on the seven weeks of essentially attritional struggle during which the Allies built up their combat power and decisively tilted the balance of forces in their favor. However, chapter 2 is largely devoted to a description of the state of armies on the opposing sides in the west on the eve of Operation Cobra, the American breakthrough toward the end of July. To understand the swift development of operations that followed the breakout, it is necessary to understand the correlation of forces that opened up the possibility of decisive operations and the strengths and weaknesses of the protagonists. This is explored in some detail, not only with regard to the quality and quantity of materiel and personnel but also, and every bit as important, in terms of logistic flexibility and sustainability, command and control, and intelligence gathering. The aim here is to counter the misperceptions and even myths that have distorted an understanding of the relative capabilities of the two sides and thus skewed interpretations of events.

My analysis of Allied operational art and command starts in chapter 3 with Cobra. This operation, aided by a British supporting attack, rapidly and seamlessly developed into a war of movement. Chapter 3 examines this breaking of the quasi-stalemate. Of course, the German defense had reached its culminating point, most importantly in the sphere of logistic sustainability, by the time Cobra struck and split the front wide open. This was, of course, the result not of an event but of a process whereby the defender grew weaker as attrition took its steady toll and air interdiction deprived the Germans of even minimum requirements of ammunition and fuel. Meanwhile, the Allies grew stronger as replacements and reinforcements poured into Normandy. It would be difficult to maintain, however, that the Allied breakthrough could not have been achieved prior to a tipping point in the last week of July. Certainly, both the American and the British armies needed to attain suitable lines of departure (in the former case, south of the Cotentin wetlands; in the latter, over the Orne and south of Caen) in order to develop an offensive with decisive aims. But could they not have accomplished this earlier, as the scales were tipping? I examine the evolution of the concepts and methods that more fully exploited American strengths and increased their operational effectiveness. The British, still largely wedded to linear, attritional methods, could not achieve comparable operational effect, although their supporting blow certainly contributed significantly to a marked deterioration of the German situation.

By early August, the means had been built up and the possibility created for operational maneuver to achieve decisive ends. Chapter 4 describes the exploitation of this opportunity. Thanks to their own initial success and potentially catastrophic German errors, the Allies were in a favorable position to achieve their stated aim of annihilating the enemy armies in Normandy and to do so, moreover, before their own looming logistic problems became intractable. This they failed to do completely because two successive encirclement operations were essentially improvised rather than planned and were then imperfectly conducted. Part of the problem lay at army level. Three of the four army commanders were, by education and experience, more tactically than operationally minded; they were happier when directing set-piece battles and relying on superior firepower than when conducting inherently less controllable operations that emphasized superior mobility to outmaneuver the enemy into a position where his destruction became certain. Alone among his peers, Lieutenant General Patton grasped both the parlous plight into which the German army had descended and the dividend that momentum, by retaining the initiative, would bring, while at the same time greatly reducing the apparent risk involved in his decisions. His boldness was not mirrored at the critical army group and theatre levels. There, caution combined with uncertain direction resulting from the essentially improvised nature of operations, exacerbated by intra-alliance rivalries and misunderstandings. The result was vacillation and compromise inimical to decisiveness in a rapidly changing, fluid situation. The Germans certainly suffered a major defeat, but within a month, the forces they had managed to extricate from disaster would play a significant role in restoring a precarious stability to the defense. Chapter 4 concludes with an analysis of Allied operational art and generalship that recognizes its achievements and deconstructs its weaknesses.

The crushing defeat inflicted on the Wehrmacht in August could (perhaps should) have been a prelude to decisive operations that would have ended the war in the west in 1944—an outcome senior German generals thought likely. Failing that, it should have placed the Allies in such an advantageous strategic position from which to resume a subsequent campaign that a coup de grâce could have been delivered earlier than the spring of 1945 and at less cost. Chapter 5 describes the Allied drive northeastward and eastward out of Normandy. The Supreme Headquarters, Allied Expeditionary Forces (SHAEF) preinvasion appreciation and, following from it, concept of operations are studied and contrasted with the unexpected situation facing the American and British army groups at the beginning of September. SHAEF plans were expeditiously adapted, and the Supreme Commander issued directives to his army groups for a general advance, with the aim of forcing the Rhine more or less simultaneously across the front. Immediately the commanders of those army groups, disliking his decisions, began to subvert his intent. I describe the development of British and American operations and the high-level compromises and fudges that were made to preserve the appearance of Allied unity as each pursued its own favored, and divergent, path to victory. In doing so, armies and army groups tended to follow a beggar-thy-neighbor approach to logistics, and both they and SHAEF shied away from making the hard choices and decisions necessary to avoid premature culmination. In late September the Allies' offensives duly culminated, without having delivered a fatal blow or seized bridgeheads over, or even reaching, the Rhine. I conclude my study with the onset of autumn because by then, the front was quite evidently congealing. Once again, the Allies were reverting, like it or not, to an attritional struggle.

A former British theatre commander wrote:

> The more I have seen of war the more I realize how it all depends on administration and transportation (... logistics). It takes little skill or imagination to see where you would like your army to be and when; it takes much knowledge and hard work to know where you can place your forces and whether you can maintain them there. A real knowledge of supply and movement factors must be the basis of every leader's plan; only then can he know how and when to take risks with those factors; and battles and wars are won only by taking risks.[6]

The most important reason for the Allies' culmination short of a strategic result was that they allowed their desires to override their knowledge of supply and movement factors, which led to mounting logistic problems. The careful calculations on which supply had been based were invalidated by unexpectedly sudden and all but complete success in Normandy and by the command decision to continue operations without the projected operational pause to build up stocks and improve infrastructure. Against minimal opposition, the armies advanced swiftly into the German depth, but it was obvious from the start of the exploitation that, within a very short period, the number of formations that could be sustained in action would shrink rapidly—to less than half in the US case. The logisticians improvised gamely, but their efforts were vitiated by SHAEF's failure to prioritize and to provide clear and consistent direction. These failings were compounded by a similar reluctance among senior commanders to accept that not all goals could be pursued simultaneously, and national and interarmy rivalries exacerbated the problem of overstretched supply lines. Chapter 6 demonstrates the inadequacy of operational level decision making in the campaign-determining sphere of logistics.

Chapters 5 and 6 outline the operational developments and parallel logistic deterioration of the late-summer campaign. Chapter 7 delves into the causes of its less than satisfactory outcome: the decisions of operational level commanders. At the beginning of September the Allies had almost everything going for them. The enemy was beaten and demoralized, forced into a purely reactive posture with force levels insufficient to react effectively. The Allies had total command of the air and vastly superior firepower and mobility on the ground. Their weakness lay in the sustainability of the force, and that was essentially calculable. As long as their commanders adopted objectives and operational plans that took adequate account of logistic constraints, they could be fairly certain of achieving their aims. For once, but only fleetingly, the enemy did not have a vote.

Various factors relating to command and control combined to rob the Allies of decisive results. One was the actual organization of command and the related issue of authority, particularly at theatre but also at army group levels. Another was a tendency to neglect the stated aim of the campaign—the destruction of the enemy—in favor of territorial gains, with disputes over where those gains would contribute most to victory. In pursuit of their divergent operational goals, the army group commanders acted in competition and did not hesitate to undermine or occasionally ignore their Supreme Commander's intent. Both Montgomery and Bradley showed much less loyalty and obedience to their superior than they demanded from their own juniors. Of course, such disagreements were partly the result of personality clashes—as Patton remarked, "all very successful commanders are prima donnas and must be so treated."[7] One of the more important responsibilities of senior commanders is the management and direction of capable but difficult subordinates, a challenge not always met by Eisenhower, Montgomery, and Bradley.

At least as important, however, were significant differences between the Americans and the British in operational doctrine and concepts. Mutual lack of understanding was aggravated by disagreements over the allocation of resources to tasks. These in turn were exacerbated by political considerations, both intra-alliance and domestic. Diverging aims prevented unity of effort, and the diffusion of effort in pursuit of multiple goals led to culmination short of everyone's objectives. Had there been more foresight and more objectivity at critical command levels, had the implementation of operational art been more uniformly effective, and, above all, had Eisenhower insisted on a consistent course of action and enforced compliance by his subordinates, greater success could have been achieved. I suggest some alternative decisions that sounder and more original operational thinking might have prompted, with beneficial results. Inevitably, the most important of these would have been made at the top. However, I recognize that the Supreme Allied Commander faced command problems that were essentially intractable. Probably no one could have done better. He deserves much more praise for his accomplishments, which were critical to the alliance, than censure for his failures.

Volume 2, *From Defeat to Victory*, deals principally with the summer campaign of 1944 on the eastern front and has its own introduction. Suffice it to say that my approach there is somewhat different. The campaign in the east was much larger in scope and scale. Consequently, I adopted a broader-brushed approach in recounting the progress of each operation. The nature of my analysis changes to an extent, becoming more mathematical. This is due to the distinctive nature of much of the Soviet source material, which is, in important respects, dissimilar to the Anglo-American. The constant between the two volumes is a focus on operational art. In the last two chapters of volume 2, I draw conclusions about the conduct of war in the different theatres and offer some reflections on its relevance for the future.

The main emphasis in chapter 4 of volume 2 is to compare and contrast the campaigns in the two theatres. It begins, however, by considering the interaction between them. Of course, the very fact that Germany had to fight a war on two fronts (arbitrarily to lump the Allied European and Mediterranean theatres together) doomed it to defeat. That doom probably could have been accomplished earlier had the Allies and Soviets cooperated more closely to achieve synergistic effect. In fact, they were as much mistrustful rivals, especially on the Soviet side, as they were partners, and practical teamwork was largely absent. Unfortunately for the Western Allies, their relationship too became increasingly antipathetic, not regarding ends but increasingly with respect to means. Strategic and operational decisions became a source of discord, prevarication, and compromise that weakened the alliance's effectiveness. Unconstrained by allies, the Soviets' decision making was simpler and more effective.

The other issues examined in the chapter relate to the conduct of operations. While the Allies achieved strategic surprise as to the Normandy location and subsequent main effort of the invasion, the Red Army made a greater effort, to greater critical effect, to practice operational-level deception and thus achieve surprise. It could also be argued that the Allies, with complete command of the air and, above all, Ultra, enjoyed better operational intelligence but exploited it less forcefully. This was partly the result of an approach to operational art that essentially saw it as merely tactics writ large—grand tactics, in British parlance. Western armies, especially the Anglo-Canadian, were inclined to focus on tactical problems to take ground of tactical significance, while minimizing casualty levels and maintaining tight control of the battle to avoid confusion. Such preoccupations tended to make commanders think small; they executed rigidly timetabled, deliberate, and consequently slow attacks to achieve limited objectives. Soviet operational ideas tended to be on a larger scale and were thought through to the desired end state. For the Soviets, destruction of the enemy was generally the main object, with the seizure of ground an important by-product. The Red Army prized tempo as a key component of success. It was seen as a force multiplier, forcing the enemy onto the back foot and keeping him there while destroying the cohesion of his formations and his ability to control them. Deliberation and caution were the antithesis of rapidity. To achieve momentum, the Soviets were prepared to accept heavy initial casualties, risk, and a degree of chaos as its price.

These differences in approach explain the contrasting development of operations in the west and east. Both the Allies and the Soviets evolved quite similar methods to penetrate the Germans' prepared positional defenses. The big difference was in exploiting a breakthrough. The Allies tended to create only small reserves for the conduct of exploitation and, moreover, to proceed with caution into the enemy's rear area; only Patton showed any real enthusiasm and flair for deep and rapid thrusts into the operational depth. They also tended, especially at theatre and army group levels, to lack consistent focus. Main efforts were seldom specified and even less often maintained, and forces were accordingly too dissipated to achieve decisive effect. The Red Army, by contrast, usually started operations with strong, armor-heavy "mobile groups" held ready to conduct operational maneuver in the enemy depth. Having contributed to the annihilation of a significant enemy grouping, these mobile groups then concentrated on key axes to forestall enemy efforts to restore the front. There was, however, one factor common to both eastern and western theatres. In both, mounting logistic problems more than German resistance often brought operations to a close.

The last chapter of volume 2 leaves the realm of the past to consider what lessons for the future can be found in these campaigns. Plainly, they do not present recipes for the conduct of future operations. Military and other technologies, and both political and social climates, have wrought a revolution in military affairs that is far greater than that of the 1930s and 1940s. Any useful lesson must focus on *how* to think, not *what* to think. The chapter examines, and questions, some common assumptions about intelligence, surprise and deception, and the utility of alliances (especially NATO) that have grown in recent decades. The historical record suggests a pause for thought on these issues, as well as in the area of doctrine. None of the armies fighting Germany in the summer of 1944 was engaged in the sort of war they had anticipated and prepared for. The Red Army came closest to having a sound doctrinal basis on which to build appropriate concepts and force structures. By 1944, it was beating Germany at its own game. The United States and Britain had to adjust from a small-war orientation to cope with a theatre-level conflict against the most sophisticated land power in the world. That adjustment took time and, arguably, was not fully successful even during the course of 1944. How well will American and British military thinkers and leaders adapt to an increasingly unstable twenty-first-century world in the throes of fundamental technological and ideological change? Even more importantly, will their political masters understand the challenges and give them appropriate direction, armed forces, and tasks? If they fail, their countries face traumatic times.

CHAPTER ONE

Immature Armies

CONCEPTS OF WAR FIGHTING

A Little Theory: Strategy, Operational Art, Tactics, and Doctrine

Nowadays, three interrelated and interdependent levels of war are identified: strategy, operational art, and tactics.[1] The operational level provides the vital connection between military-strategic objectives and the tactical employment of troops on the battlefield. It is the realm of the conception, planning, and execution of major operations and campaigns designed, through a succession of steps, to destroy the enemy's centre of gravity. In other words, it determines where, when, and to what purpose tactical units and formations are committed to battle. Probably the most succinct explanation of their relationship was provided by the Soviet theorist A. A. Svechin in the 1920s: "tactics makes the steps from which operational leaps are assembled; strategy points out the path."[2]

Strategy sets out the goal of operations in a theatre of war. In the era of major interstate conflicts, this was usually the destruction of the principal enemy grouping or the seizure of specified territorial objectives of critical economic or political importance. The aim depended on the perception of the enemy's centre of gravity—that is, which facet of his political, economic, or military power would, if eliminated, destroy the enemy's will or ability to continue the war. Until the Napoleonic era, it was sometimes possible for one climactic battle to destroy the enemy's main force or seize an objective indispensable to the enemy. This kind of decisive battle, which determined the outcome of the war, was the aspiration of most commanders in chief. In the industrial age, however, states could mobilize and equip mass armies. Their size and resilience meant the strategic aim was rarely achievable (against a major opponent, anyway) in a single operation. Rather, it required a campaign (or even successive campaigns) in which a series of operations by several major formations cumulatively led to the accomplishment of the strategic aim. Of course, the attack on the enemy's centre of gravity did not have to be direct, grinding attritionally through the strongest enemy groupings. Often an indirect approach, which dislocated the enemy by not conforming to his expectations and by exploiting his comparative disadvantage, was more economical, more effective, and, in the end, faster.

Operational art consists of the sequencing and synchronization by theatre, army groups, and armies of a series of operations and battles conducted by subordinate formations. Taken together, these must produce a whole that is greater than the sum of the parts, which results in progress toward a successful campaign and thence strategic success. Strategy makes demands on operational commanders in terms of the destruction to be wrought, the territory to be seized (or defended), and the time allowed for the accomplishment of these goals. In turn, the strategic concept must be rooted in operational reality. It is not merely pointless but fatal to set goals that are beyond the capabilities of the forces available—as Hitler often did, to the ultimate ruin of his Third Reich. That said, Allied strategists sometimes forgot that almost as important as correctly identifying the aim was choosing what *not* to do; in the event, excessive effort was dissipated on secondary or even marginal tasks. The skill of the operational-level commander lies in using deception, interdiction, operational maneuver, logistic resources, and carefully orchestrated battles to structure a successful campaign. It follows from this that operational requirements provide the sole justification for fighting battles; these requirements determine why, where, when, and how an enemy grouping is to be engaged. Fighting unnecessary battles, whether they are won or lost, inevitably absorbs valuable, usually scarce resources that might be more gainfully employed elsewhere and wears them down, to the detriment of future operations.

Tactics are employed by corps, divisions, and their subordinate units to solve the problems that must be surmounted to achieve operational goals. Tactics, in other words, is concerned with the conception, planning, and execution of current and very near future battles. The tactician does not, however, have a free hand. He is constrained by the demands of his operational superior, who lays down objectives and specifies groupings, forms of action, and their sequencing and timing. As at the higher level, the plans of major formations must be firmly based on the actual capabilities and limitations of their subordinates; without sure steps, no leaps will be possible. At the tactical level, as at the operational level, successful generalship is a function, among other things, of achieving synergistic effects. Battles, and the operations of which they are a part, must be linked in aim, timing, and geographic location, such that the totality of their achievements is greater than the sum of the individual parts.

Operational art has always been concerned with the relationships between mass, firepower, and maneuver. Its evolution has been conditioned largely by the impact of technological development and scale of deployment on these three factors, coupled with creative conceptual thinking (or, more often, its absence). By the First World War, the immense reserves accumulated as a result of conscription had resulted in armies of unprecedented size and resilience. The range and destructiveness of their firepower had increased by several orders of magnitude compared with armies of a hundred years earlier. Yet, although they could travel rapidly over long distances by railway in strategic moves (and therefore countermoves), on the battlefield they still moved at the speed of (usually excessively laden) men on foot or on horseback who were often impeded by ground torn up by shell fire or turned into a sea of mud. Moreover, armies had grown to such a size that there was no flank for the enemy to turn. The inevitable result was static (or in Russia, semistatic), trench-dominated warfare and generals who saw the grim business of attrition as the only realistic way to destroy the enemy.

The interwar years saw the development of weapons and equipment that had been in their infancy between 1914 and 1918. Tanks, combat aircraft, mechanical transport, and relatively efficient and portable radios promised at least a partial shift in the balance between firepower and mobility toward the latter. This "revolution in military affairs" (to use a term coined by the Soviets), in turn, offered maneuver as an alternative to the sterile campaigns of attrition. Instead of bludgeoning the enemy to death, and inevitably being bludgeoned back in the process, the aim was to reject battle on the enemy's terms and instead paralyze him by rapidly shifting the focus of combat to his rear areas, destroying the command and control and logistic systems on which he depended and demoralizing his troops and leaders by doing the frighteningly unexpected. Such an approach emphasized not force ratios but surprise, deception, unexpected maneuvers and tactics, and speed in the advance.[3] A rapid convergence of forces from dispersed assembly areas onto an apparently unlikely sector could concentrate sufficient strength against weakness. The superiority of this unexpected ground force could be coupled with the focused application of airpower on the chosen sector. The protracted artillery preparations that had previously been needed to penetrate a strong defense could be dispensed with. Thus, there would be no painstaking and obvious buildup for the offensive to provoke a defensive counterconcentration. Surprise is an all but essential prerequisite for unbalancing the enemy; it thus sets the conditions for the early achievement of the momentum that makes operational maneuver possible. Its restoration as a key principle was central to maneuver warfare. The wholeheartedness with which both the Wehrmacht and the Red Army accepted the logic of this revolution in warfare and changed their methods would set them apart from the British and the Americans.

Maneuver and attrition are often portrayed as opposite approaches to war fighting. This is too simplistic a dialectic. In Normandy, a preliminary wearing down of German strength was an inescapable prelude to breakthrough and the generation of operational maneuver; so too was the fixing and grinding down of the enemy's main strength by the Red Army.[4] It is also a false dichotomy: maneuver is not the opposite of attrition. Attrition's true opposite is annihilation, which is best accomplished through a judicious combination of firepower and mobility, battle and maneuver.[5] In the German and Soviet views, offensive battles were generally worth fighting only if they enabled the subsequent generation of operational maneuver. In turn, the purpose of operational maneuver was to make a major contribution to strategic success through the destruction of the enemy. This would be accomplished by disrupting the enemy's cohesion, command and control, and logistic support on a large scale by driving rapidly into his depth and causing his forces to become progressively less capable of putting up effective resistance, not least through fragmentation, psychological shock, and demoralization. It is easier to convince significant numbers of enemy soldiers that they have lost the battle, thus persuading them collectively to withdraw from combat through retreat or surrender, than it is to wear down formations in a toe-to-toe slugging match.

The term *operational art* is rightly chosen because it is not a science. There is great scope for creativity at the operational level, and the more senior the commander, the more scope there is. Many tacticians who were competent at the corps level and were promoted to army command proved capable only of massing superior forces for what was essentially an attritional contest. They lacked the necessary imagination and flair—indeed, daring—to make the transition from careful craftsman to inspired artist. Fundamentally, tactics is largely concerned with getting the most out of a combined-arms team to maximize the enemy's attrition. At least until the enemy's defense has been penetrated, most attacks are frontal. As the situation becomes more fluid, there are greater opportunities to maneuver and mount flank attacks, and even to bypass. However, the operational commander orchestrating these tactical battles often requires the destruction of the enemy facing him, at least initially, if only to create an opening sufficient for the committal of exploitation units and then whole formations into the enemy's depth. A crucial link between tactics and operational art is therefore the provision, in advance, of forces and plans to convert tactical into operational success. A division or corps might destroy the enemy to its front, seize ground vital to the integrity of the defense, and thus create a gap in the enemy's deployment. This, however, is of little operational significance if the hole is not exploited by the successive insertion of additional forces to penetrate first into the enemy's tactical depth and then into his operational rear. Moreover, against a capable enemy like the Wehrmacht, which was famous for its quick reaction to emergencies, the committal of subsequent echelons or reserves had to follow the initial penetration immediately. Delay would have given the defender time to react and restore the integrity of his defense before the damage became irreparable.

Time is a critical factor in war, especially in fluid, maneuver-dominated operations. These operations therefore assume the character of intense contests for that precious commodity. Win the battle for time, thus retaining the initiative and forcing the enemy into a purely reactive posture, and the defeat of the physical enemy becomes much easier. A rapid advance capitalizes on surprise, and speed itself is surprising—indeed, shocking—to the enemy. A formation that achieves a high tempo in the advance can generally disrupt and fragment the defense, disorient or paralyze its commander, and damage the morale of his troops; the commander's capabilities become less than the sum of the parts, and self-preservation becomes the main focus of the increasingly uncontrollable elements of his command.

Exploitation is the decisive phase of a battle or operation, the time when the fruits of hard fighting are gathered. Armies wary of exposing any significant elements to flanking counterattacks or even encirclement generally eschew vigorous exploitation or undertake it so cautiously as to give the enemy time to recover or to withdraw and restore the integrity of his defense. In this case, tactical attacks continue to be frontal, for the most part, with only limited scope for tactical maneuver. In turn, operational formations are condemned to fight attritional battles rather than keeping the foe off balance and causing his position steadily to worsen and his reactions to become increasingly belated as the tempo of the offensive mounts, until his position becomes irredeemable.

Doctrine consists of an approved set of principles and methods that provides an army with a common outlook and a uniform basis for action; in simplistic terms, it determines how an army fights. The organizational structure and equipping of an army stem from its doctrinal precepts, and doctrine provides the basis for military training and for command and control. Its importance cannot be overemphasized. If doctrine is unsound or contradictory, or if it has not been properly disseminated and thoroughly absorbed, the army will enter battle with systemic problems. At the operational level, doctrine comprises principles and guidance, as befits an art, where creativity is encouraged. At the tactical level, its character is largely prescriptive. It cannot dissipate Clausewitz's "fog of war," but it can simplify decision making under the stress of combat by limiting the range of choices that are deemed relevant in given circumstances. By ensuring that all commanders and staff officers view similar situations in broadly similar ways, it ensures that they will react in a more or less predictable fashion when faced with tactical problems. This is important for operational-level and higher-level tactical commanders, as they have neither up-to-the-minute knowledge of a situation nor the time and means to micromanage their subordinate commanders and solve problems for them. Effective common doctrine is one of the few means by which senior commanders can, albeit indirectly, influence the conduct of the tactical battle. Doctrine helps to ensure that all the moving parts work together to propel the military machine forward in a broadly predictable way, without Clausewitz's "friction" bringing it to a juddering halt.

In providing a framework of understanding, doctrine is useful as a guide to action. But if it becomes a template, it can also become a straitjacket, inhibiting some commanders. Mediocre commanders, especially if they fear the wrath of overcontrolling superiors who are intolerant of any error, commonly suffer paralysis in decision making when the textbook does not provide a clear prescription for action. In this case, they may do the safe thing, rather than boldly grasping a fleeting opportunity that could pay big dividends; worse, they may fail to act without orders from above, which inevitably arrive far too late by the time the situation is reported, a decision is made, and orders are communicated back down the chain of command. Doctrine that is allowed (or used) to stifle initiative may not prevent victories from being achieved, but it will probably result in their being more costly and less decisive.

The theoretical prescriptions outlined above are well known to today's senior officers, at least in terms of conventional interstate warfare.[6] It was not always so. All armies are prisoners of their own experience. For instance, there are some that, for societal, political, or historical reasons, will probably not progress beyond the suppression of their own populations. Others are capable of fighting one sort of war better than another, at least until they accumulate experience in the less familiar environment. Major continental armies and, in the era of universal conscription, the societies they served became used to large-scale, bloody, and sometimes protracted struggles. As a result of the climactic First World War, the French became convinced that linear-attritional warfare was inevitable in fighting their historic enemy, Germany. For the next two decades, France prepared diligently and thoughtfully to reprise the methods of 1918—failing to understand the implications of the revolution in military affairs that took place during that period. This failure led directly to its catastrophic defeat in 1940.

The Germans and the Russians had different experiences in the vast, featureless expanses of the Russian front, where trench deadlock was less intractable. Even more formative for the fledgling Red Army was the civil war that swung to and fro over all of Russia before the Soviets finally triumphed. Given creativity, it was clear that maneuver could be decisive. Moreover, both these powers were losers in the First World War, which gave impetus to thoughts about the future of warfare. How to avoid the pitfalls of the last war and do better in the next one became the obsession of their General Staffs. It was this imperative that led to their separate arrivals at the concept of operational art. The British and American victors had no such incentive to develop military theory. Both their societies, though for different reasons, rejected the very idea that there might be another such cataclysmic war, and both denied their armies the incentive and the resources to fight one. Thus, it is not surprising that the theoretical developments that did take place (for instance, the British *Field Service Regulations* of 1935) proved inadequate when exposed to the test of another major war.

Principles of War

While superior technology, numbers, and various other advantages may contribute, victory depends ultimately on sound generalship. Successful generalship requires adherence to certain principles. Those enunciated by the British Army after the First World War and elaborated on below are almost identical to those cited in US doctrinal publications (albeit with slightly different phrasing). They are very broad in nature—so broad, in fact, as to be universal; as such, they are far from being a recipe for victory. Rather, they provide some guidelines that must underpin decision making and planning. They vary in relevance and importance from one situation to another, and their application requires judgment and intelligent interpretation.[7]

Selection and Maintenance of the Aim. The aim of any operation must be carefully selected to contribute toward the attack on the enemy's correctly identified centre of gravity. It must also be clear and unambiguous. The commander must have no doubt about what he is trying to achieve, and his subordinates must be equally clear so that all their efforts are directed toward the desired end. Moreover, the aim must be realistic and achievable with the forces and in the time available. Conversely, consistency in pursuing the aim does not require bullheaded persistence in carrying out a plan that has proved far from optimal; the aim is constant, but the means employed to achieve it may—indeed, should—change to fit altered circumstances.

Maintenance of Morale. One of Napoleon's aphorisms was that the moral is to the physical as three is to one. High morale is probably the most important factor in war. It leads to an offensive spirit and the will to win. By contrast, however numerous and well equipped, a dispirited army that lacks faith in its leadership is unlikely to succeed. High morale stems from good leadership at all levels and the trust and confidence that this engenders; strong discipline, which is as necessary as leadership to overcome fear; unit cohesion, which comes from fostering comradeship (another facet of leadership) and, to an extent, from unit tradition; the self-respect of the individual soldier; a sense of purpose, reinforced by propaganda (although, as successful motivators, ideology, religion, and patriotism vary from time to time and from army to army); success in battle (the surest way to achieve high morale); and the material well-being of the soldier, so far as wartime conditions allow—he needs to feel that his leaders are doing their best for him in the circumstances.

Offensive Action. The offensive confers the initiative and, with it, freedom of action. Being able to dictate the course and pace of events is another prerequisite for victory: if the enemy has his hands full reacting to attacks, he will usually lack the opportunity, resources, or time to hit back effectively. The greater the rate of advance, the more belated and ineffectual the reactions of the defeated side are likely to be. Win the battle for time, and the defeat of the physical enemy becomes markedly easier. Moreover, the side enjoying the initiative establishes a moral ascendancy over the enemy; the force that is continually on the defensive will find it increasingly difficult to keep its morale intact. Observance of this principle does not, however, require an army to be always and indiscriminately on the attack. A few repulses or some partial, expensive successes may sow seeds of doubt in the soldiers' minds, leading them to believe that their lives are being put at risk by uncaring leaders for unimportant objectives. Morale will then suffer.

Concentration of Force. It is necessary to concentrate at the decisive place and time a force of sufficient superiority to carry an attack through to the specified objective without an operational or tactical pause that gives the enemy time to restore the integrity of his defense. Ideally, usually through the achievement of surprise, strength is concentrated against weakness. It should also be used to turn or envelop the defender, as such maneuvers do more to unbalance and demoralize him than frontal attacks. Concentration is a necessary but insufficient condition to be tolerably certain of success. An obvious and leisurely buildup merely prompts the enemy into a counterconcentration and thus hardens his resistance. The battle then inevitably becomes an attritional affair, with the attacker gnawing through the defense at a heavy cost in men, equipment, and time. Therefore, concentration must be either covert or accomplished rapidly from dispersed locations, with forces arriving at the selected attack sector only shortly before H-hour. The former approach is usually very difficult (and the greater the scale, the more problematic it becomes). The latter requires fine judgment and timing and good communications and traffic control; it is very vulnerable to Clausewitzian friction.

Economy of Effort. This principle is the corollary of the concentration of force. It is impossible to be strong everywhere. Thus, whether in attack or defense, the greater the concentration desired, the more secondary sectors must be extended in length, stripped of troops, or both. This can create a vulnerability (though the risk may be mitigated by deception). It is also possible, *pace* Clausewitz, to be too strong at the point of main effort. Attempts at excessive concentration for an offensive will probably attract the enemy's attention and lead to a counterconcentration. They may also give rise to congestion, which impedes mobility and thus the achievement of tempo. On the defensive, an excessively weakened sector may invite an unexpected attack that proves difficult to repulse. In either case, overinsurance diverts troops from other efforts where they might be better employed. Secondary efforts are supporting and not necessarily unimportant.

Surprise. With hard work and imagination, surprise in the offensive can always be achieved, at least at the tactical and operational levels. The higher the level at which surprise is achieved, the more profound its effects. It requires painstaking attention to camouflage, concealment, secrecy for the buildup, and usually deception too, to attract the enemy's attention and forces elsewhere. Surprise can take several forms, including location of attack and axes of advance, timing, and new techniques (perhaps involving new capabilities). When achieved, it causes disorientation, even paralysis, in the enemy chain of command and induces "big-picture blindness" in and consequent poor decision making by senior commanders. It harms the morale and cohesion of enemy units or formations, often causing panic. Some analysts believe it is the greatest single contributor to success, with an impact more profound than a numerical superiority of ten to one.[8] Ipso facto, where the attacker can be confident of achieving surprise, he can afford to reduce the force superiority required for success and therefore the scale of the surprise-compromising prior concentration. Surprise is, however, a wasting asset. Its effects do not last long against a capable enemy. It is therefore vital to capitalize fully on its achievement, seize the initiative while the enemy's equilibrium is upset, and exploit vigorously; a rapid advance deep into the enemy's rear prolongs the effects of surprise and is, indeed, surprising in itself.

Security. Security means the creation and maintenance of an operating environment that confers freedom of action at the necessary place and time to achieve the aim. Enemy efforts to prevent the achievement of the aim can be thwarted only if security—in its widest sense—is assured. Operational (including communications) security must be tight. Bases and lines of communication must not be subject to serious disruption by nonmilitary means or by physical attack. A favorable air situation must be achieved: "since . . . 1939, no country has won a war in the face of enemy air superiority, no major offensive has succeeded against an opponent who controlled the air, and no defense has sustained itself against an enemy who had air superiority."[9] Balance must be kept so that any countermove can be defeated without diverting forces, or even serious attention, from the aim: thus, flanks must be protected and a reserve maintained. As the offensive gathers momentum and the initiative is firmly held, the requirements for flank protection and reserves to cope with enemy reactions dwindle as the enemy's freedom of action becomes increasingly curtailed.

Flexibility. Possession of the initiative is fundamental to success. It is, however, a mistake to think that imposing one's will on the enemy is synonymous with imposing one's plan on him. The elder Moltke's aphorism that no plan survives contact with the enemy is a profound truth. The aim must remain constant, but the plan to achieve it must be open to modification in the light of changing circumstances—and the commander must have the elasticity of mind to recognize altered circumstances and speedily reach a decision and adapt his plan accordingly. For instance, unexpected resistance or the appearance of a fleeting opportunity in one sector may require the shift of effort to another, more promising one. This requirement for flexibility means that a plan must be simple; a complicated plan is unlikely to survive the stress and friction of battle and cannot be easily or quickly adapted to meet unforeseen developments. It also underscores the need for balance, including, above all, the possession of a reserve, so that any change in the chosen course of action can be accomplished rapidly, without time-consuming regrouping. The ability to commit a reserve is usually the most significant way a commander can influence the course of a battle, whether to exploit an opportunity or deal in good time with an unexpected threat.[10] Not infrequently, the outcome of an operation depends on which side runs out of reserves first. The need for flexibility also puts a premium on having an efficient staff directing well-trained, agile, and responsive forces with good communications and a high level of mobility.

Cooperation. At all levels, the foundation stone is a clear and common aim coupled with a clear division of responsibilities. US doctrine stresses unity of command as essential. At the tactical level, this principle implies little more than ensuring that the combined-arms team works smoothly without interarm or interservice rivalries or conflicts to prevent the synergies that make the whole so much more effective than the sum of the parts. This is, of course, far easier to demand than to achieve. Even in the relatively simple Napoleonic period, Clausewitz was driven to observe: "Everything in war is very simple but the simplest thing is difficult. The difficulties accumulate and end by producing the kind of friction that is inconceivable unless one has experienced war."[11] The number of parts in the military machine that have to interact harmoniously has increased logarithmically since those days. At the operational level, the increasing size and complexity of formations and their logistic support create greater scope for cooperation to falter. This is the case even when everyone wants the machine to run like clockwork and agrees on what is required. This was far from the case with the land-air interface during the Second World War, where senior soldiers and airmen, especially British ones, had both philosophical and practical disagreements about the purpose and control of airpower. Introduce the complicating factors of clashing personalities and coalition operations, where national prejudices combine with a mutual lack of comprehension, a different way of doing things, and often disparate goals, and the opportunities for breakdown become legion. Allied operations in northwest Europe in 1944 were frequently marred by poor interservice and inter-Allied cooperation.

Sustainability. The outcome of many battles and an even greater number of operations has been decided by logistic considerations, what in the Second World War was termed "administration." A clear appreciation of supply and transport constraints is every bit as important to success as a commander's correct estimate of the operational situation. Logistic resources take time to accumulate, and time is a scarce commodity for an army desirous of retaining the initiative and freedom of action. Thus, while it is necessary to predict accurately how much of everything will be required to sustain an operation through to its planned conclusion, it is undesirable to overinsure; doing so wastes time, possibly prejudicing surprise, and leaves some other part of the force deprived of assets it could use to good effect. Logistic economy is as necessary as economy of effort; therefore, to ensure flexibility in the deployment and timely switching of resources to meet the unexpected, control must be exerted at the highest possible level To achieve the level of foresight required, the logistics staff must be taken into the commander's confidence early in the planning process, and must work closely with the operations staff.

To some readers, the principles outlined above may seem unhelpfully general, even platitudinous. Yet disregard of one or more of them runs the risk of failure. As will be seen, the summer campaign of 1944 provides many examples of generals who were guilty of such disregard, with predictably adverse consequences. Subjected to the pressures of high command, even the most intelligent, professionally well educated, and experienced commanders could make the misjudgments examined in subsequent chapters.

Although official manuals describe the foregoing principles rather grandly as principles of war, they are in fact only principles of operational art and tactics. By this misnaming, the British and Americans armies showed that they conflated war and battle. This is not merely a matter of semantics. It is important to differentiate between the two, as they require different approaches, different thinking. Battle is simply a matter of how to apply military force. The prosecution of war involves a whole range of nonmilitary instruments such as economic, financial, political, ideological, and informational, which are often more important than the military. Moreover, principles that may apply to the conduct of an operation or a battle are an insufficient guide to the formation of a strategy or even the preparation and conduct of a campaign. First, the enemy centre of gravity must be correctly identified. Given that it is rarely reachable through a single operational gambit, the possible routes to that centre must be determined; then the least unsatisfactory course of action must be found, based on assessments of the relative risks and costs in lives and time and the amount of each that can be expended. Then it is necessary to determine the optimal sequence in which operations and battles should be conducted to maximize the damage inflicted on the enemy while minimizing the loss to friendly forces. Because they failed to differentiate between campaigning and battle, the Western Allies sometimes failed to identify a clear and consistent operational aim and to synchronize their actions to optimal effect, avoiding unnecessary combat. General Montgomery himself illustrated this doctrinal failing in his damning verdict on the Italian campaign: "The High Command . . . embarked on a major campaign on the continent of Europe without having any clear idea or plan as to how they would develop and fight the land battle. There was no object laid down. The whole affair was haphazard and untidy—in fact typically British."[12]

THE CHALLENGES OF COMMAND

Numbers and equipment, doctrine and training are all important determinants of an army's performance in war. Even more important is the ability of its commander. A mediocre general can achieve less than stellar success with a fine force. An inspired and inspiring commander can coax astonishing feats from an apparently tired or merely workaday army. This section examines the requirements of generalship, primarily at the operational level and primarily from the point of view of the side holding the initiative, the happy position of the Allies in the late summer of 1944.

Tactical command, even at the highest level (generally corps), is a relatively straightforward business, however confusing, uncertain, and disorganized battles turn out to be. The commander is bound by the resource, time, and space constraints imposed by his superior. His task is the conceptually simple one of bringing superior firepower to bear on the enemy in close proximity to destroy him or to take ground (or both), synchronizing his fire and movement capabilities to optimal effect to do so. His sole concern is the immediate battle, with the limited terrain and time horizons this implies.

His unit or formation is a cog in a larger machine, and it must behave at least predictably (if not completely like a cog) to avoid throwing the machine into disarray.

Operational command is more complex and taxing. The higher the level, the less clear-cut the aim and the more numerous the possible paths to realizing the ambitions of strategy; ambiguities and uncertainties abound. The spatial scope and time scale of operations are much wider than at the tactical level. Instead of merely destroying the near enemy's short-term capability in battle, the commander has to disrupt the plans, future as well as current, of the enemy's higher command. He has to seize and hold the initiative, force the enemy into a merely reactive posture, and then keep him there. He has to do so over a wide area by orchestrating over the mid to long term a whole series of land-air battles and operations; these must be synchronized and sequenced in such a way as to create synergies that are greater than the sum of the parts. Moreover, factors other than purely military ones can affect decisions, planning, and the conduct of operations. And failure has repercussions that are much more severe; it is always possible to recover from a tactical defeat, but an operational reverse can lead to campaign failure. In other words, it is not an incremental but a step change from corps to army command and an even bigger one from army to army group.

It is sufficient for the tactical commander to be a sound, determined, and unflappable technician of battle. He deals with the here and now and does not require vision (although, like any craftsman with architectural ambitions, he would be better for it). The operational commander, however, must be able to apply the principles of war imaginatively and long-sightedly. He must be able to calculate and balance time and space factors several weeks in advance; like a grand master in chess, he must be able to look several moves ahead, anticipating enemy reactions to each possible move. He must shape the situation in the area of operations so that he can inexorably push the enemy into a position that will be his downfall. Moreover, he needs to be long-sighted because his decisions will take time to implement, and any misjudgment will take even longer to rectify. Thus, command at the operational level generally requires not only ability of a high order but also education and training to harness and direct that ability down the most productive path. But, unlike the German army and the Red Army, no operational theory or doctrine had been propounded by the American and British armies. They had no academies teaching operational art to ensure that formation staffs had the expertise to understand operational demands and translate them into appropriate orders. These armies promoted technically competent commanders with proven leadership skills from the tactical to the operational level and hoped they would rise to a challenge that was only dimly understood. Some did, but many subconsciously regarded an army or even an army group as little more than a corps writ large. Understanding battle but not war, they planned operations that were often little more than a series of disconnected battles lacking a unifying logic—essentially an attritional approach. Of course, such an approach can—and did—bring success, but at a greater cost in casualties and time than a more imaginative one would have involved.

The Commander

In his chapter on command ("On Military Genius"), Clausewitz considers the various attributes that make a great general. As a starting point, he reminds the reader: "Four elements make up the climate of war: danger, exertion, uncertainty and chance. If we consider them together, it becomes evident how much fortitude of mind and character are needed to make progress in these impeding elements with safety and success."[13] It is also clear that there can be no template, no rules and regulations for the art of generalship. To an extent, it is a product of experience, education, and training.[14] But of equal or greater importance are the facets considered below, which are, inevitably, both complementary and overlapping. Though all are significant, the greatest are arguably personality and originality:

> [The commander] is the personification of the force he commands. His aptitude for war and his character, his morale and his will to triumph are the essential ingredients that weld and focus the will and effort of his command to win. The commander is the source of the command's driving logic and the application of this logic to the achievement of its object. It is he who makes the military decisions . . . [and] is responsible for the outcome, win or lose.[15]

A successful practitioner thus encapsulates the crushing burden of responsibility that weighs on the operational commander. It is a responsibility he cannot share, although many lesser generals try. Of course, style of command is an intensely personal, indeed, idiosyncratic business, and generals vary widely in their approach. To be successful, however, all need to have in substantial measure the qualities enumerated below.

Leadership and Command. At the operational level—army, and especially army group or theatre—the commander has a more difficult task than his subordinates. As a somewhat Olympian figure, he cannot personally lead troops. A commander may be able to select those who do so and send them into battle familiar with his ideas and ways; more often, perhaps, he inherits those selected by others. In any case, he must first make a definite decision and then articulate it with clarity and ensure that his subordinates understand the goal and the path to its achievement. He must ensure that they have the necessary competence and leadership abilities to get their men to achieve the aim. Inevitably, however, some subordinates will possess inadequate intelligence, or they may have been promoted beyond their level of competence, or they may lack the character to provide forceful and consistent leadership. The commander is not always able to sack them (or have them moved, or even promoted, to jobs where they can do no harm). He must work with the tools he has been given, being careful to assign missions that are within the abilities of each executor.[16] Having done so, he must be constantly ready to exercise "grip" to prevent his operation from going off the rails or floundering through insufficient effort or lack of understanding on the part of his subordinates. How much initiative he allows each one and how much detailed direction he provides should vary according to their individual abilities, but he always needs plenty of drive to get things done despite the friction of war and the failings of the executors of his will.

Another failing that can be just as dangerous as a lack of grip is overcontrol:

> The advantage that a commander believes he achieves through continuous personal intervention is mostly only an apparent one. He thereby takes over functions for whose fulfillment other persons are designated. He more or less denigrates their abilities and increases his own duties to such a degree that he can no longer fulfill them completely. . . . It is far more important that the higher commander retains a clear perspective of the entire state of affairs than that any detail is carried out in any particular way.[17]

In this way, Moltke, three-quarters of a century before the campaign analyzed in the following chapters, described the twin dangers of overcontrol. Subordinates are disempowered and thus discouraged from using their own judgment to exercise initiative and make independent, timely decisions. And the commander becomes immersed in tactical minutiae rather than giving his full attention to the operational problems that only he can deal with. It was these considerations that led the German to his dictum: "In general one does well to order no more than is absolutely necessary and to avoid planning beyond the situations one can foresee." The commander should focus on the tasks that only he can do. Everything else should be left to his staff and the leaders of subordinate formations and units. Partly through tradition and partly because of doctrinal shortcomings, the commanders of army groups and armies of the Western Allies were prone to the faults against which Moltke warned.

The commander must also inspire his subordinates' trust and confidence in him, in the aims he has set, and in his readiness to support them on the way. "It is the leader who applies force on the battlefield, but it is the commander who unleashes and directs it—and all those in his command must trust that his understanding of force will allow them to conquer."[18] Each commander differs in character and personality, but each in his own way must achieve "that mixture of example, persuasion and compulsion which makes men do what you want them to do."[19] Some put more emphasis on the power to dominate, whereas others stress persuasion, but whichever route is followed, the commander must inspire a sense of purpose and confidence among not only senior subordinates but also troops. "The commander is the primary source of morale for his men. . . . Equally, the commander must sustain his own high morale—for it is that which will help him endure the isolation of decision, and those grinding days and nights during which he assumes the risks and uncertainties."[20]

Professionalism and Judgment. Naturally, the senior general must be knowledgeable about his trade, and by 1944, that included the air dimension as well, since battles and campaigns had become three-dimensional. But the knowledge required is that of a generalist who understands the capabilities and limitations of his own and enemy forces, has a feel for the military implications of terrain, and, especially, has a grasp of the mechanics of movement and supply.[21] Moreover, the commander's level of knowledge must be appropriate to his level of command; too many competent corps and army commanders, for instance, have been promoted to the next level without the necessary education, understanding, or ability to cope with problems that are more challenging by an order of magnitude. But he does not need to be an expert and should not become involved in arcane detail. He will have experts on his staff, and he must be able to recognize when their advice is necessary, to judge its soundness, and to identify and concentrate on the essentials of any problem. While professional knowledge is obviously necessary, it is not sufficient. Many generals have possessed it yet lacked the judgment to use it effectively. "War," as Clausewitz pointed out, "is the realm of uncertainty; three quarters of the factors on which action in war is based are wrapped in a fog of greater or lesser uncertainty."[22] The commander needs common sense and a clear mind to sort out the possible from the unlikely, to distinguish essentials from the mass of details offered to him, to identify fundamental problems and find workable solutions. There will inevitably be competing priorities and uncertainties in the planning and command process, not to mention unwelcome and too often fudged logistic constraints. Sound judgment (even educated intuition) is required to find the best compromise in the circumstances (for all plans are, at bottom, compromises). Judgment is also essential in the selection of key staff officers and subordinate commanders, in assessing their characters and abilities, and in apportioning tasks to capitalize on their strengths and compensate for their weaknesses.

Courage and Resolution. In the era of machine-age mass warfare, physical courage is a less important qualification for high command than it was when personal leadership in combat was de rigueur. It does, however, influence the degree of risk a senior officer is prepared to take to see for himself what is going on and to motivate the men serving under him. Moral courage is vital to make the difficult decisions that will cost men's lives in the uncertain situations that characterize war. It is also desirable for a general to speak up when he disagrees with his commander or has doubts about the wisdom of a proposed course of action. It is all too easy for a command to succumb to groupthink and to overlook better courses of action because of subservience to a forceful boss. Obstacles, setbacks, criticism, and prophecies of failure attend all operations. A general must have the robustness of character to take these in his stride without vacillating or losing his grip. Moreover, he must exude self-confidence and a will to win, whatever his private doubts. Those who become depressed under stress or when things are going badly lose their positive influence over subordinates; indeed, they can damage morale because nothing is more infectious than pessimism, which can easily lead to a self-fulfilling prophecy. Equally fatal to success is a lack of drive to get things done. As General Patton pointed out, "Commanders must remember that the issue of an order, or the devising of a plan, is only about 5 per cent of the responsibility of command. The other 95 per cent is to insure, by personal observation, or through the interposing of staff officers, that the order is carried out."[23] Even worse is a lack of resolution to see a chosen course of action through to the end. Any signs of wavering or hesitation will be picked up and will adversely affect the whole formation.

Stamina and Vitality. The uncertainties of war and the tremendous intellectual and moral stresses of command require that generals be physically healthy as well as mentally robust—if only because the latter state is largely dependent on the former. A sick or even a very tired commander cannot be relied on to make sound decisions and plans and see them through to fruition with the necessary energy and determination. And only when a commander is clearly fit and radiating confidence, determination, and energy can he do one of his main jobs—inspiring his subordinates and his soldiers to the exertions required of them. As Patton pertinently wrote: "There are more tired division commanders than tired divisions. Tired officers are always pessimists."[24] It is the task of the army commander to supply the necessary drive when fatigue and doubts start to sap the energy of his subordinates. To do this he must remain fit and properly rested and must avoid being worn out by doing others' work either as displacement activity or through lack of trust in his staff.

Decisiveness and Boldness. A commander generally lacks certainty about the situation thanks to an insufficient amount of reliable, objective, and up-to-date intelligence about the enemy or even about his own forces. The reports that underpin his understanding are frequently late or partial and intentionally or unintentionally misleading; they always reflect individual interpretations (perhaps exaggerating dangers or cavalierly overlooking them) and thus are often contradictory. Moreover, he has little time for the calm reflection that is desirable when making important decisions. Nevertheless, from such obscurity he must reach, or infer, an understanding of the situation and make a decision. Rushed decisions are often mistaken, but usually much worse is prolonged, especially agonized hesitation (often disguised as waiting for the situation to be clarified). Perhaps the worst fault of all is indecision. Many battles and operations are decided by which side makes the best use of the limited time available. Beating the enemy to the punch is often a better determinant of outcome than superior numbers or weaponry. Decisions, right or wrong, must be made in a timely manner, allowing the staff to prepare and pass down orders and for minor formations and units to go through proper battle procedures; otherwise, things are likely to go wrong. Moreover, decisions ought to be bold (which, of course, requires moral courage).[25] Unless the commander possesses overwhelming combat power, in which case generalship becomes less important, all operations entail risk. Very often, the potential reward is proportionate to the level of risk the commander is prepared to tolerate. He must have the nerve to take a calculated risk, albeit one based on sound military judgment and not mere foolhardiness. Audacity is a good way to surprise the enemy, put him on the back foot, and thus accomplish the commander's first task—imposing his will on his opponent. By contrast, the general whose watchword is safety first rarely catches and keeps the enemy off balance. Caution may ensure against failure, but it will not bring great victories either, probably only an attritional grind.

Imagination and Flexibility. To rise above the mediocre, generalship requires more than professional knowledge and everyday competence—more than an adherence to the proven ways of the past taught in staff colleges everywhere. At the operational level, it presupposes creativity, an ability to cope with the challenge posed by an abstract aim and to assemble a variety of tactical and operational events to make a coherent whole that is greater than the sum of the parts. Creativity, including the ability to avoid stereotype and think laterally, is of an altogether higher order than initiative. It requires imagination to read the mind of the enemy commander, predict his reactions, deceive him, exploit his weaknesses, and foresee possible developments in an operation. This insightfulness is the basis of the creativity and originality that are central to generalship.[26] In any plan, these are the qualities that, when coupled with bold and vigorous execution, surprise and outwit the enemy, gain the initiative, and win the battle for time. At the same time, foresight born of insight helps planners minimize the element of chance that causes so many plans to unravel (especially the complex ones that are most vulnerable to the effects of friction). Foresight is particularly important in ensuring that the logistic demands of an operation are anticipated and provided through to its intended conclusion; too often, tactical and initial operational successes are squandered by logistic failure. Flexibility, too, comes from insight and a creative, agile mind. It is usually required at some point, possibly to modify the plan to seize an advantage offered by an unexpected opportunity, possibly to circumvent an unexpected difficulty, possibly even, in extremis, to change the decision on which the operation is based if developments show that it is inappropriate. The border between praiseworthy resolution in adhering to a course of action and obstinate refusal to change it, whatever the circumstances, can be quite fine; usually such obduracy is the result of a closed mind that refuses to admit error, however obvious it becomes.

Integrity and Realism. To make sound decisions, the commander must be honest with himself. He must face up to and deal with the situation as it is, not as it ought to be. It is all too tempting to accept without challenge reports that are pleasing and reject those that are uncongenial; it is all too easy to establish, even unconsciously, a reputation with subordinates and staff that one wants to hear only good news and is critical of those who bring bad. The commander who encourages his subordinates and staff to be yes-men is setting himself up for failure. One particular problem involves the area of greatest uncertainty—a realistic assessment of the enemy's capabilities and intentions. In the absence of hard intelligence, it is easy to "situate the appreciation," to make assumptions about the enemy that accord with preconceived ideas and impart legitimacy to a desired course of action. Thereafter, plans tend to specify what the enemy will do in each phase of an operation, forgetting that the enemy actually has a vote too.

The commander must be straightforward with his superiors, being prepared to report the bad news as well as the good, his failures as well as his successes. The more senior the commander, the more critical it becomes for him to have a true picture of the situation as it unfolds.[27] Honesty (or at least the ability to fake it convincingly) and moral courage are critical in another way, too. Preparedness to take responsibility for failure and loyalty to both superiors and (just as important, but much rarer) subordinates are the foundations of mutual trust. It is trust that welds the links in the chain of command and ensures its durability when adversity is encountered. Careerist opportunism, flattery, and back-stabbing have enabled officers to rise to senior positions but have never made for success in war.

Political Understanding and Sensitivity. The more senior a commander, the more important it is that he understand and be sensitive to political considerations, both interservice and governmental. At army group and especially at theatre level, this is a sine qua non. Battles and campaigns are fought by land-air (and often maritime) forces, and even when the army leads, proper consideration must be given to the needs and desires, as well as the contributions, of the other services. And while battles are fought for military objectives, war is waged for political ones. In the strategic arena, and at its interface with operational art, the commander must remember and accept, however galling, the primacy of political direction over his perceived optimal military solution. Political requirements trump the militarily desirable every time. "War," wrote Clausewitz in one of his most quoted aphorisms, "is an act of policy . . . a true political instrument, a continuation of political intercourse carried on with other means. . . . The political object is the goal, war is the means of reaching it, and means can never be considered in isolation from their purpose."[28] Obstinate insistence on a politically unacceptable course of action will inevitably result in dismissal or, at best, loss of credibility and influence. To further complicate the life of the commander, political aims are sometimes vague or subject to modification, or his political masters may have more than one desired end that are, moreover, incompatible or impractical. Allies present another problem, one that sometimes exceeds an alliance's military value. Poor management of relations with allies can compromise combined operations. Even when an allied formation is under command, its commander usually has to be persuaded rather than merely ordered to fulfill his allotted role, for if antagonized, he can disobey as long as he has the backing of his government.

In myriad ways, command is a qualitatively different, altogether more difficult business at the theatre or even army group level compared with the operational-tactical interface. It is hardly surprising that many successful tactical and even army commanders cannot rise to the demands of high command.

The Staff

Given the size, complexity, and geographic spread of modern armies, the commander is dependent on his staff for support and assistance. He exercises command and is responsible for the outcome of an operation. However, to reach his decision, he depends on information and advice from a formidable array of experts and specialists in everything from intelligence and logistics to communications and meteorology. Having reached a decision, perhaps after considering a variety of possible courses presented by the staff, he produces a concept of operations and an outline plan and sets priorities. Careful, accurate staff work then fleshes out his plan into clear and comprehensible orders to the numerous components of the military machine that will execute it. As the staff works out all the details related to execution, the commander can turn his attention to other, more important and (it is hoped) more creative matters. Once the operation is set in train, he largely relies on his staff for control—that is, the organization, direction, coordination, and supervision of the formation's actions. The staff continually monitors the development of the operation and the fighting condition and material welfare of the troops, keeping the commander informed so that he can modify his concept and assignments in a timely fashion. The staff is also—or at least it ought to be—the servant of subordinate formations and units, ensuring that the commander is aware of their problems and requirements and coping with these issues itself, insofar as it can. Thus, the commanding general is the brain of the military body, and the staff acts as the nervous system. For the body to respond to the commander as he would wish, the staff must be fully apprised of the commander's intent and must work in an efficient, cooperative, and timely fashion to realize it.

The commander has to be able to trust his staff and should never try to do his own staff work.[29] One of the staff's main jobs is to give the commander the time and space to carry out his two most important tasks—to think, and to visit and exert influence on his subordinate commanders as he comes to understand their problems, concerns, and states of mind, their strengths and their weaknesses. The general should do only the things that only he can do. If he spends most of his time at his main headquarters immersing himself in the details of planning and control, he is forgetting both his function and that of his staff, which is there to serve him. He lays himself open to the charge of "château generalship."[30] Moreover, he sets a bad example for commanders of lower formations, who will think it is both excusable and necessary to be forever at the end of a telephone or radio link when they should be leading.

The lynchpin of the system is the chief of staff. It is he who organizes and directs staff activity, ensuring its smooth running and its responsiveness to direction and to developing situations by providing feedback and help to subordinate formations and units. The chief of staff must always be in his commander's mind and share his vision of operations. He is the commander's closest adviser. He must be able and trusted to act in the commander's name, including making decisions when the latter is absent.[31] Thus it is essential that there be a close working relationship, based on mutual understanding and trust, between a commander and his chief of staff.

Staffs should be kept as small as possible while adequately covering all necessary functions. This allows more rapid movement and displacement, not to mention easier concealment. Most important, the more staff officers there are, the greater the likelihood that the disadvantages of excessive bureaucracy—empire building, jurisdictional quarrels, buck-passing, the generation of nugatory work, confusion, and, above all, delay—will adversely affect the work of the headquarters (HQ). The larger the staff, the greater the control but the lower the probability that the commander's intent will be implemented correctly; the potential for error and deviation increases as more people are involved. And a large staff takes more time to do things. Thus the Americans' generous provision of resources was not without a downside when it came to staffs; an infantry division in 1944, for instance, contained one-third more officers than its German equivalent, and the disparity grew with the size of the formation. The HQ of Second British Army in Normandy comprised 189 officers and 970 other ranks, while that of First US Army grew to 375 officers and 639 of other ranks. By contrast, the staff of a German army was about 300 of all ranks, including everyone from radio operators and technicians to drivers and cooks.[32]

A more serious cause of delay was the mind-set of the majority of Allied commanders, who were generally reluctant to empower their subordinates. Decisions during the course of operations that the Germans would have left to the judgment of subordinates were referred upward by the Allies; following due deliberation, fresh orders would be issued (often elaborate by German standards) and transmitted downward for action. All this took time, even when communications were working smoothly. These things matter in the battle for time, which is exceedingly important, especially in mobile operations. Tempo is not purely a function of how fast units and formations can move in relation to the enemy. Often more important is how fast they can react to altered circumstances. The speed at which a headquarters can respond is a significant factor in determining the pace of operations. For instance, an attacker who has the enemy off balance may fail to retain his advantage if the defender can get inside his intelligence-decision-action cycle when committing a reserve or redeploying to plug a gap. In a meeting battle, where both sides are attempting to achieve their aim through offensive action and they clash on the move, relative reaction times become critical. When it comes to maneuver warfare, the side that practices decentralized command, granting wide latitude for the exercise of initiative, enjoys an advantage that can sometimes compensate for a lack of numerical strength. The summer of 1944, as will be seen, provides several examples of this factor at work.

The Chain of Command in the Allied Expeditionary Forces: Theory, Practice, and Personalities

The ability of a general to display generalship depends greatly on the responsibilities he is given and the extent to which he is allowed to exercise his talents, unfettered by his superiors. It is thus important, before venturing an assessment of any commander, to probe beneath the theoretical chain of command to see how the system actually worked, what freedoms he was allowed, and what constraints were imposed on him. In theory, it was very straightforward. The theatre level provided strategic direction, specifying the aim and objectives and producing a campaign plan that set out how these goals would be achieved. This included the roles of all three armed services, measures to ensure cooperation among them and between army groups, political or other constraints, and the provision of logistic support. Army groups decided, in cooperation with the relevant air and maritime components, what operations were required to fulfill their part of the campaign plan and whether they would be sequential or simultaneous. Broad directives were then issued to the various armies. Armies were tasked with executing a series of operations and allocated the resources deemed necessary to do so. The army commander, having analyzed his task, broke it down into missions for each of his corps, assigned formations and combat and service support to each, and set out the parameters within which each would operate; he also arranged the air contribution, which he worked out with his supporting airman. The army commander's main concern was not the immediate battle but the whole operation, each comprising a series of maneuvers and battles stretching two to three weeks into the future; he had to be able to look ahead to ensure that his command was as well placed to fight the last of these battles as it was for the first. The army level was also the primary focus of administrative and logistic efforts. The corps then executed the movements and fought the tactical battles required by the army. Corps commanders were not required to look any further ahead than the current battle, perhaps two or three days, and they were largely absolved of logistic responsibilities. At each stage, the missions became narrower and more specific, and the method similarly became more prescriptive with more constraints (e.g., as to timing, ammunition and fuel availability, boundaries). In the operational if not the strategic arena, this was supposed to be an iterative process, responsive to changes in the situation. Theory, however, was not always mirrored in practice.

The British gained considerable experience from both world wars in organizing operational command. Many failures were experienced and many casualties suffered before reasonably efficient army and superior headquarters emerged and their commanders and staffs learned to work together. Even then, they were more ponderous, bureaucratic, and slow moving than those of the agile German enemy. The US Army had only four months of combat experience in 1918 to provide a doctrinal basis for the creation and running of such entities. Prior to the establishment of 12 Army Group in July 1944, the Americans had had no involvement at all at that echelon (Pershing had been in the process of setting up such an HQ when the armistice intervened in 1918). The Americans, even more than the British, suffered from a shortage of fully trained and competent staff officers, and many senior and general officers were catapulted into ranks and jobs that stretched their knowledge, experience, and competence. Although some who had learned through doing at the corps and division levels in North Africa and Sicily (and, in a very few cases, the Pacific) went into the armies of the European theatre of operations (ETO), most came directly from the United States. When these inescapable problems and limitations of personnel and doctrine are taken into account, the inadequacies, mistakes, and failures are far less remarkable than the extraordinarily high overall level of proficiency achieved by operational HQs and, to a varying extent, their commanders. Plainly, the pre–senior command experience of the latter, especially practical experience in exercising significant responsibility in real battle, had a bearing on their later performance.

The theatre commander, Dwight D. Eisenhower, was born in 1890. He did not become a soldier from any sense of vocation; he was attracted by the free college education afforded by West Point. He became an infantry officer and then an early and enthusiastic member of the new Tank Corps. In 1918 he was about to leave for France with his unit as a National Army lieutenant colonel when the war ended. Reverting to his peacetime US Army rank of captain, he initially retained his enthusiasm for armor, though this faded in the face of establishment disapproval. He spent the interwar years pursuing a military education, formal and otherwise, and performing staff jobs, once again becoming a lieutenant colonel in 1936. He had, however, been noticed by the future Chief of Staff of the Army, George C. Marshall, who considered him an officer with great promise. With another war approaching, Eisenhower was given a succession of good staff appointments and, briefly, command of a battalion. But he had never commanded troops above that level until he was appointed commanding general of the ETO in June 1942 as a lieutenant general. In November he was appointed Supreme Allied Commander in North Africa, and three months later he was promoted to four-star rank. A champion of inter-Allied cooperation, Eisenhower worked hard to create a genuinely binational headquarters. He persuaded British and American operational commanders to work together to implement a campaign for the Mediterranean theatre, although the actual military-technical side of the planning process was dominated by his British component chiefs. His success in this very problematic endeavor ensured his choice, at the start of 1944, as commander of the ETO and Supreme Commander of the Allied Expeditionary Forces (AEF). Preparing for the invasion and overseeing its execution through the Normandy phase involved balancing the views, requirements, and prejudices of the national political leaderships, both nations' chiefs of staff, and the three component commanders on issues of strategy, operational concept, and command. While this was his primary challenge—one that must have seemed like trying to square a circle—he also had to attend to ETO business and manage his more important subordinates, most of whom had inflated egos and very decided views.

Eisenhower proved to be an exemplary staff officer and a man of great charisma and ability, although he lacked boldness and originality. Above all he demonstrated a rare competence in the areas of alliance management and the political-military interface.[33] But his thorough education in military affairs and patronage by Marshall did not make up for his deficiencies in experience. When dealing with operational questions, he lacked both a firm grasp of the practical and the natural authority conferred on a successful practitioner by past achievements—and he was aware of this weakness.[34] This shortcoming, coupled with the inclination of the successful political manager to seek compromise and consensus, probably accounted for his occasional inconsistency and lack of decisiveness when faced with operational decisions. Whatever the reason, the direction coming from Supreme Headquarters, Allied Expeditionary Forces (SHAEF) in the summer of 1944 was not always firm enough to keep Eisenhower's willful army group commanders, particularly Montgomery, in line and to keep their eyes fixed on a common aim. The aim itself, as set down by the Combined Chiefs of Staff, consisted of "operations aimed at the heart of Germany and the destruction of her Armed Forces." Yet this aim became somewhat mutable. From the later days of the Normandy fighting, the destruction of the enemy's forces seemed to take second place to the conquest of territory, not all of it leading to Germany's political or economic centre of gravity. Operational concepts were also subject to modification or change, not only because the situation had changed but also because Eisenhower was being urged in different directions. His army group commanders had very different ideas about how the campaign should be prosecuted. Their professional disagreements were increasingly fueled and aggravated by doctrinal and cultural differences, mutual incomprehension and distrust, and by personal and national rivalries and antipathies. They did more than lobby vigorously for their concepts; they were quite prepared to subvert their Supreme Commander's direction. And there was another problem that loomed over all their arguments, threatening to invalidate operational decisions: the unyielding tyranny of logistics.

Direction from the top became uncertain, and in the absence of a firm grip by the Supreme Commander, his wayward principal subordinates were not going to cooperate of their own volition. Their operational aims and axes diverged, and as a result, effort was dissipated; logistic objectives vital to the Allied cause were sidelined, despite their urgency. Unity of effort was lost at the operational-strategic level, but the army group commanders were determined that it would be enforced at the operational level. Their operations would be executed according to a unified concept because they would personally ensure it. Particularly in the case of 21 Army Group, this led to another straying from theory in the direction of overcontrol, a tendency that was exacerbated when personal prejudices were allowed to intrude on command relationships.

Bernard L. Montgomery had gone to war in 1914 as a twenty-seven-year-old lieutenant. By the war's end he was an acting lieutenant colonel and division chief of staff. After an interwar career that involved the usual British mix of command and staff jobs both at home and in the empire, he was given a division to command in 1938. He commanded another in France in 1939–1940, impressing his superiors by his role in covering the retreat to Dunkirk. There followed a corps and then a district command defending southern England. Strongly backed by his mentor General Brooke, the Chief of the Imperial General Staff (CIGS), Montgomery was sent to command the Eighth Army in Egypt in August 1942. His great victory at Alamein and the subsequent Tunisian campaign made him a national hero, and his pedestrian performance in Sicily and Italy did nothing to shake that reputation. He was appointed interim commander of land forces for the Normandy invasion on the back of this formidable prestige. Montgomery had boundless faith in his own abilities. No other general—certainly no American, he believed—could match his level of understanding and professionalism. He directed the land campaign in Normandy with much-needed consistency and firmness but without flair (though well read, he was no original military thinker), and he rationalized the inevitable failures on the way to victory or blamed them on subordinates. He was deeply resentful when Eisenhower ended his role as interim ground commander and took charge personally in early September. Montgomery tried to bully or occasionally cajole the Supreme Commander into adopting and enforcing his favored operational concept, until he was threatened with dismissal in December.

As commander of 21 Army Group, Montgomery believed that only his personal direction and supervision of all significant operational and even many tactical actions could guarantee success at an acceptable cost in casualties. With only some exaggeration, he could be described as trying to run 21 Army Group as if it were Eighth Army writ larger. His HQ was writ very large indeed, having almost 750 officers to do much of the work that, in theory, should have occurred at the army level.[35] In key areas, he decided on the concept of operations, which battles to fight, when to fight them, and, to a large extent, how they should be fought (often bypassing the chain of command and going straight to corps commanders). In major operations, his army commanders were left with relatively few and often less important decisions. Their HQs were required merely to flesh out the staff work done at the army group level, implement the logistic decisions made from above, and supervise the execution of operations; they were not trusted to accomplish this last task without close supervision. The General Headquarters (GHQ) Liaison Regiment (known as Phantom) and Montgomery's staff of personal liaison officers continuously and extensively monitored activities throughout the army group.

Montgomery tended to form strong prejudices about people, particularly those who were not his own selections. He insisted, whenever possible, on employing only those who accepted without reservation the Montgomery legend and his way of doing business. He had only qualified confidence in his Second Army commander, Dempsey, and very little in First Canadian's commander, Crerar. The latter he dismissed as an inadequate leader with no experience of senior command. Crerar had been foisted on him by the Canadian government for political reasons and was irritatingly insistent about his national responsibilities. While Dempsey, Montgomery's protégé, showed more promise, he was new to army-level command in Normandy and could not approach the skill and understanding of the master. Montgomery frequently encroached on the areas of authority that properly belonged to his British and Dominion subordinates.[36]

Until 1 September, when Eisenhower assumed the role of chief of land forces, Lieutenant General Bradley also came under Montgomery's authority, first as commander of US First Army and then as 12 Army Group commander. Montgomery was just as convinced of his vastly superior generalship over Bradley as he was with regard to his British and Canadian underlings—more so, in fact, as he believed, like most senior British officers, that the Americans were essentially untutored amateurs. He recognized, however, that alliance considerations, not to mention Bradley's powerful patrons, required that the American be treated with more circumspection. Montgomery did not—indeed, could not—order Bradley about as he pleased and intrude on his areas of responsibility. Montgomery dealt with Bradley with unusual tact and consideration, but also with an assumption of superiority and an air of patronizing condescension that the American found increasingly insufferable. Bradley was able to dissemble his growing dislike, just as he had concealed the grudges that developed in the wake of the Sicilian campaign. When a breach between the two men became inevitable, it proved all the more shocking to Montgomery, who had expected Bradley to be an ally in persuading Eisenhower to adopt his concept of operations and not an opponent with ideas of his own.

Like Eisenhower, his West Point classmate and fellow infantryman, Omar N. Bradley did not fight in the 1914–1918 war and became a regular lieutenant colonel in 1934. Also like Eisenhower, he was picked out by Marshall as capable, dependable, and a future leader during his interwar round of teaching, being taught, and doing staff jobs. Bradley got his chance in early 1942 when he took command of an infantry division. A year later, after successfully preparing two divisions for war, he was posted to Tunisia, where he would soon succeed Patton as commander of II Corps. He led the corps through the rest of the North African campaign and then the one in Sicily before being moved to England to take over First Army for the invasion of France. He proved capable enough at that level, consolidating his part of the lodgment, taking Cherbourg, and then expanding southward, albeit much more slowly than hoped for and at far greater cost. A cautious, conservative-minded general, Bradley was slow to realize that American methods were neither cost-effective nor decisive. On 1 August Bradley took command of the new 12 Army Group. After just over seven weeks of commanding an army in combat, he was stepping into a job unfamiliar to any American officer. Unsurprisingly, he made a somewhat uncertain start and provided weak direction for the rest of the Normandy campaign. He would grow in confidence over time and eventually developed his own views on the desirable direction of post-Normandy operations, in opposition to Montgomery's. Bradley attempted to persuade his old friend Eisenhower to go along with his ideas and was not above subverting the Supreme Commander's purpose when he did not.

Interwar theory suggested that an army group HQ should be concerned purely with operational matters, leaving logistics and other administration to the theatre and army levels, lest it become too large, cumbersome, and bureaucratic. Moreover, it should direct but not control the operations of its armies, issuing mission-type orders and eschewing detail. Bradley departed from both aspects of this theory. Before the end of 1944, his staff had grown from about 200 to 900 officers and was as engrossed in detail as an army-level staff.[37] Bradley, like Montgomery, was not the man to take a broad-brushed approach to command, trusting his subordinates to achieve his intent without close supervision. However, Bradley (unlike Patton) never developed the sort of close monitoring capability that Montgomery created in 21 Army Group. He spent much of his time trying to rein in his erstwhile boss, Patton, and ensure that his Third Army stayed within cautiously defined bounds. Reticent, straitlaced, even somewhat puritanical, Bradley perceived the flamboyant, profane, extroverted Patton as a glory hunter who was prone to ignore necessary detail and take unjustifiable risks. Bradley was much more sympathetic to his old friend Hodges, who had replaced him at First Army. They were temperamentally similar, both being conscientious, dependable, cautious, and somewhat dull, and they shared the same managerial approach to command. Nevertheless, Bradley saw Hodges as an understudy who lacked experience as a formation commander in combat and needed continuing mentoring and supervision.

Miles Dempsey, nine years younger than his boss, Montgomery, went to the western front in 1915 as a regular army infantry subaltern and ended the war as an acting captain and company commander. After an unexceptional postwar career as a regimental soldier, he was a lieutenant colonel leading a battalion in 1938. Shortly after he returned to France in 1939, he took over a brigade and was commended for his part in covering the withdrawal in 1940. Back in England, he took over a division in mid-1941 and then, at Montgomery's specific request, went to Egypt in late 1942 as an acting lieutenant general to command XIII Corps. More than a year of battlefield successes in North Africa and a plodding advance through Sicily and southern Italy followed. Having been confirmed in his rank and once again requested by Montgomery, Dempsey assumed command of Second Army for the cross-Channel attack. He brought considerable and invaluable experience to bear in preparing it for the invasion. He failed to take Caen on 6 June (an unrealistic D-Day objective anyway) but capably consolidated the lodgment achieved. He then methodically executed Montgomery's concept for the capture of Caen and at the same time pinned the Germans' armored strength in the eastern sector; the cost in casualties, though heavy, was probably as low as British methods could achieve. Dempsey, unsurprisingly, proved to be a very conventional army commander (though his plan for Operation Goodwood was novel); he was efficient, quietly effective, and flexible, even when burdened with the management of five corps. Self-effacing to an extraordinary degree, he was utterly loyal to Montgomery and suffered his superior's meddling with great patience.

H. D. G. (Harry) Crerar was born in 1888 and became a Non-Permanent Active Militia artillery officer. He was deployed with the Canadian Expeditionary Force in 1915 and had risen to the rank of lieutenant colonel just before the end of the war. He decided to remain in the tiny Permanent Force in 1919. Becoming an increasingly shrewd political operator, he worked his way up through a succession of staff jobs to become, in 1940, a major general and chief of the General Staff. He was, however, anxious for a field command. Originally slated to take over 2 Infantry Division, instead, as a newly promoted lieutenant general, he went straight to Canadian I Corps in England in late 1941. The corps HQ was sent to Italy late in 1943, but after only one month of command in a rather quiet period, Crerar was summoned back to England to head First Canadian Army. His HQ opened in Normandy only toward the end of July because Montgomery, distrusting his abilities and judgment, delayed deploying him for as long as possible. Crerar had very little practical, high-level operational experience, but he took a somewhat pedantic delight in the details of staff work. He lacked boldness and creativity but was loyal to Montgomery. He was also inclined to devote much of his time and energy to matters of purely national significance, to the detriment of operational matters and a good relationship with his army group commander.

On Bradley's elevation, he was succeeded at US First Army by his deputy, Courtney H. Hodges. Born in 1887, his ambition for a military career received an early setback when he was dismissed from West Point for failing in mathematics. Undeterred, he joined the army as a private soldier and obtained a commission as an infantry officer through competitive examination. During the First World War he distinguished himself through his bravery, leadership, and tactical ability, ending the war as a National Army lieutenant colonel commanding a regiment. Between the wars Hodges worked his way up to the rank of brigadier general in 1940, during the process becoming a friend of Bradley and winning the confidence of Marshall. In 1942 he took command of X Corps and the next year, as a lieutenant general, assumed command of its parent formation, Third Army. In January 1944 he became Bradley's deputy and understudy, taking over First Army when the latter moved up. During his career, Hodges acquired a great reputation as an infantry tactician. He carried this low-level, slow-moving mind-set with him into the operational sphere. He was undoubtedly dependable and industrious; he studied his problems with great care, but his solutions were neither bold nor creative, and he lacked flexibility in execution. A reserved, taciturn man, Hodges was far from an intellectual and lacked charisma; he was a manager rather than a forceful leader. Indeed, he left too much of the running of the army to his chief of staff while still managing to overcommand, interfering in tactical details rather than taking the broad view needed at the army level. Nevertheless, he was able to retain Bradley's good opinion and support throughout the campaign.

Two years older than Hodges, George S. Patton was also determined to have a military career. After academic failure required him to repeat a year at West Point, he was commissioned into the cavalry. During 1917–1918 he trained the US Army's first tank brigade, bravely and successfully commanding it in battle until being wounded. He finished the war as a National Army colonel. In the interwar years he continued to champion armor in the face of an official lack of interest. Disliking the nature of staff work, he avoided it as much as he could, preferring study (he was very well read in military history) and command. During a spell as commanding officer of a cavalry regiment, he came to the attention of General Marshall, who marked Patton's potential as a future senior commander especially well suited to mobile operations. During 1940 Patton was a leading figure in the creation of American armored forces. He took command of 2 Armored Division as a major general in April 1941 and nine months later of I Armored Corps. In early 1943, after II Corps' major defeat in Tunisia, he turned it around and led it to victory in the rest of the campaign. Commanding Seventh Army (really just a large II Corps) in the campaign in Sicily, he displayed great vigor and dash and some questionable judgment in conducting successful operational maneuvers. After a disgraceful incident in which he slapped two hospitalized soldiers, Patton's career was saved by Eisenhower, but the scandal may have cost him command of America's spearhead First Army and thereafter 12 Army Group. Patton's Third Army was not committed until late July. Bradley, his erstwhile subordinate but now army group commander, distrusted Patton and considered him a flawed leader, an imprudent loose cannon who was liable to make expensive errors. Patton accomplished some impressive feats after the breakout from Normandy, and some of them could have been even more impressive had he not been reined in by the cautious Bradley. He also displayed the faults that gave rise to the latter's doubts about him.

General Montgomery's concept for the Normandy campaign proved sound and successful, but it was a very broad-brush approach. The post-Normandy campaign, based on a general preinvasion appreciation, was largely extemporized, with its operational idea subject to debate, consequent modification, and even change. Only to a limited extent in the summer of 1944 were higher formation plans elaborated to provide in advance a clear link from battle to battle and operation to operation so that the effects of each were cumulative. Instead, tactical plans were worked out with great thoroughness, but success was necessarily followed by improvisation. Improvisation and the lack of a clear, consistent vision shared by all the operational commanders led on occasion to unnecessary battles, one fatally delayed battle (to open Antwerp's port), a loss of tempo, and the dissipation of forces. Given the lack of a common Anglo-American understanding of the principles governing the planning and execution of army group and army operations, major formations acted more like semiautonomous players than a close-knit team. National and personal antagonisms and prejudices among their commanders ensured that this was the case.

Higher command has never been solely about the technicalities of warfare. Political pressures—unreasonable, even irrational, as well as justified—have always limited generals' freedom of action. This factor assumed hitherto unprecedented sharpness in the Second World War (especially in the democracies). There were two connected reasons for this: With technological developments in communications (air transport, radio, and film), politicians were rapidly and intimately apprised of the actions of field commanders. And the press gave them an important reason to make sure they knew what was going on in the field. Newspapers were far more questioning and far less trusting than they had been during the First World War. They exercised a profound influence on popular support for the war. And public relations became important to generals' careers as well as to those of their political masters. The rivalries and personality clashes that always exist between strong and ambitious characters were often sharpened by the media spotlight. So influential was the press that, rather than shunning it or attempting to muzzle it, as they had a quarter of a century before, generals now courted it. Montgomery was perhaps the most zealous cultivator of newspapermen, but he was not alone; those, like Dempsey, who shunned publicity were an endangered species by 1944. Eisenhower spoke for most generals when he later wrote: "I believed that the proper attitude of the commander toward representatives of the press was to regard them as quasi-staff officers; to recognize their mission in the war and to assist them in carrying it out."[38]

In most respects, the media were helpful to the war effort; but they did, in some ways, exercise a baleful influence. In glorifying the achievements of their own armies, British and American journalists (sometimes inadvertently) belittled those of their ally. Nor did they grasp the finer points of the campaign plan—to them, failure to take ground was failure, even if that had not been the offensive's principal rationale. Thus, the American press and, importantly, many American generals did not grasp Montgomery's operational idea; they exaggerated the operational significance of the early failure to take Caen and territory south of it on the road to Falaise, and they believed the British were not pulling their weight. Increasingly, British newspapers speculated about the possibility of a stalemate, and there was a growing danger that the troops would lose faith in their commander in chief, with adverse consequences for morale. Less excusably, the armchair critics were joined in condemning Montgomery by many at SHAEF, including Eisenhower's deputy, Air Chief Marshal Tedder.[39] The Supreme Commander was repeatedly urged to sack his ground forces commander. The issue eventually went as far as Downing Street and the White House. This mattered. It was part of a process of souring relations between the Allies and between SHAEF and 21 Army Group (or at least its boss), which increasingly and adversely affected decision making and cooperation during the post-Normandy campaign and for the rest of the war. With his prestige and authority tarnished, Montgomery could not ruthlessly impose his will as ground commander, even before he was relegated to army group command and Eisenhower assumed his role. And, given Eisenhower's hands-off, essentially managerial style of leadership, there developed a less than decisive approach to command that relied, essentially, on achieving a consensus. The Supreme Commander was, for various reasons, unable or unwilling to grip his strong-willed subordinates. This, as much as conceptual and doctrinal limitations, contributed to the renewed semistalemate that began in the autumn of 1944.

The post-Normandy operations that had begun with such high hopes and expectations would peter out a month later in general disappointment and mutual recrimination. Plainly, German resilience had much to do with this failure to complete the victory in the west; so, too, did the onset of autumn weather and sheer bad luck. But the main cause involved shortcomings in Allied generalship, as the following chapters will show. Before that can be explored, however, it is necessary to more fully understand the armies commanded by the generals. The next section deals with their doctrine and consequent organization and training. These are critical components of capability, for armies fight as they are trained.

THE AMERICAN, BRITISH, AND CANADIAN ARMIES IN 1944

The US Army's Approach to War

The United States was primarily a maritime power. Throughout the nineteenth century it had maintained a very small volunteer army. Its primary task was to wage essentially colonial campaigns to realize the country's "manifest destiny"—the extension of American power westward at the expense of Mexicans, Native Americans, and, in Cuba and the Philippines, Spaniards.

The United States did, however, experience one horrendous clash of arms—the Civil War of 1861–1865. With a population of approximately 27.5 million (not counting slaves), the Union and Confederate states together mobilized more than 3.5 million men (volunteers and conscripts, including short-timers); around 620,000 of them died (excluding civilians). The Civil War (especially its final year) shaped America's attitude and approach toward large-scale war. After three years of heavy casualties in indecisive fighting (at least in the East, which was the focus of President Lincoln's attention, for good political reasons), General Ulysses S. Grant was given command of the Union armies. Unlike his predecessors, he realized that the days of the one great Napoleonic-style victory that brought war to a triumphant end were over. The enemy armies, both in Virginia and in the West, were too strong, too well armed, too good at maneuver, and too resilient to be destroyed in one or two battles. Over the course of a campaign (eventually lasting nearly a year), superior numbers would have to grind them down by continuous fighting until the Confederates accepted surrender as inevitable.[40] Grant's grueling campaign of attrition, rather than his earlier, brilliant maneuvers against Vicksburg or Sherman's actions in Georgia and the Carolinas, became the focus of American theory and the foundation of doctrine (even though the success of the Virginia campaign depended to no small degree on Sherman's depredations in the Confederate rear). The First World War confirmed the linear, attritional nature of modern warfare; armies were large, well armed, and, thanks to a combination of conscription to provide the numbers and advances in medical science to prevent them from wasting away from disease, resilient. They could form continuous fronts that were difficult to penetrate. Only through a prolonged period of wearing down could the enemy's will to fight be broken.

With the Civil War still within living memory, Americans found the sanguinary campaigns of the Great War less traumatic than did their British cousins; that was the nature of war. Moreover, although the United States formally participated in the First World War for nineteen months, it engaged in serious, sustained combat for only the last four months, and only 116,700 individuals of all services died from all causes.[41] Thus, in the Second World War, US generals (and, for that matter, politicians and the general public), though naturally keen to limit losses as much as possible, were prepared to accept them as regrettable but necessary. As a *Military Review* article of June 1940 affirmed, "Blood is the price of victory. One must accept the formula or not wage war."[42]

Of course, in the two decades after 1918, little thought had been given to the possibility of participating in another titanic European struggle: never again would the country involve itself in the wars of the irredeemably wicked Old World. In the 1920s and 1930s the US Army was neglected. Economic stringency ensured that its strength, equipment, and training were inadequate to meet the challenge of modern warfare. The regular army's strength seldom topped 135,000 men until September 1939, when it crept up to 190,000. The large, trained reserve envisaged by the National Defense Act of 1920 was stillborn. Although the National Guard was about 200,000 strong, its state of training was even more woeful than that of the regular force.[43] With only a constabulary role and no clear enemy, doctrinal development was confused and somewhat contradictory.

The 1930 *Manual for Commanders of Large Units* emphasized maneuver and the speed, agility, and flexibility it requires. The army restructured with this focus, as well as an offensive orientation, in mind. Under the guidance of Lieutenant General Leslie J. McNair, from March 1942 commander of the Army Ground Forces, the process reached its apogee. McNair's basic concept was that the table of organization and equipment (TO&E) of units and divisions should contain only those men and that equipment required to be self-sufficient while fulfilling the most undemanding role—in reserve or defending in a quiet sector. Thus, by July 1943, the large, square infantry division (with over 27,000 men) that had been designed for the attritional campaign of 1917–1918 was replaced by the lean, triangular division with 14,253 men of all ranks (three infantry regiments, each with three battalions, and four artillery battalions, each with twelve howitzers). This force had much greater tactical agility and, just as important, strategic mobility, requiring minimal shipping space, consistent with military effectiveness on arrival. When the division was committed to the offensive, or even to the defense in a critical sector where an attack was expected, it would be reinforced with units from the GHQ pool of independent tank and tank destroyer battalions (with seventeen light and fifty-three medium tanks and thirty-six tank destroyers, respectively) and supported by several battalions from the substantial artillery holdings at the higher formation level. The size and composition of the augmentation were tailored to the task and sometimes included a major element of an armored division as well. If it was considered necessary to motorize the marching infantry component of the division (other components were already truck-borne), the addition of six quartermaster truck companies would do the trick. Armored divisions, at just over 11,000 men, were quite small. They (with two exceptions) comprised three tank, three armored infantry, and three self-propelled artillery battalions that were flexibly organized and reorganized according to task in two or three combat commands: Combat Command A, Combat Command B, and a small Combat Command R (not always formed). They too were often beefed up with attachments of tank destroyers, sometimes tanks, and occasionally infantry regiments. Armored divisions, being specifically designed for exploitation, were not supposed to be involved in an attritional grind. In practice, owing to a shortage of infantry formations, they were frequently used as such, often with combat commands detached to reinforce the latter so that there were no forces left for exploitation.

The armies that advanced through France and Belgium and into Germany were thus designed for maneuver warfare. By the end of operations in Normandy, one US division in three was armored, and there were nine (mechanized) cavalry groups as well. However, the foundation manual, *FM 100-5 Operations*, was much more ambivalent about the nature of operations. Its 1939, 1941, and 1944 iterations continued to stress that "the ultimate objective is the destruction of the enemy's armed forces in battle," and it stated that, while "an objective may sometimes be attained through maneuver alone; ordinarily it must be gained through battle." The US Army certainly did not deny maneuver a role, but it did assert that there was no alternative, relatively painless path to victory other than long, hard fighting. Grant's approach continued to hold sway. Developments on the Soviet-German front seemed to confirm this. By the middle of 1943, the quick and apparently easy victories the Wehrmacht had achieved from 1939 to 1942 looked atypical of modern war. The Soviets' long road back was proving hard and costly, an experience the Americans were sharing in the Italian campaign.

The logical corollary to the acceptance of a long period of attritional struggle was the need to field a mass army. This was indeed the original intention. The Victory Program of autumn 1941 foresaw the US Army fielding 213 divisions—a seemingly achievable figure from a population of more than 132 million. Various influences combined to pare this target back. On the positive side, increasing faith was placed on the Red Army after it started to fight back from the disasters of 1941–1942, on the other Allies, and on the ability of airpower to cripple Germany's capacity to wage war. Other factors combined perforce to limit the army's ambitions: other countries' reliance on the "arsenal of democracy" to provide the arms and equipment they could not produce themselves in adequate quantity; the manpower demands of industry and of the other services; and the problem of equipping, training, and shipping large numbers of divisions overseas. By the summer of 1943, ninety divisions had been formed, and the fifteen planned for 1944 had been eliminated from the program. In May 1944 General Marshall, Chief of Staff of the Army, made the decision to stop at that figure, believing (albeit with some trepidation) that it would suffice.[44] On VE-Day there were forty-six infantry and fifteen armored divisions in the ETO, roughly the number that Marshall had estimated would be sufficient, given all the other factors at work. It must be remembered, of course, that no one was forecasting on the eve of D-Day that the war would be over within a year. Indeed, everyone was surprised to find the Allied armies on the German frontier in mid-September, on a line the planners had reckoned on achieving by around D+350.

Of these sixty-one divisions eventually deployed in the ETO, however, just over half were available to fight the summer-autumn campaign. By the end of November 1944, only twenty-seven American infantry and eight armored divisions had entered combat in the theatre.[45] Given the problems of raising large numbers of formations from a very small base,[46] equipping and officering them, training them, and transporting them overseas (and not just to the ETO), this was a creditable achievement. However, the number was not adequate to meet the needs of operations. On few occasions did a corps or even an army go into battle with a whole division in reserve. This meant there was no dedicated force of significant size immediately available to convert tactical into operational success. Deep battle was thus generally precluded, absent a general collapse of the enemy such as that which characterized the immediate post-Normandy operations, when the bold handling of armor was a hallmark of Patton's pursuit in particular. There were notable exceptions, of course. In Operation Cobra, for instance, there were no fewer than two armored divisions and one fully motorized infantry division to exploit the breakthrough—which they did to great effect. When Third Army's XII Corps eventually forced the Moselle in September, 4 Armored Division executed a classic example of exploitation that collapsed the defense from within. But these examples were exceptional: linear, attritional methods were the norm in Normandy and became so again in the autumn, when armored divisions were used along with infantry to grind down the defense. But for attrition to bring a swift end to hostilities by breaking the enemy's will (the doctrinal aim), the enemy's losses must be more unbearable than one's own. Arguably, the paucity of divisions in the ETO made this a touch-and-go situation.

There was a problem of resilience, primarily in the infantry divisions. It was partly an issue of their organizational structure. McNair's theory was sound, and although the division was initially well balanced, it soon became unbalanced in combat as the riflemen took casualties much faster than did the other arms, requiring the relief of the entire division when most of its components were still capable of further effort.[47] However, because there were too few divisions to rotate them in and out of the line, allowing refurbishment, retraining, and rest for tired formations, each tended to remain in battle until its combat effectiveness was impaired, sometimes verging on ineffectiveness.[48] Units' strength was supposed to be kept up by a constant flow of replacements, circumventing the problem. However, in the most critical area—the infantry—the system worked badly and wastefully. Casualties among riflemen were much higher than anticipated. The ETO had decreed that 70.3 percent of replacements should be infantry, but in Normandy, about 85 percent of the losses fell into that category.[49] Thus, after the pool of 76,000 replacements (52 percent of them infantry trained) that had been built up in Britain prior to Overlord was exhausted (which occurred by the end of the Normandy campaign), the supply of combat infantrymen replacements routinely fell short of demand. The problem was compounded by their usually inadequate training (officers included) and by the callously indifferent, morale-sapping treatment they endured in transit through the communications zone (COMZ). The unlucky joined their new units in the midst of combat—pitched straight in, knowing nobody, and understanding nothing. All too often, their first battle became their last.[50] Increasingly, desperation born of a lack of replacements led to an alternative resort: retraining surplus specialists, especially air defense gunners, as riflemen to remedy shortfalls in numbers. This too tended to produce low morale, resentment, and inferior infantrymen. And because units were kept in battle, or at least in the line, for too long, there was a mounting toll of psychological casualties in addition to those wounded in action—up to one for every three physically injured during periods of heavy fighting.[51] Cohesion is essential to a unit's combat effectiveness. The steady, sometimes swift drain of casualties, the shortcomings of replacements, and the lack of time to integrate them properly, combined with the growing fatigue that also eroded morale, reduced US combat power alarmingly.

US tactical doctrine was basically sound. The foundation manual's "Doctrine of Combat" emphasized that the "ultimate objective of all military operations is the destruction of the enemy's armed forces in battle.... Through offensive action a commander exercises his initiative, preserves his freedom of action, and imposes his will on the enemy.... The selection by the commander of the right time and place for offensive action is a decisive factor in the success of the operation."[52] It goes on to stress the importance of concentration and its corollary, economy of force employed on secondary missions; the desirability of surprise in its various guises; unity of command; and a combined-arms approach, using fire and movement. Chapter 10, "The Offensive," reiterates that the enemy's destruction is the essential purpose and is usually attained by battle, and it develops the theme of the territorial objectives that can lead to its achievement. The manual is full of impeccable sentiments: a main attack characterized by a narrow frontage; a strong concentration of all arms, with the attack organized in depth and backed by reserves; a secondary, weaker attack to fix the enemy; air superiority and the close air support that follows from it; and the importance of maneuver, especially with a view to envelopment (though, significantly, it warns of the risk inherent in such a gambit).

In the first several weeks of the Normandy campaign, and too often in subsequent operations as well, doctrine was applied not creatively or thoughtfully but mechanistically and inappropriately. Formation commanders were keen to appear relentlessly aggressive and determined to seize and hold the initiative. They often saw their task as attacking more or less continually, on a broad front, even when the lack of surprise, inadequate concentration, or even insufficient preparation should have suggested the likelihood of the heavy casualties and meager gains that actually resulted. To the Americans, the principle of concentration meant the application of maximum force, attacking almost everywhere all the time. This traditional, attritional approach seemed both possible, given their superior and growing resources, especially in artillery and airpower, and less difficult and risky than radically denuding passive sectors to enable a greater concentration of force that would allow a breakthrough and subsequent, risky operational maneuver. Of course, the terrain in Normandy generally militated against a rapid penetration, and the Germans developed tactics to maximize the defensive value of the ground and to minimize the devastating potential of superior Allied firepower through camouflage, depth, dispersion, and maneuver. For some of the time, the enemy's force density also prevented a rapid penetration; either a wearing down or a diversion of German strength would have been necessary before a breakthrough could be achieved. However, Operation Cobra demonstrated what could have been done somewhat earlier and what certainly could have been accomplished later in the campaign when it once again assumed an attritional nature. One cannot blame difficult ground, weather, or enemy defenses for the lack of maneuver.[53] The Soviets often faced these same problems but created their own opportunities for deep operations by conducting Cobra-like breakthrough battles followed immediately and energetically by deep-thrusting armored formations. Of course, they had developed the doctrine for it, refined by (often painful) experience, whereas the Western Allies had not.

On many occasions, especially early in the campaign, the American army suffered tactical failure through its inexperience and faulty training. Though repeatedly stressed in theory, the need for a combined-arms approach took a long time to become effective in practice. This was not entirely the fault of units. Time to train before the invasion had been short, and the terrain in Normandy posed novel and unexpected challenges. Be that as it may, the rifle units of infantry divisions and the independent tank and self-propelled tank destroyer battalions, whose rationale was to support the infantry, had trained separately. It took exposure to combat, casualties, and tactical failure to resolve the technical problems inhibiting cooperation, such as finding compatible means of communication and working out suitable all-arms tactics. The problem was largely caused by the concept of pooling the comparatively limited number of independent battalions for temporary attachment to whichever divisions were currently part of the main effort. Had each infantry division possessed an organic tank battalion (a structure introduced after the war), this problem would have been avoided. It never plagued the armored divisions, which fielded task-organized combat commands and task forces from the start. As it was, combat experience imbued both arms with a common understanding that led to a semiofficial policy involving the semipermanent allocation of certain tank battalions to individual divisions. Tank destroyer units never got to perform the function allotted to them: the concept was anachronistic even before the invasion, as the Germans no longer mounted massed, tank-heavy attacks. These units largely ended up being used as self-propelled artillery for both direct and indirect fire. In contrast, the artillery worked well with supported units from the start, thanks to a better common understanding and longer-term relationships. Lastly, getting ground-air cooperation to work smoothly and effectively took longer than tank-infantry cooperation, as different environments and services were complicating factors.

Overestimation of the effects of artillery contributed to indecisiveness in the offensive, especially in the first few weeks, when the nature of hedgerow fighting limited its impact. There was a pronounced tendency for infantry and infantry-tank teams to rely on the gunners to solve most of their tactical problems. Even when light opposition was encountered and fire and movement using the units' organic weapons would have made an advance possible, it was common for them to stop, go to ground, and call for artillery support. There was a corresponding reluctance to press forward when that support was not forthcoming in quantity. Both American and German sources frequently commented on this aspect of tactical performance. This was an understandable response, given doctrine's emphasis on using the weight of firepower to save lives. But on many occasions, it was inappropriate: it sometimes expended ammunition to little effect, leading to temporary shortages, and artillery was of limited use in dealing with reverse slope positions and with well-protected targets such as fixed or even field fortifications. Moreover, a methodical advance, the pace of which was determined by artillery fire, combined with an inflexible adherence to plans and an overdeveloped sense of caution, was often counterproductive. Even in the *bocage*, there were times in battle at all levels when the defense was stretched or crumbling and sheer momentum would have carried the attackers forward, giving the enemy no time to rally, organize, or bring up reserves.[54] The use of speed as a weapon was too often neglected; in consequence, the defense was given the breathing space it needed to restore its integrity. Fighting through a defense that is balanced and psychologically prepared is always slower and more expensive, in lives as well as shells, than progressively breaking up an increasingly disorganized enemy whose thoughts are turning from resistance to self-preservation.[55] Along with the often excessive reliance on artillery, the ground forces consistently exaggerated what close air support could accomplish on their behalf (with the crucial exception of maneuver periods of the campaign). This was a continuing delusion that wasted resources and lives throughout; even in October, for instance, air attacks were relied on to suppress fortifications at Metz, despite proof from Cherbourg in June and Brest in September that they would accomplish almost nothing.

At the root of this sometimes disappointing performance lay personnel, especially leadership, issues.[56] The overall quality of US infantrymen was not high enough. The US Navy, Air Corps, Marine Corps, and, within the army itself, the Services of Supply and specialist arms were all allowed to cream off the best of the personnel pool; huge numbers of potentially invaluable infantry noncommissioned officers (NCOs) ended up in dead-end jobs that wasted their talents. The humble rifleman was regarded—quite wrongly, given the demands of the modern battlefield—as requiring little skill, education, or even intelligence. The result was a tendency toward phlegmatic inactivity unless constantly stirred to action, a predisposition that their generally insufficient training did little to remove. The American subunit was generally much less inclined than its German equivalent to attempt to accomplish its mission when its leader was incapacitated or deprived of guidance from above; this trait was particularly evident in the unfamiliar and challenging environment of the *bocage*. Platoon, company, and battalion commanders had to lead by example, and this often resulted in heavy casualties and a consequent loss of drive; by 31 July, for instance, officer casualties had reached an average of 79.5 percent in each of three infantry divisions.[57]

Thus, the quality of officers and of their training was critical to battlefield performance—even more so than in an army consisting of long-service regulars. Alas, it was not considered satisfactory by several senior officers. Patton, for instance, wrote in November 1944: "Our chief trouble in this war is the lack of efficiency and lack of sense of responsibility on the part of company officers."[58] Prewar American society was possibly the least militarized in the world. In the space of about two years, from the beginning of rearmament in 1940, the 20,000 or so officers of the regular army expanded thirtyfold. Their training was, for the most part, somewhat sketchy and theoretical. As with the other ranks, some preference was given to specialist jobs at the expense of the teeth arms. Many men progressed too rapidly through the ranks, gaining insufficient experience and understanding as they did so; they occupied positions that proved to be beyond their competence. Inevitably, many failed as leaders, as even the official history admits.[59] In the process of failing, they compromised the mission and the lives of their soldiers.

Plainly, hastily trained, inexperienced officers need all the help they can get from doctrine in fulfilling their professional responsibilities. This was especially true for those faced with the problems of hedgerow fighting and its unusual demands on subunit leadership. On the subject of command, *FM 100-5* was full of admirable sentiments, many (like the following) lifted straight from *Truppenführung* (the German army manual):

> A willingness to accept responsibility is the foremost trait of leadership. Every individual from the highest commander to the lowest private must always remember that inaction and neglect of opportunities will warrant more severe censure than an error of judgment . . . a commander cannot plead absence of orders as an excuse for inactivity. If the situation does not permit communication with the superior commander and the subordinate commander is familiar with the . . . mission of the whole command, he should take appropriate action and report the situation as early as practicable.[60]

The manual thus demanded initiative from both officers and NCOs, but unlike *Truppenführung*, it did not go on to say: "The commander must allow his subordinates freedom of action so long as it does not adversely affect his overall intent."[61] Neither the education nor the training of the American junior officer, let alone the NCO, equipped him intellectually for independent action. The German emphasis was on *how* to think, whereas the American was on *what* to think. Instead of accepting that battle would inevitably develop in unpredictable ways and empowering the junior leader to deal with problems as they arose, US doctrinal publications attempted to foresee each possible situation and provide a stereotypical answer in exhaustive detail. Against an enemy as clever, experienced, and flexible as the Germans, this approach was inadequate.

Significantly, *FM 100-5* omitted the more philosophical elements of *Truppenführung*—that is, those bits that explained the logic of the German command style. Following Clausewitz, they stressed that the battlefield was the realm of chaos, uncertainty, and chance as well as danger and exertion.[62] It also rapidly became an increasingly empty place as troops dispersed and sought cover to evade the firepower of a well-equipped, modern enemy. Tactical situations were usually obscure and often changed fast. Reliance on line communications, even supplemented by bulky and temperamental radios that were susceptible to overloading, interference, jamming, and intercept, made it impossible for the senior commander to maintain a strong and detailed grip on his battle, however much he desired to do so. Accepting the inevitable, German doctrine required that he devolve tactical decision making down to those closest to the problem and therefore in the best position to deal with it in a timely fashion. There was no viable alternative to the system of *auftragstaktik*.[63] The senior commander laid down an aim and ensured that his subordinates clearly understood his intent. He formulated a broad plan, allocated resources tailored to accomplish it, and then, as the fog of war inevitably descended, trusted his subordinates to act autonomously in the spirit of their missions when the letter proved to be unachievable. The factor that unified their efforts, ensuring that their different, semi-independent actions contributed to the overall goal, was the commander's intent. Officers and NCOs were habitually told what to accomplish, not how to do it. They were trained to size up any situation rapidly, make a quick decision based on their superior's intent, issue brief orders, and then execute vigorously. It was an approach to command that not only partly compensated for the friction of combat but also ensured speedy and decisive action. This received great emphasis, as surprise was regarded as an important force multiplier, and it had to be exploited rapidly and energetically before the enemy could recover his psychological and physical balance (hence the emphasis on the immediate counterattack as the key to defense). Against an enemy whose reactions were often sluggish because the locus of decision making was higher up and somewhat out of touch, this approach was likely to confer and retain the initiative.[64]

The American vision of the battlefield was, at bottom, fundamentally different from the German. Victory would come through the unrelenting application of superior force until the enemy buckled under its weight: what counted above all else in battle were quantities of men, weapons, equipment, and ammunition. Americans counted on efficient production to provide raw, overwhelming power. Surprise received lip service, but save for some special occasions, such as D-Day, it was not regarded as essential and was certainly no substitute for mass firepower. Few resources were devoted to deception, and it was not regularly practiced. Command was primarily a managerial problem, one of assembling this crushing firepower, usually over a broad frontage, and orchestrating it to smash the enemy. When the enemy had been ground down, the army's great mobility would enable it to roll forward, again on a broad front, to complete the business of destroying the enemy's army and occupying areas critical to his ability to wage war. This approach befitted the most advanced industrial economy in the world and was suited to its advanced and centralized approach to management. It was clear and simple and well suited to an army raised in haste and consequently in possession of relatively limited skills. Units were like cogs in the gigantic war machine, and as such, they were required only to do their business (mainly of attrition) predictably and without deviation. Thus, the young officer rapidly learned that there was a disconnect between the theory of command laid out in *FM 100-5* and US Army practice. In practice, most American commanders attempted to overcontrol their subordinates. Fearing they would be held responsible for the mistakes of the latter, they tended to issue detailed orders and closely supervise their execution. The mutual trust between senior and junior commanders and the acceptance—indeed, encouragement—of risk that characterized the German system in its heyday and was crucial to its success were much less evident in the US Army. If it did not succeed, initiative tended to be punishable.[65]

Of the fourteen infantry, two airborne, and six armored divisions that fought in Normandy, only two infantry, one airborne, and one armored division had prior combat experience. No corps HQ had been in battle. Thus, for the most part, neither troops nor staffs had the requisite knowledge and understanding to modify the approaches they had learned during their somewhat sketchy theoretical training. The enemy they faced was skillful and determined; although many German formations were new to battle, most had a cadre of experienced officers and NCOs that had learned their trade in the hardest school imaginable—fighting the Red Army. It is thus hardly surprising that the tactical combat performance of First Army was initially plodding, particularly in view of the unfamiliar and unexpectedly difficult terrain it faced. What is impressive is the rapidity with which the Americans learned, adapted, and retrained in the field.[66] Both minor tactical and technical innovations such as *bocage*-specific tactics and the Rhinoceros hedge-buster came from the bottom up, and most divisions quickly developed a system for learning and disseminating lessons. Corps also raised their game, learning to concentrate more, attack in some depth, and apply artillery firepower more effectively. Over time, tactical airpower was effectively integrated into the combined-arms team. There remained some lacunae; for instance, the Americans were generally reluctant to employ night attacks or infiltration tactics, perhaps regarding both as unnecessary or even counterproductive for an army with such massive firepower at its disposal. But the formations that broke out after Cobra and exploited so vigorously were vastly more effective than those that had entered combat a scant few weeks earlier—though, of course, each new division that arrived in theatre had to undergo its own learning experience, which was mercifully somewhat shortened by that of its predecessors. Progress in tactics and techniques was not matched, however, by a maturation at the operational level—a theme of the chapters that follow.

The British Army's Approach to War

Britain's power was based on maritime superiority and, by the early nineteenth century, supremacy. Its army was small and volunteer, used mainly for colonial campaigning to defend and expand its empire. Its participation in the great wars of Europe had generally been peripheral and limited, even in the struggle against Napoleon. In the century after Waterloo, Britain had not fought on the Continent at all, save for the midcentury Crimean War. This, too, was limited. The troops came from the 140,000-strong regular army, and although about 22,000 died, fewer than 5,000 of them did so as a result of combat. The British were thus totally unprepared psychologically for the appalling casualties of the First World War. In over four years they suffered about 750,000 military deaths and 1.5 million permanently handicapped, the vast majority of them on the western front. This left a deep scar on the national psyche—deeper than that experienced by most continental countries, which were used to conscription (introduced for the first time in Britain in 1916) and the mass casualties resulting from mass warfare. Reacting to the perceived horror and futility of the bloodletting in the trenches, the British Army of 1939–1945 was much more sensitive to the issue of losses than it had been in 1914–1918—and much more so than the Americans. British generals and their government were accordingly more casualty-averse than their ally, and this would have repercussions with regard to the way war was waged.

The mood of Great Britain in the 1920s was profoundly different from that of the prewar years. Victory had been won at such a high price that it was soon regarded as not being worth the cost. Pacifism became widespread. There was a revulsion against war as an instrument of policy, and a naïve belief in the League of Nations and the negotiated settlement of differences took its place: faith in the former lasted until 1936, while faith in the latter persisted until as late as March 1939. Moreover, the war had massively undermined Britain's economic strength; this problem was compounded both by a failure of industry and commerce to recognize irrevocable change and by mistaken government policies. The troubles of the 1920s were followed by the onset of the Great Depression, the effects of which were felt right up to the outbreak of the next war. Unsurprisingly in the circumstances, defense was neglected as unaffordably burdensome and largely unnecessary. The savage postwar cuts of the "Geddes Axe" were followed by the "ten-year rule," under which appropriations and planning were based on the mantra that there would be no major war for at least ten years. The rule was restated annually until 1932, but even then, its abandonment brought about no appreciable change, despite the growing power and aggressiveness of Japan, Italy, and Germany. Rearmament did not get under way until the late 1930s; even as late as 1938, defense received barely 8 percent of Britain's gross domestic product, and a major, sustained effort had to wait until the following year. Moreover, priority was given to repairing the deficiencies of and then building up the Royal Navy and the Royal Air Force (RAF); the army was a poor third in the queue for manpower and investment in equipment. This state of affairs remained constant throughout the war. There was no stomach in the country for fielding an army the size of Field Marshal Haig's in the First World War to shoulder a commensurate share of the burden of defeating the Germans on land.

Throughout the interwar years, of the three armed services, the British Army fared worst. It reverted to being little more than a collection of battalions; the efficient formation staffs of 1918 were allowed to disappear, as was much of the expertise required to re-create them. Penury precluded the development of weaponry and organizations (the Experimental Mechanized Force, for instance, was disbanded in 1929 after only two years). Of course, neither size limitations nor increasingly obsolescent weaponry precluded the development of theory about future warfare that took full advantage of the scientific and technical developments leading to a revolution in military affairs. Both the German and the Soviet militaries embraced new ideas that left them doctrinally well prepared when political and economic circumstances permitted the modernization of equipment and force structures. But the British Army faced more immediate and pressing concerns that absorbed all its attention. The first was the fear of revolution at home. Even before the war, the army had become increasingly involved in the suppression of strikes, which occasionally required the use of lethal force. After the war it faced a three-year-long insurgency in Ireland, the culmination of political conflict that had been heading for civil war since before 1914. In addition, the prospect of Bolshevik contagion spreading to the British Isles seemed very real at the time. In January 1919, 10,000 troops with tanks and artillery were deployed to forestall a rising in "Red Clydeside." Soldiers were frequently deployed in response to industrial unrest, culminating in the General Strike of 1926. The army's leadership displayed a distaste for such "duties in aid of the civil power," but it had to take the communist threat seriously until the approach of another war took precedence. The other preoccupation was imperial policing and campaigning, the traditional role at the heart of soldiering for generations. The expansion of the empire as a result of the war was accompanied by growing political and military problems within it. Insurgencies in the new Middle Eastern mandates of Iraq and Palestine were added to the traditional burdens of controlling the region, and in India, the jewel in the empire's crown, nationalist unrest was on the rise. The waning of British economic power and psychological dominance presaged troubled times for the empire.

An even more important brake on progress was intellectual stultification. Being dominated by gentry who regarded the career of an army officer as an agreeable and honorable one devoid of troublesome mental challenges, the military held few attractions for bright and progressive middle-class minds inclined toward pacifism. Nor was an officer's education calculated to stimulate professional debate. At Sandhurst, the Royal Military College, almost 40 percent of a would-be officer's time was spent learning to be the perfect private soldier.[67] At the Staff College, rote learning was the norm, the staff's solution to problems was sacrosanct, and questioning was discouraged. There was none of the doctrinal ferment that characterized the Reichswehr and the Red Army. There was no need for it. The notion of a renewed continental commitment was roundly rejected, treaty obligations notwithstanding. When asked by the French about fulfilling Britain's Locarno promise to prevent German reoccupation of the Rhineland in March 1936, the British prime minister admitted that it would take weeks to scrape up a single infantry division and cavalry brigade. In January 1936 the army's total strength, at 191,000, was almost 20 percent less than it had been in July 1914.

It was only in early 1939 that the British government accepted that it could not escape a commitment to deploy an army on the Continent. The regular army was increased to 225,000, and the establishment of the Territorial Army (TA) field force was more than trebled to 340,000 (with another 100,000 air defense gunners). In March peacetime conscription was introduced for the first time, though it was intended to supplement, not replace, voluntary service. The goal was, over two years, to produce a field force of six regular and twenty-six TA divisions (with another fourteen from the Dominions and four from the Indian Army). Thus, only on the very eve of war was any effort initiated to turn a small regular army, with its mental horizon bounded by colonial soldiering and a TA that was hardly trained at all, into a military machine capable, once again, of defeating the German army. Moreover, the Treasury argued that equipment could not be found to realize such an ambitious plan, so it was scaled back to thirty-six divisions in two years.[68]

Unsurprisingly, it took three months to produce a British Expeditionary Force (BEF) of only three divisions, although the nine-month-long "Phony War" provided time for a buildup to thirteen divisions (ten of them deemed ready for combat). Then in a mere three weeks the BEF was driven from the Continent, abandoning nearly all its equipment except for small arms.[69]

By June 1940, Britain had mobilized an army of 1.65 million. Twelve months later it had grown to 2.2 million. All these men had to be equipped and trained. The process started from a small and unpromising base and was massively set back by the disastrous defeat in France. The BEF had to be reequipped virtually from scratch, and the defeat raised fundamental questions about doctrine and training to which there was no unanimous response. Nor was the army vouchsafed a period of calm and order in which to create an effective offensive military machine to stem and then reverse the tide; it had its work cut out to defend both the British Isles and imperial possessions in Africa, the Middle East, and eventually the Far East as well. The financial neglect and intellectual barrenness of two decades and the persistent failings of the training system (such as it was) could not be turned around rapidly or without further humiliations. It is hardly surprising that the task took almost three years and was characterized by (often gallant) failure and outright disaster. However, to its credit, by the time of El Alamein, the British Army demonstrated that it could win battles against the Germans, albeit clumsily at times and by dint of reliance on superior numbers and attrition. After Alamein it maintained an unbroken record of success across North Africa and into Italy. Achieving success in secondary theatres, however, was no guarantee that it could be replicated in France against the enemy's main effort in the west.[70]

As Britain's most successful field commander, General Montgomery enjoyed the confidence of the prime minister and the CIGS, Field Marshal Sir Alan Brooke. Montgomery was effectively given free rein to mold the British invasion force as he wished. In doing so, at the forefront of his mind were two related issues: manpower and morale. Manpower—or rather its shortage, especially of infantry—was an obsession from the moment he took command of the invasion force. His Anglo-Canadian contingent was small, and he had been warned before D-Day and again in July that no more formations would be created; indeed, when the flow of replacements began to run dry, he would have to break up one or more existing units to keep the remainder up to strength.[71] So it came to pass. In August an infantry division and brigade were disbanded, followed by the equivalent of more than two armored brigades and, in November, another infantry division.[72] Montgomery was thus acutely aware of two factors bearing on his decision making: his army group was the foundation of British military power and influence in the grand alliance in Europe, and it was a wasting asset. The need to minimize casualties to conserve the force became almost a principle of war. Nevertheless, Montgomery's force was too small to play the leading role he desired for it. It was increasingly dwarfed by the Americans, who went from being less than one and a half times as strong at the conclusion of the Normandy campaign to three times as strong in 1945. Consequently, Montgomery's (and Britain's) influence on the conduct of campaigns waned steadily as American strength and self-confidence grew.

A second concern influencing Montgomery's approach to operations was the fragility of his army's morale. This concern was commonplace among Britain's generals. The soldiery, it was said, was nowhere near as tough as it had been in 1914–1918, and the officers had been softened by the luxury, not to say decadence, of the postwar years; the loss of the flower of the nation's manhood in the First World War had weakened the army for the Second. The amount of truth in this contention is difficult to assess. Certainly Germany, despite its much higher losses, both absolute and proportional, was demonstrably able and willing to fight another round. Perhaps the generals were blaming the failures of 1939–1942 on their soldiers rather than recognizing their own professional shortcomings and the army's structural and doctrinal failings (which were their responsibility).[73] Be that as it may, 21 Army Group was designed to win a campaign as economically as possible, in terms of casualties, through the execution of a series of carefully managed set-piece attacks followed by cautious, minimal-risk exploitation. Montgomery believed the troops' confidence that their commanders would not unduly risk their lives, coupled with assurances of success, would create the high morale essential to victory. Other factors were also important: firm but fair discipline, good leadership, effective and realistic training, comradeship, confidence in the quality and quantity of equipment, and good and considerate administration.[74] Montgomery did his best to deliver on all of these and was conspicuously successful on the last, but he could not avoid setbacks. By mid-July there were obvious symptoms of declining morale, especially in the veteran divisions of North Africa and Italy, as the casualty toll mounted with little ground gained.[75] These warning signs reinforced the commander's tendency toward caution. In fact, doctrinal inhibitions on exploitation and operational maneuver chimed perfectly with his desire to avoid risk.

Montgomery's personal imprint on the way his army fought was unmatched by any other general in any nation's forces. In the few months available to him, he sought to replicate the successful model of his Eighth Army. Wherever he could, he brought in his own staff officers and protégés from the Mediterranean. He also imposed his own interpretation of doctrine. This was beneficial to the forces that were training to reenter the Continent, as they were mired in doctrinal confusion. In its *Field Service Regulations* and other pamphlets, the War Office published the official version. However, it also produced army training instructions and memoranda that propounded doctrine in all but name, and various formations produced their own idiosyncratic variations. There was, in other words, a surfeit of doctrine, some of it contradictory—just as there had been in the previous world war. Many officers who were imbued with the traditional British dislike of doctrine and were grappling with the immediate problems of mastering a new job simply eschewed the lot of it. Unfortunately, there was also a downside to Montgomery's attempt to create doctrinal order. Some of the Eighth Army's practices suited neither the terrain conditions in Normandy nor the enemy's evolving concepts about defense, and there was not enough time for his concepts to be fully grasped and reflected in training practices.[76] More fundamentally, the whole British concept of how to fight on land and, consequently, how to prepare to do so was open to question.

Montgomery's approach to doctrine was, of course, influenced by his own professional development. The First World War had been his formative experience. Having gone from subaltern in 1914 to General Staff officer (GSO) 1 (chief of staff) of a division in 1918, he had participated in everything from the destruction of the old professional BEF through the growing pains of the citizen army to the final victorious campaign. Haig's army of 1918 was actually a very progressive and effective force for its time. It had developed sophisticated artillery techniques undreamed of three years earlier and used them to support massed tanks working closely with infantry and (a harbinger of the future) ground attack aircraft in a combined-arms team. This winning formula provided the basis of Montgomery's doctrine. He would use the latest available weaponry and methods of employing it tactically to produce an updated version. In other words, unlike many of his colleagues, Montgomery was far from being a reactionary who failed to see the possibilities of the new or experimental; however, unlike some Soviet and German generals, his vision did not extend to accepting that a whole new and conceptually different way of waging war had been opened up by technological change. This limitation was not the product of ignorance (he studied his profession assiduously). He did not believe in some British equivalent of *blitzkrieg* because he understood the considerable limitations of the wartime army and the need to minimize its casualties.

The commander in chief stressed the set-piece battle to the neglect of other forms of offensive action; meeting battles were no longer taught, and the quick attack and pursuit were skimmed over. Although the army had invested massively in mobility, maneuver (as opposed to controlled, organized movement to battle) was not central to Montgomery's thinking. His forte was the deliberate attack, where the key to success was concentrating the strongest possible force on the chosen sector and assigning limited objectives to be achieved through overwhelming firepower (including massed bomber formations whenever possible). Thus, each infantry division's attack was usually mounted on the frontage of a single brigade attacking "two up," about as much width as the divisional artillery could cover using the gunners' favorite technique of a rolling barrage. The first echelon and its supporting tanks were required to achieve only a modest penetration before the second passed through, followed by the third. In this way, momentum was maintained by the sustained application of fresh combat power. Once the enemy's main line of defense was penetrated, the corps reserve, an armored division, could be committed for a limited exploitation. The theory was vitiated by several factors, however: some were due to inadequacies in training that could be eliminated with experience; some, more serious, were the result of shortcomings in doctrine; others were the product of systemic faults in the army.

The Normandy fighting revealed many tactical deficiencies (at least some of which should have been corrected after lessons learned in Italy). Foremost among them was the failure to integrate all arms in the attack. The artillery was excellent, but the rolling barrage was ill suited to the close country of the *bocage*, and its effectiveness was lessened by developments in German tactics (increased depth and dispersal of defending formations and the use of maneuver). When the gunners failed to neutralize the defense completely or left the assaulting troops behind, both armor and infantry were generally reluctant and too poorly trained to continue the attack relying on their own firepower and minor tactics. They had been taught to expect artillery to solve their problems, so it became a crutch; they would not contemplate an advance without it.[77] The time it took to rework the fire plan was not considered dangerous, even though it was, in fact, a precious gift to the German defenders. Moreover, failure to train together meant that tank-infantry cooperation was mostly poor, even in the case of the independent armored brigades whose raison d'être was infantry support; both suffered in consequence. Finally, consolidation on the objective was frequently belated; consequently, the troops were driven off by the Germans' habitual immediate counterattack. Most of these problems in the deliberate attack were overcome as the campaign progressed. More serious were the problems inherent in the concept.

The buildup for a set-piece battle was usually slow, not least because of the amount of artillery ammunition required (e.g., 282,200 rounds for the initial barrage alone in Operation Totalize—before counterbombardment and other tasks were considered—in addition to an air preparation in which 3,458 tons of bombs were dropped). This could compromise the element of surprise, which was dear to Montgomery's heart, although it was in fact achieved remarkably often. There were inescapable drawbacks due to the very nature of the offensive. The vast quantity of guns and shells required generally confined attacks to one or, on occasion, two corps (i.e., with only two to four divisions in the first echelon, each with one leading brigade). Then the barrage defined the width of the blow and its direction. This helped the Germans determine what counterpenetration measures were required to block the spearhead and bring flanking fire to bear on the inevitably narrow and congested salient that was being created. Developing the attack in depth was exceptionally difficult (especially in the *bocage*); there were simply too few routes and not enough space in the burgeoning salient to accommodate all the elements that had to get forward—antitank and resupply for the consolidating first echelon, artillery to ensure continuous fire support, and the second echelon trying to conduct a passage of lines. Opportunities to generate tactical maneuver, thus avoiding continual frontal attacks, were limited. When attacking tanks and infantry moved beyond the range of the supporting artillery, all momentum would be lost. Realizing this, as they had done in the First World War and were doing in the east, the Germans adopted an elastic defense deployed in considerable depth.

The systemic problem lay in the contradictions in the British command and control philosophy, similar to those found in the US Army. The battlefields of the First World War had been a chaotic environment shrouded in the fog of war. The German reaction had been to accept this as inevitable and to manage the chaos by devolving decision making downward and relying on subordinates using their initiative to further their commanders' intent. In their *Field Service Regulations* of 1935, the British seemed ready to follow the same route. Indeed, theory continued in this vein. The 1941 *Operations* pamphlet stated: "Modern warfare demands considerable decentralization and every subordinate must be encouraged to make his own decisions on no more than very general instructions."[78] However, the army's massive expansion beginning in 1939 rekindled the regular officers' old fear and distrust of amateur officers and NCOs. They believed such people lacked sufficient knowledge and drive to be trusted to use their initiative in the stressful confusion of modern combat; moreover, the soldiery lacked the fighting quality found in the last war. Commanders believed they could rely on good results only if they set simple, limited tasks and closely supervised their execution. This prejudice almost certainly sold short the human material available.[79] The problem was only partly the men themselves, as the intelligence of the average wartime soldier and officer was higher than that of their prewar, regular counterparts. It was more the product of the generally blinkered, unimaginative, and regressive approach to doctrine and training that characterized the British Army. In contrast, the Germans enjoyed conspicuous success in producing a victory-winning military machine that had expanded from a tiny 100,000-strong Reichswehr in only five years.

Montgomery had other doubts as well. He deprecated the abilities of most of his generals. Indubitably, this was in some measure due to his arrogance and overweening sense of self-importance. He was not, however, alone in his assessment of weakness in British generalship. Brooke confided in his diary: "Half our corps and divisional commanders are totally unfit for their appointments, and yet if I were to sack them I could find no better! They lack character, imagination, drive and power of leadership."[80] Whether Montgomery was unduly harsh in his judgment is beside the point (although several commanders, some of his own choosing, proved themselves downright incompetent in Normandy). His lack of faith in their tactical acumen and leadership inclined him to exert tight control over their actions; the need for "grip" was one of his favorite themes. To accomplish this, he used both the Phantom GHQ Liaison Regiment's patrols and his own team of personal liaison officers (his eyes and ears) to monitor activity at division level or below. This (not unjustified) prejudice contributed to his conservative approach to the conduct of operations at both tactical and operational levels of war. Inevitably, as commanders feared being held responsible for the failures of their subordinates, his approach was reflected down through all levels of command.

The tried, tested, and limitedly effective methods of the last war were resorted to again in the hope that improved communications would make traditional, centralized control more effective. The senior commander would produce a plan, usually worked out in considerable detail, specifying what every formation or unit would do in each of several phases. Undeviating adherence was demanded of each subordinate level, quite often including rigid timings required by the fire and/or air support plan. There was very little room for the exercise of judgment. It appeared, in other words, that the army wished to have its cake and eat it: initiative was desirable when things went wrong, but the risk of its unauthorized exercise upsetting the plan must be avoided. Unsurprisingly, initiative could not be turned on and off like a tap, and little was shown when, as frequently happened, the plan went awry or communications broke down. Instead, subordinates preferred the safe option of referring the changed situation back to a higher authority and waiting for fresh orders, which always took precious time to arrive. In the meantime, ephemeral opportunities slipped by unexploited, and the enemy was given breathing space.[81]

Montgomery-style set-piece battles almost always achieved a penetration. They never achieved a breakthrough. Deliberate attacks stressed a measured (and, by the enemy, measurable) fire plan–led advance, thoroughly clearing the axis and consolidating at the end of each phase before beginning the next. This was an essentially attritional approach that sought victory through physical destruction rather than disruption, negating any advantage offered by superior mobility and, as such, unlikely to gather much tempo. Fast German reactions, even when surprise had been achieved, generally got inside the British decision-action cycle and enabled the defense to repair any developing rupture. As a result, openings for the generation of operational maneuver were rarely created and even more rarely seized on. This did not seem to bother Montgomery. He was a realist who accepted the limitations of the army at his disposal, made all too apparent during the years of defeat. All his experience inclined him to believe that a steady, even plodding advance suited his command (and his command style), while fluid operations did not; besides, he doubted the abilities of his main maneuver element, the armored divisions, and he refused to form a *corps de chasse*.[82] For good reason, he was risk-averse, concerned with avoiding both casualties and even the hint of failure. He wanted to fight only battles he was sure he could control, at all times retaining the "balance" he so prized so that the enemy stood no chance of regaining the initiative. For these reasons, his battles remained essentially attritional and therefore indecisive.

The Anglo-Canadian force that fought in Normandy was thus far from perfect in terms of equipment, doctrine, training, and leadership, but it was workmanlike—if small. After several misguided organizational and doctrinal experiments, it had settled on structures and concepts that would endure for the rest of the war. Its foundation was a formidable artillery arm (18 percent of 21 Army Group manpower, as opposed to 14 percent in the infantry), much of it in the thirty-seven artillery regiments of the six Army Groups, Royal Artillery (AGRAs).[83] Each of the ten infantry divisions, the basic building block of operations, was 18,347 men strong, with three infantry brigades of three battalions each, a machine gun–heavy mortar battalion, and three artillery regiments with 72 guns; there were 110 antitank guns as well, and enough trucks to transport all except the rifle component (which was lifted by plentiful higher-formation transport whenever a quick move was necessary). There were eight independent armored brigades, each with generally three armored regiments (US battalion equivalents, each with sixty-one medium or infantry tanks and eleven light tanks); these were intended primarily to support the infantry divisions, but under the Montgomery doctrine, they could also operate in a more maneuver-oriented fashion. The armored divisions, five of them, comprised 14,964 men each, with four tank-equipped regiments and four infantry battalions (one in armored half-tracks, three motorized) and two artillery regiments with forty-eight guns (and seventy-eight antitank guns). The army group thus had one armored for roughly every two and a half infantry brigades and twice as many artillery regiments (including AGRAs, but excluding air defense and antitank) as maneuver brigades—a clear reflection of its desire to fight with firepower, equipment, and mobility rather than with men's lives. The campaign, however, quickly revealed contradictions within the doctrinal framework that impelled the army in the direction of an attritional struggle, albeit of a much less manpower-profligate nature than in the previous war.[84]

The British Army raised its tactical game as the Normandy campaign progressed. Cooperation between units of infantry divisions and their supporting tanks from independent brigades improved greatly, and artillery support plans became more flexible and responsive to changing situations. Belatedly, at the end of July, armored divisions started to form tank-infantry battle groups for the first time.[85] Air support also became better integrated; however, thanks largely to RAF resistance to any devolution of control, it did not match the Americans' concept of armored column cover. The cramping effects of overcentralization were mitigated somewhat as growing skill and experience gave rise to greater trust and delegation of responsibility in many formations. However, heavy casualties among battalion-level officers and the arrival of new and often indifferently trained replacements limited this trend. At the higher tactical level, corps became slicker in mounting battles and more flexible in their conduct, though caution continued to trump drive when operations became more fluid and mobile in character.

The Canadian Army's Approach to War

Despite its lack of a military tradition and small peacetime cadre, the Canadian Dominion had fielded a volunteer corps that was among the best in Haig's army. As in the mother country, however, there was a reaction to the war's losses (about 65,000 military dead and 150,000 wounded from a population of 7.2 million in 1914). The "never again" ethos flourished in Canada too, and the Great Depression, not to mention the remoteness of Europe and the comforting protection of the Royal Navy, fostered an inward-looking sentiment. The military was even more neglected in Canada than in Britain, and preparations for war started even later. The peacetime Permanent Active Militia (PAM, Canada's regular force) numbered around 4,000, and the Non-Permanent Active Militia (NPAM, the equivalent of Britain's TA) numbered 34,000; military service was so unprestigious and unappealing and money was so tight that these strengths were only about one-third of establishment.

When the Dominion committed to fighting with Britain in 1939, the government of Prime Minister Mackenzie King initially sought to limit Canada's liability largely to air and maritime involvement, with a rather token ground force. Reaction to the cost in casualties of the last war had been as acute in Canada as in the United Kingdom. The fall of France and Dunkirk wrought a significant change of attitude, but there was no universal consensus. Limited conscription was introduced in mid-1940 and extended a year later, but it was not for general service. The expanded PAM and NPAM combined, which formed the Canadian Army Overseas (CAO), was confined to volunteers. At its peak in early 1945, it totaled almost 288,000 officers and men, and the army as a whole numbered almost half a million. All of them had to be made into soldiers from scratch and with a negligible training base, a far bigger challenge than that faced by the British or American armies. Canadian war industries were virtually nonexistent, and the CAO had to rely on Britain for virtually all its equipment—equipment that was slow to arrive, as the British prioritized making good the losses at Dunkirk and supplying their own greatly expanded armed forces. Lacking both institutional memory of the lessons of the last war and any conceptual basis for the next, the Canadian army had to rely on the British for both doctrine and all but the most basic training, as well as the means to fight. Given the circumstances, it is little wonder that it took three to four years to mold the splendid human material of the CAO into effective units, let alone formations, and there was still work to be done, especially at division and corps levels, when they went into battle.[86]

When it was decided that Canada would make a land contribution commensurate with that of the First World War, a force with a cutting edge of three infantry and two armored divisions, two armored brigades, and two AGRAs was raised for the CAO. This was quite an achievement, given that the prewar Canadian army was just a collection of units with no field formation headquarters and only forty-five staff college graduates in the whole PAM (British help was necessary to create useful staffs). The supply of volunteers largely dried up in 1943, and no further formations could be raised. Indeed, even before the invasion of Normandy, the replacement pool was well short of a war establishment that experience would expose as inadequate. Even at the start of the campaign, and despite the conversion of men of other arms into infantrymen, there was a shortage of infantry that began to impact combat effectiveness from late July.[87] There were also morale implications for soldiers engaged in or destined to join severe fighting in foreign lands, without leave home, while limited-service conscripts avoided danger and hardship.

It was originally intended that Canada's substantial contribution would be organized as an army of two corps under Canadian command. Perhaps inevitably, this plan proved impractical. Canadian troops could not stand by for years while the whole force was formed in the United Kingdom and trained to the requisite standard. Military and national pride, combined with the need for combat-experienced personnel to leaven untried units, led first to the use of 2 Infantry Division in the debacle of the Dieppe raid and then to the committal of I Canadian Corps to the Italian campaign in 1943. King was happy for the corps to stay there, as he suspected the campaign in northwestern Europe would be bloodier; in any case, the scarcity of shipping precluded the return of the whole force in time for the invasion of France. Thus, only II Canadian Corps, consisting of one armored and two infantry divisions, an armored brigade, and an AGRA, fought in Normandy. To make up First Canadian Army, a British corps had to be placed under command.

The Anglicization of the army had its advantages. Just as limiting casualties was a major concern of General Montgomery, it was a high priority for the Dominion as well. Common doctrine, equipment, and training enabled Canadian divisions, then corps, to fit into larger British formations without misunderstandings and nationalist angst to prevent generally smooth cooperation. However, Canadian formations also displayed most of the faults of their British counterparts. They were slow and ponderous, often poorly coordinated. The enthusiasm and high morale of the troops and their quickness to learn lessons were impressive, but the on-average lower level of professional education, understanding, and skill of officers, especially on the staff and at formation command level, resulted in heavier than necessary casualties and frequent tactical failure. At a crucial point of the Normandy campaign, in the early days of August, these weaknesses would have adverse operational consequences.

CONCLUSIONS

General Montgomery had always seen the Normandy campaign as going through the three phases of all his previous battles: the break-in, the "dogfight," and the breakout. Having established themselves ashore, it would take the Allies some time to build up superior combat power, gaining ground incrementally and wearing the enemy down as they did so. In the event, this second, essentially attritional phase proved more difficult, costly, and time-consuming than anticipated. The ground was eminently defensible, and the Germans defended it expertly. The attackers discovered tactical limitations in their forces, especially in conducting the combined-arms battle. The length and costliness of the dogfight were exacerbated by the fact that most of the commanders and units involved were discovering the hard way the difference between theory and training and the realities of battling a first-class enemy. It took time to rectify matters, although many of the problems should have been foreseen and dealt with in training, as four years of pre-Normandy fighting had exposed most of them. However, tactical lessons were duly learned, and performance improved. Even as both the British and the Americans, especially the latter, were gaining in experience and skill and growing numerically, the Germans were being worn down and their logistic support failing. The defense culminated in late July, and Operation Cobra would see the beginning of the third phase. In the event, thanks largely to major German errors, this phase progressed much faster than originally anticipated, with the Allies closing up to the Seine earlier than expected and the Germans in considerably worse shape.

The post-Normandy situation offered the Allies an unforeseen and wonderful opportunity to deliver a strategically crippling and, when combined with even greater Soviet successes in the east, possibly fatal blow to the Reich's ability and will to fight on. Yet they would fail to take full advantage of the possibilities opened up by the great victory achieved in August. The causes were various. Some systemic problems remained throughout the campaign and beyond. Fear of heavy casualties and their adverse effect on morale continued to inhibit commanders. Resultant overcaution meant that opportunities were sometimes missed. This was probably inevitable in the armies of the democracies, especially the British, whose experiences in the First World War had made them skeptical of authority. Less inevitable was the persistence of overcontrol and lack of trust on the part of senior commanders, which frequently led to missed opportunities and a slowing of tempo. Ever present and more problematic were the inadequacies of doctrine. Operations beyond the Seine were more improvised than the coherent, doctrinally informed approach demanded by the Combined Chiefs of Staff. And they lacked firm, consistent direction and adherence to many of the principles of war to which both Allies subscribed. These themes are developed in subsequent chapters.

CHAPTER TWO

The Tipping Point

THE FIRST SEVEN WEEKS, 6 JUNE–25 JULY 1944

The Strategic Aim

After much wrangling between the British and the Americans, the Combined Chiefs of Staff (CCS) agreed on a directive that was issued to the Supreme Commander, AEF, on 12 February 1944. General Eisenhower was told: "You will enter the Continent of Europe and, in conjunction with the other Allied Nations, undertake operations aimed at the heart of Germany and the destruction of her Armed Forces." Eisenhower clarified this mission by stating that "the purpose of destroying enemy forces was always our guiding principle; geographical points were considered only in relation to their importance to the enemy in the conduct of his operations or to us as centers of supply and communications in proceeding to the destruction of enemy armies and air forces."[1] The Germans' centre of gravity, the seizure or destruction of which would end their ability and will to fight, was thus assessed as being their armed forces rather than the national capital or areas of economic importance. Straightforward as this aim may have been, there was much disagreement over how and where it should be accomplished, and at times, it seemed as if it had been lost to sight. The operational-strategic path that would lead to the enemy's destruction was far from clear when the invasion forces were still building up in England. First, the Allies had to establish a firm bridgehead in France, a sine qua non that was expected to be very difficult, with no certainty of success.

Establishing a Lodgment: Successes and Disappointments

On 15 May 1944 General Sir Bernard Montgomery, the interim Allied land forces commander in chief (C-in-C), had outlined his "master plan," the concept of operations for Operation Overlord, to Eisenhower; the principal land, sea, and air component commanders of the AEF; and some of the political leaders who would oversee and execute the invasion.[2] Following the achievement of air superiority, the isolation of the invasion area by air interdiction, and the fixing of German forces in the Pas de Calais by deception (Operation

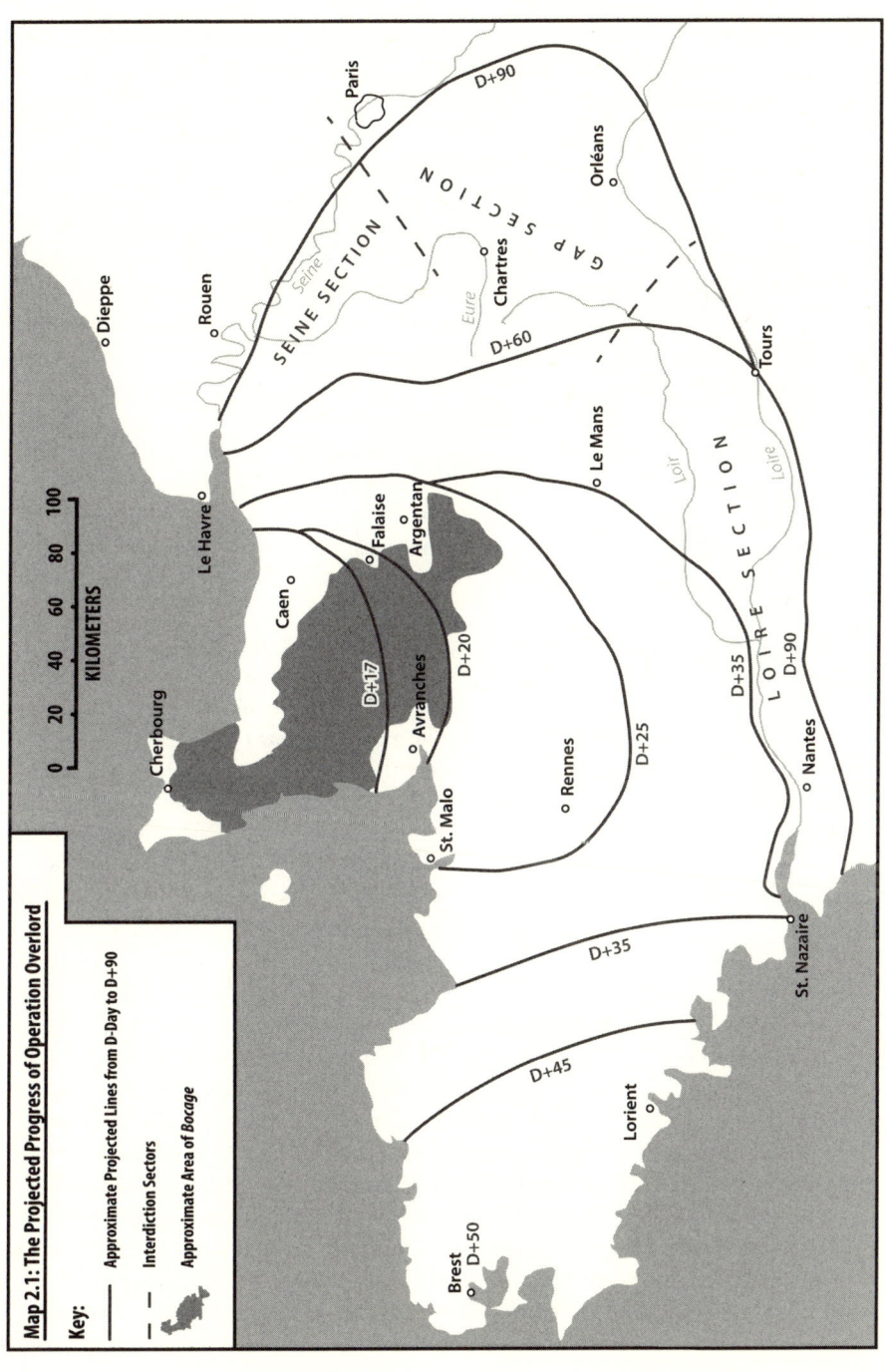
Map 2.1: The Projected Progress of Operation Overlord

Fortitude), the Normandy campaign would evolve in three broad phases. The projected progress of the invasion is shown in map 2.1.

In the first phase, the Allies would establish a substantial bridgehead. They would land on an 80 km (50 mile) frontage with Lieutenant General Sir Miles Dempsey's Second British Army to the east and Lieutenant General Omar N. Bradley's First US Army to the west. By about D+15, the Americans would have taken Cherbourg, an indispensable deep-water port. By D+20, it was envisaged that the Allies would have advanced to a line about 50 to 60 km (30 to 40 miles) inland and 150 km (90 miles) long, running roughly from Avranches on the Atlantic coast to Domfront and Falaise and then to Cabourg on the Channel coast. This would create a bridgehead with sufficient depth and maneuver room to be defensible and sizable enough to allow for the transfer of substantial forces and their necessary administrative support from the United Kingdom. It would also provide the airfield sites (especially on the Caen-Falaise plain) required by the air forces to support and defend the ground troops effectively: as long as fighter-bombers had to traverse the Channel at its widest, their response and loiter times would be unsatisfactory, as would be their depth of penetration into the enemy rear areas.

Before the start of phase two, there might be an operational pause to allow for the buildup of combat power and logistic resources to enable offensive operations to continue; ideally, however, the development of operations would be seamless. The British would push eastward and southeastward to the river Touques and Argentan, fixing the main enemy forces by aggressive action and shielding the Americans' left flank while they drove south to the Loire and cut off Brittany from the hinterland. Then the newly introduced Third US Army under Lieutenant General George S. Patton would clear the Brittany peninsula and thereby secure the ports deemed essential by SHAEF logisticians to allow fresh formations and supplies to flow into the theatre directly from the United States.

In the final phase the whole Overlord lodgment area—as far west as Brest, as far south as the Loire, and as far east as the Seine—would be occupied by around D+90. With that achieved, the Normandy campaign would be over, and the Allies would concentrate overwhelming strength for the power drive that, starting around D+120, would carry them into the heart of Germany. The main effort would focus on the Ruhr industrial area.[3] The enemy would endeavor to retain this most important centre of war-related production and, in doing so, would be brought to battle and destroyed. By which armies, where, and how this would be accomplished would be determined when the operational situation was clarified.

Thanks to the Fortitude deception plan, the defenses on Normandy's shores were far less developed and dense than those in the Pas de Calais;

moreover, the landings on 6 June achieved both operational and tactical surprise. Furthermore, the German High Command (Oberkommando der Wehrmacht [OKW]) suspected that the assault against Normandy was a feint to lure forces away from Fifteenth Army, which was defending against the real main effort expected to come against the Pas de Calais. Accordingly, it was slow to release the reserves that might have defeated the invasion, especially if aided by a period of bad weather, before the Allied buildup became too strong to overcome. In the first week alone, the Allies landed 326,000 men and more than 2,000 tanks. This was, in fact, a rate of reinforcement that the Germans, given the limitations of rail and road transport capacity and the Allied air interdiction effort, would have been hard-pressed to match.

By 13 June, a continuous if shallow bridgehead had been established. However, progress had fallen short of Allied hopes. On the left, the British had failed to take Caen, a vital road centre with crossings over the river Orne to the south that had been unrealistically designated as a D-Day objective. Their foothold over the river to the east was very restricted. The enemy thus enjoyed an uncomfortably generous view of a critical part of the British sector, denying them the space to build up necessary forces and administrative areas and to establish airfields. The danger remained of a German counterattack to roll up the bridgehead from the east. The problem at Caen was to determine the operations of Dempsey's Second Army for the next few weeks. In the west, the Americans were still more than 20 km (12 miles) from Cherbourg and somewhat less distant from the key junction of seven roads at St. Lô, significantly short of the expected rate of advance. First Army and the right wing of Second Army had encountered a complication for which they were unprepared. Very soon after landing, they found themselves moving into the *bocage*.[4] Although the Allies had an abundance of preinvasion air and ground photography and excellent maps of Normandy, for some reason, the military implications of this difficult, defensible terrain had not sunk in. The ground, skillfully exploited by a determined enemy, prevented the advance from gaining momentum.[5]

Montgomery had always accepted that the preponderance of German combat power was likely to be committed against Second Army. Simple geography placed it on the more threatening and, at the same time, more accessible axis (the shortest and easiest route to Paris and thence Germany). Faced with an initial and important failure at Caen, he developed his operational idea to meet the unwelcome circumstances (though maintaining, in the face of evidence to the contrary, that all was going according to his master plan). The British would mount a series of attacks with two aims in mind. The first was to take Caen and gain a favorable line from which decisive operations could be launched when the time was right. The other, more important one was to attract as much German strength as possible into Panzer Group West, facing Second Army, and fix it: this would enable Bradley's First Army to advance more rapidly against the German Seventh Army to seize Cherbourg and, having done so, break out in the west, thus paving the way for Third Army's thrusts into Brittany and eastward.

OKW remained concerned until the end of July that the main invasion would come in north of the Seine, mounted by the mythical First US Army Group (FUSAG). Accordingly, it kept its Fifteenth Army strong.[6] However, forces in Brittany, the southwest and south of France, and Scandinavia were depleted to reinforce Normandy, and the strong II SS Panzer Corps was sent back from the Russian front.[7] These reinforcements were not enough to recover the initiative or seriously threaten the viability of the lodgment, but they were sufficient to, in Montgomery's words, "rope off" the invasion force and create what looked like a stalemate. Until July was all but over, attritional battles like those of the First World War, with casualty rates reminiscent of the Somme and Third Ypres, remained the norm.[8] By 25 July, the Americans had lost more than 70,000 men, and the Anglo-Canadians more than 46,000 (excluding battle exhaustion cases). The pace of the advance was painfully slow. Anglo-Canadian troops finally took the southern suburbs of Caen on 20 July (D+43), and they were still almost 25 km (15 miles) north of Falaise, a D+17–20 objective. Cherbourg fell to the Americans on 26 June (D+19) but was unusable until September, and when they at last captured St. Lô on 19 July, they remained more than 30 km (18 miles) from their intended D+17 line Granville-Vire.

The slowness of the advance and its rising casualty toll gave rise to dissatisfaction and dissension within the Allied ranks. American soldiers, encouraged by a press that was every bit as chauvinistic as the British, decided that their ally was not pulling its weight and not taking its fair share of the pain.[9] A scapegoat was sought by some, and thanks to his arrogance, insensitivity, and apparent assumption of infallibility, Montgomery was a popular choice. Most American generals, including Bradley and Patton, had heartily disliked him since the previous spring for his patronizing attitude toward the US Army and his disregard for its needs and interests. Many senior airmen, including the Deputy Supreme Commander, Air Chief Marshal (ACM) Sir Arthur Tedder, also harbored grudges that were now reinforced by Montgomery's failure to provide much-needed airfield sites. Senior officers (including British ones) at SHAEF were anxious to see him sacked by the Supreme Commander. Discontent spread as far as Prime Minister Winston Churchill and the US Chief of Staff of the Army, George C. Marshall. What many perceived, with little justice, as the repeated failures of the land forces commander culminated in Operation Goodwood, which ground to an expensive and ignominious halt on 20 July. Montgomery was thought to be overcautious, and this, combined with his irritating insistence that all was proceeding without a hitch according to his master plan, sharpened existing enmities. There were, however, other reasons for the lack of progress. Both Allied armies suffered from deficiencies in doctrine and training, exacerbated in some areas by equipment that was inferior to the enemy's. Only painfully acquired experience would enable them to rectify these weaknesses and capitalize fully on their strengths, including particularly a growing superiority in men and materiel, to defeat their highly capable enemy.

THE LAND SITUATION ON THE EVE OF THE BREAKOUT

Not that he had received much recognition, far less thanks, for it, but General Montgomery's operational idea had, by 25 July, created the conditions for a transition to more decisive operations than had been possible in the buildup phase of Overlord. For a start, both armies had fought their way through to acceptable lines of departure from which such operations could—at least in theory—be mounted.[10] And the inexorable agglomeration of Allied fighting power had created the numerical superiority to do so. Moreover, British efforts to attract the bulk of German armor onto the eastern flank and thus enable an American breakthrough in the west had borne fruit (at the cost of casualties and the frustration of their own plans).

The Correlation of Forces on 25 July

With the disembarkation of 5 US Armored Division on 25 July, the Allies had assembled thirty-three divisions in Normandy—eighteen of them American, and fifteen British and Canadian.[11] They were opposed by twenty-four German divisions and some parts of divisions (excluding troops still tied down in static coast defense). Some authors have used this 1.4:1 correlation of formations to suggest that the Allies did not enjoy a substantial numerical advantage. However, this ignores two factors in particular: most German divisions were substantially smaller than their Allied (especially British) counterparts, and many were understrength even before they suffered attritional losses that were not made good. The Allies also held a much greater proportion of their strength as corps- and army-level assets. The British had almost twice as many tanks in their eight independent armored brigades as they had in armored divisions, and about one-third of their artillery was found in Army Groups, Royal Artillery (AGRAs) at the higher formation level; about half of US field artillery and tanks and tank destroyers were found in nondivisional organizations. By contrast, less than 9 percent of German armor, 11 percent of German artillery (i.e., guns and howitzers), and 23 percent of manpower (including only 16 percent employed in service support tasks) were found in GHQ units. Nor does the fact that the Germans had a lower proportion of their men employed in combat and service support roles indicate greater fighting power; German infantrymen would become acutely aware of their inferior artillery and logistic support.

In all, by 25 July, the Allies had deployed 1,452,000 soldiers—812,000 American and 640,000 British and Canadian;[12] 6,757 tanks and tank destroyers—3,371 American and 3,386 British-Canadian (excluding replacements for about 2,100 already lost); and 3,240 artillery pieces—1,720 American and 1,520 British-Canadian. The Germans had committed about 490,000 men to Normandy but had taken almost 117,000 casualties and received only 10,078 replacements; their strength by 25 July was therefore approximately 380,000. They had sent 1,869 tanks, assault guns, and self-propelled (SP) antitank guns (including replacements) but had written off about 450 (and another 450 or so were in workshops). They had also sent 1,672 artillery pieces; the number lost is unknown, but the figure was probably considerable. It is noteworthy that, despite this wasting of strength on the invasion front, Normandy continued to be starved of the troops needed to hold the German line. There were twenty-four divisions (most of them tired) or parts of divisions in Normandy, eighteen between the Seine and Amsterdam awaiting a second cross-Channel assault, and eleven elsewhere in France (another invasion, in the south of France, was expected imminently). The seriousness of the German maldeployment is well illustrated by the fact that in Normandy, the only active front in the west, the Allies enjoyed a 3.8:1 superiority in manpower, 4.7:1 in armor, and about 3:1 in artillery. The last figure is seriously misleading, however, as German ammunition supply was woefully inadequate; American guns, for instance, were firing four times as many shells per day.

Force ratios are important, but they do not tell the whole story when assessing relative strength. Qualitative factors can be very significant too. Several historians have explained the initially slow progress of the Allied armies in Normandy, especially the British, by reference to German technological superiority in combination with terrain that was ideal for defense. This contention deserves some consideration.

Infantry. British small arms were more suited to colonial combat, the army's accustomed milieu, than to modern continental warfare. The infantryman's rifle was still, essentially, the bolt-action weapon first used in the Boer War at the turn of the century. It was supplemented by two submachine guns (SMGs): the heavy American Thompson, and the world's cheapest, nastiest, and most unreliable, the Sten. The US infantry fared better, as its basic weapon was the excellent Garand automatic rifle; its high rate of fire (thirty rounds per minute) persuaded the army, somewhat dubiously, as it transpired, that it needed fewer machine guns. Those Americans whose primary job was not shooting with a personal weapon carried a carbine or SMG. The Germans had a bewildering variety of weapons, including vast arrays of captured ones of differing calibers and reliability. Most riflemen carried bolt-action rifles, while a fair proportion of the men in more favored or simply luckier units carried semiautomatic rifles or machine pistols. However, personal weapons are considerably less important than crew-served ones in deciding combat outcomes—a fact the Germans took to its logical conclusion by turning most riflemen into little more than ammunition carriers for the machine guns. These plentiful and frightening German machine guns had an adverse effect on the morale of British and American infantry, as evidenced by every infantryman's account of the campaign. They also had much to do with the Allies' reluctance to advance without plentiful artillery support.

Most German infantry battalions had eight to twelve 81mm mortars and between forty-three and sixty-three general-purpose machine guns (MG-34/42). Both British and US battalions had six such mortars, comparable in range and bomb weight; an American battalion also possessed nine company-level 60mm mortars, and a British battalion had seventeen platoon-level 2 inch (50mm) mortars. A British battalion had forty-one Bren light machine guns (LMGs), and an American battalion had forty-five Browning automatic rifles (BARs); the US battalion also had twenty .30 caliber and six .50 caliber machine guns.[13] The rate of fire of the belt-fed MG-34/42 was roughly double that of Allied machine guns (and treble that of the BAR). The Germans could thus generally generate higher volumes of fire at unit level, especially compared with the British; but this was also true of the semiautomatic Garand rifle on which the US infantry relied as a substitute for machine guns. Some Wehrmacht divisions also fielded varying numbers of heavy machine guns and mortars (105mm and 120mm) and short-range infantry guns (75mm and 150mm, usually used over open sights) in support units to augment the firepower of battalions. Of course, Allied formations did likewise, albeit less generously. The British infantry division's machine gun battalion, for instance, was a formidable asset with its thirty-six Vickers medium machine guns and sixteen 4.2 inch (105mm) mortars. The US Army infantry division's chemical mortar battalion fielded thirty-six 4.2 inch mortars.

On the defensive, even a few MG-34/42s surviving an artillery preparation or barrage were capable of bringing attacking infantry to a juddering halt, pinning the riflemen, with their inadequate (as they perceived them) LMGs and BARs, to the ground. Sometimes, a flurry of mortar bombs inflicted casualties and disorganization in the forming-up place before the attack had even begun. Often, the advance was halted in an area already registered as a target (a preselected killing zone) by the defender's mortars, which then worked over the unfortunate would-be attackers. And, of course, the Germans immediately subjected their defensive positions, once captured by the enemy, to intense, accurate fire before consolidation could take place. The mortar and its artillery cousin, the *nebelwerfer* multibarreled rocket projector, were the most effective infantry killers in Normandy. A 30 July report by the British No. 2 Operational Research Section (ORS) showed that over 70 percent of British casualties were caused by these weapons. Until both infantry and, more importantly, combined-arms tactics matured from the rather simplistic methods of the early days, attacks would too often prove expensive failures.

Armor. The Sherman, in one of its various marks, accounted for two-thirds of the Allied medium tanks in Normandy.[14] Both it and the British Cromwell, which made up another 20 percent, were seriously underarmored. The vast majority of German 75mm tank and antitank guns could penetrate any aspect of their armor out to about 1,500 m (1,640 yards), and the Panther long-barreled 75mm and Tiger 88mm guns even further (although engagements over 1,000 m were rare). Moreover, the Sherman had a distressing tendency to burst into flames when penetrated (in 73 percent of cases, according to operational analysis).[15] They were also undergunned, at least for combating enemy tanks. (In the American view, the purpose of tanks was not to fight other tanks but to support infantry and exploit success.) Their 75mm medium-velocity (MV) guns could defeat the strongest protection of most German armored fighting vehicles (AFVs) out to over 1,000 m, but they were effective against the Panther at only half that distance or less and against the Tiger at point-blank range, if at all. The only really effective tank gun was the 17-pounder on the British "Firefly" variant. This could knock out the best German tanks at over 1,000 m. The Sherman had its virtues, though. It enjoyed a good range of action—about 200 km (125 miles); it was maneuverable; its high-explosive (HE) performance was good (the reason for choosing an MV gun); and, above all, it was mechanically reliable, ensuring high levels of availability.

While most British independent tank brigades were equipped with Shermans, three had Churchill infantry tanks. These were armed with the same 75mm MV gun but were thickly armored to enable them to close onto defensive positions with the infantry they supported. They could withstand hits by the standard German 75mm at ranges over 500 m, but both Panthers and Tigers (and 88mm antitank guns) could kill them out to 1,500 m. The Churchill was excellent across difficult terrain, but it was slow, as befitted its role.

The last major category of Allied AFVs was the tank destroyer. These vehicles were the product of a flawed American doctrine. They were intended to be massed and used as a mobile reserve to defeat attacks by concentrated armor. Enemy tanks were supposed to be stalked and destroyed by these SP antitank guns, so the M-10 and M-18 were very mobile but even more lightly armored than the Sherman, whose chassis they shared; however, they had somewhat more effective antitank guns (the 3 inch and 76mm, respectively).[16] Although they could penetrate most enemy armor out to well over 1,500 m, these guns would defeat a Panther only at about 700 m and a Tiger at 500. The British began to rearm their tank destroyers with the 17-pounder, but only about 100 saw service in Normandy.

Clearly, German units equipped with Panthers and Tigers enjoyed a significant combat advantage, provided, of course, they managed to reach the battlefield. The Tiger had less than half the range of the Panther or of Allied tanks, and both were mechanically unreliable; the Tiger, in particular, spent a significant amount of time in workshops.[17] And only 650 Panthers and 138 Tigers saw service in Normandy (along with 25 Panther-based SP antitank systems). The vast majority of the 2,248 AFVs present at one time or another (including replacements) were Mark IV panzers (900), roughly equal to the Sherman; turretless StuG III assault guns (550), inferior to the Sherman; or one of the other 200 assault or SP antitank guns (mostly inferior) that were around in small numbers. In all, the Allies committed about 6,300 tanks and tank destroyers (excluding 2,300 light tanks and all replacement tanks): 2,600 US and 1,820 British Shermans (the latter including 420 Fireflies), 570 Churchills, 340 Cromwells, and 756 American and about 200 British M-10s (including more than 100 armed with the 17-pounder). This means that about one-third of German AFVs were superior to their Allied counterparts, and roughly the same proportion were inferior. Or, to put it another way, for every eight Allied AFVs, there was one better-armed and better-armored German one.[18]

Of course, because the Allies were mostly on the offensive, they had to fear German antitank guns as well as armor. Most (but far from all) divisions had twelve to twenty-four 75mm or 88mm guns, some had eight to twelve 88mm flak and/or 88mm guns in the artillery regiment, and many infantry divisions possessed up to thirty-six *panzerschreck* (manpack 88mm antitank rocket launchers); the infantry was also plentifully supplied with the *panzerfaust* (a one-shot antitank grenade launcher).[19] In addition, five GHQ antitank battalions had another 138 75mm or 88 mm guns. It appears, however, that towed guns, perhaps because of their vulnerability to artillery and tank HE rounds, were much less effective than armor as tank killers. Based on admittedly incomplete and possibly unreliable evidence, it appears that, in Normandy, they accounted for about 25 to 30 percent of Allied tank kills; close combat (presumably mainly with *panzerfaust* and *panzerschreck*) accounted for almost as many, and the rest were attributable to AFVs. The Allies, particularly the British with their 17-pounders and APDS ammunition for their 6-pounder (57mm) antitank guns, were at least as well prepared as the Germans to repel armored attacks.

Most British sources stress the presence, in their sector, of the bulk of III Flak Corps, with its 108 to 116 88mm flak guns. However, it seems that these guns were used in the antitank role only in extremis (though they were sometimes used as conventional artillery because GHQ artillery was in short supply). Indeed, the cumbersome nature and great weight of the 88mm flak limited its mobility; its high silhouette rendered digging in and concealment difficult, and it was vulnerable to artillery and tank HE fire. These factors, and the lack of crew training for antitank combat, were good reasons to keep these weapons to the rear; a brief experiment in the use of eight 88mm flak guns in *flakkampfgruppen* (antitank groups) was not considered a success. Moreover, the Germans needed all the air defense they could muster, given the omnipresence of Allied bombers and fighter-bombers. The corps itself claimed only ninety-two tank kills, twelve of them with the *panzerfaust* (out of a total army-SS claim of 3,663 destroyed tanks).[20]

Among the British AFVs were the "funnies" of 79 Armored Division. Sherman "Crab" tanks opened paths through minefields relatively rapidly and under armored protection, doing away with the need for slow hand clearing by vulnerable sappers on foot. The Churchill "Crocodile" mounted a flamethrower as well as main armament and greatly eased and expedited the business of house and hedgerow clearing by the infantry; the defense frequently folded when these vehicles put in an appearance. The Churchill AVRE (engineer tank) carried a fascine or short bridge for ditch crossing and was armed with a demolition gun whose massive charge was very effective against houses, concrete emplacements, and other fortified positions. These specialist vehicles added considerably more combat value to combined-arms teams than their numbers would suggest. Many Anglo-Canadian units had good reason to be grateful to Montgomery for his farsightedness in backing their development and production; by the same token, American units could be forgiven for deploring their rejection by Bradley.

Having looked at the overall balance of armor and put the German qualitative advantage in perspective, it is necessary to note the profound sectoral imbalance by late July. The success of Montgomery's operational idea resulted, on the eve of the American breakthrough, in First Army facing only two panzer and one panzer grenadier divisions with around 200 tanks and SP guns (excluding those in workshops). The Second and newly activated First Canadian Armies had seven panzer divisions on their front and the three heavy panzer (Tiger) battalions, for a total of more than 600 operational AFVs. In fixing the preponderance of German armored strength, British and Canadian soldiers paid a heavy price to set the conditions for American success in Operation Cobra.

Artillery. Earlier in the war, the Wehrmacht had relied heavily on air-delivered firepower rather than artillery, and priority was given to the production of AFVs over guns. By the time it was losing air superiority, the priority in artillery production had shifted to flak to protect the homeland from increasingly devastating attacks in the combined bomber offensive; by June 1944, there were no fewer than 55,000 antiaircraft guns in service. Despite this relative neglect of the field artillery branch, the Germans deployed a considerable quantity in Normandy. It did not, however, make a commensurate contribution to the defense. This was not, for the most part, a reflection on the quality of the weaponry. The Germans' field and medium (mostly 105mm and 150mm) guns and howitzers were roughly comparable to their American equivalents, and the 105mm was almost half as powerful again as the standard British divisional fieldpiece.[21] The Allies, however, possessed much larger quantities of medium and heavy artillery with a good combination of reach and punch. Unfortunately for German gunners, a significant proportion of their pieces were of foreign, captured stock—Soviet, Czechoslovak, French, and Italian. Apart from the Soviet weapons, these were generally inferior to German-made guns; more important, ammunition resupply rapidly became intermittent, problematic, or downright impossible, and even German shells became increasingly hard to come by. The maldistribution of dumps, a growing shortage of trucks and their inability to move by daylight in clear weather, as well as the multiplicity of ammunition natures (types) required all conspired with potent Allied counterbombardment to severely limit the effectiveness of German artillery. For every four American shells fired, the Germans replied with one at best. Nor could the Germans make optimal use of radio communications, which were technically excellent but woefully inadequate in quantity.

A hangover from the days of blitzkrieg, when air largely substituted for corps artillery, the vast preponderance of German artillery was found at the divisional level. Only about 180 guns and howitzers were present in the fifteen GHQ artillery battalions (which were not organized in larger units and included a mere 19 long-range, comparatively heavy 170mm guns). By contrast, taking the entire summer-autumn campaign into account, over one-third of Anglo-Canadian artillery (544 guns) was found in the corps-level AGRAs, typically around 64 medium and heavy guns in each, and over half of all US field artillery (about 1,440 weapons) was found in nondivisional units.[22] The Allies also increased their artillery strength considerably by reassigning heavy antiaircraft units to the ground role once the German air threat diminished. Moreover, each ally had worked out a very effective, flexible command and control system that the Germans, despite recognizing its advantages, could never even begin to match for want of materiel. Command of artillery was focused at the corps level, but control was decentralized to the lowest possible level. For instance, a British forward observation officer (FOO), usually a captain, was empowered to call down the fire of an entire divisional artillery regiment consisting of 72 25-pounders on an "Uncle" target of his own choosing. He could even direct his entire corps as well as divisional artillery (at least every gun in range) onto a "Victor" target. The time between the FOO's fire order and the arrival of the shells was normally about five minutes for an Uncle (divisional) target and as little as eight minutes for a Victor (corps) target.[23] Furthermore, fire could be arranged "time on target" (TOT), so that the first round from each gun arrived at the same instant, maximizing effect through a combination of surprise and concentration. Accurate survey and meteorology updates every six hours, together with periodic calibration, also improved the prospects of a first-round hit. The Germans could not match such accomplishments.

It is difficult to overstate the importance of these developments, given that the artillery was the most effective part of both Allies' combat arms and had to make up for some deficiencies in the others. In the attack, the ability to produce quick fire plans to maneuver massed fire around the battlefield at short notice often mitigated unexpected problems that threatened to hold up the advance. Just as important was the gunners' ability to break up attacks and counterattacks even before they could close with the defenders; many a precarious gain was held thanks to defensive fire tasks arranged to meet the inevitable counterattack. Only rarely did the enemy manage to defeat attacks with his artillery defensive fire, due in part to the Germans' problem with ammunition supply. More often, though, the enemy's failure was the result of Allied counterbombardment measures. Benefiting from good air photography, sound ranging, and other techniques and, above all, from air observation posts in good weather, the Allies could usually locate enemy batteries quite quickly, and plentiful medium and heavy artillery, not to mention fighter ground attack, delivered crushing weights of fire. Usually, the appearance of a light aircraft in the sky was enough to cause nearby German batteries to fall prudently silent. Of course, the Germans did their best to minimize the effect of Allied superiority through the skillful use of camouflage and dispersion, roving tactics with their small numbers of SP guns, and the studied use of pauses in Allied fire to redeploy; they succeeded in keeping their casualties remarkably low, but at the price of being largely unable to influence the outcome of the battle.

As previously noted, German mortars and the 350-plus *nebelwerfers* (mostly six-barreled 150mm, with a fair number of five-barreled 210/300mm) were actually more troublesome than conventional artillery. They were short-ranged but light, small, and easily concealed and deployable on inaccessible reverse slopes due to their high-angle fire. The mortars possessed a high rate of fire, and a battery of *nebelwerfers* could deliver (albeit rather inaccurately) simultaneous salvos of thirty to thirty-six rounds; both were thus excellent weapons for "shoot and scoot" tactics to avoid counterfire. However, by August, the problem was being mastered. The British, for instance, had introduced a countermortar organization in each formation that linked target acquisition means (including, for the first time, radar) and a dedicated communications system linked to likewise dedicated fire units of heavy howitzers or mortars, medium artillery, or heavy antiaircraft artillery firing airbursts.[24]

Increasingly, Allied artillery dominated the battlefield. In set-piece battles, it was a battle winner. However, when operations became progressively more mobile and fluid in August and September, as the German defense collapsed, the gunners had problems keeping up with the rapid rate of advance. Towed, road-bound artillery cannot match the speed and flexibility of armor and mechanized or even motorized infantry; nor could its ammunition supply. Moreover, as commanders sought to meet the voracious demands for fuel created by pursuit, they were forced to leave most nondivisional assets behind as their transport was commandeered for logistic purposes. When pursuit ended and heavy fighting again became an issue, there would be an inevitable delay while the medium and heavy guns and their ammunition were brought forward.

Reflections on Allied Materiel Shortcomings

In view of the widespread concern expressed in both American and British infantry circles about their firepower deficiency in the face of the enemy's numerous MG-34/42s and mortars, it is perhaps surprising that neither army saw fit to increase the number of Brens, BARs, and .30 caliber Brownings and mortars issued. Even if it were too great a challenge to double the number in each company, a firepower reserve of a platoon with half a dozen LMGs and another with light mortars, deployable to thicken the base of fire to support maneuver, would have lessened subunits' dependency on support weapons and arms. As a self-help measure, some formations stripped out machine guns, bazookas, and mortars from noncombat units and used them to beef up the fighting infantry. In addition to taking the initiative and increasing their holdings unofficially, some units used captured German weapons for their own purposes (though this involved problems of ammunition supply and the danger that, given the distinctive sound signature of the German machine gun, they would be mistaken for the enemy). But that was hardly an excuse for official inaction.

The Americans and British both decided to stick with their older tank designs, despite their obvious inferiority as fighting machines, because they valued quick mass production. Within a fortnight of D-Day, concerns were being expressed at senior levels in 21 Army Group about the inferior firepower and protection of most British tanks (a postcampaign study revealed that German gunners required only 1.63 hits to knock out a Sherman, while it took 2.55 to deal with a Panther and 4.2 for a Tiger).[25] General Montgomery's response was to block the publication of "alarmist" reports, lest they damage morale, and to issue disingenuous reassurances. But facts that were self-evident to tank crewmen likely did the job of lowering morale well enough, without adding official blinkers. At least the War Cabinet decided, early in the year, to concentrate in the future on producing Fireflies, heavy Churchills, and eventually the excellent Comet.[26] The Army Ground Forces (AGF) command in the United States, headed by Lieutenant General Leslie J. McNair, was just as disinclined as the British to acknowledge the immediate need for a better-gunned and better-armored tank. The excellent new M-26 Pershing was ready to go into series production in early 1944, but the AGF insisted on persevering with the Sherman (some with 76mm guns), and Pershings started to take the field only in February 1945. Nor did the army see fit to upgrade M-4s with the powerful 90mm gun, comparable to the Firefly's 17-pounder.[27] The AGF also continued to propound the discredited tank destroyer concept, and the upgunned (90mm) M-36 version was not provided in any quantity until the autumn of 1944.

When contemplating the British and American failure to respond to the problems posed by the enemy's superior machine guns and tanks and numerous mortars, it must be remembered that these weapons were not encountered for the first time in Normandy. Experience in Tunisia, in Sicily, and on the Italian mainland should have given rise to a more timely response. The Germans managed it, after all. The Tiger and Panther tanks were both developed rapidly in response to the technological surprise achieved by the Soviets' T-34 and KV-1.

The limitations of their weapons, combined with inadequate tactical doctrine and training, tended to discourage aggressiveness in Allied infantry and armored units. They preferred to rely on the excellent and abundant Allied artillery rather than their own firepower combined with maneuver to win ground. Although this certainly reduced casualties in individual tactical actions, it also meant that attacks were necessarily methodical and slow, too seldom achieving a rapid penetration by catching the enemy by surprise and thus off balance. The resultant gnawing through the defense prolonged battles and produced a steady drain of casualties. However, once the character of operations transitioned from attritional to maneuver, the high level of mechanical reliability of the Sherman and Cromwell tanks and their good road range enabled a sustained pursuit with a low dropout rate (as long as fuel resupply continued).

Mobility and Logistics

Never the mechanized juggernaut of legend, by late 1943, the Wehrmacht was well down the road of demotorization. Truck losses in North Africa, Italy, and, above all, Russia had reached critical dimensions. The decision was made to increase production to the maximum possible for 1944: 167,440 trucks. However, only 53,949 were manufactured in the first half of 1944, despite the fact that the bombing of relevant factories did not really start until the second half of the year. In all, 88,088 trucks were produced in 1944 (compared with 595,330 in the United States); these had to supply all fronts and the economy. As the loss rate of motor transport was considerably higher than the replacement rate—by a ratio of 3:1 between January and April—the situation continued to deteriorate. Moreover, the failure to produce sufficient spare parts resulted in high levels of nonavailability, as did fuel shortages.[28] Many German quartermaster and repair elements also had to cope with the problems created by the use of captured vehicles of many nationalities for which spare parts were lacking, thus aggravating the issue of unreliability.

One consequence of this progressive demotorization was an almost total dependence on railways. Of course, rail was normally the fastest and most efficient method for moving formations or bulk goods over long distances without inflicting wear and tear on vehicles or exhausting the troops. Before the invasion, the Germans had been impressed by the extent (indeed, redundancy) of the French rail system and were not unduly worried about this reliance. However, they soon discovered that the rail net was much more vulnerable than the roads to disruption from the air, and the Allied air interdiction effort in France hugely reduced its capacity. The Germans found that they could not reinforce Normandy on the scale and at the speed required to win the race to build up superior forces and thus seize the initiative. When formations arrived, usually by a combination of road and rail movement, they did so in dribs and drabs, tired and late. Furthermore, prioritizing troop movements over resupply ensured that the defense would become crippled by ammunition and fuel shortages when the inadequate preinvasion stockpiles were used up. From mid-June, the Germans were living a hand-to-mouth existence with no reserves to cope with any surge in demand.

A low level of mobility characterized most German formations. The twenty-two static infantry divisions present in France and the Low Countries on D-Day were capable only of defending in place, unless and until they received transport. The other infantry divisions were reliant primarily or entirely on horse-drawn transport, although some had motor vehicles to haul their artillery or antitank guns and to provide for some of their logistic needs. Many possessed nowhere near their prescribed complement of about 4,600 horses. The infantry, of course, marched everywhere, save for the one battalion per formation that had bicycle mobility. In theory, armored formations were fully motorized. In practice, several of the ten panzer and one panzer grenadier divisions that served in Normandy suffered from severe deficiencies when the invasion started. Despite efforts to repair these, in mid-July more than half of them had only between one-third and two-thirds of their vehicular establishment. This limited their flexibility and tactical effectiveness.[29]

While the motor transport available to combat formations was inadequate, that devoted to their logistic support was derisory; for instance, the quartermaster general of Seventh Army had at his disposal a lift capacity of a mere 500 tons in early June. This was the inevitable result of giving priority to combat formations in the allocation of transport assets (a reflection of the traditional German tendency to exaggerate the importance of the fighting arms at the expense of their sustainability). The problem was worsened by the unanticipated need to switch considerable resupply efforts onto the roads when the railways failed to cope. This in turn drove up fuel consumption, aggravating the fuel shortage, and hastened the decline in vehicle numbers as breakdowns and accidents increased (only darkness and bad weather permitted driving on the roads without drawing the attention of Allied fighter-bombers). Vehicles were lost much faster than they could be replaced (4,200, including 1,866 trucks in Army Group B, in June alone). And the denuding of higher-formation transport pools became self-defeating as divisions were increasingly forced to use their own transport to fetch supplies from rear dumps rather than having them delivered forward.[30]

By contrast, the Allies enjoyed a high level of mobility. By 24 July, for instance, the Americans alone had delivered 56,468 wheeled vehicles to Normandy. Both US and British armored divisions were fully motorized or mechanized. Each infantry division, too, was highly motorized, although transporting all its infantrymen in one lift required temporary reinforcement by three truck companies from the plentiful pool held at higher levels; this was frequently done.

The Allied logistic system was as generous as the Germans' was inadequate to support operations. To illustrate this, consider the divisional slice (a division's manpower plus its proportionate share of corps, army, and theatre troops). An average US infantry division with normal combat attachments numbered 15,600 men; in addition, there were 14,958 corps and army troops (6,223 combat and 8,735 service troops) and 9,787 communications zone (COMZ) personnel—a divisional slice in July 1944 of 40,345. A British division had a similar slice (with about 8,000 vehicles, less than half of them organic to the division). In fact, the British army group had a bare majority of combat troops—56 percent—with 44 percent supporting them (even the infantry, at 14 percent of the total, was outnumbered by the Royal Army Service Corps' 15 percent).[31]

The result of this asymmetric development of logistic capabilities would be disastrous for the Germans. When First Army launched Operation Cobra on 25 July, it did so with seven or more units of fire for all the important ammunition natures, barring only two. About 13 million gallons of fuel had been delivered into bulk storage, and decanting into jerry cans was taking place on the Continent.[32] The German Seventh Army facing it was all but out of critical categories of ammunition (e.g., 88mm armor-piercing) and was down to 0.7 of a ration allotment of fuel.[33] At the same time the Allies had attained a potentially decisive superiority in combat power, the German defense was culminating.

Command and Control

Tanks, mechanical transport, and aircraft were essential to restoring some sort of balance between firepower and mobility after the stalemate in the west during the First World War. At least as important in enabling armies to conduct maneuver warfare once again was the radio. As armies increased in size and were equipped with faster-firing, longer-ranged weaponry, firepower forced dispersion. Thus, Wellington's army of almost 68,000 men had defended on a 3 km (2 mile) frontage at Waterloo; by 1944, that was the approximate doctrinal frontage of a single German infantry regiment, and such a unit would often be required to hold more than twice that. Whether in defense or, even more so, in attack, the successful command and control of modern forces could not be done with only messengers, visual signals, or inflexible and easily cut telephone lines. While line remained the preferred means of communication, especially in relatively static situations, efficient radios became the principal means as battles developed. *Efficient* is, of course, a relative term. In the days of vacuum tube technology and weak chemical batteries, radios were much more fragile and less reliable than they are today, and they had a very limited range. They were also bulky, heavy, and temperamental. Even so, those of 1944 were a far cry from the more or less immovable sets of the First World War, useful only at the level of high command. Vehicle-mounted radio sets (voice or Morse key) generally had a range of 16 to 24 km (10 to 15 miles), and there were manpack or at least man-portable radios (usually weighing about 15 to 20 kg [30 to 40 pounds]) with a range of up to 8 to 12 km (5 to 7 miles) for use at the battalion level and below.

Radios were essential if commanders wanted to keep abreast of the changing tactical and operational situation and direct their forces accordingly; the more dynamic and rapidly developing the battle, the more vital efficient communications became. Here again, the Allies enjoyed an advantage over their enemy. They provided radios in increasing numbers to lower and lower levels; in the US Army and often in the British and Canadian armies as well, they percolated down to even platoon level. This enabled intimate support from the artillery, often en masse, at all stages of combat. By late July, compatible sets were being placed in tanks to make tank-infantry cooperation more effective, and VHF sets were being fitted in tanks or other "contact cars" to enable forward air controllers to direct close air support onto targets very close to their own troops. The Germans, overstretched and short of resources, could not even replace losses, much less improve their radios or expand their distribution. This was a growing tactical handicap that precluded the sort of flexible and devastatingly effective maneuver of massed artillery fires that did so much to ensure Allied success.

At the end of the day, of course, command and control is about concepts, doctrine, and command philosophy. Arguably, the Germans were more in tune with the demands of the contemporary battlefield, and this helped them offset, to an extent, the Allies' materiel advantages. For instance, German headquarters at each level of command were smaller, less bureaucratic, and therefore faster to act and react in fluid and fast-developing situations than their Allied equivalents.

The Land Situation: Conclusions

There is some truth to the contention that the German land forces possessed better weaponry—but only in some respects, and not at all in the crucial area of artillery. And although the Germans made excellent use of the terrain's defense-enhancing characteristics, it is clear that the Allies were slow to adapt their operational concepts and tactics to overcome these German advantages. For too long, they were willing to play to the enemy's strength. While the fighting in Normandy was restricted to an area in which the terrain was largely inimical to maneuver and the frontage was a mere 120 km (75 miles) or so, the Germans' lack of mobility was a severe but not a critical limitation. They were able to impose a linear, attritional nature on combat—an approach that actually suited both American and British doctrine, with its emphasis on overwhelming firepower rather than maneuver. Of course, the Germans were bound to lose in an attritional struggle, given the Allies' growing superiority in numbers and firepower (including air-delivered firepower); it merely took longer because the Allies were unable to maximize all their advantages. Once the Allies broke the quasi-stalemate (as happened after Operation Cobra) and the campaign entered a maneuver phase, the Wehrmacht's inferior mobility and dire supply situation became campaign-losing handicaps. The Allies' ability to outflank rapidly any effective defense and to outpace and cut off enemy forces attempting to withdraw made it possible to destroy whole formations.

AIRPOWER AND THE LAND CAMPAIGN

From Air Superiority to Air Supremacy

Air superiority is achieved when the degree of dominance is such that freedom of friendly air and related land and sea actions is assured at an acceptable cost while the enemy's is drastically reduced. Ideally, achievement of superiority is followed by air supremacy, which renders the enemy air force incapable of any effective interference. Winning air superiority was the priority of the Allied air forces and a prerequisite for their other missions and for the success of the invasion. It was essentially a business of attrition, and there were two traditional approaches. Local, possibly only temporary, air superiority could be achieved by winning a succession of aerial combat encounters, forcing the enemy to abandon operations; this was how the RAF won the Battle of Britain. Regional superiority could be established through an offensive countercampaign aimed not only at winning air battles but also at systematically and progressively destroying the enemy's air infrastructure (runways, fuel and ammunition supplies, maintenance facilities, and command and control systems, as well as aircraft on the ground). If these tasks could be accomplished over a sufficiently wide region, the enemy air force could be prevented from interfering with sea and land operations in a chosen area within it; this was how the Allies prepared for the 1943 invasion of Sicily and the subsequent campaign there and in Italy.

The Allies agreed on a far more ambitious approach at their Trident conference in May 1943. Subsequently christened Operation Pointblank, their combined bomber offensive had as its principal objective no less than the destruction of the Luftwaffe, primarily by smashing fighter-producing factories, repair shops, ball-bearing plants, and other essential facilities; there would also be airfield and depot attacks, especially within Germany, and, of course, aerial combat throughout the enemy's depth as the Germans responded to attacks on critical targets.[34] Continent-wide air superiority would enable the Allied air forces to go about the business nearest to their hearts: destroying all German war-related production and the morale of the civil population. And, particularly important as far as the CCS was concerned, Pointblank was an essential prelude to Operation Overlord.

The offensive against the German aircraft industry failed to prevent an increase in the number of fighters produced, a fact unappreciated by overly optimistic intelligence assessments. But the Luftwaffe was unable to translate this overall increase into a growth in front-line strength. Losses on all fronts (taken together) modestly outweighed gains. More important, aircrew casualties, combined with shortsighted training policies, meant that there were insufficient replacements, and their quality declined markedly (in mid-1944 Allied pilots received three to four times the 100 training hours of German pilots). In the first half of 1944 the Luftwaffe lost 9,648 aircraft, 6,648 of them while defending the west and the Reich itself. This, of course, reduced the Luftwaffe's effectiveness and led to increasingly one-sided aerial battles and a fast-growing casualty bill—a vicious circle that got worse over time. Meanwhile, the Allies had geared up for a long war and were producing better aircraft at a much faster rate than their losses; they enjoyed a superfluity of aircrews as well.[35]

The Allies expected the Germans to react to the invasion by conserving their forces out of reach of tactical airpower until the landings took place. Then they were expected to pour squadrons into air bases within easy reach of the chosen sector and contest local air superiority, with all the advantages deriving from proximity; meanwhile, the Allied fighters would have limited loiter time as a result of having to fly from bases in faraway England. This approach was countered first by the Pointblank assaults, which kept the German fighter force fully stretched defending vital assets. Second, there was an offensive counter–air effort to establish regional as well as general air superiority by eliminating the Luftwaffe's positional advantage. Thirty-four out of fifty major operational air bases and associated satellite airfields within 210 km (130 miles) of the invasion beaches were subjected to attacks that left their radar, communications, maintenance, and storage facilities and operating surfaces incapable of supporting normal operations. After the landings the campaign was stepped up, and all airfields within reach were similarly wrecked, with severe effects on serviceability and sortie rates. Lack of sufficient usable bases combined with continued, increasingly effective air attacks on Germany to pin and destroy Reich air defense fighters and with the disruption of rail transport required to equip and supply bases prevented the Germans from carrying out an effective surge to combat the invasion.

At the time of the invasion, the correlation of air forces was overwhelmingly in the Allies' favor. Together, in combat squadrons in the United Kingdom, they fielded 3,467 heavy bombers, 1,545 light and medium bombers, 5,409 fighters and fighter-bombers, and 2,316 troop carriers and transports.[36] To oppose them, the Luftwaffe's strength in all of France and in the Low Countries amounted to 325 medium bombers (with undertrained crews), 75 ground attack aircraft, 325 fighters (170 of them single-engined), and 95 reconnaissance machines; serviceability rates were low. To reinforce this meager array, the Germans managed to find another 300 fighters and 135 bombers to provide about 1,000 aircraft of all types actually opposing the Overlord forces in the crucial first week. This was clearly inadequate to meet the weight of the Allied onslaught, and from the very beginning the Luftwaffe was on the defensive; indeed, it was soon struggling to remain in existence, never mind aiding the hard-pressed ground forces. In addition to repeatedly bombing air bases that showed signs of repair, the Allies maintained standing patrols over those bases closest to the bridgehead to prevent them from generating sorties. The defenders were forced to operate out of bases in the Paris area and even further back. Even their reconnaissance efforts became sporadic, and concerted fighter or bomber operations virtually ceased. Apart from tip-and-run raids and the harassment of Allied artillery spotters, the Luftwaffe's efforts to combat the invasion were reduced to night bombing from high altitude (to avoid dense flak concentrations) and then, starting on 12 June, aerial mine laying; the former did negligible damage, and the latter caused only some relatively minor difficulties and delays.[37]

As June gave way to July, Allied air superiority transitioned to air supremacy. German antishipping forces, having accomplished very little, were withdrawn and then disbanded. Fighter units were hollowed out by mounting casualties and declining serviceability. They were unable to give top cover or air support to the army, even when it was vitally needed to avert the collapse of the front. By early August, the Allied attacks on the oil industry, begun in mid-May, were having a severe impact on fuel supplies, and a general curtailment of Luftwaffe operational activity was imposed (further weakening an already inadequate training regime). However, as the plight of the ground forces steadily deteriorated from bad to desperate, six new fighter units were committed to help save something from the wreckage. They made no difference. The pilots were as new as their aircraft; they were inexperienced and only superficially trained. Their ground support organization was disrupted by the need to pull back to avoid being overrun. Casualties were heavy, and nothing was accomplished.

Allied mastery of the air was the result of a long attritional struggle, not only in the west but over Germany and in the Mediterranean and eastern theatres as well. (And conversely, the Anglo-American assault on the Luftwaffe and German war production was of great benefit to the Red Army as it progressively smashed the main forces of the Wehrmacht.) This command of the air was a sine qua non, setting the conditions for eventual success on the ground. Without it, German reconnaissance aircraft would have detected the preinvasion buildup and probably would have penetrated the elaborate Fortitude deception that helped pin so many formations to the Pas de Calais. Without it, enemy airpower might have reacted effectively to the landings and against the shipping that supported them in the decisive early days. Without it, the interdiction campaign would not have been possible, and the enemy would have won the race to build up forces in Normandy, making a decisive counterattack possible. Had it not been maintained, the Germans would have been able to supply their forces properly and maneuver them in a timely and effective manner in reaction to Allied moves detected by air reconnaissance. Air supremacy also kept enemy air off the backs of the Allied armies, save for nuisance raids and ineffectual close air support. This was critical in many ways. Having failed to expand the bridgehead at anywhere near the desired rate, it became a target-rich environment crammed with fighting troops, headquarters, administrative areas, airfields, and the like. As it was, the Allies found that dumps and massed artillery, out in the open and uncamouflaged; nose-to-tail columns many kilometers in length; and other potentially lucrative targets could be offered without penalty. While denying effective and frequent air reconnaissance to the enemy, air mastery enabled the Allies to obtain timely intelligence at great depth. It also enabled artillery spotters to direct gunfire while denying this advantage to the enemy, an important combat multiplier. And it made possible the concentration of massive air-delivered firepower in close air support wherever it was desired on the battlefield.

Air Interdiction

Interdiction operations are mounted to destroy, neutralize, or delay enemy forces and supplies en route to the battlefield at such a distance from friendly troops that detailed integration of air and ground movements and fires is unnecessary. It was clear to the Overlord planners that such an air interdiction operation would be second in importance only to the achievement of air superiority; it would be a necessary prelude to and accompaniment for the invasion. Landings on an increasingly fortified hostile shore were going to be challenging, and even if they were successful, the enemy could build up his force levels faster by rail and road than the Allies could by sea across beaches without the benefit of a port.[38] It would be necessary to disrupt and delay German reactions, compel the enemy to commit his forces piecemeal, and degrade their logistic support. To this end, both Air Marshal Sir Trafford Leigh-Mallory, C-in-C of the Allied Expeditionary Air Forces (AEAF—US Ninth Air Force and British 2 Tactical Air Force), and the Deputy Supreme Commander, ACM Sir Arthur Tedder, championed the Transportation Plan. This envisaged a sustained attack throughout Belgium and France to reduce the overall capacity of the railway system and all but prevent enemy rail movements. Such a massive undertaking could not be accomplished by the AEAF on its own; it would require the involvement, for a considerable period, of the heavy bombers and fighters of the United States Strategic Air Forces in Europe (USSTAF—Eighth Air Force based in the United Kingdom and Fifteenth Air Force in Italy) and the heavies of British Bomber Command.

Neither the C-in-C of British Bomber Command, ACM Sir Arthur Harris, nor the C-in-C of USSTAF, Lieutenant General Carl A. Spaatz, believed that the invasion of France was necessary to win the war. They thought bombing alone would bring Germany to its knees in a matter of weeks.[39] For this reason, although they were enthusiastic about Operation Pointblank, they were reluctant to see any of their 5,000 heavy bombers and 2,000 long-range fighters diverted, as they saw it, to tasks in support of the invasion, as demanded by Leigh-Mallory and Tedder. In their view, attacks on the Luftwaffe in France, and especially the Transportation Plan, would simply provide breathing space for enemy fighter production to recover and detract from the campaign against what was now seen by Spaatz as the Germans' key vulnerability: natural and synthetic oil production (in defense of which German fighters would have to accept battle and be written down). Eisenhower, who had a realistic understanding of both the limits of airpower and its indispensable strengths, was convinced that the invasion was necessary and that the proposed air interdiction operation was essential to its success. He had to fight a hard political battle to establish the principle that creating a firm Overlord bridgehead would take priority in the allocation of all theatre air resources until it was achieved.[40] However, Spaatz's arguments for the Oil Plan carried conviction. A significant reduction of German fuel production would impact both the army's and the air force's ability to fight; the great unknown was, given the indeterminate size of German reserves, how soon the plan would start to seriously curtail German operations. Spaatz was given the go-ahead for the Oil Plan's implementation, provided it did not work to the detriment of the transportation attacks. Another less welcome diversion of effort was Operation Crossbow, wherein both strategic and tactical forces were increasingly sucked into attempts to suppress the enemy's long-range (V) weapons targeted against England.

The Transportation Plan focused on railway marshaling yards and, especially, repair centres. The goal was to destroy locomotives and rolling stock en masse and thereby disrupt, reduce, and canalize rail activity and prevent its regeneration, creating a "railway desert."[41] These strategic air attacks would be complemented by the destruction of bridges by medium and fighter-bombers and the strafing of trains to further reduce capacity. German reinforcement and supply efforts would be forced to rely increasingly on inadequate road transport; however, road bridges would also be dropped, and armed reconnaissance would prey on vehicular columns. All German activity would progressively be slowed down and curtailed, fatally weakening the defense. Furthermore, attacks on ammunition and fuel dumps would deprive the enemy of prestocked reserves to live off while attempting to restore the logistic system.

By early June, the AEAF staff had concluded that fifty-one of the eighty rail centres on the target list for the Transportation Plan had been so completely destroyed that they required only the occasional dive-bombing to prevent repair. These systemic attacks were supplemented by armed reconnaissance sweeps throughout France and Belgium and even into Germany to locate and destroy trains. From late May, daylight movement was all but precluded. By 15 July, only 33 percent of locomotives in the French railway system were still usable, and it was impossible to employ the dwindling stock of undamaged locomotives effectively owing to the destruction of switching facilities and bridges. The second strand of the air interdiction operation was the dropping of bridges on two lines of interdiction, reattacking when required. The outer line ran east of Paris, from Étaples on the Channel coast, through Fismes, to Clamecy (about 120 km [75 miles] northeast and 240 km [150 miles] southeast of the capital, respectively), and the inner line ran along the Seine from Le Havre almost to Paris and along the Loire from Nantes to Orléans. The latter bridges were not hit until D-Day, for fear of compromising the Fortitude deception. There remained the problem of the Paris-Orléans gap, where the minor Eure and Loir Rivers were obviously less formidable barriers.[42] Bridge bombing, especially on the inner line of interdiction, proved successful at an unexpectedly low cost. The Seine bridges were closed for 94 percent of the campaign (measured in "route days"), the Loire ones for 85 percent, but the "gap" bridges for only 56 percent.[43] Rail traffic in France fell off dramatically as a result of air attacks. By 9 June, it was at 38 percent of the January–February level, and by mid-July, it was at 23 percent and practically at a standstill in northern France.[44]

The first, obvious impact of air interdiction was on the Germans' ability to concentrate in an effort to repel and then contain the invaders. It appears that the casualties inflicted on German formations and units moving into Normandy were generally not significant (the memories of some German generals to the contrary notwithstanding).[45] The delays were. The disruption of railway links with the region slowed their movement, usually severely; it forced some reinforcing groups onto the roads, where lengthy detours to avoid destroyed bridges, the inability to travel by day in flying weather, and fuel shortages combined to prevent their timely arrival or their arrival as formed units ready for combat. For example, 3 Parachute and 77 Infantry Divisions each took six days to complete marches of about 150 km (95 miles) from Brittany to the American sector of the front. II SS Panzer Corps, dispatched from around Lwow on 7–9 June for a decisive counterattack in the Caen area, did not arrive until the end of the month; it took as long to move the last 320 km (200 miles) as it had to cover the first 2,000 km (1,240 miles) from Poland. On average, marching troops could move only 24 km (15 miles) per day, and vehicle-borne ones around 50 km (30 miles).[46] By the end of the first fortnight of the campaign, it was clear that the Allies would win the race to build up force levels. By 25 July, they had established a decisive superiority, thanks largely to air interdiction.

The second major effect of air interdiction was seen in the realm of logistics. The preinvasion buildup mandated by Hitler in his November 1943 directive had resulted in an influx of formations (of varying quality and freshness). This was not matched by an adequate logistic effort to sustain them. Ammunition was stockpiled for static, coastal defense, and port (fortress) divisions for three to four weeks of combat and for mobile divisions for two weeks (assuming rather optimistic rates of expenditure); fuel reserves were sufficient for two weeks. This relative deficiency did not trouble the high command, which believed it could rely on the railways. The air interdiction operations proved this belief fallacious. Moreover, Allied intelligence succeeded in locating many dumps, and air attacks destroyed them. For instance, the loss of the Domfront fuel depot on 13 June meant the loss of 40 percent of the fuel in Normandy; the Genvillers dump near Paris went up on 22 June with a POL (petrol, oil, and lubricants) reserve equivalent to the entire preinvasion stocks in Normandy, and more than one-fifth of the supplies shipped to the battle area were destroyed in transit. By the second week of the campaign, German Seventh Army was living hand to mouth, depending on daily deliveries from outside—a position officially acknowledged to be "catastrophic." Army Group B estimated that it would run out of fuel by 20–25 July.[47]

The progressive disabling of the French railway system in critical areas forced the Germans onto the roads for resupply. There was insufficient mechanical transport available—perhaps half the required lift. Furthermore, to avoid the almost certain air attacks by marauding fighter-bombers, road movement was possible only in bad weather or during the six or so hours of darkness on June nights. Truck losses mounted, not only from air attacks but also from the increasing number of accidents and breakdowns (often irreparable, thanks to a shortage of spare parts). The need to use trucks to substitute for rail movement also increased fuel consumption. As the meager lift available to the army group's quartermaster general eroded, combat formations had to send their own truck columns to the rear to collect supplies that should have been delivered forward, further limiting the mobility of front-line units and using more fuel.

By the opening of the Americans' campaign-transforming Cobra offensive, the logistic situation of Fifth Panzer Army was far from comfortable but gradually improving. In fact, any failure to repulse the Anglo-Canadian attacks would not be attributable to inadequate resupply. There was no comparable improvement in the west, however; there, the situation continued to deteriorate. German Seventh Army's stockpiles had been exhausted, a major reason for the eventual American capture of St. Lô. The army was more distant from its sources of supply, and fewer trains could be run across the Loire than through the Paris-Orléans gap; ferrying was also less well developed over the Loire than the Seine. And in the critical period immediately preceding Operation Cobra, air interdiction had once again cut the vital railway bridges at Tours and smashed the city's marshaling yards; Seventh Army's lifeline had been severed, and its restoration on 23 July was too late to replenish even minimal reserves of fuel and ammunition. Details of unit holdings have been largely lost—not surprising, given the chaos about to engulf Seventh Army—but several revealing statistics remain. When the American blow fell, 17 SS Panzer Grenadier Division was down to 1,000 rounds per machine gun and 30 per rifle; LXXXIV Corps had run out of critical 88mm armor-piercing ammunition by the end of the first day; 2 SS Panzer Division could not counterattack owing to empty fuel tanks in its panzers (which led to two Panther companies being abandoned by their crews and subsequently captured).[48] The contribution of airpower to the success of Bradley's army went far beyond the close air support emphasized by most soldiers.

Once a breakthrough was achieved and the Germans could no longer maintain a stable, positional defense but had a war of maneuver forced on them, the situation developed quickly. Given their low level of motorization, the Germans were ill equipped to cope with this increase in tempo. Allied air interdiction compounded their problems, whether by delaying reinforcement or, as they accepted defeat, hindering withdrawal. Either they confined their movement to the eight hours of darkness each August night or to days of bad weather—making them akin to a chess player able to make only one move to his opponent's two—or they risked daylight movement, which almost always involved an air attack. Critical fuel shortages worsened as every unit had to displace and supply dumps and columns were hit. Air attacks destroyed few AFVs but significant numbers of soft-skinned vehicles (SSVs), and many more armored and unarmored vehicles were lost because their crews abandoned them in a panic or they ran out of fuel and were overrun by their pursuers.

Close Air Support

Close air support comprises air attacks on enemy targets that are in such close proximity to friendly ground forces that each air mission must be carefully integrated with the fire and movement of those forces. It stood a poor third in the list of air force priorities. Most senior RAF and US Army Air Force (USAAF) commanders regarded it with a degree of distaste as the most costly, the most difficult to control, and the least effective use of airpower. Moreover, most of the senior air commanders, particularly in the RAF, distrusted or were on poor terms with their land forces counterparts. For instance, Air Marshal Sir Arthur Coningham, commander of 2 Tactical Air Force, charged with supporting 21 Army Group, detested Montgomery; Coningham gave two of his three group commanders a hard time for being too close to the soldiers, and he managed to dismiss Air Vice Marshal (AVM) L. O. Brown on grounds of his "subservience" to the army.⁴⁹ It was therefore fortunate that, at a critical operational level, relations were good: in First Army, General Bradley and later Lieutenant General Hodges worked well with Brigadier General Elwood R. Quesada of the supporting IX Tactical Air Command, and Lieutenant General Patton of Third Army got on famously with Brigadier General Otto P. Weyland of XIX Tactical Air Command; similarly, Lieutenant General Sir Miles Dempsey of Second Army and Lieutenant General Sir Harry Crerar worked well with the commanders of 83 and 84 Groups, AVMs Harry Broadhurst and L. O. Brown, respectively. Relations at lower working levels were generally excellent, as junior officers were less burdened by the baggage and prejudices of the past.

Despite its low position in the order of priorities, close air support became a normal feature of air operations in 1944. The decline of the Luftwaffe and the growing strength of the Allied air forces meant difficult choices were seldom necessary; there was usually enough airpower available to maintain air superiority or supremacy, carry out interdiction, and still allocate a generous amount of airpower to close air support. Thus, to take the example of a "typical" day, 18 July, IX Tactical Air Command and First Army allocated air effort for the next day as follows: 40 percent for close air support for First Army, 30 percent for close air support for Second Army, 20 percent for offensive fighter sweeps and combat air patrols, 10 percent for attacks on rail lines and other lines of communication.⁵⁰ However, the mutual suspicions and even hostility of air and ground forces, dating back to the earliest days of airpower, led to divergent ideas on doctrine and prevented or delayed the creation and adoption of the joint concepts and organizational and equipment developments needed to ensure effective air-ground battle. Neither soldiers nor airmen really understood the problems and requirements, capabilities and limitations, of the other, Mediterranean experience notwithstanding. Coordination measures were generally inadequate and often misunderstood or abused. It took a long time to adopt a responsive, flexible system for the timely provision and direction of close air support. Thus, it was only in late July that IX Tactical Air Command and First Army adopted the concept of intimate cooperation between fighter-bomber and armored units in a joint team—armored column cover—and the means to implement it. Even then, despite its proven success, it was decried by traditionalists as doctrinally unsound and wasteful of resources.⁵¹ The British took even longer to adopt a similar system, the "cab rank."

The main provider of close air support was the fighter-bomber, and in the P-47 Thunderbolt and the Typhoon in particular, the Americans and British had excellent delivery systems. However, in the semistatic or, at best, slow-changing conditions that prevailed in Normandy until Cobra, the weapon was of limited effectiveness. The Germans had become expert at concealing and camouflaging defenses dispersed and in depth to minimize the effect of both artillery and air attack. The ground, particularly the *bocage*, helped them. Lucrative targets were rarely on offer, and it was difficult to identify and then strike point targets with inherently inaccurate bombs and rockets. As the campaign wore on, with little in the way of gains, both ground and air commanders became concerned that close air support was not the important force multiplier they had expected it to be. On 6 July Brigadier General Weyland estimated that 80 percent of missions were falling short of expectations.[52]

It was another matter when the enemy could be detected concentrating for a counterattack. Massing made units vulnerable. Even then, however, the physical destruction fell far short of air force claims. For instance, during the Mortain battle of 7–10 August, in circumstances very favorable to the air attacker, IX Tactical Air Command and 2 Tactical Air Force together claimed 196 AFVs and 168 other vehicles destroyed and an additional 56 AFVs and 60 other vehicles damaged. In fact, detailed postbattle analysis on the ground showed that air attack accounted for only 21 AFVs and 12 other vehicles destroyed (although a few of the 15 armored and 26 other vehicles lost to unknown causes could probably be attributed to the fighter-bombers, and many of the 13 AFVs and 18 others abandoned intact or destroyed by their crews were probably given up owing to fear induced by the air attack). In other words, the pilots claimed they had destroyed roughly four times as much as they actually did (as well as more tanks and SP vehicles than the 177 actually possessed by the attacking XLVII Panzer Corps).[53] This is not to suggest that airpower had only a minor effect on the battle. The prolonged presence of fighter-bombers over the battlefield exercised a profound adverse effect on German morale and was a major contributor to the halting of the attack and the enemy's decision to take cover rather than advance. The same can be said of several other abortive German counterattacks.

There were other days when the Germans were compelled to offer dense targets for air attack. During the retreat that started in mid-August, the only alternative to being encircled in the Falaise pocket was the daylight movement of columns through the narrow gap that remained between its jaws and then back to the Seine. Unfortunately for them, there were several successive days of good flying weather, and the tactical air forces took full advantage. More than 7,500 AFVs and SSVs were lost. However, only a proportion of these were disabled by air-delivered weapons. For instance, of the 885 vehicles examined in detail in the pocket, only 359 had been damaged by air attack, and 526 had been abandoned or destroyed by their crews. Of course, many of those in the latter category had been given up because of congestion or panic caused by the fighter-bomber attacks, but a significant proportion, probably the majority, were out of fuel. Even in the most favorable circumstances for ground attack, air interdiction seems to have accounted, albeit indirectly, for more enemy losses than did direct strikes.[54]

Where the fighter-bomber really came into its own was during highly mobile operations, particularly the pursuit. Armored column cover and the British cab ranks meant that spearheads had an effective substitute for artillery, especially medium calibers, which were heavier and had a difficult time keeping up with high rates of advance. Once the systems were established, the speed, flexibility, and responsiveness demonstrated by tactical airpower proved to be a trump card. No longer did ground units have to wait at least an hour for requested air support to appear overhead. Hasty defensive and delaying positions could be hit from the air as soon as they were located and then attacked on the ground immediately afterward. Alternatively, the fighter-bomber flights could range ahead of their supported columns, seeking opportunity targets and providing useful intelligence at the same time. The seemingly ubiquitous presence of Allied aircraft was as demoralizing to the Germans as it was cheering to the British and American troops. To deal with larger or more difficult, more important targets, forces could be quickly diverted from other missions and firepower concentrated. Such a rapid response saved time and therefore increased the tempo of operations, keeping the enemy off balance and saving lives. Moreover, Quesada's persistent efforts to develop a radar system for vectoring fighter-bombers onto ground targets paid off in August. During that month, IX Tactical Air Command aircraft were grounded for only three days, compared with eleven in July, even though the weather was no better.[55]

There was another, far more controversial form of close air support—the use of heavy and medium bombers to blast a passage through enemy defenses with carpet bombing to facilitate a breakthrough or take a fortress. Generals were in awe of the amount of high explosives that could be delivered from the air in a short time, with corresponding shock effect. A single Lancaster heavy, for instance, could deliver 6,350 kg (14,000 pounds) of bombs, the equivalent of a regiment of 5.5 inch guns firing for almost five minutes. Such aircraft seemed (rather superficially) to be the mid-twentieth-century equivalent of the siege artillery used to breach the fortifications of old. Despite the unpromising precedent of its counterproductive use at Cassino in March, this tactical employment of Bomber Command, Eighth Air Force, and tactical air forces' medium assets was tried in six major operations in Normandy: Charnwood on 7 July, Goodwood on 18 July, Cobra on 24 and 25 July, Bluecoat on 30 July, Totalize on 7 August, and Tractable on 14 August. Ground commanders persistently claimed that their attacks had been significantly aided by the bombing. The fact that each operation, except for Cobra, ran into difficulties and fell far short of expectations was attributed to factors unrelated to the aerial bombardment; of course, if the commanders wanted to ensure future air support, they had to argue that. In reality, the physical results in terms of men killed and equipment destroyed were generally disappointing and not significant. When German defenders were dispersed in depth and well dug in, even accurate bombing lacked the density to cause significant losses. The disruption of command and control caused by cutting telephone lines and damaging radios was far more serious. Most damaging of all was the demoralization of those unfortunate to be caught within the bomb carpet. Provided the ground attack exploited these effects as soon as the bombing ended, before the enemy could restore cohesion, it had a good chance of making initial progress.[56] This was often problematic, however, as the safety distance required to avoid casualties to forward Allied units was almost 3 km (2 miles); the attackers needed time to cover this safety zone and then negotiate their way over the moonscape created by bombing. Even carefully negotiated bomb lines did not eliminate short bombing, which, due to a variety of errors during Cobra, Totalize, and Tractable, killed a total of 299 Allied soldiers and wounded another 1,125.

Operation Cobra did achieve a breakthrough, which was subsequently attributed in large part to the saturation bombing of a box measuring about 3 by 7 km (2 by 4 miles) by 1,490 heavy and 380 medium bombers. The target area was defended by the Panzer Lehr Division, and the views expressed by its commander, Lieutenant General Bayerlein, in 1949 have been cited extensively in support of this contention. His memory, however, was fallible on some points, and his replies to questions were probably influenced by the desire, not uncommon among German generals, to attribute their defeat to airpower as a factor beyond their control. He exaggerated his AFV losses and probably personnel losses as well, although he was undoubtedly right to stress the air bombardment's effect on morale. And it must be remembered that the initial German resistance was so effective that nowhere did the attacking Americans achieve their first-day objectives.[57] The breakthrough probably owed less to the Eighth and Ninth Air Forces' bombers than to the fact that Panzer Lehr—indeed, the whole German Seventh Army—was understrength, lacking both defensive depth and reserves, and critically short of ammunition. The powerful, concentrated attack by VII Corps on a narrow front and backed by more than 500 guns probably would have achieved a penetration without the bombing (which caused about as many American casualties [757] as German).[58] The conversion of the penetration into a breakthrough and the subsequent maintenance of momentum that kept the Germans off balance owed much to IX Tactical Air Command. The system of armored column cover created by its commander, Quesada, played a key role in ensuring a high tempo of operations. Indeed, it would not be surprising if the generals mentally blurred the difference between the massive but possibly inconclusive bombardments of 24 and 25 July and the highly successful application of armored column cover from 26 July onward.

Air preparation was now regarded as an essential prelude to penetration of the enemy defenses when serious opposition was encountered. It would continue to be employed in clearing the Channel ports and the Scheldt estuary, breaching the West Wall (Siegfried Line), and forcing the Rhine. In his memoir, Eisenhower wrote that, by the time of Operation Cobra, "the emergency intervention of the entire bomber force in the land battle had come to be accepted as a matter of course."[59] Acceptance by senior airmen (except for Leigh-Mallory), however, was usually obtained with extreme reluctance and under protest. When the ground forces failed to achieve the promised breakthrough (everywhere except for Cobra), the air chiefs complained forcefully. The tactical failure of Operation Goodwood, despite 1,855 bombers (more than 80 percent of them heavies) dropping 7,700 tons of bombs, led ACM Tedder to write to Lord Trenchard on 25 July and admit they had been "had for suckers."[60] He urged Eisenhower to dismiss Montgomery as ground forces commander, a weakening of the latter's authority that would have repercussions as the campaign wore on. Already resentful at the diversion of their resources from strategic targets under the Transportation Plan, the airmen regarded the employment of their aircraft as artillery on the battlefield as a misuse. As Tedder wrote to the Chief of the Air Staff on 25 October: "the British Army have for months now been allowed to feel that they can, at any time, call on heavy bomber effort and it will be laid on practically without question. . . . I am doing my best to get things straight, but I am sure you will realize that, the Army having been drugged with bombs, it is going to be a difficult process to cure the drug addicts."[61]

In truth, air preparation by bombers was of doubtful value. The airmen were probably right to regard it as wasteful, as a panacea sought by soldiers ignorant of the limitations of the instrument but anxious to find some deus ex machina to break the stalemate and save them from additional losses. The number of occasions on which strategic airpower was diverted to tactical missions was relatively small, so the opportunity costs were not really significant. However, Tedder and the "bomber barons" were right to fear and resist the trend to involve it more and more, especially as the approach of autumn, and then winter, promised fewer flying days in which pressure could be maintained against the Luftwaffe and the critical oil industry targets. They were also correct to argue that the Oil Plan and disruption of the transport infrastructure within Germany were exercising a more powerful influence on the Wehrmacht's ability to continue the war than any amount of bombing of the front line ever could. The relentless attack on synthetic oil production, combined with the loss of the Ploesti oil fields (the source of 25 percent of German oil supplies), overrun by the Soviets in August, reduced the production of aviation fuel from 175,000 tons in April to a trickle of 7,000 tons in September. This forced the Germans to withdraw their fighters from the battle fronts in a vain and costly effort to protect this vital resource.[62] Dwindling supplies of fuel also severely hampered ground maneuver at a time when it was more important than ever.

Reliance on massive aerial preparations was often counterproductive for the ground forces as well. It could exercise a pernicious effect on planning. Air participation was very weather sensitive, both over the bombers' bases and over the target areas. If a plan was dependent on thousands of tons of bombs, low clouds at the wrong time could wreck it (and an average of one day in three saw poor flying weather in France, let alone in the United Kingdom). The timing of bomber intervention in the ground battle had to be set in stone from an early stage. Bearing in mind the elder Moltke's dictum that no plan survives contact with the enemy, this imposed a rigidity on the ground battle that boded ill for a successful outcome. This was particularly true of those phased operations in which a second bombing was planned for attacks on enemy positions in depth. This problem posed difficulties during Operation Bluecoat and ruined the promising Totalize offensive.

Airpower: Conclusions

Winning air superiority was a sine qua non for the invasion to succeed. Probably the least influential factor in the successful campaign to do so (directly, at least) was the bombing of factories responsible for fighter production. In 1943 the Germans turned out 10,059 fighters of all types, and 24,981 rolled off the production lines in 1944. The Luftwaffe's major problem became not the availability of aircraft but the availability of adequate aircrews. Experienced, and therefore effective, pilots were lost much faster than they could be replaced, and the novices were poorly trained as instructors were pressed back into front-line service and the already truncated training programs, intended to produce more pilots faster, were further curtailed by fuel shortages. The offensive counter–air effort against air bases throughout the enemy's depth, the later attacks on the oil industry, and the Germans' forced acceptance of aerial combat even in adverse circumstances proved to be campaign winners.

Air interdiction likewise had a profound effect on the land campaign. The Allies had won the competition to build up combat power in Normandy by mid-July. Of course, this was not attributable solely to air action. The Fortitude deception inhibited the Germans' ability to reinforce Normandy in time to make a difference. More important, though, was the fact that the Red Army had fixed the preponderance of German land combat power. At the end of May there were 54 divisions in France and the Low Countries (almost half of them static), 27 in Italy, 25 in the Balkans, and 22 in Scandinavia (including 7 in Finland, facing the Soviets), but 157 in the USSR.[63] When the Germans sent reinforcements to Normandy in June and July, few could be spared from the eastern front (in fact, only II SS Panzer Corps was sent). But even if they had attempted to deploy more forces and sooner, air interdiction would have imposed severe limits on what they could achieve.

OPERATIONS BEHIND GERMAN LINES

Airpower was the principal means of carrying the struggle into the German rear areas, but it was not the only one. Underground resistance movements grew up in the occupied countries, and the Allies encouraged them. The Special Operations Executive (SOE) was set up in July 1940 on Churchill's orders to "set Europe ablaze." Its remit was twofold: to spread propaganda in occupied countries and to equip and train resisters. It was joined in its activities by the US Office of Strategic Services (OSS), established in June 1942 (although this forerunner of the CIA had additional responsibilities, including espionage). With the invasion of France in the summer of 1944, the British and Americans endeavored to support and direct the efforts of the resistance to aid the AEF, principally by interfering with German lines of communication. In acknowledgment of the important role the French resistance was expected to play, SHAEF, shortly after the landings, recognized the Forces Françaises de l'Intérieur (FFI) as a regular armed force of de Gaulle's legitimate government of France.

Resistance Movements and Their Allied Helpers

Much myth, born of the desire to bolster national self-respect, has grown up about resistance movements in the Western countries conquered by the Germans. In truth, although only small numbers enthusiastically welcomed the conquerors, not insignificant sections of society were happy about the triumph of extreme right-wing ideology and the political and economic opportunities presented by occupation. By far the largest segment rejected active collaboration but would not go so far as to engage in active, or even passive, resistance. Most people preferred to get on with their lives and ignore the authorities, to the extent they could do so without inviting adverse consequences. Only a very small minority chose to join the underground, at least before the German defeat appeared imminent. Fear of betrayal and savage German responses to perceived terrorist acts, especially indiscriminate reprisals, certainly helped limit the number of resisters and make them unpopular.[64] However, passive resistance became increasingly widespread as time wore on. This most commonly took the form of subtle, minor sabotage—mislaying files, frustrating telephone calls, misdirecting trains by relabeling freight trucks, and so on. As more time passed and people were emboldened by German reverses, this sometimes escalated into overt noncooperation, slowdowns, demonstrations, and strikes.

For the first three years or so of the occupation, resistance movements were small, inchoate, fragmented, and localized; many were communist inspired, although diverse political and social (indeed, criminal) elements were eventually drawn in.[65] This limited flowering did not take place until later in 1943, when the German introduction of forced labor compelled young men to choose between unpalatable compliance and disappearing from official view; the growing intensity of the labor drives fed the underground with recruits from the *réfractaires*, although the vast majority were more concerned with remaining hidden than with fighting. However, as the Germans' fortunes declined and the prospect of Allied victory grew, participation in the underground also grew, as did passive resistance. The ranks of the "September resisters"—those who joined as the Germans retreated—dwarfed those who had shown commitment while the outcome was still in doubt. For many, fighting the occupiers took second place to settling scores with collaborators and political or personal foes and establishing a favorable postwar political position. It was with this aim in mind, for instance, that the communist resistance precipitated the uprising in Paris on 19 August. Fearing both German reactions and communist success, de Gaulle and his military commanders urged an immediate American move on the capital.[66]

In the Soviet Union and the Balkans, the combination of mountains, forests, swamps, vast expanses, and low population densities made it possible for units of partisans, often of substantial strength, to undertake operations. An increasing flow of recruits and general cooperation from the population were guaranteed by the brutal ideological and racial policies adopted by the Germans in the east but not mirrored in the west (save, of course, for the "final solution" of the "Jewish question"). The geography of France and the Low Countries, and the much more selective use of terror by the occupiers, militated against the flourishing of the sort of partisan warfare that characterized the war in the east and southeast. In northwestern Europe only the terrain of the Vosges and the Ardennes was suited to guerrilla activity, and both regions were limited in terms of area and importance. The rugged and thinly populated Massif Central and the alpine plateau of Vercors near Grenoble were more suitable, and Maquis activity was greater there; however, both were far from any important German lines of communication. The only attempt to rise up against the occupiers was made in Vercors in mid-June, but it was savagely crushed in July. In regions of more immediate interest to the invaders, Normandy's underground was very weak; by and large, the Germans and the Normans got along pretty well before the landings. For both historical and terrain reasons, there was a much stronger resistance movement in Brittany, which would become very active and be of much help to Third Army.

SOE and OSS propaganda had some influence in the occupied countries, and this increased as the war wore on and Germany's fortunes declined. Their active branches provided arms for nearly half a million Frenchmen (and for fewer Belgians and Dutchmen), as well as training and communications. To support the invasion directly, ninety-nine three-man Jedburgh teams, trained in guerrilla warfare, were inserted between June and September to step up efforts. They were tasked with liaising with (and, if necessary, leading) resistance groups and organizing equipment drops so they could conduct actions designed to aid the field armies. Each army group and army headquarters had a Special Forces (SF) detachment to coordinate Jedburgh operations. They did not, however, have direct communications and had to work through SFHQ at SHAEF.[67]

To intensify pressure on the enemy rear, a British Special Air Service (SAS) brigade was deployed in support of the invasion. It consisted of two British and two French battalions and a Belgian squadron. Its tasks were to arm and train resistance groups, locate targets for the Allied air forces, and delay and disrupt enemy reinforcements and logistic activities. To these ends, the brigade conducted forty-three operations. The SAS came under the command of 1 Airborne Corps, not SFHQ.

Results of Special Forces and Resistance Activities

The SAS claims that it reported 400 targets for air attack; inflicted more than 12,500 casualties; destroyed or captured 640 vehicles; achieved 164 cuts of railway track and 33 derailments; and destroyed 7 trains, 29 locomotives, and 89 rail trucks. The casualty claims are probably exaggerated, and the other achievements added little to the destruction wreaked by the air forces. Nevertheless, the brigade fulfilled its mission. It is impossible to quantify the damage and casualties inflicted by the Jedburgh teams; their achievements are not amenable to objective analysis. However, it is clear that many of them had an impact, some of it considerable. More could have been achieved if the Jedburghs' insertion had been more timely; the rapid advance that followed the breakthrough meant that several teams had hardly landed before spearheads arrived in their operating area.[68] Both types of SF provided a level of professionalism that made the resistance groups they worked with much more effective. Their operations helped boost the morale of the occupied population, at least when they did not result in savage reprisals, and lowered that of the enemy; they also helped tie down German troops (albeit not of front-line caliber) and equipment.

The accomplishments of the resistance in aiding the Allied landings and advance are difficult to assess, as they are encrusted with legend and distorted and exaggerated by special pleadings, often politically motivated. The intelligence provided by the resistance was occasionally of great value (e.g., on the V weapons), but most of it was either too partial (in both senses of the word) or imprecise to be useful or of uncertain reliability. Sabotage of rail, power, and telephone lines was a useful supplement to aerial bombing, but only the latter could destroy high-value targets such as bridges or locomotive repair sheds. Ambushes and raids on German units were only harassing in nature, although they no doubt lowered enemy morale somewhat.[69] Probably more important than sabotage in disrupting German communications was passive resistance—the subtle, often imperceptible sabotage by railway and communications workers described earlier.[70]

Behind German Lines: Conclusions

General Eisenhower has been quoted as saying that active resistance efforts were worth half a dozen divisions to him.[71] This was probably an exaggeration designed to please the prickly de Gaulle. Despite the high level of publicity accorded to these activities during and after the war, they accomplished relatively little of direct operational significance. There were exceptions, however, in the wake of the German retreat—for instance, bridge seizures like that at Morlaix and Verdun in August and, notably, the securing, intact, of the Antwerp docks by the Belgian resistance before the arrival of 11 Armored Division. Tactically, resisters were frequently of value to the Allies in providing local knowledge that helped speed the advance.

The FFI, embodied as paramilitary units, proved most useful as an adjunct to Allied armies as the enemy withdrew. In Brittany 20,000 former resisters helped Third Army mop up the Germans left in the peninsula and mask the "fortress" ports into which most of them withdrew—indispensable help, given the early shift of Patton's main effort to the east. During the army's subsequent, rapid drive to the Meuse, a combination of XIX Tactical Air Command and FFI forces covered its long, exposed Loire flank. The most important contribution of the FFI occurred in the south, where the more favorable terrain, combined with massive withdrawals from Army Group G to feed the Normandy battle, offered great scope to the estimated 75,000 resisters and the reinforcing Jedburgh, SAS, and OSS operational groups. On 7 August Colonel General Blaskowitz had to report that he was no longer coping with merely a terrorist movement but with an organized military force in his rear; a week later, when the invasion started, he controlled only the Rhône valley and a coastal strip. The FFI helped prevent his demolition of the Mediterranean ports, and it harassed and speeded the German withdrawal. The decision was then made to integrate FFI units into First French Army to replace North African troops before the onset of winter, and by the end of October, more than 60,000 had been absorbed.

Even if later claims of their contribution were overblown, the Allies received a good return on their investment in SF. It could have been greater, however. Higher-level commanders did not really appreciate the potential of this new capability; in addition, insertion generally took place too late, and there were frequent communications and resupply problems. As a result, the operational-level impact of the Jedburgh teams was less than it could have been. Moreover, a faulty command and control structure prevented the synergistic coordination of SAS and Jedburgh actions. The fact that formations greatly appreciated the teams' tactical assistance upon linkup (e.g., acting as guides, providing local knowledge and liaison with FFI contingents) was of only some consolation to the originators of the concept.[72]

OPERATIONAL-LEVEL INTELLIGENCE

In most armies before World War II (with the exception of the Red Army), senior generals had some degree of prejudice against intelligence. It was still associated, by implication, with the dirty business of spying—not an activity for gentlemen. Nor was it a likely path to promotion for talented and ambitious officers—indeed, it was a notorious dead end for military careers. Of course, there were some natural intelligence officers and some mavericks attracted by the seedy glamour and mystery who turned out to be good at it, but on the whole, intelligence was the destination of the mediocre. This was true of the prewar regular armies, but massive wartime expansion, especially in the democracies, brought in a whole lot of amateurs, many of them academics, who had fewer inhibitions about the job and proved very capable. But they usually had a difficult time establishing the idea that they were worth heeding. Most commanders did not expect much of their intelligence staffs, and their intelligencers reacted accordingly, hesitating to push unwanted appreciations onto strong-willed, irascible, and opinionated commanders; it was much safer to tell the old man what he wanted to hear, as Brigadier Charteris had done with his C-in-C, Field Marshal Haig, in the First World War.

This situation continued throughout the war in the Wehrmacht, where operational-level intelligence was generally poor to disastrous—especially on the all-important eastern front. To a significant extent, this was due to cultural factors. Germans—especially Nazis, whose thinking was skewed by ideological prejudices—looked down on Russians as *untermenschen*, racially inferior and therefore incapable of outsmarting the master race. As a result, the Wehrmacht continually fell for Soviet deception and was wrong-footed by most major Red Army offensives. (On average, during the third period of the war [1944–1945], the Germans missed over 50 percent of the Soviet buildup for each offensive and thus underestimated the attacker's strength by a critical 25 percent.)[73] That said, the Germans usually did little better against the Western Allies.

For the British and Americans, in contrast, operational-level intelligence blossomed as the war went on. This was due to a rarely interrupted run of successes that earned intelligencers the right to be listened to. It must be said, however, that intelligence became much weaker and patchier below army level. Tactical signals intelligence (SIGINT) was efficient, especially in gathering order of battle (ORBAT) material, but it was hampered by the German preference at division and corps levels for teletype or radio telegraph rather than voice radio communications (these low-power systems were more difficult to direction-find and intercept, and messages were usually encoded). Of fundamental importance, at the tactical level, intelligence was woefully slow to grasp some of the enemy's concepts for defense (especially its depth and the distribution of resources within it). There was a comforting stereotype of the enemy as somewhat rigid, inflexible, and lacking initiative, a misperception that was almost 180 degrees removed from the truth. The result was a persistent underestimate of the Germans at the tactical level. This frequently led to attacks falling well short of expectations. Of course, the tactical failure of a corps or even a division, due at least in part to a faulty understanding of the enemy, could contribute to the failure of a theoretically sound army plan.

Allied Sources of Intelligence and Its Exploitation

The key to these operational successes was Ultra—the exploitation of the penetrated secrets of the German Enigma cipher machine used for top-secret radio traffic. Ultra decrypts, along with those from Magic (Japanese messages from Berlin to Tokyo), established a reputation for accuracy that could not be gainsaid. Ultra was probably of more intelligence value than all other sources combined. Once they overcame their inbuilt prejudice against intelligence in general and doubts about Ultra in particular, most generals came to rely on it (although Bradley did so somewhat late and with qualifications, as it seemed too good to be true).

Often sensationally, Ultra revealed enemy dispositions, formation strengths (personnel and equipment), supply states, and casualties. Even more important, it often revealed, at least by inference, enemy intentions and actual plans (with alternatives, should things go wrong). Never before in war had one side been given such insights into the enemy's hopes and anxieties, strengths and vulnerabilities, resources and constraints, even his commanders' habits of thought and their relationships with one another. The battlefield, Clausewitz pointed out, is "the province of uncertainty and chaos," with "a great part of information being obtained being contradictory, a still greater part false and by far the greatest part of doubtful character." Ultra removed much of that uncertainty for top Allied commanders, giving them an inestimable advantage over their German counterparts.[74]

This inexhaustible supply of priceless information, to switch analogies, put the Allies in the position of a poker player keeping his own cards concealed while being able to see those of his opponents. Had the Germans ever suspected that the enemy was reading their top-secret traffic, the supply would have dried up instantly (or after some spectacular piece of disinformation). For this reason, the distribution of Ultra-derived intelligence was restricted to army-level commanders and above. No reactions were permitted if the only source of information could have been Ultra. And great pains were taken to conceal the source of any information passed down to lower levels. (This suited commanders like Montgomery and Bradley, enabling them to claim to both subordinates and posterity insight and boldness where none actually existed.) Both for this reason and (though increasingly less often) because of time delays between German transmission, decryption, and dissemination to Allied HQs, Ultra was largely of operational value. However, there were times (more often, as the war wore on) when it was able to influence tactical actions too.

Still, Ultra had its drawbacks. German senior commanders had a natural preference for face-to-face meetings or telephone or teleprinter communications. When these means were used, Ultra was silent, but silence did not mean decisions were not being made and orders issued. Early on, there could be a massive time lag between a communication being intercepted and decrypted. But by the time the Normandy invasion was under way, decryption problems had mostly been overcome (especially for Luftwaffe traffic, which often revealed much about the ground forces). However, the process of decryption, translation, evaluation, and dissemination to army groups and armies always took time; for the information to be turned into intelligence and acted on required even more time. Events, especially in rapidly developing situations, could render the product passé—particularly at the tactical level. German intentions could change, or commanders might disobey orders, meaning that Ultra had apparently been misleading. And Ultra often gave only a partial picture—for example, an intercepted communication could be the answer to a question asked by telephone, or it could be the question, with the answer delivered by other means. It could not provide answers about states of training, morale, and combat effectiveness and other important intangibles, and if the wrong assessment was made, it could lead to costly failure (e.g., in operations to open up the Scheldt to make Antwerp usable and in the execution of Operation Market Garden).

In other words, Ultra told the truth, but not always the whole truth. Ultra was not the sole answer to all intelligence problems. Complementary sources were needed to produce a balanced picture or, in some cases, any picture at all. The principal source was air reconnaissance, both visual and photographic. With command of the skies, Allied aircraft could go pretty much wherever they desired, and their product was vital, both operationally and tactically; it included counterbombardment planning and mapmaking, pinpointing supply dumps and troop concentrations, and surveilling destroyed bridges. The army and air force Y Service provided radio direction finding and intercept—a very valuable source, but largely at the tactical level. The French and Low Countries' resistance movements provided inevitably patchy information of widely varying quality; it was usually difficult to assess and often dubious. Otherwise, there was the usual variety of tactical assets, such as sound ranging to locate enemy artillery and mortars, patrolling, interrogation of prisoners, and so forth.

Allied Intelligence Successes in Normandy

Before the 6 June invasion, Ultra was of more limited value, as the enemy was able to rely on telephones or teleprinters, couriers, and personal meetings for a lot of communications that later required the use of radios.[75] Nevertheless, it was important in providing some partial intelligence and in reinforcing other sources. After the landings, Ultra was the main source of operational intelligence and an often significant source of tactical intelligence.

Before 6 June the Allies built up a fairly comprehensive and accurate picture of German dispositions and strength in France and the Low Countries, especially (and especially important) of the mobile formations. Knowledge of which airfields were in use often defeated enemy camouflage measures; after the invasion, advance notice of movements and raids, including their timing, made specific, targeted counteractions possible. Revelations about casualties and manpower, equipment, and fuel shortages were very important in assessing general capabilities and in encouraging the AEAF to persist in the correct course of action. The success of Operation Fortitude in concealing the likely invasion sector was apparent. And most important to the conduct of the campaign, Ultra continued to confirm until late July that the Germans still expected the fictional FUSAG to launch a second, probably main assault, most likely between the Seine and the Scheldt. This, of course, was of inestimable help to the Allies. German armored formations that could have mounted damaging counterattacks in the buildup phase remained pinned for a time, as did, later on, infantry divisions that should have relieved them to provide mobile reserves. (The beauty of an unimpeachable source like Ultra is that you *know* the enemy has not seen through your bluff and is not stringing you along until he can pull off some terrible surprise.)

Field Marshal von Rundstedt and his successor as C-in-C West, von Kluge, misunderstood Montgomery's operational idea. They both believed that the US sector was of secondary importance to the British sector in the east. They thought the main effort lay in the British offensive on the Caen-Falaise-Paris axis, which would be supplemented imminently by a FUSAG landing north of the Seine and also aimed at Paris.

Ultra and the Y Service kept tabs on Luftwaffe reinforcements, intended movements (including timing), basing, strengths, casualties, and supply states (not to mention intentions and battery locations for III Flak Corps), down to the small details; this enabled quite precise targeting of the offensive counter–air campaign and defensive actions. It thus helped ensure that the Allies enjoyed not just air superiority (which numbers would have assured) but air supremacy by early July. It also produced the exact locations of POL and ammunition dumps, enabling air attacks that quickly reduced the enemy to a hand-to-mouth logistic situation.

Throughout the period, intelligence generally had a good grasp of ground forces' deployments, strengths, growing supply problems, and intentions. The continuing presence of the bulk of the German armor in the British sector showed that Montgomery's scheme to pin the enemy's main strength in the east to facilitate a breakthrough in the west was actually working. It was also clear that Army Group B was being ground down mercilessly: by 16 July, it had lost about 100,000 men and received replacements for only 12 percent of this wastage; by 6 August, losses had reached 141,000, although the replacement rate had doubled.

There was usually adequate warning of even tactical counterattacks. More dangerous operational-level blows were almost always anticipated and responses prepared. The earliest was disrupted and delayed by the bombing on 10 June of HQ Panzer Group West. The biggest, by the newly arriving II SS Panzer Corps, was defeated by the timely transition to the defense during Operation Epsom (from 28 June).

The intelligence picture on the eve of the breakthrough, starting 25 July, was both accurate and comprehensive. The locations of all but two divisions were known, and the deployment of German Seventh Army facing the Cobra attack was known in some detail, including the lack of even tactical reserves and ammunition and the commander's belief that the defense would crack under serious pressure.

As Cobra developed, Ultra revealed three interesting things: the chaos into which Seventh Army quickly descended, its show-stopping shortages of ammunition and fuel, and the slowness of Army Group B to react effectively (insofar as it could, of course). It also suggested, if only by the lack of traffic, that the Germans would be surprised (as they were) by the British Bluecoat offensive designed to complement Cobra.

The (quickly fatal) error committed by the OKW was the launching of a counteroffensive from Mortain to the sea at Avranches. Although Ultra failed to give unambiguous warning of the attack until shortly before H-hour on 6 August, it did flag the prior concentration of four panzer divisions in the area just north of Mortain. The formations used in this failed attack remained in the area, and on 10 August it was revealed why: Hitler had ordered another, stronger attempt. The positioning of the bulk of German armor in an exposed salient at the farthest extremity of their line positively begged the Allies to embark on an encirclement operation. Both Ultra and other sources kept track of German reactions to the growing crisis and chaos as they tried to extricate themselves from disaster. The demise of the Luftwaffe in western France was also tracked.

Failures of German Operational Intelligence in Normandy

At the operational level, German intelligence failed in Normandy (as it did in most campaigns).[76] This was partly a cultural problem based on the German assumption of superiority ("they can't fool us"; "they can't decrypt our Enigma messages"); the mediocrity of most intelligence officers; commanders' unwillingness to listen to those who threw cold water on favored projects or prophesied doom; and a degree of gullibility and ignorance in crucial areas that contributed to poor appreciations. And, of course, Hitler increasingly monopolized operational decision making, and he was not going to listen to naysayers who argued with his famous intuition. But the Germans' intelligence failure was also a result of relying on poor sources and a lack of good ones.

The Germans had no equivalent of Ultra. They did have a generally efficient SIGINT setup, equivalent to the British Y Service. It provided 70 percent of their ORBAT intelligence and, owing to poor Allied communications security, frequent warnings of the timing and nature of attacks. Their patrolling, sound ranging, and other tactical means were also good. Although these were no substitute for operational-level sources, the Germans were frequently able to defeat, or at least contain, attacks at the tactical level and thus frustrate Allied operational plans.

Allied air supremacy denied all but the most fleeting and shallow penetrations of air reconnaissance. This changed on 2 August when the Germans' new jet, Arado 234, flew the first of thirteen fast, high-level photoreconnaissance missions that month (apparently unnoticed by the Allies' air defense). But this reconnaissance breakthrough was too late; the Germans had irretrievably lost the initiative and, indeed, any ability to substantially affect the outcome. Their photography produced only historical snapshots of the forces destroying the Army of the West.[77]

For higher-level intelligence, the Germans relied on agent reconnaissance. The Abwehr inserted scores of spies into Britain, but they were staggeringly ill trained and amateurish; MI5 rounded up all but one (he committed suicide). Those that could be were turned, and the others were imprisoned or executed. The double agents, manipulated by the XX Committee, were used to feed disinformation to the Germans. They, together with open sources, signals deception, and tolerated air reconnaissance of dummy concentrations, were the tools of Operation Fortitude—the deception plan for the invasion. This was so successful that it continued to influence German actions until late July. When Operation Cobra started on 25 July, the Germans believed there were still forty-two Allied divisions in FUSAG ready to land north of the Seine. (Like all successful deception plans, Fortitude played to enemy expectations rather than trying to create new ones.)

Army Group B intelligence reports tell the story of the German failure. Right from the outset, the Germans got things wrong. When the Allies started to land on 6 June, they achieved surprise as to both location and timing. Agent reports, confirmed by SIGINT and some air reconnaissance, had indicated that the main landing would be done by Patton's FUSAG (concentrated in the southeast of England) between the Somme and Dunkirk. In addition, the Allies would need four consecutive days of good weather to land, and that situation did not pertain on 5 June (the Germans could not, as the Allies did, study weather patterns out in the Atlantic, so they were less well informed).

The fate of the invasion would depend on the relative rates at which the two sides built up their combat power. The Germans imposed a crippling handicap on themselves that ensured they would lose the race. OKW was slow to release the panzer divisions that might have been able to drive the invaders back into the sea. Hitler saw the Normandy landings as a secondary effort designed to draw forces away from the Pas de Calais, where FUSAG would make the main effort. The Germans continued to believe in the FUSAG threat until the last week in July, when a second landing disappeared from Army Group B's intelligence appreciations. This persistence was partly due to the reluctance of intelligence officers and their commanders to admit mistakes and abandon preconceptions that formed the basis of a whole campaign plan; it was also due in part to grossly inflated estimates of Allied strength. Before the invasion, the Germans believed there were seventy-nine divisions in the United Kingdom; the actual number was thirty-seven, and most of the phantom forty-two were in the mythical FUSAG. Army Group B's weekly report of 17–23 July maintained that the Allies had "at least 40 divisions" in Normandy (there were actually thirty-two, including two in the process of landing) and another fifty-two in Britain, of which forty-two were deployable.

Army Group B did no better when it came to assessing the intentions of 21 Army Group. Naturally, the Germans expected there to be a synergy between Montgomery's army group and those of FUSAG. The main effort was believed to lie with Second Army (and later First Canadian Army), which would seek a breakthrough on the Caen-Paris axis. At the right moment, FUSAG would land in one of three places: between Calais and the mouth of the Somme, astride the Somme, or between the Somme and Le Havre. The last would form the other wing of a thrust on Paris, which was seen as a politically important objective in its own right. More importantly, its seizure would isolate Seventh Army in Normandy and open a short route over good terrain to Germany. Moreover, the start of the long-range weapons (V1 and later V2) offensive against London would compel FUSAG to make the Pas de Calais launching sites one of its objectives. Accordingly, the main effort of the defense, including its best formations and armor, was deployed on the eastern flank of the bridgehead to stop the British.

German intelligence failed to see the big picture, but it achieved some tactical successes. The most notable was predicting the axis and timing of Second Army's Goodwood offensive on 18–20 July—although this was helped by protracted and ponderous preparations that were difficult to conceal. After this defensive triumph, there followed a string of more or less disastrous failures.

The next American offensive was expected, and it was fully appreciated that German Seventh Army, facing US First Army, was on the brink of collapse. What was not divined was the change in American methods. Instead of continuing to attack across the front, Bradley chose a Montgomery-style concentration on a restricted frontage with a large armored exploitation echelon. Operation Cobra, launched on 25 July, achieved the hitherto elusive breakthrough that marked the beginning of the end. Rather too late, two panzer divisions were committed to stop the rot, but ignorant of the size and shape of the problem, they were sucked piecemeal into an attritional grind.

On 30 July Second Army mounted its supporting offensive, Operation Bluecoat. This achieved surprise with regard to axis, being on the west end of 21 Army Group's sector instead of the usual east side. II SS Panzer Corps was hastily pulled out of the line and redeployed to counterattack and restore the defensive front. It too attacked blind and failed to recover a favorable line, becoming bogged down in an attritional struggle.

Faced with an American breakout from Normandy into good tank country, Hitler decided on a counteroffensive from Mortain to the sea at Avranches to cut off those elements of Third Army that had broken out.

Again, the 6 August effort had to be launched into the blue, as intelligence had only the haziest notion of which US formations were located where. The American forces (including air) were far too strong to be overcome by unfocused attacks, and the venture failed. In doing so, it left the cutting edge of Army Group B stuck in a salient and positively asking to be encircled.

An encirclement usually needs two wings, and First Canadian Army attacked on 8 August to provide the second. The Germans fully expected another imminent thrust down the Caen-Falaise axis, so surprise was not possible. In Operation Totalize, however, the Canadians achieved surprise through the use of novel tactics, undetected by German intelligence. Fortunately for the defenders, the initial success was not properly exploited, and the offensive largely failed.

By mid-August, Seventh and Fifth Panzer Armies were in headlong flight, having implemented the drill for escaping encirclement that had been worked out through repeated, painful experiences in Russia. Some idea of how, where, with what, and how fast the Allies intended to close the trap would have been very useful. However, intelligence provided little information of any value. It certainly failed to obtain any clue as to which of the three courses assessed by Army Group B would actually be adopted by the Allies.

Given the Allies' intelligence dominance in Normandy—unparalleled in military history—the Germans did pretty well to keep going as long as they did. The fact that so many German soldiers escaped to fight another day (and fight hard, at that) was a tribute to the skill and determination of those soldiers and their leaders; it owed nothing to their intelligence support. But it did owe quite a lot to the failings of Allied generalship and to faults in British and American doctrine and training, which will be discussed in the next chapter.

CONCLUSIONS

Even before the opening of the Cobra offensive, the Allied armies firmly held the initiative, and they had attained a potentially decisive superiority in combat power to exploit it. Their air forces had total mastery of the skies and could deliver formidable firepower wherever and whenever they chose (subject only to the weather). Their supply state was healthy. They had a clear, often detailed intelligence picture. The Germans, by contrast, had many hollowed-out formations. Their defense was stretched very thinly, especially facing the Americans in the west; they lacked operational reserves, and even tactical ones were inadequate. The front-line troops never saw a German aircraft. The logistic situation was poor in the east of Normandy, and serious combat could be sustained for no more than a few days in the west. The

Germans were blind as to enemy intentions and were forced to rely on precedent, prejudices, and guesswork to prepare for the next Allied onslaught.

Seventh Army was bound to crack, probably sooner rather than later. An American breakthrough would lead to operations that assumed a fast-changing, maneuver character. Once the stability of the defense was lost in one sector, maintaining a positional defense in the other would become steadily less tenable as its flank became more and more exposed. But the Wehrmacht was no longer capable of conducting maneuver warfare. A lack of mobility and fuel would inevitably lead to many German units being caught in encirclement or overrun by their more mobile opponents.

However, the Allies would face problems as well. They had built up impressive stocks in the bridgehead but, because of their own air interdiction, would lack railway transport. These stocks would have to be moved timeously and in adequate quantities to support a long pursuit followed by renewed heavy fighting. The logisticians fully appreciated the problem and repeatedly reminded commanders and their G3 staffs about this reality. The SHAEF plan for post-Normandy operations was predicated on the possession of Brest and other Breton ports, in full working order, and an operational pause of about thirty days while forces, supplies, and the means to move them were built up for the war-winning offensive. Absent these preconditions, the culminating point of the offensive would come quickly.[78] General Eisenhower fully understood the concept of the culminating point (he had read Clausewitz's *On War* not once but three times and had been examined on the content by his mentor, Major General Fox Connor).[79] He also understood logistic constraints. His stated strategic aim (as a good Clausewitzian) was destruction of the German armed forces, which, in the west, were grouped mainly in Normandy. Logically, given the imminence of Allied culmination, these Germans would have to be destroyed in Normandy and its immediate environs, not merely pushed back with heavy but possibly restorable losses. If the war was to be concluded rapidly, it would require a single-minded concentration on the annihilation of Seventh and Fifth Panzer Armies before the Allies' offensive impetus ran out of steam, as it inevitably would due to logistic overstretch and fatigue. It is unclear whether Eisenhower or his principal subordinates fully grasped this point. Certainly, in the event, the AEF failed to achieve this goal as a result of the dissipation of their efforts.

CHAPTER THREE

July: Breakthrough and Near Breakthrough

OPERATION COBRA

Background

The Overlord plan anticipated that, by the end of June, the Americans would be in possession of the entire Cotentin Peninsula and would be preparing to break out. Actually, they had pushed only halfway down the peninsula and were making heavy weather of advancing further. The British were not in possession of Caen, and attempts to outflank the city had been frustrated. Consequently, the airmen were still denied the airfield sites they craved, and both armies were running out of space to accommodate both newly arriving formations and the administrative buildup. A month after the invasion, there was real fear of a World War I–type stalemate developing. This would have been a potentially disastrous setback with far-reaching operational-strategic consequences. Morale, civil as well as military, would have been seriously impaired. The Germans probably would have ceased to fear a second landing as the summer weather window closed and would have risked thinning out their defenses elsewhere on the coast to reinforce Normandy; more infantry divisions would allow a relief in the line of panzer formations for a counteroffensive role. At the same time, logistic sustainment for the invasion force would have been imperiled. Although Cherbourg had been captured at the end of June, the port had been so thoroughly ruined that it would not be fully functional until August, and even at maximum capacity, it could support only fourteen divisions. By the end of July, the Allies planned to have more than twice that number ashore. Logisticians discounted the possibility of continuing to reinforce and supply over the beaches and via the mulberry harbors during the autumnal gales; the "great storm" of 19–21 June had already wrecked the American mulberry harbor and stranded, badly damaged, or destroyed more than 800 landing craft and other vessels—a foretaste of trouble to come. The Allies had to acquire additional ports quickly, and they were still a long way from Brittany—their preferred source of such ports.[1]

American progress remained agonizingly slow. To shake clear of the Cotentin's swamplands, reach even part of the Lessay–Périers–St. Lô road, and take the critical communications hub of St. Lô on 19 July, First Army took seventeen days to advance 5 to 14 km (3 to 9 miles) and suffered 40,000 casualties (more than 50,000, if cases of combat fatigue are included).[2] Had the Germans been much stronger, the advance would surely have ground to a halt. Fortunately, however, Field Marshal von Kluge, C-in-C West and of *Army Group B*,[3] remained convinced by Second Army attacks that the main danger was on the Caen front. All four of the fresh infantry divisions released to him in the first three weeks of July were deployed in *Panzer Group West's* sector. Montgomery's operational concept was bearing fruit, although it was all taking much longer and costing much more than anticipated. At least in part, this can be attributed to the Americans' dubious operational approach of attacking more or less continuously and more or less everywhere. Patton deprecated this dissipation of combat power in his diary entry for 14 July: "Bradley and Hodges are such nothings. . . . They try to push all along the front and have no power anywhere. All that is necessary now is to take chances by leading with armored divisions and covering their advance with air bursts. Such an attack would have to be made on a narrow sector, whereas at present we are trying to attack all along the line."[4] Yet Patton's criticism does not take into account the inhibiting effects of the terrain. Marshes and numerous ditches, many of them wide, canalized movement. There were few good roads, and the *bocage* compartmentalized the ground into a series of natural strongpoints that the skillful Germans exploited to the full. Even after the Americans had worked out effective combined-arms tactics, generating momentum would continue to be a problem as long as the defense maintained an adequate density and depth. Given the ground and its development by the enemy, Patton's supposed answer was simply fatuous, although he was right about the need for concentration.

There are several different explanations of the genesis of the Cobra concept. Bradley suggests that it was his own brainchild, which he had worked out, unaided, by 10 July.[5] He had realized that the methods used so far would not bring victory quickly and at a reasonable cost; mere combat power alone would not suffice as long as it was dissipated in broad-front attacks. What was needed was concentration, although this could not be achieved until his army had reached suitable terrain where the Americans could mass their resources. But according to Dempsey (commander of Second Army), Bradley had lamented his failure to break through at the 10 July conference of ground forces commanders, and Montgomery had been understanding, saying: "Never mind. Take all the time you need, Brad. . . . If I were you I think I should concentrate my forces a little more," putting two fingers together on the map.[6] Whether it was Bradley's inherent flexibility of mind or whether it took a nudge from his army group commander for Bradley to adopt a more "British" approach is an interesting question for the student of generalship; unfortunately, it cannot be resolved definitively.[7]

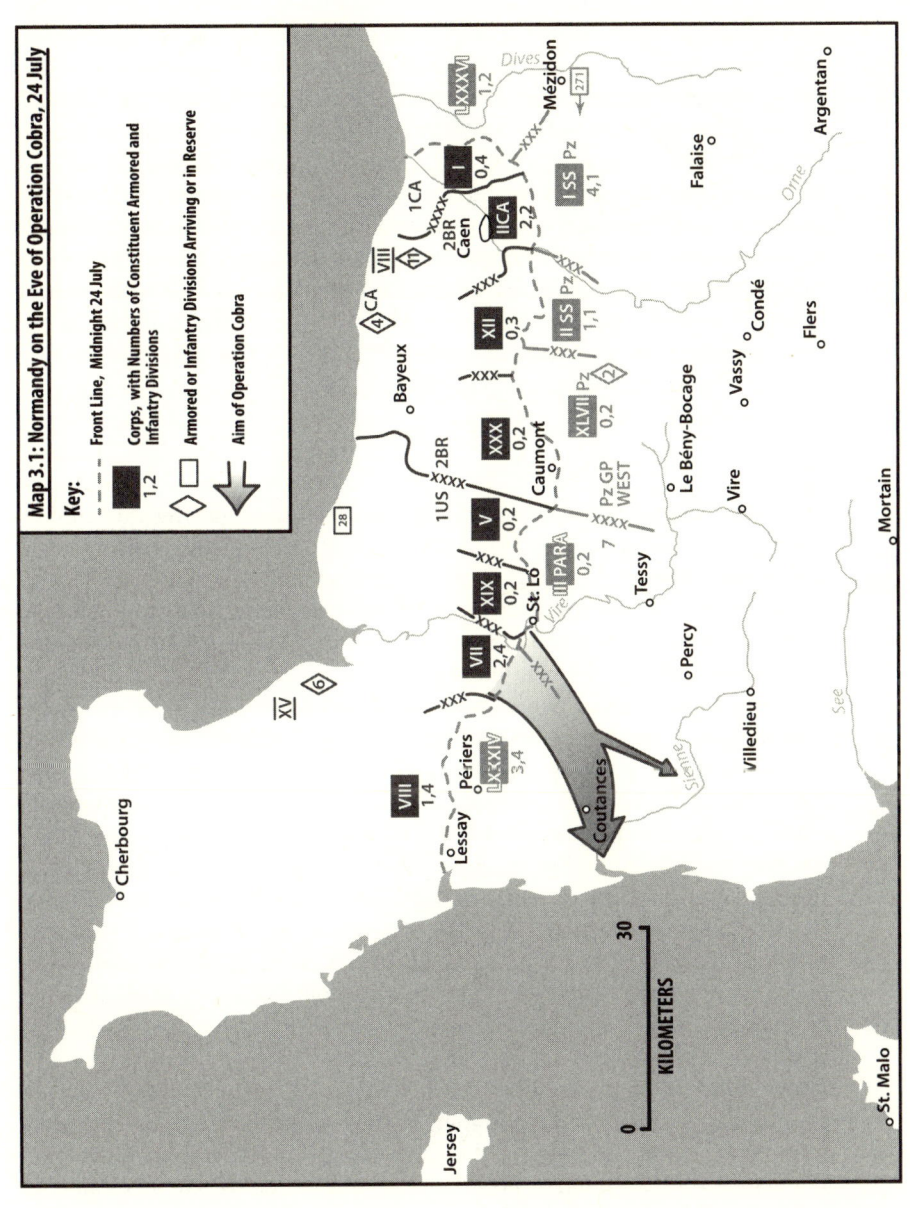

The concept called for an unprecedentedly heavy preliminary aerial bombardment. Then a strong, infantry-heavy first echelon would drive a penetration through the defense on a narrow front in the centre of the army's zone. Giving the enemy no time to react, a second echelon, strong in armor, would drive through the clear breach created by the first and envelop the forces facing the army's right wing. Early momentum would ensure that the pace of operations was dictated by the more mobile Americans. Having destroyed the enemy's left wing and advanced as far as Coutances, a subsequent operation could then be mounted to carry the offensive into Brittany, the objective of Third Army (forming), and eastward toward the Paris-Orléans gap. Critical to the success of this offensive, originally scheduled to begin on 18 or 19 July, would be the continued pinning of the German armor by Second British Army. To this end, Operations Goodwood and Atlantic were to be mounted on 17 July. Map 3.1 shows the situation in Normandy, down to corps level, on the eve of the twice-postponed Operation Cobra.[8]

Terrain

Obstacles. The river Vire, a considerable barrier, flowed northward from the town of the same name through St. Lô, offering obvious flank protection and a boundary. There were four rivers athwart an advance to the south. The Soulle flowed into the sea at Coutances, as did the Sienne to its south, before it turned to go due north to the same estuary; both valleys were steep-sided and difficult. The Sée, which flowed due west to Avranches, was not much of an obstacle, but the ridge to its south was. The Sélune, 7 to 15 km (4 to 9 miles) south of the Sée and the last barrier before Brittany, was relatively formidable and could be made more so by blowing the dam near Ducey (about 6 km [3.5 miles] from the Pontaubault crossing into Brittany). High ground could also be exploited for its defensive value. There were west-east ridges running roughly from Coutances to Caumont, interrupted by the valley of the Vire; from Gavray to Percy to south of Caumont; south of the Sienne to Vire; and south of the Sée to Mortain. Once past Coutances, however, there was fairly flat ground in a coastal strip. Around 15 km (9 miles) north of Avranches, the *bocage* gave way to open country favorable to armored operations.

Routes. Once the Americans had reached the Lessay–St. Lô road, there were several major north-south roads going to the base of the Cotentin Peninsula more than 70 km (45 miles) distant. One road from Lessay and one from Périers went to Coutances; both then continued the 40 km (25 miles) to Avranches. The town of St. Lô was a hub from which five roads went more or less in the desired direction. One went westward about 30 km (18 miles) to Coutances; two went southward to Vire and Mortain; one passed between Avranches and Mortain; and one, branching off the latter, joined a road going from Coutances to Avranches about 12 km (7 miles) north of that town. Numerous minor roads traversed the area, but most could not support military traffic of any volume, many of them being little more than farm tracks. Roads were even more important than usual, as the *bocage* country greatly hindered cross-country movement for infantry and tanks and made it impossible for SSVs. Although more than half the American tanks were equipped with "Rhino" cutters, making the hedgerows passable, delays were inevitable. Accordingly, major crossroads and communications centres would assume great importance for a rapid advance, especially those at Coutances, Torigni-sur-Vire, Tessy-sur-Vire, Gavray, Percy, Villedieu-les-Poêlles, Vire, Avranches, Brécey, and Mortain. Those at Torigni, Tessy, Vire, and, eventually, Mortain would be important not only for a southward advance but also for a push to the west and for any German counterattack.

The defensibility of the ground and the paucity of routes made it essential to achieve a clean breakthrough and the rapid committal and advance of exploitation forces. If a high tempo of operations were not achieved, German formations redeployed from the British sector or even further afield would be able to occupy blocking positions at obstacles on the fast routes, and low-mobility divisions in the front line would be able to withdraw in good order to establish a new line. As is often the case, the possession of ground and the fate of its defenders would depend primarily on who won the battle for time.

The German Defense

First Army had taken heavy casualties to reach the Lessay–St. Lô road. But the Germans, too, had suffered grievously from attrition, and unlike the Americans, they had not received a constant stream of replacements to keep units up to strength. Nor had they benefited from a steady accretion of new units and formations as the buildup progressed. Although the Americans were obsessed with taking ground and were frustrated by their slowness, they had in fact succeeded in hollowing out the defense. By the time of Cobra, *Seventh Army* comprised ten divisions. Of these, only the two panzer divisions were rated at combat-effectiveness levels I (*2 SS*) and II (*Lehr*)—that is, at full or limited offensive capability. These classifications were somewhat optimistic, however, with the former division at just over half its TO&E in armor and the latter at around one-quarter. The remains of *17 SS Panzer Grenadier* were rated at level IV—of limited defensive value—as were all the infantry divisions save *3 Parachute*. Actually, these so-called divisions were the shattered remnants resulting from weeks of unremitting combat; they consisted of amalgamated elements and the remains of another six divisions, some of which were rated ineffective. In fact, the strength of the infantry formations was the equivalent of less than three divisions at full TO&E. About 190 tanks and SP guns and 370 or so towed guns remained. POL and artillery ammunition were in very short supply, and air support was totally absent.[9]

SS Colonel General Paul Hausser, *Seventh Army*'s elderly but capable and energetic commander, faced the unenviable task of holding Bradley's army at bay. Many indicators told him to expect an attack between the Taute and the Vire: a strong armored concentration (2 and 3 Armored Divisions) was evident in the area, enemy air reconnaissance and air interdiction efforts had been increasing, artillery registered targets, mines were being removed, and prisoner interrogation suggested the imminent committal of elements of Third Army. Quite probably, the enemy would link a fresh offensive with airborne or seaborne landings to the south of the Cotentin or in Brittany.[10] Though he did not know the full measure of the problem, Hausser was outnumbered by approximately 4–5:1 in infantry and guns and perhaps treble that in tanks and SP guns.[11] His force was very weak, but he enjoyed two advantages: his front was short, rather less than 50 km (30 miles), and much of the terrain was defensible. Hausser was confident that General Meindl's two divisions of *II Parachute Corps* could hold, or at least aggressively delay, in the broken ground east of the river Vire. On the far-western sector of his front, the swampy ground made cross-country movement so difficult that the Germans called it the *wasserstellung* (water position); the weakest elements of *LXXXIV Corps* would suffice there. The central sector, between the Vire and the Taute and in the Périers area, was the weak spot. Should the army be forced back, there was defensible high ground in the ridges north and east of Coutances to the Vire and then on the Sienne and the ridge north of Percy. However, Hausser was constrained by von Kluge's concern that any withdrawal would expose the flank of his defenses south of Caen, not to mention Hitler's abhorrence of giving any ground at all. Besides, withdrawal could be dangerous, given both the fragile nature of his infantry formations and the vastly superior mobility of the Americans and their air support; *Seventh Army* could not conduct a war of movement.[12] The army commander opted for a positional defense consisting of a series of strongpoints barring the routes south. He placed his two panzer divisions in the line because he realized they were the only effective formations he had, and the line would not hold without them. There were only tactical reserves amounting to two infantry divisions, each at about 40 percent; these imparted a small measure of depth to the defense.[13] The only significant operational reserves in Normandy were 2 *Panzer Division*, beginning a refit, and *116 Panzer*, just arriving from *Fifteenth Army* (and not yet reported by Ultra). Both were assembling in the eastern sector. Thus, *Seventh Army*'s combat formations were in poor shape to withstand a well-conducted offensive. Even more ominously for Hausser, his logistic situation was dire, thanks to effective air interdiction. Fuel and ammunition of all natures were in short supply, some critically so.

On 20 July Hausser presented an estimate of the situation to von Kluge: "because of our losses suffered during previous actions, the fighting quality of our units has been, in places, lowered to such an extent that, in the event of enemy attacks supported by strong artillery, penetrations by the enemy cannot be prevented." He requested additional artillery, replacements, reserves, resupply, and air support. The C-in-C was not unsympathetic, but von Kluge feared an attack in the east even more and had no resources to spare. The next day he wrote to the Führer, warning: "the moment is fast approaching when this overtaxed front line is bound to break up. And when the enemy once reaches the open country, orderly and effective conduct of the battle will be almost impossible because of the insufficient mobility of our troops."[14] Hitler had no troops to offer to shore up the defense. Nor, in the wake of the attempt to assassinate him on 20 July, was he in the mood to listen to the negative views of those he suspected of treachery or to countenance defeatist suggestions of retreat.

First Army's Plan

First Army's mission had been set by Montgomery in a directive dated 30 June.[15] Pivoting on its left in the Caumont sector, the army was to wheel south and east in a wide turn until it attained a line approximating Caumont-Virc-Mortain-Fougères. This would open the way for Third Army, activated for the purpose, to seize the Brittany ports. While Patton was securing the Americans' logistic base, First Army, along with the British and Canadians on its left, would push eastward to the Seine and Paris to complete the Overlord lodgment area. As a first step toward the breakout, Bradley had hoped to attain the line of the Coutances–St. Lô road, but the heavy costs of the July fighting persuaded him to accept the St. Lô–Périers–Lessay road as his line of departure (LD). The aim of Operation Cobra was to advance to the former road and achieve the destruction of the German left wing by encirclement.

American intelligence maintained a good picture of *Seventh Army*'s OR-BAT and the battle-worthiness of its components. It was also clear that *Army Group B* could not readily lay its hands on much in the way of reinforcements, and those that could be found would take some time to arrive. Thanks to German tactical skill, however, the exact locations of the main line of resistance and tactical reserves were unclear. These last deficiencies were important, but on the whole, the Americans enjoyed an enviably accurate grasp of their enemy's situation. Bradley produced his original, tentative plan on 13

July. As a result of discussion, particularly with the principal executor of the plan—Major General J. Lawton Collins, the commander of VII Corps—it was significantly modified and developed. There were four elements in First Army's operational grouping—the pinning force, the pressure force, the penetration force, and the exploitation force—and their composition and tasks were set out in the army's field order.

The pinning force comprised V Corps on the army's left flank and XIX Corps on the centre-left, both east of the Vire. The four infantry divisions of this grouping were to pin the enemy to their roughly 25 km (15 mile) front.

The pressure force, consisting of VIII Corps (commanded by Major General Troy H. Middleton), had four infantry and two armored divisions. It would be deployed on the right, between the river Lozon and the sea. Initially, this corps would also pin the Germans on the almost 30 km (18 mile) sector facing it. Upon the success of the main attack, the corps would attack to crush the enemy against the barrier created by the exploitation force on the Coutances-Marigny line.

The penetration force from VII Corps (commanded by Collins) consisted of three reinforced infantry divisions (9, 4, and 30), which were to open a breach in the defense on a narrow, 7 km (4 mile) sector occupied largely by the *Panzer Lehr* division between Marigny and St. Gilles; their priority task was to clear the roads and hold open a corridor for the follow-on forces. On penetrating to the depth of the enemy's tactical zone of defense, the two flank divisions were to wheel outward to the rivers Lozon and Vire, respectively, to secure the flanks of the penetration against enemy tactical reserves. Originally, Bradley had allocated only two infantry divisions, but Collins argued that this was insufficient to ensure a rapid penetration, and Bradley gave him his army reserve.[16]

The exploitation force, with three fully mobile divisions, was also part of VII Corps. The motorized 1 Infantry, reinforced by Combat Command B (CCB) of 3 Armored and a cavalry squadron, as well as the usual attachments (tank and tank destroyer battalions), was to advance through Marigny to seize the high ground north of Coutances and provide the anvil on which VIII Corps would smash the enemy's left flank grouping. Third Armored Division, with an infantry battalion in exchange for its detached combat command, would advance through Carantilly, south of the river Soulle to the south of Coutances, to cover 1 Infantry Division's left flank and strengthen the anvil as necessary. These two divisions would thus execute a shallow encirclement of the enemy's left wing. Meanwhile, 2 Armored, augmented by a motorized regiment from 4 Infantry Division, was to advance through St. Gilles and establish blocking positions on roads into the battle area from Cérences to Tessy-sur-Vire and prevent enemy reinforcements from interfering with the main effort; its presence in the enemy's depth would also have a significant disruptive effect. Of course, intensive air interdiction would also disrupt and delay any enemy forces coming up from the depth or from the east. Two novel methods would help expedite the advance of the exploitation elements. Rhino hedge cutters on one-third of the tanks would facilitate more rapid cross-country movement (but would not, of course, obviate the need for combined-arms teamwork). Armored column cover would increase the firepower available to the spearheads and compensate for non-SP artillery's difficulty in keeping up with the rapid advance. Three fighter-bomber groups, each with forty-eight aircraft, would be dedicated to the role, providing continuous reconnaissance and ground attack for each advancing column; additional aircraft would be kept on strip alert, ready to respond to requests for close air support. In all, between 27 and 30 July, IX Tactical Air Command would fly 5,105 sorties in support of the accelerating exploitation.

Bradley considered the air plan critical to Cobra's success. A speedy breakthrough and early achievement of momentum would be possible only if the enemy in the chosen attack sector was largely neutralized from the start. This could not be accomplished by artillery alone, although First Army did achieve an unheard of concentration of more than 750 guns for the battle.[17] The main weight of fire was to be delivered during an extraordinarily heavy aerial preparation against a box measuring about 7 by 2.5 km (4 by 1.5 miles) over two and a quarter hours. This would involve 350 fighter-bombers and 380 medium bombers of Ninth Air Force and approximately 1,500 heavy bombers from Eighth Air Force. The unfortunate *Panzer Lehr* would be buried under 4,700 tons of bombs and a deluge of shells. The various components of the air bombardment were carefully organized and sequenced. Comprehensive suppression of the defenders had to be ensured while minimizing the danger to American troops. The latter were to withdraw only about 1,200 m (1,300 yards) from the bomb line (the northern edge of the target area)—half the minimum distance deemed prudent by the airmen.

It was hoped that the success of Operation Cobra would result in the substantive destruction of *Seventh Army*'s left wing. This would enable Patton's Third Army to break out of Normandy and into Brittany to take the ports deemed so important by SHAEF logisticians.[18] This phase of the operation was expected to take place without an operational pause.[19] It was not, however, preplanned. Given the uncertainties about how events would develop, this was not considered possible.

Execution

Delayed by weather, the operation got under way on 24 July.[20] It was a false start—and a bad one. At the last moment, it was postponed due to overcast skies in the target area, but many of the heavy bombers failed to receive the recall order, and short-bombing caused 170 casualties to 30 Infantry Division. Despite the possible loss of surprise and Leigh-Mallory's insistence that time constraints meant that the same fatal approach would have to be used by the bombers, Bradley decided to renew the operation on 25 July. Again, short-bombing resulted in another 600 casualties (including 495 in the unfortunate 30 Infantry Division); all three assault divisions suffered a degree of disorganization. Recriminations followed: The soldiers maintained that they had expected the attacking bombers to fly in parallel to the road, not at right angles to it, and they blamed the approach for the disaster. The airmen retorted that they had always pointed out the impracticality of the parallel approach and the soldiers' lack of appreciation for the limited visibility of the smoke- and dust-obscured battlefield from the cockpit.[21]

Initially, the bombing was thought to have had only limited effects. When the infantry advanced, it found, in the words of a division historian, "the enemy doing business at the same old stand with the same old merchandise—dug-in tanks and infantry."[22] By nightfall on 25 July, the infantry divisions had advanced only 700 to 1,500 m (765 to 1,640 yards) over the St. Lô–Périers road, well short of their objective for the day. Ninth Division on the right, with only the usual augmentation and the greatest distance to go, was 3.5 km (2 miles) short of Marigny. Thirtieth Division on the left was still 2.5 km (1.5 miles) from St. Gilles (although it was the only formation that attempted to press forward until midnight). The infantry had expected to make easy progress through a defense obliterated by the weight of high explosives rained down on it. When that did not happen, all three divisions, now veterans of *bocage* fighting but disorganized and shaken by short-bombing and trying to absorb numerous replacements, reverted to their usual caution. However, their unit-level command and control and tactics had matured considerably over the previous six weeks, and their attacks did not stall. Map 3.2 shows the development of Cobra from its hesitant beginning to its successful conclusion five days later.

Gloom pervaded VII Corps and First Army headquarters at the poor progress achieved on the first day. No clear breach for the exploitation forces had been created. Should the penetration force be given another day to complete its task? If so, the mobile divisions would not achieve the early momentum needed to cut off the retreat of the enemy's left wing at Coutances. And every day that progress was measured in yards rather than miles was a gift of time to the Germans, allowing them to find and move reserves or redeploy formations to preserve the front; the Germans were famously quick to react. Collins decided to risk the early committal of 1 Infantry and 2 Armored Divisions to complete the breakthrough and begin the exploitation phase immediately (3 Armored would wait for the clearing of Marigny, lest the volume of traffic through the narrow, incomplete breach lead to gridlock). That decision

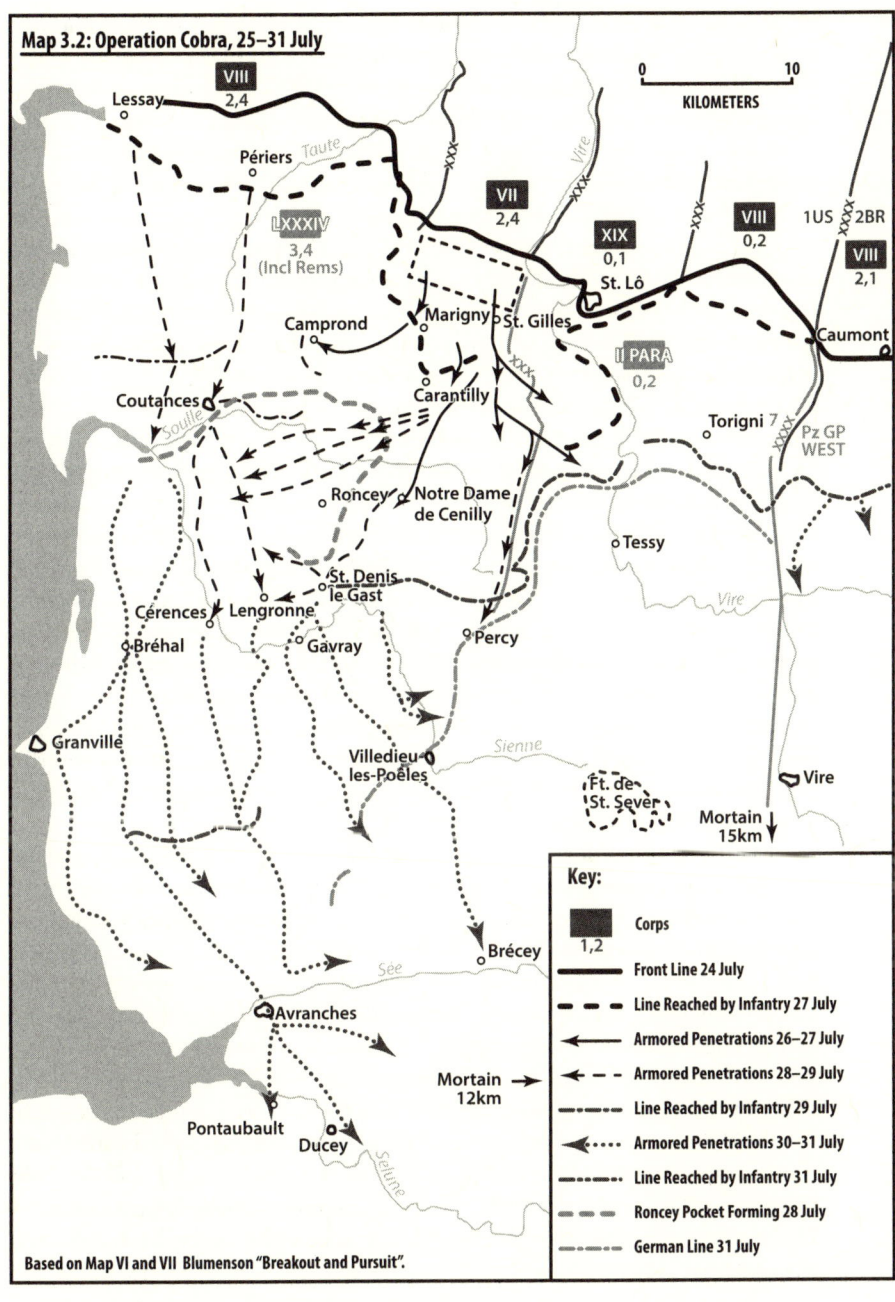

displayed a fine feel for the way the battle was developing, notwithstanding appearances.[23] Collins noted the encouraging results of air reconnaissance; the content of initial prisoner interrogation reports, which suggested the defense was merely a thin crust; and the seeming lack of coordination in the Germans' response, manifested by an absence of the usual local counterattacks. Orders for committal were issued just after 2000 hours on 25 July (the divisions were at two hours' notice to move).

Collins was correct in his belief that *Panzer Lehr*'s defense was irredeemably shattered. The Germans thought a major air effort on 24 July had been followed by an attack that fizzled out; they were not expecting a renewal the next day. This mistaken appreciation was compounded by their underestimate of the strength of VII Corps, which they assessed as four divisions rather than six.[24] When the attack went in on 25 July, the only fully functional element of the defense was the outpost line, which had been little affected by the bombing. In the main defensive zone, casualties were not insignificant (though much less than the division commander claimed and the Americans subsequently believed, as detailed in chapter 2). The main effect, however, was the psychological impact on the soldiery and, above all, the disintegration of command and control. Resistance came only from uncoordinated pockets of defenders, and the defense had little depth to slow and disrupt the attackers' progress. Well-executed counterbattery work suppressed the enemy artillery, depriving the defenders of essential fire support. Moreover, the German logistic position was dire. As described in more detail in chapter 2, right from the start of Cobra, *LXXXIV Corps* was suffering from such crippling shortages of fuel and ammunition that its ability to maintain a defense would have been compromised even if *Panzer Lehr* had not collapsed.

The German commanders (von Choltitz in *LXXXIV Corps* and Hausser at *Seventh Army*) reacted with their customary vigor. In the late afternoon of 26 July, the two reserve divisions were committed, but together they mustered only nine very weak battalions, with little antitank and artillery and very few tanks. Subjected to intensive air interdiction by swarms of fighter-bombers and 216 medium bombers, they were insufficient and too disorganized to conduct an effective counterattack or even a successful counterpenetration. When the weight of the offensive became clearer during the evening, Hausser requested permission to pull his left back to Coutances to reestablish the defense on a shorter line. Von Kluge authorized a limited withdrawal (he was afraid a full-scale withdrawal would turn into a rout and uncover the flank of *Panzer Group West*) and requested that OKW release 9 *Panzer Division* from the south of France and four infantry divisions from *Fifteenth Army*; Hitler agreed to give him 9 *Panzer* and three infantry divisions. But once his line had been penetrated, the way was open to American operational maneuver, and given the time it would take 9 *Panzer*, let alone the infantry, to arrive, he lacked the mobile forces to check it. When he belatedly recognized the seriousness of the threat posed by First Army's offensive, von Kluge ordered more immediate countermoves at around noon on 27 July. The HQ of *XLVII Panzer Corps* and *2 Panzer Division*, refitting southwest of Caen, were dispatched to fill the growing void between *LXXXIV* and *II Parachute Corps*. The next morning, *116 Panzer Division*, newly assembled as a reserve south of Caen, was also ordered west. Ultra and air reconnaissance monitored these moves.

The US offensive gathered momentum on 26–27 July, helped by the committal of all Ninth Air Force's available aircraft to air interdiction and the close support of VII Corps. Nevertheless, the immediate aim—the encirclement of the enemy's left flank grouping—was not achieved. Tactical problems, errors, and a predictable dose of Clausewitzian friction delayed the advance of 1 Infantry Division (reinforced) and 3 Armored Division (commanded by Major Generals Clarence R. Huebner and Leroy H. Watson, respectively), allowing the Germans to slip out of the net. The former intended to bypass Marigny with its attached armored combat command while the village was taken by the leading infantry regiment. The bypassing maneuver was hampered by difficult terrain, made worse by the cratering caused by the bombing, and the armored force ran into elements of *353 Infantry Division* with a few tanks. It proceeded slowly, reaching Camprond—7 km (4 miles) to the west and the previous day's objective—only on the afternoon of 27 July. Nor did it advance immediately from there toward Coutances. The plan was for the combat command to wait until it was relieved by the leading infantry regiment; however, that unit was embroiled in Marigny and did not achieve a linkup until midnight. Meanwhile, Collins, misled by an overly optimistic report on 26 July that Marigny had been taken, ordered 3 Armored Division to pass through the next day. The result was a massive traffic jam as the armor competed for road space with the follow-up regiments of 1 Infantry Division (a mess that Watson singularly failed to cope with). Although Watson's lead task force managed to pass around Marigny, he halted it just beyond the village, well short of Cerisy-la-Salle, for fear of blundering into defensive positions in the dark. The net result was that the fast-reacting von Choltitz had just enough time to throw together a scratch force from *2 SS* and *17 SS Divisions* and some assorted infantry to establish blocking positions from just west of Camprond (4 km [2.5 miles] east of Coutances) to Cerisy-la-Salle. These covered the German left wing's withdrawal through Coutances, as VIII Corps failed in its pinning mission. The German left, aided by minefields, demolitions, the *bocage*, effective rear guards, and American caution, started withdrawing on the night of 26 July and was clear by the evening of 28 July.

Whereas the main effort on the US right proceeded more slowly than planned, the attack on the left went well initially. It would decide the fate of the Germans' west flank grouping. Aided by the success of 4 Infantry Division on its left, Major General Leland S. Hobbs's 30 Infantry Division, after a slow start, fulfilled its mission of penetrating the defense and then swinging outward to clear the west bank of the Vire to halfway between St. Lô and Tessy-sur-Vire. Passing through, Major General Edward H. Brooks's reinforced 2 Armored Division took St. Gilles in the midafternoon of 26 July; by the end of the next day, it was only about 4.5 km (3 miles) from Tessy-sur-Vire and, at Notre-Dame-de-Cenilly, had covered half of the approximately 30 km (18 miles) to Cérences. Brooks, unlike the commanders on the Coutances axis, pressed his armor forward by night as well as by day.[25]

The slow progress of the shallow encirclement and Middleton's failure to pin the enemy, coupled with a more rapid advance on the left of the breakthrough, including by XIX Corps, persuaded Bradley to modify the Cobra concept. His Ultra-fed knowledge of the enemy's plight and reactions helped considerably. First Army would widen and deepen the gap created in the enemy front, with the aim of collapsing the entire left wing of *Seventh Army* and opening the way into Brittany. A new field order was issued on 28 July. It assigned fresh missions, but only in general terms, as the fluid situation did not lend itself to detailed, prescriptive tasking. VII and VIII Corps would cooperate to complete the destruction of the enemy in the Cotentin. The former would shift its main effort to the south, partly to avoid intermingling with VIII Corps, which would advance down the coastal strip. Bradley shifted the boundary between VII and XIX Corps about 4 km (2.5 miles) west of the river Vire and detached 30 Infantry Division and Combat Command A (CCA) of 2 Armored to the latter. XIX Corps (commanded by Major General Charles H. Corlett[26]) was instructed to push down the west bank of the river, outflanking *II Parachute Corps*, taking the high ground of the Forêt de St. Sever, and capturing Vire, a critical road and enemy supply centre, from the west. In doing so, it would cover the flank of the upcoming thrust into Brittany.

Adapting less readily to altered circumstances, Collins still hoped to pull off the shallow encirclement. He believed that a vigorous attack on the original axis by 3 Armored Division would both close the trap and loosen the enemy resistance in front of 1 Infantry Division so that it could hit the retreating enemy's flank. Again, however, Watson failed to act expeditiously. His advance was slowed by difficult terrain, giving the SS troops time to establish a scratch defense, though on favorable ground. Despite Rhinos and close air support, 3 Armored, necessarily launching a frontal attack, failed to penetrate; the division geared up for a deliberate attack on 29 July. When the renewed attack went in, however, it hit air. During the night of 28 July, the Germans had slipped away from the Coutances area, as Middleton's and

Collins's forces discovered when they met and found the net empty. That meeting resulted in gridlock, which Watson, who was at his command post rather than leading forward, failed to untangle.[27] A new corps boundary was drawn east of the Coutances-Cérances road. However, Collins's misguided perseverance with a plan whose prospects had passed had cost precious time. His formations had not (with one important exception) achieved the tempo necessary to impose a battle of maneuver on the Germans.

The Germans had escaped one trap only to fall into another. On 28 July 2 Armored Division advanced in fine style, refusing to be slowed by confusing encounters with the enemy or by open flanks; it occupied, after an initial overextension, a series of blocking positions about 13 km (8 miles) long, on a line Lengronne–St. Denis-le-Gast–Notre-Dame-de-Cenilly. Brooks intended to deny the Germans access to crossings of the river Sienne and escape to the south. His 2 Armored Division (less its CCA and the attached infantry from 4 Division) went from having a protective mission—guarding against enemy relief forces from the south or southeast—to performing the role originally allocated to Huebner's and Watson's divisions. Of course, being a much smaller force, it was lucky the Germans could not organize to fight their way through to comparative safety.

Although *LXXXIV Corps* had escaped immediate destruction in the Coutances pocket, it was in a terrible state of disorganization. Communications had collapsed, and neither von Choltitz nor Hausser knew the whereabouts of all their own troops, let alone those of the enemy. They realized there were Americans to the south of the main body; indeed, *Panzer Lehr's* commander had narrowly escaped capture, the commander of *2 SS Panzer Division* had been killed by an American patrol just north of St. Denis-le-Gast, and Hausser had been fired on. What they did not know was that this was merely the thin screen of CCB. On 28 July von Choltitz received a new mission from his army commander that he felt compelled to challenge, but to no avail. The forces retreating southward from Coutances were to break out toward the southeast, to the Percy area. Hausser feared that his army was being split down the middle and wanted to concentrate; a later counterattack westward could restore a line to the sea. No sooner had orders been issued to *LXXXIV Corps* than von Choltitz received a counterorder from von Kluge, who was horrified at the prospect of leaving open the coastal route southward; a line must be established from Bréhal along the Sienne to Percy and Caumont. Some elements received the counterorder or acted on their own initiative and successfully extricated themselves to the south. Others tried to break out in the area of Notre-Dame-de-Cenilly on 29 July, but the lack of prior reconnaissance and organization resulted in a repulse. This grouping pulled back to try again through St. Denis-le-Gast, but it was detected in the Roncey area and subjected to six and a half hours of sustained attack by Ninth

Air Force and air-directed artillery fire.[28] Then a night breakout southward was attempted, but in the confused and fragmented battle, only disorganized remnants succeeded in exfiltrating.

Developments in *Seventh Army's* centre were somewhat less catastrophic. Around midday on 27 July, von Kluge had released HQ *XLVII Corps* and *2 Panzer Division*, which had been refitting southwest of Caen since its relief on 23 July (probably about 100 tanks and SP guns were ready for action). The goal was to restore the situation in the Marigny–St. Gilles area by counterattack, and forward elements were crossing the Vire at Tessy-sur-Vire that evening. By the next day, von Kluge realized that more combat power would be needed, so he sent the just-joined *116 Panzer Division* (146 combat-ready AFVs) to reinforce the corps; it started arriving late on 29 July (suffering considerable losses from air attacks on the way). The counterattack from Tessy, switched from a northwesterly axis to the west to assist the escape of *LXXXIV Corps'* left wing, went nowhere. The two divisions were fed in as they arrived, and they ran into XIX Corps' own drive south, strongly supported by IX Tactical Air Command's fighter-bombers, which came out in force to hit the newly arrived armor. A line was stabilized from less than 3 km (2 miles) north of Tessy to the southeast through Percy and to the crossroads town of Villedieu-les-Poêles. Beyond that town there was no coherent defensive line. As 30 July dawned, there was a yawning 30 km (18 mile) gap from Villedieu to the sea, and VII Corps, turned ninety degrees, was moving into it; the powerfully reinforced, motorized 1 Infantry Division passed west of the town and reached the river Sée. And to Huebner's west, VIII Corps, now under Patton's supervision and led by 4 and 6 Armored Divisions rather than the infantry, raced down the coastal strip and passed through Avranches. The corps picked up about 7,000 demoralized prisoners as it advanced. The routed enemy had become so ineffectual that VIII Corps suffered less than 700 casualties between 28 and 31 July. On the last day of the month, CCA of 4 Armored Division took the bridges over the Sélune at Pontaubault and the dam upstream near Ducey.

This was a disaster for the Germans and a turning point in the campaign.[29] The routes into Brittany, and to the south and west, were open. No longer could the Germans maintain a linear, positional defense in favorable ground and thus impose an attritional nature on the campaign. Their western flank had been turned, and the Americans could, and would, exploit their vastly superior mobility, enhanced by their mastery of the air, to conduct wide-ranging maneuver against the German flanks and rear. The whole position of *Army Group B* was fatally compromised, as map 3.3 clearly illustrates.

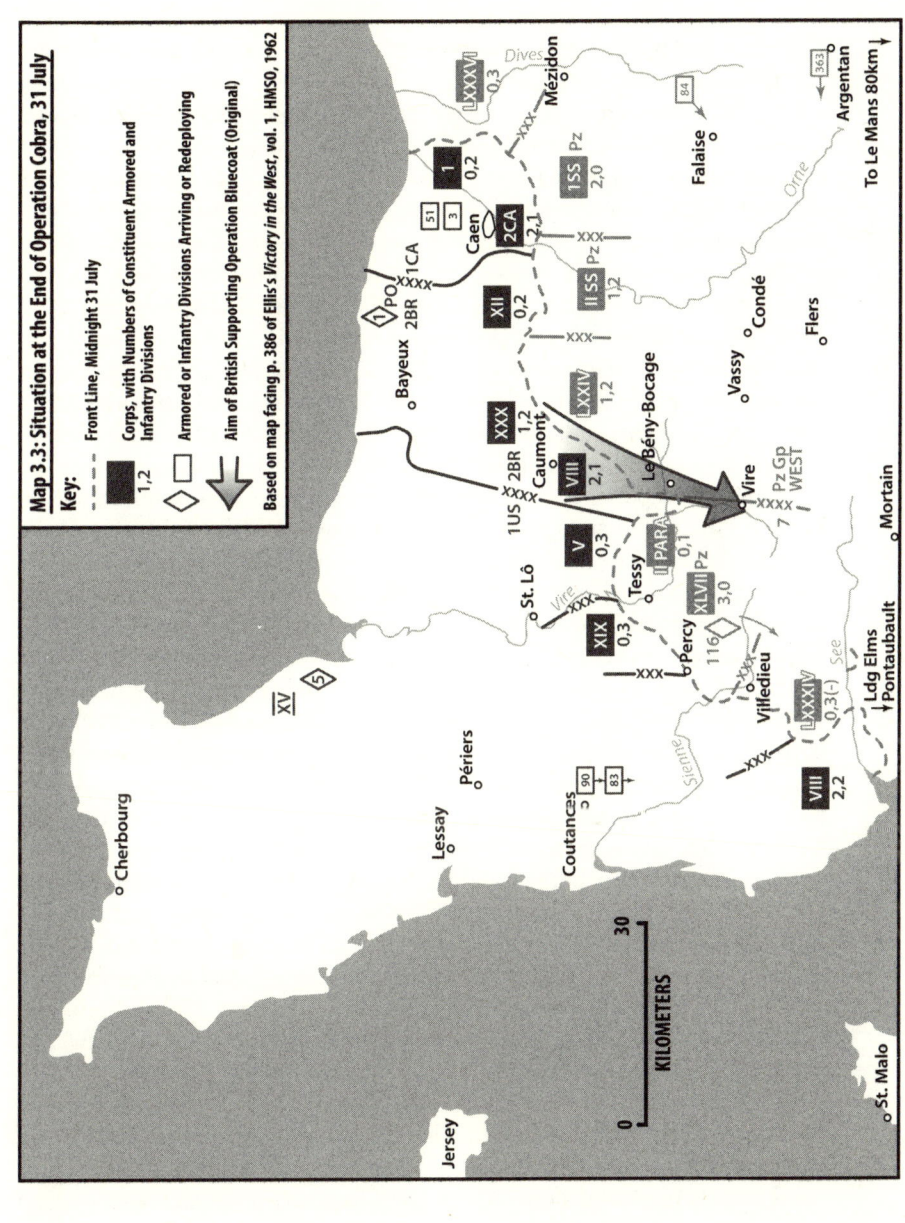

IMMEDIATE POST-COBRA OPERATIONS: 1–6 AUGUST

On 1 August HQ 12 Army Group became operational, with First Army and the newly activated Third Army under command.[30] Bradley moved up to army group command and was replaced by his deputy, Lieutenant General Courtney H. Hodges; Bradley left the First Army staff in place to avoid unnecessary disruption in the midst of fluid, fast-moving operations. The new army group set about exploiting the breakout from Normandy and the success being enjoyed by British Second Army's offensive alongside the boundary between 21 and 12 Army Groups, which had started on 30 July.

Third Army initially comprised VIII Corps and the newly arrived XV Corps (Major General Wade H. Haislip commanding the latter), which initially shared the former's six divisions. As additional forces arrived, both original corps would be reinforced, and XX and XII Corps would join Third Army. The army's principal task, mandated by the Overlord plan, was to capture the Brittany ports, especially St. Malo, Brest, and Quiberon Bay (for development as a port). Its subsequent mission was to push south to secure the Loire flank and simultaneously move eastward as the right wing of the great wheeling movement that Montgomery envisaged, crushing the Germans against the Seine barrier.[31] Patton's natural boldness was encouraged by his Ultra-derived knowledge of the weakness of *XXV Corps* in Brittany; it had been stripped of field-capable divisions and battle groups to feed the maw of Normandy (the four immobile, low-quality formations remaining were capable only of holding the port "fortresses"), and the reinforcements belatedly heading for *Seventh Army* were too distant to affect his operations. He ordered his two armored divisions to ignore the danger to their flanks and rear and to seize distant objectives; the infantry would follow. On 1 August 4 Armored advanced 64 km (40 miles) to bypass Rennes, Brittany's capital; thereafter it invested Lorient and St. Nazaire but, lacking enough infantry and artillery, did not capture them. Meanwhile, 6 Armored's objective was Brest, about 240 km (150 miles) distant; in a spectacular cross-country dash, it reached the city on 7 August but found that it could not be taken from the line of march. The two infantry divisions of VIII Corps (later reinforced) followed up and set about the long and costly business of reducing the key ports.[32] For Patton, the corps' achievements, however spectacular, were insufficient. Once it was clear that the ports could not be rushed by armored divisions, he wanted to extricate them for more suitable armored tasks in the east, where the possible destruction of major enemy formations now beckoned; on 11 August he alerted 4 Armored to prepare to join XV Corps and begged unsuccessfully for 6 Armored as well.

In accordance with Montgomery's scheme of maneuver, First Army wheeled eastward. However, the gap that had been ripped open on *Seventh*

Army's left did not mean an easy advance for most of the US forces. The Germans, aided by defensible terrain, the shortening of the line in the centre, and the arrival of two fresh infantry divisions, conducted an organized, fighting withdrawal. It would take First Army six days to advance approximately 20 km (12 miles) to a line roughly Vire–St. Pois–Mortain, although progress was easier between the Sée and the Sélune. This was hardly spectacular progress. Neither Hausser nor von Kluge could take much comfort from this, however. There was still the problem of their open flank, which the Americans were beginning to exploit. VII Corps started to feel round the German left. More significantly for the future, as soon as the first elements of XV Corps came up on 2 August, they started toward the Mayenne River. Initially, this was a move in anticipation of the main effort of Third Army being shifted eastward. Bradley, more concerned about security than an offensive eastward at this stage, merely wanted 79 Division inserted into the Fougères area on First Army's right to cover both VII and VIII Corps against counterattack; simultaneously, Patton had ordered 5 Armored into the same area for the same reason. Significantly, Haislip's men encountered no resistance as they advanced southward.

By 6 August, VII Corps had taken the high ground and crossroads town of Mortain; reached southeast to Barenton, 10 km (6 miles) southeast of Mortain; and pushed forward elements onto the river Mayenne, just north of the eponymous town. To its south, XV Corps, advancing with all three divisions in a single echelon, had advanced 50 km (30 miles) in two days to reach a line Mayenne–Laval–Château Gautier and established four bridgeheads over the river. There was no resistance. Patton requested and received permission to press on to Le Mans, about 70 km (45 miles) to the east.

The massive intervention by Eighth Air Force was the most spectacular but, at the end of the day, not the most important contribution of the Air Corps to the success of Cobra and, especially, its decisive exploitation. The Ninth Air Force played a vital role once operations became mobile. It kept the Luftwaffe at bay, preserving (along with plentiful antiaircraft artillery) the critical bridges over the Sée and Sélune and the vulnerable columns that would flood south. Armed reconnaissance, ranging far ahead of advancing ground forces, interdicted enemy movement (which was increasingly out of rather than into the battle area). Armored column cover provided a rapid, responsive source of fire support when, thanks to the tempo achieved, medium and heavy artillery could not keep up. It was available in profusion, usually with an entire fighter group assigned to support each column to provide continuous squadron coverage. By 1 August, only two fighter groups were still flying out of bases in England, so loiter times were not foreshortened, and the response time to requests for surges in air effort was commendably short.

From the end of July, Hausser and von Kluge were clear about the extent of the disaster. Powerful, highly mobile American formations with abundant air support would break out into open country and conduct a deep or shallow encirclement of *Seventh Army* while simultaneously advancing eastward. The only force that could fill the yawning gap between Mortain and the Loire, a distance of about 130 km (80 miles), was *LXXXI Corps*, with the low-quality, garrison *708 Infantry Division* and the understrength *9 Panzer Division*, just arriving on the Loire. The situation would have to be restored by counterattack. On 1 August von Kluge ordered that all possible panzer forces be relieved in the line and concentrated for a drive on the Mortain-Avranches axis to restore a short, defensible front in *bocage* country and cut off Third Army elements pouring into Brittany.

Time was not on the German side. It would take until 6 August to replace the attack formations with newly arriving infantry and concentrate them under *XLVII Panzer Corps* in the Sourdeval-Mortain area. Four developments in those five days doomed the concept. First, British Second Army mounted Operation Bluecoat, which required three panzer divisions to halt it. Second, VII Corps advanced to Mortain, widening the Avranches corridor to 32 km (20 miles); capturing Mortain and the high ground around the town deprived *XLVII Panzer Corps* of its favorable LD. Third, American formations moving up for committal found themselves within easy reach of the battlefield between the Sée and the Sélune. Finally, elements of both First and Third Armies advanced to and over the river Mayenne, outflanking the attack grouping, and they showed no signs of remaining passive. Both sides were intent on offensive operations, but the Americans had superior strength in the vicinity, the ability to bring devastating airpower to bear, and an enemy open flank to exploit. *Army Group B*'s position was about to go from bad to desperate.

OPERATION BLUECOAT

Background

If the first six weeks of the Normandy campaign had been largely disappointing for the US Army, they were even more so for the British. At least the Americans had had the tangible satisfaction of taking the port of Cherbourg. The British had struggled until 9 July to take Caen; then it had taken another two weeks to clear a limited space south of the city from which a further offensive could be mounted on the Falaise-Paris axis. It is true that the main purpose of British operations had been achieved: the bulk of German combat power, including almost four-fifths of the armor, was pinned in the east. That was of little consolation to the overwhelming majority of officers and men not privy to the campaign plan. To them, and even to some who should have known better, something akin to stalemate seemed to be setting in. Morale was beginning to suffer in several formations, and Montgomery was under personal attack for the expensive lack of progress in geographic terms.

To Montgomery, it was quite clear that the only sector in the British area of operations that offered the potential for decisive results was on the left, in the direction of Paris. However, as Operations Goodwood and Spring had shown, the very success of his operational idea (pinning German armor in the sector) had made a breakthrough there all but impossible. The Germans had built up formidable combat power to bar the way; on the eve of Cobra, the Germans had ten divisions, including seven panzer and all four GHQ heavy tank (Tiger) battalions, between the sea and just west of the Orne. Montgomery resolved to deliver a sharp blow where it was least expected, on Second Army's right (but it was Dempsey who selected the Caumont sector specifically), where there were only two overextended infantry divisions. This offered several gains: it would support the Cobra offensive by taking ground important to the defender as he adjusted to a new and adverse situation; it would also unbalance the enemy, forcing him to weaken both his reaction to Cobra and his defense south of Caen in order to shore up his line in the centre. Then 21 Army Group, employing the newly operational First Canadian Army, could resume its main effort in more advantageous circumstances. On 27 July Montgomery and Dempsey discussed the upcoming Operation Bluecoat, an attack by six divisions, with Bradley. Following their discussion, Montgomery signaled Eisenhower and Brooke: "I have ordered Dempsey to throw all caution overboard and to take any risks he likes, to accept any casualties he likes, and step on the gas for Vire." The attack was scheduled to start on 2 August. However, the CIGS was concerned that, whereas First Army had broken through and was advancing rapidly, the British were in danger of conforming to their stereotype—passively waiting while the Americans did the heavy work. On 28 July he urged Montgomery to bring Bluecoat forward, and it was duly advanced to 30 July. Eisenhower too expressed the need for urgency.

Terrain

The battle area was defined in the east by the Anglo-American boundary—the little river Drôme and then the much larger Vire south of where it turned temporarily eastward about 4 km (2.5 miles) from Le Bény-Bocage, 12 km (7.5 miles) from Tessy-sur-Vire—and in the west by the river Orne. The *bocage* was at its most dense in this area south of Caumont, and it was more hilly and wooded than elsewhere, which helps explain why it had been a quiet sector for five weeks; it also lacked an attractive geographic objective to make it worth fighting through. Only Vire, 30 km (18 miles) south of Caumont, was of significance. It was a major German logistic centre, and the road running due east from it to Falaise was a main supply route. The obstacles running west to east roughly halfway between Caumont and Vire would, however, become ground of operational value as a result of the unfolding success of Operation Cobra.

Obstacles. Running more or less west to east from the Forêt l'Evêque to Thury Harcourt on the Orne was a high, steep-sided ridge covered by woods for most of its length. About 10 km (6 miles) from the Orne was Mt. Pinçon, the highest hill in what is aptly called the Suisse Normande (the very hilly area astride the gorge of the Orne). The other dominating height, 12 km (7.5 miles) northwest of it and 8 km (5 miles) south of Caumont, was Hill 361 (today's Bois du Brimbois).[33] About 10 km (6 miles) north of Vire, also running west-east across one-third of the sector, the river Souleuvre and its tributaries flowed, also surrounded by high, steep-sided, wooded ridges. These were only the most prominent defendable positions, however. There were two other minor ridges before the Vire-Falaise road was reached, and streams ran in every direction; their banks were often too soft or too steep to be fordable without preparation by armor, and the bridges over them were not sturdy enough to bear heavy vehicles. The generally close, hedgerow-strewn country and the frequent woods, copses, and orchards hampered movement; they also afforded good concealment that made it hard to use artillery and airpower to full effect unless and until combat assumed a more fluid character. The numerous stoutly built farms, hamlets, and villages provided good strongpoints for defense.

Routes. There were few metalled roads, and only two, which merged into one, were capable of taking two-way traffic and ran in the right direction—from Caumont through St. Martin-des-Besaces to Vire. That road was joined 13 km (8 miles) short of Vire by another from Caen via Villers Bocage. There were a few departmental roads, but most were one-way, tortuous, local lanes or farm tracks. Many were too narrow for tanks, with ditches or high banks topped with hedges on either side. Traffic management could easily break down, with long tailbacks clogging movement.

All movement in such country was bound to be slow and difficult. Off-road movement, even for tanks, was all but impossible much of the time (British tanks did not have the benefit of the Rhino hedge cutter). Infantry found the going slow, especially if lumbered with heavy weapons. Navigation—even ascertaining one's location with any precision—was frequently problematic, with all that implied for arranging fire and air support and cooperation. With often restricted fields of vision and fire, the ground in many areas lent itself to infiltration tactics.

The German Defense

LXXIV Corps defended the left of *Panzer Group West*. The country greatly favored the defense. During the weeks in which it had been a passive sector, the Germans had worked effectively to improve on nature and prepare excellent positions. Both sides had carried out extensive mining to improve the security of their fronts (but when the British took over the Caumont sector, the Americans were unable to produce minefield maps to show what they had done). Because it was an apparently unpromising area for an offensive, and because *Panzer Group West's* reserves in the area south of Caen could reinforce quite speedily, the overstretched Germans had thinned the sector out. Holding a passive front that was not expected to burst into life, the corps was very weak and, with a frontage of about 30 km (18 miles), overextended.[34] Another problem would beset the defense: the British attack was delivered down the enemy's interarmy boundary.

The corps had two static, occupation infantry divisions (each of around 11,500 men), with limited artillery and antitank capabilities; the latter included a few assault guns and attached tanks for stiffening. Only about half of *276 Infantry Division* would be subject to the initial attack. Two British corps delivered the main blow on *326 Division*, which had not yet seen combat and had relieved *2 Panzer Division* in the line only on 23 July, taking over 16 km (10 miles) of front. The entire corps reserve consisted of a heavy SP antitank battalion with twenty-one *jagdpanthers*. Nor was a strong army reserve available to compensate. Once *2* and *116 Panzer Divisions* had moved west to face the Cobra offensive, only *21 Panzer Division* was left uncommitted in *Panzer Group West*. This tired, understrength division had been in the line virtually continuously since 6 June and was relieved only on 28 July; it possessed forty-one Mk IV tanks and thirteen attached Tigers in running order (another nineteen Mk IVs and sixteen Tigers were in workshops), and it was trying to absorb about 2,400 indifferent ex-Luftwaffe infantrymen. The division was refitting in the Forêt de Cinglais, more than 30 km (18 miles) to the west. It would be the first reinforcement committed to the battle, arriving on 31 July.

Second Army's Plan

Operation Bluecoat was intended to support the American Cobra offensive and weaken the enemy defense in the Caen sector so that the offensive there could be resumed with better prospects of success.[35] The aims of Bluecoat were threefold: to fix the enemy armor in the British sector; to prevent the Germans from establishing a defense anchored on the high ground south of Caumont in order to maintain a solid line swinging southeastward (along the river Vire) in the face of American pressure—that is, to knock away the hinge; and to threaten the right rear of the enemy attempting to check the US breakthrough.

Second Army was responsible for an approximately 40 km (25 mile) sector. Dempsey had three armored and five infantry divisions, one infantry brigade, and four independent tank/armored brigades.[36] He allocated forces and tasks as follows.

Pinning Force. An essentially passive sector of about 20 km (12 miles) west of the Orne was held by XII Corps (commanded by Lieutenant General Neil Ritchie) with two infantry divisions, each reinforced by a tank brigade, and an AGRA. The corps was expected to fix the enemy to its front, then advance in conformity with XXX Corps on its right.

Main Effort. XXX Corps (Lieutenant General Gerald Bucknell commanding) in the centre had a 13 km (8 mile) sector, of which 9 km (5.5 miles) would be attacked, nearly 3 km (2 miles) on the principal axis. The corps' component formations, and their missions, were as follows: 43 Infantry Division, most of 8 Armored Brigade, and special armor were tasked with seizing Hill 361 and the spur to its east, about 11 km (7 miles) distant, by H+10 and securing the division's left flank; 50 Infantry Division and 56 Infantry Brigade with supporting armor were to take the village of Amaye-sur-Seulles and the nearby high ground, an advance of around 7 km (4 miles); 7 Armored Division was "to be prepared to move forward on any of the axes available to XXX Corps"; and a reinforced AGRA would provide fire support.

Secondary Effort. On the right was VIII Corps (Lieutenant General Richard O'Connor commanding), filling the remaining 7 km (4 miles) or so: 15 Infantry Division with 6 Guards Tank Brigade was to protect XXX Corps' right by advancing 8 km (5 miles) to take Hill 309 (or Quarry Hill), the high ground 2 km (1.25 miles) to the northwest of Hill 361; 11 Armored Division was to cover its right; the Guards Armored Division was in reserve; and a reinforced AGRA would provide artillery support. The corps was to be prepared to exploit toward Point Aunay on the western side of the Forêt l'Evêque.

Reserves. Although Second Army had no dedicated reserve, the army group had just pulled back two infantry divisions and an armored brigade in the Caen sector, and they were only a 40 to 50 km (25 to 30 mile) road march away.

A complicated three-phase plan, supported by a heavy bombing program, was prepared for the reinforced 15 and 43 Divisions' capture of the high ground deemed so important to the enemy. In greatly simplified form, it went as follows. The attack was organized in depth, with each division being in three echelons (including the brigade holding the LD, which subsequently became the divisional reserve).

Phase one was a preliminary operation to overcome the presumed outpost position of the defense. This would be preceded by fighter ground attack and executed by the first echelon of the leading reinforced brigade of each division, with the aid of on-call artillery concentrations. The two battle groups (BGs) would advance about 2 km (1.25 miles); then the two follow-up BGs would perform a passage of lines and prepare for the next phase. This would begin at X-hour, three hours hence, on an army LD (drawn, it must be noted, on no obvious terrain feature).

Phase two would be preceded by a sixty-minute aerial bombardment: 693 heavy bombers would carpet-bomb areas about 2 km (1.25 miles) in front of XXX Corps, and 650 medium bombers would do the same for VIII Corps. At X-hour, a creeping barrage would start, moving forward up to 2.5 km (1.5 miles) at rate of 90 m (100 yards) every four minutes to carry the tanks and infantry onto the intermediate objectives.

Finally, in phase three, second-echelon brigades would pass through, picking up armor from the first-echelon brigade, and follow another similar barrage to within 600 m (650 yards) of the objective. After a pause to tie up the final assault, they would take the hills with the support of heavy artillery concentrations. In 15 Division's sector, there would be a second sixty-minute bombing by 216 mediums on Hill 309 six hours after the end of the phase two bombing. (This second air strike was a result of lessons learned from Operation Goodwood, where German depth positions, out of range of divisional artillery, had halted the attack.)

After the high ground was taken, 15 Division was to patrol to the river Souleuvre and link up with 11 Armored in the area of Forêt l'Evêque; 43 Division would patrol to the east and southeast. Deeper objectives, if any, were not specified in corps orders. These would most likely be determined as the operation unfolded. There was no mention of Vire, despite Montgomery's "step on the gas" assurances to Eisenhower and Brooke.

Execution

Substantial regrouping was required, particularly of VIII Corps, which had to move formations between 32 and 80 km (20 and 50 miles). This was conducted entirely during the night 28–29 July over perpetually congested routes. Meanwhile, normal patterns of activity were maintained on the hitherto passive Caumont sector, as was strict communications security. Dummy radio nets and tank movements successfully masked VIII Corps' move from the Caen area. When Bluecoat opened at 0655 hours on 30 July, it caught all levels of German command, from division upward, unawares.

Having achieved operational surprise, Second Army enjoyed a massive numerical preponderance for at least the first few days of Operation Bluecoat. Factoring the overextended *326* and *276 Infantry Divisions* and *21 Panzer Division* into the calculation of *LXXIV Corps'* strength, and ignoring XII Corps, the force ratios favored the British by 4.4:1 in men, 10.5:1 in tanks and SP guns (excluding British light tanks and special armor), 3.6:1 in guns and mortars over 80mm, and 5:1 in towed antitank guns (excluding *panzerschreks* and *panzerfausts*). This superiority excluded the firepower of the massive preliminary air bombardment. The fundamental question would be whether the British could translate their advantages of surprise and initial strength into a rapid advance, despite the difficulties posed by the terrain. Map 3.4 shows the objectives and actual evolution of Operation Bluecoat.

The bombing was effective in damaging the morale of the newly arrived, green troops of *326 Division*, and it destroyed its HQ. This significantly aided VIII Corps' advance. On the main axis, however, bombing made little difference, as the attack stalled barely 1 km (0.5 mile) beyond its LD.

In view of the surprise factor and the weakness and overextension of the defense, it is perhaps strange that XXX Corps' main attack (by 43 Infantry Division and most of 8 Armored Brigade) was still nearly 3 km (2 miles) short of Hill 361, its H+10 objective, at the end of the second day of operations and that the supporting attack by 50 Division was still only 2.5 km (1.5 miles) beyond its LD. In the neighboring VIII Corps, however, 15 Infantry Division and 6 Guards Tank Brigade achieved their first-day objectives on time. Various histories explain XXX Corps' failure by pointing out that the enemy had greatly improved a minor obstacle, carried out extensive mining, and deployed well-concealed and dug-in antitank and machine guns (hardly unique problems). Then his reinforcements arrived. The corps continued to make disappointing progress for the next three to four days, despite the committal of 7 Armored Division and in marked contrast to VIII Corps. On 4 August XXX Corps' and 7 Armored's commanders were finally dismissed after six weeks of underperformance.

Predictably, given the terrain and the initially stubborn resistance, adherence to the timings specified in VIII Corps' plan of attack proved impossible. Although the infantry of 15 Division worked closely and effectively with the tank guardsmen, they took two to five hours longer than planned to clear their phase one objectives, and clogged routes combined with the *bocage* prevented follow-up units from getting forward. The "bold" decision was made to send the tanks forward without infantry in phase two, so as not to lose the benefit of the barrage. The same decision was perforce adopted for the capture of the final objective; the attack had to be launched from the northwest rather than the northeast, as originally planned, and an armored battalion had to wait on the objective for almost four hours before infantry

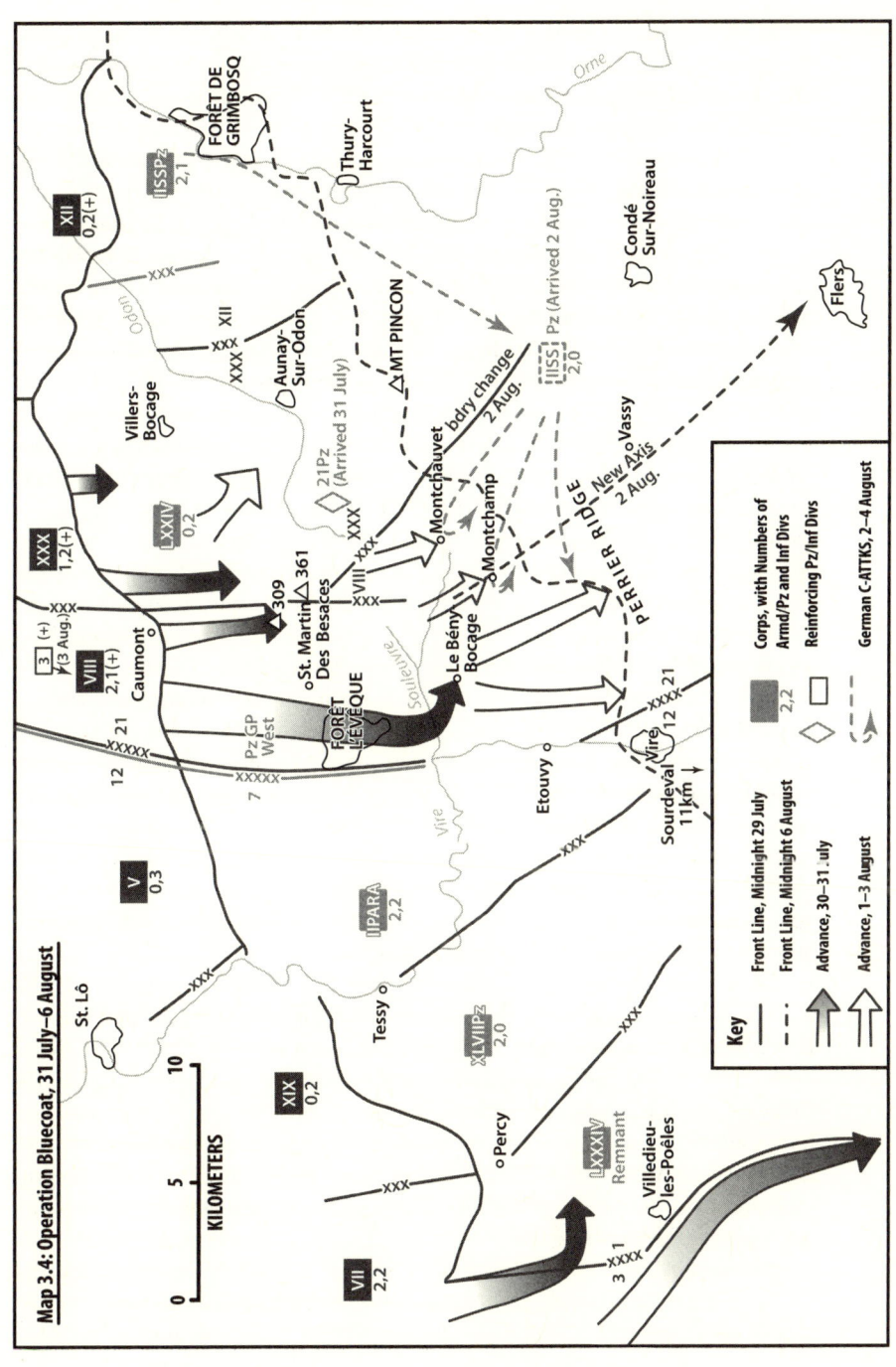

could come up. Learning a lesson from Goodwood (even more applicable in the *bocage*), 11 Armored Division was organized and trained for the first time in balanced BGs comprising equal elements of tanks and infantry. Its advance was hindered as much by the absence of any decent routes and by frequent mines as it was by the enemy. It required a night infiltration attack to ensure the timely capture of St. Martin-des-Besaces; this was forced on a reluctant Major General Roberts by O'Connor, his corps commander.

On 31 July VIII Corps exploited its success, even though its open left flank (thanks to the failure of XXX Corps) caused concern. As 15 Division and 6 Guards Tank Brigade consolidated their gains, the Guards Armored Division was directed on Le Bény-Bocage via St. Martin. The Guards immediately ran into trouble. This division (under pressure from O'Connor) had only the day before adopted a combined-arms organization similar to that of 11 Armored Division. It was hampered by the unfamiliarity of this arrangement and by its lack of training in tank-infantry cooperation. It also ran into elements of the newly arrived *21 Panzer Division*. However, 11 Armored advanced through the undefended Forêt l'Evêque. Roberts exploited medium reconnaissance's discovery of an intact, undefended bridge over the river Souleuvre on the enemy's interarmy boundary. He immediately sent six handy tanks to seize it, followed, as soon as it could be organized, by a mixed BG that established a firm defense by the early evening of 31 July. By midafternoon on 1 August, the whole division was consolidated on the Le Bény-Bocage ridge, the last significant obstacle before Vire. A mere 112 men and twenty-six tanks had been lost for an advance of about 17 km (10 miles), so slight had been the enemy resistance. O'Connor ordered the division to consolidate and, next morning, to seize bridges over the Souleuvre from the south to aid the advance of Guards Armored, which was stuck in the area of Le Tourneur. Meanwhile, reconnaissance patrols probed as far as Vire without encountering any enemy; the town itself, it was discovered, was defended only by logistic troops and a couple of flak batteries.

In view of its success, Dempsey shifted the main effort to VIII Corps and, on 1 August, allocated the reserve 3 Infantry Division and 4 Armored Brigade to it. However, his army's advance was not to be directed on Vire. Montgomery, for reasons never adequately explained, altered the axis southeastward, with Flers (about 20 km [12 miles] southeast of Le Bény-Bocage) now specified as an objective.[37] Moreover, it was not until fresh orders were received on 2 August that 11 Armored resumed its advance, now with the immediate mission of cutting the Vire-Vassy main supply route by establishing itself on the Perriers ridge.

Panzer Group West had reacted promptly. At 1700 hours on 30 July, *21 Panzer Division*, its last reserve, was ordered to restore the situation. The division was delayed by air interdiction and arrived too late to hold Hill 309 or recapture it before its defense was consolidated; *LXXIV Corps* insisted on a counterattack, but predictably, this failed in the face of an adverse force ratio and massed fire by the corps artillery. Although *21 Panzer* was able to check the advance of 43 Infantry and the Guards Armored Divisions, this was no longer enough. The 11 Armored had split *Seventh Army* and *Panzer Group West* apart by advancing down the boundary, and it had established itself in strength on the last obstacle before Vire. In the late afternoon of 1 August, *II SS Panzer Corps* (9 and *10 SS Panzer Divisions* and *102 SS Heavy Tank Battalion*) was ordered out of the line south of Caen to stop XXX Corps and retake the Le Bény-Bocage ridge. Thanks to mission command accompanied by slick staff work, *II SS Panzer Corps* had leading elements on the move within two hours of receiving the order, and the main body had disengaged and was redeploying within six hours.[38] It could muster forty tanks and SP guns in *10 SS*, seventy-six in *9 SS* (although twenty-three were lost to air attack during the redeployment), and about twenty Tigers. The strength of the two divisions' six infantry battalions was below 75 percent of TO&E.

The arrival of *10 SS Panzer* to reinforce *21 Panzer* and the remnants of *326 Infantry Divisions* on 2 August prevented the Guards Armored and XXX Corps from gaining momentum. It was not until the end of 3 August that the Guards Division reached Montchauvet, 8 km (5 miles) south of Hill 361 and 10.5 km (6.5 miles) short of Vassy. This left 11 Armored, which had reached the Perriers ridge on 2 August, in a salient. Moreover, starting late on 2 August, *9 SS* mounted minor probing attacks into the division's flank. With O'Connor's concurrence, Roberts transitioned to defense until such time as the Guards Armored could catch up. At this stage, 11 Armored had lost 31 medium tanks destroyed and was down to 114 runners (excluding the armored recce regiment, which was carrying out a flank security mission 8 km [5 miles] to the west). However, it would soon receive several repaired tanks from workshops, and 3 Infantry Division, together with 4 Independent Armored Brigade, was arriving to reinforce VIII Corps; its lead brigade came under the command of 11 Armored when it reached Caumont at 0800 on 3 August.

Arriving in an unfamiliar sector and with no reliable intelligence, *9 SS Panzer* set about trying to retake the Le Bény-Bocage ridge on 2 August. BG Weiss, based on *102 SS Heavy Tank* and divisional reconnaissance battalions, was dispatched to restore contact with *3 Parachute Division*'s right (the flank of *Seventh Army*) and attack from the southwest via Vire. The rest of the division spent that day and the next conducting reconnaissance in force-infiltration attacks on a wide front against 11 Armored's left flank, presumably to identify suitable weak spots for a concentrated attack. It became clear that force ratios would not support a recovery of the Le Bény-Bocage ridge. Moreover, by the end of 3 August, air interdiction and ground combat had reduced 9 SS to thirty-four tanks and SP guns and each of its panzer grenadier battalions to company strength. On the positive side, the afternoon of 3 August saw the arrival of BG *Olboeter* from *12 SS Panzer* (consisting of thirteen Panthers, an infantry company, and a battery) and an army engineer battalion to prevent a thrust across the Vire-Vassy road toward Flers.

On 4 August *9 SS Panzer* made another effort to close the gap between *Seventh Army* and *Panzer Group West*, this time on the less ambitious Etouvy-Montchamp line (about 5 to 8 km [3 to 5 miles] north of the Vire-Vassy road). This was a more focused effort, with *9 SS* attacking from the east and BG *Weiss* from the west, but lack of strength compelled the continued use of infiltration tactics. Given the British sensitivity to threats to their flanks and rear, the Germans probably hoped they could persuade 11 Armored to fall back to keep the forces on the Perriers ridge from being cut off. However, by this time, Guards Armored and 15 Divisions were making some progress, and 11 Armored had been reinforced by an infantry brigade of 3 Division. The attack failed.

Being even less ambitious on 5 August, *9 SS* attempted to push the British off the Perriers ridge, recalling BG *Weiss* to help (it had been relieved by elements of *3 Parachute Division* to face the advancing 3 Division and 4 Armored Brigade in the west). The attack was beaten off, partly by concentrated artillery and air. By now, *9 SS* had shot its bolt offensively and had to take over much of *10 SS*'s defensive mission as well. The final effort to retake the ridge was mounted on 6 August by *10 SS Panzer*, pulled out of the line to the north the day before. The division had been ordered south to join *XLVII Panzer Corps* for the Mortain counterattack, and this was the last chance to reestablish a defense forward of the Vire-Vassy road before it left. This attack, too, was launched with insufficient reconnaissance and forces and was repulsed with considerable losses. However, 11 Armored Division suffered too. The division had lost 31 tanks destroyed in its advance to and seizure of the Perriers ridge. It lost another 130 tanks and 500 casualties in holding the ridge over the next four days. The full casualty bill for VIII Corps up to 6 August was 5,114.

By the end of 6 August, 3 Division and its supporting armored brigade were only about 1.5 km (1 mile) from the Vire-Vassy road, 11 Armored still owned much of the Perriers ridge, and the other two divisions of VIII Corps were within 2.5 km (1.5 miles) of closing up to its left flank. The salient was all but eliminated. Even XXX Corps had made progress, thanks to the withdrawal of *10 SS Panzer*, taking the dominant Mt. Pinçon feature on 6 August.[39] With that, Operation Bluecoat was effectively over, although XII Corps (two infantry divisions and two tank brigades) achieved a potentially important success with its supporting advance in forcing the Orne and moving into the Forêt de Grimbosq. The dual threat of an advance down the east bank of the Orne and southeast toward Falaise was taken seriously, and a battle group of *12 SS Panzer Division*, the depth formation of *I SS Panzer Corps*, was sent from south of Caen to deal with the small bridgehead before it became too well established.

At the start of Bluecoat, the Germans' left wing, *Seventh Army*, was in the process of disintegration. The British offensive then drove a wedge between it and *Panzer Group West* (renamed *Fifth Panzer Army* on 6 August) and threatened the town of Vire. The town was important in its own right as a communications hub and supply centre, but its significance increased on 2 August when Hitler ordered a counterattack into the flank of the US breakout from the area Sourdeval-Mortain. The former was less than 11 km (7 miles) south of Vire, and the latter 18 km (11 miles). If the British offensive were not contained, the counterattack would be stillborn at best; at worst, *Seventh Army* would be faced with a double envelopment by the Americans from the south and the British from the north. No wonder the Germans reacted so strongly, even at the risk of weakening the Caen sector and, indeed, the Mortain counterattack!

OPERATIONAL ART AND GENERALSHIP

Operation Cobra

The weakened state of *Seventh Army*, its parlous logistic plight, and the absence of reserves that could quickly intervene to close any breach meant that First Army was pushing at a flimsy door that was barely closed, never mind locked. This was partly due to the fact that the offensive achieved strategic and operational surprise: the former in that the Fortitude deception had, until too late, denied *Army Group B* in Normandy the infantry divisions that would give depth to the defense and release panzer divisions from a frontline, static defense role;[40] the latter because the Americans had adopted an unexpected approach as to method. It was also a tribute to the success of Montgomery's operational idea of pinning the enemy's main strength on the left in order to break out on the right.[41] And, of course, it was a consequence of the heavy attrition inflicted on *Seventh Army* over the previous weeks.[42] Of particular importance was the systematic weakening over time of the Germans' ability to fight. By 25 July, air interdiction had left most units so short of fuel and ammunition that prolonged resistance was no longer possible. For all the attention paid to the massive preliminary air bombardment, the air arm's most important contribution to victory had been cutting the bridges over the Loire and all but closing down rail traffic to *Seventh Army* dumps.

To admit the weakness of the defense is not to denigrate the American achievement, which was unprecedented in the Normandy campaign:

the Americans advanced almost 60 km (40 miles) on the critical west flank, opened the way into Brittany, and inflicted about 10,000 losses on the enemy (killed, wounded, and captured), all in the space of seven days. It is the vigorous, flexible exploitation that makes Cobra notable as an example of operational art, not the breakthrough. The unfolding of the operation illustrates the importance of tempo to success. The initial failure to achieve it in VII Corps' main effort, first in the penetration and then in the advance to Coutances, doomed the shallow envelopment to failure. This was redeemed by the rapidity with which 2 Armored Division formed a deeper encirclement. First Army's timely change of concept was complemented by the speedy reorganization and change of axis of VII Corps. As a result, *XLVII Panzer Corps* arrived too late to restore the integrity of the defense; all it could achieve was a very limited counterpenetration, which was outflanked to decisive effect. VII Corps' accelerating advance was coupled with the Patton-driven acceleration of VIII Corps, which turned retreat into rout on the coastal axis. Crossings over the last obstacles before open country was reached were seized before demolition could be carried out and defense organized.

Bradley generally showed a sure touch in the planning and execution of Operation Cobra. His change in approach to operations, whatever the inspiration, was undoubtedly correct; he concentrated massive force on a well-chosen and narrow front (40 percent of combat power on 11 percent of the American sector) and prepared to exploit rapidly with a strong armored-motorized grouping, with the aim of destroying the enemy through maneuver and not merely taking ground and relying on attrition.[43] His willingness to discuss the plan with its principal executor and accept major modifications displayed a flexibility of mind not always evident in Montgomery's British forces. Bradley displayed moral courage when he accepted not only the likely loss of surprise after the 24 July false start but also the inevitability of the same (again fatal) plan for the preliminary air bombardment.[44] When the breakthrough got off to a slow start and hesitant exploitation combined with prompt enemy reactions to invalidate the initial plan, he displayed good generalship by altering his concept for the operation. Remembering that the aim was to destroy as much of *Seventh Army's* left wing as possible and take the Brittany ports quickly, he ordered the widening of the penetration to the whole space between the sea and the Vire and a switch to parallel pursuit. He also recognized that the fluid, fast-changing situation made tight control at army level inappropriate, and he trusted his corps commanders to exercise sound judgment. Perhaps, however, he should have made sure that Collins grasped the fact that the shallow encirclement was destined to fail. Arguably, of course, such a shallow encirclement was ill-advised from the outset; a deeper move was more likely to trap even a fast-reacting enemy by fully exploiting the two forces' disparity in mobility and airpower. With good reason, however, all the Allied commanders had considerable respect for the Germans' ability to pull something out of the bag and confound their hopes. Many Americans were considerably more adventurous than their British counterparts in their willingness even to contemplate the prospect of armored divisions advancing ahead of the main forces and exposing their flanks.

Bradley showed good judgment in entrusting the main effort to Collins, who improved the plan and imparted drive to its execution. On the one hand, his decision to commit most of the exploitation force early, despite the apparent failure on 25 July, was evidence of a fine feel for the way the battle was developing and for the vital importance of tempo. On the other hand, this sense seemed in abeyance when, despite the new army order, Collins persisted in adhering to the original scheme of maneuver, even though enemy reactions, coupled with the failure of VIII Corps' pinning mission, had invalidated it.[45] After that blip, though, Collins managed his large corps with skill in a fluid, fast-changing situation and got the best out of his subordinates.

No plans were laid to exploit the success of Cobra. In view of the uncertainties surrounding the post-Cobra situation, improvisation was presumably considered the only possible course of action. It was considered sufficient to have a general operational idea that Third Army would break out into Brittany and take the ports while First Army, later reinforced by Third, wheeled eastward to push the enemy back to and over the Seine. It would have been better to develop contingency plans with branches and sequels to meet foreseeable developments, even the less likely.[46] The elder Moltke's reminder that no plan survives contact with the enemy is no reason to eschew planning; it is a reason to produce several variants. Preplanning always produces quicker, more effective reactions that preserve both the aim and unity of action, even if the variant adopted is itself subject to variation. To achieve the aim of Operation Cobra—destruction of the Germans' left wing—a major rent would have to be created in the enemy front. This is what actually happened, but there was no scheme waiting to be implemented to make the transition to pursuit. It took until 3 August for Bradley (and, for that matter, Eisenhower and Montgomery) to seize on the chance to modify the Overlord plan—and even then, although Patton's drive into Brittany was vigorous, the exploitation of the enemy's open flank in Normandy was initially hesitant. As *Seventh Army*'s chief of staff later commented: "In the area of the breakthrough precious time had been gained by the enemy's hesitation on 31st July and during the first days in August."[47] The fact that the Germans lacked the resources to make more effective use of that time was the Allies' good fortune.

The success of Cobra was not due solely to better operational performance. It would not have been possible without the great improvements in the American ground forces' tactics, techniques, and procedures over the

148   Chapter Three

previous seven weeks. Combined-arms groupings from battalion to division, flexibly tailored and retailored according to mission and terrain, had become the norm in experienced formations. They were emboldened to conduct vigorous offensive actions without the usual concern for flank security. Improvements in tactical air support, especially in the form of armored column cover, increased the contribution of the air dimension to increasingly mobile operations. In fact, tactical airpower had an operational impact on the development of operations. As *Seventh Army*'s chief of staff pointed out:

> [Countermoves failed] on account of the enemy's air force, which prevented any movement of large extent on the battlefield. Covered by their air force, the enemy troops who had penetrated into the line affected the rear of the German units to such an extent that the unity of the defense deteriorated and the battle finally turned into separate fights for hills, localities and individual farms. The command was almost entirely dependent on radio communications, since all wire lines had been destroyed and messengers shot in the enemy-saturated terrain. The separate units fought on their own as small combat teams, and had hardly any contact with neighboring troops.[48]

Without these developments, no operational idea, however good, could have been implemented successfully.

Tactical successes are the necessary building blocks of operational success. Having achieved a penetration and unbalanced the defense, tempo is critical to keep the enemy off balance and defeat him through maneuver. VII Corps' failure to achieve sufficient momentum was the primary cause of the failure to achieve the encirclement at Coutances. This was partly Collins's fault. He allocated too little additional combat power to 9 Infantry Division to ensure its early capture of Marigny. The lack of initial impetus meant a loss of time that was never made up, even though the corps commander's committal of the reinforced 1 Infantry Division without a clear breach, taking the risk that congestion would stall the advance, was a bold move to try to compensate. However, Collins did not ensure that Huebner's plans and subsequent implementation were compatible with the requirement for a rapid advance. Huebner intended to advance in column of regiments led by his attached combat command, with each unit moving forward only when relieved by the following one in a caterpillar-like movement. This cautious stop-wait-start approach, inching into the enemy's depth, was unlikely to gain tempo; nor did it. Consequently, the main effort of the encirclement allowed the enemy enough time to redeploy much of 2 *SS Panzer*'s mobile capability to take up blocking positions on favorable ground. The committal of 3 Armored Division in the mistaken belief (not verified) that Marigny had been taken ensured that it would not attain early momentum either. Then Watson proved to be overcautious, moving slowly and not all at night and eventually running into the relocated SS.

There was a contrast between the bold handling of 2 Armored Division by Brooks and the safety-first approach of Huebner and Watson. Brooks's Combat Commands B and R together advanced rapidly by night as well as day, fully exploiting the enemy's confusion. An unbalanced defender cannot organize effective resistance, and their scythe-like sweep into the enemy rear cost only 200 casualties and three tanks. These combat commands performed a decisive role in destroying the enemy left wing. The grouping was powerful—an armored regiment and an armored infantry regiment, two SP artillery battalions, and reconnaissance. Yet the force was spread over 10 km (6 miles) to block the Germans' escape, a dispersion that would have seemed unacceptably risky, especially in the absence of intelligence as to the enemy's strength and capabilities, to a less bold commander. A well-organized breakout attack through the stop line would probably have succeeded, inflicting considerable damage in the process. This, of course, was the very feat the Germans could not pull off. They were too ignorant of their enemy's strength and deployment. They were short of fuel and ammunition and had no prospect of resupply, as the Americans were sitting athwart their lines of communication. Their forces were disrupted and demoralized by the events of the past few days. HQ *LXXXIV Corps* had inadequate knowledge of the situation of its own forces and lacked the means to transmit orders. Von Choltitz, faced with orders and counterorders from his army and army group commanders, seemed to have given up trying to cope. The Germans' combat power was, in short, far less than the sum of its parts. This is usual in forces that have been badly defeated. In these circumstances, it becomes progressively easier to convert the enemy's retreat into a rout, and routed troops do not put up effective, or often any, resistance.

There is all the difference in the world between following up an organized, deliberate enemy withdrawal with rear guards (as VIII Corps did when the Germans pulled back from the St. Lô–Lessay road) and pursuit. The latter is characterized by the steady deterioration of the defeated side's organization and command and control, and by the demoralization of his forces, which become more concerned with escape than with checking the victorious advance. Pursuit is the time when the rewards of victory are harvested: retreat is transformed into rout, destruction is inflicted with little fear of immediate retribution, and ground is taken before its defense can be organized. During its conduct, the enemy's ability to react effectively (in the absence of reinforcement) becomes marginal; accordingly, actions that would normally be considered risky become essentially risk free. Open flanks, gaps in combat formation, and bold forward thrusts by even small units are unlikely to be exploitable by the enemy. Speed itself becomes a weapon, one that gives the enemy no time to implement a scorched-earth policy that will hamper the future development of the campaign.[49] VIII Corps' rapid, Patton-driven, armor-led advance to the Sélune and seizure of the Pontaubault bridge, taking thousands of prisoners on the way, is an object lesson in converting tactical into operational success, retreat into rout, and the thrust into Brittany into operational-level exploitation. The rapidity with which Brittany was overrun failed to take major ports from the line of march, but it did prevent the Germans from destroying the railway bridges and tunnels that would be vital to the employment of those ports when taken.

Patton also urged a bold drive eastward with XV Corps, to be joined by the others as they came up. In this case, his operational thinking was ahead of that of his army group and ground forces commanders. Hodges, by contrast, persisted in making his main effort against the enemy between Vire and the Sée, where the Germans were strongest and enjoyed the most defensible terrain. Of his eight infantry and two armored divisions, only 1 Infantry Division and CCA/3 Armored had been inserted to round the German left flank by 6 August, and their role was conceived as flank protection. Given First Army's superior mobility and air support and Bradley's delineation of the army boundary (just north of Mayenne), Hodges could have taken the opportunity to redeploy more force, especially armor, more rapidly from his left and centre to the right (and thus largely out of *bocage* country). Hodges displayed what proved to be an enduring trait—a preference for frontal attacks relying on superior firepower over maneuver.[50] For all his deprecation of Montgomery's alleged tendency toward overcaution, Bradley was slower to recognize the desirability of exploiting the breakout with an immediate, vigorous push eastward. Initially, he mandated merely the security-oriented deployment of XV Corps to Fougères. However, he rapidly came to agree with Montgomery on two points: that Brittany would require less force than originally anticipated, and that, as Ultra had revealed on 2 August and air reconnaissance tended to confirm, the enemy facing his right wing was utterly inadequate to restore the situation and would continue to be so for some time to come. He authorized the advance to the river Mayenne and thence, on 6 August, even farther east. Bradley demonstrated an open mind, flexibility about plans that easily could have been set in concrete, and a reasonable balance between prudent regard for any potential threat to the narrow Avranches choke point on which exploitation depended and boldness in seizing an opportunity.

The operational commander with imagination and a feel for the battle recognizes opportunity and accordingly takes risks that would be foolhardy in other circumstances.[51] Ideally, he anticipates such opportunities. In these circumstances, the advice of Patton is indubitably correct: "In planning any operation, it is vital to remember two things: 'In war, nothing is impossible, provided you use audacity' and 'Do not take counsel of your fears.'"[52] A good general is always thinking about what he can do to the enemy. Most spend too much time worrying about what the enemy might do to them.

Operation Bluecoat

Historians, especially American ones, have dismissed Bluecoat as a failure. This is far too harsh a verdict. By the standards of the Normandy campaign to date (excepting only Operation Cobra), it accomplished much and achieved more than it set out to do. It was a limited operation (mounted with a rapidity that surprised the Americans, who deprecated their ally's usually slow and methodical buildup), and it fully achieved its aims. VIII Corps advanced about 25 km (15 miles) through difficult country, forcing two major obstacles and several minor ones, all but the first from the line of march; XXX Corps eventually made nearly 19 km (12 miles). These advances deprived the enemy of the Mt. Pinçon–Le Bény-Bocage ridge hinge, on which he could have pivoted to conduct an orderly withdrawal of *Seventh Army*.[53] The fact that the Germans chose another, ultimately fatal alternative—the Mortain counterattack—does not detract from the achievement. In addition, the important Vire-Vassy main supply route was rendered unusable. Significant enemy forces were firmly fixed to the British front at a critical time. Hitler had wanted to add the relatively powerful *II SS Panzer Corps* to the forces for the counterattack but was unable to do so. Instead, the corps was written down while trying to restore the defensive front in the centre. Moreover, the diversion of that corps to cope with Bluecoat left the Caen sector weakened, setting favorable conditions for the next Allied offensive, Totalize. Finally, the advance of the British so near to Vire made that town indefensible, aiding the Americans in its capture on 6 August. Furthermore, the threat posed by VIII Corps exercised a powerful influence on the German command. Its proximity to the concentration area for the Mortain blow was a major factor in the hasty mounting of that operation before the requisite forces had been fully assembled and prepared and before reconnaissance had been conducted. Operation Bluecoat was not a failure—but it could have been more successful. It was prevented from being so by deficiencies in doctrine, or at least in its practical application, and by the mind-set of commanders, particularly a tendency toward overcaution and "playing by the book."

Good operational security and the rapid redeployment of more than half the force involved, combined with Dempsey's selection of an unexpected attack sector, ensured operational surprise.[54] In addition, and largely because surprise was achieved, the two attacking corps enjoyed very favorable force ratios, and the enemy was spread too thinly to achieve much depth to the defense. These factors ought to have ensured a relatively high rate of advance, the difficult terrain notwithstanding, at least until enemy reinforcements arrived. This was indeed the case with the secondary effort, but the main effort failed to gather early momentum. As usual, British sources are coy about failure, let alone the reasons for it.[55] One factor was clearly inadequate command. On 3 August the commanders of both XXX Corps and 7 Armored Division were relieved, followed soon thereafter by other senior officers. The chief of staff of XXX Corps wrote: "The dismissal of Bucknall and Erskine was fully justified—they made no effort to push hard or carry out their orders."[56] Failure by commanders is to be expected in war, but these two had been underachieving badly since mid-June, and Dempsey (no doubt strongly influenced by Montgomery) had tolerated it, to the detriment of the campaign. And 43 and 50 Divisions' poor performance at the start of Bluecoat probably owed much to excessive reliance on artillery and air-delivered firepower against well-prepared reverse-slope positions, combined with an inflexible plan and a lack of initiative in its execution, not to mention indifferent tank-infantry cooperation—common British vices.

Another cause of XXX Corps' failure, as well as the difficulties experienced by VIII Corps (which only its flexibility and initiative overcame), was a flawed plan. The plan was typical of the very prescriptive, methodical British approach to battle, which relied, at the expense of maneuver and momentum, on the delivery of massive artillery and air-delivered firepower to solve all tactical problems. The plan was excessively complicated and thus vulnerable to the effects of inevitable friction. It depended on inflexible timings for the air attacks, which, to have any value, had to be followed up immediately by a ground advance. This ground advance, in turn, depended on the timely completion of a preliminary attack, followed by a reorganization in difficult terrain on an ill-defined LD. Even more problematic was the scheme to have a second bombing start nine hours into the battle, which required a second-echelon brigade to be ready on yet another LD. The same problem attended the artillery barrages, although these could at least be amended, albeit at the expense of time. The planning seemed to be based on the assumption that the enemy would accept his allotted role of passive victim rather than reacting violently and possibly unpredictably. It also made little allowance for the difficulties posed by the close nature of the country and its lack of usable routes. For instance, 15 Division's attack on the right in the preliminary operation had to cross about two dozen *bocage* hedges and pass by or through about ten orchards or copses to attain its second (i.e., army) LD, all in three hours. And 43 Division's objective for the first day, almost 11 km (7 miles) deep, was supposed to be attained by H+10—the acme of wishful thinking. Seven weeks into the campaign, it is difficult to excuse such unrealities in planning by Dempsey's Second Army and its corps, even allowing for the great haste with which the plan had been thrown together. Nor is the hallmark of a good plan: vague intentions after the immediate objective is seized; subordinate commanders need something on which to set their sights. Plainly, the British were slower to learn from experience, and to modify doctrine accordingly, than their American ally.

The hapless, green, and greatly overstretched *326 Infantry Division* was surprised and disrupted by the loss of its commander and HQ to air attack. It was unable to stop VIII Corps because the corps and divisional commanders had developed effective combined-arms teams and displayed not only determination but also a willingness to be unconventional and to take risks. There were three occasions when, by ignoring excessively conservative tactical doctrine, a shock effect was created that fully justified the risks: the decision to send much of 6 Guards Tank Brigade ahead to the objective, even when temporarily deprived of infantry protection; the night infiltration by infantry of 11 Armored to capture St. Martin, departing from the usual (and often questionable) practice of halting the whole division to harbor at night; and, similarly, 11 Armored's dash, showing scant regard for open flanks, through the Forêt l'Evêque and over the Souleuvre to occupy the Le Bény-Bocage ridge in strength early on 1 August.[57] Each of these actions displayed proper boldness and paid handsome operational-level dividends in terms of significant features taken and, above all, tempo gained at minimal cost. The last action removed at one stroke the possibility of *21 Panzer*, or even of a larger force, restoring the integrity of the defense on the last good defensive line before Vire. The essence of risk taking in battle, as exemplified by these actions on 30–31 July, ought to be twofold: it should be done early, when the enemy is too shocked and out of balance to react effectively—that is, risk should be calculated and not a mere gamble (like the hasty, unreconnoitered *21 Panzer* counterattack against a defense that had had time to consolidate); and it should gain tempo and present the enemy with a fait accompli that he cannot reverse except by extraordinary effort.

In Normandy, following the practice of his mentor Montgomery, Dempsey always kept a tight grip on his corps commanders. To keep his finger on the pulse of the battle, Dempsey had located his tactical HQ less than a mile from those of the two corps involved and frequently visited his corps commanders twice daily. As during Goodwood (when he colocated with VIII Corps' HQ), his desire was to detect immediately any signs of enemy disintegration so that he could direct and control the subsequent exploitation. When Bluecoat developed in an unexpected way, he was admirably quick to amend his plan in light of the contrasting accomplishments of his two attacking corps. Switching the main effort to VIII Corps, he gave it the task of exploiting beyond the Le Bény-Bocage ridge and ordered forward the reserve 3 Division and 4 Armored Brigade to reinforce that advance. However, presumably on instructions from his C-in-C, he changed the axis of the corps to the southwest. On the positive side, this meant the two attack corps were advancing on parallel rather than divergent axes, but on the downside, it failed to exploit success and seize the most operationally significant objective on the army's front after the Mt. Pinçon–Le Bény-Bocage ridgeline. It would take the Americans until 6 August and many casualties to take Vire, a critical town that had been essentially undefended and ripe for the taking on 2 August.

After a promising start, caution and a desire for a "tidy" battlefield intervened. O'Connor ordered 11 Armored Division to consolidate on the Le Bény-Bocage ridge and help Guards Armored across the Souleuvre (the latter was being hampered by poor tank-infantry cooperation in coping with the seasoned *21 Panzer*). Whether the decision was prompted or merely endorsed by Dempsey is unclear; certainly, the responsibility for it belonged to the army commander. A better option might have been to have the division further disrupt the enemy by driving deeper into his rear and, ideally, taking Vire. This would have had an operational-level impact, threatening to roll up *Seventh Army*'s line, and it would have helped the Guards just as much. As a Soviet military adage puts it, "The best aid to a unit in trouble is the headlong advance of its neighbor." Indeed, the rapid progress of 11 Armored Division speeded up that of US V Corps on its right, compelling the withdrawal of *II Parachute Corps* by threatening its flank. It could be argued (though no British studies agree) that Roberts and O'Connor (plainly with Dempsey's approval or insistence) were again overly conservative on 2 August in halting the advance on the Perriers ridge after another 7 to 8 km (4 to 5 mile) advance without real opposition.[58] General Eberbach, the commander of *Panzer Group West*, commented on the British pause: "*II SS Panzer Corps* could not cover the distance of the approach march, carry out all attack preparations and establish contact with the enemy before the afternoon of 2 August. The enemy therefore had at least 24 hours of complete freedom of action. But it was our luck that the British, in general, stood still during this period."[59]

The hesitant nature of the exploitation of initial success certainly conformed to the British concern for secure flanks, a tidy battlefield, and the avoidance of risk. Probably the knowledge that *II SS Panzer Corps* was being brought in to stabilize the situation by counterattack suggested prudence to Dempsey, who was privy to Ultra intelligence. But by transitioning to the defense, VIII Corps also ceded the initiative to the enemy when there was nothing between 11 Armored and the next important road centre of Flers, about 20 km (12 miles) beyond the ridge and 28 km (17 miles) behind the concentration area for the Mortain counterattack. True, the division was in a salient, was strung out, and had vulnerable supply lines. The enemy would come against that open flank. But had the corps really culminated? At last light on 3 August, 11 Armored alone still enjoyed a 3:1 superiority in tanks over *9 SS*

Panzer.⁶⁰ Further, 3 Infantry Division and the attached 4 Armored Brigade were coming up rapidly (its leading brigade, at Le Bény-Bocage that afternoon, had already been detached to Roberts's division). VIII Corps could have reinforced success by downgrading to a pinning action the grim, frontal, attritional battle then being fought by Guards Armored and 15 Infantry Divisions along with 6 Guards Tank Brigade; it then could have switched forces to reinforce success (one good route and several minor ones were available). It is worth noting, in this context, that one of the Guards' strongest battle groups remained unused for four days, and its (medium tank-equipped) armored reconnaissance regiment was idle for six.⁶¹ Even if (relatively small) enemy forces had got behind the spearhead, would the latter's temporary isolation really have mattered, especially given the proximity of corps artillery and Allied command of the air, with the attendant possibility of close air support, not to mention other forces coming forward?

The committal of *21 Panzer* and subsequently of *II SS Panzer Corps* were both cases of too little, too late. German efforts to restore the front, first in the area of Hills 309–361, then on the Le Bény-Bocage ridge, then on a line south of it, and finally on the Perriers ridge, failed for a number of reasons. Having achieved surprise, VIII Corps at first exploited it to the full, prolonging its effects by vigorous exploitation. The corps' momentum ensured that it consistently beat the enemy to key terrain, aided continually in this endeavor by air interdiction. Belated reactions meant that the Germans forfeited the benefits of holding ground favorable to the defense and instead had to counterattack across it. They had little knowledge of their enemy's situation (often consolidated and ready) and little time for reconnaissance or preparation. German strength was consistently inadequate for the task set by the senior commander, a problem made worse by a lack of situational awareness, which made the choice of *schwerpunkt* (point of main effort), a critical decision, a matter of guesswork. In their desperation, the Germans ignored the principle of realism and assigned unachievable objectives. They repeatedly failed to recognize the culminating point of the defense and to adjust plans accordingly. Of course, senior German commanders frequently recognized the impracticality of their missions but were constrained by orders issued from the remote fastness of the Führer HQ in East Prussia.⁶²

Caution is often well advised, but not in the circumstances that pertained throughout the first few days of Bluecoat. The Germans were overstretched both tactically and operationally. They were grievously unbalanced and had no reserves, and they still had to worry about a now-weakened Caen sector as well as the American breakout and the new rupture between the two German armies. Except on their right flank, the Germans were no longer fighting from strong, prepared defenses; they were forced to fight at least partly offensively (tactically) in the face of Allied superior mobility, armored strength, and air supremacy. Avoidance of risk is simply sacrifice of opportunity when the enemy lacks the means to exploit a vulnerability that is largely theoretical. British doctrinal conservatism, even perhaps timidity at the operational level, resulted in a failure to translate tactical into operational success. By continuing to see ground as something to fight *for*, methodically, rather than something to fight *over* to encompass the enemy's destruction, Second Army passed up the chance to capitalize on what should have been a breakthrough by vigorously exploiting into the enemy's depth in parallel with the Americans. This failure condemned its troops to a reversion to attritional battle once the Germans had taken advantage of the breathing space vouchsafed them to restore the integrity of their front. The contrast between First Army's determination to create a breakthrough in Operation Cobra, despite a disappointing first day, and the British hesitancy in developing a clear, early breach in Bluecoat is striking.

Had the British possessed the will to exploit the unexpectedly great success achieved by 2 or 3 August, more troops could have been found, and quickly, even without canceling the upcoming and arguably more important Canadian attack toward Falaise. XII Corps did not need two full-strength infantry divisions and the 300 or so tanks of 31 and 34 Tank Brigades to hold its 20 km (12 mile) front. Given the low level of threat, one infantry division and an armored brigade, or even a regiment, would have sufficed: the Germans were in no condition to attack, and even if there had been some small threat, fresh armored divisions (first the Canadian and then the Polish) were landing and concentrating behind the corps. The rest could have been used to reinforce Bluecoat's success.[63] As it was, XII Corps was too strong for its basically defensive mission but too weak to pose more than a tactical, local threat to the enemy to its front. It was able to do only what it actually did: follow up the enemy withdrawal made inevitable by the successes of Cobra and Bluecoat. (Admittedly, though, the forcing of the Orne and the establishment of a small bridgehead in the Forêt de Grimbosq on 6 August helped unbalance the German defense of the Caen sector just prior to the Canadian offensive on 8 August, but little was made of this.) The misuse of XII Corps flouted the principle of economy of force.

Even without reinforcement, VIII Corps and XXX Corps between them had four infantry and three armored divisions and three independent armored brigades. This gave them a considerable numerical advantage over *II SS Panzer Corps*, with its three very understrength panzer divisions, the remnants of *326 Infantry Division*, and much of the battered *3 Parachute Division*, which had redeployed to defend from Vire to Viessoix, 7 km (4.5 miles) to the west. Nor did the enemy enjoy the benefit of prepared positions. From the start of Bluecoat, Dempsey followed the principle of concentration admirably, but he failed to reap its fruits. After 11 Armored Division (reinforced by 185 Infantry Brigade) and VIII Corps surrendered the initiative on taking the Perriers ridge, the division fought off counterattacks for four days until its flanking formations came up. Given the nature of the ground, the force ratio, the support of corps artillery, and close air support, it held the ground it had gained. The enemy, however, was able to restore a stable defense line, albeit at a price. When VIII Corps resumed the offensive on 11 August in Operation Grouse, it did so against first-class (albeit worn) formations that were, by then, prepared and alert. It did so with another ambitious, complex, three-phase plan. The main attack by 3 Infantry and Guards Armored Divisions, both reinforced, stalled more or less on their LDs, with heavy casualties. The initiative had been ceded and modest gains accepted back on 2 August, when more could have been accomplished. The decision to renew the offensive when the advantages of surprise and momentum had been given up more than a week earlier was questionable.

The culmination of Operation Bluecoat in the first week of August coincided with the expansion of the US offensive into both Brittany and the east. Montgomery had decided, "The time had now come to deliver the major attack towards Falaise, which had so long been the fundamental aim of our policy on the eastern flank. . . . I envisaged this operation as a prelude to subsequent exploitation of success." On 4 August Montgomery ordered that "the northern flank [sic] of 12 US Army Group should operate on the axis Domfront-Alençon."[64] By 6 August, American forces were already up to the river Mayenne. In the circumstances prevailing in early August, there seemed to be every reason to shift the main effort of 21 Army Group to First Canadian Army for its thrust on the potentially decisive Caen-Falaise axis.

CHAPTER FOUR

August: Incomplete Encirclements

OPERATIONS OF 12 ARMY GROUP:
FROM COBRA TO THE FALAISE POCKET

The Mortain Counterattack and the Decision in Favor of the Short Encirclement

The German army in the west now faced defeat on a scale comparable to that being endured at the same time in Belorussia (covered in some detail in volume 2).[1] While the Germans were still fighting a coherent battle north of the Sélune, giving ground only grudgingly, their left wing had apparently disintegrated so that, with the crossing of the Sélune, their southern (no longer western!) flank was effectively in the air. The Germans, it appeared, no longer possessed the balance required to conduct the deliberate withdrawal to the Seine that the Allies had anticipated. Nor did they have sufficient forces remaining in Brittany to undertake an effective defense. These favorable developments had been anticipated in one of SHAEF's postinvasion contingency plans, code-named Lucky Strike, and its broad outline was now enthusiastically implemented. It would no longer be necessary to devote the whole of Third Army to the reduction of Brittany. Its main effort could be devoted to an advance toward the Paris-Orléans gap, exploiting the open flank in a deep turning movement. There seemed to be no significant enemy forces south of the Loire to threaten such a maneuver. If the Germans could be destroyed in Normandy, or at least bundled out in shortish order, the Seine ports of Le Havre and Rouen could be captured before they could be demolished.

Initially, as Patton's VIII Corps was crossing the Sélune, Eisenhower and Bradley were still thinking in terms of a major commitment in Brittany. The latter was also concerned about securing its rear and the flank of VII Corps, which was tasked with widening the Avranches corridor. Thus, on 2 August Bradley ordered 79 Infantry Division to Fougères, in the belief that Patton was neglecting flank protection (actually, Patton had already tasked 5 Armored to move into the same area). Then, on 3 August, persuaded about the virtues of a bolder, more wide-ranging maneuver, Bradley ordered Patton to leave Brittany to "a minimum of forces." He was to press forward and cross the river Mayenne with his XV Corps and, when XX Corps came up, extend southward. These deployments were but a prelude to a further advance to the east that began on 5 August in response to Montgomery's M516 directive of the previous day. This set out the plan to crush the enemy against the Seine barrier, where all the bridges were down, and thus destroy him. A new army group boundary was drawn on a line Vire–south of Flers–Sées–Dreux–Mantes-Gassicourt on the Seine. North of it, 21 Army Group's First Canadian Army and Second Army would wheel to the left (the former after reaching Falaise) to close on the river between Rouen and Mantes. On the right, 12 Army Group would also wheel eastward to the Seine, with Third Army executing a long envelopment round the German open flank and sweeping as far south as the Loire to block crossings over that river while the main effort headed in the general direction of Paris. An airborne corps would drop or airland in the Chartres area to block off any enemy attempt to retreat through the Paris-Orléans gap.

The plan was predicated on the Germans doing the sensible thing: cutting their losses and retreating as fast as possible out of Normandy. Instead of escaping from the trap before it could be set, however, they thrust deeper into it. On 2 August von Kluge received the Führer's order for a counterattack to close the Avranches corridor. Hitler made clear his determination to supervise the execution from his HQ in far-off East Prussia, as he did not trust the many generals he presumed to be defeatist or potentially or actually treacherous (whose number included von Kluge). The Führer insisted that every armored formation in Normandy be concentrated for the blow. This stipulation was deeply unrealistic. Already, three panzer divisions were necessarily committed to preventing a British breakthrough on the Caumont sector. Denuding the Caen sector would assuredly lead to its collapse, so at least one had to be left there. Sixth August was the earliest possible date that the remaining four panzer divisions intended for the strike grouping, *XLVII Panzer Corps*, could be relieved by infantry divisions sent from *Fifteenth Army* and concentrated for the counterattack.[2] By that date, the outlook for not only the counterattack but also the entire front looked decidedly bleak. By advancing to Mortain and taking the high ground immediately to the east, the Americans had widened the Avranches corridor to about 32 km (20 miles) and deprived the Germans of their desired LD. The attacking force had neither completed its concentration (indeed, its concentration area was under threat from the ground and the air) nor conducted adequate reconnaissance and battle preparation. Strong American forces had advanced as far as the Mayenne River and were plainly not going to stop there; they would soon be in the left-rear of the strike grouping, overrunning German supply bases in Le Mans and Alençon. Moreover, it was only a matter of time before 21 Army Group renewed its offensive on the Caen-Falaise axis to form another wing of encirclement. From von Kluge downward, senior commanders wanted to withdraw, not attempt an advance to retake ground they probably could not gain and certainly could not hold. But the Führer was adamant. Indeed, his ambition had extended from merely restoring a short, defensible line on favorable ground, and at the same time cutting off Patton's army, to the utterly delusional one of rolling up the Allied line.[3]

When the German attack started shortly after midnight on 6 August, it achieved tactical surprise against 30 Infantry Division and consequently a 9 km (5.5 mile) penetration, though on only two narrow sectors. It had stalled by noon in areas vulnerable to counterattack. The attack had been hastily put together and was thus ill coordinated; not all units arrived in good time, and an American unit retained the high ground at Mortain (though surrounded) from which it directed damaging and disruptive artillery concentrations onto the German columns. Then, with the lifting of the morning fog, swarms of fighter-bombers converged on the battlefield, from 2 Tactical Air Force as well as IX Tactical Air Command; they flew almost 500 close air support sorties against *XLVII Panzer Corps* that day. The Luftwaffe had promised a maximum effort in support—300 fighters—but the Allied offensive counter-air operations were so effective that not one reached the battlefield. Hitler, of course, blamed von Kluge for the failure (attacking too early, with insufficient force, and in unfavorably clear weather). He insisted the offensive be resumed on a slightly different axis, this time commanded by the presumed to be fervent Nazi general Eberbach, after *Fifth Panzer Army* had been denuded of yet two more panzer divisions to reinforce it. Von Kluge was fully aware of the futility of continuing this course of action, but he dared not disobey an unequivocal order from the Führer.

There was no chance of a renewed attack succeeding, given German casualties and the loss of surprise. In fact, the original attack could never have progressed as far as Avranches and held on to its gains.[4] Facing the attack were 30 Infantry Division and most of 4 Infantry Division, with CCB/3 Armored in depth and CCB/2 Armored coming in from the north, all part of VII Corps. En route to join Third Army's eastward thrust was XX Corps, with 2 French Armored Division just south of Avranches, 35 Infantry Division near St. Hilaire in the attack sector, and another division that would arrive at Avranches on 8 August; yet another was at Fougères. (Patton claimed credit for halting XX Corps as a precaution, accounting for its ideal position to resist the counterattack.[5]) Of this plethora of forces, only 35 Division actually needed to be diverted to join the battle. By 8 August, XV Corps had already advanced to Le Mans with three divisions, putting it 100 km (60 miles) in the left-rear of the German attack grouping. The follow-on force, XX Corps, was in the Laval area. Meanwhile, the First Canadian Army offensive, Operation

Totalize, had made a promising start on the Caen-Falaise axis against a defense weakened by detachments to the Caumont and Mortain sectors.

Bradley was quick to grasp the opportunity presented by German foolishness in retaining their main grouping in a salient on their extreme west wing. On 8 August, convinced that the reinforced VII Corps could hold at Mortain, he proposed to Eisenhower and, with the Supreme Commander's approval, Montgomery that the Allies modify the operational concept outlined in M516 and execute a short encirclement of *Seventh* and much of *Fifth Panzer Armies*. Twelfth Army Group would provide the southern jaw of a vise to crush the Germans. Third Army's main effort would be shifted northward. XV Corps would turn through ninety degrees at Le Mans and advance north via Alençon to the army group boundary Carrouges-Sées (about 70 km [45 miles] north of Le Mans). First Army would eliminate the penetration in the Mortain area, relieving the unit encircled on the high ground; at the same time, it would sideslip to the right to attack on the Domfront-Flers axis. Providing the northern jaw, 21 Army Group's First Canadian Army, whose attack started on 8 August, would push through Falaise southward to Argentan and thus close the last major west-east road out of the trap being set for the Germans. Second Army would continue on its assigned axis toward Flers. Montgomery so directed, with Eisenhower's endorsement.

Montgomery conferred with Bradley and Dempsey (though neither Hodges nor Crerar were invited) to coordinate the details. Plainly, however, Montgomery had some doubts about the likelihood of destroying the bulk of the German force in a shallow encirclement and wished to hedge his bet. His M518 of 11 August restated the aim of closing the encirclement along the Falaise-Argentan-Alençon road but speculated about a German breakout eastward (Ultra reported this intention on 12 August) and the necessity of being "ready to put into execution the full plan given in M510 [for the long envelopment] should it appear likely that the enemy may escape us here."[6] He was pleasantly surprised by the rapidity with which XV Corps advanced north to and over the army group boundary but was disappointed at the Canadians' failure to emulate its progress. Map 4.1 gives a broad overview of the development of the breakout between 1 and 13 August within the overall context of the theatre. Map 4.2 illustrates developments in Normandy up to 16 August in more detail, showing the creation of the Falaise pocket and the beginnings of American exploitation to the east.

The Southern Jaw of the Vise:
American Operations to 20 August

In executing its role in the encirclement, First Army was to continue through the *bocage* and across wooded ridges and small rivers on its eastward march.[7]

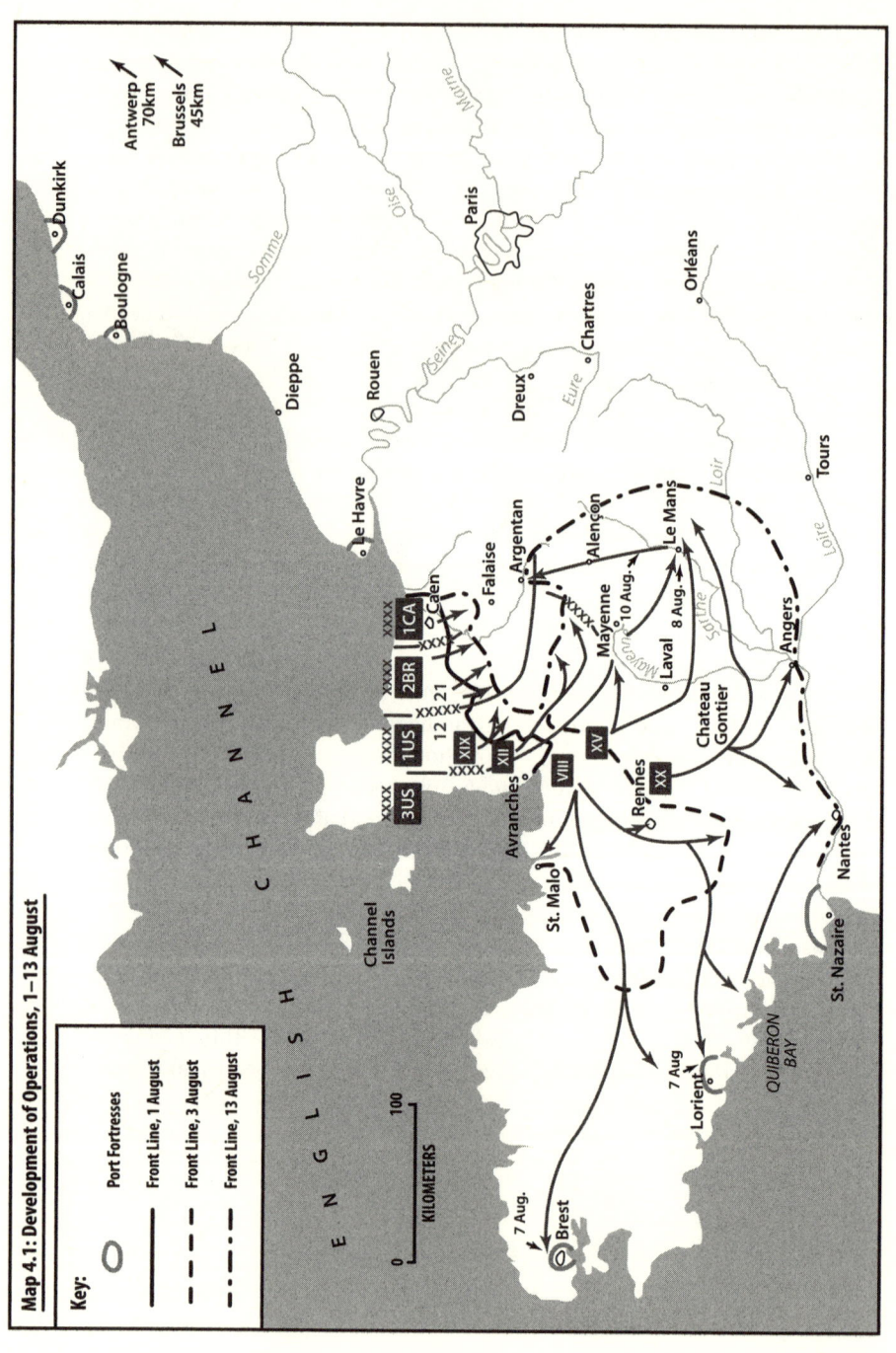

Map 4.1: Development of Operations, 1–13 August

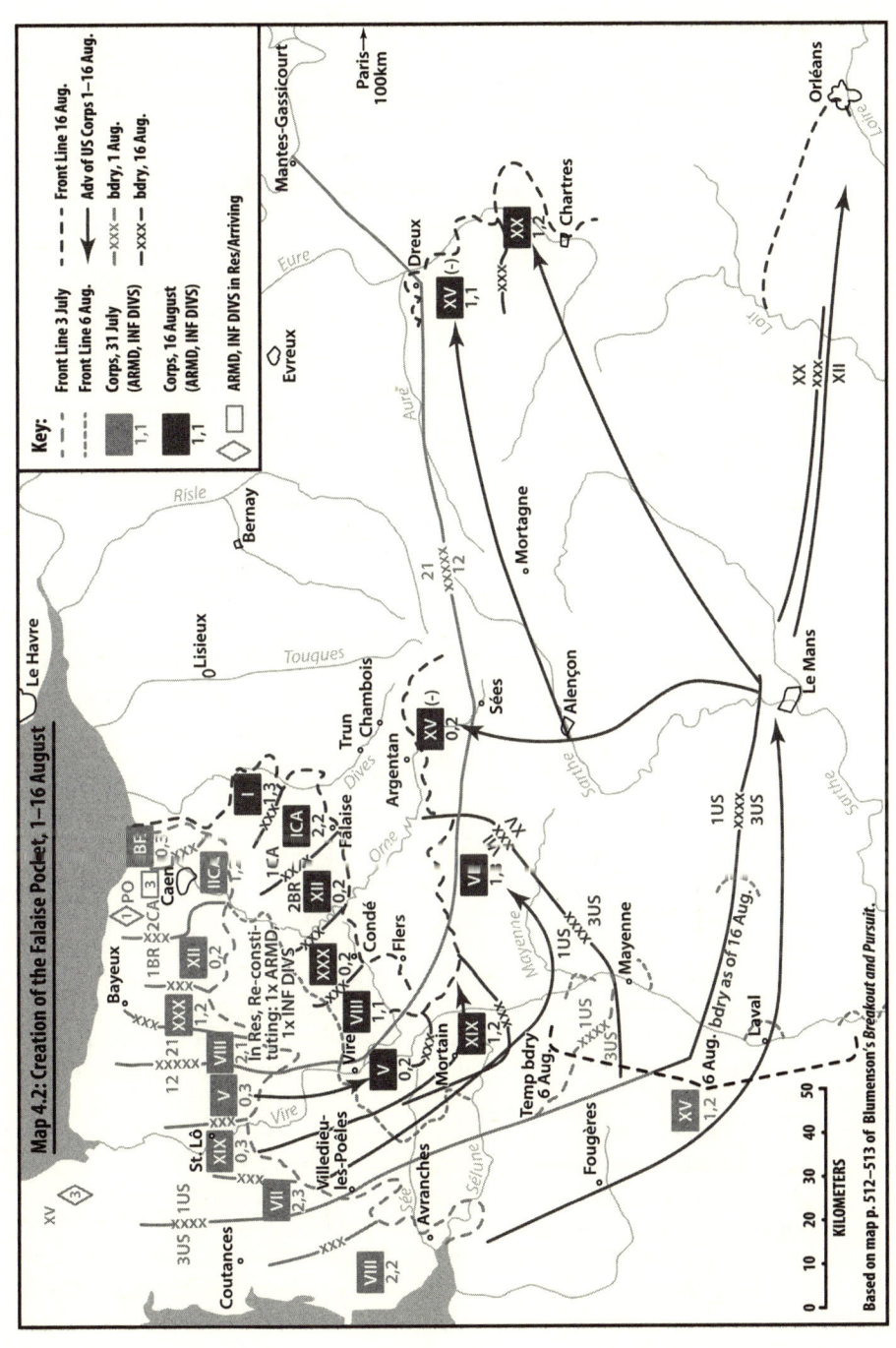

The enemy made his usual good use of the ground. Third Army's advance, however, took place over altogether more favorable terrain. It was generally south of *bocage* country, and when elements were turned north from Le Mans, through Alençon to Argentan, the hedgerows were to the west. The going was generally easy; there were minor rivers, ridges, and woods and one significant obstacle, the river Eure, before Paris and the Seine were reached. But even if the ground had been more defensible—indeed, even where it was—the Germans simply lacked the forces to utilize it.

Haislip's XV Corps was allotted a key role in the encirclement. It was strengthened for its task to two armored and two infantry divisions by the addition of Major General Leclerc's 2 French Armored Division, with its veterans of North Africa. The corps advanced in two columns led, Patton style, by the armored divisions. Open flanks were ignored save for armored cavalry patrols, and possible areas of resistance were bypassed. In its advance to and then past Alençon on 11 August, it encountered ineffective opposition from the screen established by the overextended *LXXXI Corps*.[8] Interpreting Patton's instructions creatively, Haislip ordered a further advance to Argentan, more than 10 km (6 miles) beyond the army group boundary. On 12 August the corps reached the undefended town and would have taken it, once lead elements of 5 Armored Division arrived, had Leclerc not ignored his orders and interposed one of his columns in the American line of march, thus preventing the timely refueling of the American spearhead. As a result, enough of *116 Panzer Division* arrived in time to contest the town. Its spectacular advance had nevertheless put XV Corps 40 km (25 miles) due east of Flers and almost 60 km (40 miles) behind the enemy forces fighting in the Mortain-Domfront area and supposedly preparing a renewed thrust on Avranches. It had also overrun two major supply and administrative centres in Le Mans and Alençon, dramatically worsening the already precarious logistic situation of *Seventh Army*. And while XV Corps was cutting a swath through enemy territory to the north, XX Corps was building up behind. By 13 August, 35 Infantry Division, which had been pulled out of the battle around Mortain, and the newly arrived 80 Infantry and 7 Armored Divisions were in the Laval–Le Mans area, ready to advance to the left of Haislip's force that day.[9] Another infantry division had been sent south to take Nantes and Angers and guard the Loire flank.

While the American jaw of the vise was proceeding satisfactorily, 21 Army Group's contribution was not. Second Army's advance was slow and deliberate against a balanced and dogged defense in favorable terrain. More important by far, First Canadian Army's attack had ground to a halt 10 km (6 miles) north of Falaise (and thus more than 30 km [18 miles] north of Argentan) on 10 August. It was not scheduled to resume until 14 August. The Americans were skeptical of the Canadians' ability to take Falaise, let alone advance south of the town, in time to prevent a German escape from the pocket. Patton and Haislip were all for pressing on to take Falaise for themselves, and very early on 13 August Patton ordered XV Corps to continue cautiously northward. On hearing of this, Bradley overturned the decision and ordered a halt, an order with which Patton argued and only reluctantly complied. The Americans would wait at Argentan for their allies to link up with them. This started the unraveling of the short hook plan that Bradley himself had proposed. Patton then suggested a return to the eastward orientation of Third Army interrupted on 8 August. Bradley concurred. The army (except, of course, for VIII Corps, which was still embroiled in Brittany) left three divisions of XV Corps in defense in the Argentan area, lest the Germans attempt a breakout to the southeast and thereafter thrust eastward into the Dreux-Orléans area. The Dreux-Chartres-Orléans line was reached on 16 August, and Patton proposed a swing north to seal off German escape routes over the Seine.

West of the army boundary, which Bradley had drawn on a line from Mayenne to Carrouges, First Army continued frontal attacks to wear down and drive back the enemy in the salient. Then, on 16 August, V and XIX Corps found themselves facing the British, who had crossed their front as the German pocket shrank. Second Army too had been pressing southeast, and five American divisions had been progressively pinched out as the armies converged. As the army's front shrank on the left with the contraction of the pocket, Bradley extended it on the right by changing the boundary to Alençon-Sées-Gacé. V Corps HQ was sent on 17 August to take command of the formations left in the Argentan area. Then, extending First Army's responsibility to the Seine, XIX Corps was switched to the eastern flank with three divisions, a march of at least 150 km (90 miles) across the rear areas of VII and V Corps, which involved a great deal of good staff work and flexibility in the organization of transport. This move was completed by 19 August. The two remaining infantry divisions were moved west to join the siege of Brest, rather than east with their erstwhile corps; they replaced 4 Armored Division, ordered east from Brittany on 15 August, but Bradley would not sanction the redeployment of 6 Armored because, according to Patton, he feared a German attack from south of the Loire.[10]

VII Corps had been given the role of advancing on the Mayenne-Domfront-Flers axis, driving into the enemy flank, and closing the gap that had opened between the two US armies. First Infantry Division and most of 3 Armored Division were already in the Mayenne area, 30 km (18 miles) south of Domfront, when the decision for a shallow encirclement was made. However, despite the dearth of enemy on the designated axis, there was no advance beyond Domfront until the corps had been built up by the side slipping of 4 and 9 Infantry Divisions. The corps pushed forward on 13 August, meeting so little resistance that 1 Division advanced more than 30 km (18 miles) that day; at 2200 hours Collins was calling for more "territory to take" and claiming that he could take Falaise before the British even started to move.[11] The time required to concentrate on the new axis meant that there was initially a 50 km (30 mile) gap separating VII Corps from XV Corps, but this had lessened to about 30 km (18 miles) by 13 August. By the next day, the interval was only 10 km (6 miles) and closing fast.

After the disappointing start to Operation Tractable, the successor to Totalize, which is discussed in the next section, Montgomery decided that the pincers should close not on the Falaise-Argentan road but farther east on the river Dives. The Americans would attack northeastward toward Trun (about 10 km [6 miles] northeast of Argentan) to link up with the renewed Canadian offensive now primarily directed thence. There were, however, only three divisions left in the Argentan area (including the recently transferred and green 80 Infantry Division), and they faced considerably stronger opposition than had existed three days before; moreover, they still had no corps HQ to command them. Patton was instructed to remedy the latter situation, and he dispatched his chief of staff with a small team to form a provisional HQ, pending the arrival of Bradley's choice, Major General Gerow's V Corps HQ (pinched out farther east). However, no sooner was the attack ready to mount than Bradley postponed it in reaction to an enemy spoiling attack. Bradley then redrew the boundary between First and Third Armies, moving it farther east; Hodges was now responsible for the Argentan sector. Moreover, Gerow was not prepared to implement someone else's plan over ground he had not studied (indeed, when he arrived, he was ignorant of even the location of his own divisions); muddying the picture further, he was unsure which army was his superior HQ. Confusion and delay thus prevented the attack from getting under way before 18 August. In addition, Leclerc wholeheartedly refused to commit his 2 French Armored Division to fulfill its allotted role in the battle because he aspired to march on Paris and seize the city for his political master, de Gaulle. The V Corps advance failed at Argentan, but its right reached Chambois on the river Dives during the late afternoon of 19 August. There, elements of 90 Infantry Division met part of the Polish Armored Division of II Canadian Corps to close the Falaise pocket.

While vacillation and confusion delayed the completion of the short encirclement, Patton, given his head, demanded a bold, rapid advance eastward. There was no effective opposition on Third Army's new main axis, and this goal was easily accomplished almost everywhere. Advances of 100 to 150 km (60 to 90 miles) and more were achieved in three days, rendering irrelevant the projected plan for an airborne assault in the Paris-Orléans gap. XV Corps took Dreux on 16 August (crossing the river Eure). The two divisions of XX Corps (Major General Walton H. Walker commanding) advanced in parallel and, after a bit of a fight, took Chartres on 18 August. By the end of the same day, XII Corps (from 19 August, commanded by Major General Manton S. Eddy), the last to come up (also with two divisions), was about to enter Orléans. There was very little in front of these three armored and three infantry divisions of Third Army. The recently arrived *First Army* HQ, with only *LXXX Corps* under command, had improvised battle groups from four divisions stretched across a 70 km (45 mile) front and could do little more than establish roadblocks across primary routes. The only real check was imposed by Bradley's hesitancy owing to his concerns for Third Army's flanks, especially if the Germans in the pocket attempted a breakout through the Paris-Orléans gap, along with growing difficulties with fuel supply. These circumstances, primarily the latter, led to another halt order on 15 August that remained in force for two days. On 18 August Bradley gave permission for XV Corps to advance to the Seine at Mantes-Gassicourt, though only reluctantly did he authorize the establishment of a bridgehead over the river; this was easily accomplished on 20 August. Then on 21 August he sanctioned the resumption of an eastward advance to seize additional bridgeheads south of Paris at Melun and Fontainebleau. Opposition was minimal.

OPERATIONS OF 21 ARMY GROUP: FROM
BLUECOAT TO THE FALAISE POCKET

The Northern Jaw of the Vise: Anglo-Canadian
Operations to 20 August

After Operation Bluecoat ground to a halt in the face of *II SS Panzer Corps*, 21 Army Group's main effort continued to lie with Second Army.[12] Dempsey retained nine divisions and four independent armored brigades to Crerar's seven divisions (including a weak airborne division) and three brigades. However, against a stronger enemy and with surprise no longer a force multiplier, the heady early days of Bluecoat were not replicated. Operation Grouse, which started on 11 August, failed to reach the ambitious objectives of Flers and Tinchebray and resulted in heavy casualties, showing that the British were back to an attritional grind. The main effort was switched from right to left to exploit a 7 August crossing of the Orne at Grimbosq for a drive on Falaise. However, XII Corps was not reinforced for the task. The following week registered an advance averaging 10 km (6 miles) in total across the front.

The British advance was very deliberate, with little dash or élan being displayed at any level, even after the enemy started a deliberate withdrawal on 13 and 14 August and therefore lost the advantage of fighting from prepared positions. Thus, "orders [were issued] to the effect that any enemy withdrawal would be closely followed up."[13] There seemed to be no attempt to do more than follow up. According to its war diary, 6 Guards Tank Brigade spent 14–16 August with "nothing to report." Revealingly, 29 Guards Armored Brigade's diary entry for 14 August read: "Orders to units are that it is not the intention to push on as quickly as possible but to mop up every position as they are discovered. . . . [At 2300 hours the divisional] GOC phoned to say 'form for tomorrow is soft pedal—maintain contact, follow up if enemy withdraws but units not to get involved.'" Eleventh Armored Division reverted to its old habit of stopping for rest and maintenance during the hours of darkness and missed a chance to destroy *10 SS Panzer Division* as it pulled back over the river Orne at Putanges on 17–18 August.[14] On 18 August 59 Infantry Division was withdrawn for disbandment to provide replacements for other formations. No wonder a captured German commander remarked during his interrogation: "The British did not follow up very vigorously from the west."[15] They preferred to rely largely on artillery and air strikes on increasingly congested traffic.

As the heavy fighting subsided, it was obviously considered desirable to rest and refurbish some formations that had taken significant casualties and, as the line of contact shrank as a consequence of the German retreat, other formations were pinched out. On 10 August 15 Infantry and 7 Armored Divisions were withdrawn into reserve. They were followed on 16 August by the Guards Armored, which spent the next three days doing mundane tasks, resting and sightseeing, attending an investiture parade, and listening to a speech by Montgomery. Only one of these formations, 7 Armored, was sent to reinforce First Canadian Army, and then only on 15 August.

Canadian Army Operations to 20 August

Initially, Canadian First Army's parallel offensive on the Caen-Falaise axis, Operation Totalize, seemed more promising. Its primary objective, as set out in Montgomery's M516, was "to gain such ground in the direction of Falaise as will cut off the enemy forces now facing Second Army and rendering their withdrawal eastwards difficult—if not impossible." If that aim had been desirable on 4 August, it was becoming potentially decisive by 8 August (H-hour having been advanced by twenty-four hours).[16] This would become the northern wing of the encirclement that, coupled with the southern wing comprising the American Alençon-Argentan thrust, would trap the Germans in what came to be called the Falaise pocket. Crerar's First Canadian Army had only limited resources, however. His I British Corps, with only an infantry and an airborne division and a tank brigade, was committed to defending the bridgehead's left flank. That left Lieutenant General G. G. Simonds's II

Canadian Corps as the sole executor. He mustered three somewhat tired infantry divisions (one British), two green armored divisions (one Polish), and two independent armored brigades (one British).

The Canadian corps faced the daunting prospect of attacking over the same ground that had witnessed the expensive tactical failures of Operations Goodwood and Spring. The terrain was bounded on the west by the river Laize, a tank obstacle; there was no comparable obstruction to the east until the Dives was encountered 20 km (12 miles) or so from the Laize. From the LD to just short of Falaise, the ground was gently rolling, with several ridgelines and small hills that gave fine fields of fire over an almost prairie-like emptiness, except for the villages, hamlets, and small woods that dotted the landscape every 1 to 3 km (0.5 to 2 miles) or so. The only break in the country as it rolled south from the front line was about 15 km (9 miles) distant—the wooded valley of the Laison; the stream itself was believed to be an insignificant obstacle.

The Germans of *I SS Panzer Corps*, which faced the renewed effort on the Falaise axis, were markedly weaker than those that had so effectively defeated attempts to thrust southward in July. Four panzer divisions had been drawn off to stop Bluecoat and mount the Mortain counteroffensive, leaving only the small, inexperienced, newly arrived, and low-quality *89 Infantry Division* and, in depth, *12 SS Panzer Division* to hold the threatened sector. This meant that the Allies had a superiority of about 7:1 in men and armor and 5:1 in artillery (excluding mortars, where the ratio was about 2:1). The attack would be supported by two massive heavy bomber strikes.

Simonds, however, was not relying on mere numerical advantage (which, in any case, he believed was smaller than it actually was). He saw his trump cards as being surprise and airpower. Surprise could not be achieved with regard to either axis or timing, given the well-known German sensitivity about the sector and developments elsewhere, but it could be achieved with regard to method. Goodwood and Spring had been repulsed by skillful German use of carefully concealed mortars, machine guns, and long-range antitank weapons deployed in great depth, especially in fortified villages, to dominate the open ground that characterized the battlefield. Simonds proposed to overcome the first defensive position with an armored attack at night by massed tanks and infantry carried in armored half-tracks and SP guns converted into armored personnel carriers (APCs). A rolling artillery barrage and darkness would neutralize the defending mortars, machine guns, and antitank weapons, thus enabling the mechanized force to penetrate rapidly to the depth of the first defensive position. Meanwhile, heavy bombers would destroy the villages on the flanks of the main attack so that they could speedily be mopped up by infantry. Simonds expected the second position to be a harder nut to crack, for here he would encounter the better part of *12 SS* and part of *1 SS Panzer Divisions*, and the position was out of range of all but the medium and heavy artillery of the AGRAs. This, in his view, necessitated a second massive air strike to suppress the defenders so they could be overrun by the second echelon, comprising the two armored divisions, in what would amount to a second breakthrough battle.

The N158 Caen-Falaise road would be the centre line. In phase one, attacking in the first echelon on the left would be 51 Infantry Division and 33 Armored Brigade. To the west would be 2 Canadian Infantry Division and 2 Canadian Armored Brigade. In each division, one brigade would hold the LD and be ready for phase two tasks, and one would clear the villages bypassed by the main effort and those on the flanks. Massive strikes by 1,019 British heavy bombers would obliterate the four flanking villages with 3,462 tons of bombs, and they would thus fall easily to the infantry. The main effort would be mounted by the two armored brigades accompanied by the third, now-mechanized infantry brigade of each division. To achieve surprise, there would be no preliminary bombardment. The advance, starting at an H-hour of 2345 on 7 August, would be preceded by a 4 km (2.5 mile) wide and 6 km (4 mile) deep, fast-moving rolling barrage (lifting 180 m [200 yards] every two minutes). In all, 720 guns, each with an allocation of 350 to 650 rounds, would support the attack. The barrage would be hugged by six tightly packed tank and armored infantry columns driving forward to seize a series of village objectives 5 to 6 km (3 to 4 miles) from the front line. As the first echelon consolidated on its objectives, providing a firm base for phase two, the second would move up and artillery would displace forward. There would be a five-hour gap between the end of phase one and the second bombing.

Phase two would be preceded, from 1226 to 1355, by 678 American heavy bombers striking the assessed main locations of the panzer formations. Tactical air elements would carry out battlefield interdiction to the south (but only in the afternoon). Immediately following the air bombardment, the armored divisions, 4 Canadian to the west and 1 Polish to the east, would attack together, each unavoidably on little more than a 1,000 m (1,100 yards) frontage, as the tip of the night's penetration had been necessarily narrow. Fourth Division would take a series of objectives on either side of the N158, ending up holding the high ground west of Potigny, 8 km (5 miles) north-northeast of Falaise. The Poles would do likewise to the east on a parallel axis, taking the high ground overlooking Falaise and 3 to 5 km (2 to 4 miles) northeast of the town—a very ambitious objective. To secure the flanks of the second echelon, the infantry brigades that secured the LD for phase one would come up and take the villages there.

Third Canadian Infantry Division would be in reserve, prepared to mop up positions bypassed in phase two. I British Corps on the left and XII Corps to the west would pin the enemy to their fronts, the latter pressing forward

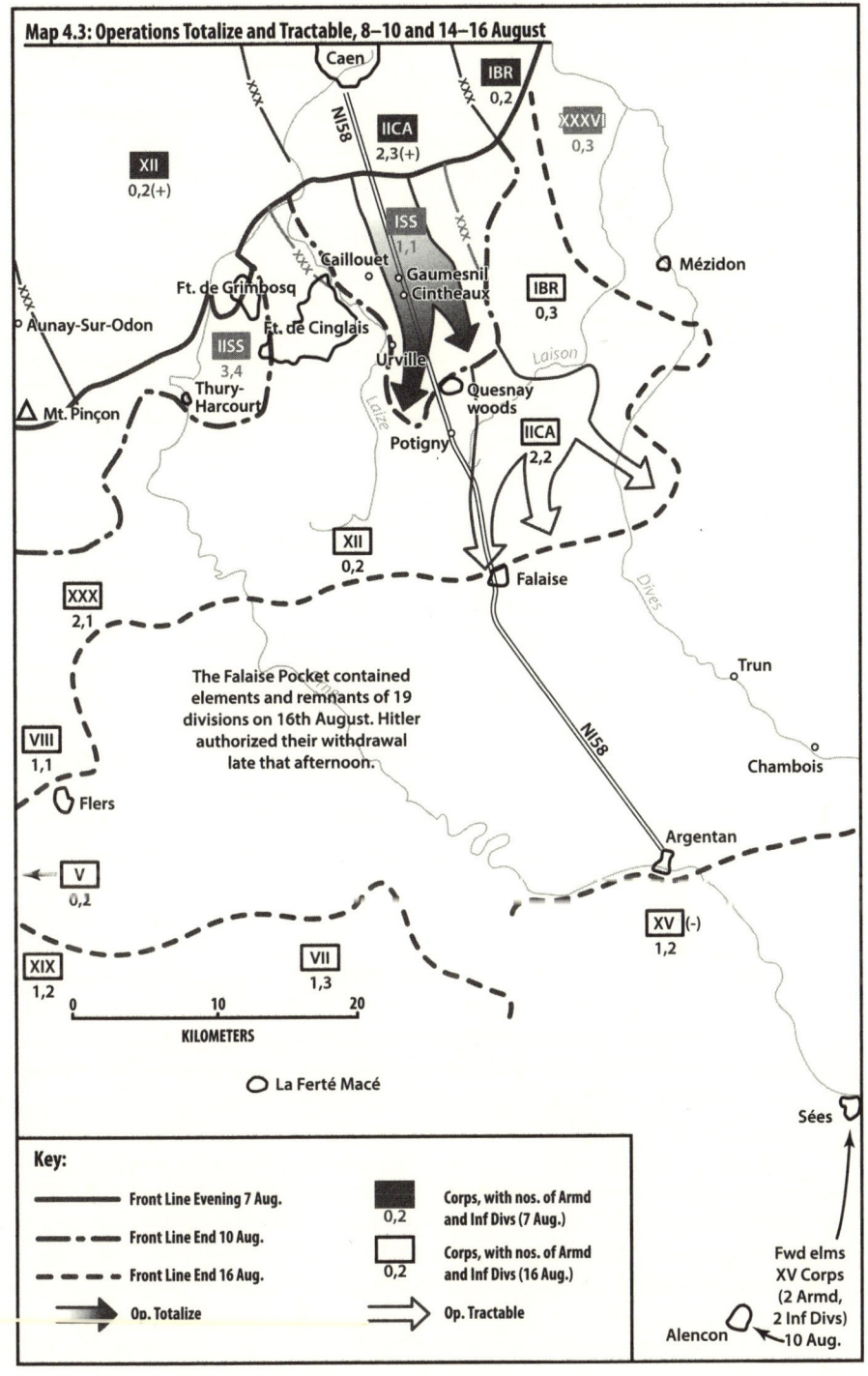

from the Grimbosq bridgehead toward Falaise as part of Second Army's wider push on the town.[17] The actual development of Operation Totalize and its successor, Tractable, is shown in map 4.3.

The deep penetration effort in phase one went well. Most of the careful provisions for night navigation worked—more or less—and by 0800 on 8 August, the two armored and two infantry brigades had penetrated a surprised and bewildered enemy and captured most of their objectives, with only light casualties. The only objectives that remained untaken were Caillouet's quarries and the hamlet of Gaumesnil; both, through an error in staff work, were within the bomb line for phase two. Clearing the villages to the flanks and those bypassed proved four times as costly and took until early or midafternoon. One-third of the heavy bombers had to abort their missions because of target obscuration, and most of the rest were somewhat off target, at least in 2 Canadian Division's sector. Consequently, infantry without artillery or (initially) tank support did not enjoy the expected walkover. Moreover, bypassed and even overrun elements of *89 Infantry Division* did not, as intelligence had opined, give up without a fight. The forward move of the second-echelon divisions was thus hampered by enemy stay-behind groups and by massive traffic congestion worsened by the attempted redeployment of first-echelon artillery. Nevertheless, they were ready on their phase two LD in time to follow on immediately after the end of the second bombing.

Only 75 percent of the American heavy bombers actually dropped their loads (some of them fell short onto Canadian and Polish units). The results were very mixed. Two targets on the flanks were squarely struck (one of them a German dummy concentration left to confuse Allied intelligence when BG *Wünsche* deployed to try to eliminate the Grimbosq bridgehead). Those near the centre line were only lightly affected, and in any case, German armor had preemptively moved out of the impact area. SS Senior Colonel Meyer, the young (thirty-five years old) but immensely experienced commander of *12 SS Panzer Division*, did not conform to the Canadian plan. Realizing that *89 Division* was under attack, he went to the key, now front-line, village of Cintheaux on the centre line; meanwhile, he ordered his immediately available armor (seventy-four tanks and SP antitank guns, including eight Tigers) to concentrate further south under SS Major Waldmüller. He made a quick appreciation of the situation and saw that the enemy had obviously broken through the forward division. Meyer saw what he estimated at up to two armored divisions to his front (the first echelon's tanks, as it happened). Time had to be won for the forty-four tanks and accompanying infantry of BG *Wünsche* to disengage and return and for *85 Infantry Division*, coming from *Fifteenth Army*, to arrive (it was two night marches away and could not be expected before 10 August). He ordered BG *Waldmüller* to mount a spoiling attack. While the enemy was delayed, BG *Wünsche* and some 88mm antiaircraft guns would establish a defense astride the N158 and in the key Quesnay woods to bar the road to Falaise. When *85 Division* arrived, it could extend the line up the Laison valley. Then Meyer traveled nearly 3 km (2 miles) south to *89 Division's* HQ at Urville to confer with its commander and General Eberbach, the army commander, who had come forward to make his personal assessment of the situation. Eberbach confirmed Meyer's plan and, at around 0800, returned to drum up reinforcements (including the return of BG *Olboeter* and *102 SS Heavy Tank Battalion* from *II SS Panzer Corps* and others promised by von Kluge, even though *Army Group B* reserves had long since been exhausted).

When it went in around noon, the *12 SS* counterattack accomplished little against the consolidated forces of the Anglo-Canadian first echelon and took significant casualties (though it escaped from the impact area of the second heavy bombing). It did not spoil the attack of the second echelon, which was still moving to its LD as the Germans were being repulsed. However, on transitioning to defense, BG *Waldmüller* was able to halt the attack of the Polish division, stopping it more or less on its LD with the loss of fifty-seven tanks. The air bombardment had not crushed the defense as promised, there was insufficient artillery support (the Canadian AGRA had taken severe punishment from short-bombing), and the Poles lacked maneuver room and tactical experience. Fourth Canadian Armored Division fared no better. Its advance did not even start until 1615 (almost three hours after H-hour), owing to confusion about whether it or 2 Canadian Infantry Division was responsible for taking objectives not achieved in phase one because they were within the bomb line. Its attack was cautious, and neither division nor corps commanders went forward to make personal assessments and provide leadership.[18] The division advanced 2 km (more than 1 mile) before dark; then, following traditional practice (and despite Simonds's exhortations) it, like the Poles, mostly harbored for the night. One battle group (Worthington Force) was sent forward to establish itself on the divisional objective, but errant navigation led it onto a ridge 6 km (4 miles) to the east.

During the evening and night, the Germans restored a coherent if perilously thin defensive line. The remains of *89 Infantry Division*, now at about 50 percent, held the left flank. BG *Wünsche* was established in the Quesnay woods area, and BG *Waldmüller* was supposed to extend the line eastward along the ridge that formed the northern side of the Laison valley. Actually, Worthington Force had stumbled onto the centre of this position, and its elimination required precious time and resources. Fortunately for *I SS Panzer Corps*, the second echelon continued to disappoint Simonds and Crerar on 9 August. Somewhat disjointed efforts and mostly poor tank-infantry cooperation, combined with stubborn German resistance, prevented momentum from being achieved. The Poles did not advance until 1100, and

4 Canadian Armored Division's attempt to bypass resistance and proceed straight to its objective resulted in failure, with heavy casualties, when *Wünsche*'s tanks belatedly convinced the Canadians that the Quesnay woods were vital ground. Then, that evening, BG *Olboeter* arrived in time to limit the one Canadian success of 9 August—the casualty-free capture, in a silent, nighttime infiltration attack by infantry, of the northern half of 4 Canadian Division's objective. Tactical airpower had a very limited effect on the battle, thanks to 2 Tactical Air Force's cumbersome system for air-land cooperation (so different from the intimate American armored column cover).

By 10 August, Crerar's and Simonds's ambitions had moderated to the point where the objective became to push through the Quesnay woods and reach the Laison with 3 Canadian Infantry Division, supported by the tanks of 2 Canadian Armored Brigade and all the available artillery; following success, the Poles would cross the Laison to the east. This attack failed too, thanks to poor tactical intelligence, inadequate preparation, and German determination. Operation Totalize was over.

If anything, the importance of progress by Crerar's army increased once the short encirclement became the formally stated operational goal. Accordingly, Montgomery issued his M518 on 11 August: "We shall now concentrate our forces in order to encircle the main enemy forces so that we can destroy them in their present location. . . . First Canadian Army will capture Falaise. This is a first priority and it is vital that it should be done quickly. The army will then operate with strong armored and mobile forces to secure Argentan. A secure front must be held between Falaise and the sea." To underscore the importance of a rapid advance on the Falaise-Argentan axis, Montgomery shifted Second Army's main effort from its right flank to its left—the XII Corps thrust from the Grimbosq bridgehead over the Orne toward Falaise.

Again, planning and execution of the next operation remained largely in Simonds's hands. Orders for Operation Tractable were issued on 13 August, for implementation the next day. Bypassing Quesnay woods to the east, Tractable was essentially a rerun of Totalize. Tractable, however, would be executed in daylight, with smoke substituting for darkness in providing concealment. Heavy bombers would neutralize the enemy on the right flank, barring the Caen-Falaise road. The air strike would be followed by a pinning attack by the Poles. Medium and fighter-bombers would soften up the enemy defending the Laison valley. Then two divisions, each with two infantry brigades and one armored brigade (the infantry borne by APCs), would attack in a concentrated phalanx on a narrow frontage to break through the antitank screen, cross the Laison (believed to be no obstacle), and take the high ground on the other side. Third Division would then close on Falaise from the northeast, while 2 Canadian Infantry Division did so from the northwest. On Crerar's orders, it had crossed the Laize on 11 August to cooperate with

XII British Corps in its drive on Falaise; by 14 August, it was still more than 10 km (6 miles) from the town, though opposed only by part of the somewhat worn *271 Infantry Division* holding about a 15 km (9 mile) frontage.

Operation Tractable, like its predecessor, saw short-bombing, bringing the total Canadian and Polish casualties from that cause to just over 800. And like Totalize, it started well and then lost its way. When the Laison proved to be fordable only in some places, confusion reigned and units intermixed as they departed from the parade ground formation mandated for the advance and sought ways forward. Momentum was lost, and the situation was not helped when 4 Canadian Armored Brigade's commander was killed and the chain of command broke down. Confusion and lack of urgency and initiative helped an increasingly enfeebled defense fight a successful delaying action. Falaise was finally entered on 16 August and was not totally cleared until two days later.

Even as Tractable was getting under way, however, some confusion about First Canadian Army's priorities was setting in. At the beginning of the month, Falaise was a Second Army objective, and the Canadians were supposed to cut the approaches to and exits from the town and then take it. Later, concerned that the Germans were withdrawing from the pocket, Montgomery expanded the Canadian mission to take Trun, a crossing of the Dives 16 km (10 miles) west of the town. In fact, although it was too late to change the Tractable plan, the latter became the new main effort after Falaise's capture was certain. And Montgomery demanded that I Corps begin its drive toward the Seine on an axis Mezidon-Lisieux as soon as 7 Armored Division arrived from Second Army. At a 16 August meeting with Bradley and Dempsey (again excluding Crerar and Hodges), he suggested to Bradley that the Trun-Chambois area should be the revised junction of the Allied forces: the enemy who succeeded in retreating east of the N158 could still be trapped west of the Dives. In anticipation of meeting up with American forces, Crerar suggested on 16 August that the US and Canadian First Armies exchange liaison officers as part of an effort to prevent fratricidal clashes between Allied units. He received no reply until 18 August and was then informed that, apart from corps artillery, liaison could take place only at army group level. Despite this rebuff, he sent hourly situation reports to the Americans but received none in return.[19]

Simonds was already implementing the Canadian part of this new variant on the operational idea. On 15 August he had started 1 Polish Armored Division on the new axis, and by the next day it was across the Dives and about 12 km (7 miles) from Trun. To join them, he turned 4 Armored 90 degrees, although the advance could not begin before 17 August, and the Poles could not proceed any further until the Canadians came up. When 4 Armored eventually got started, its advance was badly bungled, and Trun was not taken until midday on 18 August, when 3 Canadian Division came up. The Poles pressed on but did not reach Chambois until the evening of 19 August, when they linked up with elements of US 90 Division. The trap was finally closed, but the gate was not reliably robust; the Canadian and Polish elements blocking the last escape route south of Trun were thinly spread. A breakout on 20 August, assisted by a *II SS Panzer Corps* counterattack from the east, was partially successful.

THE FALAISE POCKET AND THE DEEP ENCIRCLEMENT

The Falaise Pocket

All the senior German commanders were fully aware of the futility of renewing the offensive toward Avranches and of the mortal danger facing *Seventh Army* and *Panzer Group Eberbach*.[20] They were equally aware of the pointlessness, even personal danger, of suggesting retreat to the Führer. Von Kluge found a way out. With the unanimous backing of his army commanders, he persuaded a reluctant Hitler that a preliminary operation would be necessary before resuming the attack to the west. XV Corps, marching into the rear of the attack grouping, would have to be dealt with first, and a critical supply route (and, by the same token, withdrawal route) would have to be reopened. Hitler agreed and, on 11 August, ordered a counterstroke on a southeastward Carrouges–Le Mans axis. So fast did Haislip's force advance, however, that von Kluge was compelled to change the axis to an easterly direction and to divert forces to stop the American drive at Argentan. The move to the assembly area was chaotic and slow (Eberbach's HQ took six hours to move a mere 30 km [18 miles]), as routes were congested and littered with the wrecks left by air attack, fuel was in short supply, and organization and communications were breaking down. Then an enemy column overran the assembly area even as the concentration was getting under way. The panzer group had to transition to defense to sustain the southern shoulder of a closing trap.

The Germans had very little offensive capability left. Their command and control and logistic systems were in dire straits, and *1 SS, 2 SS, 10 SS*, and *2 Panzer Divisions* could muster a total of only seventy-three combat-ready tanks by 11 August.[21] Of course, the C-in-C of *Army Group B* had not wanted to mount a counterstroke at all; he merely needed an excuse to disengage from the Mortain area and withdraw to the east, sure in the knowledge that events would overtake the whole notion of further offensive action. The Canadian offensive toward Falaise and XV Corps' advance north from Alençon had begun forming an encirclement that was frighteningly familiar to many veterans of the Russo-German front. It was time to get out while that was still possible. Nonessential administrative elements were unofficially dispatched eastward. Plans were readied, based on experience gained in the USSR: more capable formations would hold the flanks of the pocket to protect the retreat; a corps HQ would divest itself of troops and devote itself full time to traffic control; and *II SS Panzer Corps*, with two divisions (actually, only two small, tired battle groups with twenty to twenty-five tanks between them), would assemble at Vimoutiers, outside the pocket, to counterattack and reopen an exit when the Allied jaws snapped shut. But Hitler still clung to the illusion that the counteroffensive could be resumed. He did not authorize withdrawal until the late afternoon of 16 August.[22] By then, it ought to have been too late. The pocket was 56 km (35 miles) deep (i.e., west of the Dives) and 20 km (12 miles) wide at the neck (the Canadians having taken Falaise on 16 August). No major east-west road was left to the Germans. The retreat, taking place under conditions of acute logistic shortages and chaos, would have to be over hilly terrain and two rivers, with Allied artillery and fighter-bombers able to reach every nook and cranny of the shrinking pocket. But the Allies gave the Germans the one thing they needed to get significant elements out of the trap: time.

The Allies were not unaware of the German plight. Ultra, tactical SIGINT (Army Y), and air reconnaissance, supplemented by other sources, followed the abortive plans to renew the Avranches counteroffensive, the changing groupings and movements, and the Germans' increasingly precarious logistic situation. During the period 12–15 August, all intelligence sources suggested that the enemy, understanding the threat of a double envelopment, had contemplated a counterattack against XV Corps to check the southern pincers. It became increasingly evident, however, that tank, fuel, and ammunition shortages and general confusion had forced the abandonment of this plan in favor of a counterpenetration. It was also apparent that, although tactical withdrawals were being carried out, the bulk of German combat power remained west of the Falaise-Argentan road, with a defense building up on either side of Argentan to protect the south side of the salient.[23] Then, on the evening of 16 August, Ultra reported von Kluge's morning request for permission for a general withdrawal, followed by *Army Group B*'s order to start such a withdrawal to the Orne that night and to the Dives the next. Late that night, Montgomery told the CIGS there was good reason to believe there were still six panzer and SS divisions inside the pocket (an assessment with which First Army's intelligence concurred). There was, in short, still ample incentive on 16 August to make vigorous efforts to close the pocket along the Dives.

On both the northern and southern wings of the encirclement, a combination of delays, inadequate forces at the decisive place, and poor tactical handling, not to mention effective German reactions, prevented the effective sealing of the pocket before 20 August. Even so, *Seventh* and *Fifth Panzer Armies* were shattered. Constant air attack and artillery fire inflicted enormous and growing casualties. A partial count of equipment losses amounted to more than 300 tanks and SP guns, 200 light AFVs, 2,500 SSVs, and 300 guns.[24] Of the approximately 100,000 men left in the pocket at the beginning of the withdrawal on 14 August, approximately 10,000 were killed and more than 40,000 were missing or captured. However, up to 40,000 escaped, as Ultra reported on 22 August. To that number must be added those units that had been withdrawn before the encirclement got under way and those outside the intended pocket. Intelligence estimated that there were 250 tanks and SP guns and 75,000 troops still west of the Seine (actually, there were about 115,000 men). These forces had to be destroyed before they could cross the river. If they were merely driven eastward, Allied logistic constraints (evident as early as 16 August) would soon limit and then halt further efforts and give the enemy the opportunity to rebuild his strength, using the escaped elements as cadres.

The Deep Encirclement

Even as the pincers were closing on the Falaise pocket, the minds of the Supreme Commander and the army group commanders were turning to post-Overlord campaigning. There was, however, unfinished business: the considerable enemy force still attempting to escape the Normandy catastrophe. On 19 August Montgomery met Bradley, Hodges, Dempsey, and Crerar to plan their destruction. US combat power was building up on the south side of the salient, with XV Corps already at Dreux and XIX Corps completing its concentration 15 to 30 km (9 to 18 miles) west of the town. Third Army had its XX and XII Corps halted in the Chartres-Orléans area. There was thus no prospect of a German breakout to the southeast through the Paris-Orléans gap on the most direct route to the Reich. That left only one exit, subject to interdiction by the AEAF: northeastward over the Seine between Vernon and the estuary. Late on 17 August, Ultra reported a list of ferry sites in operation in that sector.

The solution agreed on was a thrust down the west bank of the Seine for a second encirclement. To accomplish the task, Bradley offered transport to shift two Second Army divisions round US First Army via Avranches to its right flank. However, the necessary forces were already there, with two divisions of XV Corps at Mantes and XIX Corps' three divisions in the area west of Dreux. The inter–army group boundary was temporarily redrawn to run north from Verneuil to west of Rouen to allow the two US corps to sweep north toward Elbeuf and cut off the fleeing enemy for 21 Army Group, advancing eastward, to crush him on an American anvil.[25] Meanwhile, Third

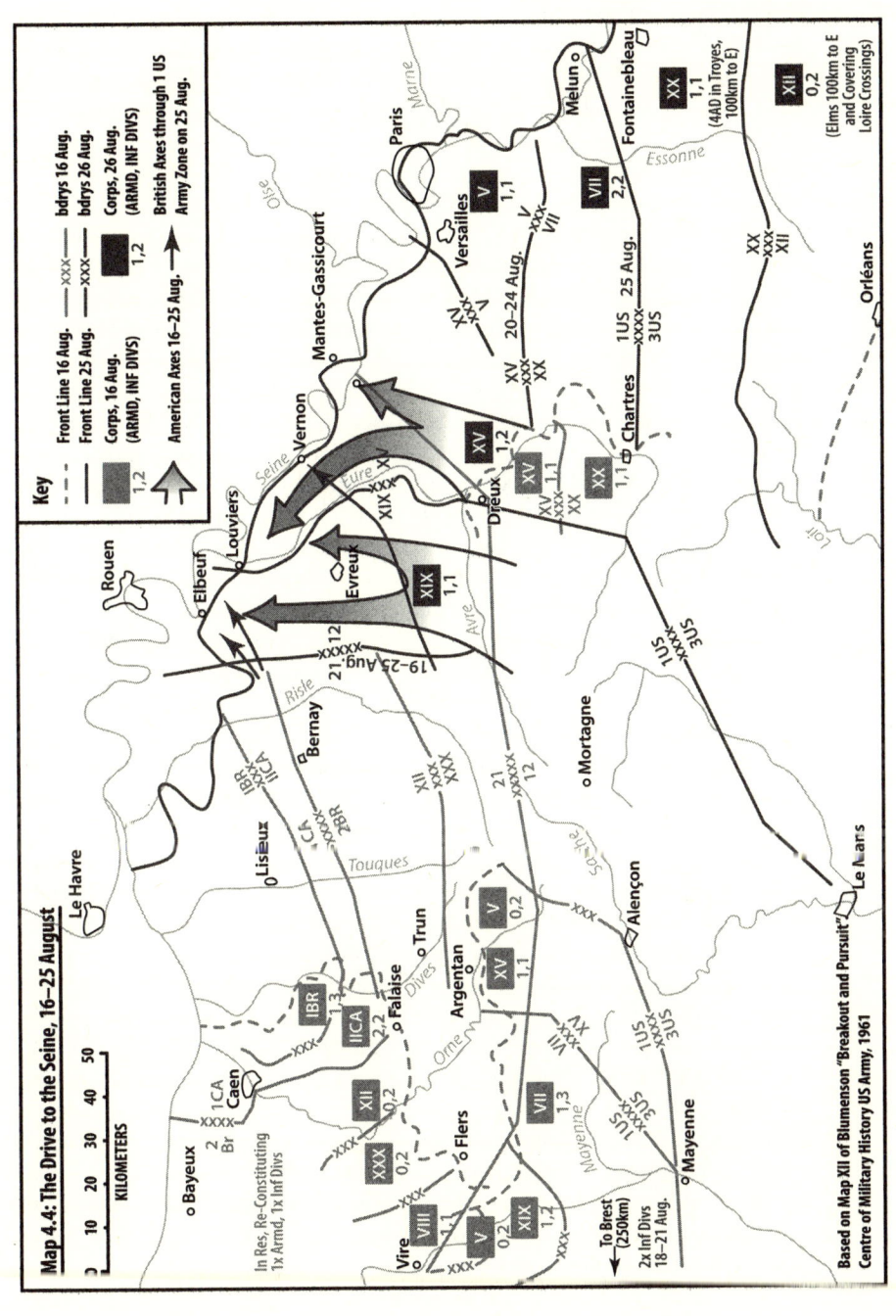

Army would advance to the east and seize bridgeheads over the Seine south of Paris, in addition to the one to the north at Mantes. These Seine bridgeheads would render the river useless to the Germans as an obstacle and provide a springboard for a 12 Army Group advance on Germany. The conclusion of the Normandy campaign with the Allied drive to the Seine is shown in map 4.4.

On 21 August Third Army duly resumed its eastward push against light opposition. By 25 August, XX Corps had advanced 90 to 120 km (55 to 75 miles), seizing three bridgeheads over the Seine 40 to 70 km (25 to 45 miles) upriver from Paris. XII Corps' lead division went even further to take Troyes, 170 km (105 miles) from Orléans, 145 km (90 miles) southeast of Paris, and only 250 km (155 miles) from the Rhine. For all his spectacular seizure of ground, however, Patton had not lost sight of the original aim of operations—destruction of the enemy. On 23 August, with his forces rapidly closing on the river, the general proposed that XX and XII Corps turn north from their bridgeheads, together with XV Corps (already across at Mantes), and head north toward Beauvais to trap those Germans who had escaped over the Seine. Bradley rejected the idea in favor of a continued thrust to the east, despite a looming crisis in fuel supplies as the increasing distances between depots and the front stretched available transport resources.

Although the German forces attempting to retreat over the Seine were still numerous, their state of organization, equipment, and command and control was very weak (save for *LXXXVI Corps* on the coastal sector), and they had no prepared positions to fall back on to facilitate an organized withdrawal. *Seventh Army* was unable to prepare even an approximate strength return, and *Fifth Panzer Army*, apart from two infantry divisions recently arrived on the Seine from *Fifteenth Army*, produced only a partial one for *I* and *II SS Panzer Corps* on 21 August. This showed that the five panzer divisions remaining west of the Seine could muster only five understrength infantry battalions, about sixty tanks and twenty-six guns. This was the core of the organized rear guard covering the withdrawal over the Seine. *First Army* defending Paris and all the land east to the Rhône-Saône corridor was similarly lacking in combat power: it possessed two poorly trained, ill-equipped infantry divisions; shattered elements of three formations that had survived Normandy; some security units; and, arriving too late to defend the Seine line, two SS panzer "divisions" that were actually understrength infantry regiments without armor. Nor was there any relief from constant air attack. The Luftwaffe dispatched an extra 800 fighters to cover the retreat, but their largely novice pilots were no match for the Allies and did not affect Allied air supremacy; in a short time, about half of them were shot down, destroyed on the ground, or overrun on their airfields.

Starting on 20 August, 5 Armored Division of XV Corps advanced between the Eure and the Seine, reaching Louviers on 25 August. The corps' other division, 79 Infantry, was left to hold the Mantes bridgehead. Its neighbor to the west, XIX Corps, advanced with an armored division and an infantry division up and a third initially refused to the left. The Americans advanced on a front of 45 km (30 miles), going down to 25 km (15 miles), and to a depth of approximately 35 to 50 km (20 to 30 miles) in five days to come up to Elbeuf and Louviers. Ten British and Canadian divisions were involved at one stage or another in a frontal pursuit from the Dives, over the Touques and Risle, to the Seine, advancing up to 80 km (50 miles) in five to ten days. There was an inevitable entangling of US formations establishing the stop line and Anglo-Canadian ones advancing from the west; however, generally good staff work and inter-Allied cooperation prior to and after the meeting enabled the Americans to withdraw south of the army group boundary and their allies to complete the clearing of the west bank and establish bridgeheads over the river before the month was out.

Paris

While First Army's XIX Corps and newly acquired XV Corps were having another stab at cutting off the German retreat, this time on the Seine, its VII Corps and V Corps, pinched out by the elimination of the pocket, were reorganizing.[26] They would now advance on the army's right. The boundary with Third Army was redrawn on a line from Chartres to Melun, removing Paris from Third Army's zone of advance and placing it in Hodges's (specifically, in V Corps'). As an objective in its own right, Paris had not loomed large in SHAEF thinking; however, as the most significant communications hub in all of France, its possession would be essential to any push to the east. Eisenhower had initially intended to bypass the city and capture it through encirclement, without the need for costly street fighting or the earlier-than-inevitable diversion of the 4,000 tons of supplies per day the logisticians believed the food- and fuel-starved city would need. Accordingly, the FFI, recognized by the Allies as the official face of French resistance under SHAEF control, ordered the resistance in Paris to maintain a low profile and avoid provoking the Germans. This purely military calculation took no account of French political realities. The enduring truth that he who holds Paris controls France meant that both Gaullists and leftists were eager to claim credit for the capital's liberation, and no faction would be content to play a passive role. By 19 August, encouraged by the approach of American forces, the disintegration of the Pétain government, and the feebleness of the German reaction to widespread strikes and defiance of authority, the city was in a state of insurrection. Lacking both the fighting power to crush the uprising and the stomach to implement Hitler's order to reduce the city to ruins, the military commandant agreed to a rather ill-defined truce with the insurrectionists. This was due to expire at noon on 23 August.

De Gaulle had been lobbying for the early liberation of Paris, to be led by 2 French Armored Division. Leclerc, a fervent Gaullist, had been pressing the same demand with his unheeding corps and army commanders, refusing to allow his division to become decisively engaged with the enemy in the Falaise encirclement battle, whatever the orders issued by Gerow or Hodges. By 22 August, influenced by French political pressure and by the growing belief that the Germans would not contest the city, which was now believed to be largely in FFI hands, Eisenhower had changed his position on Paris. Leclerc was sent to liberate the city, reinforced by 4 Infantry Division, when, yet again, the French general ignored his corps commander's orders as to axis. On 25 August Paris was surrendered to the provisional government of France, thus realizing de Gaulle's ambition to preempt a communist seizure of power and to present a fait accompli to a somewhat unfriendly US government.

The Extent of the Disaster Suffered by *Seventh* and *Fifth Panzer Armies*

Allied air interdiction efforts combined with the long envelopment proved to be less decisive than hoped. On 21 August AEAF's main effort was shifted from interdicting the Seine to attacking retreating forces north of the river and preventing the establishment of a defensive line on the Somme; Leigh-Mallory equated the destruction of the permanent bridges with the sealing of the barrier. The ground forces advanced with more circumspection than vigor and failed to close the crossing sites, even though significant numbers were still on the left bank. Montgomery did not seem unduly perturbed by these developments or by the failure of the ground forces to seal all escape routes over the river in good time. He had already decided, as he wrote to the CIGS on 18 August, that "all German formations that cross the Seine will be incapable of combat during the months to come."[27] All the same, suspecting that significant numbers of the enemy had managed to cross the river, Montgomery ordered an inquiry into the magnitude of the escape. The conclusion confirmed his suspicion: between the Dives and the Seine, about 240 tanks and SP guns, 250 light armored vehicles, 4,450 other vehicles, and 230 guns had been destroyed or abandoned; about 80,000 men had been killed or captured. But the inquiry also established that in the last twelve days of August, approximately 240,000 men, 28,000 vehicles, and 195 tanks and SP guns had managed to cross the Seine. Clearly, air action had not made the river an impassable barrier (a fact made obvious even before the retreat by the number of divisions from *Fifteenth Army* that had reinforced *Seventh* and *Fifth Panzer Armies* in July and August). A partially destroyed railway bridge in Rouen, three pontoon bridges, about sixty ferry and boat crossing sites, and many more small, improvised crossings had enabled considerable numbers to avoid death or capture.[28] The bulk of those that escaped the trap did so over 26–27 August—that is, after First Army's sweep north closed off 60 km (40 miles) of river but stopped at Elbeuf.

British and American works on Normandy are meticulous when dealing with Allied casualties during the campaign. From D-Day until the end of August, these totaled 209,672 among the land forces (about 60 percent of them American). They tend to be more cavalier about German figures. The commonly quoted total is 450,000 casualties (about 240,000 killed and wounded and 210,000 prisoners), statistics that probably originated in unreliable wartime estimates. A study based on a careful examination of the documentary evidence suggests that German losses actually amounted to 288,695 (including 198,616 missing), although this figure is for the whole of Oberbefehlshaber (High Command) West and includes well over 65,000 lost in the south of France and the retreat from the south and southwest. Given that as many as 640,000 Germans fought in Normandy, it is clear that substantial numbers were going to be available to reconstitute formations—given time.[29]

Five severely mauled divisions had to be sent to Germany for rebuilding. The remnants of the other eleven infantry divisions provided only four improvised, underequipped divisional battle groups, and the eleven panzer and panzer grenadier divisions had only some five to ten tanks and one battery each.[30] Both of the Normandy armies were, over the course of only four weeks, rendered combat-ineffective. Only the scratch *First Army* and the much-depleted *Fifteenth Army* remained to contest an Allied eastward march on Germany. It would take time to summon additional forces from other theatres (and none could be diverted from the eastern front, where even greater disasters had been engulfing the Wehrmacht). On the one hand, a window had been opened for a potentially decisive strategic exploitation. On the other hand, if it were not effectively utilized, the men who had escaped could form the core of rebuilt or fresh divisions. Most importantly, of the one army, seven corps, and twenty divisional HQs caught in the pocket, only one corps and three divisional HQs had been destroyed. The enemy had a substantial number of men almost immediately available in Germany—two shadow divisions (bodies of combat troops organized like divisions, but without logistic infrastructure), nine fortress battalions, and seventeen replacement battalions—but they were not an integrated force. There were also six parachute regiment equivalents, albeit without artillery or much antitank weaponry, in training in the Netherlands. The command and control elements that escaped from Normandy ensured that there would be experienced, efficient brains to direct the refitted formations and the new bodies that would be created, and some logistic and administrative structures to keep them going.

OPERATIONAL ART AND GENERALSHIP IN AUGUST

Army Level

The key decisions were made at the higher operational level, and army commanders operated with only limited freedom of action. Indeed, Bradley, and especially Montgomery, tended to exercise tight supervision and control, allowing little room for creativity. Dempsey, Crerar, and Hodges accepted this as right and proper. Patton, however, was inclined to interpret his orders as creatively as possible, exercise initiative, and exceed the goals set in his mission. It was fortunate for the Allies that the circumstances in which Patton's army entered battle were so favorable to his aggressive, risk-taking style of command. That the German defense in Normandy unraveled so completely and, above all, so quickly was due largely to Patton's energy and audacity, often in spite of the wishes of his more cautious superior.

Second British Army: Lieutenant General Dempsey. General Dempsey had spent the twelve weeks prior to Operation Bluecoat engaged in the thankless task of pinning the bulk of German combat power on the British sector of the front through an attritional struggle. Sandwiched between the newly activated First Canadian Army to the east and US First Army to the west, he had no maneuver room. He would have to create his own opportunities to carry out operational maneuver by breaking through the defense and then inserting exploitation forces through the gap. He failed to accomplish this up to and including Operation Goodwood, but he succeeded in Bluecoat. A rapid, skillful, covert regrouping of two-thirds of the attack grouping onto a quiet and weakly defended sector ensured surprise. Initially, this was fully exploited by O'Connor's VIII Corps, which eschewed customary tactical caution at critical moments and thus achieved an early breakthrough. However, fear of overextension soon reasserted itself, and exploitation gave way to the consolidation of gains. Dempsey did not press O'Connor to take risks but concentrated instead on trying to coax a more energetic performance out of XXX Corps. The opportunity to turn *Seventh Army*'s withdrawal into a rout was lost.

From the fourth day of operations, Second Army slipped away from a maneuver-based approach aimed at dislocating the enemy, forcing him into an untenable position and back into attritional operations to grind him down. There were arguments in favor of this reversion to the familiar. The primary aim of the operation had been achieved; the Germans had been prevented from shifting *II SS Panzer Corps* to the west to stop the Cobra breakthrough. Methodical operations were believed to conserve the force, a major consideration for an army facing a manpower crisis (so acute that 59 Infantry Division was about to be broken up to provide replacements for other formations). And such operations were controllable and low risk, unlike an attempt at vigorous pursuit, which could lead to confusion, uncertainty, and exposure to damaging counterattacks that could weaken morale. It is, however, difficult to shake the suspicion that Dempsey's Second Army was happy to get back into its comfort zone, despite the fact that the operational circumstances of early August had made bolder action both safer and more desirable. The Germans lacked the strength, the logistic support, and the ability to achieve even temporary and local air superiority to wrest the initiative back from the British while simultaneously attempting to stem the American breakthrough. The Allies knew this, thanks to their excellent operational-level intelligence.

Post-Bluecoat operations were not—indeed, could not be—characterized by the usual lengthy buildup to achieve strong concentrations on narrow sectors and by the expenditure of massive stocks of ammunition created over many days. Rather, following the expensive and therefore very short-lived Operation Grouse, there was pressure across the front by all three corps (until VIII Corps was pinched out by the shrinking of the pocket).[31] However, by the middle of August, pressure had largely given way to merely following up the German withdrawal. Formations were, of course, grateful for the rest and the opportunity to refit. However, the British lack of aggressiveness meant that the German withdrawal was hardly discommoded. Enemy formations were not pinned to allow more time for the encirclement to be completed and to prevent enemy disengagement in the west to concentrate for a breakout to the east. Strong thrusts were not mounted into the German northern flank of the pocket to cut off and destroy individual retreating groupings. XII Corps, decreed the main effort after the failure of the Canadians' Operation Totalize, was not strongly reinforced, and it advanced at a very deliberate pace (though, admittedly, the ground greatly favored the defense). The inevitable opportunities for the pursuer created by a chaotic retreat were not seized upon, such as when 11 Armored Division failed to prevent *10 SS Panzer*'s crossing of the Orne during the night 17–18 August. The pursuit to the Seine following the elimination of the pocket was similarly unthreatening to an even weaker enemy; the Germans were pushed toward US First Army's anvil but not hammered on it. In short, there was a persistent failure to capitalize on the enemy's weaknesses and conduct the vigorous pursuit that turns battle success into campaign victory. However, Dempsey did look ahead to post-Normandy operations and ensured that they could start as soon as his commander desired. He planned to seize bridgeheads over the major obstacle (the Seine) through forced crossings from the line of march, thus avoiding the delay that would have attended a more deliberate approach.

Dempsey was plainly right to reject Bradley's rather extraordinary offer to ferry two British divisions round US First Army to complete the wide encirclement on the Seine. The scheme (presumably designed to free all American forces for an immediate march eastward on Germany) would have been disruptive, logistically impractical, inadequate in strength, and, above all, too tardy in execution to catch many of the enemy. Altogether more sensible was the general agreement on a temporary boundary change to allow a XIX and XV Corps attack between the Eure and the Seine, across the line of the British advance. Second Army's HQ worked well with US First Army to deconflict the two armies advancing on converging axes. (Of course, there would have been no problem to solve if the US thrust had been directed up the east bank of the Seine.) Dempsey's incautious (and possibly misquoted) remarks about being delayed by American slowness in clearing his line of march were unfair and out of character; he was normally the soul of tact. Montgomery, demonstrating a sensitivity that was often lacking in his own dealings with the Americans, smoothed over the affair, and no lasting harm was done to Dempsey's relations with his allies. It did, however, illustrate the level of dislike, even hostility and distrust, that was increasingly infecting Anglo-American relations, to the detriment of sound decision making.

In late August the much weakened, disorganized, and logistically starved enemy was in the most vulnerable state imaginable, but Second Army appeared happy to leave his destruction largely to the Allied air forces and other armies. This assertion presupposes, of course, that Second Army was capable of acting in any other way. It was well trained to conduct the set-piece battles on which doctrine placed so much emphasis, and it had acquired much practical experience in putting that training to good use. However, in its long working-up period in Britain prior to the invasion, it had not been prepared for maneuver warfare and pursuit—certainly not at the formation level. For the most part, commanders, staffs, and formations were used to relying on massive, sometimes unnecessary and logistically unsound use of firepower and very deliberate, overly cautious tactics. Unlike the Germans, they lacked sufficient relevant training and experience to conduct fluid battles, and neither HQs nor their commands displayed the agility demonstrated time and again by the Wehrmacht.[32] Awareness of this disparity in capabilities reinforced the British inclination toward caution. This was unfortunate, for by mid-August, caution was no longer an appropriate response to developments. When the enemy is badly damaged, unbalanced, in logistic difficulties, under great psychological pressure, and forced into increasingly belated and therefore ineffectual improvisations, that is the time when ruthless exploitation of the initiative and risk taking pay the greatest dividends.

It is the time when the main concern should be not what can the enemy do to us but what can we do to him. In August, Second Army seemed unable to rise to the occasion. It had not yet become the somewhat more versatile and agile force that would fight the post-Normandy campaigns.

It seems that Dempsey did not encourage, or display himself, the boldness and ruthlessness that characterize an effective pursuit—either that, or he was restrained from doing so by Montgomery. Powerful influences undoubtedly constrained him, including an instinctive reaction to the prospect of casualties and knowledge that the British component of the AEF was reaching the bottom of the manpower barrel. But the real reason was his very British desire for a tidy battlefield, along with the concomitant impulse to exercise tight control through detailed, prescriptive orders and close supervision of subordinates. This was the very antithesis of the mission command style that brought such great victories to other very mobile, armor-heavy armies enjoying unlimited air support.

First Canadian Army: Lieutenant General Crerar. Like Operation Bluecoat, Totalize achieved more than its predecessors in Normandy. II Canadian Corps drove a salient up to 15 km (9 miles) deep and 8 km (5 miles) wide into the German defense. In doing so, it reduced a fresh infantry division to 50 percent, inflicted significant losses on *12 SS Panzer Division*, and greatly alarmed *Army Group B*. With his Caen hinge weakened to breaking point and the Americans advancing almost unopposed northward from Le Mans, von Kluge could see that his worst fear—encirclement of most of *Seventh* and *Fifth Panzer Armies*—was about to be realized. Nevertheless, the operation failed to achieve its aim of cutting the German withdrawal route through Falaise. This failure, coupled with the operational pause before the effort was resumed in Operation Tractable, would have far-reaching repercussions.

Despite some halfhearted claims to ownership by Crerar, it is clear that Operation Totalize was the brainchild of II Canadian Corps' GOC Lieutenant General Simonds. He had reflected on the causes of the expensive failure, a fortnight before, of his Operation Spring. The Totalize plan contained novel features designed to negate those aspects of the German defense that had made previous attacks so costly and inconclusive: heavy night bombing in close proximity to ground troops; an attack by massed armor at night; and the use of APCs to get infantry rapidly into the enemy's tactical depth, undisrupted and with only light casualties.[33] These innovations ensured surprise and, in consequence, a speedy penetration of the defense. Phase one was completed at low cost and largely according to plan. However, the battle started to go wrong immediately thereafter. Momentum was lost and never regained.

One reason for this turn of events was the effective way the Germans reacted. Although untested and now shocked and disrupted, units of *89 Infantry Division* fought on, despite being overrun or bypassed. Even more critical in the battle for time was the speed and tactical acumen with which German commanders at all levels reacted. Meyer and Eberbach both made early, on-the-spot appreciations and decisions, saving precious time in the decision-action cycle. Their characteristic, reflexive counterattack failed to recover ground and resulted in irreplaceable casualties, however. Simonds had anticipated this, and the first echelon was consolidated and ready. Conversely, the subsequent delaying action won the time needed to establish a defense in the Potigny area and, eventually, on the line of the Laison. The defensive action that followed the spoiling attack was also active and maneuver based. The tanks were not deployed with the infantry to stiffen the defense but concentrated in the Quesnay woods for countermoves, as Worthington Force found at the cost of its destruction. That the Germans would react so quickly and effectively was, of course, predictable, even in the case of a poor, green division like *89 Infantry*. That had been the pattern throughout the campaign, most recently in their response to the initial penetration in Bluecoat. Even at this late date, intelligence and commanders often failed to understand the enemy.

Imaginative and innovative as it was, Simonds's plan contained major flaws that gave the Germans a chance to recover from their surprise and reestablish a coherent defense. Many of these flaws were inherent in British operational and tactical methods and thinking. In other words, they were systemic. The first flaw involved the faulty use of airpower. There was a growing reliance on the massive use of heavy bombers to supplement artillery in the task of burying resistance under hundreds of tons of high explosives. In neither Goodwood nor Bluecoat had this been the hoped-for panacea. In Totalize, the effect was adverse. The preliminary night bombing was only partially successful, but dependence on it meant that initial infantry attacks on fortified villages were mounted in inadequate strength and without artillery and tank support; consequently, casualties were significant, and the flanks of the advance were not cleared on schedule, impacting the forward displacement of artillery for phase two. Critically, the second bombing was counterproductive. It had little effect on the defense, largely hitting empty ground and the dummy concentration at St. Sylvain, but it inflicted serious damage and disruption on the two AGRAs supporting the phase two attack. Most significantly, the afternoon air strikes were considered so essential to the breakthrough of the second position that a long tactical pause was deemed acceptable; as it turned out, it was six to eight hours before the Polish and Canadian armored divisions crossed their LDs. That was just enough time for the Germans to restore the integrity of the defense. An air plan involving the employment of Bomber Command and Eighth Air Force was necessarily inflexible, being set in stone well in advance of the operation and not subject to any change after H–5 or cancellation after H+8. Even if ground operations were proceeding well, they would still have to stop and wait for the air attacks to go in, and neither the air plan nor ground plan could be adjusted if the enemy did the unexpected. Both these things happened on 8 August.

During the planning stage of Totalize, Crerar had noted the lengthy interval between phases one and two. This violated the principle of maintaining momentum and the initiative. However, he did not press the issue, even after Ultra's revelation that much or most of *1 SS Panzer Division* had been redeployed.[34] It was unfortunate that Crerar, the man with the authority to cancel the second bombing, lacked the courage of his convictions, was somewhat intimidated by the forceful and more experienced Simonds, or feared offending the senior airmen, to the possible detriment of future support from the heavy bombers. He had, after all, expended political capital to arrange it.

An obsession with the firepower delivered by strategic bombers obscured more successful and less controversial air techniques. Actually, airpower could have made a decisive contribution to Operation Totalize had reliance been placed on its tactical arm, properly used. Continuous air interdiction of the battlefield would have severely delayed the march of BGs *Krause* and *Olboeter*, the battle groups principally responsible for repulsing the Canadian attacks on 9–10 August. Close air support could have contributed mightily to deepening the penetration. With artillery unable to displace forward in time to give continuous support, fighter-bombers would have provided an alternative source of firepower. Their effectiveness against point targets, especially vulnerable ones like antitank guns and artillery, would have been greater than in previous battles, as the Germans would be neither well dug in nor camouflaged during an increasingly fluid battle. To ensure immediate responsiveness, some fighter ground-attack units could have been continuously in the air over the battlefield, using the cab-rank concept developed by AVM Broadhurst in late 1943. Any necessary surge effort could have been mounted at short notice from other squadrons held on cockpit alert and ready to fly on order.[35]

Had Simonds and Crerar reposed the confidence in the break-in plan that it actually merited, they would have dispensed with the crutch of the second heavy bombing. This would have left II Canadian Corps with the flexibility to exploit the initial success immediately (although broad preplanning of this exploitation would have been necessary to avoid delay and confusion).[36] At the very least, elements of the first echelon could have pressed forward with the barest of pauses for reorganization. Better still, predesignated combined-arms battle groups of reinforced battalion strength, probably drawn from the second echelon, could have pushed south on either side of the N158 in advance of their formations' main bodies to seize the high ground just west of Potigny and a crossing over the Laison immediately to the east. They would have enjoyed a high priority for air support. The aim would have been to preempt the enemy onto key points on the favorable defensive line in his depth and hold them until the second echelon could deploy and make its way forward to reinforce the leading units. Disruption of the German defense and a speedy advance to render nugatory his reactions would have reduced the time required and thus the element of risk.[37] It is likely, too, that the armored divisions could have come forward more rapidly had there been greater urgency about the move; as it was, there was no need to be on the LD much before the H-hour determined by the air effort.

In the event, when the second-echelon attack went in, it was against a first-class enemy that was beginning to recover his balance. The two armored divisions would have to fight their way forward. The Germans, however, were still vulnerable to well-conducted attacks mounted by a force that enjoyed considerable numerical superiority. Though this was especially true on the afternoon of 8 August, it remained so through the next day. It was therefore unfortunate that both second-echelon divisions were inexperienced and thus prone to the failings of green formations. The Poles had not grasped the importance of fighting in combined-arms battle groups, and Canadian inter-arm cooperation was weak. Neither formation was prepared for night fighting (with especially tragic consequences for Worthington Force). Both were guilty of poor battle procedure and committed tactical errors. Simonds and Crerar blamed the very disappointing results not only on inexperience but also on commanders' lack of drive and incompetence; Simonds castigated commanders down to the unit level accordingly. Their failure, however, was due in large measure to faults in the plan. That 4 Armored Division left its LD almost three hours late owed much to the poor staff work that placed Gaumesnil inside the bomb line and allocated it as an objective (in phase one) to two different divisions; the egregious failings of Brigadier Booth, commanding 4 Armored Brigade (which did not result in his dismissal), were merely a complementary factor. Moreover, each armored division was allotted a narrow zone of advance (scarcely more than 1 km [half a mile] wide) and therefore lacked the maneuver room to bypass opposition as Simonds demanded. Yet II Canadian Corps could have expanded its actions considerably to the east. The weak German *LXXXVI Corps*, which held the right flank facing I British Corps, held a 20 km (12 mile) frontage from the sea to La Hogue.[38] This was increased overnight by 7 km (4 miles) by 51 Highland Division's advance. It would be extended that same distance again with the German night withdrawal on 8–9 August. Stretched, lacking mobility, and with almost no armor, *LXXXVI Corps* was poorly placed to elongate its defensive flank southward in sufficient strength to repulse an Allied effort to turn the right flank of the main defense.

Crerar's failure to exploit the boundary between *I SS* and *LXXXVI Corps* is hard to explain and harder to excuse. From the end of phase one, 51 Division and 33 Armored Brigade played only minor roles. Reverting to I British Corps' command on the afternoon of 9 August, they merely kept up with the Canadian advance and covered its flank. They, together with one of the armored divisions, could have been used under either corps to widen the operation's spatial scope and overstretch the defense while the rest of I Corps pinned the enemy to their front. Such a task would have been consistent with preparing the way for a thrust toward Rouen, which Crerar believed would be the post-Totalize role of his army. This would not have overstretched Crerar's forces, as he still would have had 2 and 3 Canadian Divisions and an armored division and brigade in hand for the direct attack on Falaise.

The outcome of the attacks on both 8 and 9 August was far below expectations. The lesson not learned was that a thrust narrowly confined to a few kilometers on either side of the N158 would become subject to diminishing returns. The plan for 10 August was based on a belated recognition of the central importance of the Quesnay woods to that axis. A predictable, frontal attack by 3 Canadian Division was repulsed. This failure was an expensive reminder that, without surprise, careful planning, and a well-constructed fire plan, an improvised attack was unlikely to succeed against a capable enemy that had been given time to prepare.

With that sharp reminder of the force's limitations, it took two and a half days to generate the fresh set-piece attack that Simonds and Crerar deemed necessary, despite Montgomery's demand for urgency. Neither general accepted that the Totalize plan had been flawed in any way, ascribing failure to the incompetence of their subordinates. Thus, Operation Tractable was largely a reprise of its predecessor. It once again relied on the use of heavy bombers (a reliance that was not fully justified by results and not without serious consequences); it saw the same use of tightly massed tanks and APC-borne infantry; it substituted obscuration through smoke for the cover of darkness; it was tightly controlled, leaving little room for initiative when the plan went wrong. And go wrong it did when the river Laison proved to be a tank obstacle in many places (a fact that better intelligence work would have revealed). The attack lost cohesion and, with subordinate commanders having no idea how to react when the unexpected happened, fizzled out in a mix of confusion and passive waiting for fresh orders.

Rather than persisting in frontal attacks against an increasingly coherent defense, it might have been better, even as late as 10–11 August, to seek a solution on either flank. A subsidiary attack was started on the west bank of the Laize on 11 August by 2 Canadian Division to complement the thrust southeastward from the Grimbosq bridgehead by XII British Corps—an effort that gained momentum with the departure of BG *Wünsche* on 8 August. The ground, however, was not favorable to a much larger deployment and a rapid increase in tempo. On the left, had Crerar willed it, there was a possibility that II Canadian Corps, in cooperation with I British Corps, could have broken through the now grossly overextended *LXXXVI Corps* and turned the flank of *I SS Panzer Corps*. Of course, at this stage of the offensive, having failed to exploit earlier opportunities, the Canadian army really could have used additional formations to regain momentum. Probably because he rated Crerar so lowly, Montgomery was not inclined to reinforce him as readily as he would the more trusted Dempsey. This lack of esteem led to his exclusion from critical C-in-C's meetings to discuss the operational situation. For instance, this happened when Montgomery met with Bradley and Dempsey on 13 and 16 August and made decisions that directly affected First Canadian Army.

Operations Totalize and Tractable demonstrated the flaws and limitations in both Canadian operational thinking and tactical competence. Surprise was seen as a combat multiplier, but there was insufficient appreciation of the transience of its effects; every hour that passed without exploitation was pure gain for the enemy. At bottom, Simonds and Crerar thought there was no substitute for sheer volume of fire—the more the better.[39] This led to overreliance on the effects of bombing, carefully prepared fire plans, and impractically rigid timetables. Tempo was a secondary consideration that was apparently considered to be of secondary value, even though the enemy had amply demonstrated time after time that momentum (and the paralyzing shock it induced) was the main weapon of armored forces. As Kurt Meyer scathingly remarked: "A tank attack which is divided into phases is like a cavalry charge with meal breaks." He also pointed out: "You just cannot lead a tank battle from behind an office desk. The place for the responsible unit commander has to be with the foremost elements of his attacking spearhead so as to be able to take decisions according to the situation and to deliver annihilating hammer blows."[40] This was not the way of Canadian divisional commanders, who tended to be desk bound, planning off the map rather than going forward to see the ground for themselves, assess how their units were faring, and provide leadership. They took their lead from their seniors.

While Simonds spent considerable time with his division commanders, it was because he (rightly) reposed little trust in their tactical competence. His cold, critical presence inspired mainly fear. He commanded forcefully, rather than led. Crerar preferred to stay at his main HQ, generally 60 km (40 miles) from corps HQs, where he involved himself in the details of staff work and frequently had problems distinguishing among the essential, the important, and the trivial. He made forward visits, usually daily, but did not go below corps level. Both Crerar and his HQ lacked experience of actual battle, and in August it showed. His generalship was immature and flawed, being prone to half measures because of a mixture of fear of failure and overoptimism (as well as some dubious British doctrine). The planning of the operation was left largely to Simonds, the man Montgomery would have preferred as army commander. For the most part, Crerar found that he was reduced to being a conduit between Montgomery and Simonds, and he was sometimes bypassed even in that role. His contribution was largely exhortatory, although he did play an important part in obtaining heavy bomber support from the air forces. Both Crerar and Simonds were firmly wedded to British concepts of secure bases and flanks; massive fire plans (including air) to avoid unnecessary casualties; tight, centralized control; and balance—that is, the avoidance of risk as an important principle of combat. Neither displayed a feel for the way battle developed, insisting on sticking to the complex plan and blaming subordinates when that plan went wrong. Simonds, however, would eventually develop a "fingertip feel" for battle, which Crerar never did. Simonds's judgment was both sounder and far more creative.

US First Army: Lieutenant General Hodges. Hodges's first real test as army commander came five days after he assumed command. Ultra gave only a few hours' notice of the beginning of the German counterattack at Mortain, insufficient for any tactical preparation. Bradley and Hodges had been concerned about the threat to Avranches yet, curiously, had missed warning signs in the first of several bouts of overconfidence.[41] From 1 August onward, Ultra had recorded the Germans' dismay at *Seventh Army*'s open flank. Yet Allied generals did not ask themselves why the Germans were taking the risk of fighting so hard west of the river Vire when timely retreat would be the more prudent option (as Montgomery had pointed out in his M516); indeed, as reinforcements arrived at long last from *Fifteenth Army* and more from the south of France, they were fed into the forward battle instead of preparing a fallback line to cover a withdrawal. Nor did the generals pick up the hints provided by intelligence in the first week of August. A series of SIGINT reports on 4–6 August about a growing armored concentration under *XLVII Panzer Corps* on the enemy's left wing should have suggested that the Germans intended to restore the situation by counterattack, especially as fresh infantry divisions were relieving panzer units in the line. Air reconnaissance also detected elements of the counterattack grouping.

Fortunately, First Army was well placed to repulse the blow. The Avranches corridor had already been prudently expanded to a comfortable width, and the high ground around Mortain was firmly occupied. With more than six US divisions (including one French) in or near the battle area and massive air support, the weak, hastily organized, ill-reconnoitered German attack was doomed from the start. The unfussed, efficient reaction by First

Army in harnessing maximum air and artillery support helped VII Corps ensure that the enemy made a minimum of progress. It was clear by early on 8 August that the attack had run out of steam, with Hodges reporting as much. Though the possibility of renewal could not be discounted, it was clear that without surprise and substantial reinforcements, which were simply not available, the German counteroffensive had culminated. Now badly unbalanced, damaged, and crippled logistically, and with command and control becoming increasingly precarious, the Germans were vulnerable to further Allied attacks.

At the higher operational level, the Allies were determined to exploit the Germans' open southern flank by executing an encirclement of the attack grouping to close the pocket on the line of the Falaise-Argentan road. At his lower level, however, Hodges seemed slow to exploit the same vulnerability. Frontal pressure was exerted against the main strength of the German grouping all the way from Vire round to Mortain and Barenton, rather than conducting primarily pinning attacks and economy of force measures while pulling formations out of the line and sending them, as fast as possible, round the German left. In fact, V Corps and then XIX Corps were not redeployed until they were pinched out by the British advance across their front. Similarly, VII Corps attacked into the strongest part of *LVII Panzer Corps* until 12 August when, pinched out by XIX Corps' advance, it started to sideslip 4 and then 9 Infantry Divisions to the southeast. Meanwhile, 1 Infantry and much of 3 Armored Divisions waited in the Mayenne area and were not committed to a thrust on the Domfront-Flers axis until a week later, on 13 August, by which time the Germans' withdrawal had apparently started. Hodges presumably wished to wait until he could launch a powerful, concentrated, flank-secured VII Corps in a northerly direction. This gave the enemy the breathing space he badly needed to adjust his dispositions. It also rendered nugatory the mobility advantage enjoyed by the Americans (enhanced by mastery of the air, which inhibited enemy maneuver) and thus sacrificed the tempo of which the American forces were capable and which would have kept the enemy off balance. Moreover, it delayed closing the gap between First Army and XV Corps, attacking on the Alençon-Argentan axis. Instead of putting maximum effort into attacking where the enemy was absent, into his flank and rear to disrupt the defense, Hodges preferred head-on attacks into strength over ground favorable to the defense and improved by mining. The casualty rate from 6 to 11 August was over 1,000 per day, with a peak of 1,796.

Had relations between Hodges and his allies been more collaborative than competitive, he could have sought to take advantage of British Second Army's early success in Operation Bluecoat. The Americans' V and XIX Corps had been making heavy weather of their advance on Vire until the British advance compelled *XLVII Panzer Corps* to withdraw from Tessy-sur-Vire on 31 July; by 2 August, the critical town itself was defenseless against attack by VIII Corps from the north. Hodges could have welcomed a British seizure of this important road centre and thrust into the flank of the enemy opposing his army's advance; then he could have used the opportunity to shift his focus to the right to further unbalance the Germans. Later on, he refused Crerar's eminently sensible offer of an exchange of liaison officers and information as elements of First US and Canadian Armies closed on Trun-Chambois, raising the specter of fratricidal clashes. It was perhaps typical, and certainly small-minded, to take refuge in bureaucratic excuses to explain his noncooperation. Hodges was understandably angry at Leclerc's persistent avoidance of his orders and importunate demands to be allowed to liberate Paris, but he seemed not to appreciate that, while under his command, the Frenchman presented a special case. As the senior military representative of an ally, he could not be disciplined or ordered around as if he were an American. When he had to do so, however, Hodges could work with his allies. The complicated work of coordinating with Second British Army and its XXX Corps to disentangle American and British forces after the former had taken Elbeuf and the latter had closed up to the army group boundary was accomplished efficiently and relatively smoothly.

By 16 August, Bradley had decided to hand over American responsibilities for closing the pocket to First Army. The subsequent mix-up between V Corps and the provisional corps at Argentan and the slow resumption of attacks northward were due to Bradley, not Hodges. The latter was presiding over the complex and impressive maneuver of XIX Corps from the army's left to the extreme right wing and the start of its attack on the Elbeuf axis. However, the advance of both XIX and XV Corps to the west of the Seine was, at 7 to 8 km (4 to 5 miles) per day, not fast enough, given the weakness and disorganization of the enemy, and it was too slow to trap the remnants of the two pocketed German armies. Army HQ had considerable communications problems as a result of the great distances involved, but it is hard not to conclude that Hodges failed to press his subordinates (as Patton did) to eschew plodding, deliberate methods in favor of improvisation, vigor, and risk taking. This was certainly not because he did not go forward to assess the situation for himself. Early in the campaign, he frequently visited corps and division commanders (although such forays tailed off as time went on). His presence, however, was not inspirational; indeed, his incessant worrying about detail made such visits something to be endured rather than welcomed. His absence did not mean that his subordinates were left to execute their missions as they saw fit. Hodges had little trust in any of his commanders, save for Collins at VII Corps. He demanded minutiae in reporting that was more appropriate to an HQ one or two levels below army, and he issued detailed, prescriptive orders. He was another commander who could not live comfortably with the chaos of war.

Hodges has frequently been referred to as the US Army's foremost tactician. Unfortunately, he did not rise above tactics to become a practitioner of operational art. First Army's war diary has a revealing entry for 30 July: "General Hodges . . . felt since the beginning that too many of these battalions and regiments of ours have tried to flank and skirt and never meet the enemy straight on . . . believing it safer, sounder, and in the end quicker, to keep smashing ahead, without any tricky, uncertain business of possibly exposing yourself to being cut off."[42] He was most comfortable at infantry unit level, conducting attritional battle. Concepts such as surprise, Cobra-like concentration on narrow sectors and economy of force elsewhere, maneuver in which open flanks were an acceptable risk, and clever sequencing of battles were on the margins of his military thought, crowded out by an obsession with a methodical approach and minor tactical details. The idea that battle might best be avoided in favor of maneuver to place the enemy at a disadvantage did not seem to cross his mind. His judgment was suffused with caution, even when boldness would be appropriate, and he lacked the ability to think beyond the current battle. At best, Hodges was a competent plodder and a safe if uninspiring manager. Neither professional growth nor imagination and flair had qualified him to command an army by August 1944.

US Third Army: Lieutenant General Patton. The principal mission originally envisaged for Third Army had been the capture of the Brittany ports. Even though this had been reduced from an army to a corps task, Patton set about it in a typically bold but not foolhardy fashion, given the enemy's weakness and Allied air supremacy. Dispensing with phase lines, intermediate objectives, and other appurtenances of linear battle, he instructed his armored division and corps commanders to bypass opposition and seize distant objectives without fretting about their flanks. Though striving to achieve his assigned operational goal, Patton, like Montgomery, had doubts about the operational idea from the outset. He questioned whether Brittany had become a distraction, given the opportunities opening up to the east. Like Montgomery, Patton favored a long hook round the open southern flank to trap the enemy at the Seine. This demonstrated a sound appreciation of the operational situation and an instinctive feel for the way it was developing. He was accordingly delighted when Bradley, on Montgomery's prompting, limited the Brittany operation to a single corps and directed the main body of Third Army in the general direction of Paris.

Haislip was imbued with Patton's way of warfare. His XV Corps advanced from the Fougères-Vitré area to Le Mans at 30 km (nearly 20 miles) per day, placing it in a favorable position to execute Bradley's post-Mortain idea of a short hook. Patton (like Montgomery) had doubts about the northward swing from Le Mans, though. He believed the original long envelopment to the Seine would have a better chance of trapping significant German forces. Given the superior mobility and mastery of the air enjoyed by the Allies, he was probably right. However, he implemented Bradley's instructions with his customary vigor. When ordered north, XV Corps moved more than 25 km (15 miles) per day to Argentan, 10 km (6 miles) beyond the army group boundary. This tempo in the advance scattered the few forces the Germans could muster to oppose it before they could organize into an effective delay force. It wrecked the remains of the logistic organization of *Seventh Army* and massively disrupted its command and control, placing the whole army in considerable peril. The very speed of the American advance brought security. The enemy was given no time to redeploy against it, even if sufficient forces had been available and had been able to move expeditiously (neither condition pertained, given the unrelenting pressure exerted by the other three armies and the omnipresent Allied fighter-bombers).[43] However, Patton was mindful of the need for concentration, as XV Corps was being placed across the line of retreat of a major enemy grouping. Before the operational focus was unexpectedly changed, he had intended to send XX Corps (reinforced by 4 Armored Division from Brittany) north on Haislip's left to partially fill the gap between First and Third Armies. But he would not risk losing the initiative by slowing the tempo of his operations to wait for Walker to come up. He ordered Haislip to continue this advance north from Argentan, believing, probably correctly, that XV Corps could take Falaise before the Canadians, stalled since 10 August, could do so. Patton was correspondingly irritated by Bradley's vacillation when the stop order was issued. The principle of maintenance of the aim had been jettisoned because of, he wrongly believed, British jealousy or ignorance of the situation as well as Bradley's fears.[44]

Thwarted at Argentan, Patton was nevertheless determined to maintain unrelenting offensive action to prevent German recovery and the reestablishment of a viable defense. He believed the best course of action was a reversion to the long envelopment, and he urged this course on Bradley. Receiving permission to head east again with part of XV Corps and all of XX and XII Corps (the latter now to include 4 Armored Division), he again stressed the preemptive value of speed. The rate of advance to Dreux, Chartres, and Orléans, establishing bridgeheads over the Eure, was at least 35 to 50 km (20 to 30 miles) per day (although it took two days to completely clear the latter two cities).[45] Then Bradley, who was assailed by doubts, according to Patton, again applied the brakes. After a two-day halt, XV Corps was allowed to advance 40 km (25 miles) to Mantes-Gassicourt and (with Bradley's reluctant consent) establish a bridgehead over the Seine; the task was accomplished in two days. Then on 21 August the brakes were taken off and XX and XII

Corps advanced at 25 to 40 km (15 to 25 miles) per day to force the Seine at Melun and Troyes, taking the bridges intact. These were spectacular rates of advance, and Patton, always looking forward to the next operation, was determined to establish bridgeheads over any obstacle he reached, not merely stop on it. Any chance the Germans might have had of establishing a defense along the Seine was forestalled.

Bradley deprecated Third Army's achievement. In his memoirs he wrote:

> But while the world gaped over the speed of Patton's spectacular advance to the Seine, it was Hodges's almost anonymous First Army that sweated through the laborious in-fighting against the Falaise pocket. . . . Patton measured his successes in miles; Hodges in enemy dead. . . . If casualties offer an index to the rigors and ordeals of combat . . . First Army can claim to have borne the brunt of our advance. . . . First Army suffered 19,000 casualties . . . almost twice the number sustained by Third Army on the enemy's open flank.[46]

In so writing, Bradley suggests a clear bias toward the traditional American approach of grinding the enemy down through frontal attacks in overwhelming force. This illustrates his imperfect grasp of the potential payoff from operational maneuver. It is true that the conditions for Patton's success were set by the other three armies fixing the bulk of the enemy force, enabling his maneuver. It is also true that mere occupation of ground is seldom worthwhile as an end in itself. However, Third Army's seizure of terrain contributed decisively to the physical destruction of the enemy, even when centres of resistance were bypassed, as was Third Army's wont. Patton's deep and rapid advance netted a claimed 73,000 prisoners by the end of August, almost twice the number taken by the Allies in the Falaise pocket. More important, it dealt a fatal blow to the logistic infrastructure of *Seventh Army*. It severely disrupted the command and control of the enemy's major formations (e.g., by causing the precipitate flight of *Seventh Army* HQ from Le Mans and of *Army Group B*'s from near Mantes). It preempted the possibility of the Germans forming a succession of depth defense or even delay lines, up to and including the Seine. It demoralized their forces and commanders. And it created conditions for the physical destruction through encirclement of the entire Normandy grouping.

Patton displayed greater operational vision than his army group commander. He was quick to recognize the error of committing too strong a force to Brittany in pursuit of the outdated Overlord plan. Instead, he (like Montgomery) envisaged a long envelopment to destroy the enemy on the Seine. He believed in a concentrated effort and was frustrated by Bradley's insistence on guarding against illusory threats at the expense of the main effort. He was less convinced than Bradley about the wisdom of going for a short hook in the changed circumstances of the German defeat at Mortain; if the Germans had reacted more quickly and initiated an earlier withdrawal, too many would have escaped. However, Patton threw himself boldly into the new maneuver. Whether the envelopment was short or long, the key to its success would be speed in execution to keep the enemy off balance, in a reactive posture, and always a step behind. He saw that speed, and the surprise it engendered, could be used as a weapon in maneuver warfare. When Bradley terminated XV Corps' drive north but allowed much of XV, XX, and XII Corps to thrust eastward to the Dreux-Chartres-Orléans line, Patton renewed the suggestion of a wheel down the river to seal German exits from Normandy over the Seine. In doing so, Patton was keeping the operational aim firmly in mind: destruction of the enemy, rather than the mere conquest of territory. The same is true of his 23 August suggestion for yet another envelopment, this time on the Beauvais axis. It was not Patton's fault that Bradley fumbled the opportunity to complete both the short envelopment and then the long one.[47]

Patton has often been criticized for his reckless conduct of offensive operations. This accusation, leveled by those who were still thinking in terms of the tempo achievable by infantrymen on foot, was unfounded in Normandy. Although he saw that speed in the advance would be the main protection for open flanks, he employed forces where necessary (the minimum possible). For instance, on 2 August he dispatched 5 Armored Division to protect the flanks of both VIII and VII Corps during the breakout into Brittany. When XV Corps was moving alone into the enemy flank on the Le Mans–Argentan thrust, he sought security by having the corps advance two-up, with two divisions trailing and thus ready to drive into the flank of any enemy attempting to exploit the first echelon's flank. (This was his favorite operational formation.) He also had 80 Infantry Division deploy in a screening role between Mayenne and Le Mans, and before the halt order led to a change in operational focus, he had intended to commit XX Corps into the gap—offensively, of course. When his army's main thrust was redirected toward the Seine after the short hook was stopped, the axes of his corps' advance were within mutually supporting reach. However, Patton deprecated overinsurance, as he rightly interpreted Bradley's demand for ground forces on the Loire flank and the overly long retention of 6 Armored Division in Brittany; sufficient security could be derived from demolished bridges covered by FFI elements and IX Tactical Air Command and Ultra's early warning. In general, he thought that Bradley, like Hodges, was too cautious, too conservative, insufficiently appreciative of the fact that flanks could look after themselves if the enemy was unbalanced, and thus unable to exploit theoretical vulnerabilities.[48]

Patton was unique among Eisenhower's principal subordinates in being prepared to accept, even welcome, the chaos of a fast-moving war. Others attempted to impose order and tidiness on the battlefield and were continuously concerned about operational security. Patton preferred to remind himself of his own maxim not to take counsel of his fears; he always pondered what he could do to the enemy, not what the enemy could do to him. This sangfroid stemmed from an unusually keen, instinctive understanding of and feel for the battlefield, as well as his grasp of the devastating potential of maneuver and speed in the advance. It also reflected his grasp of another demand of generalship at the operational level. He was concerned not with *how* to beat the enemy tactically—that was the task of his subordinates—but with *where* to beat him in order to gain positional and temporal advantage. Patton was not one to pore over the large-scale maps so beloved by his fellow army commanders.

Army Group and Theatre Level

The first of August brought two major changes to the Normandy campaign. Montgomery's operational idea of fixing the enemy on the left and breaking through on the right finally came to fruition. Third Army was out of the Cotentin Peninsula and the *bocage* and was free to advance west, south, or east with no immediate, organized opposition to overcome. And with the activation of 12 Army Group, the Americans were no longer directly under Montgomery's command. While he remained the temporary head of the land forces (a position Eisenhower intended to assume himself on 1 September), he was in practice only a primus inter pares. Bradley was now a fellow army group commander, with a larger and still growing force under him and a much closer relationship with the Supreme Commander. Bradley's view of the relationship was clear:

> I had not [earlier] asked to be freed from Montgomery's British Group command. He had neither limited our authority nor had he given us directives that might have caused us to chafe. As long as Montgomery permitted this latitude in US operations, we were content to remain under his command until the tactical situation necessitated a change. . . . Until SHAEF was permanently established in France Eisenhower directed that Monty would act as his agent, exercising temporary operational control over the US Army Group. The Briton's authority would be limited primarily to coordination and the settlement of boundaries between our Groups. Despite this delegation of powers to Monty, Eisenhower would captain the team. . . . After having granted me so free a hand as an army commander, there was no reason to believe that Monty would now curtail me at Army Group.[49]

The sudden collapse of the German western flank took the Allied commanders by surprise. How should they continue the campaign, now that the original plan had suddenly become obsolete? There was now no need for a plodding expansion of the Overlord lodgment area south to the Loire and east to the Seine, no need to open the ports in Brittany, and no need for an operational pause to allow a steady logistic and force buildup for the next stage, the march on Germany. The stated aim of theatre strategy remained the destruction of the German armed forces and an advance into the heart of Germany. How should this be achieved in the light of these changed operational circumstances (including the successful Allied attack on the enemy's southern flank, which began on 15 August with landings on the French Riviera)? Where should the main effort now lie? Which offensive action should be supporting, and where should economy of force be practiced? How could surprise continue to be achieved and prolonged to keep the enemy wrong-footed? What security measures would be necessary during exploitation to ensure that the enemy could not recover the initiative? What steps would be needed to obtain close cooperation among armies, army groups, and air forces and ensure that their combined achievements were more than the sum of their individual parts? How could logistic sustainability be ensured for weeks and months to come, now that the operational pause originally envisaged to allow for a buildup would no longer take place? Senior operational commanders and staffs would have to address all these questions in August if the campaign were to come to a rapid, complete, and triumphal conclusion. The opportunity was there. How well did Montgomery, Bradley, and Eisenhower grasp it?

21 Army Group and Land Forces Command: General Montgomery. Montgomery was the first senior commander to appreciate that the suddenness and completeness of the breakthrough had changed the operational calculus of the campaign. Completion of the Overlord lodgment west to Brittany's shores, south to the Loire, and east to the Seine could be done concurrently rather than consecutively because Brittany was now largely defenseless, having been denuded of troops to feed the battle for Normandy.[50] The contingency foreseen in SHAEF's Lucky Strike option had come to pass, and its concept could be adopted. On 1 August, after discussing the situation with Bradley and Dempsey, Montgomery directed the former to limit operations in the province to a single corps (he would have sent a smaller force, but SHAEF logisticians insisted that the ports would still be needed). Bradley was to make Third Army's main effort a wheel toward Paris; this would be aided by an airborne operation in the Chartres area to cut the enemy's line of retreat. The success of this long envelopment, an idea already mooted by 21 Army Group planners as early as 10 July, would clearly depend on fixing the bulk of the enemy forces and preventing them from establishing a viable fallback line of defense. Montgomery was already setting these conditions. US First Army was ordered to swing eastward, Second Army was already knocking away the hinge of one potential line on the Le Bény-Bocage–Mt. Pinçon ridge, and the Canadians would soon deal with another in their attack on Falaise, ordered on 3 August.

Montgomery formalized and elaborated his ideas in his M516 directive of 4 August, promulgated after discussion with Eisenhower and Bradley. Correctly, he wrote that the enemy front was "in such a state that it could be made to disintegrate completely." If the Germans devoted sufficient forces to holding firmly on their right flank in the Caen sector, they would be unable to restore their left wing (now open for about 130 km [80 miles] from Mortain to the Loire). If they attempted to build up their left, they would find their right collapsed by the upcoming Canadian attack toward Falaise (to be mounted no later than 8 August); this attack would preclude an enemy delaying action on the substantial obstacle of the Orne and might trap significant elements. The only course open to the enemy, he opined, was to execute "an orderly, staged withdrawal to the River Seine." Montgomery wanted to ensure that the withdrawal was neither orderly nor deliberate. If possible, he wanted to convert retreat into rout, giving the enemy no opportunity to carry out a scorched-earth policy in the vacated area and, especially, preventing the same type of destruction of the Seine ports that had left Cherbourg handling only 80 percent of its planned capacity as late as 4 August (thirty-five days after its surrender). Accordingly, minimal forces would be devoted to Brittany, as "the main business lies to the east." The whole Allied force would press the Germans back to the Seine, with Patton's army exploiting their open flank to conduct a long envelopment to expedite the process. The enemy would be crushed on the obstacle.

Montgomery's appreciation was logical—but wrong. As happens so often in war, the enemy chose the one course of action that had not been considered—on this occasion, because of its likely disastrous consequences for the Germans. The Allies were fashioning a noose, and the enemy, obligingly, placed his head in it by mounting the Avranches counterattack. After discussing the matter with Eisenhower, Bradley proposed the short hook on 8 August as a variant on Montgomery's operational idea. The latter willingly adopted it, at least provisionally, with the proviso that the long envelopment option be retained in case a speedy junction could not be achieved in the Falaise-Argentan area.

In the early days of August, Montgomery displayed sound operational judgment and, at the same time, flexibility in his approach. He kept the principal aim firmly in mind: destruction of the enemy's main forces. Territorial gains, even those that were central to the Overlord plan, such as the Brittany ports, were secondary considerations; they would be achieved, sooner or later, with the enemy's elimination. The implied gamble—that sufficient Channel port capacity could be taken quickly—was worthwhile, given that delay in taking the ports would be no worse than waiting for the Brittany alternatives, and at least the Channel ports were considerably nearer to Germany. Relentless offensive action was to be maintained, with an emphasis on hitting the enemy where he was most vulnerable, on his weak flank. This would retain the initiative, prolong the effects of surprise, and keep the enemy off balance. It was, however, debatable whether there was a sufficiently clear delineation of main and supporting efforts, both within the land forces as a whole and within 21 Army Group, and the consequent requirements for concentration. It is, of course, arguable that such distinctions carried less weight during pursuit, when attacking all along the front is more justified than when the enemy is balanced and in the possession of reserves. An economy of force approach was obviously intended for Brittany.

Unfortunately, Montgomery appeared to lose some focus and clarity of purpose as the month wore on. By unexpectedly switching 21 Army Group's attack from the left to right flank at the end of July, he had achieved surprise and sufficient concentration to make gains on an axis and at a time that greatly helped the development of the Americans' Cobra offensive. However, Second Army's attack had definitely culminated by 11 August at the latest, despite its reinforcement by an infantry division and an armored brigade a week before. Moreover, with the adoption of the short encirclement, the main effort clearly should have shifted back to the east. If Canadian First Army's attack to close the pocket at Argentan from the north were to succeed quickly, it needed weight. This point was emphasized when Operation Totalize ran out of steam by 10 August, when it was still more than 30 km (18 miles) short of the town. It would be renewed under the new designation Tractable on 14 August, a day after XV Corps reached Argentan (and six days after the German effort at Mortain failed). That day, too, Montgomery directed that in addition to taking Falaise, the offensive would be extended almost 20 km (12 miles) to the east to include Trun. The next day, offensive action would also be mounted by I Corps, which was to attack toward Lisieux, 40 km (25 miles) due east of Caen. Thus, First Canadian Army would be responsible for approximately 60 km (40 miles) of frontage and attacks on two divergent axes.

The preponderance of 21 Army Group's strength still lay with Second Army, even though it had only about half the frontage of First Canadian Army and its attacks, if effective, would drive the enemy out of the trap being set by the latter. In the middle of the month, Dempsey had six infantry and three armored divisions and four independent armored brigades; Crerar had four infantry, a small airborne, and two armored divisions and three brigades. Not until 15 August was one division sent from Dempsey's Second to Crerar's First Canadian, and that was the sum total of the shift of emphasis (even though two other divisions were out of the line, resting). Montgomery told Dempsey to move his main effort to his left flank, to support XII Corps' drive on Falaise, but that was an inadequate response to the problem, given the nature of the terrain it had to cross and the limited number of routes and deployment room. First Canadian Army was plainly overtasked, and the limited help it received from its right was barely a palliative.

Montgomery must therefore take considerable responsibility for the failure to seal the Falaise pocket in good time and in adequate strength, whether in the Falaise-Argentan area or the Trun area. Crerar could have made good use of another corps HQ and four to five divisions or brigades to widen and accelerate his offensive southward. It is possible, of course, that Montgomery never really believed in the short hook idea or that he became disillusioned by the slow, halting nature of the Canadian advance and was therefore unwilling to invest heavily in it. It is noticeable that, when meeting with Bradley and Dempsey on 11 August, he did not suggest an alternative method of closing the pocket—shifting the army group boundary northward and calling for a reinforced US First Army effort in an attack north from Argentan. His M518 of that date certainly suggested doubts about the short encirclement and a renewed interest in the long envelopment, "should it appear likely that the enemy may escape us here."

If he had really given up on the short hook, he should have put more combat power into the northern wing of the deep envelopment on a general Mezidon-Lisieux-Rouen axis to play his part in sealing German exits over the Seine. The very weak and increasingly overextended *LXXXVI Corps* would not have been able seriously to delay a force more than twice as strong as the I Corps drive. Moreover, he could have contemplated an airborne operation on the east bank of the Seine to interrupt *Fifth Panzer Army*'s resupply and escape routes and establish bridgeheads for a subsequent advance to the north. Montgomery failed to recognize that, even before the middle of August, Second Army had become an operational backwater, and decisive effect could be achieved only on 21 Army Group's left. This failure to assess priorities correctly was a serious lapse in judgment.

It is, of course, appropriate for a land forces or army group commander to be less concerned with current operations than with the big picture and the development of optimal concepts for the next one or even two operations. Thus, from his 17 August conference with Bradley until the end of the month, Montgomery was increasingly preoccupied with shaping the post-Normandy campaign according to his preferred course of action. Already afflicted with "victory disease"— the belief that whatever the Germans salvaged from the wreck of *Army Group B* would be of no future significance—he regarded the ongoing battle as having a foregone conclusion that required no further input from him. In lobbying to get his way in the next round of the game, he took his eye off the ball in the current round. Given his subordinates' dependence on his guidance—a reliance he had assiduously fostered—this proved unfortunate. His armies pursued territorial gains, not the destruction of the enemy, and they did so with habitual caution and only a moderate expenditure of effort (and therefore casualties). Similarly, he allowed the air forces to lose the correct focus for their activities; interdiction on the Seine was largely dropped in favor of deeper missions, allowing the Germans to carry out crossings in broad daylight. The long envelopment fell short of annihilating the enemy.

Most of the desirable attributes of command are evident in Montgomery's handling of the climax of the Normandy campaign. However, his character prevented him from being a good coalition commander or, in many ways, even a good subordinate. He had a natural talent for getting people's backs up, especially the Americans'. He did make an effort to deal with his US ally with more sensitivity and less arrogance than a year or even a month or two earlier (i.e., before his prestige, and with it his security of tenure, had been shaken by the Goodwood failure). This, for instance, was apparently the cause of his sudden and arbitrary change of the inter–army group boundary on 1 August, preventing VIII British Corps from taking the important and defenseless town of Vire.[51] Later he handled Bradley with admirable tact, consulting him before issuing directives, and he exhibited patience and discretion in view of Bradley's vacillations. Montgomery was also reasonably patient with and supportive of Crerar, although the latter had no doubt that his army group commander wanted to replace him, ideally with Simonds. Certainly Montgomery had small faith in Crerar's abilities and reposed much greater trust in Dempsey. Alas, it was impossible to erase the negative perceptions built up since the campaign in Tunisia eighteen months before. Most Americans, including his Supreme Commander and especially his fellow army group commander, had developed a strong distaste for Montgomery's arrogance, his refusal to admit error, and his style of discussion, which always sounded didactic at best and insufferably patronizing at worst. Characteristically, he did not understand the antipathy generated by his manner and dogmatism until post-Normandy operations were well under way. This failure would have unfortunate repercussions.

It is possible that his distrust of Crerar dissuaded Montgomery from reinforcing First Canadian Army to the level required by its necessarily enhanced role beginning on 8 August. If that is the case, then he allowed prejudice to distort his understanding of the operational situation (including the unfortunate truth that a less experienced or less able subordinate often needs more resources to accomplish a mission than a more gifted colleague would require). Certainly, his insight, professional judgment, and flexibility were deficient in the critical last three weeks of August.

Montgomery was frequently criticized by Americans for his excessive caution. Though he was generally risk averse (and not without reason), this criticism was not wholly justified. It is perhaps easy to note the deliberate, often plodding tactical methods favored by the British and extrapolate an equal lack of operational imagination and risk taking (as there had been in North Africa and Italy). However, Montgomery's early modification of the Overlord plan was audacious, especially logistically, as well as decisive and perceptive. So, to an extent, was the concept of the long envelopment, and he always approved of Patton's bold, sweeping advances, whereas Bradley expressed concern and suggested the desirability of pauses. In September Montgomery would display a daring that the uncharitable could describe as rash, but other than that, he rarely departed from the tried, tested, and conventional. It can be argued, of course, that, given the Allies' overwhelming strength, there was no need for risk taking—but that would overlook the fact that greater operational daring might have brought an earlier victory at less cost and with a more advantageous postwar political situation.

12 Army Group: Lieutenant General Bradley. Bradley's elevation to command of the newly activated army group could not have come at a more promising or challenging time. The development of Operation Cobra had created the longed-for breakout, ending weeks of semistalemate, and Third Army was about to enter the fray to exploit. Bradley was not as quick as Montgomery to conclude that Brittany was now a less critical objective and, in fact, one that was unlikely to pay a worthwhile dividend if the Cherbourg experience was any guide. By 3 August, though, the ease with which 79 Division had executed its flank-defensive deployment to Fougères had convinced him that XV Corps could push southeast to the Mayenne River. He was soon receptive to the idea of only a minimal deployment into Brittany and a Third Army drive on the Seine, as propounded in Montgomery's M516.

There is little doubt that Patton could have closed on the Seine in plenty of time to seal the river against retreating German forces. After all, XV Corps could have advanced from Le Mans to reach Mantes-Gassicourt in a mere six days or less, had it not been diverted north and thereafter received two stop orders. From Mantes it could have turned north up the east bank, perhaps to link up with an airborne corps drop on its lower stretch (north of Louviers or Elbeuf). The rest of Third Army, reinforced at the expense of First Army, would form the inner southern wing of encirclement and strike into the flank of the retreating Germans. Any attempted breakout would be unlikely to succeed in the face of superior American mobility, armored strength, and airpower, not to mention British and First Army pressure to fix the defenders. While First Army would lose a corps to Third Army in this scenario, it could have assumed control of VIII Corps operations in Brittany as a replacement.

The concept of the short hook, born of the Germans' colossal error of judgment when they attacked at Mortain, also had some merit. It was a "shallower and surer move," as Bradley described it, and it would not strain the logistic system as much as the long one would. It was undoubtedly less radical than the envelopment at the Seine and perhaps more likely to fail. If the enemy perceived his peril in good time and reacted expeditiously (which was likely), he might well succeed in pulling most of his forces the 60 km (40 miles) back over the Orne before XV Corps could advance the 80 km (50 miles) from Le Mans to Argentan—assuming *I SS Panzer Corps* could prevent a reasonably brisk Canadian advance of 50 km (30 miles) from Caen to Argentan. This plan also ignored the fact that the continuing attacks by First and Second Armies would, if successful, drive the enemy out of the pocket before it was fully formed. In the event, however, the Germans, thanks to Hitler, were very slow to respond to the threatened encirclement; this failure was offset by the poor progress of the Canadians, who took nine days to advance just under 30 km (18 miles). Many Americans unfairly blamed Montgomery's perennial caution, but Patton was convinced, correctly, that XV Corps could have pressed on to Falaise to close the pocket if it had not been denied permission to do so by Bradley. The latter produced various unconvincing rationalizations for his 13 August stop order: the sacrosanct nature of the army group boundary (which had already been crossed and was clearly negotiable); reluctance to take Falaise for fearing of offending British sensibilities (risible); the fear of a fratricidal meeting between Americans and their allies (avoidable with good staff cooperation, Phantom patrols, and special liaison officers and, in practice, a nonproblem at Chambois and later on the Seine); and, contradictorily, the idea that too many German formations had already escaped (not what most intelligence was reporting at the time). The true reason was his preference "for a solid shoulder at Argentan to the possibility of a broken neck at Falaise. . . . Nineteen German divisions [*sic*] were now stampeding to escape the trap," and Haislip's corps would not have been able to hold them.[52] XV Corps would transition to the defense, relinquishing the role of hammer for one of anvil while waiting for the Canadians to turn up. If the encirclement failed, it would not be Bradley's fault.

The fact that XV Corps was somewhat out on a limb actually *was* Bradley's fault. His short hook scheme of maneuver was not part of a holistic army group plan. It merely involved a change of axis for some of Third Army. He should have ordered First Army to ease up on its frontal attacks to create a new attack grouping, based on 1 Infantry and 3 Armored Divisions, which were already in the Mayenne area; this grouping then should have attacked as early as possible on the la Ferté axis to close the gap with Haislip, strengthen his flank, and broaden the threat to the enemy's. This was not done in a timely fashion, and Bradley would not yet countenance the release of 4 and 6 Armored from Brittany or the early return of 35 Division to Patton. Worse, he dispatched the two pinched-out infantry divisions of V Corps to besiege Brest, more than 300 km (185 miles) to the west, despite previously acknowledging the greatly reduced relevance of Brittany operations and the need to concentrate on destroying the enemy in Normandy.

Actually, by 13 August, VII Corps was belatedly advancing from Mayenne and meeting so little resistance that its progress was rapid; by the next day, it would close the gap to a mere 10 km (6 miles). This ought to have caused Bradley to rethink the stop order. So too should have the available intelligence, most of which indicated that the enemy had not begun a major withdrawal. The Germans had been contemplating a counterattack to the southeast, but their command and control was patchy, their logistic situation was dire, their every daylight move was subject to air attack, and their armored strength was reduced to fewer than eighty tanks and SP guns, all of which Bradley knew. With well over 500 tanks and tank destroyers, superior artillery, and abundant air support, not to mention elements of XX Corps behind it and VII Corps coming up fast on its left, was XV Corps really in mortal danger of being "trampled . . . in the onrush"?

In vetoing a further offensive American role in the short hook, Bradley was, as Patton would have put it, "taking counsel of his fears." Whether or not the judgment was correct, it was surely wrong of Bradley not to discuss one of the most critical decisions of the Normandy campaign and its implications and alternative courses of action with his land forces commander when he met with Montgomery and Dempsey just after noon on 13 August. Instead, prompted by a frustrated Patton, he plumped the next day for a reversion to the march on the Seine by half of XV Corps and all of XX and XII Corps. Their six divisions set off at ninety degrees to the northerly axis agreed on with Montgomery, and by 16 August, Patton had four divisions in the Dreux-Chartres area and another two approaching Orléans. Bradley was presumably embarrassed when, on 15 August, Montgomery proposed a new junction for the Canadians and Americans at Trun, as well as continuing with the long hook. By this time, only three divisions were left in the Argentan area. In implementing his part of this renewed attack, Bradley so confused the arrangements for command and control that it went in only on 18 August—five days after a stronger blow could have been delivered against a weaker enemy, and two days after the Germans had been allowed to begin a full-scale retreat (untroubled, since 17 August, by Allied air attack, now that the pocket was too small to allow the drawing of bomb lines)."

Bradley seemingly alternated between boldness and doubt, between force-oriented and terrain goals. His vacillation resulted in a dispersal of effort, with no clear operational focus. At the decisive place in mid-August—the Argentan area—there were only three divisions out of his immediately available eighteen, and only one of these managed to advance far enough to link up with the Canadians. Bradley's hasty, poorly thought-out improvisations had dissipated his forces and thus condemned his own proposal—the short hook—to at least partial failure as enemy forces belatedly flooded through the open neck of the pocket.[53]

The long envelopment had not been invalidated by the short alternative, however. Had Bradley been single-mindedly focused on the primary aim of destroying the German forces, he could have proposed a thrust up both sides of the Seine to Rouen or beyond (as Patton wanted), possibly augmented by an airborne corps assault on key crossing sites. XV and XX Corps could have executed such a maneuver, with XIX Corps from First Army following and refused to the left (the same switch from one flank to another it would perform slightly later). Meanwhile, XII Corps could have established additional Seine crossings in the Paris area, reinforced in time by VII Corps, thus setting the conditions for a subsequent march on Germany. The Germans could not muster any serious force to stop such a powerful Third Army attack into their rear. Such a decision would have had the additional merit of putting the main effort under the command of the most thrusting, maneuver-minded of the Allied commanders (though it would have necessitated some reshuffling of command responsibilities). With *Seventh* and *Fifth Panzer Armies* annihilated west of the Seine, there would be nothing of significance (save for sacrificial port-fortress garrisons) to prevent the Allies from picking up territorial gains in any direction. There is little doubt that Montgomery would have endorsed such a plan with enthusiasm (especially if it would have committed large American forces in the direction he favored for post-Normandy operations). Patton's Beauvais maneuver would have done this, which was presumably the reason behind Bradley's refusal to countenance it.

Thus, through belated doubts about his short hook proposal, Bradley need not have awarded the Germans an opportunity to rescue something from the wreck of *Seventh* and *Fifth Panzer Armies*. His conduct of operations became no more decisive, however, in following the new course of action. He imposed a second, two-day operational pause on Third Army when nothing of significance lay in front of it. He sanctioned the establishment of a XV Corps divisional bridgehead over the Seine at Mantes-Gassicourt only reluctantly, and he made no use of it to develop the offensive northwestward to destroy the Germans' crossing means and their reception centres on the right bank. He devoted only four divisions to the attack up the left bank. The rest of First Army and Third Army (less the now reinforced VIII Corps in Brittany) were switched from the task of encircling and destroying the enemy to that of forcing and then advancing from the Seine above Paris and taking the city. Bradley preferred seizing ground to decisive operational maneuver. He had lost sight of the stated aim of Operation Overlord: destruction of the German forces. He was happy to own up to this, even in retrospect. In his memoirs he wrote of the thrust up the left bank: "Had we not turned that pincer to Dempsey's aid, we could have swept far east of Paris for more spectacular gains in terrain. But once again we were willing to forego ground in an effort to kill Germans."[54] Presumably afflicted by victory disease, believing that the enemy in Normandy was finished, his focus had already shifted to post-Overlord operations, and his sights were set on an advance to Germany by the shortest route. This would explain why he peremptorily rejected Patton's 23 August proposal for a Third Army thrust northward to try yet again to pocket the fleeing Germans, this time in the area from Beauvais to the Channel (another proposal he did not see fit to discuss with his land forces commander).

Yet even the eastward thrust was pursued only in fits and starts. This was partly the result of Bradley's ever-present concern about possible enemy countermoves and partly because of the logistic pinch that was beginning to be felt at the front. A transport shortage produced fuel supply constraints, which had already contributed to the pause imposed on Patton's eastward pursuit. As it happened, on this occasion the Germans derived little benefit from this gift of time, as they had utterly inadequate forces with which to restore the front. However, Bradley was flouting a principle when he checked a successful advance to maintain the efforts of another formation that was largely involved in an attritional grind. Logistic problems would rapidly become worse until, within a week or two, they would temporarily close down much of 12 Army Group's offensive effort.[55] The sure and certain knowledge that this was going to happen should have been a powerful argument in favor of completely destroying the enemy forces in Normandy before pursuing distant objectives.

Bradley did not adjust quickly to his step-up from army to army group. Somewhat pedestrian competence at the lower level was insufficient at the higher. He lacked imagination and breadth of operational vision, responding instead to the ideas of others (mostly Montgomery and Patton). This was probably one reason for his failure to pursue a single aim consistently. He was a naturally cautious commander possessed of limited insightfulness and foresight, and he lacked the ability to put himself in the enemy's shoes. Consequently, he persistently overestimated German capabilities, especially their ability to inflict damaging counterblows. Threats, such as the putative *Fifth Panzer Army* attack southeast to escape the pocket or the attack from south of the Loire against either Third Army's flank or into Brittany, were allowed to delay or prevent action. They were invariably greatly exaggerated or even illusory. These traits contributed to his reluctance to commit wholeheartedly to a single concept of operations and to his frequent vacillations. He would embark on a course of action and then be assailed with doubts, checking or halting moves recently put in train or changing direction. The result was a lack of decisiveness in American operations.

Just as Montgomery's personality limited his effectiveness as a commander, so too did Bradley's. His allowed his dislike of Montgomery—a natural reaction to the latter's attitude and manner, compounded by grievances nursed since Sicily—to warp his judgment somewhat. He was disinclined to work constructively with the land forces commander, preferring to undermine him with the Supreme Commander behind his back. His distaste for and distrust of Patton, combined with his cautious streak, also led him to favor his old friend Hodges. Both prejudices were periodically detrimental to operations. By keeping Montgomery in the dark and cooperating and coordinating only intermittently with 21 Army Group, Bradley diminished the effectiveness of both encirclements and ruled out a third (Patton's Beauvais maneuver). Although Third Army was conducting potentially more decisive operations—at least until the two attempts to close successive traps on the Germans were handed to Hodges through boundary changes and troop transfers—Patton was left with fewer divisions (if those devoted to the Brittany distraction are discounted). Patton's army was checked by looming supply difficulties, while First Army was allowed to expend ammunition in indecisive, attritional battles. And Patton was indisputably the more dynamic army commander, better suited to encirclement maneuvers than the pedestrian Hodges.

The Northwest European Theatre: General Eisenhower. Once the plans for the Normandy campaign had been agreed to by Eisenhower and his command team and approved by the CCS, the Supreme Commander found himself a frustrated observer rather than a player in the first couple of months of battle. He had agreed to the appointment of the vastly experienced Montgomery as interim commander of land forces and to his concept of operations. He rightly resisted the temptation to attempt remote control from the wrong side of the English Channel. This did not stop him from fretting about slow progress in what appeared to be a succession of indecisive operations, especially in the British sector, where the repeated failures in the Caen area limited the Allies' flexibility and grasp of the initiative. Of course, his worries were inevitably more acute and wide ranging than those of any other officer in the theatre, for he had larger concerns weighing on him—concerns of which most others were only dimly aware. Eisenhower knew that, despite the Allies' declared policy of defeating Germany first, any appearance of stalemate in France might lead to an even greater diversion of American resources to the supposedly secondary Pacific theatre. He was also aware that distant logistic problems could affect his operations, from a looming shortage of replacements to a shortfall in some artillery ammunition natures due to the War Department's underestimate of needs. And at the forefront of President Roosevelt's mind, and therefore the mind of Eisenhower's boss, General Marshall, was the November presidential election and the need to ensure that public opinion was squarely behind their approach to waging war. Eisenhower was badgered by increasingly vociferous complaints about Montgomery's leadership from most US generals, from his own SHAEF staff (including his chief of staff, Bedell Smith, and British officers from his deputy downward), from Washington, and from the American press. Increasingly they blamed him for his failure to grip his subordinate.

Eisenhower was also in dispute with his British ally over a major strategic issue. The often vituperative argument dragged on for seven months and involved not merely Eisenhower, Marshall, Montgomery, and Brooke but the prime minister and the president as well. Though committed to Overlord, the British also wished to maintain a strong (British-dominated) Italian campaign. The Americans saw this as lacking much strategic relevance once Italy had been driven from the war and heavy bombers had access to Italian bases from which they could pound the Reich; they suspected a British plot to drag them into a Balkan campaign. The Americans wanted to concentrate on the battle for France, complementing the main effort in Normandy with Operation Anvil, an assault on the Riviera coast followed by a thrust up the Rhône valley. They adduced strong arguments: a commitment had been made to Stalin at the Tehran conference; such an offensive would divert substantial German forces by threatening their rear; the liberation of France would be the most logical and politically acceptable use of the substantial French forces being equipped and trained by the United States (while simultaneously exploiting the resistance movement, which was particularly strong in the south); and the possession of Mediterranean ports (especially Marseilles) would greatly ease the logistic situation and speed up the arrival of American reinforcements by avoiding entry bottlenecks.

Launching Anvil at the same time as Overlord plainly had many advantages, but a shortage of assault shipping precluded simultaneity. When this became clear, Eisenhower, left with the decision, prevaricated as long as he could before coming down firmly in favor of Anvil, even at a later date. By 2 July, stasis in Normandy made a fresh landing, even one scheduled for as late as 15 August, attractive as a means of breaking the looming stalemate. With the post-Cobra breakout under way, however, Anvil (now renamed Dragoon) seemed redundant to the British, and Prime Minister Churchill made a last, desperate effort to have it canceled in favor of a smaller, improvised assault in Brittany. Eisenhower, bolstered by Marshall and Roosevelt, remained immovable on the issue. It was a fundamental tenet of American doctrine that the maximum possible force be brought to bear on the enemy's main forces to smash them by sheer overwhelming weight, and the Riviera campaign was part of that process. It proceeded as planned and was a great, and inexpensive, success. In retrospect, it clearly did not contribute significantly to victory in Normandy. However, it was not obvious at the time that this would be so, and the logistic conduit of the Rhône corridor and the arrival of strong Allied forces in Alsace had a favorable effect on the campaign in the west. (The fact that its gains were not fully exploited was Eisenhower's fault.) Whether anything substantial could have been accomplished in Italy had forces not been diverted from there is open to debate: Brooke, a vehement opponent of Anvil/Dragoon, doubted it.[56]

By late July, climaxing with the perceived failure of Operation Goodwood, Eisenhower was under much pressure to assume personal command of the land battle. His worry about the semistalemate that had seemingly settled in was compounded by Montgomery's refusal to recognize (or perhaps admit) that all was not proceeding according to his master plan. It is also possible that, despite his earlier endorsement of the operational concept propounded by his land forces commander, Eisenhower had lost sight of its logic and believed that failure was becoming endemic. He certainly complained to Churchill and Brooke and urged Montgomery to make greater efforts, despite the cost in casualties. But Eisenhower realized there was no room in the bridgehead for his vast, cumbersome SHAEF HQ; in addition, alliance politics made it almost impossible to sack Montgomery, and in any case, it would have been highly undesirable to alter the command structure at a critical time in the campaign. Probably just as important as these calculations was Eisenhower's habitual reluctance to make decisions before events compelled him to do so. On this occasion, operational developments relieved him of the need to make a decision and endure the consequent confrontation—something he always strove to avoid. The Cobra breakthrough rapidly led to breakout and brought an early victory in Normandy within the Allies' grasp.

Toward the end of July, Eisenhower was still stressing the importance of the Breton ports. "We must get the Brittany Peninsula," he wrote to Montgomery. "From an administrative point of view that is essential. We must not only have the Brittany Peninsula, we must have it quickly. So we must hit with everything."[57] Nevertheless, he enthusiastically endorsed first Montgomery's decision to downgrade Brittany's priority in the Overlord plan, then his long envelopment concept, and then Bradley's short hook response to the opportunity offered by the Germans' Mortain counterattack. On 7 August he moved to an improvised SHAEF forward HQ in Normandy to keep in closer touch with operations as they developed. However, he had never commanded so much as a battalion in combat and had no feel for battle. He was thus ill equipped to judge the advisability of Bradley's stop order of 13 August. He backed it, retrospectively endorsing Bradley's hollow arguments to excuse it.[58] He raised no objection to the later operational pause either, nor to Bradley's dispersal of effort in search of territorial gains at the expense of encirclement. This was despite warnings from his logistic experts that pursuit beyond the Seine in any significant strength would be impossible because of a severe shortage of motor transport. The obvious conclusion was that the enemy had to be annihilated in Normandy, not just damaged and pushed back. Just as he made no attempt to ensure that Bradley's operations dovetailed with Montgomery's, at no stage did he try to refocus the actions of the latter. Instead of closely complementing each other, the operations of the two army groups drifted apart.

Eisenhower had both the clear authority and the responsibility to ensure that cooperation and coordination between the Allies remained close and that their efforts were focused on the declared aim. Because he failed to grip his subordinates, the destruction of enemy forces was only partially accomplished. In effect, Eisenhower remained a spectator throughout August—the Supreme Commander who did not command.

It is possible that Eisenhower's failure to exercise his powers was attributable to his lack of practical understanding—understandable, given his training and limited experience—of the demands of the operational level of war. This lacuna was certainly there in the opinion of the CIGS, who confided to his diary on 27 July: "There is no doubt that Ike is all out to do all he can to maintain the best of relations between British and Americans, but it is equally clear that he knows nothing about strategy [read higher operations] and is quite unsuited to the position of Supreme Commander as far as any of the strategy of the war is concerned." Brooke may have been right, but he was also biased by the fact that Eisenhower did not simply accept British guidance uncritically; he was probably unconscious of the irony when he bemoaned the way "national spectacles pervert the perspective of the strategic landscape." It is likely, too, that Eisenhower's lack of combat experience made him diffident, or at least cautious, when arguing with those who had a great deal of experience in battle, such as Montgomery. It is quite noticeable how much more confident and assertive Eisenhower became as time wore on and his experience grew. During the Germans' December 1944 offensive through the Ardennes, he was much more sure-footed, more self-confident, and more decisive than Bradley.

Professional shortcomings aside, Eisenhower's character and command style (the former determining the latter to a considerable extent) contributed to a lack of decisiveness in Normandy. He wanted to be popular; he preferred to persuade interlocutors to reach compromises and consensus, rather than compel obedience. This approach, combined with his seemingly inexhaustible patience, equable temperament, and goodwill, was the only way to manage the alliance. The Supreme Commander needed to be a diplomat as well as a soldier. The British and American governments, military commanders, and popular press were touchy, convinced of their own infallibility, and suspicious of others. Eisenhower had to act as chairman of the board, a symbol of unity who shaped policy by persuasion, rather than an autocrat who ruled by decree.[59] He had to practice a high degree of decentralization to obtain cooperation and to avoid wasting time dealing with destructive squabbles between nationalities and services. He was often accused of agreeing with whomever he had last spoken. This appearance of bending with the wind was often necessary until he could work someone around to his point of view or at least to a compromise. Command of a coalition force is at least as much a political matter as a military one, and politics has been aptly defined (by Otto von Bismarck) as the art of the possible. Eisenhower also had a politician's tendency to postpone decisions until further delay became dangerous; events often rendered unpopular decisions unnecessary or at least made them appear inevitable. When required, however, he was capable of decisiveness with regard to such diverse issues as command of the strategic air forces, the date of the invasion, and Anvil/Dragoon.

Eisenhower earnestly strove to maintain unity of purpose in his coalition command while pursuing what he believed to be the best course of action or, rather, the best compromise available. Yet he was inevitably influenced by his military upbringing and by his personal likes and prejudices. These had molded his military brain into certain well-defined channels, and despite his honesty and integrity and his efforts to accommodate others' points of view, he was inclined to heed some people's opinions more than others; he was only human. Eisenhower was imbued with the Leavenworth teaching that victory in major war stemmed from continuous offensive action across the front until, by dint of superior resources, US forces so wore down the enemy that he cracked and could then be destroyed in pursuit. So it had been in the Civil War and the First World War, and so it would be in 1944. His views were naturally shared by his closest subordinate commander, his old friend Omar Bradley. Eisenhower spent long hours discussing the campaign and making plans with Bradley during his seventeen often lengthy visits to Bradley's HQ during the Normandy campaign. In contrast, he saw Montgomery, his principal subordinate, only nine times, and then for the briefest periods possible. Eisenhower disliked the man, was uneasy in his presence, and shied away from confrontation; for the most part, they communicated by letter and telegram. And while Eisenhower was critical of Montgomery's perceived failures around Caen, his excessive caution, and his sensitivity to casualties, he was indulgent of Bradley's errors in the west, including the delay in taking Cherbourg, the failure to foresee and then deal with the problem of the *bocage* and achieve the tempo envisaged in preinvasion planning, and his vacillations in mid-August.

Eisenhower's approach to command thus had a great deal to recommend it, as long as the strategic and operational situation developed gradually and his principal subordinates were in broad agreement about the concept of operations. It was ill suited to achieving decisive effect in fast-developing situations such as those that pertained in August and September, when those commanders were at loggerheads over the direction the campaign should take. It also required his army group and army commanders to be men of goodwill, prepared not only to compromise but also to live up to the commitments they made, to suppress their egos and prejudices and act in the spirit of his directives, and to cooperate constructively to further the common aim. In the late summer of 1944, this could not be said of Montgomery, Bradley, Patton, or J. C. H. Lee (the chief American logistician).

CONCLUSIONS

The stated aim of Allied operations was the destruction of the enemy's army. Although very heavy damage was inflicted, that aim was not achieved. It could have been. This would have enabled Anglo-American forces to march into Germany by any or, if they chose, every axis with minimal opposition; they could have closed up to the Rhine along its entire length, taking key economic objectives, in particular the Ruhr, and perhaps threatening Berlin. The stretching of the logistic system would have been a matter of only minor importance if there were no prospect of hard fighting. The Allies could have afforded to advance without bringing their full combat power to bear until at least those immediate objectives had been secured. But if the Germans were able to scrape together enough formations from the strategic depth to provide a screen behind which the remnants from the Normandy catastrophe could be reconstituted, a Teutonic version of the "Miracle of the Marne" (or of Dunkirk) would be possible. Then the Allies would find that their looming supply crisis, despite ample warning by the logisticians, would force an early culmination of their offensive. The enforced operational pause would give the enemy yet more time to field freshly raised and rebuilt forces and prolong the war. The Germans had lost whole armies before—for instance, at Stalingrad and in Tunisia—and had traded space for time to rebuild them. It was about to happen again.

Montgomery was overly optimistic (and had forgotten his painfully acquired knowledge of the Wehrmacht's resilience) when he assured Brooke in mid-August that German formations that crossed the Seine would be incapable of combat during the months to come. Indeed, more than a dozen divisions that had escaped the Normandy envelopments, albeit much the worse for wear, contributed to the checking of the Allied advance in September. Two of them, *9* and *10 SS Panzer Divisions* of *II SS Panzer Corps*, would, a mere four weeks after evading destruction at Falaise, ensure the defeat of Operation Market Garden, Montgomery's attempt at a knockout blow. *Army Group B* had suffered a disaster in Normandy, but it was not the utter catastrophe it could and probably should have been. In the end, the losses in personnel and equipment were serious but not decisive. The *Army of the West* retained its cohesion and ability to regenerate. The HQs that escaped the partial encirclements in August provided the command and staff expertise necessary to rebuild formations, and fourteen of the surviving divisions (eight of them panzer) were reconstituted and provided most of the combat power for the Germans' Ardennes offensive in December.

After the war, General Eberbach mused: "I still don't know why the Allies did not crush us at the Seine."[60] There were several reasons for this failure, but one was fundamental: unity of command was lacking in Normandy. Eisenhower was the titular supremo, but he preferred to fudge issues, delay decisions, seek consensus, and believe (or hope) it had been found; he did not exercise a firm grip. Whether he could have done so effectively if he had been so inclined is another question, but given the waywardness of his subordinates, especially Montgomery, this was a recipe for the indecisiveness that vitiated the campaign. Each operational-level commander lost sight of the declared theatre aim—the destruction of enemy forces—at least sometime during the month of August. Furthermore, national rivalries, occasional mutual incomprehension, and simple personal dislikes limited inter-Allied cooperation. Consequently, there was sufficient dispersal of effort to allow the Germans to avoid complete disaster.

Another important Allied weakness was the lack of awareness in the senior echelons—inevitable, in view of the lack of theoretical foundations or training—of either the possibilities or the demands of the operational level of war. Only insights born of a study of military history, experience, or both provided guidance for the more perceptive generals. Bradley, Hodges, Dempsey, and Crerar never really grasped that army, let alone army group, operations were not simply a matter of tactical solutions writ large. The problem (not that one was recognized) was compounded by the unexpectedness of the breakout. Only the most general planning had been done, and it had not foreseen the very advantageous circumstances in which the breakout took place. The campaign became one of hasty improvisations, and these were not always based on a holistic appreciation of the situation and its possibilities. As a result, battles were not always purposefully sequenced or synchronized, and some were fought unnecessarily. The desirability of maneuver in place of attack was frequently ignored, and the dividends to be gained from deep battle and deep operations were generally passed up in favor of a risk-averse, security-first approach to the exploitation of success. The effects of decisions and actions thus added up to less than the sum of their parts.

CHAPTER FIVE

September: Operational Ideas and Developments on the Ground

RIVAL CONCEPTS OF OPERATIONS

The SHAEF Preinvasion Appreciation

In May 1944 SHAEF planners looked forward to post-Normandy operations.[1] Of course, they had not the remotest idea how the Overlord campaign would develop; they could not even be sure the invasion would succeed in establishing forces ashore. They clarified the mission received from the CCS and studied the nonvariables that would affect the way the military situation developed—the terrain, the weather, and the logistic requirements of the forces. They assumed that the advance would be achieved at a relatively even tempo, rather than by fits and starts, and that the Germans would retain their cohesion and effectiveness while being driven back. They made a very simplistic and speculative stab at calculating relative strengths (suggesting it could be as long as eight months after the landings before Allied superiority became potentially decisive); this, however, was no more than guesswork and had little influence on their recommended lines of operations. The conclusions they drew suggested a concept of operations that was outlined in very broad terms. This was not circulated below the level of SHAEF, AEAF, and Allied Naval Expeditionary Forces (ANEF), although this does not mean that Montgomery, the land forces commander, was unaware of its contents.

Objectives. The CCS directive to the Supreme Commander, AEF, instructed him to "enter the Continent of Europe and, in conjunction with the other United Nations, undertake operations aimed at the heart of Germany and the destruction of her armed forces." Analyzing the mission, the SHAEF staff concluded that Berlin, the political heart of Germany, was too distant to be an immediate strategic objective; however, the Ruhr, the country's economic heart, was within the grasp of the Western Allies. The region was believed to provide 50 percent of the Reich's steel and 38 percent of its coal. (Northern France and Belgium, which would be overrun en route to the Ruhr, provided 15 percent and 18 percent, respectively, so an advance to a triangle of roughly Wesel-Hamm-Cologne, a penetration of up to 80 km [50 miles] over the Rhine, would deprive German industry of 65 percent of its steel and 56

219

percent of its coal.) The Wehrmacht would have to stand and fight to retain the Ruhr or lose the very sinews of war on which it depended. Having been brought to battle, it could be largely destroyed, the principal object of the campaign.

The only other area in the west that had any economic importance was the Saarland, about 250 km (155 miles) south of Cologne. This region, together with Lorraine and Alsace, contained only 16 percent and 14 percent, respectively, of Germany's steel and coal resources. The Rhine cities south of Cologne were, at that time, of little or no economic significance. It was obvious that the Ruhr had to be the principal geographic focus of any operations designed to have a decisive effect on the course of the war.

Topography and Weather. The SHAEF planners studied four avenues of approach to the Rhine, with particular regard to the Ruhr objective. They did not consider the terrain much beyond the Rhine in any serious way, and their survey was a purely map appreciation, devoid of any operational context. Map 5.1 illustrates their conclusions.

The plain of Flanders. This approach (through northern Belgium and southern Holland) was very flat, with a good road net, making it conducive to mechanized maneuver. There were numerous airfields and sites for even more.[2] However, the planners noted the numerous water obstacles—canals and streams both large and small—that intersected the region. These were in addition to the major obstacles of the Albert Canal; the rivers Meuse (Maas), Waal, and Rhine; and the West Wall,[3] which more or less petered out north of Roermond. Moreover, the polders and the complex system of drainage ditches would allow the enemy to flood large areas and further impede mobility. The possibility of an amphibious assault on the Dutch coast to outflank defensive lines was denied by the enemy fortifications created as part of the Atlantic Wall; these were especially strong at the huge ports of Antwerp, Rotterdam, and Amsterdam. Accordingly, SHAEF rejected this avenue of advance.

The Maubeuge-Liège/Brussels-Maastricht-Cologne axis. This approach was flat, well-provided with roads and airfield sites, and crossed by fewer rivers and canals en route through Belgium. It was true that the Roermond-Liège-Duren triangle would pose problems. Both the Meuse and Rhine, and the dense area of the West Wall between them, would have to be crossed, and minor built-up areas, often linked by ribbon development and the villages studding the area, would somewhat impede maneuver. Though bypassing was possible both to the north and to the south, Aachen would need to be taken because it was a road hub; the West Wall was relatively deep in the vicinity of the city. Overall, this route through central Belgium and the so-called Aachen gap offered the best and fastest going (as it had for

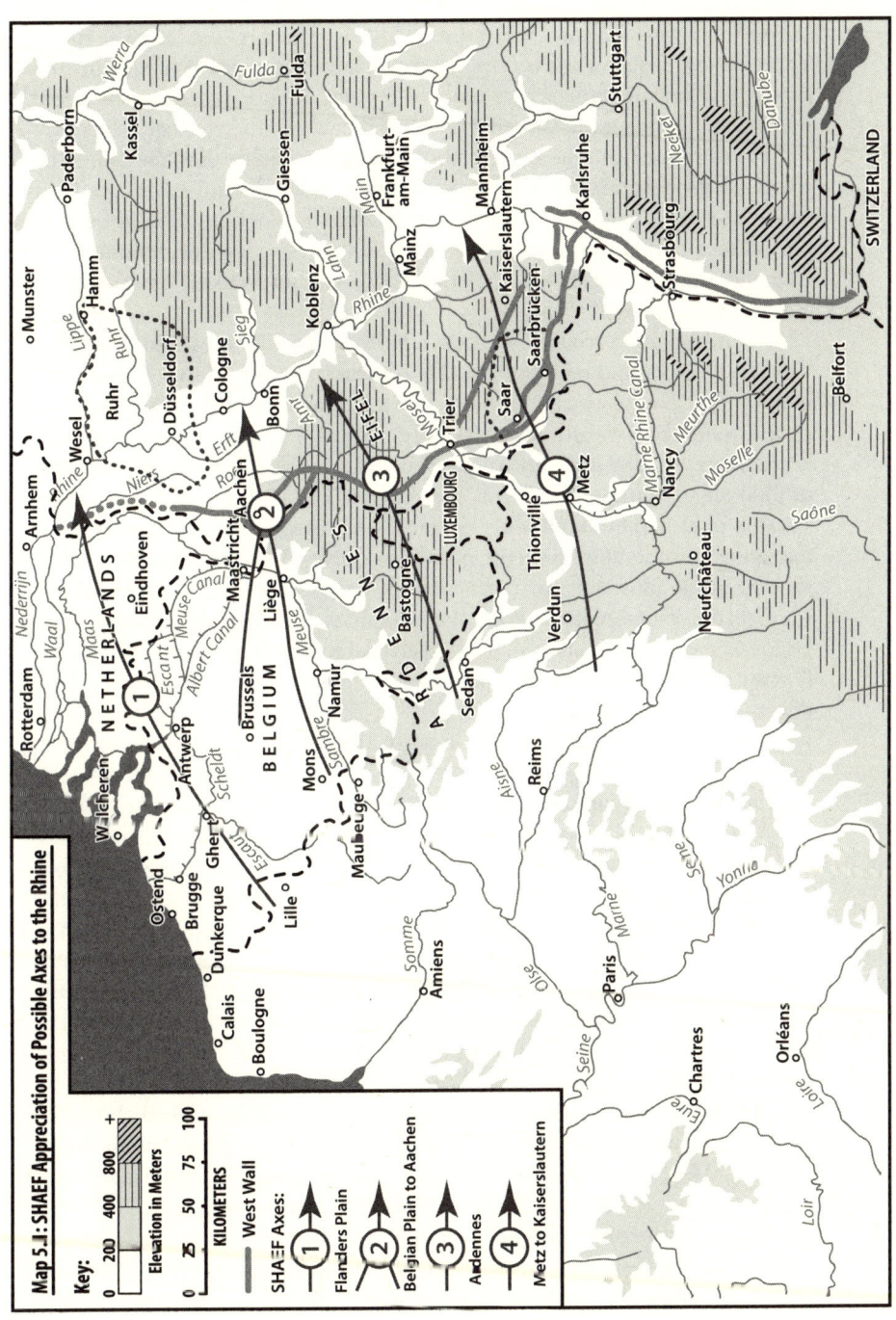

centuries of warfare), and it led directly to the Ruhr by the shortest route. The distance factor was every bit as significant as the going in view of the prodigious logistic demands of modern armies. A northerly advance would successively capture the Channel ports on the way to the strategic objective, and the distance from the biggest port, Antwerp (capable of maintaining the whole AEF on its own), to Cologne was a mere 200 km (125 miles). Another advantage of placing the main effort in the north was that it could be supported more effectively by air force tactical bomber elements still based in England and by First Allied Airborne Army, a major SHAEF asset of operational significance.[4]

The Ardennes. A triangular region about 120 km (75 miles) wide along the German frontier and tapering roughly 140 km (90 miles) into southern Belgium, the Ardennes became steadily less mountainous, broken, and forested as it extended westward. The river Meuse was a major obstacle bisecting it; the many smaller streams were often considerable obstacles too because of their steep banks and difficult approaches. The road net was sparse, and suitable places to build airfields were rare. Moving eastward into Germany, the going became more difficult, even discounting the West Wall (which was thinner in the mountains), all the way up to the Rhine and Moselle valleys. Though not a complete barrier, the Ardennes was seen as challenging to large-scale military maneuver and easily defended. The planners rejected it as an avenue, even though it had been adopted for the Wehrmacht's main effort in 1940.

The Metz-Kaiserslautern gap. East of the Meuse, an advance south of the Ardennes progressed into increasingly broken and wooded country. The road net was adequate to support maneuver, although it would be difficult to progress far without either the Metz or Nancy hubs. Airfield sites were relatively lacking. The rivers Moselle and Saar were major obstacles before reaching the Rhine, and one of the West Wall's denser sections was in the Saarland. Though a reward for crossing both fortifications and the river would be access to the Saar industrial area, it was of comparatively less importance than the Ruhr, and the cities of the middle Rhine lacked economic significance. An invading army turning north for the Ruhr would face the uninviting choice between pushing up the narrow Rhine valley and plunging northeast into much more difficult terrain. Distance too militated against a southerly approach. It was almost 900 km (560 miles) from Cherbourg to Saarbrücken and another 300 km (185 miles) from there, down the Rhine, to Cologne. The SHAEF staff identified the approach as worth exploiting as an axis but considered it secondary to the one north of the Ardennes.

If the Nazi regime continued to fight after the loss of the Ruhr, Berlin was less than 500 km (300 miles) away, across the flat, largely armor- and air-power-friendly northern German plain (and most of the Reich's synthetic oil production and refining plants were also there). A direct drive on the capital from the middle Rhine—the Mannheim area, for instance—would be almost 700 km (430 miles) to the northeast through difficult country. The south of Germany offered, at that time, no particularly valuable military objective and a lot of very difficult terrain.

As the campaign progressed, changing weather would have several implications for the conduct of operations, none of them good. The growing frequency and severity of storms in the English Channel would reduce and then preclude the use of the Normandy beaches for resupply. It was therefore an urgent imperative to acquire ports to supplement Cherbourg, both for logistic sustainment and for landing fresh divisions from the United States. Furthermore, the demand would be for deep-water ports, both because they could accommodate ships straight from America and because the availability of coastal shipping was limited. In the autumn, overcast and rain became the norm rather than the exception, and air operations would be increasingly curtailed. The troops would no longer be able to rely so heavily on close air support. Moreover, inclement weather and steadily lengthening hours of darkness would greatly decrease the effectiveness of air interdiction; German operational mobility would increase accordingly. Airborne operations would be more subject to chance and would eventually become impossible until spring. Moreover, increasing rainfall would worsen the going, especially across the Flanders plain. Allied mobility would be circumscribed, and the construction and maintenance of airfields would become more difficult and time-consuming.

The SHAEF Operational Concept

It was expected that the Seine would be reached around D+90. That being the case, the advance from the river would be able to start on about D+120, after a month's operational pause to build up logistic capabilities and force levels for the drive on Germany. The advance would be conducted on a wide front, utilizing both of the so-called gaps into Germany, as well as the Riviera-Alsace/Lorraine axis. This would conceal whether the main effort was north or south of the Ardennes, enabling the achievement of surprise. It would compel the enemy to overstretch his resources and raise the possibility of defeating him in detail. Because of their high level of mobility, flexibility, and mastery of the air, the Allied forces would be able quickly to switch emphasis from one axis to another to take advantage of enemy vulnerabilities revealed as the campaign progressed. It would be imperative to exploit the Allies' superiority in armor, forcing the enemy to fight on terrain favoring mechanized maneuver and preventing him from conducting a deliberate withdrawal from one river line to another at a pace he could determine. Airborne forces would be used to preempt the establishment of a firm defense on selected lines and expedite the advance. These advantages of a broad-front approach were predicated on the belief that the Allies would not achieve decisive numerical superiority against the canny Germans until the American buildup was well advanced, probably not until 1945.

Logistic support from the beaches and mulberry harbors would become increasingly interrupted as inclement weather accompanied the approach of winter. To supply 21 Army Group's advance, the British would take Le Havre and then the smaller Channel ports as they advanced on the Allied left. They would need to capture Antwerp (the third largest deep-water port in the world, after New York and Rotterdam) as soon as possible because it would be necessary to carry the Allied offensive into Germany. Initially, 12 Army Group would draw its supply from Cherbourg; then it would obtain more and more supplies from the Brittany ports as they were opened, from St. Malo and Quiberon Bay (a deep-water anchorage to be developed as a port), and from Brest. Once they no longer needed it, the British could hand over Le Havre to meet growing American demands and provide a port closer to the front line as it moved eastward. Finally, 6 Army Group would draw its sustenance from Marseille; with a capacity similar to Antwerp's, it would also be able to meet some of the needs of forces advancing south of the Ardennes.

The Growing Conceptual Divide

As the Normandy campaign approached its unexpectedly imminent climax during the second half of August, the thoughts of theatre and army group commanders turned to the best way of converting operational success into strategic victory and a quick end to the war in the west. Clearly, immediate exploitation would be crucial. On 19 August Eisenhower announced his decision to forgo the operational pause envisaged in the Overlord plan to build up forces and logistic capabilities for the drive on Germany. Instead, the AEF would immediately implement the preinvasion SHAEF concept for subsequent operations. The SHAEF concept for an advance across a broad front is contrasted with Montgomery's operational idea of a concentrated thrust on a single strategic axis in map 5.2.

Not knowing what was in Eisenhower's mind (they had not spoken since 13 August, and Montgomery was not officially privy to the SHAEF plan), Montgomery put his own concept for future operations to Bradley on 17 August. He hoped to secure Bradley's agreement for a joint proposal to the Supreme Commander. After forcing the Seine, the two army groups would advance abreast "in a solid mass of 40 divisions" deployed between the North Sea and the Ardennes.[5] The British would clear the Channel ports

Map 5.2: Opposing Operational Concepts: Broad versus Narrow Front

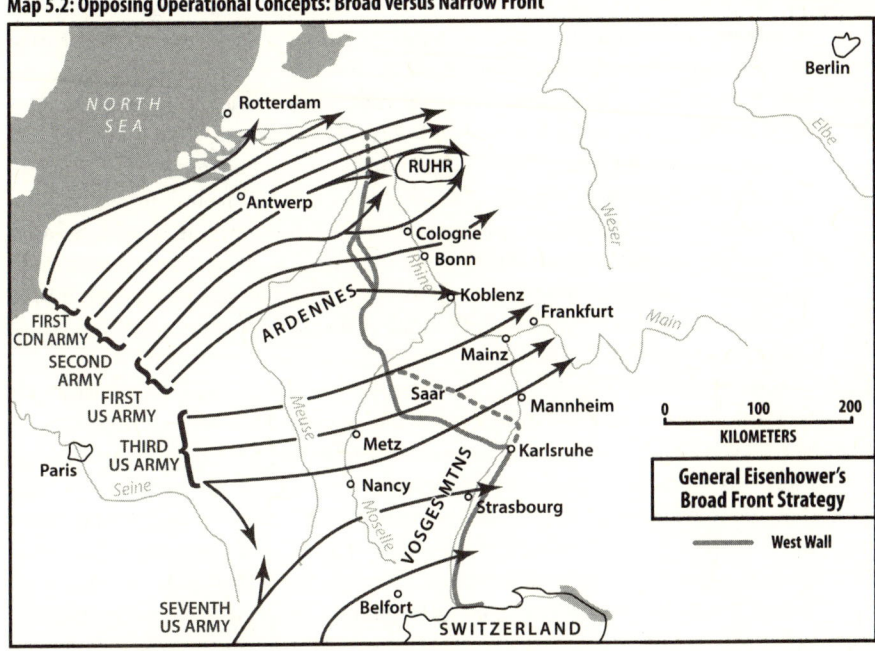

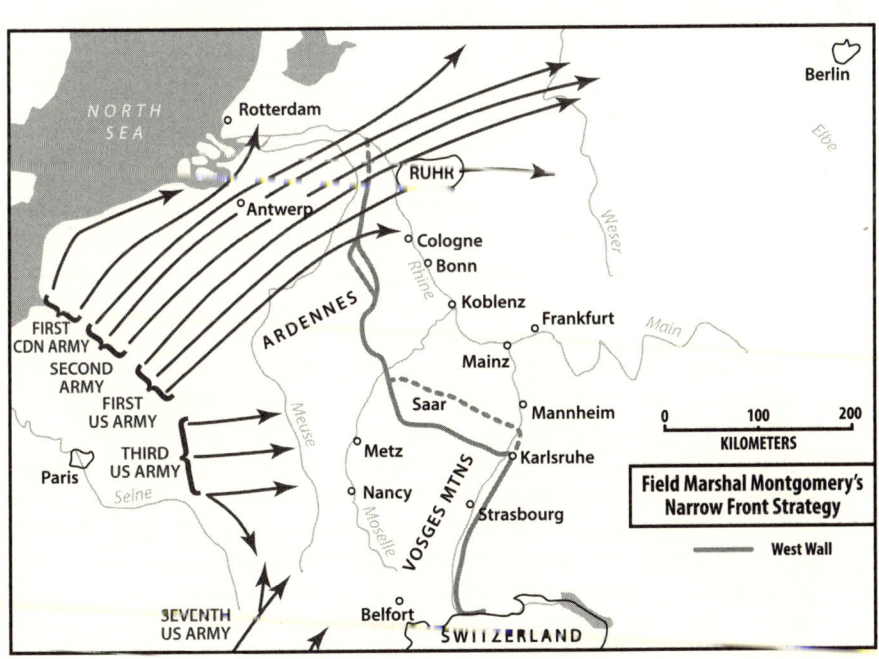

and take Antwerp while 12 Army Group moved against the Ruhr. Supported by strong air groupings based in Belgium, this single, concentrated thrust would destroy the enemy before it, force the Rhine, and take the Ruhr before bad weather intervened. It would receive first priority for logistic support. A strong American force would deploy as far forward as Reims-Troyes to protect the right wing. The Dragoon forces would advance into Alsace to threaten the Saarland, but there would be no attempt to link up with them. As Montgomery described this concept in his memoirs, it was "a Schlieffen plan in reverse," but this time executed against a shattered enemy.[6] He also looked ahead to subsequent operations aimed at Berlin, in preparation for which 21 Army Group would envelop the Ruhr to the north and seize bridgeheads over the river Weser.

Bradley listened to Montgomery in silence, which the latter mistakenly took for agreement. Bradley, however, had his own idea for a campaign plan, one that he had concocted with Patton. Following SHAEF's May concept, there would be a double thrust on a wide frontage. In the north, the Canadian army would take the Channel ports and Antwerp while Second Army headed straight for the Ruhr. An equally important thrust would be made by the entire 12 Army Group straight through the Saar region to Frankfurt. Recognizing that the British army group might lack the strength to clear the politically sensitive V-1 "rocket coast" and take the ports (which would be as vital for the sustainment of 12 Army Group as for its ally), he proposed a modified plan, more likely to appeal to Eisenhower, in one of their frequent meetings. A single US corps would be sent on the Maubeuge-Aachen axis, directed on Cologne, to support Montgomery's advance. The notionally subsidiary effort of 12 Army Group would take place south of the Ardennes, but it would actually be of equal size. Third Army (less VIII Corps, which now consisted of four divisions in Brittany) and two-thirds of First Army would take the Saar and then cross the Rhine between Mannheim and Mainz to advance on Frankfurt. Meanwhile, 6 Army Group would try to force the Rhine farther south around Strasbourg. In setting out the advantages of his "American plan," Bradley noted that it was the shortest, quickest route to Germany; it was aimed directly into the enemy heartland across an undefended sector; and it would take the "important Saar basin." Twelfth Army Group would link up with 6 Army Group and cut off the enemy withdrawing from southwestern and southern France. This would leave 21 Army Group with enough strength for its task, provided Montgomery "would take a chance and attack without insisting upon an overwhelming preponderance of force."[7]

On 20 August Eisenhower held a staff conference to discuss the way ahead and concluded with two decisions: he would assume personal command of the land forces on 1 September, and his two army groups would advance on separate axes, with 12 Army Group moving in the direction of

Metz-Saar. Disturbed by these unexpected developments, de Guingand, 21 Army Group's chief of staff, suggested that Eisenhower wait until he had discussed both matters with his boss, Montgomery. Despite agreeing to do so, on 22 August Eisenhower informed the CCS that he would assume personal direction of the land battle on 1 September. He was directing the Army Group of the North, under Montgomery, to secure the Channel ports, including Antwerp; having done so, it would eventually go east to the Ruhr. To accomplish its primary mission, it would have First Allied Airborne Army at its disposal. The Army Group of the Centre, under Bradley, would advance east and northeast of Paris; from there, it could either go into Belgium and help Montgomery or, more likely, strike south of the Ardennes through the Metz gap. The eventual course of action would depend on the enemy's strength on each axis. Bradley's speed of advance would depend on how quickly the Brittany ports could be opened and the supply position improved, an urgent SHAEF priority. The Army Group of the South, when it came under the Supreme Commander, would support the central group.[8]

Disagreeing vehemently with both ideas, Montgomery sent Eisenhower the proposal he had outlined to Bradley; when the response was negative, he requested a meeting. On 23 August they had a one-to-one discussion, at Montgomery's insistence. Montgomery sought to persuade the Supreme Commander that the main effort needed to be in the north, and not in name only; that 21 Army Group lacked sufficient strength (even with the addition of airborne forces) to take both Antwerp and the Ruhr without First Army's help (he needed at least twelve divisions); that until the port capacity closer to Germany was increased, any advance across the whole front would peter out for want of supply; and that Third Army should therefore be reined in. Montgomery also argued that the current command arrangements should continue—that is, with himself acting as land forces commander under the general strategic direction of Eisenhower.

The British argument had some effect, but much less than Montgomery had hoped. In a letter of 24 August, formalized in an instruction to his principal subordinates issued on 29 August, Eisenhower set out his decision. This had plainly been influenced by his discussions on 26–27 August with Bradley and with senior SHAEF staff officers. Eisenhower would assume control of ground operations as planned, as of 1 September. The Army Group of the North would destroy the enemy south of the Somme and then secure the Channel ports, Belgian airfields, and Antwerp, overrunning the V-1 launch sites in the process. The airborne army would be available to help attain those objectives. The eventual objective would be the Ruhr. The Army Group of the Centre would make its main effort north of the Ardennes to support 21 Army Group, but only "for the moment." Hodges would not be put under British operational control; Montgomery was given authority only to coordinate the American's actions with his own army group's (no simple matter, given that he could communicate only through Bradley's HQ, which was moving on a divergent axis outside the limits of radio range). Patton would prepare an offensive on the Paris-Metz axis. The opening of the Breton ports was again emphasized, with the corps involved then rejoining Third Army. Priority for logistic support would be accorded to the northern thrust, with First Army receiving 5,000 of the 7,000 tons expected to be provided daily by COMZ; however, it was important that both start as soon as possible to forestall enemy attempts to restore a cohesive front. Clearly, Eisenhower intended to stick with offensive action across the whole front but was prepared to give temporary priority to operations north of the Ardennes, at least until key operational objectives, the deep-water ports, were taken; after all, no advance into Germany would be possible without them.

The situation evolved radically over the next ten days. Instead of continuing to lag behind the Americans, Second Army made a spectacular advance to take Antwerp. On 4 September, emboldened by success and German weakness, Montgomery again proposed that all resources be concentrated immediately on a strong, single thrust on the Ruhr and thence to Berlin to end the war. There was insufficient supply to support offensive action on both the Ruhr and the Saar axes, he argued, and the former was far more likely to be decisive. Eisenhower seemed to draw a different conclusion from the way operations were developing. Moreover, he had already started to have doubts about his decision of eleven days before, inaccurately referring to the proposed northern thrust as "pencil-like"—hardly an apposite metaphor for the proposed eighteen divisions of Second and First Armies combined, and growing to twenty-four once the Canadian army had completed its mission to take the ports. Members of his staff, including four British generals, were telling him that Montgomery was too cautious to prosecute a bold offensive (when Eisenhower issued his 29 August directive, Second Army was only starting the breakout from its Seine bridgeheads), and in any case, the suggested march on Berlin would be logistically infeasible until much more port capacity was available for use.

Eisenhower had already discussed the future with Bradley, Hodges, and Patton on 2 September. His American subordinates expressed their unhappiness with the emphasis on operations in the north, reducing them to a supporting role for Montgomery. This indubitably influenced the new directive Eisenhower issued on 4 September. The enemy front was collapsing, he maintained, and the primary aim of AEF operations was to complete the destruction of the enemy's main forces west of the Rhine. This would be accomplished through a simultaneous, not sequential, double thrust. The main effort would remain in the north, but 12 Army Group's allocation of supply for its two armies would now be equalized at 3,500 tons per day (though

COMZ failed to live up to its promises and managed to provide only about 3,300 tons to First Army and 2,500 tons to Third Army during the first half of September). The objective of Army Group North and Army Group Centre remained seizure of the Ruhr, and the airborne army could be used to speed the process. First Army, however, was to shift its emphasis southward. While two corps advanced on a general Maubeuge-Namur-Aachen axis, one corps would be sent through the Ardennes to prevent a dangerous gap from opening between it and Third Army. As well as capturing Brest (a top priority), the latter would advance immediately past the Saar to take Frankfurt, linking up in the Dijon area with Seventh Army, which was progressing fast up the Rhône-Saône corridor.[9] To strengthen Patton's thrust, Bradley switched an infantry division from XIX Corps to Third Army (a move of about 400 km [250 miles] during a fuel shortage). Second French and 6 Armored Divisions were also sent to Third Army from Paris and Brittany, respectively, thus raising its strength to nine divisions, compared with First Army's eight going east.

On 9 September Eisenhower reported to the CCS, laying out his broad-front approach with the main effort toward the Ruhr. On the subject of the need for more ports, he emphasized that Army Group Centre's priority was the capture of Brest, but otherwise he confined himself to saying, "During our advance to the Ruhr and Saar the deep water ports of Havre and Antwerp or Rotterdam will be opened." He also maintained that despite the poor logistic situation, "an advance beyond the Siegfried Line involves a gamble that I am prepared to take in order to gain full advantage from the present disorganization of the German armies in the west." This presumably indicated that he was unwilling to lose what might be a transient opportunity for exploitation by prioritizing the capture of the Antwerp approaches. The CCS approved his report and stressed that the main effort had to be in the north; Antwerp or Rotterdam had to be opened before the onset of bad weather.

Meanwhile, Eisenhower had replied to Montgomery's letter of 4 September in the terms outlined above. Such was the chaotic nature of SHAEF communications that his message of 5 September arrived in two parts, the second before the first, on 7 and 9 September. Unsurprisingly, Montgomery was dissatisfied with the content, which he regarded as being effectively a repudiation of the course of action already agreed. He more or less demanded that Eisenhower visit him to discuss the matter further. They met at Brussels airport, their first meeting in fifteen days; they talked on the aircraft, as Eisenhower had an injured knee and could hardly walk. Montgomery insisted that the Supreme Commander leave his principal logistician out of the meeting but brought his own. He proceeded to hector Eisenhower about his error in dispersing AEF effort and allowing Patton to continue to receive supply while XIX Corps on the British flank was both halted and deprived of one-third of its strength to bolster the secondary axis in the south and while the rest of First Army was stalled for want of fuel, about 100 km (60 miles) short of the Rhine. Such dispersal of effort would enable the enemy to improvise a defense and impose a new stalemate. Pointing out the unsatisfactory command arrangements for operations north of the Ardennes, Montgomery also proposed his reinstatement as land forces commander. Showing considerable forbearance, Eisenhower rebuked him gently: "Steady, Monty, you can't speak to me like that. I'm your boss."[10] Still, Montgomery insisted that the offensive north of the Ardennes, the main effort, ought to be given absolute priority for supply. He outlined his expanded plan for a thrust by Second Army to outflank the West Wall and the Ruhr by forcing the Rhine at Arnhem, an axis given additional importance owing to the V-2 rocket offensive on London that had just started from bases in the Netherlands. To give momentum to this thrust, he proposed to employ an entire airborne corps of three and a half airborne and one air-landing divisions to "bounce" bridges over all the major water obstacles between the Dutch frontier and Arnhem. This would provide a springboard for a thrust on the Ruhr. At least there was no more talk of an advance on Berlin without a pause, a prospect Montgomery now recognized to be logistically infeasible.[11] The German capital remained the ultimate geographic objective—a goal agreed on by Eisenhower—but its attainment would be achieved in a subsequent phase of the campaign.

Eisenhower accepted that Montgomery's arguments had some cogency, however arrogantly and insensitively he had presented them. Of course, the situation had changed dramatically since Montgomery first proposed his single-thrust concept: the British advance had outstripped even Patton's; Antwerp and the Belgian rail net had been captured intact, and the other Channel ports were under siege; the British supply position was better than the American; and intelligence suggested the enemy north of the Ardennes was still weak. Though he would not lessen his commitment to the broad-front advance, Eisenhower also reaffirmed the primacy, at least for the near future, of the effort north of the Ardennes. In that spirit, he told Bradley on 12 September that if Patton had not managed to cross the Moselle with the bulk of his army by 14 September, he would have to transition to defense. Eisenhower assigned to Montgomery the airborne force requested, his sole operational reserve, to pave the way to and over the Rhine at Arnhem. To strike for the Rhine while the iron was perceived to be still hot, Eisenhower was willing to give temporary priority to the Arnhem operation over Antwerp. He also responded promptly to Montgomery's request for additional American air and land transport to support the logistic buildup for and execution of the operation, code-named Market Garden. This would enable the start date to be brought forward from 23–26 September to 17 September, thus minimizing the operational pause. Montgomery would also be allowed to deal

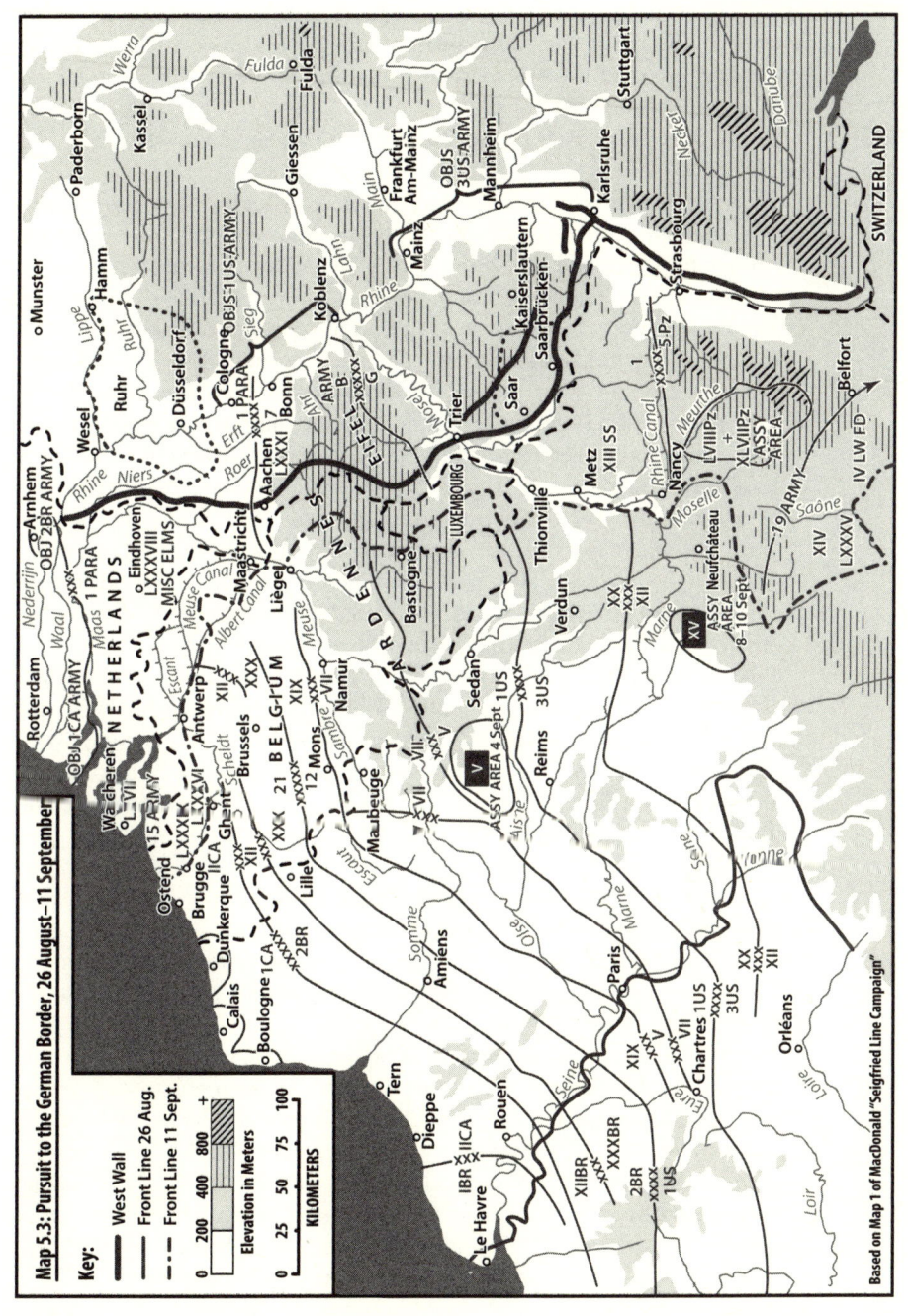

directly with Hodges rather than through 12 Army Group. Map 5.3 shows the Allied advance to the German frontier over the period 26 August–11 September, creating the situation to which the Supreme Commander responded with his next directive.

On 13 September Eisenhower issued a new directive that stated:

> The general plan is to push forward our forces to the Rhine, secure bridgeheads over that river, seize the Ruhr and then concentrate our forces preparatory to a final non-stop drive into Germany. During this time we must secure the following bases: Northern Group of Armies must secure the approaches to Antwerp or to Rotterdam quickly so that one of these ports . . . can provide adequate maintenance for them deep into the heart of Germany; they must also secure other Channel ports. Central Group of Armies must reduce Brest promptly so that this place may be available for staging our troops. It is important too that physical junction should be established between Southern Group of Armies in their advance from the south and the right of Central Group of Armies so that the supply lines from Marseilles may assist in supporting the right of Central Group. . . . My plan of maneuver is to push hard over the Rhine in the north with the Northern Group of Armies, First US Army and First Allied Airborne Army, while Third US Army, except for a limited advance . . . [is] to hold adequate bridgeheads beyond the Moselle thus creating a constant threat to the enemy and preventing him from reinforcing further north by transferring troops from the Metz area. As soon as this is accomplished all possible resources from Central Group of Armies must be thrown into the support of First Army's drive to seize bridgeheads near Cologne and Bonn in preparation for assisting in the capture of the Ruhr.[12]

After bridgeheads were secured in the north, Third Army was to advance through the Saar and establish its own bridgeheads across the Rhine. Logistic priority would go to securing bridgeheads on the left, save for providing adequate security and reconnaissance on the right and securing and developing ports.

Bradley had objected strongly to Montgomery's plan and was not pleased with this new directive. He still wished to make his main effort south of the Ardennes on a general Metz-Frankfurt axis. To this end, he had altered the 29 August allocation of scarce fuel supplies to favor Third Army and reinforced it at the expense of Hodges's left wing. He now set about persuading the Supreme Commander to modify his decision again. On 14 September Bradley announced that Patton had crossed the Moselle in force and suggested that Third Army be allowed to continue its advance; if it made little progress over the following forty-eight hours, he could shift its efforts northward. Eisenhower agreed that, provided Montgomery received the maintenance promised him and Hodges was sufficiently supplied to reach his first principal objective, there was no reason why Patton should not continue acting offensively, as long as conditions were favorable.

Of course, Montgomery was concerned that such concessions to 12 Army Group were diluting the declared main effort and ran the risk that no blow would be hard enough to be decisive. Perhaps somewhat disingenuously, Eisenhower reassured him. Montgomery was not reassured, especially after he received a letter on 15 September in which the Supreme Commander considered which courses would be open once the Ruhr, Saar, and Frankfurt areas were taken—events he considered imminent. While Berlin was still the most important target, the objectives and axes of operations subsequent to achieving the Rhine would be determined when the situation, in the east as well as the west, was clarified. But the broad-front approach would continue. "It is my desire to move on Berlin by the most direct and expeditious route, with combined US-British forces supported by other available forces moving through key centers and occupying strategic areas on the flanks [the Augsburg-Munich area], all in one coordinated, concerted operation. It is not possible at this stage to indicate the timing of these thrusts or their strengths." Eisenhower concluded by inviting his principal subordinates to come forward with their comments and suggestions.[13]

Montgomery replied on 18 September, implying that despite Eisenhower's mantra that the main effort was north of the Ardennes, he was allowing Bradley too much freedom to divert forces and supplies to the south. When it came to future operations, both time and logistics would determine what was and was not possible. These factors would preclude a general advance across the front without an operational pause, and that was undesirable because it would give the enemy a chance to recover. What was needed was a single, powerful Anglo-American thrust by 21 Army Group and First Army in the north to seize the Ruhr and subsequently drive on to Berlin across the north German plain—a mission achievable by such a force as long as it had unqualified logistic support. Objectives in southern and central Germany were a mere distraction. If (perversely, he implied) the Supreme Commander saw the Frankfurt-Berlin axis as preferable, then the whole of 12 Army Group should concentrate on that thrust and 21 Army Group should fulfill a secondary or passive role. Either way, logistic limitations would require the curtailment of offensive action by either Third Army or most of 21 Army Group to enable the other to deliver a decisive blow. Any attempt to advance on all axes simultaneously would be doomed to failure. The decision could not wait, Montgomery warned; it was required immediately to put the necessary arrangements in place. Time was the key factor; indecision or half measures would lead to disappointment.

Eisenhower replied on 20 September to this restatement of Montgomery's ideas. He affected the attitude that there was no great difference between their concepts: "Never at any time have I implied that I was considering an advance into Germany with all armies moving abreast." But he again rejected as impossible what he described as Montgomery's "knife-like drive towards Berlin." He reiterated his commitment to the broad-front advance. The main effort would be on the Ruhr-Berlin axis, but supporting attacks were necessary to pin German forces and prevent a counterconcentration. The main effort could not be the sole one, however, as it would "have to drop off so much of its strength to protect its rear and its flanks that very soon the drive would peter out." On the question of timing, he became slightly more specific: "We must marshal our strength up along the western borders with Germany, to the Rhine if possible, insure adequate maintenance by getting Antwerp working at full blast . . . and then carry out the drive you suggest."[14] To build up the Allied left, he had ordered Ninth Army to redeploy with the divisions freed up by the fall of Brest the previous day and to hold a defensive region east of Luxembourg. This would allow Hodges to concentrate his full strength for a drive on the Rhine.

Montgomery's response was immediate, blunt, and uncompromising. His letter of 21 September rejected the idea that their concepts were similar and condemned Eisenhower's allowing Third Army to go so far that it had outrun its logistic support and deprived all forces of flexibility. He opined that it should be halted immediately and all resources concentrated on the left hook; otherwise, the offensive would be stopped short of the Ruhr. Clearly, a conceptual impasse had been reached, and the Supreme Commander decided to hold a conference to end the increasingly acrimonious bickering, clear the air, and clarify a definitive plan for the conduct of future operations in Germany. As was his wont, Montgomery begged off attending the Versailles conference on 22 September, maintaining that the Market Garden situation required his undivided attention. As usual, he sent his chief of staff to represent him. Delightedly, de Guingand reported back: "Eisenhower had supported my plan 100 percent and [agreed] that the northern thrust was to be the main effort and get full support."[15]

In fact, the decisions were more nuanced. A distinction had to be made between the logistic requirements of current and future operations. An additional deep-water port in the north was an indispensable prerequisite for the final drive into Germany; thus, the opening of Antwerp could not be left on the back burner indefinitely. The operations against the Ruhr were the current, but not necessarily the future, main effort; Antwerp was, in effect, an equal priority. Bradley would aid these operations by taking over VIII British Corps' sector, allowing 21 Army Group to concentrate. He would also continue his thrust toward Cologne and Bonn as far as resources allowed

September: Operational Ideas and Developments on the Ground 235

and be prepared, when supply permitted, to seize any opportunity to force the Rhine and attack the Ruhr from the south. The logistic requirements of the main effort would have to be met in full before Third Army received any supply. Relying on its own logistic chain, 6 Army Group would continue operations into Alsace to take Mulhouse and Strasbourg. First Army would not be placed under British command, but in emergencies Montgomery would be allowed to communicate directly with Hodges. In a follow-up letter to the field marshal, Eisenhower stressed that Bradley was being required to support 21 Army Group efforts, as well as how stretched the Americans were becoming south of the main effort and thus vulnerable to a German counterattack if they chose to concentrate for that purpose. He concluded by suggesting that misunderstandings were at the root of their disagreements and that Montgomery should feel free to say so whenever he felt things were going wrong; SHAEF would do whatever it could to rectify matters. And, he reiterated, Antwerp was needed.

Eisenhower convened another conference at Versailles on 4 October. It was attended by the three C-in-Cs, the army group C-in-Cs, and even Brooke (whose presence explains Montgomery's). There was vociferous agreement that Antwerp must be given absolute priority because any serious theatre operations depended on its opening. In the face of this unanimity and the uncertain situation in his area of operations, Montgomery had no alternative but to suspend his drive to the Ruhr (now, after the failure at Arnhem, on a Nijmegen-Wesel axis). He was still reluctant to switch his first priority to the Antwerp approaches, however. He wanted to give equal emphasis to necessary Second Army preliminary operations to strengthen the Nijmegen bridgehead and clear the enemy from the west bank of the Meuse. It took a 9 October telegram and a 13 October letter from Eisenhower, in language as near to being peremptory as he ever got, to modify his approach.

The first Versailles conference took place at a time when Allied confidence in early victory had been shaken for the first time. By the time of the second, the cold fact of the Allied culmination was becoming clear. A combination of stiffening enemy resistance and, even more, logistic facts that could no longer be ignored or wished away made it clear that their offensive was running into deepening trouble everywhere. At least in retrospect, the conceptual debate that preceded this culmination is somewhat surprising. Although it took place against the background of a rapidly evolving operational and logistic situation, developments on the ground seemed to have relatively little impact on the thinking of British and American senior commanders. Their proposals, priorities, and arguments hardly changed between the beginning of the pursuit in late August and its culmination; indeed, they would continue essentially unchanged well into the winter. This aspect of generalship, and the increasingly acrimonious arguments about command it engendered, are considered in chapter 7. In the meantime, the rest of this chapter outlines the intelligence that influenced decisions (though only selectively) and then the events themselves. The following chapter examines the elephant in the room that all the senior commanders tried to ignore or to exploit selectively in argument: logistics.

ALLIED INTELLIGENCE AND THE GERMAN SITUATION UNTIL MID-SEPTEMBER

With the end approaching in Normandy, the general tone of Allied intelligence estimates had become increasingly euphoric.[16] On 26 August SHAEF intelligence maintained: "The August battles have done it; the German army in the west has had it. . . . Two and a half months of bitter fighting have brought the end of the war in Europe in sight, almost within reach." On 2 September it became more specific: "The German army in the west is no longer a cohesive force but a number of fugitive battle groups, disorganized and even demoralized, short of equipment and arms. . . . no longer in a position to offer serious resistance on any line short of the West Wall." On 9 September SHAEF estimated that, after allowing for reinforcements and the recovery of troops cut off in Belgium and the Riviera, Germany might soon have fifteen divisions, including four panzer, to hold the fortifications; the total might rise to a still inadequate twenty by the end of the month. At a higher level, the British Joint Intelligence Committee noted on 5 September: "Whatever action Hitler may now take, it will be too late to affect the issue in the West, where organized German resistance will gradually disintegrate under our attack." On the same day, Eisenhower noted: "The defeat of the German armies is complete and the only thing now needed to realize the whole conception is speed."[17] Such optimism was fueled by events on other fronts too. By 5 September, Seventh Army spearheads had reached Besançon, almost 700 km (435 miles) from the beaches where they had landed a mere three weeks before. In Italy, the Allies had started to penetrate the Gothic Line in a number of places and hoped to break into the Po valley soon. In July and August, in successive offensives, the Red Army had advanced 350 to 600 km (215 to 370 miles) across a frontage of almost 2,000 km (1,240 miles) to the border with East Prussia, the Vistula, and the Carpathians and driven Romania from the war, thus opening the way into Hungary and the Balkans. Allied commanders in the west were hoping for, even expecting, a replay of the events of autumn 1918, when the defeat and rapid retreat of the German army had led to pleas for an armistice that amounted virtually to surrender. Some believed that the disastrous failure of the generals' 20 July plot to kill Hitler and seize power was not the end of the matter and might be reprised.[18]

They overlooked, perhaps willfully, or at least downplayed the signs of both German recovery and their own fast-approaching culmination.

So sudden and so devastating had been the German defeat in Normandy that the *Army of the West* had been rendered almost combat-ineffective in the short term. *Army Group B* informed the OKW on 29 August that, after the rearward dispatch of five infantry divisions for refitting, the remaining eleven from Normandy could form about four ill-equipped battle groups; from eleven panzer formations (each now with five to ten tanks and a battery), only a single regimental group could be formed, and it would need fresh men and equipment. A note of 4 September listed as fit for action about four infantry divisions in *Fifteenth Army* (excluding fortress troops); in *Fifth Panzer Army*, three-quarters of a panzer division and less than two infantry divisions; in *First Army*, three panzer–panzer grenadier and four and a half infantry divisions; and in *Nineteenth Army*, withdrawing up the Rhône valley, one panzer and three infantry divisions, with another division equivalent and tens of thousands of noncombat personnel retreating from the southwest.[19]

From the end of August, the speed of the advance and the degree of confusion and collapse in the *Army of the West* made the creation of any detailed and up-to-date intelligence picture impossible. German higher HQs lacked both a clear picture and the ability to exercise effective and continuous command and control. Thus, their intentions were even less grounded in reality than during the later stages of the Normandy campaign, and decisions on defense or delaying actions on successive lines were repeatedly overtaken by events. Indeed, the very survival of attenuated formations was often accomplished through the initiative of subordinate commanders, without reference to army group let alone the high command. Ultra, however, continued to be a prolific source of information as German line communications ceased to function. Useful order of battle material continued to be acquired; the orders of senior HQs were often based on wishful thinking, which was both interesting in itself and revealing as to aspirations and actual capabilities. From mid-September, the volume of Ultra traffic began to tail off somewhat in *Army Group B*'s area—Holland and Belgium—leaving the Allies better informed about *Army Group G* facing Third and Seventh Armies in eastern France.[20] As before, Luftwaffe communications proved a reliable source of intelligence on unit basing and strengths, on which offensive counter–air operations were based, not to mention a German fuel crisis of growing proportions.[21]

Lists of formations withdrawn for refitting were provided, together with their concentration areas. The latter were mostly too far forward, owing to the pace of the advance. By early September, any hope of establishing intermediate lines had been abandoned, and the Germans had become belatedly concerned about restoring the West Wall, stripped since 1940 of weapons and everything else of use to create fixed defenses elsewhere, especially the Atlantic Wall.[22] There was particular anxiety about the Aachen section and the area from Trier to Metz, the entries to the Reich under the most imminent threat at the start of the month. In fact, the whole 120 km (75 mile) long First Army sector from Luxembourg City to Lunéville was worrying both von Rundstedt, restored to the position of C-in-C West on 5 September, and Model, who remained at *Army Group B*. If Third Army continued to advance as rapidly as it had since crossing the Seine south of Paris, it would link up with Seventh Army coming from the Riviera and cut off the mix of 100,000 or so Wehrmacht soldiers and civilians fleeing from the Bordeaux area and up to 300,000 men of *Nineteenth Army* retreating with agonizing slowness up the Rhône valley. Losses of trained personnel on top of those in Normandy were to be avoided, if possible, and Alsace had to be defended to prevent the West Wall from being turned. Accordingly, Ultra reported that the veteran *3* and *15 Panzer Grenadier Divisions*, redeployed from Italy, were sent to Lorraine at the end of August, along with two new grenadier divisions and a panzer brigade; *17 SS Panzer Grenadier Division* absorbed two new, ill-trained, and underequipped SS formations and was dispatched to Metz, and three shattered panzer divisions were sent to the Saar to refit. On 13 September it was reported that three additional panzer brigades were joining *Fifth Panzer Army*; its HQ had opened in southern Lorraine on 9 September to command a Hitler-decreed and unrealistically ambitious counterattack into Patton's right flank.

Farther north, the other immediate concern was Allied pressure toward Liège, threatening Aachen and the Ruhr industrial region. On 7 September von Rundstedt reported that all the forces at his disposal had been sent to the Aachen area: an inadequate, weak, and delayed *9 Panzer Division*; three small brigade-sized units; and *12 Volksgrenadier Division* (which would not arrive before 12 September). *Army Group B* could only play for time to put the West Wall into a state of defense and garrison it. Yet that task would require six weeks, and the resources allocated were utterly incommensurate with the task. Model insisted on 8 September that without an immediate reinforcement by one panzer and three infantry divisions, *Seventh Army* would be shattered and a strategic breach opened on the German frontier.

West of Maastricht, Hitler ordered *First Parachute Army* (hitherto a training command) to hold the line of the Albert Canal as far as Antwerp. It would have under its command three understrength, underequipped, and hastily improvised parachute and two infantry divisions; battle groups from a miscellany of training units; and ten heavy flak battalions hastily switched to a ground role. By 9 September, Second Army had identified elements of four more divisions or divisional battle groups and noted strong resistance that prevented it from enlarging its bridgeheads over the canal. Hitler displayed a keener sense than Montgomery and Eisenhower of the importance of the Scheldt estuary when, on 3 and again on 7 September, he stressed the absolute imperative of holding not only the fortresses of Boulogne, Calais, and Dunkirk, but also what would become known as the Breskens pocket and Walcheren Island at the mouth of the Scheldt. The last two measures would not only deny the Allies the use of Antwerp but also provide an escape route, via the South Beveland peninsula, for remaining *Fifteenth Army* formations to defend the western end of the Albert Canal—and potentially threaten the flank of any advance on the Eindhoven-Arnhem axis. On 9 September Second Army duly noted the first appearance on the Albert Canal of a formation extricated from south of the Scheldt. Ultra provided ample details about this almost three-week-long evacuation, ending with a report on 23 September that 82,000 men, 530 guns, 46,000 vehicles, and 4,000 horses had crossed to safety. It also revealed that in the first days of September, *II SS Panzer Corps* had been sent to refit somewhere in the Venlo-s'Hertogenbosch-Arnhem area, astride or very near the axis of Operation Market Garden's "airborne carpet." It was unclear whether the corps moved from there before the operation started, although on 13 September it was reported that "one broken panzer division" had been sent to the Arnhem area to refit, and the presence of *II SS Panzer Corps* was suspected. An air photographic reconnaissance mission on 15 September confirmed the presence of at least some AFVs near Arnhem, reinforcing reports from the Dutch resistance. Ultra reported on both 14 and 15 September that the enemy expected a large-scale airborne operation in Holland and an attack on Second Army's chosen axis. A SHAEF intelligence summary of 16 September noted that *9* and *10 SS Panzer* were in the Arnhem area.[23] Ultra also placed an *Army Group B* HQ at Oosterbeek, just west of Arnhem, confirming resistance reports.

Clearly, Ultra produced much valuable intelligence. It painted a broad but accurate picture of the disintegration of *Fifth Panzer* and *Seventh Armies* and German fears for the largely nonexistent front in each sector. It also revealed that, to restore the front, *Fifteenth* and *Nineteenth Armies* would have to be extricated before they were cut off by the advancing wings of the Allied forces. The enormity of the challenge the Germans believed they were facing was obvious in the report sent by von Rundstedt to the OKW on 7 September. The Allies were assessed as having on the Continent about fifty-four motorized and mechanized divisions, with strong army troops and another thirty or more in England, including six airborne, all ready to deploy. The British army group was assessed as having twenty-five to twenty-seven divisions; eight to ten of them, with 600 tanks, were being employed to cut off *Fifteenth Army*, and another group was preparing to force the Albert Canal and advance on Rotterdam and Amsterdam. An additional six to eight divisions, probably with 400 tanks, were coming up and could be employed to either help destroy *Fifteenth Army* or to augment the thrust into Holland. It would take some time for the forces currently attacking *Fifteenth Army* to reduce Le Havre, Boulogne, Calais, and Dunkirk. The US army group, with fifteen to eighteen divisions and about 1,000 tanks, was attacking eastward on a broad front from Hasselt to Toul—objective, the Rhine. Three to four units were being brought up on the northern flank, and about five divisions were tied down besieging Brittany fortresses. All German forces were committed, under heavy attack, and partly exhausted. They lacked artillery, armor, and reserves. *Army Group B* was reduced to approximately 100 tanks. The enemy had air supremacy and was conducting deep interdiction. The few forces sent as reinforcements had been ordered to the Aachen area, where the threat was most acute and the West Wall was directly and immediately threatened. They would delay for as long as possible while the inadequate manpower allocated did what it could to rehabilitate the West Wall. Reinforcements and equipment to refit shattered formations were urgently required.[24]

Von Rundstedt was very pessimistic about the ability of his forces to stop the Allied offensive. He was right. In July sixty-two divisions had failed to hold a 160 km (100 mile) front in Normandy. By 5 September, seventeen to eighteen divisions, mostly worn down and largely deficient in armor and artillery, including the four nonfortress formations of *Fifteenth Army* in danger of encirclement, were being asked to hold a sector well over 450 km (280 miles) long. His estimate that twenty-five fresh divisions and an operational reserve of five to six panzer divisions were necessary to stabilize the situation was entirely realistic. Although reinforcement on that scale remained a pipe dream, the picture for the Germans had brightened somewhat by midmonth. *Fifteenth Army* had successfully extricated itself from the Scheldt estuary, less the two divisions left to hold "Fortress Southern Holland" (now so christened by Hitler) and Walcheren. Some reinforcement of the Aachen sector had been reported, including *12 Volksgrenadier Division*, and the presence of *21 Panzer Division* and three panzer brigades with *XLVII* and *LVIII Panzer Corps* of *Fifth Panzer Army* had been noted in Lorraine.

Ultra did not give the whole picture. It could not describe the rapid restoration of discipline and morale in an army that was apparently in the process of dissolution. Nor did it reveal the impressive organizational improvisation that enabled cadres to collect and weld remnants, stragglers, and a miscellany of undertrained and underequipped training and replacement organizations together with convalescents and overage or medically unfit security and occupation troops into moderately effective combat units and formations.[25] The proportion of substandard personnel making up some of these ad hoc formations should not, however, be exaggerated. As the sharper

Allied intelligence officers noticed, most of the thousands of prisoners swelling the Allied cages were from rear-echelon, air defense, security, and Luftwaffe ground staff units; experienced combat troops and units were making a determined effort to extricate themselves to fight another day, and these provided the cadres for improvised and refitting formations.

This manpower was supplemented by an increasing flow from within the Reich. At the beginning of September, Göring surprised the General Staff with the announcement that he had 20,000 paratroopers more or less ready for front-line duty, and he could add another 10,000 from air and ground crews made redundant by the shortage of aviation fuel and aircraft (together with the nucleus of *First Parachute Army*). The Reinforcement Army, dimly understood by Allied intelligence, turned out thirty-one newly organized *volksgrenadier* divisions, twelve of which went to the west, and ten panzer brigades, four of which went to the west.[26] Although manpower, albeit of variable quality, could be found quickly, weapons and equipment were more problematic. For instance, on 15 September von Rundstedt's command mustered only 392 serviceable tanks and SP guns, with 144 under repair and 411 in transit (including the new panzer brigades). Nevertheless, some of these new formations, especially the simpler infantry ones, were surprisingly effective, given their speedy generation. The Germans rapidly built these improvised, regenerated, and new formations into an integrated force capable of creating not merely islands of resistance or a thin screen but a new front. Firm command and control was restored and logistic problems were eased by the fact that the Germans were falling back on their lines of communication. At the same time, Allied pressure diminished or became sporadic as their own logistic problems impacted operational plans. Allied attacks now frequently met with resistance whose coherence and determination made up for any lack of unit-level combat power and tactical competence. The Allies were beginning to pay the price for failing to destroy German formations, and particularly their command and control entities, in the Normandy encirclements.

FROM PURSUIT TO CULMINATION

By 25 August, Second Army was starting to force the Seine; the Canadians, against greater opposition, would do likewise on 30 August. Third Army already had bridgeheads above and below Paris; the liberation of the capital was largely accomplished, and an assault on Brest was about to begin. First Army was regrouping for a further offensive. This situation was not at all what SHAEF had envisaged as the likely conclusion of Overlord. Although the enemy had not managed to execute an orderly withdrawal to the Seine, his battered forces were still deemed sufficiently strong and balanced to fight for successive lines back to an eventual stand on the West Wall. During the four weeks following Cobra, operations had developed with unprecedented and unanticipated speed, inflicting unexpectedly massive damage on the enemy. All agreed that immediate exploitation was called for to prevent his recovery. There could be no operational pause to improve the logistic position of the armies, even though none of the Breton ports required to support post-Normandy operations was yet in use. Even though it had been designed to meet very different circumstances, the Supreme Commander resolved to implement the SHAEF concept, outlined in May, of a broad-front advance to take the Allied armies up to and even into Germany. This decision would spark the often acrimonious wrangle between British and Americans outlined earlier, which contributed to the squandering of the fruits of victory in Normandy.

As early as 7 August, Eisenhower had clearly been thinking boldly and broadly about the development of the campaign. He wrote to Marshall and explained that it was his intention to destroy as much as possible of the German forces west of the Seine, cross it before the river's defense could be organized, and annihilate the rest of the German forces between it and the Somme, picking up the Seine ports on the way. On 17 August he promulgated the decision to continue the pursuit without implementing the Overlord plan for an operational pause for consolidation and logistic buildup. In doing so, he was disregarding the advice of his American logisticians. They had originally estimated that it would be possible to maintain only twelve US divisions as far forward as the Mantes-Gassicourt-Orléans line by D+90, and this was assuming that at least some of the Brittany ports would be open and feeding in supplies. In addition, a shortage of around 10,000 logistic trucks (127 companies) precluded an immediate advance beyond the Seine until railway repair had been pushed much further east to reduce overstretch. Eisenhower proved right in rejecting the advice of his experts, who were unduly pessimistic, at least in the short term. In the event, the logisticians rose to the challenge. By D+79, sixteen US divisions were being maintained on the Seine and five in Brittany; in mid-September the sixteen were 320 km (200 miles) beyond the Mantes-Orléans line.[27]

Although the planners had underestimated the latent capabilities of the supply chain, they were right to point out that, at least later if not sooner, the cost of ignoring logistic realities would catch up with the field commanders. Moreover, problems would grow exponentially as the various expedients adopted to keep the show on the road became the source of greater future difficulties. This was primarily an American predicament, at least at first. They had larger and more dispersed forces moving further and further from the ports that fed them, whereas the more concentrated British picked up some useful port capacity on their way north and found that the parts of the railway system they overran were easily and quickly rehabilitated. But eventually, they too would find that their ambitions outpaced their ability to supply them. Eisenhower was aware of the looming danger. On 4 September he wrote to Marshall:

> We have advanced so rapidly that further movement in large parts of the front, even against very weak opposition, is almost impossible. . . . The closer we get to the Siegfried Line the more we will be stretched administratively and a period of relative inaction will be forced upon us. The potential danger is that while we are temporarily stalled the enemy will be able to pick up bits and pieces everywhere and reorganize them swiftly for the defense of the Siegfried Line or Rhine. It is obvious from an overall viewpoint that we must now as ever keep the enemy stretched everywhere.[28]

Given the outcome of operations in the late summer, the Supreme Commander was right to worry. The culmination of the offensive was entirely predictable, as the next chapter demonstrates. If there was any surprise at all, it was that the logistic system took so long to fail.

In August the victory in Normandy appeared to be decisive. The ease and rapidity of the subsequent pursuit over the next fortnight confirmed this impression in the minds of the Allies, from junior officers to generals. The sense of self-confidence engendered by this experience was reinforced by intelligence assessments that fed "victory disease." These assessments consistently emphasized the positive signs and downplayed factors that failed to accord with the optimistic groupthink that had taken hold. Most commanders and staffs failed to recognize the warning signs that the culminating point of the offensive might be approaching, even when their troops' daily experience of combat was increasingly at odds with higher-level intelligence (which, in any event, was becoming more cautious). They persisted in employing operational and tactical methods that were inappropriate and therefore counterproductive, in the hope that one final effort would bring final victory. By the end of September, however, hubris was giving way, slowly and reluctantly, to an understanding that there was a new reality: German resilience had been seriously underestimated, the Allied ability to cope with the looming logistic crunch through improvisation had been overestimated, and the war would not be over by Christmas.

21 Army Group

In his last directive as land forces commander, issued on 26 August, Montgomery drew the inter–army group boundary but shifted it eastward and then

244   Chapter Five

southward at Bradley's request, so that it ran roughly east of Amiens–Tournai to turn more easterly and run south of Brussels–Hasselt–north of Maastricht.[29] Montgomery stressed that, given the enemy weakness: "The proper tactics now are for strong armored and mobile columns to bypass enemy centers of resistance and push boldly ahead, creating alarm and despondency in enemy rear areas. Enemy bypassed will be dealt with by infantry columns coming on later. I rely on commanders of every rank and grade to drive ahead with the utmost energy; any tendency to be 'sticky' or cautious must be stamped on ruthlessly."[30] He was right. By and large, the enemy was much more interested in retreating than in fighting (so much so that the air forces largely switched from close air support, which was no longer needed, to interdiction). Indeed, German operational and often tactical command and control seemed to have disintegrated. Their mostly shattered and disorganized formations, now reduced to battle groups largely devoid of heavy weapons and mechanical transport, were in no condition to fight. Covered by occasional rear guards, they sought to exfiltrate as best they could back toward the West Wall. Only *Fifteenth Army* (five infantry divisions strung out between the Seine estuary and southern Holland) had any cohesion and, albeit limited, combat power.

Montgomery ordered 21 Army Group to destroy enemy forces in northwest France and Belgium and to secure the Pas de Calais area, the Belgian airfields, and Antwerp as a prelude to a drive on the Ruhr. He was determined to "bounce" a crossing of the Rhine before the Germans could organize the defense of that formidable obstacle. The V-1 launching sites would be overrun on the way. First Canadian Army was tasked to take Dieppe and Le Havre, but "the main business lies to the north and in the Pas de Calais." I Corps was sent to capture Dieppe; the larger II Canadian Corps, with its main weight on its right flank to outflank resistance, was to destroy all enemy forces in the coastal belt up to Bruges and take the Channel ports. The army group's main effort would lie with Second Army on the right, to which 7 Armored Division would revert, thus bringing its total strength to three armored and three infantry divisions and two armored brigades in XII and XXX Corps.[31] It was directed to destroy the enemy encountered within its boundaries, seize crossings of the Somme, and capture Antwerp, Brussels, and bridgeheads over the Albert Canal. By executing the mission at a high tempo, the army would prevent the enemy from holding on any of the defensible river lines and also the eastward withdrawal of *Fifteenth Army*, trapping it against the sea. Montgomery issued a subsequent directive on 3 September, during and clearly influenced by Second Army's spectacular advance across Belgium. This envisaged Dempsey continuing on to the Ruhr. Owing to the likely logistic constraints caused by Eisenhower's failure to give 21 Army Group absolute priority, Crerar would hold in the Bruges-Calais area until the maintenance situation allowed First Canadian Army's employment further forward.

The Canadians made a promising start when 2 Canadian Division took Dieppe on 1 September, finding this useful port largely undamaged. With a well-planned and well-executed deliberate attack, Crerar's I Corps took Le Havre on 12 September, after which the corps' two infantry divisions and armored brigades were allowed to rest and refit while much of their transport was stripped out to augment the logistic support of II Canadian Corps. The latter thrust into southern Belgium with the two armored divisions leading and the infantry formations peeling off to take the French ports. Facing stronger resistance than Second Army, the corps made slower progress. Boulogne and Calais were invested on 4 and 5 September but were found, unlike Dieppe, to be strongly held. Ostend fell on 8 September. Dunkirk's defenses were probed by 2 Canadian Division from 6 September, but a deliberate attack was canceled, and the decision was made to mask it instead; the Germans held Dunkirk until the end of the war. The Canadians' advance temporarily ended on 7 September, when their attempt to close up to the Scheldt estuary ran into more than a rear guard on the Bruges-Ghent Canal.

Second Army's XXX Corps, with XII Corps echeloned to its left rear, raced north. It advanced by night as well as by day to deny the possibility of an eastward retreat by *Fifteenth Army*. This endeavor was successful. Opposition, especially in front of XXX Corps on the right, was light and poorly organized; the corps was advancing through a gap between *Fifteenth Army*, trapped on the seaward flank, and the shattered remnants of *Seventh Army*, retreating toward the Reich. The Germans were given no breathing space to organize even an effective rearguard action. The Somme was bounced, and on 3 September the Guards Armored Division took Brussels; the next day it advanced another 20 km (12 miles) to cross the Dyle at Louvain. On 4 September 11 Armored, with significant help from Dutch resistance, captured Antwerp; the division stopped there after capturing the docks and all their supporting infrastructure virtually undamaged. Had it pressed on for another 24 km (15 miles)—there was little opposition at the time—it would have cut off the South Beveland peninsula and any possibility of a withdrawal northward by *Fifteenth Army*. On 5 September XII Corps' 7 Armored Division reached Ghent. XXX Corps had advanced 400 km (250 miles) in six days (averaging more than 66 km [40 miles] per day); the armored divisions fragmented the opposition and, as ordered, bypassed pockets of resistance for the following infantry to mop up. The rate of advance would have been even higher had it not been for an almost day-long pause to allow for an airborne drop at Tournai, an operation rendered unnecessary by the speed of the ground advance and accordingly aborted. The most important accomplishment during the pursuit was the securing of the vast dock facilities of the deep-water port of Antwerp. But their seizure intact did not mean that the port was instantly usable. First, the Scheldt had to be cleared to its mouth, about 90 km (55 miles) distant, and Walcheren island and South Beveland had to be taken—points forcefully made by the Allied naval C-in-C, Admiral Ramsay.

Though according to its commander, Lieutenant General Horrocks, XXX Corps still had enough fuel for another 150 km (90 miles) or so, a two-day halt was ordered to rest, refit, bring up more supplies, and allow XII Corps on the left and US XIX Corps on the right to come up. Horrocks resumed his advance on 7 September on the Brussels-Arnhem axis. Field Marshal Montgomery's eyes were firmly fixed on the Rhine and the Ruhr; opening Antwerp was important, but he considered it a secondary goal and could not or would not find the requisite forces or logistic support for simultaneous operations. There would be no exploitation of German weakness north of Antwerp and no advance to seal off the South Beveland peninsula and trap *Fifteenth Army* on the wrong side of the Scheldt.

XXX Corps found that the Germans had used the pause to scrape together some forces. As a result, 11 Armored failed in a somewhat belated attempt to force the Albert Canal, and the Guards had to fight hard to secure a small bridgehead at Beeringen, around 50 km (30 miles) from Louvain. In view of the renewed resistance shown by the enemy, Dempsey shifted XII Corps eastward to take over responsibility for Antwerp and Brussels, allowing XXX Corps to concentrate for its continued advance. When fully relieved by elements of Canadian First Army, XII Corps would conduct a supporting attack on the left of XXX Corps, protecting its flank. There was stiffening resistance between the Albert and Escaut Canals, estimated by 9 September at sixteen battalions, several of them paratroopers, reinforced by fifty tanks. It took the whole of XXX Corps five days (rather than the one day expected) to establish a firm bridgehead over the Escaut Canal just north of Neerpelt, even though it was only 25 km (15 miles) from Beeringen. Because of both weather and this renewed and unexpected opposition by the Germans, Operation Comet, a reinforced divisional airborne assault on the Rhine bridge at Arnhem and its approaches, was canceled on 10 September. The days of quick, easy gains were over.

On 14 September Montgomery issued another directive: 21 Army Group would envelop the Ruhr to the north and cut it off by a thrust through Osnabrück, Münster, and Hamm on the eastern side. This axis would achieve operational surprise, outflank the West Wall, overrun the V-2 launch sites (a major concern to the British government), and be within range of a proposed supporting airborne operation. "But on the way to it we want the ports of Antwerp and Rotterdam, since the capture of the Ruhr is merely the first step on the northern route of advance into Germany." The task of First Canadian Army was to "complete the capture first of Boulogne, and then Calais. . . . The whole energies of the Army will be directed towards operations designed to enable the full use to be made of the port of Antwerp."[32] Following completion of that task, and when the maintenance situation allowed, the army would advance on an axis Breda-Utrecht-Amsterdam (the last a port comparable in size to Antwerp). Crerar was being required to take two strongly defended Channel ports, mask a third, and clear the Scheldt estuary without reinforcement or logistic priority. Indeed, when he recovered his I Corps from Dieppe, it was to relieve Second Army of its responsibility for Antwerp and the line to its east. For the army group, the main effort would be with Second Army, which, with the assistance of an airborne corps consisting of three airborne divisions and one air-landing division, would secure crossings over the Rhine, Waal, and Maas in the Arnhem-Nijmegen-Grave area and establish its strength on a general line Zwolle (Zuider Zee)–Deventer–Arnhem, facing east and with bridgeheads over the river Ijssel. The advance would be rapid, without regard to happenings on the flanks. US First Army would establish a deep bridgehead over the Rhine between Cologne and Bonn and then advance round the south face of the Ruhr in close coordination with the operations of Second Army.

Montgomery, desperate for ports near the main action in Belgium, was disappointed at Canadian First Army's slowness in securing them. Well fortified, Boulogne did not fall to 3 Canadian Division until 22 September. The division then went on to attack Calais, which was similarly strong and surrendered on 30 September. Second Division was committed to masking Dunkirk until late in the month, when it was relieved by a special service brigade and ordered to Antwerp to relieve elements of XII Corps. The rest of II Canadian Corps was unable to attack in any strength over the Leopold Canal to clear the south shore of the Scheldt, never mind Walcheren island, until after the Germans had successfully consolidated and organized Fortress Southern Holland (the Breskens pocket). Serious operations to open the Scheldt did not begin until 1 October. The south shore was finally cleared, after difficult fighting, only on 31 October, and the island was taken in a combined operation on 8 November. The first ship into the port arrived only on 28 November, as de-mining took three weeks. The whole process had taken an unconscionable amount of time and cost almost 13,000 casualties. The ports had to be assaulted successively, as the medium and heavy artillery, tanks, and special armor necessary to reduce fortifications were insufficient for concurrent operations. The allocation of ammunition was inadequate for assaults on fortified areas. Poor weather, precluding the aerial bombardment considered necessary, forced a two-day delay in the attack on Boulogne, and this had a knock-on effect on Calais.[33] Given the fact that I Corps was first grounded and then (reinforced by the Polish armored division) diverted

248   Chapter Five

to the support of Second Army, there was insufficient infantry available to mount an early attack toward the mouth of the Scheldt over canal obstacles rendered even more challenging by deliberate inundation. XXX Corps had missed the opportunity for an unopposed advance north from Antwerp on 4–5 September, and Crerar's paucity of resources meant that no attack to isolate the South Beveland peninsula was mounted until early October. This made it possible for the bulk of *Fifteenth Army*, less the two divisions left behind to defend Fortress Southern Holland and Walcheren, to escape over the Scheldt, down the peninsula, and onto the flank of Second Army's thrust toward Arnhem.

The stated aim of Operation Market Garden was for Second Army to position itself astride the rivers Maas, Waal, and Neder Rijn (Lower Rhine) in the general area Grave-Nijmegen-Arnhem and to dominate the country north as far as the Zuider Zee. The axis from the Neerpelt bridgehead to Arnhem was difficult, as SHAEF's preinvasion appreciation had recognized. There were six significant water obstacles to be crossed, including three very wide rivers.[34] The task of the airborne corps in Operation Market (the vertical envelopment part of Market Garden)—the successor to the canceled Operation Comet, but on a three times greater scale—would be to seize the bridges to enable the ground forces to advance rapidly without having to mount major crossing operations. British 1 Airborne Division, reinforced by the Polish airborne brigade, would establish bridgeheads at Arnhem, 120 km (75 miles) north of Neerpelt; US 82 Airborne would take the Nijmegen and Grave bridges, 100 km (60 miles) and 90 km (55 miles) distant, respectively, and the canal crossings between them; US 101 Airborne would take those over the Aa and Dommel Rivers and the Willems and Wilhelmina Canals and the town of Eindhoven, the latter 30 km (18 miles) from Neerpelt. The corps also had an air-portable division that, if all went according to plan, would be flown in to Deelen airfield, north of Arnhem, at around D+5–6. Both operations were to be mounted simultaneously and at short notice. D-day was moved forward from a tentative 23 to 17 September, once Eisenhower had promised American transport to augment 21 Army Group's logistic lift.

The ground offensive, Operation Garden, was to be executed by XXX Corps, with the Guards Armored and two infantry divisions, in the centre; XII Corps, with one armored and two infantry divisions, would be on the left; and VIII Corps, with one armored and one infantry division, would be on the right, mounting supporting attacks to widen the corridor of advance and protect the flanks of the main effort. However, only XXX Corps could complete its assembly and hasty battle preparation by 17 September; neither of the secondary efforts could begin before the nineteenth. The terrain facing Second Army presented considerable difficulties. XXX Corps was to advance on a very narrow frontage, with only one two-lane highway going all the way to Arnhem, one minor through route that actually merged with the main one for a time, and country roads and tracks for the rest of the way. Cross-country mobility south of the Waal was somewhat circumscribed by drainage ditches and soft going. If anything, it became worse north of that river, where much of the main road and other tracks were carried on embankments flanked by deep, wet ditches that also intersected the generally sodden land in great numbers; straying from the narrow, muddy roads was to risk becoming irretrievably mired. Numerous small woods and orchards gave cover to enemy guns commanding the roads. The corps would be compelled to advance not merely in column of divisions but, for much of the time, on a battle group frontage. The possibility that the airborne troops would fail to prevent the demolition of bridges meant that a massive engineer effort had to be laid on: 9,000 men and 2,300 trucks. In all, XXX Corps had 20,000 vehicles to move up the one decent road. Traffic control would be a challenge, and getting units, such as bridging and ferrying elements, up past their forerunners to respond to emergency demands would be problematic.

The flanking corps faced even greater terrain challenges. Neither had any decent north-south routes, and both, but especially VIII Corps, faced marshy ground intersected by frequent wide ditches with soft banks. Neither corps could be ready to attack alongside XXX Corps on D-day. XII Corps forced the Escaut Canal on 18 September, but with considerable difficulty, and pushed forward slowly. By 25 September, when the main effort's failure to keep a bridgehead over the Rhine was finally acknowledged, it had advanced to a point west of Veghel, about 20 km (12 miles) short of the Waal. VIII Corps' infantry division had been hastily brought up from the Seine, but it was unable to attack before 19 September; it then made relatively good progress and reached Boxtheer, approximately 30 km (18 miles) south of Nijmegen, on 25 September. Thus, the flanking corps widened the salient driven into German-held territory but were unable to advance sufficiently far and fast to secure XXX Corps' narrow corridor from the flank attacks that would cut its principal route on three occasions.

Success would plainly depend on a number of factors: the achievement of surprise by the airborne operation (it would be impossible for Operation Garden), leading to a preemptive seizure of the bridges; a rapid buildup of airborne combat power to ensure the retention of gains; and a high tempo of advance by the ground forces to prevent the enemy's recovery before the Rhine was crossed. Montgomery stressed that XXX Corps' offensive should "be rapid and violent, without regard to the flanks." If at all possible, it was intended to reach Arnhem within forty-eight hours, and certainly within three days. Lieutenant General Frederick "Boy" Browning, commander of the airborne corps, believed that 1 Airborne Division could hold its bridgehead for up to four days. The Zuider Zee, it was believed, could be reached by D+6. Thanks to a gross underestimate of German capabilities, these were seen as realistic targets. The information available about the enemy was used very selectively to produce intelligence that proved what the commanders wanted to hear. Eisenhower was continually being prodded by Marshall and Arnold, the Chiefs of Staff of the Army and Army Air Force, to use the airborne forces (in which they had made a massive investment) in a deep operational role; the five aborted operations (and another thirteen planned and abandoned) were becoming an embarrassment. Moreover, the window to use them was closing, as the autumn weather would soon make a large-scale operation too hazardous. Montgomery was desperate to retain his army group as the theatre's main effort, despite the powerful lobbies pressing for its shift to the south; success in Market Garden would oblige the Supreme Commander to reinforce that success. Lieutenant General Lewis Brereton, commander of the Allied Airborne Army, and Browning, the relevant corps commander, were both as anxious as Eisenhower to mount a triumphant airborne operation. Dempsey, the ground executor, did not like the concept but was, as always, loath to question Montgomery's judgment. And so the clear evidence of stiffening resistance in southern Holland was explained away as being merely a hard crust that would collapse when pierced, leaving a free run for XXX Corps' advance. The presence of *II SS Panzer Corps* was either discounted as rumor or dismissed as irrelevant because it lacked combat capability after its mauling in Normandy. Allied optimism had become an unchallengeable faith, and in any case, the most compelling evidence questioning the advisability of the operation came very late in the day—so late, perhaps, that cancellation had become unthinkable.

The Market Garden plan was imaginative and bold. It actually came quite close to success, as map 5.4 shows. But it was also deeply flawed, and this, as well as the prompt, well-judged, and fierce German reaction, doomed it to failure. First Allied Airborne Army was an air force command (and it was entrusted to a commander of debatable competence who certainly had an imperfect understanding of the essentials of operations on the ground, especially by lightly equipped airborne forces).[35] The critical decisions about the delivery of the force were made by both American and British airmen, who would not let the needs of soldiers influence their plans. The army assumed command only once the troops were on the ground. Because the Americans distrusted their aircrews' ability to navigate accurately in the dark (especially on moonless nights), it would have to be a daylight insertion; there was thus no question of doing more than one drop in a day to compensate for a shortage of transport aircraft. This meant that delivery would have to be spread over three days; actually, because of poor weather (hardly a surprise in mid-September), the third lift went in on D+5, and the final one did not take place until the seventh day. There were thus inadequate numbers of troops, particularly at Arnhem and Nijmegen, in the critical early stages when objectives had to be seized and consolidated before the enemy recovered from his surprise—a weakness exacerbated by the need to leave substantial numbers to protect the drop and glider landing zones for subsequent lifts. In the case of 1 Airborne, with a single objective, this problem could have been lessened if both the soldiers and the airmen had demonstrated a degree of flexibility with regard to the plan. Having gone forward in the afternoon of D-day to see firsthand how the attack was faring, the divisional commander found it was not going well. He could have requested that the second lift, scheduled for D+1, be moved from its intended drop zone (DZ) more than 10 km (6 miles) to the west and onto the one planned for the Polish brigade in the third lift, just south of Arnhem bridge; this would have necessitated increased air defense suppression, but it ought not to have been an insuperable obstacle.[36]

This problem could have been mitigated had the air force allowed coup de main seizures of the Arnhem, Nijmegen, and Grave bridges to forestall the defense. However, despite the extensive air defense suppression that was planned, fear of flak was allowed to trump an important principle of airborne assaults: that troops should be delivered as close as possible to the objective, and preferably on both sides of it. The British task was made even more difficult by the RAF's insistence on using drop and landing zones about 10 km (6 miles) from the objective and on only one side of the river. The enemy had enough time to establish a scratch blocking position to stop most of the single, lightly armed parachute brigade available at the start from reaching the bridge. Only one battalion was able to reach the bridge and establish a defense, though only of the northern end. The subsequent buildup of combat power was too slow to make up for the initial failure, particularly as the enemy was able to interpose forces between the bridge and the DZs and LZs before the second lift. Nevertheless, that sole battalion fulfilled a vital role. It was positioned to prevent *10 SS Panzer Division* from reinforcing the defense of Nijmegen and the river Waal and thus restoring the integrity of the German line.

The increasingly hard-pressed airborne troops would have benefited greatly from continuous close air support to compensate for their weakness in artillery. Here too, however, the senior airmen let their airborne soldiers down. Brereton displayed no interest in the subject and made no effort to discuss the issue with Coningham at 2 TAF or with Montgomery or Dempsey. The RAF's inflexibility restricted 83 Group, supporting Second Army, in its delivery of the close air support on which XXX Corps would depend. The escorts and air defense suppression for troop and supply drops were provided by the Air Defense of Great Britain, and senior air officers were so worried about the possibility of fratricidal combat that they imposed a blanket ban for long periods; nor were communications between continen-

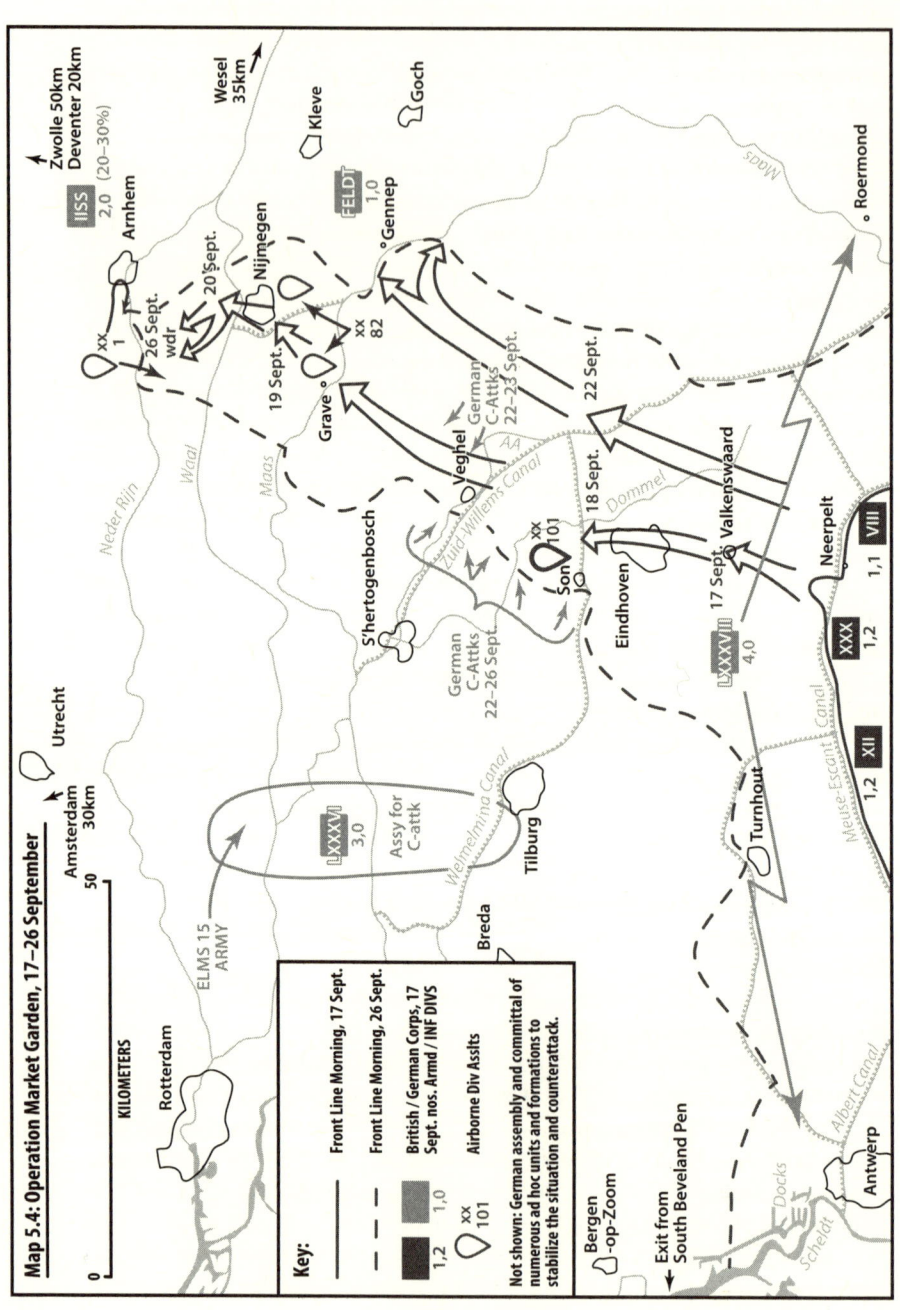

tal and British-based commands anything close to adequate. Poor weather and problems of target identification further restricted support. To make matters worse, the Luftwaffe turned out and, despite its meager strength, had an impact on the battle.

While the airmen ensured that Market got off to a compromised start, there were also some grave faults in the airborne soldiers' planning and execution of their missions. Browning wasted a battalion's worth of gliders flying in his corps HQ. Given the fact that any influence he might have exercised on the battle could have been achieved from England, this was mere indulgence; in the event, radio communications failed so badly that he could communicate only with 82 Airborne, the division with which he was colocated. More seriously, he insisted on leaving the seizure of the Nijmegen bridges (especially the road bridge) to a subsequent phase. No major effort was made until the evening of 19 September, by which time the Germans had organized a coherent defense and reinforced; the bridges were not taken until the next evening, by which time the British at Arnhem were in desperate straits.[37] As the essence of the whole operation was the early securing of bridges, especially the biggest ones, this is difficult to justify. Of course, defense of the eastern flank was important too, but it was not the primary task. The 101 Airborne similarly dropped the troops intended to capture the Zon bridge on only one side of it and about 3 km (2 miles) from the objective. As a result, the Germans were able to blow the bridge and delay the advance of the ground forces.

There was a fundamental problem with the plan: if the enemy proved stronger and quicker to respond than the optimists had assumed, the lightly armed and equipped first lift of each formation would be seriously overtasked. There could be no guarantee that the subsequent lifts would come in on time, and with the surprise factor lost, they could be (indeed, were) too late to reverse any failures. Even if 1 Parachute Brigade had arrived at the Arnhem bridge in strength, it likely would have been too weak to hold both the bridge and the essential routes to it from the DZs and LZs. The 82 Airborne could not expect to secure the Grave, Maas-Waal, and Nijmegen bridges and, at the same time, protect the eastern flank from counterattack. The 101 Airborne was expected to take and hold a strip of territory about 20 km (12 miles) long—including four bridges and the town of Eindhoven, about 10 km (6 miles) from the nearest DZ—but this area provided no depth in which to absorb counterattacks. Unsurprisingly, these counterattacks succeeded in cutting the road on which the ground advance and supply depended.

Operation Market was also plagued by misfortune. Poor weather delayed 1 Airborne's second lift by five hours and its third by two to four days; one-quarter of 82 Airborne's infantry and all of 101 Airborne's artillery were delayed four days. Weather also interfered with resupply, although in the British case, the enemy's appearance on successive DZs was largely to blame for its running out of ammunition and food. In addition, the weather limited close air support for both airborne and ground forces and the interdiction to delay enemy reinforcements. The arrogance and stupidity of an American officer also contributed to the operation's failure: he defied security instructions and took the complete corps plan onto his glider. This fell into German hands and was on the desk of the commander of *First Parachute Army* during D-day. The British division's conduct of the battle was not helped by the unfortunate absence of its commander from his HQ at the most critical time, nor by the almost complete failure of radio communications both internally with Browning and with the air forces. The latter problem also contributed to the lack of close air support.

Despite many problems and setbacks, British paratroopers clung to the north end of Arnhem bridge until the morning of 21 September. The rest of the division held an exploitable bridgehead to the west of the town that included, though just barely, a ferry site. Had XXX Corps made the linkup within forty-eight or even seventy-two hours, success would have crowned Operation Market Garden; even arrival on 21 September might have been timely enough to reinforce the bridgehead and cover the construction of a bridge. It was the failure of Horrocks's command, especially of the leading Guards Armored Division, that did the most to doom the venture. Dempsey's orders were to advance "at maximum speed," and this was plainly necessary to capitalize on surprise, cross difficult ground, and successively relieve the lightly armed airborne troops before the enemy could recover, reinforce, and reestablish an effective defense south of the Rhine.

The ground offensive by XXX Corps started at 1435 on 17 September, its timing selected to coincide with the beginning of the airborne assault. The choice of H-hour was an error. No attack from the Neerpelt bridgehead was going to achieve surprise, and its start would not compromise operational surprise as to the depth and scale of the airborne operation. A precious half day was wasted to no purpose, despite the urgent need for early linkups with successive airborne forces. Following a heavy, 1,800 m (1,970 yard) wide barrage, and with strong, continuous close air support, the leading battle group of one armored regiment and one infantry battalion broke through the weak defense; the artillery and air had destroyed the towed antitank guns and all but eight of the SP guns. At 1730 the armor entered Valkenswaard but stopped for the night to rest and perform unnecessary (at this stage of the operation) maintenance. It had advanced barely 12 km (7 miles) from the line of departure and was still 10 km (6 miles) short of Eindhoven, where the linkup with men of 101 Airborne was to take place; the two British units had suffered fewer than fifty casualties. The advance was resumed at 0700 on

18 September but did not reach Eindhoven until 1800 and the demolished Zon bridge over the Wilhelmina Canal until 2100. Nevertheless, engineers set to work immediately, and a tank-bearing bridge was opened at 0615 on 19 September. The advance restarted straight away, and Grave was reached at 1100. From there, a battle group was sent to reinforce 82 Airborne's defense of the eastern flank, which was increasingly under pressure, and a hasty infantry-tank attack on the Nijmegen bridges was improvised. The now well-organized defense repulsed this effort without too much difficulty. German counterattacks were starting against the narrow corridor, by the weak 59 *Infantry Division* from *Fifteenth Army* from the west and by a newly arrived panzer brigade from the east. Reinforced, these attacks would temporarily cut the main road again, delaying supply and the bringing up of subsequent echelons on 22 and 24 September.

The need for an assault crossing over the Waal was always likely once the decision was made to make the Nijmegen bridges a secondary objective for 82 Airborne Division, giving the Germans time to organize their defense and reinforce. It was plainly required after the repulse of the Guards-airborne attack on the afternoon of 19 September, although Browning and Horrocks apparently failed to reach this conclusion immediately. It was left to Brigadier General Gavin, 82 Division's commander, to propose it. Insufficient foresight in setting the order of march and a seeming lack of urgency meant that the assault boats were not brought up until 1430 on 20 September. At 1500 on the fourth day of the operation, an attack began to seize the Nijmegen bridges. The Guards attacked from the south, and American airborne forces attacked from the north bank after a hazardous and costly opposed crossing of the almost 300 m (330 yard) wide, fast-flowing Waal. By about 1900, both bridges were secured intact, and British tanks crossed the river. Consolidation on the objective was completed by 2015. By this time, the situation of 1 Airborne was critical and worsening with every passing hour. Nevertheless, and to the incredulity, incomprehension, and fury of the American paratroopers who had paid dearly to take the bridge, an immediate continuation of the advance was deemed impossible. Later, lack of infantry was used as an excuse, even though there was a battalion's worth on hand and a whole battle group defending the Grave bridge, where the lead brigade of 43 Infantry Division would arrive by 2300. Orders to resume the attack were not issued until 1100 the next day, and the Guardsmen did not cross the line of departure until 1330. The Germans used those eighteen hours to reinforce, a process that accelerated after they retook the Arnhem bridge. The attack was halted almost immediately. Meanwhile, much of the Polish brigade had dropped south of the Rhine, suffering heavy casualties and finding that they were too late to influence the battle. The Germans continued to compress the airborne bridgehead, taking the ferry site, and they strengthened their positions facing XXX Corps. At 0830 on 22 September, 43 Infantry Division took over the attack up the Arnhem road but was immediately stopped by a strengthening defense. The attackers displayed no inclination to heed the first part of Horrocks's somewhat contradictory injunction to "advance with all speed, but, and this is most important, . . . artillery ammunition must be used with the utmost economy." Toward the end of the day, however, a subunit managed to break out to the west and reach the Rhine opposite the shrinking airborne bridgehead; it was joined by the rest of the brigade the next day, creating a corridor to the river. It was too late to reinforce 1 Airborne, as the bridgehead had become so compressed that it was too small and swept by fire to be a viable springboard for offensive action. On the night of 25–26 September the remains of 1 Airborne were withdrawn south of the river, and Operation Market Garden was over. The culmination of the offensive left Second Army with a salient 70 km (45 miles) deep and 20 to 40 km (12 to 25 miles) wide, leading to nowhere and difficult to defend. The British had paid dearly for giving the enemy the gift of time, first at Valkenswaard, then at Zon, and finally and fatally for their prospects of success at the Nijmegen bridges.

The British were good at conducting set-piece attacks, but in Operation Garden they once again demonstrated their poor tactical performance and inadequate leadership in mobile operations. The lack of any real and sustained sense of urgency was extraordinary, given both the stress on tempo in Second Army's orders and the growing plight of their fellow British soldiers facing annihilation at Arnhem. Instead, the Guards and 43 Divisions seemed more concerned with minimizing their own casualties.[38] The Guards in particular were tactically rigid, unwilling to depart from inflexible groupings and doctrine by taking the initiative, improvising, bypassing rather than mopping up remaining resistance, and operating at night. There had been little improvement since Operation Bluecoat more than two months previously. Back then, much of the blame had been placed on the corps commander, Bucknall. His replacement, Horrocks, had demonstrated energetic and effective leadership in Normandy and the pursuit but then seemed to lose those attributes in Operation Garden; perhaps the severe wound that had incapacitated him for fourteen months was still taking its toll. He failed to press his subordinates to greater and more continuous effort and risk taking, even though they greatly needed pressing. While poor planning and tactical failure contributed to operational failure in both the airborne and ground operations, Dempsey, Montgomery, and Eisenhower made dubious decisions too. These are considered in chapter 7.

The failure at Arnhem marked the culminating point of Montgomery's drive on the Ruhr, but he refused to recognize it as such. At first, Eisenhower accepted that there was still potential in Second Army's offensive, and he agreed to let Bradley send a division to take over the east side of the corridor, freeing VIII Corps to intensify the effort. On 27 September he issued a fresh directive. First Canadian Army's main task was to complete operations to enable the use of Boulogne and Calais and "to have the free use of the port of Antwerp." The early completion of these tasks was described as vital, and they were 21 Army Group's priority. His actions belied his words, however, because Second Army was still given priority in supply, and I Corps, which would soon be augmented by the Polish armored division, was already committed on the Turnhout-Tilburg axis, rather than Crerar's desired attack on Bergen-op-Zoom to seal off the South Beveland peninsula. In practice, the army group's main effort would remain with Dempsey, but its goal would now be "to operate strongly with all available strength from the general area Nijmegen-Gennep against the NW corner of the Ruhr," with the aim of crossing the Rhine in the area of Wesel. By 4 October, Montgomery realized that he lacked the capability to mount the new offensive without preliminary operations to strengthen the defense of the Nijmegen bridgehead and clear the Germans from the west bank of the Meuse, where they threatened his right flank. He considered these endeavors at least as important as Antwerp. In his directive of 9 October he promised Crerar 104 US and 52 British Divisions, but they could not join the action for another week or two. I Corps, meanwhile, continued to support Second Army.

12 Army Group

At first, 12 Army Group was given two divergent axes. First Army with XIX, VII, and V Corps, each consisting of one armored and two infantry divisions, was to support the British by advancing in a northeasterly direction to a line Mons-Sedan.[39] This was the titular main effort, but the priority accorded to the offensive north of the Ardennes proved neither permanent nor absolute. The army group boundary was drawn Tournai–south of Brussels–Hasselt–north of Maastricht. On 4 September Eisenhower shifted the priority from the northern thrust, back to a more even approach to his broad-front concept. First Army was turned more to the east on a general Namur-Liège-Aachen-Cologne axis, the easiest terrain by which to approach Germany. It would cross the Rhine in the area of Cologne, Bonn, and Coblenz, the objectives of XIX, VII, and V Corps, respectively. The army's centre of gravity had shifted to the south when V Corps was switched from the centre to the right to advance through the Ardennes before the Germans could defend the line of the Meuse, thus covering Third Army's flank to Patton's evident satisfaction. Moreover, the allocation of increasingly scarce fuel was to be equalized between the two American armies. Within First Army, Hodges, apparently complying with Bradley's wishes, gave priority to VII and V Corps; XIX Corps on the left was halted for several days and lost an infantry division to Patton. Supporting the British was sliding down the scale of priorities. Third Army's XX and XII Corps, each with one armored and two infantry divisions, were to advance due east on a general Reims-Metz-Mannheim axis to cross the Moselle, take the Saar industrial region, and force the Rhine between Coblenz and Karlsruhe. Although returned to Patton, XV Corps HQ initially came without formations; however, it would be back in action with two divisions by the middle of September, bringing Third Army back to equality with First Army, at eight divisions each. This excluded VIII Corps (which would be transferred to the newly arrived Ninth Army HQ on 5 September), which still had the task of reducing the fortress port of Brest, as well as other formations masking other Breton garrisons. In all, there were five infantry divisions and one armored division in Brittany. Before the end of the month, two of these were reassigned to Patton's command and one to Hodges's. This did not diminish the number of formations in Brittany and Normandy; by the beginning of September, the flow of reinforcements from the United States had brought Ninth Army up to five infantry and two armored divisions, all stripped of transport to support the failing American logistic effort.

First Army faced only slightly stiffer resistance than Dempsey did. Hodges adopted the same approach to the pursuit:

> Although a study of our rapid progress during this period might seem to indicate that our forces were widely dispersed at times, units within the corps were kept within supporting distance of one another. . . . As insurance against the creation of a gap between armored combat commands forming the spearhead . . . and follow-up divisions, motorized infantry followed closely behind the armor to mop-up bypassed pockets of resistance and maintain contact between the armored columns and the slower moving infantry divisions following behind. The necessity for allowing the armored units certain freedom of action . . . was recognized in order to take full advantage of the enemy's disorganized state. Armored tactics under these conditions were bold and aggressive. The necessity for calculated risks by these units was recognized and accepted—risks which would have been unsound if the defense had been prepared and ready to meet armored threats.[40]

The enemy situation remained opaque throughout the advance, partly because constant contact with the retreating forces was not maintained. Poor weather limited air reconnaissance, and the situation was too fluid for radio direction finding and intercept to provide much tactically useful intelligence. Moreover, the relatively primitive and short-range radios of the time often delayed or precluded the passage of both situation reports and orders from fast-moving spearheads to and from formation HQs; as a rule, the larger the formation, the more intermittent and unreliable the contact with subordinates.

On 31 August Bradley shifted First Army's thrust in a northerly direction to cut the Lille-Brussels road. He hoped to block the Germans' line of retreat from France before they could defend the line of the Albert Canal–Meuse River. Real knowledge of the strength and location of the enemy was scant; all Hodges knew was that he was supposed to link up with an airborne assault planned by the high command for the Tournai area on 3 September. He ordered XIX Corps on the army's left to cross the army group boundary and advance through Tournai on Ghent, a move that would cut across Second Army's axis of advance on Brussels and Antwerp. As a result of the penetration to Tournai, of which neither Montgomery nor Dempsey had been warned, Hodges's army almost stumbled into the improvised encirclement of an enemy grouping (a surprise to both sides) in the vicinity of Mons. About 18,000 to 25,000 demoralized prisoners were taken, the sorry remnants of ten to twelve divisions, although most of the prisoners were not fighting troops.

Continuing the advance, which was now back within boundaries and heading east, First Army had all three corps in a single echelon, with no discernible main effort and no army reserve. The corps spearheads reached the Meuse on a line north of Namur and southeast of Sedan on 5 September. They had made up to 280 km (175 miles) in ten days, despite the delay caused by the profitable diversion of the Mons pocket. The state of *Seventh Army*, opposing Hodges's 110,000 men and 850 tanks in eight intact divisions, was dire. There was not a single combat-effective division left by the end of 5 September; most now consisted of HQs with only hastily formed battalions of stragglers and logistic elements. The German army had no more than 30,000 men with around 40 tanks and assault guns.[41] On 11 September leading American units crossed the German frontier: V Corps in the Ardennes and, a day later, VII Corps in the Aachen area; XIX Corps was just east of the Albert Canal on either side of Maastricht. The progress of First Army's operations from 9 to 19 September is shown in map 5.5. The tempo of the offensive was slowed only marginally by growing but patchy German resistance. The principal cause of the slowdown was a worsening problem with fuel supply. Daily deliveries of POL could no longer be guaranteed from 28 August onward (despite First Army's priority awarded by the army group, which, in any case, was canceled on 4 September). The army was living hand to mouth and unpredictably, with some formations forced to halt temporarily by a total failure to resupply them. From 29 August, First Army had only one-third to two-thirds of a single day's supply of POL on hand—sometimes less, and on several days none. It never knew what supplies to expect or when, and the new allocation of 3,500 tons per day was 1,000 tons below the minimum needed to maintain a full-fledged drive. By 6 September, the army was receiving a mere 1,500 tons daily. In fact, supply shortages became an insuperable drag on operations and could not be overcome before resistance hardened.[42]

Where VII Corps entered the Reich in the Aachen sector, the Rhine was only about 80 km (50 miles) beyond. But hard up against the frontier was the more immediate problem of the West Wall. Hodges was anxious to break through the line before the Germans could man it with more than inadequate numbers of service troops, police, home guards, and tired remnants. Nevertheless, he was reluctant to assault a fortified position without some of the corps artillery, grounded to provide provisional truck companies, and an adequate reserve of ammunition; that commodity had been neglected and stocks had run down over the past fortnight, as all logistic efforts concentrated on fuel. Informed that the desired minimum level for five days of continuous, heavy fighting could not be attained before 15 September, he decided to commence the attack on the fourteenth. Collins, commanding VII Corps, was doubtful about the likely strength of the defense and therefore unhappy with any delay. He suggested that he be allowed to mount a reconnaissance in force as early as the next day, 12 September. Hodges gave the go-ahead to both VII and V Corps. XIX Corps, facing the most favorable going to the north of Aachen, could not join the effort on the West Wall. That corps, deprived of POL for days, had yet to pass Maastricht.

Gerow's V Corps had somewhat contradictory instructions. His assigned objective was Coblenz, implying a drive through the Eifel Mountains—much more challenging terrain than their continuance to the west, the Ardennes. At the same time, he was expected to cover Third Army's left, which implied an advance up the Moselle valley, a poor axis more than 100 km (60 miles) south of VII Corps' Aachen-Bonn axis. He could support and protect the flank of one army or the other, but not both. With Hodges's qualified approval, Gerow made his main effort in the north of his sector, although the support to his northern neighbor was somewhat notional: the Hürtgen Forest separated his two infantry divisions from VII Corps, whose main attack was more than 30 km (18 miles) to the north, and the widely spread out armored division attacked another 20 km (12 miles) to the south. Each division achieved a penetration of the West Wall, but at a cost. Lack of artillery and air support; the terrain, which helped even a few defenders mount a resistance out of proportion to their numbers; an inability to concentrate; and the lack of axial roads all discouraged Gerow, and the attacks were called off on 16 September. He later explained that the plan agreed with the army commander had been merely to investigate the possibility of achieving ambitious objectives if the opposition proved "negligible." When the defense proved to be "stout" (somewhat of an exaggeration), First Army instructed him "not to get too involved."[43]

Collins expected to accomplish more from an attack masquerading as

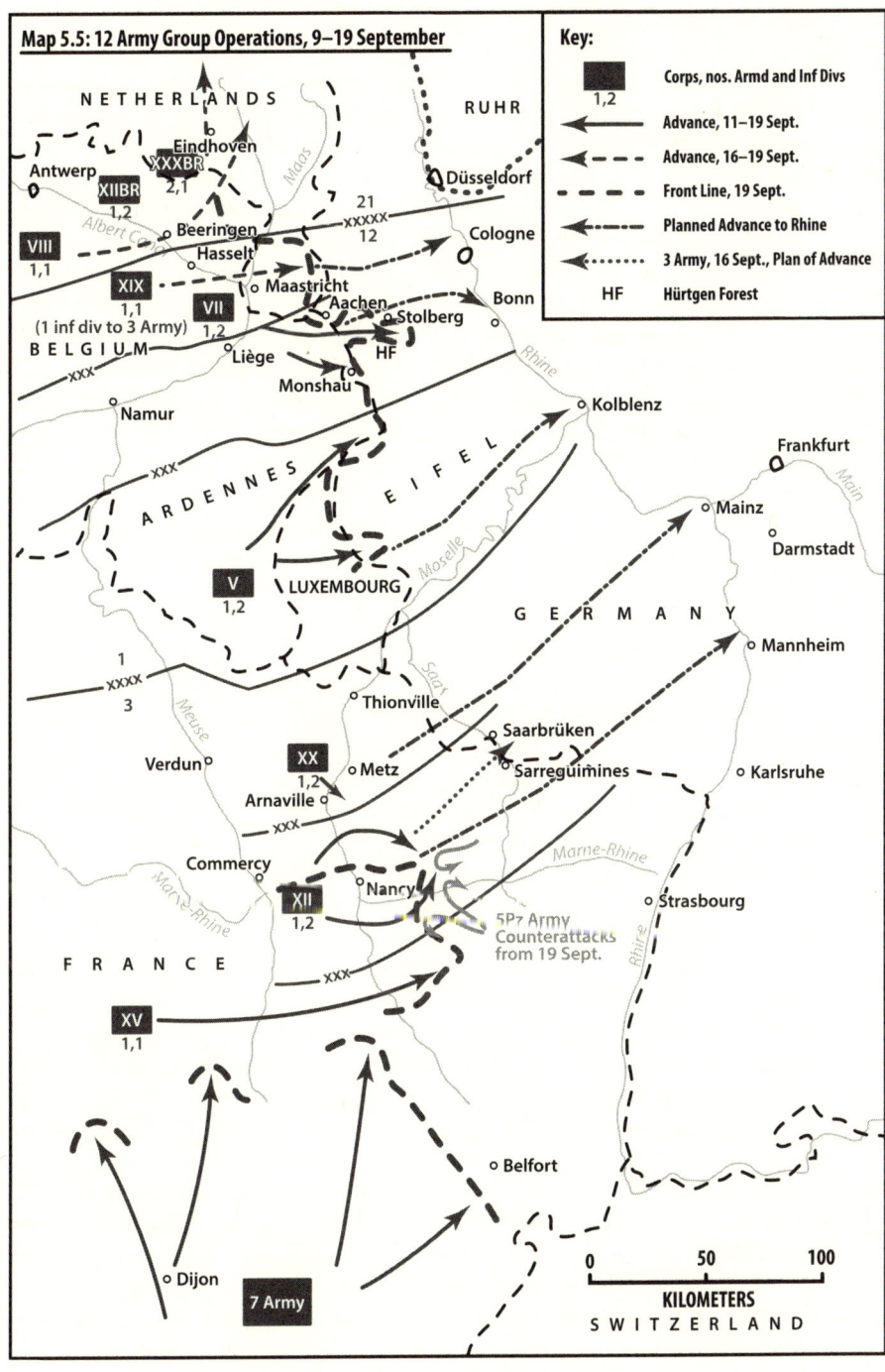

a reconnaissance in force. Although his sector was about 56 km (35 miles) wide, the only promising avenue into the enemy depth was the so-called Stolberg corridor between the city of Aachen and the Hürtgen Forest to the south and east. There was also the semblance of another narrow corridor, the Monschau, 16 km (10 miles) within the forest and parallel to it. The Stolberg corridor was generally less than 10 km (6 miles) wide, and it was intersected by two bands of the West Wall, two river obstacles, a few villages, and the congested industrial suburb of Aachen. The plan was for 1 Infantry Division to mask Aachen and take the north shoulder of the Stolberg corridor while the reinforced 3 Armored Division drove through it and a regiment of 9 Division cleared the wooded ridge on the south shoulder and pushed up the subsidiary avenue. In a week's fighting, the main effort penetrated up to 12 km (7 miles), creating a 20 km (12 mile) gap in the first belt of the West Wall and an 8 km (5 mile) gap in the second, having crossed both rivers and taken most of the villages; in the Monschau area, only a narrow breach in the first belt was achieved. It was less than Collins had hoped for, thanks to several factors: the dogged resistance of the nucleus of enemy veterans and, less so, the patchy efforts of ill-trained and ill-equipped improvised units; the growing shortage of artillery ammunition and the absence of air support, owing to poor weather; and the wear and tear on men and equipment (e.g., by 18 September, 3 Armored was reduced to 153 medium tanks, only half of them available for use). Even so, the groundwork for a breakthrough had been laid. But it was not to be achieved. VII Corps had no reserves with which to maintain momentum, and neither did First Army. There had been no commensurate effort to the north of Aachen to overstretch the enemy. From 16 September the fresh, full-strength *12 Volksgrenadier Division* arrived to stiffen a sagging defense, followed the next week by another full division as well as a depleted one. For the rest of the month, VII Corps consolidated its gains, improved its position, and transitioned to defense. The Germans had bought priceless time.

Hodges's northernmost corps was intended to play an integral role in the First Army scheme of attack. It was supposed to penetrate the West Wall north of Aachen and form a wing of the city's encirclement, the other wing being VII Corps' 1 Infantry Division from the south. But Hodges made the timely fulfillment of this role impossible. Corlett's XIX Corps was immobilized for three days in the Tournai area and then near Hasselt for another day as scarce fuel was diverted to the other corps to keep them advancing. Moreover, not long into September, XIX Corps was shorn of one of its infantry divisions, which was sent to augment Third Army (motoring almost 400 km [250 miles] to get there). When Corlett was able to resume his advance, at least he did not have to worry about forcing the formidable double obstacle facing him before he reached Aachen—the Albert Canal and the Maas River.

He was able to negotiate the use of bridges already captured by VII Corps at Liège and by XXX British Corps at Beeringen. Beginning in the middle of the month, however, he confronted another problem. Operation Market Garden took the British off to the north, ninety degrees away from his own axis eastward. By 19 September, when Corlett issued his order to attack the West Wall, the gap between the Allies had opened to 50 km (30 miles), covered only by patrols, and it would only grow wider. He was responsible for defending First Army's left flank as well as enveloping Aachen, a tall order for a two-division corps.

Leaving his corps cavalry to cover his left, Corlett intended to penetrate the single belt of fortifications facing him with his infantry division and then turn it southeast to link up with 1 Infantry Division; when possible, the armor would follow to exploit. Artillery ammunition was drastically short, which compelled increased reliance on air support. Weather precluded flying on 20–21 September, and the attack was canceled the next day. Hodges and his corps commanders discussed the prospects for a continued offensive and concluded they were poor. Ammunition was short, the troops were tired, equipment was worn out, the weather was poor, and the enemy's defense was recovering across the entire front from Arnhem to Metz. First Army would refurbish its units, improve its lines of communication, and build up stocks for a renewed drive on the Rhine.

When Eisenhower allocated the bulk of 12 Army Group's available fuel to First Army, Patton could expect an early culmination of his offensive. This did not deter him. On 28 August he proposed the river Meuse, 135 km (85 miles) from XII Corps' leading division at Troyes and more than 200 km (125 miles) from XX Corps' troops on the Seine, as his next objective. Bradley preferred the more modest goal of the Marne, but, Patton had little difficulty bringing his commander around to his way of thinking. Bradley still hankered after his own scheme of maneuver, even after Eisenhower had decided to place the main effort in the north. Patton was determined to go as far as he could before the fuel tanks ran dry; meanwhile, he hoped to persuade his superiors to alter theatre priorities. Third Army enjoyed two strokes of luck to help it on its way. First, it found more than 200,000 gallons of erstwhile German fuel, a windfall it did not declare to COMZ but kept for its own use (even so, this was only a single day's consumption). On 30 August XX Corps established a bridgehead over the Meuse at Verdun and XII Corps established another at Commercy, following advances of 45 to 65 km (30 to 40 miles) per day; then the fuel ran out. Third Army was less than 150 km (90 miles) from the West Wall and twice that from the Rhine at Mainz. However, Patton's hopes of Eisenhower and Bradley proved well placed, though not immediately. On 4 September, a new decision on fuel allocations, coupled with another discovery of German POL, enabled Patton to restart his offensive. On that day, his corps closed up to the Moselle. Both Patton and Bradley had justified the ongoing emphasis on the Metz-Saar-Frankfurt axis by arguing that it was important to forestall the enemy's efforts to establish a viable defense at the entrance to the Reich. Actually, Ultra reports in the first three days of September had warned that *First Army* in Lorraine had already been augmented with two veteran panzer grenadier divisions from Italy, two new *volksgrenadier* divisions, and a new panzer brigade.[44] And Patton's chief intelligence officer had warned even before the end of August that the enemy facing Third Army was not in a state of collapse, was being reinforced, and would fight determinedly.

The Germans were anxious to win sufficient time to put the West Wall into a defensible state. In Lorraine, unlike in Belgium, they would be aided by the terrain. The Americans faced a long natural slope crossed by two major river obstacles, the Moselle and the Saar, and three lesser but far from negligible ones; they all became more formidable with flooding. The province was dotted with tangled woods, some of which were very large, and with villages and numerous heights of tactical significance. There were two fortified areas before the West Wall would be reached. The Maginot Line, paralleling the German equivalent, was of minor importance, as it had been stripped of weapons and anything else of use in building the Atlantic Wall; in any case, it faced eastward. There was also the Metz fortress. Patton dismissed this as even more inconsequential than the West Wall (he disdained all fortifications). But he would find that although the works dated from the pre–First World War era, they were a boon to the defense. There were three principal road and rail hubs, at Thionville, Metz, and Nancy, that gave access to the Saarland. As in the north, worsening autumnal weather would hamper movement by turning insubstantial obstacles into difficult ones, reducing off-road mobility, and making minor roads impassable. And it would both reduce air support and make it unpredictable.

The German *First Army*, with six divisions (two of them with limited defensive capability only), was grossly overstretched to cover a frontage of 120 km (75 miles). However, its forces had put the five-day gift of time to good use and organized the defense of the Moselle line, even though they lacked depth and had little ability to maneuver to counter penetrations. Despite what should have been disquieting reconnaissance reports, the Americans failed to see that their fuel-starved operational pause required a rethinking of plans. When Third Army resumed its advance on 5 September, Patton's operational directive declared that the army would advance with its two corps abreast (three, after XV Corps arrived in midmonth) to seize bridgeheads over the Moselle and then the Rhine between Coblenz and Karlsruhe; it would be ready to advance on Frankfurt on order. Eyes firmly fixed on the Rhine, Patton displayed little concern for the enemy to his immediate front, although he briefly discussed methods of breaching the West Wall with his corps commanders. The Moselle obstacle would be nothing more than a speed bump on the way. The enemy, he believed, could do no more than fight a delaying battle, and he would reach the Rhine in ten days—despite having only five divisions available initially,[45] and with no guarantees that POL would arrive in adequate quantities to accomplish this. Walker (XX Corps) and Eddy (XII Corps) were similarly vague about the enemy and the terrain (they were relying on Michelin road maps, for want of anything better) and were as insouciant as their army commander.

At army, corps, and division levels, forces were deployed for a continuation of the pursuit. Reconnaissance was sketchy, no main effort was specified, and combat power was spread evenly over whole formation frontages, with no immediately available reserves. As it was assumed that the Moselle would be crossed from the line of march, neither sufficient artillery ammunition nor bridging was brought up to meet the demands of a deliberate forcing. In consequence, the offensive stalled for days more or less on the forward line of the defense. This was very dangerous for Patton's ambitions. On 12 September Bradley, reluctantly heeding the Supreme Commander's decision to give logistic priority to Market Garden, informed Patton that he would have to transition to the defense if he were unable to establish the bulk of his army over the Moselle by 14 September. Map 5.5 shows the development of Third Army's offensive from its hiatus on 9 September through the beginnings of German counterattacks on the nineteenth.

Walker's corps had battered frontally, ineffectually, and expensively at the Metz position, defended by the determined and tactically savvy officer candidate school of the improvised *Division No. 462*. It seized a precarious toehold over the Moselle south of the city but could not hold it; only by 13 September did it have another very small bridgehead that was at least consolidated. Under continual pressure by Patton for results, Walker continued his futile assaults on the forts but belatedly concentrated his efforts on the Arnaville bridgehead; a grueling attritional struggle resulted in its expansion to approximately 2 to 3 km (1 to 2 miles) wide and deep. However, it lacked exit roads that would allow for operational exploitation, and relentless rain had rendered the ground too soft for cross-country movement. To the relief of the exhausted and much depleted 5 Infantry Division, the battle was called off on 23 September when 7 Armored Division was removed, belatedly, to reinforce XIX Corps at Aachen. Had Walker disposed of just one more division, he probably would have broken through in the initial assault.

Eddy's corps suffered similar early reverses, also from the want of a reserve division when and where it mattered. He then concentrated on creating a double envelopment of Nancy. This endeavor was eased by the defense's overstretch, considerably exacerbated by XX Corps' attacks farther north, which forced the Germans to rob Peter to pay Paul in their efforts to contain the push from Arnaville. By midmonth, thanks largely to a notable example of tactical maneuver in exploitation to operational effect by 4 Armored Division, the overstretched defense of Nancy had collapsed, and XII Corps was firmly over the Moselle in strength. Moreover, XV Corps had come up on Eddy's right and established its own crossing over the river about 30 km (18 miles) south of Nancy. On 14 September this corps effected a junction with the advance elements of Seventh Army, which had come up the Rhône valley, although the link remained tenuous for several days.

Eddy's success came just in time to rescue Patton's offensive. It enabled Bradley to invoke the "get-out clause" in Eisenhower's establishment of priorities. The latter relaxed his 13 September directive, noting that if 21 Army Group could proceed with the promised supply and First Army could attain its first principal objective, there was no reason "why Patton should not keep on acting offensively if conditions for offensive action were favorable." Patton revised his plan in the light of the changed circumstances, gaining Bradley's approval and Eisenhower's endorsement. His superiors' agreement was presumably due, in significant part, to his very optimistic, possibly mendacious assessment that he had enough POL to reach the Rhine and sufficient ammunition for four days of combat. Patton's directive of 16 September narrowed the objective to Rhine crossings between Mainz and Mannheim. This would allow for greater concentration and the attenuation of his army as it advanced. XX Corps' objective remained Frankfurt, bypassing Metz if it continued to be an intractable problem and crossing the river at Mainz; XII Corps would cross at Darmstadt; and XV Corps, echeloned to the right rear during the advance, would cross at Mannheim or be prepared to exploit a bridgehead established by one of the other corps. The main effort would be with XII Corps, which would advance in column of divisions, led by 4 Armored, and drive through the West Wall between Saarbrücken and Saarguemines. In addition, 6 Armored Division, already arriving from Brittany, would join XII Corps, as would, probably, 7 Armored from Arnaville; if released as planned to Third Army, 83 Division would go to Walker's command. Patton had ordered the advance to begin on 17 September, but the ever-cautious Eddy was worried about the as yet incomplete mopping up of the enemy in the wider Nancy area. He sent half of 4 Armored back to expedite the process—an unnecessary diversion, as the bulk of 6 Armored Division was coming up fast. This delayed the start of the offensive by three days.

Hitler entertained greater ambitions than merely holding the line of the Moselle. At the beginning of September he had perceived an opportunity to cripple Third Army with a counterstroke into the American right flank on an axis south of Nancy-Reims. He ordered HQ *Fifth Panzer Army*, now under the young and dynamic leadership of von Manteuffel, to take command of the operation, which would comprise six panzer and panzer grenadier divisions (two of them actually combat-ineffective shells) and three (if possible, six) of the new panzer brigades. Always fanciful, Hitler's concept was a pipe dream by mid-September. The advance of XII and XV Corps had occupied the proposed assembly area, and all the formations earmarked except for two brigades, elements of *15 Panzer Grenadier*, and a still-to-arrive, heavily attrited panzer division had been committed to hold the line in Lorraine or elsewhere. In partial recognition of new realities, OKW scaled back the scope of the operation to a restoration of the Moselle line. Because of the high command's insistence on immediate action, and despite Manteuffel's protests, the counterstroke went off at half cock before its concentration was completed, without adequate reconnaissance, and in piecemeal fashion (not least because of American air interdiction). A sprawling, on-off battle between 19 and 29 September saw the mostly ill-trained, underequipped German formations repulsed, with heavy casualties, by a combination of excellent American maneuver-defensive tactics and plentiful close air support.

They may have been costly failures, but the German attacks forestalled Third Army's drive on the Rhine and discouraged Eddy and eventually even Patton from immediately pressing on to the West Wall. Had the Americans persevered in timely fashion with their own offensive plan, they probably would have succeeded, engaging the panzer formations as they arrived and destroying them in detail in a series of meeting battles. Their momentum could have taken them through the largely unmanned West Wall and certainly would have unhinged the defense of Metz. As it was, regardless of Patton's wishes, Third Army had culminated. The decision promulgated after Eisenhower's Versailles conference, when the Americans were still acting on the defense, meant that supply for a renewed offensive would not be forthcoming until after a lengthy operational pause.

Even if the pursuit across France and into the Low Countries ended disappointingly, in a less than decisive victory, it still accomplished much. Rather than reaching the Seine on D+90, by that day the Allies had attained a line the planners had not expected to reach until D+240. There was, however, a major exception to this generalization. In Brittany the Americans had not achieved the goals hoped for by D+50. When the Americans broke into Brittany at the beginning of August, two-thirds of the German garrison, including the best-armed and best-equipped troops, had already been committed to Normandy. The remainder quickly took refuge in the fortified ports of St. Malo, Brest, Lorient, and St. Nazaire, where they were ordered to hold out to the last man. Having downgraded the importance of these ports to the campaign, SHAEF was happy to leave their reduction, and the opening of Quiberon Bay (a perfectly sheltered deep-water anchorage situated between the last two ports) to Major General Troy H. Middleton's VIII Corps. Initially short of infantry, Middleton could tackle only St. Malo immediately, while investing the others.[46] The port fell on 18 August but was too small to make any real difference to the American supply situation, even if its full potential had been realized (its planned capacity was only half that of one of the Normandy beaches). Reinforced to three infantry divisions, the corps then went on to besiege Brest. The fortress garrison was well manned, and although most were not field troops, there was a tough nucleus of about 7,000 underequipped but determined paratroopers. Middleton was uneasy about his orders for an early assault. Instead of the 20,000 tons of ammunition he had requested, Third Army had authorized only 5,000 tons. Promised another 3,000 tons, which did not arrive in good time, the Americans began their onslaught on 25 August but shelved it after three days of heavy casualties and no progress (air and naval support was not a sufficient substitute for army artillery). Bradley granted Brest priority in supply on 10 September. It was not until 19 September, after expending 25,000 tons of ammunition, flying 6,000 sorties by Ninth Air Force, and taking just under 10,000 casualties, that the battle ended. The port facilities had, of course, been wrecked.

Already on 3 September, the SHAEF staff had abandoned plans to use Lorient, St. Nazaire, Nantes, and Quiberon Bay (even though the bay's opening would require only the clearing of the Quiberon peninsula and Belle Isle at the entrance, as well as the establishment of mulberry-type docks). Then on 14 September it decided to do without Brest as well (a curious decision, as its capture had been emphasized only the day before in Eisenhower's latest directive). Presumably, the feeling was that the war had moved on. The distance from the port to Metz was more than 1,000 km (620 miles) by truck, twice the distance from Le Havre, which had been captured on 10 September and which the Americans hoped to take over from the British as the latter took the Channel ports. The logisticians had planned to have 22,300 tons per day flowing through the Brittany ports by 4 October (having taken them much earlier, of course); however, only 4,000 tons were arriving from the two minor ports that had not been fought over and badly damaged.[47] The battle for Brittany had absorbed relatively strong forces, required enormous quantities of fuel and ammunition and a considerable air effort, and cost thousands of casualties, to little purpose. For the remainder of the war, Lorient and St. Nazaire were masked by a green infantry division and the 20,000 men of Brittany's FFI.

BACK TO STALEMATE: THE AUTUMN CAMPAIGN

By the end of September, the Allied offensive had culminated all along the front and had fallen short of all its operational terrain objectives.[48] Despite the enormous casualties incurred in restoring a cohesive front, the German army, far from being destroyed or disintegrated, was becoming somewhat stronger. None of the theatre's three top land commanders clearly recognized that their culminating point had arrived.[49] Montgomery, for one, was characteristically unprepared to admit failure. He was not even prepared to admit, however tacitly, that his main effort should now shift to opening up Antwerp. His eyes remained fixed on the Rhine; he still believed that his army group should be the main effort and that time might still be on his side if he could strike immediately. Perhaps the river could no longer be bounced, but it could be forced in a less spatially ambitious operation in tandem with an American thrust on Cologne. On 27 September he issued a new directive. Crerar's main task was to complete the capture of Boulogne and Calais and enable the Allies' use of Antwerp. Early completion of these operations was declared vital—but once again, words were not matched with resources. I Corps was to attack on Second Army's left to free the latter from the necessity of protecting its left flank; once again, the task of sealing off the South Beveland peninsula would have to be postponed. Dempsey, while holding the Nijmegen bridgehead, would attack directly toward the southwest corner of the Ruhr, forcing the Rhine in the area of Wesel. The army's right wing would not have to worry about its flanks, as 7 US Armored Division of XIX Corps would clear VIII Corps' sector west of the Maas.

By 9 October, however, reality forced a reluctant Montgomery to change his mind. The Nijmegen salient needed shoring up, and then the whole area south of the Lower Rhine had to be cleared. A single US armored division was not nearly enough to clear the west bank of the Maas; the task eventually took all of VIII Corps as well as the American division and was completed only in late November. Above all, Montgomery was under great pressure from both Eisenhower and Brooke to afford the highest priority to Antwerp in terms of both forces and personal attention. Their demands became more peremptory.[50] On 16 October Montgomery awarded it "complete priority over all other offensive operations in 21 Army Group, without any qualification whatsoever." With two additional divisions (including another American) and adequate quantities of ammunition, the battle of the Scheldt was finally brought to an end on 8 November; the first Allied ship started to unload in Antwerp on 29 November, eighty-five days after the capture of the port. The Rhine bridgehead and the Ruhr had been put on the back burner, and the autumn campaign had been reduced to a dreary grind to improve 21 Army Group's position so that the eastward offensive could be renewed in time. It would be February 1945 before the thrust on Wesel took place. It was a bitter pill to swallow, but Montgomery eventually had to adjust his ambitions to come into line with his Supreme Commander's wishes and his own lack of combat power.

Bradley's offensive had failed as surely, if not as spectacularly, as 21 Army Group's with Market Garden. He was no more daunted by what he perceived as a mere setback than was Montgomery. The German forces were still believed to be on the verge of disintegration. With luck, attacks across the front would find a weak spot that would permit a rapid advance to the Rhine. There would, however, be a need for an operational pause. The logistic situation would have to be improved to allow the deployment of grounded divisions and those freed up from Brest, as well as to build up ammunition stocks to levels required for attacks on a defending enemy rather than pursuit. Greater concentration would have to be achieved on the main axis. Hodges's offensive objectives were changed to attaining the Rhine at Düsseldorf, Cologne, and Bonn. His frontage was reduced when Bradley moved Ninth Army HQ, with two divisions of VIII Corps, into the Ardennes to take over V Corps' former sector. Glossing over a fortnight-long boundary shift to take over much of British VIII Corps' sector, this moved the army's centre of gravity northward and reduced its sector from approximately 160 km (100 miles) to around 95 km (60 miles). Its objectives shifted too, with the corps objectives now Düsseldorf, Cologne, and Bonn, respectively. At least Hodges would continue on the offensive. To his extreme displeasure, Patton's offensive was closed down—and this time, the high command meant it when it gave priority to the north. At last, the logistic facts of life had triumphed over operational illusions. There would be enough supply only for a Third Army defensive operation. Moreover, the army was to give up three divisions; 7 Armored was sent to First Army to take over responsibility for part of the British front, and XV Corps was detached to 6 Army Group, as Devers's line of supply from Marseille could support two more divisions in its attacks toward Strasbourg and through the Belfort gap.[51] For the month of October, Patton was reduced to three minor local attacks to secure a better line of departure for the future resumption of the offensive (one of them another futile and costly attempt to reduce the Metz fortifications). When the army restarted its push for the West Wall and the Rhine in November, it quickly turned into another attritional grind; attacks were spread evenly across the army zone, and there were no reserves. It was brought to an end by the December crisis in the Ardennes, when substantial forces were required to move north.

Hodges's set-piece attack at Aachen by XIX and VII Corps started on 2 October, despite the worsening supply crisis (12 Army Group reimposed artillery ammunition rationing on the same day). In the regrouping that followed Bradley's new decision, the frontage of the former corps increased temporarily to over 100 km (60 miles) when it was given responsibility for clearing the Peel marshes; although its strength was increased to four divisions, it still had only two divisions for its task at Aachen, as one division went to the marshes and one was needed for flank protection. VII Corps' sector was reduced to about 30 km (18 miles). Each assault corps devoted a single infantry division to the envelopment of the city, with the armored divisions covering the flanks. The encirclement was completed in a fortnight, and Aachen was surrendered after another week. The original idea had been for Corlett and Collins to advance together to force the Roer and thus provide springboards for an advance on the Rhine, but even the Roer intermediate objective had been abandoned by the end of the operation.

While the Aachen battle was proceeding, VII Corps started its long involvement in the Hürtgen Forest. Originally intended to secure the high ground south of the Stolberg corridor, whence a counterattack into the flank of an American advance could be damaging, the battle took on a life of its own. Collins was drawn into fights through broken, heavily forested, roadless terrain (much more challenging than the Ardennes) for a succession of hills, villages, towns, and crossroads of questionable value. For the November offensive, Ninth Army took over the sector north of Aachen, receiving a new corps as well as XIX Corps. Although it faced the best going, however, there was a return to an emphasis on the Stolberg corridor toward Düren on the Roer, with other First Army corps attacking on VII Corps' flank in support (including a continuation of the Hürtgen battle). Operations would be resumed against a reinforced and increasingly well-prepared enemy, with no hope of achieving surprise. Twelve divisions would be involved initially, but there was no greater concentration than in previous efforts, and no reserve was kept to build up the attack and then exploit success. The attacks were not sequenced or synchronized to advantage. It was another push across the front. In midmonth the Americans reached the Roer, only to halt there while their commanders pondered a problem that had been staring them in the face.[52]

Not until well into November was the vital ground first tentatively identified: the Roer River dams. When the Americans attacked over the river en route to the Rhine at Cologne and Düsseldorf, the enemy could open the floodgates and produce an inundation downstream that would grow to approximately 2.5 km (1.5 miles) wide and up to 10 m (11 yards) deep and impair movement long after the waters had subsided. Forces that had moved east of the river would be cut off and vulnerable to counterattack by the newly formed *Sixth Panzer Army*. Attempts to breach the dams from the air failed. Not until the beginning of December was V Corps tasked specifically with taking the dams preliminary to another effort to cross the Roer and get to the Rhine. The attack got under way on 13 December but was aborted on the sixteenth when the Germans unleashed their counteroffensive through the Ardennes immediately to the south.

The end of September had seen the effective end of Montgomery's operational idea. For want of a better one, the broad-front advance continued against steadily stiffening resistance by an enemy that was recovering grip, balance, and strength. The Germans were greatly aided by the dismal state of Allied supply (until it ameliorated in November), by having fortifications to fight from, by poor weather that lessened Allied close air support and interdiction, and by increasingly restricted going. As the summer crisis eased, the Führer's thoughts turned once again to the attack. On 16 September he announced his decision in favor of a counteroffensive through the Ardennes with the objective of Antwerp, the nucleus being provided by the new *Sixth Panzer Army* being built up from the refitting panzer divisions. On 25 September he explained to a select group of advisers his concept for an offensive beginning toward the end of November.[53] By 16 December, when the oft-postponed thrust through the Ardennes began, the Germans had assembled seven panzer and thirteen infantry divisions, admittedly of variable quality and with totally inadequate logistic backup. But the Germans were supposed to be nearing the end of their tether, not hitting back. The Allied autumn offensive had been intended to retain the initiative, exhaust the enemy all across the front, and move Allied forces at least up to the Rhine and in some places across it. Instead, it had failed to destroy the enemy or seize operationally important terrain, and it gave rise to US vulnerability without compensatory gain. The Germans would hit the weakest part of the line, manned by overstretched American divisions worn down in the Hürtgen battle.[54] Bradley was badly unbalanced and lacked any operational reserve to meet the blow.

On 30 November Montgomery wrote to Eisenhower, recapitulating the aims of the autumn campaign and concluding pithily and brutally: "We have achieved none of this; and we have no hope of doing so. We have therefore failed; and we have suffered a strategic reverse."[55] It is difficult to disagree with this verdict.

CHAPTER SIX

Logistic Realities

THE LOGISTIC SYSTEM

In essence, the business of logistics consisted of four parts: to identify in advance the needs of the theatre and provide for them; to develop a system that could and would respond in good time to the demands of the fighting formations; to ship what was required to the Continent, whether by ocean-going ship or coaster; and to deliver from ports or beaches what was needed where and when it was needed. Each of these steps posed its own problems, and the failure to solve each one before the autumn would have a negative effect on the campaign.[1]

Predicting and Meeting Theatre Needs

By and large, the Allies did a good job of predicting the needs of the armies and air forces in northwest Europe. However, there was a general failure to anticipate the nature and thus logistic requirements of *bocage* fighting, a problem of particular concern to the Americans. Consequently, shortages developed as early as June. The infantry wanted more mortars, grenade launchers, light and submachine guns, and bazookas in particular. It also became apparent that the army had failed its armor branch by not pushing the earlier introduction of the M-26 Pershing or upgrading at least some Shermans with the 90mm gun (as the British had with their 17-pounders), thus condemning tankers to combat against often superior tanks. Many ammunition natures, particularly 105mm and 155mm howitzer and 81mm mortar rounds, were also expended at higher than predicted rates (often because of unjustifiably profligate usage, as even First Army's chief of staff admitted). Occasional periods of poorly enforced rationing and appeals for self-restraint failed to change behavior significantly, so strict rationing was imposed in mid-July to build up stocks for Operation Cobra.[2] The success of the breakthrough and transition to pursuit eased most weapon and ammunition shortages, but only for a time. The problem then became one of fuel supply, although this was mostly an issue of moving abundant fuel stocks. The ammunition problem then resurfaced in early autumn. Moreover, it became clear that the War Department, having cut back procurement a year before in response to congressional perceptions of waste, was not providing adequate quantities of some types of ammunition—a problem compounded by COMZ's deficiencies. The sudden transition to a war of movement revealed another shortage—motor transport—which would eventually bring operations almost to a halt. Inadequate provision for a switch from semistatic to fast-moving operations was due partly to the War Department's failure to procure adequate numbers of heavier trucks. But it could also be blamed on the field commanders overriding their logistic planners and according too low a priority to the buildup of truck fleets in the first two months.

The British and Canadians were generally conditioned to expect a less generous provision of materiel and supplies (and, perhaps in consequence, were better at stock control and accounting and the avoidance of waste). They apparently made fewer importunate demands of logisticians to meet unexpected needs. They too, however, suffered from periodic ammunition shortages and restrictions on usage until well into August. And both armies suffered again from a dearth of munitions in September and October. To a large extent, this was caused by a lack of logistic lift, a problem resulting from conscious trade-offs in the planning process and greatly exacerbated by the discovery that 1,400 newly procured British three-ton trucks suffered from engine defects (which afflicted replacement engines as well).

The major failing of each of the Allies was the inadequate provision of infantry replacements. Each army faced a manpower crisis sooner or later. For the British, it was sooner. As a result of drawing faulty lessons from the North African campaign, the War Office seriously underestimated the infantry's likely casualty rate (by almost half) while simultaneously overestimating that of the other arms. Even without this miscalculation, the British had recognized a year before D-Day that they would likely face a shortage of 35,000 infantrymen by the end of September. This estimate proved to be only slightly too pessimistic. As forecast, to keep other formations up to strength, 21 Army Group had to disband two divisions (one in August and one in November) and the equivalent of two armored brigades. The Canadian army likewise suffered from shortages from August until mid-November (when a static role on a passive sector led to falling loss rates). The US War Department (and the ETO) were also far off in the prediction of infantry loss rates, especially riflemen. By the end of July, the replacement pool was almost dry of infantrymen. The transition from attritional to maneuver warfare eased the problem until November, when a full-scale manpower crisis blew up with the return of attritional warfare. This was not entirely the War Department's fault; as it pointed out, the theatre was 70,000 men overstrength, of which 32,000 were overhead, and it could and should have been retraining some of the surplus to provide the needed riflemen.[3] In the event, all three Allies mitigated the shortage by combing HQ and administrative units for potential infantry, retraining surplus air defense gunners and personnel from other overmanned combat units, and speeding up the flow of replacements. The results were not entirely satisfactory, as they produced large numbers of poorly trained and resentful riflemen. The British deficiencies also exerted a baneful effect on operational planning and execution that went beyond the disbandment of formations; commanders were so concerned with minimizing casualties that they became overcautious and sometimes missed opportunities.

While the macro-needs of the land forces were, for the most part, adequately anticipated and met, the same cannot be said for more detailed theatre plans. There was something of a logical disconnect between the structure of the Allied armies and their operational planning prior to the invasion. Although there was great emphasis on armor and mobility in their organizational development, suggesting a preparedness and a desire for maneuver warfare, the armies assumed that expansion of the lodgment to the Seine and the Loire and through Brittany would progress in a steady, predictable fashion as the enemy conducted an orderly withdrawal from one obstacle to the next. Once the Seine was reached, there would be a month-long operational pause while ports were opened, rail and pipelines extended, and more supplies and motor transport landed to establish the forward dumps necessary to support a further advance. The subsequent march on Germany was expected to take place in a similarly predictable fashion. In essence, the offensive would resemble that of the Allies in 1918 rather than the German blitzkrieg. The logistic system was configured for this essentially linear, even-paced development. To take the American model as an example, COMZ was supposed to receive supplies into the theatre (Normandy); transfer them to the appropriate dumps, duly sorted and inventoried; and forward them, on demand, through its various sections to the army rear boundary. Army would then distribute them to the divisions. The plan anticipated the creation by D+41 of an adequate reserve of fourteen days of supply for all items save ammunition, of which there would be five units of fire.[4] By D+90, reserves would be built up to twenty-one days of supply for most items and five units of fire. Army levels would be maintained throughout at seven days of supply and seven units of fire. (Of course, the number of divisions in France would go up in the interim, from fifteen to twenty-one.) To achieve such levels of reserves, supplies had to be landed at a rate exceeding current demand by at least 50 percent. That is, given that a division slice initially required as much as 800 tons per day, upward of 1,200 tons would have to be landed daily—a figure excluding the air forces' needs, coal, civil affairs supplies, preshipped equipment, materials for railway and bridge repair and pipeline construction, and other overheads. For the period up to D+41, this meant that 26,500 tons per day had to be landed. The figure would rise to approximately 45,000 tons a day by D+90.[5]

Operations did not develop as predicted. The D+17 phase line was only partially reached by the end of July. The Breton ports had not been taken by D+50. However, the sweeping post-Cobra advances carried the Allies eastward at such a speed that they went from the hoped-for D+20 line (south of the Sélune) to the D+90 line (the Seine and the Loire) in less than a month. While operational commanders were seizing the opportunities vouchsafed to them, the logisticians were increasingly pressed to adjust their plans and actions to reflect the new realities. When the offensive continued beyond the Seine without any pause, they progressively failed to cope with demand.

Systemic Shortcomings

Most shortages, including those of ammunition, arose not because of inadequate foresight by the War Department and War Office or even excessive demand but because of the difficulties of delivering adequate tonnages to the Continent and then distributing supplies to the armies.[6] This was partly a function of limited port capacity (exacerbated during the period of the "great storm" in June, when the beaches became unusable for a few days). In larger part, it was due to the unexpected and therefore unplanned rapidity with which the offensive developed in August–September. The pace of operations would have led to logistic overstretch sooner or later. The fact that it happened sooner and affected the US forces more acutely was to a considerable extent due to flaws in the setup of logistic management. For eighteen months before the invasion, there had been a struggle of byzantine complexity between competing jurisdictions over who and which organizations should command, control, or coordinate what aspects of the American logistic effort. Whatever Lieutenant General J. C. H. Lee's shortcomings as a logistician (he had a peacetime quartermaster's mentality, lacking a can-do approach, initiative, and a willingness to improvise), he was a formidable bureaucratic infighter. Even Eisenhower's directive issued on D-Day itself did not definitively settle any issues. The Americans went into the campaign with a command and supply system that could charitably be described as confused and more unkindly described as in disarray. A variety of commands existed (SHAEF, ETO, First Army and then 12 Army Group, COMZ and its ill-defined subordinates the Forward, Advance, and Base Sections), and they often expended much time and effort working against one another.[7] Institutional responsiveness to the requirements of the field forces was not among the system's defining characteristics. COMZ was divorced from the operational chain of command. Lee was responsible only to Eisenhower. Neither Smith, the SHAEF chief of staff, nor Bradley, let alone the army commanders, could issue orders to COMZ or its parts; they could only make requests. This had a negative impact on both their authority and their ability to plan with confidence. Given Lee's powerful mentors in Washington (including Marshall himself), Eisenhower never felt confident enough to sack him, even when he failed to deliver, or even to impose a more rational system on him. In stark contrast was the simple, straightforward British system, in which the army group's chief logistician was directly subordinate to the operational commander, an arrangement replicated down the chain of command.

COMZ, with its squabbling subcommands, was a complex piece of machinery supposedly designed to provide supply without waste or delay. In practice, it was overly bureaucratic and inefficient, quite unsuited to cope with the friction generated by battle and unable always to get what was needed to the fighting man in good time. The flexibility, adaptability, and responsiveness to rapidly changing circumstances required by maneuver warfare were lacking. Also largely absent was foresight, a prerequisite for effective logistic support; for instance, winter arrived long before appropriate clothing was provided because COMZ was purely reactive.[8]

The supply system was undesirably rigid in its organization of deliveries. Thus, the prescheduling of supply shipments into France for the whole of June, July, and August resulted simultaneously in shortages and unbalanced stocks. To mitigate the consequences, selective unloading was instituted to meet current priorities. This resulted in shipping lying idle, increasing turnaround times, and it meant that, at any given moment, a high proportion of theatre supplies was stuck in the pipeline. For example, the priority accorded to ammunition in July to alleviate shortages created deficiencies in other areas, such as replacement tanks and quartermaster and engineer stores. The inflexibility inherent in the system was alleviated to some extent by special express shipping services, sometimes by air, to meet unpredicted requirements.[9] The disposition of goods once they were landed was another problem. With every sort of supply competing for scant space on and near restricted docks and beaches, those responsible for handling the supplies were sometimes overwhelmed. Stocks were piled up wherever space could be found, and record keeping was often scant. Lacking a proper system of inventory and control, supply officers lost track of stores and found it easier to put in a fresh demand than to hunt for the items required. Uncertainty about depot balances, or even contents, led to massive waste; supplies that are unsorted, unrecorded, and unlocatable might as well not have been shipped in the first place. Nor did COMZ maintain close liaison with operations staffs to ensure the intelligent anticipation of needs; it was purely reactive. Moreover, the indenting system was insensitive to urgent demands and became chaotic as requisitions were resubmitted (often several times) when not honored; the problem was frequently compounded by the practice of substituting "filler" tonnage, things not requested, for the required items (both suppliers and movers were often satisfied with achieving a quantitative target, regardless of expressed needs). Waste, often incurred as a consequence of haste, was endemic. For instance, by mid-October, more than 3.5 million jerry cans supplied to the Americans in theatre and essential for the delivery of fuel from bulk storage and pipe heads to the front had been discarded, lost, or stolen, contributing significantly to the armies' fuel supply crisis. Unquantifiable but substantial amounts of POL and other attractive items disappeared into the chaos of the resurrected French railway system (both individual cars and whole trainloads) or into the insatiable black market.

US field forces prided themselves on their casual, informal approach to supply. Administration was generally seen as pedantry, producing delays and interfering with the essential business of fighting. In their disdain for records or formal authorizations, they contributed significantly to the disorder and waste that increasingly characterized the system. When the armies advanced and turned over their rear supply dumps, COMZ usually inherited a mess; supplies were scattered around with little or no supporting paperwork. The armies were also guilty of ultimately self-defeating short-termism in their resort to "moonlight requisitioning," hoarding, overrequisitioning, cannibalization, and subversion of the system through bribery, barter, and outright theft. In particular, their commanders' habit of subordinating logistic considerations to operational aspirations was bound to overstretch COMZ sooner or later. Partly because of the extraordinary demands placed on it, and partly because of its structural and command deficiencies, the crunch point came earlier than it might have. Though systemically flawed, the logistic machine managed to function for some time with remarkable if steadily declining effectiveness, working imperfectly and staggering from crisis to crisis. This was made possible by the goodwill, ingenuity, and initiative of some senior and many mid- and junior-level officers who were determined to provide for the fighting formations in difficult circumstances.

THE SYSTEM AT WORK: GROWING PROBLEMS AND FAILURES

Delivery into Theatre: Shipping and Discharging Cargo

US Army logisticians calculated that, to be fully effective in the offensive, fighting formations should be able to count on a daily supply of roughly 650 tons per divisional slice, with another 4,000 to 5,000 tons going to Ninth Air Force.[10] By the beginning of September, the planners were counting on having, in addition to the Normandy beaches, Mulberry A (which was actually destroyed in a storm after only three days of operation), Cherbourg, and the Breton ports, principally Brest, Lorient, and Quiberon Bay. This would provide a daily discharge capacity of about 46,000 tons, including an expected

25,000 tons from the beaches and Cherbourg. This tonnage was calculated to be enough, after a portion was set aside for the British, for the maintenance of twenty-one divisions, the buildup of the reserves required for a sustained offensive, and the support of the air arm. It was further calculated that discharge capacity would be sufficient to support the planned buildup as far as the beginning of September (D+90), but only by a very narrow margin, and only if the ports were taken more or less as forecast (including St. Malo on 1 July, Quiberon Bay by 16 July, and Lorient and Brest by 26 July). However, by the end of September, capacity was expected to start to fall short of requirements, with a serious deficiency continuing for several months. Brittany's perceived centrality to the success of Overlord is clear from the fact that it was expected to provide the bulk of supplies by the time the autumn weather circumscribed beach activity, with Brest being the point of entry for reinforcing formations and Quiberon Bay alone discharging 10,000 tons per day.[11] No wonder Eisenhower wrote to Montgomery in late July: "We must get the Brittany peninsula. From an administrative point of view that is essential. We must not only have the Brittany peninsula—we must have it quickly. So we must hit with everything."[12]

These expectations were not realized. In June and July, thanks to the late opening of Cherbourg, only 62 percent of planned discharges had actually been achieved, limiting the buildup of stocks; however, the much slower than anticipated rate of advance mitigated the effects initially. Thereafter, the plan to open the Breton ports as the main source of supply was progressively jettisoned. St. Malo was taken on 18 August and Brest on 19 September, but each was so comprehensively wrecked and blocked that neither was ever used. Neither Quiberon Bay nor Lorient was ever developed (the latter was never captured, and although the former had been taken on 16 July, no effort was made to seize Belle Isle, whose batteries controlled the entrance). Thus, the over 20,000 tons expected to flow from Brittany by the end of September (and 30,000 by early November) did not materialize; the 4,640 tons coming into minor, inefficient ports was an inadequate replacement, bringing the total discharges at the beginning of October to only 26,000 tons per day from all sources. To the logisticians, the upset to their plans was greater because St. Malo, Brest, Lorient, and Quiberon Bay were all deep-water ports and anchorages, and opening additional shallow-draft capabilities was pointless, as all available coasters were already in use. The port situation also contributed directly to the ammunition crisis that dominated operations in October.[13] The Canadian army took Rouen on 30 August and Le Havre (a deep-water port) on 12 September, and SHAEF almost immediately allocated these ports to 12 Army Group. Like Cherbourg, St. Malo, and Brest, however, they had been thoroughly demolished. They were not open for business until October, when they discharged close to 90,000 tons between them; they did not take on major importance until November, when they handled almost 293,000 tons. Thus, at the beginning of October, with adverse weather disrupting or preventing unloading over the beaches, the outlook for the landing of supplies was bleak. Discharges in October averaged only around 25,000 tons per day, compared with an estimated requirement of at least 38,500 tons and a planned 49,750.[14] This quantity was grossly inadequate to meet the army's needs, and the rate of discharge was too slow to clear shipping as it arrived. By early September, a backlog of over 100 deep-draught Liberty ships (each with a cargo capacity of almost 11,000 tons) was awaiting an opportunity to unload. Until then, they acted as floating storage, a waste of shipping space the system could ill afford; the only alternative to lying idle was being forced into British ports for time-wasting transloading into coasters as these became available.

There was an additional complication to calculations of port discharge rates. Supplies had to be not only landed but also cleared. Cherbourg, the Americans' only major port until Le Havre opened in the autumn, enjoyed only limited access by road and rail (and the same limitations applied to most smaller ports). Creating mountains of supplies at the dockside was arguably worse than nondelivery, as it led to further constriction, not to mention holdings of inadequately documented and therefore essentially unusable stocks. Moreover, as the demands for motor transport to move supplies to the armies escalated, trucks were taken from clearance duty, further limiting capacity.

British and Canadian requirements were proportionate to that of the Americans; fourteen divisions required 9,100 tons per day. Initially, they lacked a significant port like Cherbourg, but their mulberrry harbor was operating smoothly. By August, the average daily discharge over their beaches and through the artificial harbor was around 16,000 tons; this was sufficient to create fourteen days of reserves plus fourteen days of working margins or equivalent stocks of all commodities held in the rear maintenance area (RMA). However, the projected thrust northward would take the armies far from the RMA in Normandy, and the major obstacle of the unbridged Seine would complicate and slow the flow of supplies. On 30 August the weighty decision was made to rely on the early capture and opening of at least one Channel port and meanwhile reduce the amount of supplies and vehicles imported into Normandy to 7,000 tons per day. The first post-Normandy task of First Canadian Army was to capture the Channel ports, defended by substantial elements of *Fifteenth Army*, to support 21 Army Group's advance. But the big prize would be Antwerp, the answer to all future capacity problems.

As the Americans had found at Cherbourg, the quick capture of a port did not necessarily mean a quick opening. This was, however, achieved at Dieppe, which began receiving vessels on 7 September and quickly reached a daily capacity of 6,000 to 7,000 tons. With Dieppe in operation and Boulogne about to fall, the decision to rely on ports north of the Seine to bring in sufficient supplies to meet 21 Army Group's needs seemed justified. Both ports were much nearer the point of main effort and, being north of the Seine, enjoyed rail links northward that were only lightly damaged by the air interdiction campaign; they also joined with the Belgian system, which was untouched. However, Boulogne was not surrendered until 22 September and could not be opened until three weeks after its capture; even then, it could accept only coasters landing about 2,200 tons. It could not take substantial cargoes until two larger, deep-water quays were opened, and these were not discharging a respectable 11,000 tons daily until November. Ostend was receiving a mere 1,000 tons per day by the end of September (although it was also an entry point for bulk POL), and Calais could receive only landing ships tank (LSTs) and personnel.[15] During the Market Garden operation, the army group still depended, but to a decreasing extent, on supplies trucked north from the RMA in Normandy; it would not enter the autumn campaign with enough supplies to meet all the needs of both its armies, never mind the stores and other items required to cope with a backlog of repairs and the replacement of defective equipment.

The US port situation has been dwelled on at greater length because the Americans faced the more challenging problem. Their component of the Allied force was also larger and set to grow larger still; six more divisions would land during September and October (all, with Brest unavailable, using discharge facilities at the expense of supplies). The American beaches were more exposed to autumnal gales and their mulberry was already wrecked, so the need for compensatory port capacity was growing more urgent. And by the beginning of September, the supply line from their only major port, Cherbourg, was twice the length of the British line; another port nearer to the front would save scarce motor transport (one argument against developing the south Breton ports in favor of Le Havre was that the latter would save the equivalent of seventy truck companies for every 5,000 tons landed).[16] In addition, Marseille was expected to become another entry port for Third Army supply, although there would be no surplus capacity from the maintenance of 6 Army Group until late November. But what the Americans needed every bit as much as the British was Antwerp, captured essentially intact on 4 September and capable of handling an initial 40,000 tons daily (coincidentally, the logisticians' estimated daily requirement by early September), to be shared on a 1.3:1 American-British ratio. The port also had massive storage capacity for bulk POL; excellent clearance facilities; road, rail, and canal links with the interior; and good inland communications. In addition, it was a much shorter haul from Antwerp to the front than from Cherbourg, let alone Brest.[17] That is why Admiral Ramsay, the naval C-in-C, signaled to Eisenhower and Montgomery on the day the port was captured: "It is essential if Antwerp and Rotterdam are to be opened quickly enemy must be prevented from: carrying out demolitions and blocking ports; mining and blocking the Scheldt and the new waterway between Rotterdam and the Hook; both Antwerp and Rotterdam are highly vulnerable to mining and blocking . . . ; it will be necessary for coastal batteries to be captured before approach channels to the river routes can be established."[18]

Delivery within Theatre: Growing Land Transport Problems

Before Operation Cobra, the Allied lodgment was so small and the lines of communication were so short that delivery of POL and timely resupply were not problems for the transportation at hand (provided the items were available, which in July was increasingly not the case with ammunition).[19] Nor, given its forecasted pace of operations, did SHAEF anticipate a sudden and dramatic change. It was expected that the progress of port opening in Brittany, the repair of railways and bridges damaged by air interdiction, the construction of pipelines, and the buildup of road transport (including much more heavy lift for lines of communication work) would ensure uninterrupted supply to the armies. It was not to be like that. From the beginning of August to the beginning of September, the armies advanced from the D+20 line to that anticipated for around D+240, distances of 550 to 650 km (340 to 400 miles). While the commanders were delighted, the logisticians were appalled.

It was always intended that railways would take care of most long-distance hauling; a single train could shift more than 1,000 tons—400 2.5-ton truckloads, or the lift of eight to nine light truck companies. The aim was to provide at least one double-track line from the rear base and RMA to the rear boundary of each army. This would mean that army transport, collecting from the theatre's forward dumps, would have to haul loads only over the limited distances for which their transport was scaled. Of course, for the first two months of the campaign, the bridgehead was so constricted that the only rail rehabilitation that took place was of the yards at Cherbourg (port clearance was the first priority) and then of a line to Carentan, 50 km (30 miles) southward, hardly an economic distance for rail operations. With Third Army's spectacular advance following Cobra, though, pressure was on COMZ's engineers to abandon carefully prepared plans for lines into Brittany and to make rapid extension to the east their main effort. The five general service engineer regiments originally allocated were reinforced by another four; by the end of August, more than 18,000 men (including prisoners of war) were working on reconstructing the rail lines. They made impressive progress, restoring the marshaling yards at St. Lô (which had been so obliterated by air attacks that the engineers had to obtain the plans from SNCF, the French national rail company, to figure out what went where) and then, by 17 August, to Le Mans. By 27 August, a single-track line had been pushed forward to Chartres; by 30 August, despite the considerable damage inflicted by previous Allied interdiction attacks, it reached just west of Paris. But by that time, the American armies were already about 400 km (250 miles) further on, and the absence of bridges over the Seine and the Paris bottleneck slowed progress. Work was commenced on the only lightly damaged lines east of the city and reached Liège and Verdun by mid-September. However, rail capacity was limited by several problems. Until reconstruction of the devastated Parisian marshaling yards and the Seine bridges was completed, supplies had to be trucked from railheads at Chartres and Dreux to the other side of Paris before being reloaded onto trains. Parts of the system remained single-track for some time. Reliability was limited by several factors: the temporary nature of some urgent repairs, the meager quantities and worn condition of locomotives and rolling stock after four years of occupation and air attack (eventually, these were augmented through Cherbourg), the lack of fully functioning infrastructure (e.g., communications, signaling), and the time required to create an efficient movement staff.

The British experience, thanks partly to geography, was somewhat easier. By 1 September, a single line had been opened as far as Argentan, but operating it was complicated by limited siding and loading point capacity and a shortage of engines. A day or two later, a through rail route was discovered nearly intact between Beauvais and Brussels, although the 280 km (175 miles) included a 65 km (40 mile) stretch of single line working north of Amiens. A link between the RMA in Normandy and Beauvais had to wait for the completion of a single-line Seine bridge at Le Manoir on 22 September, but by the end of the month, there was a continuous connection between the RMA and Brussels. Even before that, on 6 September—the day before the first coaster discharged in the port—Dieppe was linked to the main route, and upward of 2,800 tons per day were being moved right up to the Brussels area. By 6 October, the railhead had been pushed forward to Eindhoven. The shortage of locomotives and rolling stock was not resolved until the opening of the Dieppe rail ferry on 29 September; by 7 October, SHAEF had met 80 percent of British requests for both. Until then, Cherbourg had been their only point of entry, and the Seine rail break prevented their import north of the river. Inefficiency in operating the system, similar to that in the US area, was also a limiting factor, and the service was unreliable up to the end of September.

Despite the endeavors of the engineers and railway operators, rail transport was beset by too many problems to contribute significantly to the supply of the armies in the first crucial weeks of September. Even in the middle of the month, it was only beginning to carry the weight the logistic theoreticians had intended—6,000 to 7,000 tons per day as far as Paris, and 5,000 to 6,000 from the east side of the city to the army rear. Moreover, the Americans were obliged to use scarce capacity to provide 1,500 tons of food and coal each day to meet the needs of the people of Paris and to move engineer stores for bridge and rail rehabilitation and pipeline construction. It was not until November that rail managed to carry half the tonnage required by the armies.

From July, most fuel was delivered to the Continent by tanker, although from mid-August, the submarine pipeline PLUTO was also pumping it ashore at Cherbourg. Having decanted POL into jerry cans for delivery to the troops, supplying units by vehicle was not a problem as long as the bridgehead was constricted. Indeed, reserves grew to very comfortable levels. The exploitation of the Cobra breakthrough changed all this. By mid-August, the increased distance from depots to American spearheads meant that twice as much time was needed by a greater number of trucks—at a time when demand showed every sign of growing exponentially. It was time to press forward with a more economical solution: delivery as far forward as possible in bulk, by pipeline. Three general service engineer regiments and other elements (almost 9,000 men, including prisoners) were put to work to construct a triple line (two for POL and one for aviation gasoline). By the end of the month, the pipe head had reached Alençon, and over the following fortnight, a single POL line was pushed forward beyond Chartres to within about 30 km (18 miles) of the Seine. At that stage, further progress was dramatically slowed as COMZ ended the brief, ten-day-long priority given to moving pipeline materials by rail and took truck units away to meet the immediate needs of the armies at the expense of long-term savings. The decision was made to concentrate on building shorter lines from Le Havre and Antwerp (in the event, purely local pipelines were built from Le Havre and Rouen, and although a line was constructed from Antwerp to Maastricht, it was not completed until December). The pipe head of the line from Cherbourg did not reach the southeastern outskirts of Paris until 6 October.

British construction, too, lagged far behind, reaching 30 km (18 miles) northeast of Rouen during September. Mid-October saw the opening of a PLUTO terminal near Boulogne, but bad weather delayed the start of pumping until 27 October. That month, too, a line was constructed between Ostend and Ghent, but not until December was another put into operation from Antwerp to Eindhoven. Ample bulk POL installations had been created in Boulogne and Ostend and were inherited in Antwerp to support operations north of the Seine, but the fighting formations needed packaged fuel. Similar to the Americans' situation, a growing shortage of jerry cans and longer vehicle turnaround times were limiting factors.

Although the pipelines cut the demand for motor transport (except, of course, the trucks supporting construction), their performance was not an unalloyed success. Much of the pipe laying was done by troops who were undertrained for the task, leading to poor workmanship. In addition, most of the pipeline was laid along the sides of hard-surface roads; leaks and breakage from traffic accidents were frequent until the engineers learned to reduce the latter by laying pipes on the other side of roadside hedgerows. There was also pilferage via deliberate punctures to feed the black market. Communications between pumping stations, let alone tank farms, to control use and report failures were also inadequate. Aspirations to move the pipe heads close to army dumps fell far short of achievement until winter had arrived. All these problems resulted in interrupted supply, increased the turnaround time for transport units, and aggravated the fuel shortage at the most critical period of the pursuit.

Before the invasion, SHAEF's refusal to provide COMZ with the 240 truck companies (averaging forty-five to fifty trucks) it had requested and allocating shipping space for only 160 seemed to entail no undue risk. In the event, the immediate needs of the restricted bridgehead and the priority accorded to the delivery of other items resulted in only 94 of those companies being in France by the time of the breakout. Moreover, the Transportation Corps sought a ratio of 2:1 between heavy and light trucks (i.e., between 6-, 10-, and 12-ton semitrailers and 2.5-tonners), but the War Department failed to provide the former in adequate quantities, and the actual ratio was 1:2.5. If operations had unfolded more or less according to forecasts, this would not have mattered. Railways and pipelines would have shifted the vast bulk of supplies from the Normandy base area to Advanced Section railheads, and motor transport would not be required to haul supplies more than 250 km (155 miles) to the army rear. The unanticipated successes of August made nonsense of these calculations. Transport provision had not been scaled for far-reaching mobile operations with longer journeys and longer turnaround times. With the aid of 300 to 360 British vehicles borrowed for a month, the Americans coped for the first three weeks. But the decision to move in strength beyond the Seine without a pause to establish intermediate supply dumps between the Normandy base area and the armies and to acquire sufficient additional transport required hasty improvisation to meet rapidly growing demand.

COMZ set up the Red Ball Express, a one-way loop highway for operation twenty-four hours a day to be used exclusively by its own fast through traffic. Starting on 25 August, the original highway ran from St. Lô through Alençon to Chartres and returned via Mayenne. Initially, 118 truck companies were employed, but that number, augmented by reinforcements, quickly grew to a peak of 132 by 29 August. They moved 89,000 tons to the dumps in the Dreux–Chartres–La Loupe service area by 5 September (the date the original mission was considered completed). Averaging this out over the twelve days, that amounted to around 7,400 tons per day. In the same period, 70 trains carried slightly more than 30,000 tons as far as Chartres, averaging 5,000 tons a day by the beginning of September. These quantities were theoretically enough to provide for the immediate needs of the sixteen divisions involved in the pursuit, cover air force requirements, and deliver forward materials for railway repair and pipe laying, but not enough to create any intermediate dumps or reserves. In practice, the unpredictability of deliveries and the unfortunate fact that they often failed to include the most needed items often left formations critically short of current requirements. And of course, by 5 September, army-level transport had a very long haul to fetch supplies from the dumps and get them to the divisions; for instance, First Army was soon trucking supplies 480 km (300 miles) from west of Chartres all the way to Liège. For this reason, armies formed their own provisional truck companies with vehicles from grounded air defense, medium and heavy artillery, engineer, and other units. They also tried to require COMZ convoys to deliver east of the Seine. Even divisions felt compelled to send their own trucks in search of supplies; for instance, trucks from 1 Infantry Division made two round-trips of 1,120 km (695 miles) each.

COMZ had to extend the operation of the Red Ball Express for an indefinite period, and the round-trip became much longer as well. By 20 September, the outward run was from St. Lô, through Versailles, and around Paris to Soissons (still 300 km [185 miles] short of Liège) in support of First Army. The route branched off from Versailles through Melun and on to Sommesous (200 km [125 miles] west of Metz and 160 km [100 miles] from Nancy) to supply Third Army. Each round-trip was approximately 1,600 km (990 miles), meaning a five-day turnaround time.[20] Because transport resources were overstretched, COMZ had to inform the armies that they would each receive only 3,500 tons per day for the foreseeable future. But even that amount—enough for five divisions, or enough for seven if the opposition was very slight—could not be achieved. By midmonth, approximately 45,000 tons in total had been delivered, not even two-thirds of the already inadequate allocation.[21] Coincidentally, Lee chose the first fortnight in September, when the transport shortage was most acute, to move his ultimately 29,000-strong HQ from its hutted accommodation in Normandy about 450 km (280 miles) to more luxurious quarters in 167 Parisian hotels.

The situation began to improve in the second half of September with the rehabilitation of the railways. A driblet of supplies started to run on lines from east of Paris on 7 September, growing to 5,000 to 6,000 tons per day as the month wore on. When there was sufficient capacity to move 2,000 tons per day to each army, it was decided that most Red Ball convoys should terminate east of Paris, where cargoes would be transferred to railcars. This would save on motor transport without penalizing the fighting formations. In all, the Red Ball Express lasted another seventy-two days, until 16 November. It transported in excess of 315,200 tons to forward depots or to Paris for transfer to railway trains. And from 6 October it was supplemented by the White Ball Express, running the somewhat shorter route from newly opened Le Havre to Reims. However, the period of greatest need, when resistance started to harden and pursuit ceased to result in easy gains, was the period when supply was at its most disorganized and inadequate.

To find the number of trucks required by the Red Ball Express (and, later, the Red Lion), COMZ reduced base area and port and beach clearance activity by 50 percent, thus adding to the backlog of coasters waiting to be unloaded and the proportion of supplies stuck in the pipeline. This reduction in activity also contributed to growing confusion as to what could be found in which dump as an increasingly harassed Normandy Base Section attempted to make space at quays by depositing supplies wherever it could find room. COMZ and the armies also formed provisional transport companies by stripping out vehicles from many service and combat units (e.g., maintenance, engineer bridging, corps artillery) and from three immobilized infantry divisions. When the pace of the pursuit started to slacken as resistance stiffened in mid-September, many of these formations and units would be missed. Despite all these efforts to find more trucks, their numbers actually started to decline as accidents, wear and tear, and lack of maintenance took their toll; by the first week in September, only 115 companies were running, almost 15 percent fewer than just a week before. Nevertheless, the improvised system was fairly effective in keeping the armies advancing with its "only just in time" deliveries, but it was not efficient. Deliveries were unpredictable, making even short-term planning somewhat speculative, and they often fell short of demand. Both armies, the Third in particular, resorted to the shortsighted expedient of hijacking convoys meant for others and even depriving COMZ trucks of fuel for their return journey; COMZ became understandably reluctant to send its vehicles into Third Army's rear. Moreover, the Express was becoming increasingly uneconomical, consuming enormous quantities of fuel—300,000 gallons (815 tons) per day, equivalent to two-thirds of Third Army's daily demand at the end of August. It was also becoming increasingly creaky and unsustainable in its demands on both troops and their vehicles.

Success came at a heavy cost to COMZ and, ultimately, to the field forces. Lack of maintenance took its toll as grossly overloaded vehicles were run into the ground and spare parts, tires, and tools ran short; driver exhaustion led to a significant rise in the rate of accidents (and minor sabotage by drivers seeking a rest was not unknown, as was the selling of desirable loads on the black market). The number of major repairs required rose from 2,500 in mid-September to 5,750 by the end of the month. This was more than the repair facilities could cope with and denuded them of spares, with debilitating effects that lingered for months. For instance, when Ninth Army received five truck companies relieved from Red Ball duty, it found that only 60 percent of the vehicles were in operable condition. The operation of the system, improvised as it was, left much to be desired, especially in its early stages. Coordination among the various sections of COMZ and with the armies was poor, and the latter's unilateral ordering of convoys further forward than planned did not help matters. Loading and unloading of convoys were unduly time-consuming (11.5 to 39 hours), thanks to the scattered location of dumps and the difficulty of finding items within them. Traffic control suffered from a shortage of military police and efficient communications, which led to time- and fuel-wasting encroachments by other units onto Red Ball routes. Sometimes, as journeys lengthened and the operational situation changed, convoys could not find army dumps and had to travel an extra 80 to 150 km (50 to 90 miles) to hawk their loads around, or they were diverted to divisional supply points over unfamiliar routes. All this substantially lengthened turnaround times.

The 21 Army Group experience was in many ways similar to that of 12 Army Group, though somewhat less fraught. The American forces were much more widely spread. The British established rail links sooner than their ally as well. There was the same heavy initial reliance on road transport, and the plan to establish road heads 80 to 160 km (50 to 100 miles) apart and stock them with up to five days' holdings of all stores immediately fell victim to the pace of the advance. Conversely, at 510 km (315 miles), the distance from the RMA to Brussels was much shorter than from the Normandy base to Liège or Metz; with the opening of Dieppe, 340 km (210 miles) distant, the problem was further eased. Though this was still double the distance used to calculate the allocation of transport, considerable reinforcements were provided to mitigate the problem. During August, Second Army increased its number of general transport companies (each with 90 to 120 trucks) from six to fourteen, and a tank transporter company was converted for load carrying as well. Like the Americans, the British needed even more; accordingly, imports over the beaches were limited, two divisions of VIII Corps and artillery and engineer units were grounded to free up transport for Second Army, and more tank transporters were pressed into service to carry supplies. After the fall of Le Havre, I Corps was also stripped of its trucks to reinforce supply efforts for the Canadians. Up to the first week in September, neither the British nor Canadian armies were seriously discommoded by a lack of transport—albeit at the cost of immobilizing substantial combat forces that would soon be needed. However, the decision to mount Operation Market Garden still threatened overstretch. From the reserves, 1,820 trucks and 154 extra POL tankers were added, and an additional seventeen general transport companies were provided on permanent loan. Unfortunately, 1,400 new trucks were found to be inoperable because of faulty engines, resulting in a transport deficiency that necessitated reliance on American help for Market Garden. On Eisenhower's command, the Red Lion Express was set up to haul 500 tons per day, mostly POL, from Bayeux to Brussels. The Red Lion ran from 16 September to 12 October; about half the amount delivered went toward the maintenance of the two US airborne divisions involved, at least partly refuting American claims that American needs were being subordinated to those of the British.

Air was routinely used to supplement the trucking effort from mid-August. But between 29 August and 3 September, First Allied Airborne Army successfully argued for the return of its aircraft (i.e., IX Troop Carrier Command and 38 and 46 Groups, RAF); after 3 September, Brereton, the army commander, had to relinquish half the force but wrested the aircraft back on the fourteenth for Operation Market. Between 20 August and 16 September, air transport (including 200 unsatisfactorily converted bombers) delivered 12,800 tons to 12 Army Group, just under 7,800 tons to 21 Army Group, and 2,650 tons of emergency supplies to Paris (the last an unanticipated drain on scarce resources that tied up land transport for some time as well). Toward the end of the month, some air transport operations in support of First and Third Armies were resumed, but only until the first week in October, when weather largely shut them down. Given the limited lift (3 tons) of the standard transport aircraft, the C-47, air transport could never be more than a palliative (save for the fast delivery of certain high-value items). As Bradley saw it, diverting the vast bulk of Troop Carrier Command to airborne operations in support of 21 Army Group also made availability unpredictable, as did the weather; these factors not only reduced the flow but also inhibited planning. Moreover, poor planning characterized air resupply. Requests were often duplicated, and motor transport was frequently delivered to the wrong airfields or was not waiting to collect at the other end. Forward airfields were in short supply, lacked adequate ground facilities, and were often summarily taken over by combat units.[22]

OPERATIONAL CONSEQUENCES OF LOGISTIC FAILURE

The logistics planners were not prepared for the sequel to breakthrough, even though that was the avowed and oft-repeated aim of offensive operations.[23] They were consistently very conservative, indeed, overcautious. They had expressed doubts about the feasibility of the deep post-Cobra exploitation without prior capture of the Breton ports and had estimated that only twelve divisions could be maintained as far forward as the Seine by D+90. By then, they argued, a shortage of 127 truck companies would preclude any additional advance until railway reconstruction had progressed much further. Actually, by D+79, sixteen divisions were being maintained in action on the Seine and another five in Brittany; three weeks later, in mid-September, sixteen American divisions were being sustained, albeit increasingly inadequately, 320 km (200 miles) farther east in addition to those in Brittany. This was despite the fact that the preconditions related to ports, railways, and pipelines remained unmet. The logisticians' achievements confounded their earlier pessimism. Their improvisations and exertions, especially the Red Ball Express, were an effective, if not efficient, response to an unforeseen challenge. But it was a response with limits. By 5 September, excluding Dragoon forces, there were twenty-four US divisions on the Continent; by 1 October, that number would rise to thirty-three (including two airborne), but only twenty of them could be maintained in combat as far forward as the Rhine, never mind farther east. Moreover, the answers to the supply crisis were short-term ones, applied at the expense of other long-term, long-lasting problems. In mid-September the system was unable to meet more than 80 percent of the minimum daily requirements of over 13,000 tons per day in the combat zone.[24] In addition, there was a backlog of 150,000 to 180,000 tons of supplies needed in the forward areas to repair or replace materiel, replenish basic loads, and build up reserves. If the Germans did not give up (as they had in 1918) as the Allies approached their border, the armies' combat effectiveness would become increasingly degraded. Indeed, if the campaign stretched into the autumn, this hand-to-mouth system would collapse. In the longer term, there could be no shortcutting of the requirement for adequate levels of all-weather, deep-water port discharge capabilities; developed railway and pipeline networks; and the intermediate, well-stocked depots and dumps between base areas and the armies that had been planned before the invasion. Albeit later than they had thought, the planners were proved correct in their assertion that logistic realities could be defied for only so long. Commanders remained willfully blind to this until too late in the day.

Concerns over ammunition stocks that had led to rationing before Operation Cobra disappeared in the wake of the breakout. They were replaced by worries about fuel supply. For instance, on no day between 26 August and 5 October did First Army have more than a one-day supply of POL on hand; on thirteen days there was half a day or less, and on sixteen days there was none at all, as it was issued as soon as it arrived. Both armies found their actions severely circumscribed by fuel shortages throughout September, on some days to the extent of almost total immobility. The crisis both coincided with the stiffening of enemy resistance and contributed to it by easing the pressure on the Germans. And once the pursuit gave way to increasingly heavy fighting, ammunition shortages and the lack of medium and heavy artillery and engineer bridging equipment caused by the diversion of vehicles to the Red Ball Express contributed to the Americans' inability to bring their full combat power to bear. By the second week in September, Third Army's emphasis in demand had switched from fuel to ammunition. First Army followed suit a week later. By the beginning of October, both had to reimpose rationing.[25] And growing shortages of spare parts and replacements for worn-out equipment and all the other items neglected in the failing effort to meet demands for fuel and then ammunition contributed significantly to the degradation of fighting power. By early September, only about one-third of 3 Armored Division's tanks were in operable condition. With the expansion and development of the railway system and, later, pipelines, the supply outlook improved. COMZ was able to raise each army's allocation to 5,000 tons per day on 23 September (still enough for just seven or eight divisions) and then to 5,400 tons on 25 September and 6,500 tons on 4 October. Targets once again proved to be too optimistic and unattainable in the short term (First Army did better than Third), but by mid-October, the firepower situation was improving. Unfortunately for the Allies, this improvement came too late to restore the tempo of the advance. The offensive had culminated and stalemate had set in once again. Not until 7 November, much later than COMZ promised, were enough stocks accumulated for 12 Army Group to resume the offensive.

The fault was not solely that of the logisticians. Field commanders persisted in producing and following operational plans that ignored supply realities and COMZ's very real problems. Hodges and Patton, far more than their more logistics-conscious British counterparts, were impatient of such considerations in their desire to concentrate on combat; the former was described by a troubleshooting War Department observer as "a man intolerant of supply shortcomings who has not studied supply and does not intend to."[26] In consequence, the combined effects of time, space, and friction slowed the advance to an intermittent crawl before the end of September. But the crisis was also caused in part and then exacerbated by an ill-thought-out administrative system poorly suited to the inconvenient realities of maneuver warfare. The armies, entirely overlooking their own contribution to the crisis, heaped blame onto COMZ and its commander for the growing difficulties. COMZ countered by blaming unforeseeable events, the failure to capture ports on schedule, the irresponsible behavior of combat formations, the shortage of service troops, and the weather—everyone and everything except itself. In truth, although these excuses had some foundation, COMZ was a bureaucratic and inefficient organization of overlapping jurisdictions and reliant on inadequate communications; as such, it was able to support only linear, attritional, relatively slowly developing warfare.

The main constraint limiting COMZ's ability to supply the fighting formations in September was the lack of in-theatre transport capacity, exacerbated by systemic failings (some of which were belatedly addressed in October). There were plenty of stocks of most items on the Continent (some ammunition natures being the most important exception) but as of 1 September, 90 percent of them were still in the Normandy base area. Even by the end of October, when the rail system was hitting its stride and shifting increasing tonnages forward, that figure had only dropped to 70 percent. In November there were still 600,000 tons in stockpiles at or near the invasion beaches and Cherbourg. Given that port capacity was not the principal bottleneck affecting supply in the late summer, the decision to abandon the project of exploiting Quiberon Bay's natural harbor and the other Brittany ports cannot be blamed for the onset of a new stalemate in October. Imports were not a major problem in the late summer of 1944. They would, however, become one if deep-water ports were not opened rapidly to ensure adequate and continuous supply of the whole Anglo-American force in increasingly demanding conditions of combat and, at the same time, cope with the growing inflow of reinforcing formations (eight US divisions in September alone). In practice, this meant bringing at least Antwerp on line. Antwerp could handle more than the Normandy beaches and all the Channel ports combined, and it was five times nearer to Aachen than Cherbourg was and more than twice as close to Metz.[27] The failure to open Antwerp until 29 November would have a profoundly deleterious effect on the campaign.[28]

The idea that only POL shortages stopped the pursuit is false. Other problems and deficiencies grew from neglect and sapped fighting power. Tanks and other vehicles became badly worn, immobilized, or total losses. In a November report, SHAEF provided the War Department with statistics on the loss of equipment: every month, 700 mortars, 375 medium and 125 light tanks, 900 2.5-ton trucks, 1,500 jeeps, and 100 cannon of various calibers had to be written off, not to mention 5,000 tires every day; theatre tank losses in August and September amounted, respectively, to 25.3 percent and 16.5 percent of establishment, and with reserves exhausted, even if the official replacement rate of 9 percent were met, it would not be enough to keep up unit strengths. Repairable items were being neglected owing to a lack of maintenance facilities and spare parts; thus, 15,000 vehicles lay deadlined in November. Advance airfields were not being built, and air units were not being moved up. Even when ammunition became available, needs could not be met in good time. Increasingly during September, the armies were forced to live a hand-to-mouth existence. This made forward planning a somewhat dubious, even nugatory exercise and led to an offensive that proceeded in fits and starts. All this allowed the enemy to rally and reconstitute some of his shattered units and formations and find fresh troops from the interior of the Reich and other fronts. It was not, by the standards of July, an impressive force in terms of size, quality, and training and equipping of the troops. But, given terrain favoring the defense, it was enough to stall weakened Allied forces, whose commanders were still infected with an optimism that was becoming harder to justify and increasingly mismanaged the campaign.

At the end of September, SHAEF and COMZ brought an overdue awareness of reality to operational planning. They calculated that the supply needs of 12 Army Group and air force essentials in the first half of October would amount to 18,800 tons per day, assuming the employment in combat of twenty-two divisions. This figure would go up to 22,700 tons by 1 November, when there would be twenty-eight divisions. The army group had also demanded another 100,000 tons over and above daily requirements to both repair deficiencies and create minimal reserves. However, deliveries in September were running at only 8,000 to 10,000 tons daily to the forward areas, and even in October it would be impossible to supply the minimum amounts necessary. It would take all of two months to improve the port and transport situation sufficiently to not only satisfy daily necessities but also create the required stocks in the forward dumps. Moreover, this mid-November target would be met only if railway rehabilitation proceeded on schedule and Antwerp started to ease the port discharge bottleneck. The possibility of restoring the momentum of August and delivering a fatal blow to the Germans before the winter had disappeared.

The autumn operational pause led to much ill feeling and recrimination between the American armies and even more between them and COMZ, which the army group did little to smooth over. The logistic crunch also contributed in no small measure to a souring of Anglo-American relations, with denigration of the Supreme Commander an unfortunate by-product. The US armies knew what they needed and, somewhat cavalierly, assumed that the required supplies were available somewhere in the system. When these supplies failed to materialize, they blamed each other for hogging supply, COMZ for its inefficiency, and the high command for diverting transport and POL to the British. Thus, one of Hodges's staff colonels declared that in his army's "race across France we were badly crippled for want of gasoline . . . [because] gasoline was diverted to the British to enable them to take the Channel ports, to capture the V-1 launch sites and to bring them faster into Antwerp." Similarly, one of Patton's officers wrote: "The situation now had all the indications of deliberate withholding of gas from Third Army. . . . Bradley told Patton that 'Montgomery had won.' That he had succeeded in inducing Eisenhower to make the main effort . . . in the strongly held and organized north instead of in the weak and disorganized south, as favored by Bradley." Patton's diary entry for 30 August echoed the sentiment: "The Brits have put it over again. We got no gas because, to suit Monty, the First Army must get most of it."[29]

LOGISTIC REALITIES AND CONCLUSIONS

The actual unfolding of events demonstrated that Eisenhower's decision in favor of an advance right across the front was mistaken. Each of the armies in his Northern and Central Groups culminated short of its assigned geographic objective, and the German army was vouchsafed enough breathing space to recover its strength and balance in the operational pause that followed. Operational and tactical failings undoubtedly contributed to this disappointing result, but the main cause of the Allied failure was the logistic system's inability to cope, especially on the part of the Americans. Difficulties in supply prevented a significant and growing proportion of US combat power from being used to maximum effect; by 1 October, only twenty of 12 Army Group's thirty-one divisions could be maintained as far forward as the Rhine, but weeks earlier, shortages and deficiencies had been acting as a brake on operations. Just as important, the resultant uncertainties complicated and distorted planning. Moreover, by trying to do too much with too little for too long, the Allies exacerbated their problems and ensured that recovering from them would be a slow process. It would take months to remedy the results of prolonged neglect of vehicles and equipment, acquire and ship forward the necessary spares and stores and replacements, and establish the intermediate depots, even minimally stocked, that were necessary for the prosecution of sustained operations. This raises the question: would two powerful but sequential thrusts, rather than a simultaneous advance, have been more logistically feasible for 12 Army Group?

Had Third Army been halted on the Meuse at the end of August (but still with its bridgeheads) and left on the defensive for a time, what lift would have been freed to support a stronger effort north of the Ardennes, the supposed main effort? Assume that XII and XX Corps, with six divisions between them, were left to defend the passive sector; assume that the Germans could not mount a serious threat against them, so POL and ammunition requirements were less than normally allocated in defense. In this case, the two corps would be able to get by on a meager average of 250 tons per division per day, a total of 1,500 tons. The theoretical allocation of supply to the two US armies was 3,500 tons apiece daily, so in theory, Hodges would be gaining 2,000 tons. In practice, however, during the first half of September, COMZ was averaging only 2,500 tons to Patton and 3,300 to Hodges, so the actual gain to First Army would be halved. Air resupply could reliably add about 650 tons per day, up to 1,000 in a surge. With 4,950 to 5,300 tons a day, First Army would be able to maintain sixteen to seventeen divisions in pursuit mode or seven to eight in attack mode, similar to its actions around Aachen in mid-September, but now properly resourced. Thus, Third Army's transition to defense probably would have enabled First Army, nine to ten divisions strong, to penetrate as far as the Rhine in September in a continuous rather than a stop-and-go push. Had the assault on Brest been abandoned, there would have been enough resources to dispatch VIII Corps with perhaps three or four divisions to augment Hodges's efforts or to reinforce the underresourced 21 Army Group.

It is likely that, having ensured that First Army had enough forces and staying power to reach the Cologne-Bonn area without giving the enemy any respite to reestablish a coherent defense, an operational pause would have been necessary to sort out accumulated problems in the logistic system. This would mean postponing Patton's offensive until well into the autumn—probably November—with all the adverse consequences that would entail. However, the offensive would have been more powerful, and adequate levels of supply would have been assured. Patton's army would not have been alone in the assault on the southern flank, as 6 Army Group, its own supply in order, would have been attacking from the south. Chapter 7 considers more fully the operational calculus involved in a phased effort to close on the Rhine.

Patton and Bradley would have preferred to put the main US effort south of the Ardennes from the earliest days of exploitation to enable Third Army to execute a quick drive across the Rhine with ten to twelve divisions. They accepted that this could be done only if Third Army were given priority on all available supplies and transport. They envisaged the British, then on the Seine, being halted in place. First Army, too, would remain inactive, with the possible exception of a limited advance to protect the northern flank. Even with this concentration of logistic effort, they recognized that the limit of exploitation would be no further than Frankfurt; this, however, was considered sufficient, as such a rapid and deep advance, penetrating into Germany itself, would likely induce collapse and frighten the enemy into immediate capitulation. SHAEF studied the concept carefully in late August and rejected it. Logistically, it was a nonstarter. The force would require 6,500 to 8,000 tons per day, more than the entire amount COMZ delivered on an average day to the whole army group through most of September. In other words, assuming Hodges's army still needed at least 1,500 tons, even seven to eight divisions in the Frankfurt area would be ambitious. The Red Ball Express would have to be extended by over 50 percent to Saarbrücken, and the increased turnaround time would require even more trucks and fuel to maintain the same rate of supply. Army transport would still have a 200 km (125 mile) haul from there to Frankfurt. The wear and tear on vehicles and men and the depletion of spare parts, tires, and so forth would increase. Long lines of communication within Germany, running through difficult territory, would be vulnerable to disruption by raids, guerrilla activity, and sabotage. Air resupply would help, to the tune of 500 to 1,000 tons per day, but only in good weather and in the absence of the Luftwaffe. The latter could not be guaranteed beyond fighter cover, and without forward airfields, that would become steadily scarcer. Above all, considering purely logistic factors for a moment, the Patton-Bradley scheme did not begin to address the issue of ports. The US forces would enter the autumn campaign still reliant on Cherbourg and the beaches, with the insignificant addition of some minor ports and the imminent closing, or at least drastic limiting, of the beaches as the weather made its impact.

Montgomery's narrow-front concept was based on a keener appreciation of logistic factors, and it was aimed at a more important geographic objective. Montgomery was famous for his conservatism in the area of logistic risk; Americans habitually accused him of overinsurance. Nevertheless, the SHAEF study of early September agreed that Montgomery's initial idea of a thrust as far as Berlin was theoretically feasible. Three British and two US corps could be employed initially, with three going all the way to Berlin (albeit on reduced maintenance), a British one being halted in the Bremen-Hamburg area, and an American one being halted in the Frankfurt-Magdeburg area. They believed, however, that several preconditions for success would have to be achieved. Both army groups would have to be on or over the Rhine by 15 September to provide an adequate LD. The Channel ports and Antwerp would have to be discharging 7,000 tons per day by that date. Railway rehabilitation would have to progress further and faster than was actually being achieved to free up road transport. Supplying the offensive would require the equivalent of 489 truck companies, but only 347 were available; air could compensate for 60 companies' worth of the deficit (they assumed a highly optimistic lift of 2,000 tons per day), but the remaining deficiency would have to be found by the wholesale deprivation of divisional organic transport. Five American corps would have to be grounded or left "quiescent."[30] As none of the SHAEF stipulations were met, Eisenhower rejected this overly ambitious scheme but later agreed to Montgomery's more modest Market Garden proposition.

With the resources available as of mid-September, was the scheme to encircle the Ruhr really as viable as Montgomery claimed? Second Army's administrative position at the time was by no means good. Commodity stocks in the Brussels area road head were low, and the road head was too far behind the forward troops, with the Brussels bottleneck intervening. A month's pause was considered necessary to reestablish administration on a sound footing, but none would be vouchsafed. That said, "at no time were there insufficient stocks in army depots to meet the requirements of Market Garden."[31] During the early period of the offensive through Holland, the line of communications' supply of the army was still largely dependent on the 500 km (300 mile) haul from the RMA to Brussels. Although this was alleviated for more than half the journey by rail transport, army transport still faced a

230 km (145 mile) lift to get to Arnhem. Nevertheless, the system coped, helped to a considerable extent by the 500 tons per day trucked by the Red Lion Express, the use of tank transporters, and air resupply, which averaged 550 tons each day for four weeks into mid-October.

Of course, the Rhine crossing at Arnhem was merely an intermediate objective, not the final one. Montgomery aimed to move round the north face of the Ruhr as far as Münster and Osnabrück via Deventer, an additional 170 to 185 km (105 to 115 miles). Could Second Army, whose nine divisions required 5,850 tons daily, be supplied over this additional distance? Several factors were favorable. By the end of September, Dieppe and Ostend were discharging up to 8,000 tons daily; by 12 October, Boulogne was adding another 2,200 tons. This would go a long way toward meeting 21 Army Group's total need for 9,100 tons. Dieppe enjoyed a through rail link with Brussels via Amiens from 6 September, and with the bridging of the Seine on 22 September, so did the RMA. The rail system would provide up to one-third the tonnage 21 Army Group required—more as time passed; moreover, Dempsey's railhead would reach Eindhoven by 6 October.[32] The road head was advanced to the Neerpelt area by 4 October, 80 km (50 miles) nearer to Arnhem than Brussels. These improvements would considerably ease, but not eliminate, the line of communications part of the problem; however, army transport would still face hauls of up to 300 km (185 miles). Fortunately, in mid-September the War Office agreed to loan an additional seventeen general transport companies (normally about 120 trucks each) to the army group, and these had all landed, preloaded with supplies, by 3 October. All this added up, in theory, to the conclusion that Montgomery's concept was logistically feasible, particularly if he continued to receive American and air force help, which together amounted to 1,000 tons daily, and sometimes more.

Theory, however, does not take into account the problem of organizing, managing, administering, and controlling a substantially improvised system over vastly increased distances, an area of growing concern. Weather would increasingly impact air resupply, and the Luftwaffe might become a factor if Allied fighters could not quickly relocate forward. Once into Germany, attempts at sabotage could be expected. The line between logistic success and disastrous overstretch was probably quite thin and vulnerable to the ever-present friction of war. As it was, the failure of Market Garden necessarily resulted in a reappraisal of the logistic situation. Second Army calculated that a resumption of the offensive would require a buildup of the Antwerp-Brussels area advanced base until it contained 20,000 tons of supplies and 40,000 tons each of ammunition and fuel, not to mention large quantities of engineer, ordnance, and medical stores. By the end of October, there were only 23,000 tons of POL and a mere 4,000 tons of ammunition, even though supply targets were almost reached.[33] Whether Montgomery's intended outcome actually fit into a wider operational perspective and whether it was therefore desirable are considered in the next chapter.

Such calculations are highly hypothetical and owe much to hindsight. Armies at the time overestimated their own capabilities and underestimated the enemy's, and neither they nor COMZ was entirely honest about the true status of supply—or even sure what that status actually was, given the somewhat chaotic nature of American logistic administration. Eisenhower lacked the necessary data to make a truly informed choice, and wishful thinking distorted the intelligence picture of the German situation. That said, one thing was crystal clear: until the port of Antwerp was discharging significant tonnages, which it could do very rapidly once the Scheldt estuary was cleared, the Americans would be unable to exploit fully more than two-thirds of their combat power. In addition, if the Germans did not collapse and sue for peace when the Rhine was reached or crossed, neither army would be in good enough administrative shape to pursue the campaign into the heart of Germany. Unless and until the Allies took advantage of Antwerp's huge capacity, the excellent road and rail links to the interior, and their relative proximity to even the most southerly portion of 12 Army Group's front, the campaign was likely to degenerate into a largely pointless, attritional semistalemate. If the Allies were not sure of their ability to bring the campaign to a successful conclusion before autumn was well advanced (as they could not be), they would have been well advised to make clearing the Scheldt estuary the first priority of post-Normandy operations. The issue could not be postponed and fudged, as had been done with the Brittany ports. The longer the supply problem was neglected, the worse it would get and the longer it would take to put it right. In the event, this was not actually achieved until well into December, by which time the Allies had lost the initiative, wrested so convincingly from the enemy back in the heady days of August.

CHAPTER SEVEN

Command, Operational Art, and Generalship

ISSUES OF COMMAND

Eisenhower budged, temporarily, from his position on the broad-front concept of operations, but not on command. From mid-August he had been under mounting pressure to assume personal command of the Allied land forces. His staff, American and British alike, as well as the American generals who disliked Montgomery and were imbued with a newfound post-Cobra confidence, urged him on. Like them, the American press questioned why a Briton was still in charge when American troops were bearing most of the burden and casualties. More seriously, Secretary of War Stimson and President Roosevelt himself felt the same way, lamenting that American arms were not being accorded the credit due them. They were keen to head off a congressional debate that could be damaging to the administration in this presidential election year. And General Marshall, Eisenhower's patron and guide as well as his boss, wanted both more recognition for the US Army and less British influence in military affairs generally. Accordingly, on 20 August the Supreme Commander announced that he would assume operational command as of 1 September.

Montgomery argued forcefully on 23 August for both his single-thrust concept of operations and, bound up with this issue, his retention of command of the land forces. He brusquely dismissed the argument that "public opinion should make us want to take military decisions which were definitely unsound." Only victory mattered: produce success, and public opinion would follow. He argued:

> [The] Supreme Commander should not descend into the land battle and become a ground C-in-C. The Supreme Commander must sit on a very lofty perch in order to be able to take a detached view of the whole intricate problem—which involves land, sea, air, civil control, political problems, etc. Someone must run the land battle for him. We had won a great victory in Normandy because of unified control and not in spite of it. I said that this point was so important that, if public opinion in America was involved, he should let Bradley control the battle and I would gladly serve under him.[1]

Eisenhower rejected Montgomery's views on command. For the latter to retain it

> was impossible, particularly in view of the fact that he wanted to retain at the same time direct command of his own army group. To my mind and that of my staff the proposition was fantastic. The reason for having an army group commander is to ensure direct, day by day battlefield direction in a specific portion of the front to a degree impossible to a supreme commander. It is certain that no one man could perform this function with respect to his own portion of the line and at the same time exercise logical and intelligent supervision over any other portion. The only effect of such a scheme would have been to place Montgomery in a position to draw at will, in support of his own ideas, upon the strength of the entire command. . . . A supreme commander in a situation such as faced us in Europe cannot ordinarily give day by day and hour by hour supervision to any portion of the field. Nevertheless he is the one person in the organization with the authority to assign principal objectives to major formations. He is also the only one who has under his hand the power to allot strength to the various major commands in accordance with their mission, to arrange for the distribution of incoming supply, and to direct the operations of the entire air forces in support of any portion of the line. The existence, therefore, of any separate ground headquarters between the supreme command and the army group command would have placed such a headquarters in an anomalous position since it would have the power neither to direct the flow of supply and reinforcements nor to give instructions to the air forces.[2]

Arguably, Eisenhower was correct in maintaining that acting as both army group and land forces commander was too big a job for one man, particularly if, like Montgomery, he had a less than broad-brush approach to the former task. Certainly, this was what von Kluge and Model found when they were in charge of both the western theatre and *Army Group B*—and they operated within a system that ceded more autonomy to subordinates. Moreover, the span of command was about to expand to encompass not two but three army groups when Devers's forces reached the area of Dijon. But Eisenhower's argument applied equally against himself. The Supreme Command was a multifaceted and onerous job requiring Eisenhower's rare combination of skills and a great deal of time. Wedding that role (and that of commander of US forces in the ETO) with the role of land forces commander would ensure that neither got the full attention it deserved. If the combined job of land forces and army group commander was too much for one man, surely the combination of Supreme Command and land command was too much as well? That had been the rationale for giving Eisenhower, when newly appointed Supreme Commander in the Mediterranean theatre in 1942, a land forces commander (in that case, Alexander, when there was only one army group to manage). Eisenhower was correct, of course, that Montgomery wanted to use the position he coveted to implement his own operational idea. But was that any more unreasonable than denying him the position because Eisenhower had an alternative idea? Certainly, it would be better to pursue a single course of action vigorously, provided it was not demonstrably erroneous, than to compromise and follow several courses and, in consequence, fall short in all—which is what actually happened.

In the debate, neither general could reveal his most fundamental reason for demurring. Montgomery forbore from pointing out his main objection to the amalgamation of responsibilities: that Eisenhower, with only staff experience, lacked the practical training, expertise, and experience to be a credible operational-level commander. Moreover, he lacked the means (such as Montgomery's Phantom GHQ Signal Regiment and system of personal liaison officers) to keep his finger on the pulse of battle. Lacking a complete and up-to-date picture of the operational situation and a true feel for combat, and continually distracted by other necessary but operationally unimportant matters, Eisenhower would perforce rely on the normal reporting chain, with all its delays, omissions, and spin imparted by self-serving subordinates. These reports would be supplemented by personal visits forward, but only when he could escape the myriad nonoperational demands competing for his time and attention. Similarly, Eisenhower could not voice his main argument: that Montgomery had to relinquish command because he was simply no longer acceptable to the US military, from Marshall downward. Montgomery's growing estrangement from American commanders stemmed from his doubts about their command abilities and theirs about his; these doubts, combined with personality clashes, required the limitation of his command to Anglo-Canadian forces. Indeed, by that stage of the war, given the preponderance of American forces and national pride, no British general would have been acceptable to the US government and to the general public.[3] Then there was the Briton's intriguing idea that Bradley be appointed in his stead—a suggestion that was likely disingenuous. Montgomery probably felt safe in his display of modesty and self-abnegation when he offered to serve under Bradley. Whether or not Bradley was seen as an unalloyed success in his brief tenure as army group commander, three weeks in the role could hardly be considered adequate preparation for further elevation, which seemed to leave no alternative to Montgomery. Regardless of Eisenhower's thoughts about Bradley's capacity for the job, he certainly knew that the general's appointment would not have settled the issue, if only because Bradley would have had difficulty controlling Montgomery and at the same time maintaining harmony between the army groups. The job required the political awareness, tact, and skills that Eisenhower possessed and his principal subordinates did not.

Montgomery was displeased as well as disappointed to be superseded as commander of the land forces, but not just for himself. He genuinely believed the campaign's command and control would suffer, not only because he deplored Eisenhower's lack of grip but also because he considered SHAEF's operational-strategic concept of the broad front to be fundamentally flawed. He could not grasp the reality that Eisenhower would necessarily remain inflexible over the issue of command; or, rather, he could not accept the implications of the irrevocable shift in the balance of power within the alliance in favor of the Americans. With the backing of Brooke, he refused to regard the issue as settled and fought on, further souring relations.[4] On 10 October, in the wake of the culmination of the Allied offensive, he produced "Notes on Command in Western Europe," the summary of which stated:

> I do not believe it is possible to conduct operations successfully in the field unless there exists a good and sound organization for command and control. I do not believe we have a good and sound organization for command and control. It may be that political and national considerations prevent us having a sound organization. If this is the case I would suggest that we say so. Do not let us pretend we are all right, whereas we are very far from being all right in that respect.

Goaded beyond his normal, tactful endurance, Eisenhower's waspish reply contained the blunt message that if Montgomery believed command arrangements were so unsatisfactory, "it is our duty to refer the matter to higher authority for any action they might choose to take, however drastic." Recognizing he had overstepped the mark and was in danger of being dismissed, Montgomery wrote: "You will hear no more on the subject of command from me."[5]

However, Montgomery did not finally give up until after a confrontation in December, which only the diplomacy of his chief of staff, de Guingand, prevented from becoming a political row at the top resulting in Montgomery's dismissal. Meanwhile, Eisenhower and Montgomery grew further apart, both geographically and conceptually. Discussing matters face-to-face might have helped, but even that was ruled out by Montgomery's stubborn and shortsighted obstinacy: he refused to travel to SHAEF or to attend any of the Supreme Commander's conferences, sending de Guingand to represent him instead. He thus missed the opportunity to influence his senior through the power of cogent personal argument.[6] Even Montgomery's consolation prize for losing the land command only made matters worse. He was promoted to field marshal on 1 September, a move that helped assuage the anger of the British press, which had become shrill over his perceived demotion. It also infuriated US generals, who believed the elevation was undeserved and, in some way, insulting to them. The whole issue of command was no longer a matter of objective calculation; it was becoming toxic, with personal and national prejudices distorting and dominating the argument.

Eisenhower did not get off to a good start in exercising direct responsibility for the land campaign. On 31 August SHAEF's forward HQ completed its move to Granville, on the Atlantic coast of Normandy, and opened the next day. In location, in structure, and in preparedness, it was singularly ill-suited to assume command of land operations. With 3,250 personnel, 750 of them officers and warrant officers, it was large. When it moved on a fortnight later, it had swelled to 5,000 with the arrival of main HQ—vast, unwieldy, and bureaucratic (though positively slim compared with the 1945 total of 16,000). Granville was a bad choice for the first location on the Continent. It was inaccessible by road, and movement by air was increasingly subject to weather-imposed delay. It also became more and more remote from the fast-moving front line (being about 600 km [370 miles] from Brussels, Verdun, and Dijon, where Seventh Army would shortly arrive). This would have been bad enough, but communications were atrocious. Skilled signals personnel and equipment that had been allocated to help the establishment of 12 Army Group were not quickly replaced; in consequence, as the deputy head of the intelligence branch admitted, "we were sort of silent."[7]

It was not only communications with the major commands that became patchy. SHAEF relied largely on COMZ HQ in its dealings with the War Department in Washington on nonoperational matters, as well as for the organization and control of supply.[8] After a mere three weeks in Normandy, and acting without even notifying the Supreme Commander, Lee, the COMZ commander, relocated his soon to be 29,000-strong HQ to Paris (flying in huge numbers of additional personnel from England) over the first fortnight in September; this required the diversion of a considerable amount of scarce transport from troop supply.[9] SHAEF's forward HQ started its own move from unsuitable Granville to Versailles on 15 September. It opened in the new location five days later. Thus, during the first three weeks of a crucial month—the climax of the campaign, when events unfolded with unprecedented rapidity—SHAEF was unable to exercise its functions effectively. For instance, on 5 September Eisenhower sent Montgomery a very important telegram concerning the future conduct of operations; this was received in two parts, the second part arriving before the first, all of four days later. When his principal subordinates began to drift away from the spirit and even the letter of his directives, Eisenhower was not well placed to recognize what was going on or to react in a timely fashion.

Eisenhower was firm in his assertion of operational command, but less so in its exercise. He was also less decisive in sorting out a critical issue within the American logistic setup (logistics were a national responsibility). The relationships between SHAEF, army group and army HQs, and COMZ had been confused well before the invasion and remained so throughout the summer and autumn of 1944. The Americans lacked the simple, straightforward hierarchical organization of the British, whose chief supply officer (Major General Graham) was a staff officer directly responsible to Montgomery. The US logistic command structure was overly elaborate, with duplication and overlapping authorities; this was matched by an equally complex supply scheme. COMZ had been established as a coequal command with the two army groups; in fact, Lee was a deputy theatre commander until 19 July, and even after he lost that title, his HQ continued to operate as a theatre HQ and remained the channel of communications with Washington on routine and technical matters. As a result of jurisdictional uncertainty and competition among the various senior HQs, administrative and logistic arrangements and responsibilities were confused. Moreover, within COMZ, the relationship between its HQ and its subordinate organizations, the Advanced and Base Sections, did not evolve as planned: there had also been a Forward Echelon Communications Zone, but this created too much confusion and uncertainty and was subsumed into COMZ's HQ when it deployed to Normandy. Indeed, the relationship between the different elements of COMZ and the field armies also evolved in an unsatisfactory fashion.[10] Given the way operations developed after the breakout, a logistic crisis was inevitable sooner or later. That it happened sooner and lasted so long was partly a product of poor command arrangements. This was the Supreme Commander's responsibility. He could not, apparently, compel or persuade Lee to introduce necessary reforms, and he would not relieve him because Lee had powerful protectors in Washington.

The spectacular territorial gains achieved between 25 August and 5 September did not consign Anglo-American misunderstandings and antagonisms to history, buried by a shared enjoyment of victory. British and American senior officers had little understanding of the other army's doctrine and culture. Each tended to recognize only shortcomings in the other and to dwell on its failures, real and perceived. The Americans, for instance, were perennially complaining about British slowness and fastidiousness over boundaries, blaming these traits for the failure to destroy the enemy west of the Seine (charges the British resented). Satisfaction born of success did not lead to a reversal of the decline in Anglo-American relations that had started in Normandy.[11] On the contrary, they worsened as competition for resources between the army groups sharpened, personal dislikes became magnified, and the desire for recognition stimulated jealousies. Especially to career soldiers, who were proud of their professionalism and ambitious for promotion and honor, it mattered greatly which army and which generals would gain the main credit for winning the war. This was particularly true for American generals, as promotion was at the mercy of politicians—the president proposing and Congress, heavily influenced by public opinion, disposing. Small problems could become larger ones, especially if the media seized on them, as had happened with Dempsey's injudicious comment in late August about Americans blocking his line of advance. There was another boundary dispute at the beginning of September, when XIX Corps transgressed at Tournai as part of the maneuver to form the Mons pocket, giving rise to a complaint by 21 Army Group. First Army staff believed, wrongly, that the boundary had been drawn by Montgomery with the deliberate intention of hogging the best routes. Deeper issues grew to undermine what little harmony existed just beneath the surface. Montgomery was increasingly at odds with Bradley and his principal subordinates, and with the Supreme Commander himself, over rival operational concepts and the associated implications for command, the subordination of formations, and the distribution of supplies.

Whereas Montgomery regarded these as professional matters, Patton and Bradley in particular took them personally, which sharpened the division. Personality clashes amplified professional disagreements and infected staffs, exacerbating prejudices. British and American operational-level commanders talked to each other less and less, preferring written communications that were, on occasion, undiplomatically blunt. Thus, they failed to iron out problems and resolve issues between them. For example, between 22 August and 3 September, Montgomery made no effort to see Bradley, even though he was still land forces commander and responsible for operational coordination. Presumably, this was a factor in Bradley's decision to order the Tournai maneuver without consultation.[12]

Inveighing against rather than seeking cooperation with one's ally had become the norm. The growing antagonisms between commanders and staffs mattered. Without a determination at the top to pull together, the campaign plan would be vitiated. And without cooperation, or at least close coordination, between the army groups and particularly on the main axis between 21 Army Group and First Army, there was a very real danger that operational-level efforts would produce less than the sum of American and British parts. This is exactly what happened. Inter-Allied tensions and a divergence of effort grew and, by lessening pressure where it could have been decisive, afforded the enemy a chance to recover, at least temporarily, from defeat. Of course, in the euphoria of an apparently unstoppable advance, when total victory seemed not only inevitable but imminent, such a possibility had seemed inconceivable.

CONCEPTS OF OPERATIONS, GENERALSHIP, AND OPERATIONAL ART

The CCS had established the strategic aim: the destruction of German military power. The SHAEF preinvasion appreciation had analyzed the mission well. It had concluded that the Ruhr industrial region was far and away the most important geographic objective, the capture of which would deprive the Germans of the means to wage war; for that reason, the enemy would have to engage in battle for its defense, thus offering opportunities to shatter his forces. This was the guiding logic that should have underpinned every decision on the allocation of resources made by the Supreme Commander. The SHAEF study of terrain, ports, and weather was sound enough, although it did not draw conclusions about how these factors would affect the primary aim set by the CCS. The operational-strategic concept stemming from the appreciation had inevitably been formed in the abstract, without any knowledge of what the actual military situation would be (especially with regard to the enemy) once a firm lodgment had been secured on the Continent. Thus, the decision to utilize both the Aachen and Metz so-called gaps and the Rhône axis, with the first of these being the main effort, was based purely on theoretical and doctrinal foundations. Whereas the aim ought to have remained immutable, the method should not have been set in stone; rather, it should have been subject to revision once the circumstances of any breakout were clear. Conducting an offensive against a strong and balanced defense, one capable of utilizing every defensible line and mounting damaging counterattacks, is very different from conducting a pursuit against a shattered foe that lacks immediate reserves to restore the situation. Moreover, the decision must be firmly grounded in logistic realities. As Heinz Guderian once pointed out, "logistics is the ball and chain of armored warfare," and no amount of tactical ingenuity or wishful thinking can circumvent the limitations it imposes.

The Supreme Commander's decision of 19 August to dispense with the operational pause posited in the Overlord plan to allow a buildup of forces, supplies, and logistic infrastructure was plainly correct. An unexpectedly complete defeat of the enemy had to be exploited as fast and as far as possible before he had a chance to regroup, bring up reserves from the strategic depth or other fronts, and restore a coherent front. There even seemed to be a chance that an immediate and vigorous exploitation could precipitate a German political collapse. The question was, where and how should the decisive blow be delivered? The answer was obvious to Eisenhower, Bradley, and most American generals whose formative experience of military education and doctrine consisted of their time at the Leavenworth Command and Staff College. The enemy must be attacked across the whole front with all available forces, smashing him by superior numbers and firepower and irretrievably breaking both his capability and his will to fight. Firmly gripped and ground down everywhere, the Germans would be robbed of flexibility and their ability to maneuver and recover the initiative. The period of semistalemate in Normandy had done nothing to shake the generals' faith in this deeply ingrained doctrinal principle. Indeed, the victory was seen as proof that the concept was correct, in spite of the British failure, in American eyes, to pull their weight by attacking with sufficient vigor and persistence around Caen. The fact that the breakthrough had been achieved by an unusual (for the Americans) concentration of forces for a surprise attack in Operation Cobra was glossed over.

To Montgomery and his acolytes, the US approach was fundamentally flawed. It downplayed the importance of surprise and maneuver and failed to exploit to the full the superior mobility and flexibility of the Allied forces; the last two attributes were being utilized only tactically, not operationally. Above all, for the war-weary British, who recalled the slaughter on the western front thirty years before and had reached the bottom of their manpower barrel, it was simply too expensive. The Camberley Staff College emphasized the virtues of the judicious selection of an aim designed to inflict critical damage; the concentration of forces at the decisive point and, if at all possible, the achievement of surprise in doing so; its corollary, economy of effort in secondary sectors; the conduct of a powerful offensive on chosen axes, thus retaining the initiative; and the creation—and, once they are committed, re-creation—of reserves to retain flexibility and the initiative. Hence Montgomery's very different concept of operations: the "full-blooded" thrust on one axis by a concentrated force (exaggeratedly posited as forty divisions strong).

There is always the danger that doctrine will lose its proper function, as a guide for the wise, and become dogma for the less intelligent or less thoughtful. There is no ready-made answer for every situation. Certainly, against a strong, well-prepared defense, especially on favorable ground, the British approach is more likely to achieve useful results at a reasonable cost in lives, ammunition, and, just as important but often forgotten, time. If the defense is in a state of imminent collapse and the enemy is becoming more inclined to flee than fight, exploitation of every avenue of attack to hasten the process of disintegration is most likely to prevent his recovery. An attack on a broad front is also to be recommended even against a prepared enemy when he is weak and overextended and lacks reserves. In making a choice, an important element in the decision—perhaps the deciding element—ought to be the sustainability of the offensive. Has a sufficiently favorable force ratio been created, including reserves that can be made available, to achieve the desired depth of penetration with the desired level of destruction of the enemy, taking into account his possible reactions? Is the logistic capability of the force, in both supplies and transportation, equal to the task of achieving the desired end state?

In the circumstances pertaining at the end of August 1944, both Eisenhower's and Montgomery's operational concepts had their attractions. Either, it seemed, could result in the implosion of the Third Reich, just as the Allies' approach to the German frontier in November 1918 had contributed to revolution in Germany. Eisenhower's approach held out the promise of fully capitalizing on the Germans' defeat: they could become so overstretched by multiple threats that they would be unable to establish a viable new line; a rapid advance could even cut off the retreat of the forces defending southern and southwestern France; the liberation of territory would be maximized, and much of it would be sufficiently rapid to preclude enemy demolition of the transport infrastructure, industrial plant, or cultural features; all Allied forces would be engaged to greatest effect, with the most emphasis being placed on the most potentially decisive (i.e., northern) axis; and the effects on military and domestic morale would be most beneficial (and political masters would be correspondingly pleased). By contrast, Montgomery's approach promised a higher degree of certainty about the rapid conquest of the principal objective, the Ruhr, whatever the enemy's reactions or reserves available from the interior or other fronts; it would place the Allies in the best position to exploit toward Berlin across the most favorable going if the Germans did not collapse; and enemy groupings situated south of the Ardennes would be so deeply outflanked by Allied advances both in the north and from the Riviera that their positions would become untenable and they would be forced to retreat anyway, enabling the Americans to transition to pursuit with a minimal expenditure of resources. The course of action that held out the least promise of achieving a prompt decision was that advocated by Bradley, even in its watered-down form. The Saar region had only a fraction of the Ruhr's importance, and the Frankfurt area was of very minor significance; the terrain between the Saar and Frankfurt was difficult and became worse beyond it, whether going north to the Ruhr or east to Berlin; supply lines would be much longer than via the easier route to the Ruhr and Berlin via Aachen; and it soon became clear that the defense was becoming stronger in Lorraine than in the north.

The last phase of the summer campaign was initially filled with promise. Thanks to the great victory achieved in Normandy, the initiative lay uncontestedly with the Allies. The Germans were forced into a purely reactive posture and could only hope that trading space for time, luck, and Allied mistakes would allow them to cobble together a viable defense somewhere far to the rear. The Allies, in other words, enjoyed an almost unfettered choice among the various courses of action open to them. There were only two major constraints on the possible operational-strategic actions available to the Supreme Commander, and only one of them was military—the limitations imposed by logistic constraints. These were fairly clear and calculable, however. As long as the Supreme Commander and the army group commanders in particular had the foresight to pay due attention to logistic realities, much remained within the realm of the possible. For once, the enemy had no vote: for an indeterminable but, to the prudently minded, possibly short period, the Germans would be in no position to punish actions that would normally be considered unacceptably risky.

Bradley's scheme to make 12 Army Group's main effort on the Metz-Saar-Frankfurt axis was rightly rejected as focusing on a secondary objective. His fallback proposal, to thrust on Frankfurt solely with Third Army, was turned down by SHAEF as a logistic nonstarter. The operational-strategic objections were just as cogent. Such a narrow thrust would be pencil-like compared with Montgomery's, and it would not destroy those forces the enemy had salvaged from Normandy or had not yet engaged. It would become increasingly vulnerable to attacks into its ever-lengthening flanks to sever a line of communication from the Seine that would be well over 500 km (300 miles) long by the time Frankfurt was reached. It would take place over terrain much more favorable to the defense and unpromising for the establishment of airfields. Another of Bradley's ideas made little sense either: he wanted his armies to "go as far as practicable and then wait until the supply system in rear will permit further advance."[13] This advocated the use of scarce movement resources to support an advance by Third Army that was avowedly going nowhere decisive, in the hope of a better tomorrow. It also implied a rejection of his responsibility to give priority to First Army on the axis deemed more important based on his superior's intent. Of course, Bradley had fashioned a rod for his own back when he chose to ignore the logisticians' warnings that they would not be able to supply his army group adequately without the timely opening of several Breton ports. The combination of Cherbourg, the beaches, and Le Havre (a present from the British) would be less and less adequate the farther east he advanced. He would become dependent on being given additional capacity nearer the front as a result of Montgomery's capture of Channel ports, especially Antwerp. Yet at different times, he proposed leaving 21 Army Group with inadequate American support to achieve the objectives set by Eisenhower or stopping it well short of the vital ports. Bradley's continued advocacy of the southern axis and his refusal to accept the reality of logistic limitations did not enhance his reputation as a practitioner of higher-level operations.

Montgomery's operational idea would have exploited the easiest and therefore fastest going for mechanized forces to reach the principal objective in the west with an Anglo-American grouping so strong that it would crush whatever defense the Germans cobbled together. He was also more inclined to take account of the constraints imposed by logistics if the Germans did not quickly collapse. The 21 Army Group administrative appreciation concluded that, with Dieppe fully functioning and the RMA, Boulogne, Calais, and Ostend contributing (the last three increasingly), there would be just enough discharge capacity to support the army group's offensive to the Ruhr. With progress being made on improving road and, especially, rail links, there would also be enough land transport capacity to keep supply lines functioning—provided air and US trucks played their part as well. This was a reasonably measured calculation of the sustainability of the proposed advance round the north of the Ruhr, although it could be accused of overoptimism, particularly because it ignored the element of friction, which was bound to degrade projected performance. However, the northeastern Channel ports would have to be taken and opened promptly, and Antwerp would be needed sooner rather than later to put Allied logistic support on a permanently sound footing. It was short-term thinking on Montgomery's part to concentrate on seizing only those ports required to meet his own immediate requirements and ignore the pressing needs of the Americans. He could not bring the campaign to a triumphal conclusion largely on his own with only limited participation by 12 Army Group. Montgomery's own chief of staff was quite clear on this point.[14]

In actual fact, Montgomery could not fulfill even his allotted role without direct help. His army group was too weak to capture the Channel ports, open the Antwerp approaches, and mount a strong offensive on the Ruhr simultaneously. To achieve his ambitions, Montgomery would have required at least an additional corps of three or four divisions, with supplies to match. Nor would a consecutive approach to these British tasks be feasible, as the enemy could not be allowed a period for recovery and consolidation on either axis.[15]

That left the SHAEF broad-front course of action. But that, too, was logistically unsustainable to the planned depth of operations if both major axes were pursued simultaneously. The point need not be elaborated, as previous chapters have already proved the point.

All things being equal, Montgomery's operational idea was the best. But all things were not equal. Another, more important limiting factor in the choice of courses of action was politics. Eisenhower was acutely aware that, especially in a presidential election year, the prejudices, preconceptions, and attitudes of the American public and political class, not to mention the army itself, were critical to his continuing command. British views and desires were not without significance, but their influence was waning as American preponderance and self-confidence grew. Eisenhower had to assume active command of operations, and he had to allocate a leading role—if not *the* leading role—to American forces. When Montgomery reproached Eisenhower for allowing political considerations to interfere with the adoption of militarily optimal solutions, he betrayed a lack of understanding that alone disqualified him for the highest command. Soldiers inculcated in the purist belief that decisions should be based solely on their military merits may find it hard to accept, but political arguments trump military ones almost every time. Making war is a political act to achieve a political end, and politics inevitably influences methods, timing, and objectives. This frequently leads to the adoption of militarily less desirable solutions, as it did in the west in the late summer of 1944. And, ironically, it also led to worse political outcomes.

The result of the tug-of-war between Montgomery and Bradley (the latter egged on by Patton), with Eisenhower acting as a somewhat ineffectual player-cum-referee, was an unfortunate lack of operational decision making. The problem was probably exacerbated by the poor state of SHAEF's communications and then the disruption caused by its displacement at a critical time. The two army groups, hardly on speaking terms, prepared to go their separate ways on divergent axes. British Second Army, with eight armored and infantry divisions and with the aid of three airborne divisions, would attempt to seize crossings over five major water obstacles and advance 120 km (75 miles) north in a mere two or three days to force the Rhine; then it would move another 70 km (45 miles) or so to the Zuider Zee and establish yet another bridgehead over the Ijssel as a springboard for an envelopment of the Ruhr. The Americans would try to advance east, despite an increasingly precarious supply position: First Army would advance north of the Ardennes on Aachen and then Cologne, and Third Army would move south of the Ardennes on Mannheim via the Saar, both objectives being about 160 km (100 miles) distant and across several obstacles, including the West Wall. Meanwhile, First Canadian Army was charged with the task of taking Boulogne, Calais, Ostend, and the Antwerp approaches—tasks on which all other operations would ultimately depend; it was also required to support its British neighbor and was given inadequate resources to do each job expeditiously. Despite growing signs of resistance, the Germans were cast in the role of victims rather than players in the thinking of all the Allied commanders. Logistics, more than the enemy, would determine progress. Little attention was paid to cooperation, even between First Army and 21 Army Group, which it was supposed to be supporting, and Montgomery made little attempt to achieve coordination with Hodges. Indeed, the rivalry between the two US armies was almost as bitter as the Anglo-American divide, and the two took pride in poaching the other's logistic support.

Was there some way Eisenhower's political imperative could be followed without incurring operational penalties? One answer lay in an approach that abandoned simultaneity, which was logistically unsustainable, and sought to achieve synergy through the strict prioritizing and sequencing of offensives.

Alternating blows on different axes was usually an effective means of disorienting the enemy and keeping him off balance. Given both the Allies' superior mobility and the Germans' limited forces and intelligence gathering, it would have been particularly effective in the late summer of 1944. Ideally, a decision based on a two-phase operation would have been made during late August, but it took the game-changing event of the fall of Antwerp, captured with docks intact on 4 September, to force a rethink. This event had such significant implications that it should have prompted a revised operational-strategic appreciation and decision. With that event, the parameters of the operational problem were crystallized. Eisenhower had made it clear that the principal immediate objective lay in the north—the Ruhr industrial complex. There were thus two issues requiring solutions. First, Montgomery's army group was overstretched by its responsibilities for both the rapid opening of ports from Boulogne to Antwerp and the establishment of at least an operational-sized bridgehead over the Rhine; neither task could wait without the loss of precious momentum. On the plus side, its supply situation looked comparatively healthy. Conversely, Bradley's army group had an abundance of formations—twenty-one divisions on 1 September, with another six due to arrive over the next few weeks, to the Anglo-Canadian fourteen—but it was already failing to sustain them all in continuous offensive operations. It urgently needed the opening of Antwerp, which would ensure not only the supply of First Army north of the Ardennes but also that of Third Army to the south.

In early September four infantry divisions of US VIII Corps, reinforced by eighteen corps artillery battalions, were engaged in the reduction of Brest; another division was masking Lorient. On 10 September logistic priority was accorded to Brest. It was not until 19 September, after expending 25,000 tons of ammunition (transported in scarce trucks), flying 6,000 sorties by Ninth Air Force, and taking just under 10,000 casualties, that the battle ended. The port facilities had, of course, been comprehensively wrecked. It was, in the end, a curiously pointless battle, for although Eisenhower had still been demanding the port on 13 September, SHAEF decided not to use it just a day later. It was already too far from the front, and its rehabilitation would take too long to be worthwhile.[16] Even as early as the end of the first week in September, it should have been an easy decision to simply contain the Breton garrisons, primarily with FFI but also with a US stiffening, and redeploy VIII Corps, with about three divisions and much artillery and air support, to the more promising task of opening the Scheldt. Had the decision been made promptly, by 6 or 7 September, substantial elements of the corps could have completed the 900 km (560 mile) march from Brest to arrive at the future Breskens pocket at roughly the same time as the main body of retreating Germans. This augmentation would have enabled First Canadian Army to attack Boulogne and Calais simultaneously and still support Second Army's operations. Such a decision should not have shocked American sensibilities, as Eisenhower had always expressed his preparedness to detach corps-sized formations to Allied command.[17]

The next element of the new decision would have been the temporary suspension of Third Army's offensive in Lorraine. Patton would be required to halt on the Moselle, and XV Corps, instead of returning to his command, would become 12 Army Group's reserve. These measures would have ensured that First Army had the logistic support necessary to sustain an offensive of nine or ten divisions at least to the immediate terrain objective and possibly beyond it. This would have been a continuous effort, capitalizing on and maintaining the momentum gained in the pursuit through Belgium, rather than the rather stop-and-go affair that actually transpired. The existence of a reserve corps would have ensured that success could be properly and timeously exploited and that the northern offensive would have adequate force to achieve the desired depth of the operation. Politically, this option would have been portrayed not as a British-led operation but as a joint Anglo-American effort in which two roughly equal armies, First and Second, attacked side by side for a common objective while First Canadian and Third Armies temporarily performed secondary tasks. The possible gains, provided Hodges did not misuse his resources and mismanage his attacks, would have been the gaining of the Rhine's west bank in the Cologne-Bonn area and probably a sizable bridgehead as well, along with a likely diversion of German forces from the defense of southern Holland, which might have enabled the British to cross the Rhine at Arnhem (or, preferably, in the area of Wesel). Of course, there was the danger that the enemy might reinforce the Aachen sector at the expense of Lorraine when he realized that Patton was subject to enforced quiescence. This eventuality could have been postponed by the use of operational deception. In September 1944, 23 Special Troops (the US deception unit) successfully simulated 6 Armored Division north of Metz.[18] A larger-scale effort, suggesting the assembly of a corps-sized formation, could have been mounted using elements of several combat units as well as the 23rd and employing a replicated corps radio net and disinformation as well. (Such stratagems were routinely used by the Red Army to wrong-foot the Germans, a point amplified in volume 2.) Moreover, by 5 September, Seventh Army, coming up the Rhône-Saône corridor, was approaching Dijon and Besançon and thus posing a threat to the Germans' flank in both Lorraine and Alsace that they could not ignore. Substantial German forces would remain pinned in the south.

Having attained the desired objectives north of the Ardennes, the second phase could have been a renewed offensive by Third Army in the autumn. This would have been expedited by the early clearing of the Antwerp approaches to ensure adequate supply and the flow of reinforcements. Worsening weather and the consequent lessening of air support and more restricted going would have made the advance more difficult and more unpleasant. An inevitable consequence of the operational pause would have been a breathing space for the Germans to organize and strengthen their defenses. It is doubtful, however, that their forces would have become appreciably stronger. The fighting in the north, the more sensitive sector, would have absorbed any reinforcements for the west and taken a heavy toll. It is highly unlikely that the enemy could have found anything approaching the extra forces needed to achieve a ratio of forces to space that would have established a stable defense in depth. German success in force regeneration was impressive, but the challenge would have been one of impossible proportions; nor, given the pressure on other fronts and Hitler's reluctance to trade space for time and forces, could significant reinforcement be expected from outside the west. In any case, the disadvantage of facing a better prepared enemy probably would have been outweighed by the additional forces available and the assurance of logistic sustainability to the planned depth of the operation. Third Army's strength easily could have been at least doubled by the addition of XV Corps and VIII Corps, the latter once the Scheldt was open. An army group reserve could have been re-created using III Corps HQ, arriving in early September, and divisions that were relieved to refit and rest could have been replaced by the several fresh formations that followed shortly thereafter. Moreover, by the time such an autumn offensive was mounted, the Germans also would have faced a synergistic, sustained attack into Lorraine and Alsace from the south by fifteen divisions as Seventh and First French Armies of 6 Army Group, their logistic problems straightened out, paid the dividends always promised by Operation Dragoon.[19]

If Eisenhower ever considered the merits of dividing his broad-front advance into sequential phases, he left no record to that effect. Perhaps he dismissed it as being just as politically inadvisable as going with the single thrust, permanently closing down Third Army's offensive. Certainly, Bradley, Patton, and their supporters in the popular press would have found it an unpalatable decision. But all operational-strategic plans are necessarily compromises, and this one surely could have been sold to Marshall, the ultimate arbiter, as militarily sensible and therefore worth imposing on fractious subordinates. Perhaps Eisenhower simply put off making a decision in the hope, or even the expectation, that it would never have to be made. A German collapse, widely predicted in early September, would have averted the divisive controversy and personal unpopularity such a decision would provoke. He was certainly inclined toward such prevarication, and taking the easy path would have been an attractive option. However, his equivocations about the conduct of post-Normandy operations amounted to a frequently changing decision or a nondecision (it comes down to the same thing). Sometimes decisions can safely—indeed, usefully—be postponed, but the method of exploiting the Normandy victory was not one of them. Logistic imperatives were remorseless drivers.

OPERATIONAL ART AND GENERALSHIP IN SEPTEMBER

Army Level

A fundamentally flawed operational-strategic idea will generally result in failure. If the concept is merely imperfect or confused, it can sometimes be rescued from failure by excellent lower-level operational and tactical judgment and execution. By the same token, its deficiencies will be compounded by poor lower-level performance, and defeat or, at best, frustration of the aim will be inevitable. Unfortunately for the Allied cause, the handling of both army groups and armies was sufficiently imperfect as to result in culmination well short of achievement of the aim.

For most Allied operational-level (and indeed, tactical) commanders, pursuit was an unfamiliar phase of war, one for which personal experience would provide no guide. As an army commander in North Africa, Montgomery had conducted an undistinguished pursuit, and Patton had experience from both Sicily and Normandy. But for many generals whose wartime experience had so far consisted of attacking determined German formations in skillfully organized defenses, it would be difficult, for the sake of speed in the advance, to overcome their sensitivity to casualties, put aside their usual reliance on heavy artillery preparations and their concerns about opportunistic counterattacks and open flanks, and operate without the normal paraphernalia of boundaries, phase lines, and terrain objectives. This caution enabled many German formations to disengage, slip away, and escape complete destruction in the later stage of the Normandy campaign. Doctrine was of limited help. Neither the US nor the British Army acknowledged the need for deep operations (so central to Soviet thinking, as volume 2 will show), save in the limited sense of special and airborne forces and air action. The subject of pursuit was studied only cursorily in Western theory (for instance, the topic was allocated just over 4 of the 318 pages of the 1944 *FM 100-5*). Meeting battles, let alone operational-level meeting engagements—which were typical when enemy reserves were encountered on the move—were not considered at all. The concept of the forward detachment, so essential to the Soviet practice of exploitation, did not exist.[20]

Once the pursuit was under way, most Allied generals became accustomed to it and acted more boldly. Indeed, overconfidence became prevalent during September. Increasingly, some commanders were prone to take short-term actions, as if tactical successes would inevitably aggregate into operational success and logistic problems would dissipate rather than inevitably grow larger. The enemy was more or less dismissed as a major factor in their calculations. With victory seemingly assured, and sooner rather than later, the main questions became which nationality and which generals would garner the main credit for it, rather than how to go about actually accomplishing it. Much decision making became somewhat slapdash and influenced by national and personal prestige and rivalries instead of by objective estimates of the situation. None of the operational commanders anticipated, or recognized in good time, the point at which stiffening opposition required them to transition from pursuit mode to less improvisational attacks off the line of march.

Second British Army: Lieutenant General Dempsey. Montgomery routinely involved himself in the details of British and Canadian operations and sometimes issued instructions directly to corps commanders. However, he rarely issued written orders. It is thus impossible to determine how much of a plan or the guidance and supervision of its execution was Dempsey's work and how much his boss's. Dempsey was a shy, modest, retiring character who hated publicity and had a very equable temperament; he was content to do his job efficiently and without fuss and let Montgomery both interfere and take the credit for success, which the latter was more than willing to do. The C-in-C was probably less controlling in the pursuit phase than had been the case in Normandy; this was partly because his protégé had proved himself and needed less mentoring and partly because events were moving much too swiftly and Montgomery had other concerns and less time to devote to each. Dempsey certainly had a feel for the battle. He was also increasingly confident of his judgment. He probably handled the pursuit with little interference or advice—and he did not need them. By the time it came to Operation Market Garden, though, Montgomery was back to his customary habit of exercising tighter control.

American generals, accustomed to regard British Second Army as methodical and slow, not to say plodding, were surprised by the high rate of advance achieved in its post-Normandy operations. This was largely due to Dempsey's wholehearted and skillful implementation from the very start of Montgomery's demand for a bold pursuit. He recognized the need to replace tactically cautious methods with audacity, ignoring the usual sensitivities about flanks and attacking without detailed preparation or strong artillery support. Relying on speed and maneuver rather than numbers, he was prepared to immobilize a quarter of his force to ensure the full motorization of the other six divisions and to allow freedom of action to Ritchie and Horrocks, the corps commanders carrying out the pursuit. The aim was to keep the enemy on the run, bypassing pockets of resistance, and to preempt any attempts to reestablish a coherent defense on the water obstacles that crossed his line of advance. Thus, foresight ensured that the Seine was forced from the line of march after an approach march organized from a depth of almost 200 km (125 miles); the same was accomplished with the Somme 110 km (70 miles) further on. Emboldened by success, Dempsey assigned far-reaching objectives, up to 150 km (90 miles) distant, shortly after the latter river was crossed. The admirably concise order issued to Horrocks on 2 September stated: "XXX Corps is to capture a. Antwerp b. Brussels."[21]

When XXX Corps achieved its objectives, taking Brussels on 3 September and Antwerp the next day, Dempsey reverted to a more cautious, more "British" approach. Balance was being lost, formations were going out on a limb, and logistic margins were tightening. Despite the fact that the corps still had enough fuel to go another 150 km (90 miles), he halted Horrocks to allow XII Corps to come up on his left and take time for maintenance and rest. Like every other senior commander, he probably was not worried about the consequences of a pause, believing the German army to be so demoralized and disorganized that it could not recover cohesion for many weeks, if at all. At the time, *Seventh Army* was in full, disorganized flight; *Fifteenth Army* was withdrawing in good order but was still far south of the Scheldt, and Second Army was moving into a gap between them. The Germans were scrabbling to create some sort of stop line along the Albert Canal, but they were far from achieving this, never mind posing a counterstroke threat to a strong armored advance; available intelligence suggested as much. It was no time to check the pursuit, however tired the soldiers or worn the tanks.[22] The Guards Armored Division should have been urged forward immediately to secure a bridgehead over the formidable obstacle of the Albert Canal before it could be defended. As it was, the three-day operational pause meant that the crossing at Beeringen was contested, giving the Germans more time to establish a defense of sorts on the Escaut Canal. Though German disorganization and Allied good fortune enabled the bouncing of a bridge at Neerpelt, it was 12 September before a shallow bridgehead was firm; it had taken the Guards five days to advance 80 km (50 miles), a distance they had become accustomed to covering in a single day.[23] Moreover, as delays accumulated, the Germans were becoming more organized farther north, as Market Garden would shortly reveal.

As well as losing momentum, Dempsey apparently lost sight of two related aims of 21 Army Group: ensuring the early use of Antwerp, and trapping and eliminating *Fifteenth Army*. His order to Horrocks failed to spell out that it was not the city of Antwerp that mattered but the docks to the north. In the event, he did not have to because Roberts, commanding 11 Armored Division, consolidated their capture by the Dutch resistance. But neither Roberts nor Horrocks, as tactical commanders, was aware of the wider concern with cutting the escape route of von Zangen's force and clearing the Scheldt estuary. Dempsey was presumably aware of this, or should have been, but he had his eyes fixed firmly on the Rhine. Had he insisted on an immediate forcing of the Albert Canal in the northern suburbs of Antwerp, he would have established a favorable position from which an advance of less than 20 km (12 miles) would have sealed the South Beveland peninsula, the withdrawal route of *Fifteenth Army*.[24] Seventh Armored Division of XII Corps, north of Lille on 5 September and in the Ghent area a day later, could have been rushed to exploit the bridgehead, perhaps in conjunction with elements of 11 Armored and then reinforced by 50 Division, which was only 30 km (18 miles) from Ghent and 40 km (25 miles) from Antwerp. Alternatively, 7 Armored and 50 Divisions could have mounted a quick thrust to the coast in the Breskens area before the retreating Germans reached it. Although Dempsey can be criticized for not at least mooting such courses of action, the main responsibility for the lack of energetic action to exploit the initial success at Antwerp must be laid at Montgomery's door. He was aware of the strategic picture. He was accustomed to exercising close control over his principal subordinates. He reserved the right to make all important decisions, and it was he who had to choose between concentrating on the drive to the Rhine or risking a temporary dispersion of effort to open the Scheldt. In making the choice, he should have at least consulted with the Supreme Commander, who had a pressing, oft-repeated interest in the early opening of Antwerp. In the event, he bullied and cajoled Eisenhower into giving priority to the Rhine.

Dempsey showed shrewd operational judgment when he expressed reservations about the offensive on the Brussels-Arnhem axis. On 9 September he noted in his war diary:

> It is clear that the enemy is bringing up all the reinforcements he can lay hands on for the defense of the Albert Canal, and that he appreciates the importance of the area Arnhem-Nijmegen. It looks as though he is going to do all he can to hold it. This being the case, any question of a rapid advance to the North-East seems unlikely. Owing to our maintenance situation, we will not be in a position to fight a real battle for perhaps ten days or a fortnight. Are we right to direct Second Army to Arnhem, or would it be better to hold a LEFT flank along the Albert Canal and strike due East towards Cologne in conjunction with First Army?[25]

Dempsey was uneasily aware that German resistance was stiffening by the day. The consequent cancellation of Operation Comet in favor of a much larger, corps-sized airborne operation, accompanied by an army-scale ground attack, inevitably meant more delay, which presumably meant further German consolidation and reinforcement. That, in turn, implied that XXX Corps' chances of advancing 120 km (75 miles) up a mostly single road in a couple of days were diminishing. The operation seemed to be predicated on the assumption that little had changed since the heady pursuit of the first days of September. In addition, Dempsey should have been perturbed by multi-sourced but admittedly inconclusive intelligence reports, although it is unclear what information he had access to and whether it was watered down.

Dempsey's favored idea for flanking the Ruhr was sounder than Montgomery's. He would have had his army advance on an easterly axis initially, crossing the Maas at Venlo and then swinging northeast to force the Rhine at Wesel (where it actually crossed six months later). Although the general terrain was little better than that going north, only two (rather than three) major water obstacles would have to be seized by airborne assault. Such an attack was also more likely to achieve surprise than a thrust from the Neerpelt bridgehead, a move that intelligence indicated was expected by the enemy. And without surprise, given the terrain-imposed limits on the strength that could be brought to bear, the Arnhem axis was unpromising for a rapid advance if the enemy had significantly augmented his force during the operational pause. Above all, it would be a shorter approach, avoiding the danger of a lengthening of exposed flanks and allowing for mutual support with the Americans. Whether Montgomery, with Eisenhower's backing, would have been able to persuade the airmen to risk the flak defenses on the Ruhr approaches that included Wesel is an open question; it certainly would have required the application of pressure not only on Brereton but also on the powerful strategic bombing champions, as the task of air defense suppression would have required a major effort by Eighth Air Force's bombers and fighters.

In keeping with his habit of reserving the major operational decisions to himself, Montgomery did not discuss the Wesel axis, summarily rejecting it in favor of Arnhem, even though he knew that most of his senior staff as well as the operation's executor were in favor of the former. The loyal Dempsey did not demur; he accepted the decision and determined to carry it out as well as he could. Arguably, he should have pressed his case more forcefully, but that was not his way. Unfortunately, as he had feared, the operational pause and the extraordinary recuperative powers of the Wehrmacht had changed the operational situation. This, combined with misfortune and numerous errors, both operational and tactical, doomed Market Garden to failure.

Some of these mistakes were forced or due to others. The important supporting attacks on the flanks could not start until D+2, but time would brook no delay of D-day. Montgomery's decision not to trap *Fifteenth Army* left it free to strike into the flanks of the uncomfortably narrow airborne corridor. Browning's failure to prioritize the taking of the Nijmegen bridge imposed a delay that, along with the malign effects of weather, ultimately proved fatal. But some blame can be laid, wholly or in part, at Dempsey's door. The plan for Operation Market was formulated by the airborne army and corps in England and contained numerous faults and deficiencies. Dempsey exerted no influence on its formulation. Although it was outside his remit, the airborne formations would come under his command on landing, and it would have been reasonable for him to request, if not demand, a say in the process; he had considerable experience of the pitfalls of airborne operations and would probably have picked up the flaws in Browning's plan. Presumably, Montgomery would have supported his trusted lieutenant, recognizing that planning a joint operation without the involvement of both services was a military stupidity; the whole point of the operation was to project XXX Corps over the Rhine with great rapidity, and a rapid advance of that corps was vital to the airborne's survival. Eisenhower too, mindful of Marshall's keen interest in the decisive employment of the airborne forces, probably would have lent his weight to overcome the objections of First Allied Airborne Army. There were faults in the Dempsey-Horrocks plan as well. Given that Adair and his Guards Armored Division had earned a reputation for a cautious, conservative, by-the-book approach to tactics, Roberts's thrusting 11 Armored Division would have been a better choice for the spearhead role, as speed in the advance was a sine qua non; it could have passed through the Neerpelt bridgehead straight into the attack, without the Guards' need for a sometimes awkward transition from defense. In addition, H-hour should have been fixed for first light to maximize the hours of daylight available during the crucial first day. And, given the overriding importance of tempo, Dempsey did not do nearly enough to spur Horrocks on. Market Garden provides several examples of poor tactical decisions having a major operational impact.

Characteristically, even though he disliked both the concept and the plan, Dempsey took full responsibility for its failure (with the exception of the performance of the commander of 1 Airborne Division, whom he excoriated). Actually, most of that responsibility was Montgomery's, even down to the tactical plan, which was much influenced by the C-in-C's ideas as expressed directly to Horrocks.

For all the mistakes revealed by hindsight, Dempsey showed a sound grasp of relevant principles in his conduct of operations in September. He kept his superior's aim firmly in sight; in retrospect, he should have exercised initiative and exploited the seizure of Antwerp immediately, but Montgomery, who usually gave very detailed orders, had not specified what he wanted. There was no lack of decisiveness, no vacillation in Dempsey's handling of his army. He appreciated the value of surprise and achieved it when he preempted German attempts to establish delay lines; his boldness and consequent speed in the advance surprised both the enemy and his allies, but ultimately (and, it could be argued, too early), the customary British caution prevailed. He demonstrated flexibility in his groupings and in the execution of decisions and gave full rein to his tactical commanders in their handling of the battle. He was always conscious of the limitations imposed by logistics and factored them into his plans. His leadership, though unspectacular to the general public, earned him nothing but praise from his subordinates. Dempsey was not an inspiring commander as far as the lower ranks were concerned; he was too reserved to play the showman. But he looked after his men well, including the avoidance of unnecessary casualties. His professionalism and judgment were sound—more so than Montgomery's when it came to Market Garden, where his feel for the enemy's recovery and its implications proved more prescient. Again unlike his master, he generally maintained cordial relations with the Americans and cooperated with them as much as possible.

First Canadian Army: Lieutenant General Crerar. Montgomery considered Crerar a mediocre general, lacking drive and unfit for army command; he made no secret of his opinion. He would have liked to replace Crerar with the imaginative and tactically able commander of II Canadian Corps, Lieutenant General G. G. Simonds. He also objected to Crerar's insistence that he had national responsibilities for which he was directly answerable to the Canadian National Defense HQ; this offended Montgomery's principle that operational command was a full-time job for one man (save, of course, for himself, as he thought he should be both land forces and 21 Army Group commander). Although it is true that his national responsibilities absorbed a significant amount of Crerar's time, the real problem was that the C-in-C was uncomfortable having a subordinate who was not under his sole control.[26] He expected poor performance from Crerar and thus accepted, without checking their accuracy, negative stories that confirmed his opinion.

On 1 September, concerned that First Canadian Army spearheads were lagging far behind those of Second Army, exposing the latter's left flank, and dismissing Crerar's excuse that he had inadequate logistic support, the C-in-C sent a barbed demand for more urgency. Dissatisfied with the response, and disbelieving Crerar's assertion of strong opposition to his now well-understrength armored divisions on the Somme and the need to give his 2 Canadian Division forty-eight hours to absorb over 1,000 replacements, Montgomery summoned Crerar to a meeting on 3 September. Crerar felt obligated to attend a memorial service in Dieppe in memory of the Canadians who had died there two years before, and he arrived too late for what he had not realized would be a conference of army commanders. Montgomery rejected Crerar's explanation, reprimanded him sharply, and declared his intention to have him replaced. Crerar replied that he rejected the criticisms of his performance and would appeal his dismissal to the government in Ottawa. Shortly after this, Montgomery backed down and sent Crerar a somewhat sickly apology, but the incident further soured relations and reinforced each man's prejudice against and distrust of the other. Montgomery continued to fret about the slow pace of Canadian operations undermining his thrust to the Ruhr and to criticize Crerar's performance. He accused Crerar of making unnecessarily heavy weather of comparatively straightforward tasks.

Montgomery's brusque dismissal of Crerar's problems as mere excuses for a lack of determination and grip was unfair. Crerar was facing tougher opposition than Dempsey, as *Fifteenth Army* had not been engulfed in the disasters that had befallen *Seventh* and *Fifth Panzer Armies*. The sector allotted to his army left little maneuver room for much of the time (it narrowed to less than 40 km [25 miles]). Moreover, it soon became clear, in part from Ultra, that the Germans were going to leave substantial garrisons to hold the Channel ports and the mouth of the Scheldt.[27] Crerar had a real worry about the loss of combat power as a result of undermanned units (his Canadian divisions were short of 4,318 men by 31 August, with most of the deficiencies falling in the twenty-one rifle battalions, and Polish replacements had totally dried up). He had resource constraints, especially in the areas of transport and ammunition. His engineers were short of bridging equipment, increasingly in demand even as preparations for Market Garden diverted it to Second Army, and engineers were required for airfield construction and line of communications road building. And it would have been wrong for him to neglect his duties toward the Canadian government and its army. Not least among these was preserving the unity of Canadian formations under Canadian command.

Montgomery's pressure on Crerar continued to grow. On 6 September the taking of Le Havre and Boulogne became a priority, as their possession was calculated to be sufficient for Market Garden to proceed. By 9 September, Montgomery was demanding Calais and Dunkirk as well, as they would be required to enable an advance deep into Germany; the Antwerp approaches were at the bottom of the list of priorities. The C-in-C was anxious to know how soon these ports would be in Canadian hands. Then, on 14 September, he suddenly started to pay more attention to the Antwerp issue. Both the CCS and Brooke, as well as Eisenhower, were expressing concerns about the early opening of Antwerp. Montgomery passed the buck to Crerar. Clearing the Scheldt was now given precedence, but an ambiguously worded order also indicated that capturing Boulogne remained a priority; Calais and Dunkirk could be put on the back burner. But as Crerar soon discovered when he sought naval advice, opening Boulogne meant that the outlying fortifications of Calais would have to be taken as well.[28] It is easier to change priorities with a stroke of the pen than it is to readjust troop dispositions and the flow of supplies on the ground, and the C-in-C offered no additional troops or ammunition. Capturing Le Havre had required a deliberate, corps-sized attack with the application of formidable air and naval firepower, all of which took time to organize. It was plain that the similarly well-prepared, strongly manned fortifications at Boulogne and Calais would require similar treatment. Moreover, whatever Montgomery's desires, their reduction would have to be consecutive, as each would require the application of the same limited supply of special armor and medium and heavy artillery and, in Crerar's view (uncontested at army group level), the same naval gunfire and heavy bomber support. The bringing up of essential resources and the provision of the necessary ammunition would require scarce transport and fuel, and the army group would not make that immediately available.

Crerar had only II Canadian Corps to take three ports (two, after Dunkirk was postponed) and to clear the Scheldt estuary. The latter task alone would require its two infantry divisions; the armored divisions were of limited utility in sodden terrain intersected by numerous canals. Yet 2 Division was not available; on relief in front of Dunkirk, it had been sent to Antwerp to release a XII Corps division to join the Market Garden operation. To clear the approaches to Antwerp and, at the same time, deal with the Channel ports, Crerar would have needed more than just Simonds's corps. Yet the fall of Le Havre did not mean that I Corps became available to match means to Montgomery's desired ends. That formation, with all its supporting armor and artillery, was immobilized, losing its transport to augment that supporting the advance on Arnhem. When its two divisions were eventually brought forward, the first of them on 23 September, they were sent to support Second Army by taking over much of XII Corps' sector and, augmented by the Polish Armored Division taken from II Canadian Corps, to support the already failing Market Garden by advancing on the Turnhout-Tilburg-s'Hertogenbosch axis.

Montgomery was highly critical of the time it took to capture the Channel ports and then open the Scheldt, a perspective repeated uncritically in many postwar studies.[29] It is hard to see how the process could have been expedited, absent the allocation of sufficient troops and ammunition to secure these objectives simultaneously. Launching attacks on strongly fortified places without detailed preparation, sufficient firepower, and special armor would have been a recipe for expensive, morale-sapping failure and more loss of time when the attacks had to be remounted. The fact was that First Canadian Army was seriously overtasked. Had Crerar been able to use I Corps immediately after it was finished with Le Havre to reduce Boulogne and Calais (or even, in the latter case, just the Cap Gris Nez batteries), allowing II Canadian Corps to concentrate earlier on the Antwerp approaches, the port issue could have been settled much more rapidly. In addition, Crerar might have been able to advance north of Antwerp to isolate the South Beveland peninsula, as he had desired. As it was, the enemy was prepared, and *Fifteenth Army* (less its two stay-behind divisions) was long gone by the time such an effort was undertaken. It is difficult to imagine how Crerar could have accomplished more than he did, or sooner. He needed more troops and ammunition, but the Canadian army received neither until more than three weeks into October, by which time Crerar had departed on sick leave.

There was, however, an even better, more radical solution to obviate the problem altogether. On the day after Antwerp fell to the British, docks intact, II Canadian Corps was 30 to 50 km (18 to 30 miles) south of Boulogne and 200 km (125 miles) or so from Bruges, save for 2 Division, which was still at Dieppe. Crerar could have suggested to the C-in-C that, as Antwerp had more capacity than all the ports between it and Cherbourg combined, it might be a good idea to simply mask the Channel ports and concentrate as much of II Canadian Corps as possible on an early clearing of the Scheldt estuary to open Antwerp.[30] Ideally, the effort would be augmented by some or even most of the more forward elements of XII Corps and an airborne and/or small amphibious operation. The idea would be to get there before the bulk of the less mobile *Fifteenth Army*, slowed even more by intense air interdiction, and certainly before a defense could be organized. It has been suggested that Simonds thought along those lines, though his biographer cites no evidence. Of course, to make this suggestion, Crerar would have needed a full understanding of the bigger picture, especially the logistic one, and this he was unlikely to have. In any case, this is just the sort of operational-strategic idea that should have occurred to Montgomery himself.

Although he can hardly be blamed for failing to accomplish the impossible, Crerar can be faulted on two counts. First, presumably because he did not want another damaging row with his boss, he did not point out with sufficient forcefulness the unreasonable nature of the demands being made of him. Nor did he highlight the fact that organizing complex interservice operations was time-consuming and weather-dependent, even if the RAF were disposed to be cooperative (which was not always the case, despite Crerar's investment of time and effort in building relationships).[31] His lack of rapport with Montgomery probably deterred him from making suggestions for fear of their likely peremptory and sarcastic dismissal.

Second, Crerar presided over a headquarters that was rather slow and ponderous in its decision-making process. Whereas most army commanders (Hodges was another exception) made their own appreciations and decisions and then trusted their staffs to work out the details, Crerar looked to his chief of staff and others to prepare and present alternative plans from which he could choose. Sometimes he would assemble his staff for a special conference to prepare presentations for himself or even for the C-in-C, and only then would he make a decision. Crerar's was an essentially managerial style, command by committee. This approach, combined with uninspiring leadership and an obsession with often minor details, caused him to sometimes lose sight of the aim and the bigger picture, and he was often buffeted by staff disagreements and conflicting agendas. The problem was compounded by Crerar's poor health; his energy and powers of decision were increasingly eroded by his illness.[32] Toward the end of September he went to England for treatment, and Simonds became acting army commander. Simonds's more decisive style infused new life and vigor into First Canadian Army HQ. Crerar thus missed the battle of the Scheldt, which was steered and driven, despite great difficulties, to a successful conclusion by his acting successor. Crerar did not return until 7 November. He had hoped to get back a week earlier, but Montgomery schemed until the last moment, trying to prevent his return altogether.

Crerar did not deviate in his efforts to achieve the goals he had been set, although, unlike Simonds, he displayed no creativity in doing so; he was a plodding commander who lacked imagination. Like Dempsey, he can be criticized for not standing up to his master. Of course, the fact that both generals had good cases to argue by no means guaranteed that the famously single-minded, intolerant, and forceful Montgomery would have listened to them. They might have concluded that argument was not only pointless but also counterproductive, souring relations to no effect; in that case, the best course was to remain loyal and suppress their doubts. Crerar probably had only one chance to surprise the enemy. In the immediate aftermath of the seizure of Antwerp, he could have had Simonds preempt the defense of Fortress Southern Holland by having an armored division race ahead of both the retreating, foot-mobile defenders-to-be and possible Canadian support to establish bridgeheads. Perhaps the move could have been combined with an amphibious assault on the fortress-to-be. Such a venture would have been somewhat risky and contrary to doctrine (by violating an army boundary), and the need to do such a thing never occurred to Montgomery, let alone his subordinate. Absent the preemption of defense of the Channel ports or the Breskens fortress, Crerar lacked the strength and ammunition to do anything other than reduce each of his several objectives in turn; he was never able to achieve the sort of concentration he would have liked and that might have speeded up the process. Indeed, he was compelled to rely on air- and sea-delivered firepower to compensate for his own deficiency and worked diligently to gain the cooperation of the other services (encountering some resistance from the RAF).

Competent enough in a pedestrian way, Crerar lacked imagination and boldness. Though perfectly sound in theory, he was never going to come up with original and daring methods to take on his more daunting tasks without relying on vastly superior firepower and numbers. As a manager more than a leader, he failed to inspire his subordinates and his soldiers. His ill health sapped his energy and decisiveness and increased his dispiriting querulousness. It was fortunate for the Canadian army that the more innovative and dynamic Simonds replaced him for the reduction of the Breskens pocket and Walcheren.

US First Army: Lieutenant General Hodges. First Army's pursuit was just as vigorous as Second Army's and duly reaped its rewards when, at the beginning of September, it caught the shattered remains of several *Seventh Army* divisions in the Mons pocket and netted up to 25,000 prisoners. It would appear that this successful maneuver had been ordered by Bradley, who had not enlightened Hodges other than to instruct him to link up with an airborne assault at Tournai. The latter accepted this northward shift of axis (across the boundary with 21 Army Group) without question and promptly switched VII Corps almost ninety degrees to the north to conform with XIX Corps' move on Tournai. When Collins pointed out that this would open a gap between his formation and Third Army to the south and asked Hodges who would fill it, the army commander replied: "Joe, that's your problem."[33] Left to exercise his initiative, Collins contemplated leaving an infantry division but rightly recognized the need for concentration and instead used merely a reinforced cavalry group. Like the 140 km (90 mile) switch of XIX Corps from the army's left to right flank in August, the Mons pocket affair demonstrated further the flexibility and agility of both US formations and First Army's staff work. It provides a good example of the use of operational maneuver during exploitation to important operational effect. The German losses delivered all but the coup de grâce to *Seventh Army* and left the road to Aachen, the best avenue to the Reich, largely devoid of troops to contest it. But Hodges was only partly the architect.

In truth, Hodges was not comfortable with fluid, fast-developing situations. He pored incessantly over his situation map, but it was with the mind-set of an infantry tactician used to relatively slow, incremental developments over limited areas. Nor did he have the means to ensure that he always had the clear, up-to-date picture he craved, having failed to develop a First Army equivalent of Montgomery's Phantom Regiment or Patton's 6 Cavalry Group. He probably would have liked to keep his corps commanders on his customary tighter rein, but communications shortcomings made that impossible when the pace was hectic. Whereas he was happy to give plenty of leeway to Collins, he trusted Gerow much less and Corlett hardly at all.

These prejudices apparently influenced his decisions when conflicting demands from above and logistic constraints forced him to make hard choices as his army approached the German frontier.

After Eisenhower modified his concept of operations on 4 September, Hodges was pulled in different directions. The main effort was in the north of his zone of advance, in support of the British and aimed to force the Rhine in the area of Cologne. At the same time, he was required to cover the left flank of Third Army as it pushed east on the Verdun-Metz axis. At around 140 km (90 miles), his army's zone was wide; his territorial objectives were also extensive, from Cologne in the north to Coblenz, 80 km (50 miles) south. With only eight divisions (after one was detached to Patton's command on 3 September), some were, of necessity, allocated uncomfortably wide sectors. Hodges chose to advance in a single echelon without any reserve, though his army was not spread evenly across the front: XIX Corps in the north had a sector only 25 km (15 miles) wide; VII Corps in the centre had 50 km (30 miles), with its three divisions concentrating in approximately two-thirds of that, while the rest was screened by a cavalry group; and V Corps was allocated about 75 km (45 miles), again, with most of the force occupying two-thirds of the space. Such a combat formation was suited to pursuit, and it was plainly desirable to penetrate the West Wall—ideally, in more than one place—before it could be properly defended. In the circumstances of early September, such a forcing from the line of march seemed entirely possible. The elimination of a substantial force in the Mons pocket, on top of the losses in Normandy, suggested that the enemy lacked the means and the strength of morale to put up a serious fight for the West Wall or, indeed, short of the Rhine. This interpretation was strengthened when both Second and Third Armies started to run into unexpected problems; clearly, the enemy could not be recovering everywhere. But once opposition stiffened, as it started to do on 11 September, the lack of a reserve would make it difficult to achieve a timely concentration. Of course, this is exactly what happened when *12 Volksgrenadier Division* started to arrive on 12 September and VII Corps lacked the combat power to overcome the strengthening defense.[34] Another division would have made the difference between completing the penetration and the failure that actually occurred. The poor lateral communications south of the Namur-Liège road would make it difficult and time-consuming to redeploy significant forces from the mountainous and forested terrain of the Ardennes and Eifel to the main axis astride Aachen, so the need for concentration had to be anticipated if momentum was to be maintained.

The warning signs of the coming logistic pinch had been clear even as First Army crossed the Seine; by the beginning of September, there were endemic shortages, particularly but not exclusively of fuel. When lack of fuel required the temporary suspension of one corps' advance, Hodges halted

XIX Corps. When required to detach a division to Third Army, he sent 79 Infantry Division from XIX Corps, one of the formations furthest from Patton's area of operations. As a result, when VII Corps was checked on 11 September at the West Wall, its left-hand neighbor was weakened and lagging several days behind and could neither cover Collins's flank nor add substantial weight to the attempt to penetrate the defenses in the Aachen area; it was still 20 km (12 miles) west of the fortifications when Collins ceased his attack. This was doubly unfortunate. The going north of the city, on either side of Geilenkirchen, was not ideal for operational maneuver, but it was better than that facing Collins in the Stolberg corridor and much better than that in the Hürtgen Forest and the Eifel, where half the army's strength was located. The enemy was indeed weak. A strong reconnaissance in force mounted on both sides of Aachen simultaneously, as urged on Hodges by Collins, almost certainly would have pierced right through the fortifications before the enemy could create an adequate defense. If Collins had been able to call on even a single reserve division, he probably would have broken through. And, for that matter, a quick attack most likely could have taken Aachen from the line of march. As it was, the Germans were able to scrape together just enough strength to hold off the sequential attacks south and north of the city to which they were subjected, mounted with an inadequate supply of artillery rounds as the supply problem transmuted from one of POL to a more long-term one of ammunition. The three separate corps attacks had petered out by 18 September, and on 22 September Hodges postponed any renewal subject to replanning and an improved logistic situation—just when Montgomery was hoping the Americans would pin forces and attract reserves away from Nijmegen and Arnhem.

First Army had suffered a setback. Although it did not appear so at the time, coupled with the already failing Market Garden, it would be the culminating point of the Western Allies' 1944 campaign. The failure was a consequence of being given a mission that pulled the army in different directions with objectives that were too spread out and with inadequate resources, especially in logistics, to accomplish it. This fundamental problem of overtasking was down to Bradley, though Hodges accepted his mission without demur or even question; apparently, given the overconfidence of early September, he had no doubts about its feasibility. Nevertheless, Hodges was not absolved of the responsibility for clarifying his mission. Was the Rhine crossing in the Cologne area the most important of his three tasks, as appeared to be the case even after Eisenhower's temporizing of 4 September? If so, the main effort should have been toward the Aachen gap, with that axis weighted accordingly. This would have meant a happy coincidence of the main effort with the exploitation of the fastest, least defensible avenue to the Rhine and therefore the best chance of sustaining a high tempo of operations, retaining the initiative, keeping the enemy off balance, and reaching the objective before the enemy could reinforce, at the very time supply was about to become problematic. Moreover, a very rapid US advance would have left Aachen vulnerable to a coup de main, which would have solved the problem of trying to funnel forces round either side of the city with limited maneuver room (especially to the south). This would have required a northward shift of emphasis—the opposite of what happened—perhaps with a reduced V Corps being responsible for the entire Ardennes sector. Given the terrain, Allied air supremacy, and the Germans' great weakness, this would not create a dangerous vulnerability, at least in the short term; indeed, it would be surprising if the Germans risked the loss of scarce formations in an attempt to hold an ever-deepening salient in the Ardennes as an investment in a very doubtful future.

Hodges resolved the challenges facing him in the pursuit in a way that undermined the Supreme Commander's stated intent. The extent to which he was a free agent is not entirely clear, however. How far was he permitted to exercise his discretion in choosing his operational formation and priorities (for example, from which corps to detach a division to Third Army, to which corps to direct scarce fuel)? Was he guided or, more likely, directed in some of these decisions by his immediate superior, Bradley? If that was the case, it speaks ill of the army group commander's generalship, both in his subverting of Eisenhower's intent and in his interfering micromanagement.

Not all Hodges's errors were forced, however. Even if V Corps was required to emphasize support for Third Army, there was no need to spread VII Corps' effort into the Eifel to try to force the West Wall on a broad front. In the circumstances pertaining in September, a reinforced 4 Cavalry Group could have screened a 30 to 40 km (18 to 25 mile) sector, allowing the three divisions to concentrate on forcing the Aachen gap even if XIX Corps were wrongly held back from a simultaneous attack. Moreover, the coming logistic crisis was largely predictable.[35] It required choices to be made, rather than attacking everywhere in the hope that the enemy would collapse somewhere under the continuous pressure. And the first choice should have been to concentrate on the supposed main effort, especially since the worsening weather was increasingly depriving the Americans of the close air support on which they relied. Hodges was too concerned with maintaining an even advance, and thus a fairly straight front line, and with avoiding risks, even if they were very small, given the Americans' combat power, mobility, and command of the air. This was inimical to concentration and the maintenance of a reserve and thus to rapid progress where it really mattered. Indeed, even if the Stolberg corridor had been fully penetrated, the lack of depth in which the attack was mounted suggests that it would have run out of steam before carrying across the Roer. The inevitable corollary of Hodges's lack of concentration of logistic as well as combat resources was a loss of momentum and the accomplishment of only minor penetrations through weak defenses. As a consequence, the Germans gained precious time. Hodges was to repeat the error again and again as summer gave way to autumn.

The Germans made good use of the gift of time to improve their defenses and reinforce as best they could. They also started the process of re-creating an operational reserve in the shape of the new *Sixth Panzer Army*, built from the shells of divisions smashed but not annihilated in Normandy. They were still weak and vulnerable—so much so that the Americans generally disparaged the Germans' efforts and in consequence underestimated the significance of a mere ten-day operational pause. They were wrong to do so, as history could have taught them. The result was that Hodges still did not concentrate sufficiently; nor did he organize his main attack in enough depth to ensure that its weight was sufficient to carry it through to the Rhine objective—either that, or he was incapable of giving up attacks over his whole zone of advance. Each of his three corps, including V Corps on the subsidiary axis in the Eifel, had almost identical allocations of artillery and other army assets. Each of the two corps tasked with encircling Aachen used just a single infantry division, with the armored divisions carrying out flank protection. Meanwhile, Collins, with his other infantry division, embarked on an effort to clear the Hürtgen Forest, based on a false analogy with the Argonne Forest problem that had so vexed the US Army in 1918 and the highly dubious assumption that the Germans would be able to assemble sufficient forces therein to threaten the southern flank of a thrust toward Cologne. The Hürtgen battle would drag on into December, again with no concentration but rather a succession of seven divisions following one another sequentially through attritional battles that bled them white. It is hard to imagine any terrain more defensible or worse suited to the equipment and training of US forces. The Germans, thanks mostly to long experience in Russia, were better at forest fighting, and American advantages in armor, mobility, and artillery, not to mention the air, were largely negated. The original object, dubious as it was, would have been achieved by simply attaining the first ridge, but the advance crawled deeper, as if hills, villages, and road centres had some intrinsic value. Most of the 33,000 American casualties were suffered to little purpose. Had Hodges not become fixated on using the Stolberg corridor to get to and across the Roer in the area of Düren, he might have thought about shifting the main effort north of Aachen and crossing lower down, thus attacking through terrain where superior American firepower and mobility could be properly utilized and a German infantry sally need not be feared.

Ironically, there was good reason to become involved in the Eifel, at least to a limited extent. The Germans' control over the Roer dams gave them the ability to disrupt any attempt to exploit a crossing downriver: the longer it took to force the river, the greater the danger of a significant force being cut off on the east bank by floods and destroyed by a growing *Sixth Panzer Army* before reinforcements could be fed in. Although warnings were sounded at a lower level from the beginning of October, Hodges willfully ignored and then downplayed the danger. It was not until well into November that he recognized there was a problem, and not until December that the dams figured prominently in First Army planning. And the best route to the reservoirs was up the Monschau corridor, not across the ridges of the Hürtgen Forest. In September, or even in early October, V Corps probably could have taken them if it had been given some of the infantry being squandered farther north in the Hürtgen. There was otherwise very little point in Gerow's attacks.

Some generals, after initially fumbling or hesitantly grappling with an unfamiliar and more challenging level of command, grow into the job. Hodges did not. His professionalism remained at the tactical level, and he was unable to raise his sights to the operational dimension. Obsessed with tactical detail—his comfort zone—he lacked the breadth of vision, understanding, foresight, imagination, and flexibility of mind required for army command. He was uncomfortable with maneuver conducted at a high tempo in open warfare and preferred the methodical linear and attritional approach.[36] He was impatient with logistic constraints, and he made short-term decisions characterized by micromanaging tendencies; he often avoided the hard choices and ruthless prioritizing that higher command requires. He lacked boldness, even in situations of low risk. For example, his concern to get V Corps over the Meuse before the river could be properly defended was at the expense of XIX Corps on the fast avenue and main axis, and he ignored the fact that the axis through the Ardennes into the Eifel was slow going and too easily blocked. He tried to keep all three corps attacking simultaneously, even when incipient supply shortages indicated that all three would inevitably fall short of their objectives, including those on the main axis. He persistently failed to ensure adequate concentration, enabling even a weak defense to resist penetration of the West Wall through its entire depth, let alone open up possibilities for exploitation. He oversaw disjointed attacks that were not coordinated in time and space and, as a result, were not synergistic, leading to failure on the main axis. He regularly overburdened his subordinates, berating Corlett and Gerow when they failed. He had a penchant for doing the obvious, conducting uncoordinated frontal attacks and routinely ignoring the combat-multiplying effects of surprise. He could not conceptualize subsequent operations that built on the one currently under way; indeed, as with the Roer dams, he could not look ahead and identify a sound basis on which follow-on operations could be mounted. He did not learn from experience, as his dismal repetition of futile attacks into the Hürtgen Forest made clear.

A shy, remote, and austere figure, Hodges did not provide inspiring leadership, increasingly remaining in his HQ and conferring with a select few. He grew out of touch with and estranged from two of his three corps commanders. He did nothing for the morale of his troops or their leaders; rather, he became a depressing influence as his nerves, health, and stamina visibly declined and his pessimism grew. He was reputed to care greatly about his men, but the best way to do so is to minimize casualties by eschewing unnecessary battles and ensuring that those that must be fought are fought on favorable terms and to a successful conclusion.

US Third Army: Lieutenant General Patton. As First Army advanced beyond the Seine, Patton's maneuver strength was reduced to six divisions when VIII Corps became tied down in Brittany and XV Corps was resubordinated to First Army. He was determined to make the most of what he had and practiced strict economy of force for flank protection: by the time the army was preparing to cross the Moselle, a single division of XII Corps was echeloned to the right rear to cover the 350 km (215 miles) from Orléans to Neufchâteau.[37] In the last few days of August, Third Army had advanced at a spectacular rate of 45 to 65 km (30 to 40 miles) per day to bounce crossings of the Meuse at Verdun and Commercy on 30 August. This was accomplished by driving forward until the last vestiges of fuel were exhausted, despite the objections of both corps commanders. Patton, who recognized the importance of continuous operations, was demonstrating greater boldness than the cautious Dempsey, who stopped short of the major obstacle of the Albert Canal with fuel for another 150 km (90 miles) still left in his tanks. The spearheads were less than 300 km (185 miles) from the Rhine, half that from the West Wall, and half as much again from the Moselle (not that Patton expected a battle to cross that river, good defensible obstacle though it may be). But no POL was to be had for another five days. To Patton, with his keen understanding of the importance of momentum to keep the enemy off balance and unable to establish defensive lines in depth, the delay was intolerable. When the fuel shortage eased (though not, he was warned, ended), he anticipated a resumption of his rapid pursuit. After all, the enemy was beaten and too demoralized to make a stand.

On 28 August Third Army's perceptive intelligence chief, Oscar Koch, warned that the German retreat did not exhibit the characteristics of a mass collapse or rout. The enemy, he said, "has been able to maintain a sufficiently cohesive front to exercise overall control of his tactical situation." A day later he warned that "numerous new identifications in contact in recent days have demonstrated clearly that, despite the enormous difficulties under which he is operating, the enemy is still capable of bringing new elements into the battle area and transferring some from other fronts."[38] This appreciation became increasingly valid as the days passed, German reinforcements arrived, and enemy organization improved in Patton's sector. It was, however, at odds with the picture being painted at higher levels and, more significantly, with Patton's instinct that "the Boche has no power to resist." Patton discounted the importance of the five-day operational pause forced on him by the fuel drought. He also deprecated the value to the enemy of the fortifications of Metz and the West Wall, sweepingly dismissing all fixed defenses as useless.[39] He expected to resume a pursuit on 5 September, as his operational directive of that date made clear. His eyes were fixed on his Rhine objectives, and he fully expected to cross the Moselle, Saar, and West Wall from the march and reach the river in ten days. This underestimation of the enemy led him, as it did Hodges, to neglect the principle of concentration and the creation of a reserve in favor of spreading his forces equally over his whole sector to make hasty, improvised, and piecemeal attacks. And, as with First Army, the consequence of doing so would be an operational setback.

The initial error—discounting the Germans' ability to put their breathing space to good use and prepare the Moselle line for defense—can perhaps be forgiven, despite warnings from intelligence. Others made the same miscalculation, and failure to regain momentum through an excess of caution would have been poorer generalship. However, Patton could have taken the precaution of creating a reserve to exploit the expected success without pause or to redeem unexpected failure. Less easy to excuse is Patton's slowness to adapt to the new situation. After the first three or four days of the renewed offensive, it was clear that the enemy had indeed reestablished a coherent and effective defense on the Moselle. It was time for flexibility, for a rejigging of the concept of operations. Even if Patton was more than half right in dismissing this defense as a thin crust without depth, a decision on the direction of the main effort, followed by more concentration, would be needed to ensure a speedy breakthrough at an acceptable cost. It was also time to remedy the lack of a reserve to add depth to the attack. Indeed, had either of his corps possessed even one more division, their initial attempts to force the Moselle almost certainly would have been successful against a very overstretched defense. As if to emphasize the need for a change in approach, on 12 September Bradley issued his ultimatum that Third Army's offensive would be closed down unless Patton could cross the Moselle in strength within two days.

There was no timely change. Patton let Walker's XX Corps continue to batter away at the Metz fortress in frontal attacks while two divisions expanded his small bridgehead to the south. Heavy attrition did not lead to a breakthrough, and the Arnaville bridgehead, which did not provide access to decent routes for exploitation, became an even more unsuitable springboard for further advance when the autumnal rains precluded off-road movement and turned the river Seille, athwart his line of advance, into a significant obstacle. Eddy, however, continued to develop his attack in the less strongly defended southern sector. A brilliant armored exploitation crumbled the defense, Nancy fell, and an opportunity for a deep thrust by XII Corps presented itself, with XV Corps now across the Moselle on its right. It was enough to persuade Bradley and Eisenhower, his declared priority for operations in the north notwithstanding, to approve Patton's modification of his operational concept. Third Army's objective would remain Rhine crossings, but in a reduced zone from Mainz to Mannheim. This more than halved the width of the objective, allowing greater concentration. Patton intended XII Corps, reinforced with the already arriving 6 Armored Division and perhaps later by 7 Armored, to advance in column of divisions and force the West Wall in a narrow sector near Saarbrücken. The thrust would start on 17 September. Haislip's XV Corps would be echeloned to the right to cover the flank of the main effort, and the arrival of Seventh Army from the south, with which XV Corps made a firm junction on 14 September, would protect the army's right and further stretch the German defense. But it was not until 20 September that Patton finally abandoned attempts to take Metz and reverted to an economy-of-force action in the area and released 7 Armored Division.

Patton was insistent that XII Corps' attack start on time, but he did not go himself to ensure that Eddy did so. The result was delay while that evercautious infantryman diverted armor to tidy up the situation north of Nancy instead of simply bypassing an enemy that posed no offensive threat. The enemy used the three-day pause to bring up fresh forces and mount their own attack with *Fifth Panzer Army*. This ill-conceived effort, decreed by Hitler, predictably failed to restore the line of the Moselle: the force ratio was inadequate, the formations employed were inadequately equipped and trained, their concentration area was partially overrun by XV Corps, and those not pinned were committed piecemeal as a result of delays and casualties inflicted by air interdiction. The German attacks were defeated, with heavy losses, in an on-off battle that lasted more than a week. Nevertheless, tactical defeats had an operational effect that decisively aided the defense of Lorraine. It appeared to higher command that Third Army's offensive was mired, the initiative lost or at least compromised. The tendency in intelligence circles now swung away from downplaying the enemy's capabilities to looking for more threats—and finding them. On 23 September, on Eisenhower's explicit instructions, Bradley closed down Third Army's offensive and ordered Patton to go over to the defense.

Clearly, Patton was too slow to recognize the change wrought by his forced operational pause on the Meuse. By the end of 13 September, XX

Corps was struggling to consolidate a bridgehead south of Metz, and Walker was only just getting around to achieving greater concentration, whereas XII Corps was beginning its exploitation from its bridgeheads and was about to take Nancy. There were no good exits from Walker's crossing point, and Metz was still strongly held; however, an excellent road net spread out from Nancy to the east and northeast (offering the prospect of coming at Metz from behind, if that was desired). Patton would have been better off if he had acted as he had contemplated on 16 September: transitioning to the defense immediately with XX Corps and taking its armored division, probably reinforced, and much of its corps artillery to reinforce Eddy's efforts. Synergy would have been achieved with XV Corps, which by then was making headway on the right flank; when 6 Armored Division arrived from Brittany, it could provide a reserve. Thus assured of reinforcement, Eddy would have been emboldened to mount his northeastern drive without pause. As it was, the window of opportunity was closed by delay. Patton lost his last chance to bring his Lorraine operation to a successful end in September by failing to act according to his own precept—that 95 percent of a general's job is to ensure that his intent is being properly and fully implemented. He did not personally intervene when Eddy did not immediately implement his 16 September order for a powerful thrust on the Nancy-Saarbrücken-Mainz axis. Had this main effort been undertaken promptly, the disjointed counterattacks by *Fifth Panzer Army* (which so powerfully influenced higher command) would have been preempted and its elements defeated in meeting battles during the course of the advance. Such an outcome could have convinced Eisenhower, as it certainly would have convinced Bradley, that Third Army's offensive should continue. The West Wall, about 80 km (50 miles) distant, might have been breached from the line of march if supply had been ensured. Although such a result would have greatly delighted Patton and Bradley, it would have done nothing to redeem the situation on the theatre's main axis in the north.

There was obviously a more fundamental problem with Patton's Lorraine operations than mere tardiness in adjusting to operational setbacks. It had become abundantly clear even before 12 September that the expenditure of logistic resources and the time required to force the Moselle were going to be greater than envisaged in more optimistic moments. This should have caused a rethinking of the likelihood of bouncing intermediate defensive lines without much of a fight and therefore about the achievable depth of the operation. If Frankfurt had ever been a feasible objective—an idea dismissed by SHAEF on logistic grounds in late August—it was now looking increasingly unrealistic. Patton did not revise his appreciation, however; instead, he exhorted his subordinates to do better and importuned his superiors for more troops and supplies. He also painted an altogether too rosy picture of his existing ammunition situation and future prospects in an effort to extract more logistic support from SHAEF via the army group.

Patton's record in observing the principles of operational art was mixed. He was certainly able to think in broader terms with regard to space and time than was the tactician Hodges, and he kept his aim firmly in focus. But as time wore on, it was clear that he was deluding himself about its realism, in terms of both sustainability and the time required for its accomplishment. His single-minded devotion to offensive action without letup and with all the forces he could bring to bear, practicing economy of force, was admirable, but he was slow to adjust to the unexpected and to concentrate when it became necessary. His renewal of the offensive in November, when the enemy had enjoyed a breathing space of almost six weeks, was mounted on a broad front with inadequate reserves and reverted to focusing too much attention on Metz. He had achieved surprise in the pursuit from the Seine principally through speed in the advance. One of the reasons for the comparative lack of success in early September was that he failed to compensate for the loss of momentum by doing something unexpected. Later in September, however, he successfully employed deception to wrong-foot the enemy, and in November he achieved a measure of surprise through his timing of the renewed offensive, if not its focus.

Some historians, and some of his contemporaries, have argued that Patton would have been the best man to command 12 Army Group. It is true that his generalship displayed many positive features. His leadership coaxed or compelled greater results from subordinates than they thought they were capable of; Eddy, for instance, irritated Patton with his ingrained caution and conservatism and corresponding lack of enthusiasm for audacious maneuver, but he surely would have exercised even less initiative had he been under Hodges's command. Patton also inspired loyalty from his staff and subordinate commanders, and this enhanced Third Army's performance. His stamina, courage, and relentless optimism had much to do with this. His boldness and decisiveness were legendary. However, he had serious shortcomings. He was altogether too abrasive to enjoy a fruitful and cooperative relationship with his principal ally (a problem compounded, of course, by the fact that Montgomery's character was, in that respect, all too similar). He showed little loyalty toward his superiors; for instance, he constantly carped about the Supreme Commander's alleged pro-British bias and at one time urged joint resignation on Bradley if Eisenhower proposed putting any American formations under Montgomery's control. He deliberately tried to deceive Eisenhower, ignored his intent, and endeavored actively, with Bradley's collusion, to undermine the Supreme Commander's campaign plan and reorient the American effort southward. He then relished his defiance of orders to wind down offensive action. His acumen did not extend beyond operational to logistic matters: logistic realities were not malleable to his will and shaped and constrained his actions in a way that he found unacceptable, so he tried to ignore them or perhaps overcome them by exhorting others to make the problem go away. Above all, perhaps, he (again with Bradley) displayed a lack of strategic vision and judgment. Seizure of the Saarland and the Frankfurt objective would not decide the war: they were of minor economic and political importance, and the routes from there to really worthwhile objectives—the Ruhr and Hitler's capital—were 300 km (185 miles) and 500 km (310 miles) away, respectively, and across generally difficult country. Like SHAEF, Bradley and Patton knew the Ruhr was the heart of the German war economy, just as Berlin was Germany's political heart, and the easiest, fastest, and least defensible routes to them lay north of the Ardennes and across the north German plain. It would be justifiable to advance on both avenues simultaneously only if doing so were logistically feasible and only if success in the north were certain. But both generals were more concerned about competing with their ally than cooperating with him; their goal was to achieve American and personal triumphs, regardless of whether these contributed significantly to campaign objectives.[40] By championing the southern approach to the "heart of Germany," even though they knew the essential precondition had not been met, Bradley and Patton demonstrated a lack of operational-strategic judgment that ought to have disqualified them both from army group command.

Army Group and Theatre Level

The great, albeit not decisive, victory achieved in Normandy meant that the problem to be overcome in September was radically different from that of August. The Germans' ability to shape events had been largely eliminated by the effective destruction of *Fifth Panzer* and *Seventh Armies*. How could operational success be turned to strategic advantage in a way that would end the war, or at least bring its end much closer? How could the enemy's ability to wage war be decisively crippled? Was there some other way to deliver such a shock to the enemy's political system that his will to fight would collapse? The SHAEF preinvasion appreciation had provided a broad goal that, one way or another, would probably have the desired effect. It did not provide a blueprint, but it would be treated as such.

12 Army Group: Lieutenant General Bradley. The SHAEF directive of 4 September, Eisenhower's first since assuming the role of land commander as well as Supreme Commander, allocated four tasks to Bradley's Central Group of Armies: as part of the theatre's main effort, to breach the Siegfried Line (West Wall) covering the Ruhr and seize the industrial region; to capture Brest; to breach the sector of the Siegfried Line covering the Saar and take Frankfurt; and to protect the Allies' flank. Priority was given to operations north of the Ardennes, but the offensive south of that area was to start as soon as possible to forestall the establishment of a stable defense and possibly trap enemy forces withdrawing from southern and southwestern France. Any commander would have found it difficult to find the optimal balance of combat and logistic resources to achieve these somewhat contradictory and widely dispersed objectives. The first step should have been to clarify the mission, compelling the Supreme Commander to establish a clear order of priorities. Bradley did not do this, and he made two decisions that were questionable at best.

The first of these involved Brest. The SHAEF planners had originally calculated that sustaining US forces and building up adequate stock levels would require discharges of 45,000 tons per day by D+90.[41] As Cherbourg and the beaches would provide only about 28,000 tons per day, they looked to the Brittany ports of St. Malo, Brest, and Lorient and an artificial port in Quiberon Bay to make up the shortfall (the latter being especially important to cover the interval between the capture and opening of the others). But none of the ports had been taken by D+60, the date specified to meet the required lead time for opening them in early September. In the event, St. Malo fell on 18 August and Brest on 19 September, but neither they nor Quiberon Bay were ever opened to Allied supply traffic: they were too thoroughly demolished, and the front had moved too far east to make commissioning them worthwhile. Given that Le Havre was invested on 1 September and taken on the tenth, and Antwerp was captured undamaged on the fourth, why did neither Bradley nor Eisenhower immediately rethink the requirement for Brest? Indeed, why did Bradley give VIII Corps priority for supply on 10 September to expedite the port's capture? The Americans expended 25,000 tons of ammunition (and the trucks and fuel to haul it), flew more than 6,000 sorties (by Ninth Air Force), and suffered almost 10,000 casualties to take a port that SHAEF officially decided not to utilize on 14 September. Bradley argued that Brest could not simply be masked like other Brittany ports because Ramcke, commander of the large German garrison, was aggressive and fanatical and would have attacked American lines of communication.[42] This reasoning was specious. The Germans lacked armor, field artillery, and motor transport, and only about one-third of the 20,000 troops were paratroops, the rest being of low quality. American supply lines in Normandy were almost 200 km (125 miles) east of Brest. Containment using a combination of a division or even a separate brigade, some cavalry, FFI, and airpower would have been a perfectly viable option. Patton's explanation for persevering with this costly siege, despite the fact that the port was useless, was more credible. "He [Bradley] said to me . . . we must take Brest in order to maintain the illusion of the fact that the US Army cannot be beaten . . . I fully concur in this view. Anytime we put our hand to a job we must finish it."[43] Such reasoning is the negation of generalship. One of the responsibilities of those exercising senior command is to know where, when, and how to seek battle. Another is to know when to finish it. Like any other enterprise, combat is subject to the law of diminishing returns and may eventually become counterproductive. A general must know when perseverance ceases to be a virtue and becomes a costly vice.

The American high command made a progressive decision during the first half of September to forgo the use of any significant Breton port. Given the increasingly urgent need for greater capacity, the fact that the seizure (never mind opening) of such ports was far behind schedule, and the unexpectedly swift acquisition of alternatives in Le Havre and Antwerp, the decision made sense—on one condition: that serious steps were taken to ensure the latter's early use. Both Bradley and Eisenhower seemed to assume that exhortations to Montgomery would accomplish the task. Neither thought to offer material assistance, even though both were aware of Montgomery's other priorities and his lack of resources to accomplish them all simultaneously. In late September the Americans made a slight effort to alleviate Montgomery's problem, sending 7 Armored Division and, a month later, 104 Infantry Division. This was too little, too late to maintain the momentum of Second Army or, of crucial importance to the Americans, ensure the timely opening of Antwerp. The British field marshal was rightly criticized for his neglect of the Antwerp problem when it was amenable to an early solution, before the defense of the Scheldt estuary solidified. But Eisenhower and Bradley showed a lack of foresight—indeed, poor judgment—in acting as passive spectators. In this, as in their reactions to the culmination of First and Third Armies' September offensives, they failed one of the tests of generalship—the ability to anticipate developments and take timely action to reinforce success or avoid failure.

Bradley's second lapse lay in his interpretation of the Supreme Commander's broad-front operational concept. Even after Eisenhower equalized the distribution of still inadequate supplies and agreed to shift V Corps into the Ardennes, it was clear from his 4 September directive that the main effort was supposed to be directed against the Ruhr, with First Army supporting the British. It was clearly a breach of at least the spirit of his commander's intent when Bradley ordered or allowed Hodges to detach a division from his left wing and starved XIX Corps of fuel in order to strengthen Third Army's drive on the Saar. Moreover, on 9 September Bradley promised that two divisions released from VIII Corps, 6 Armored and 83 Infantry, would go to Third Army, not First Army (let alone 21 Army Group). On 13 September Eisenhower reiterated his intention: "all possible resources from Central Group of Armies must be thrown into the support of First Army's drive to seize bridgeheads near Cologne and Bonn in preparation for assisting in the capture of the Ruhr." He could not have been clearer, but again Bradley worked on his superior to qualify this injunction and thus give him an excuse to continue to support Patton, even when Hodges was failing because of inadequate logistic backup and faulty dispositions. This preference continued even after the Versailles conference of 22 September again emphasized the effort in the north; in fact, it continued until Eisenhower issued an explicit order. By the end of the month, both of Bradley's armies had culminated short of their immediate objectives.

Bradley actually acknowledged in his memoirs the primary importance of the Ruhr objective.[44] But an objective operational thinker who accepted this premise would not have arrived at Bradley's position—doggedly arguing for equal treatment of the secondary axis in the face of a steadily worsening supply position and an enemy he allegedly did not believe was in a state of collapse.[45] It appears that Bradley's main motivation was to escape from under Montgomery's shadow and win a striking success on an axis that was clearly his own. As long as his main effort was merely in support of the British, he would not be recognized as a great or even independent commander. He feared that First Army, perhaps even his whole army group, would once again be placed under 21 Army Group's command, and he would be reduced to a subservient position and deprived of the glory that victory would bring.[46] Regardless of what he wrote later, like almost every other senior officer in the Allied camp, he believed the Germans were finished, at least as far as resistance west of the Rhine was concerned. He probably reasoned, consciously or unconsciously, that with the pursuit becoming more and more like a victory parade with every passing day, neither the enemy nor logistic limitations could stop the advance short of the river. That being the case, 12 Army Group's triumph in conquering the Saar could be portrayed as a decisive contribution to the end of the war—a goal worth striving for, even in the face of the Supreme Commander's perceived pro-Montgomery bias.

Bradley's personal dislike (even detestation) of Montgomery, burgeoning since Sicily and increasingly unmitigated by respect for his achievements, was a powerful motivating factor discernible in Bradley's actions at the time, in his subsequent writings, and in the comments of others in a position to know. However human or understandable, these feelings provided a poor basis for operational calculation and were inimical to cooperation between the Allies. For instance, there was no attempt to synchronize or sequence the actions of the two army groups to the advantage of both, and there was no serious attempt to coordinate the actions of First and Second Armies. This was, of course, every bit as much the fault of Montgomery as of Bradley—indeed, more Montgomery's fault, as he was the designated leading player on the northern axis. Poor interpersonal relations at the top also contributed powerfully to deteriorating relations between the Allies at formation level generally, greatly reducing the synergy between their operations and thus their effectiveness. In his handling of both the Brest and the main effort issues, Bradley demonstrated a serious lack of judgment and operational-level perspective and thinking. He also showed a lack of loyalty to his Supreme Commander, an American and a man he counted as a friend, by conspiring with Patton to undermine Eisenhower's intent and circumvent his directives.

Bradley failed to make hard choices on other important operational issues. Indeed, he treated them like scaled-up tactical problems and not qualitatively different issues requiring a wider and more forward-looking perspective. Presumably because he failed to think through his post-Normandy operation to its entire depth, he reacted to events rather than shaping them in advance, and he was happy to let his army commanders conduct somewhat disjointed operations that descended into a series of separate corps battles. Moreover, this lack of foresight, combined with an innate caution, caused him to hesitate when decisiveness and boldness would have yielded rich dividends. And like his protégé Hodges, Bradley's actions exhibited the less progressive side of Leavenworth doctrine. There was an uncritical acceptance that this doctrine was both timeless and unchallengeable, rather than a product of history that needed to be amended in light of technological developments and changing enemy capabilities. It encouraged senior commanders toward a linear-attritional model of offensive operations that was inimical to broad maneuver.

Thus Bradley was content for each of his armies to advance with all their corps in a single echelon, with no reserves at army group or army level or even within the corps themselves, and to direct them to capture quite widely spaced objectives—First Army to Cologne, Bonn, and Coblenz (90 km [55 miles]), and Third Army to Mainz, Mannheim, and Karlsruhe (100 km [60 miles]). Inevitably, this resulted in a dispersal of forces across his entire frontage with precious little concentration. As long as the enemy was trying to flee rather than fight, this operational formation carried no penalty. It was, indeed, beneficial to the extent that it exploited all available tactical avenues, kept the enemy on the run everywhere, and held out the hope that his command and control, cohesion, and will to continue the war would all disintegrate. However, if the Germans were able to check a thrust on an important axis, the lack of concentration and depth in the offensive would necessitate a time-wasting regrouping before momentum could be restored. Time would afford them a chance to restore some semblance of a defense and to reinforce it. Moreover, an advance with every available division in a single echelon was inevitably going to overstretch the logistic system. This unpalatable fact was evident as early as the beginning of the general advance across the Seine. And this, of course, is exactly and predictably what happened.

With the supply he hoped to receive, Bradley could maintain a maximum of ten to twelve divisions on reduced scales (excluding those involved in the reduction of Brest). This was not necessarily a drawback, as long as the pursuit continued. Pursuit uses less ammunition and fuel than combat against a defending enemy (a point amplified in volume 2). Arguably, he would have been better off keeping those divisions in action, perforce resting the other one-quarter to one-third, which would become a reserve ready for committal once more supply became available or was transferred from active formations if the situation changed. The uncertainty of commanders and their staffs would have been removed, and they would have been able to plan with confidence rather than rely on hope fed by specious promises and then be forced belatedly to cut their coats according to the amount of cloth they found themselves with. This, of course, would have precluded advancing everywhere all the time. Bradley and his army commanders would have had to decide how best to deploy their limited resources. This ought to have led to a concentration on the main axis at each level. An inevitable corollary could have been an uneven development of the front, with the creation of salients as enemy positions were bypassed. It was doubtful, however, that the Germans would risk the encirclement and destruction of remnants left in a salient forward of decent obstacles rather than try to rescue the remains of their shattered armies.

The Germans also had to take into account the rapid progress of Devers's forces, which would threaten their left flank. In any case, with its vastly superior combat power, mobility, and command of the air, 12 Army Group would have had little to fear from countermoves in September. As long as the Americans held the initiative through vigorous and continual offensive action that kept the enemy in a reactive posture, they could afford to undertake what in less favorable circumstances would seem a risky maneuver. Caution is desirable when facing a balanced, offensively capable, and aggressive enemy; in the circumstances of the late summer, it led to a waste of resources. It is possible that even if he had concentrated earlier and kept and properly employed a reserve, Bradley would not have been able to force the Rhine in the Cologne area before logistic constraints curtailed his operations in the autumn. But even if he failed to cross the river, he surely would have reached it and compelled the Germans to commit their last reserves to piecemeal destruction in stopping him: *Sixth Panzer Army* would have been stillborn. The Supreme Commander would surely have considered that a satisfactory outcome.

21 Army Group: Field Marshal Montgomery. From as early as mid-August, Montgomery had a clear and firm idea of how post-Normandy operations should be conducted to convert operational into strategic, war-winning success—his Schlieffen plan in reverse. All that was required was a quick decision to implement it. He was surprised and perturbed to find that neither Bradley nor Eisenhower accepted what he regarded as the only sensible way ahead. From their 23 August meeting through to October, he worked ceaselessly to convince the Supreme Commander to subscribe without qualification to his operational-strategic idea and to check perceived backsliding from even the watered-down version accepted by Eisenhower after the beginning of September. Indeed, it was probably Montgomery's unwavering determination to have his concept adopted more than self-aggrandizement or vanity that drove him to argue so vehemently and persistently for his appointment as ground forces commander. It is true that Montgomery's concept was more completely thought through than Bradley's and more likely to achieve the intent of the preinvasion Joint Chiefs of Staff and SHAEF directives, but his single-minded insistence on this plan was not merely obsessive but also to the exclusion of other necessary considerations.

The capture of Antwerp with all its port facilities intact should have been recognized as an event of such significance that it merited a recasting of plans. This did not happen at either theatre or army group level, despite the insistence of the Allies' naval commander in chief on the urgent logistic necessity of opening this major deep-water port and his warning to both Eisenhower and Montgomery on the very day of the city's fall that opening the port was dependent on clearing the Scheldt estuary. Though warned by 21 Army Group's 12 September intelligence summary that the Germans had determined that the best way to defend the Rhine was to prevent the opening of Antwerp, Montgomery affected to believe the task could be quickly and easily accomplished by Crerar. He paid only lip service to the problem. He was determined not to weaken or delay his drive on the Ruhr, already much diminished from its original "full blooded thrust" by the diversion of supply to Third Army and the consequent drastic slowing of US XIX Corps' advance on his right. He made the self-centred calculation that with "one good Pas de Calais port," an airlift of 1,000 tons per day, and additional motor transport, he could reach the Rheine-Osnabrück-Münster area. With Dieppe, Boulogne, Calais, and Dunkirk and 3,000 tons moving through Le Havre, he suggested that he could even support an advance on Berlin.[47] It was the US army group, not his own, that really needed Antwerp. Although he was prodded into action by yet another directive from SHAEF on 13 September, it only took the form of urging Crerar to greater efforts while still confusing the issue with continued demands for Channel ports and the suggestion of a thrust north from Antwerp, without any additional troops or artillery ammunition for these tasks. Meanwhile, he gave Eisenhower disingenuous assurances about reinforcing efforts to open Antwerp.[48] In fact, Montgomery's neglect of the Antwerp problem, coupled with reassurances to Eisenhower and exhortations for Crerar, persisted until long after the culmination of his main effort at Arnhem. He did not deploy a force adequate to the task of opening the port until 16 October, six weeks after Antwerp's capture. Guilefully, he tried to divert Eisenhower's attention from the issue by holding out the prospect of seizing Rotterdam, another huge inland port, as a result of the success of Market Garden. But Rotterdam is more than 110 km (70 miles) west of Arnhem and just under 100 km (60 miles) from Antwerp, and with all his forces fully committed, it is unclear which formations were going to perform this feat. It is clear that by allowing *Fifteenth Army* to withdraw all the way back to the Scheldt and then over the estuary, leaving strong fortresses on Walcheren and in the Breskens pocket and reinforcing the line with the remaining formations, as early as the first week in September, Montgomery had sown the seeds of failure for both his own and the theatre's operational concepts.

With the Supreme Commander's 4 September directive fresh in his mind, Montgomery could and should have immediately ordered Crerar merely to mask the Channel ports and concentrate on this task; he could have temporarily detached to Crerar 7 Armored Division, already in Ghent by 6 September, or, better still, the whole of XII Corps to initiate such an operation before the defense could form. Such a quick response would have both trapped the unmotorized *Fifteenth Army* and opened the Scheldt rapidly. Inevitably, there would have been a period in which XXX Corps was advancing unsupported. However, the bulk of First Canadian Army would have become available to join the advance on Germany in a matter of days, rather than many weeks. Crucially, enough supply and transport would quickly have become available to allow all British and American ground units and formations, as well as reinforcements as they arrived, to move forward.[49] Possession of Antwerp as a working port would have been a combat multiplier, making it possible to increase considerably the weight of the main effort. Montgomery apparently failed to appreciate such factors, regarding the issue as a simple binary choice between Antwerp and the drive on the Rhine.[50] This was at best a gross oversimplification. In making this choice, he showed a lack of foresight and judgment, arrogance, and disloyalty both to his Supreme Commander and to his subordinate in the way he blamed Crerar for the lack of progress resulting from his overtasking. It is difficult to avoid the suspicion that Montgomery, like Bradley, regarded the war as almost won—hence his implication that Second Army, with some help from First Army, could penetrate not only as far as Osnabrück but also, with sufficient port capacity, all the way to Berlin (a delusion that was of brief duration, being dropped by the time he met with Eisenhower on 10 September and repudiated in the Versailles conference of 22 September, the very time Eisenhower was espousing it).[51] And like his American opposite number, he wanted to hog the honor and glory of victory.

The vision the field marshal pursued with myopic intensity was no longer the advance on the Ruhr with Hodges's army alongside—that had been scuppered by Eisenhower's permitting the dispersion of 12 Army Group's effort—but a lightning thrust on a divergent axis to cross the Rhine at Arnhem and advance north of the Ruhr. Market Garden was solely Montgomery's brainchild. His senior staff and the operation's executor, Dempsey, were all dubious about the plan. It has often been described as a bold, calculated risk that, though operationally sound, failed owing to tactical error and sheer bad luck. There were indeed major errors in planning and execution at the tactical level, as well as some bad luck.[52] Despite these problems, the operation came within a measurable distance of success. Montgomery argued: "the operation was justified because, had good weather obtained, there was no doubt that we should have attained full success." It was also unfortunate that "the enemy managed to effect a surprisingly rapid concentration of forces to oppose us. In face of this resistance the British . . . [were] not strong enough to retrieve the situation created by the weather by intensifying the speed of operations on the ground. We could not widen the corridor sufficiently quickly to reinforce Arnhem by road."[53] There is some truth in his assertions, but closer analysis suggests that it was conceptually questionable, actually more of a gamble based on dubious operational assumptions.

Market's predecessor, Comet, was mooted on 3 September, confirmed on the sixth, postponed three times because of Second Army's loss of momentum, and then canceled on the tenth. The Neerpelt bridgehead was not established until 12 September, after five days of heavy fighting to advance about 30 km (18 miles). Owing to this evident enemy recovery, the forces assigned to Market were increased to an airborne corps, with D-day on 17 September. Given the knowledge that *Fifteenth Army* formations had withdrawn into western Holland and growing suspicions between 13 and 16 September that *II SS Panzer Corps* was in the area of the projected advance, the enemy situation should have been reassessed. This, in turn, should have given rise to severe doubts about the whole concept. Would an airborne force that would take at least three days to deliver (several more if the weather turned poor) be able to seize all its objectives and build up fast enough to hold them? Spells of poor weather, either over the drop zones or over the air bases, were to be expected in September. In any case, if it had taken the ground forces four days to advance the last 16 km (10 miles) from Beeringen to Neerpelt, could they gain and maintain sufficient tempo to cover the 120 km (75 miles) to Arnhem in two or three days, even if helped by airborne assaults? The latter assumption might have been justified if the enemy had been continuing his withdrawal, but his resistance was stiffening considerably, and the ground both favored the defense and, crucially, limited the amount of combat power that XXX Corps could bring to bear. Moreover, the flanking corps, facing even more difficult ground, would not be ready to mount their supporting attacks to protect the flanks until D+1 or 2. In other words, terrain would go far to negate Second Army's superior combat power. Clausewitz's friction, not to mention the enemy, interferes with the execution of every plan, and this one had no tolerances to allow for setbacks. Montgomery's decision to leave the objectives and timetable unchanged smacks of wishful thinking. Any operational plan in which everything must go off without a hitch in order to succeed must be considered flawed.

Even if the Rhine could be bounced and a bridgehead could be established over the Ijssel in the Deventer area, would 21 Army Group have sufficient strength remaining to advance another 150 km (90 miles) round the north of the Ruhr to sever its communications with the rest of the Reich? First Canadian Army would be more or less fully occupied reducing the Channel ports and the defenses of the Antwerp approaches for weeks to come (the latter task was not completed until late November). That would leave Second Army with a maximum of only eight to ten divisions (even after poaching from First Canadian) to march deep into enemy territory, securing steadily lengthening open flanks and a vulnerably narrow "airborne corridor" as they did so—a truly "pencil-like thrust" far removed from Montgomery's August proposal and a violation of his own most cherished principle of concentration. Air support, on which the Allies relied so heavily, would diminish because of the increasing distance between the front and airfields and the worsening autumn weather. There would be no help from friendly resistance movements once the German frontier was crossed; on the contrary, sullen, uncooperative hostility from the civil population and growing acts of sabotage could be expected, including by stay-behind troops who would blend into the population. Moreover, it was extremely unlikely that even this smallish force could be adequately supplied absent the opening of Antwerp, which was plainly not imminent. The Channel ports would discharge enough, but not until well into October. Then there was the even greater problem of transport from the ports to the front. It was 440 km (275 miles) from Boulogne to Deventer, for instance. Railway rehabilitation, especially signaling, communications, and bridge repair, could not keep up with a rapid advance, and it would take time for links to achieve significant capacity. There could be no pipeline constructed in any realistic time frame. Even if 21 Army Group were allowed to keep its eight American truck companies on loan and a monopoly of air resupply (increasingly subject to interruption by weather), it would find itself subject to logistic overstretch.

If Second Army succeeded in forcing the Rhine at Arnhem, its line of advance would be almost ninety degrees divergent from First Army's. A gap about 80 km (50 miles) wide would have developed between spearheads at Arnhem and Aachen. By the time Second Army turned east from the Deventer area, with ever more precarious supply, it would be on its own, separated from the Americans in the Aachen-Cologne area by 150 km (90 miles) and the Ruhr conurbation, and out of reach of support. If the Germans could find the forces from other fronts and the Replacement Army, there was a real danger that they could at least delay First Army on the Rhine while cutting Second Army's communications and defeating it in detail. Montgomery's arguments in favor of the Arnhem axis had some merit. However, the incomplete West Wall at its northern extremity was not much of an asset to the defense. The V-2 menace, a purely British problem, should not have been allowed to influence operational-strategic decisions that could have led to an early end to the war. In any case, the separation from the Americans should have weighed more heavily in Montgomery's decision making. He must have known that he would not be able to persuade Eisenhower to switch 12 Army Group's effort in a more northerly direction, even if it had not been fully committed. Nor did he try. Dempsey was right to favor the Eindhoven-Wesel axis. Had the British so advanced, it might have been possible to persuade Eisenhower that the Americans should put serious weight behind a thrust on an axis Maastricht-Geilenkirchen-Düsseldorf and/or Cologne, instead of through the Stolberg corridor and the Hürtgen Forest.

Absurdly, Montgomery claimed that Market Garden "was 90 percent successful," as it left his forces in possession of crossings over four major obstacles, and the ground taken north of Nijmegen later provided the jumping-off area for the March 1945 Rhine crossing (at Wesel).[54] In reality, the operational aims were not achieved: the West Wall was not turned, and the time spent failing to do so was used by the Germans to strengthen the defense. The Arnhem bridge was a sine qua non, given that the whole point of the operation was to achieve a favorable position from which to mount an attack to envelop the Ruhr. The opportunity costs were also high: the priority given to Market Garden allowed *Fifteenth Army* to escape being pinned against the sea and destroyed, and it diverted effort away from the early opening of Antwerp. All that had been accomplished was the acquisition of a salient that led nowhere and would prove costly to hold by forces that would have been better employed attacking alongside First Army on the Venlo-Wesel axis (which, at the time, was very lightly defended, unlike Holland, which had *Fifteenth* as well as *First Parachute Army*). As it was, Montgomery's attempt to spin away defeat only lowered his credibility and reputation with the Americans, with a resulting loss of influence. As in the wake of Operation Goodwood, he appeared to be a strident loser wont to oversell his ideas in excessively intemperate terms. Both the failure of Market Garden and the denial of that failure led to the loss of Eisenhower's trust. Even when sound, Montgomery's opinions about the best course of future action were treated with ever greater skepticism.

Although his attempt to force the Rhine in September had culminated in failure at Arnhem, Montgomery insisted that he could still succeed by switching the axis of the offensive. Operation Gatwick, a follow-on to Market Garden scheduled to start on 12 October, would comprise a Second Army thrust on Krefeld (just north of Düsseldorf) via Eindhoven and Venlo. This would enjoy logistic priority over Canadian efforts to open the Scheldt. In his obsession with the Ruhr and his arrogant, self-absorbed refusal to admit failure, Montgomery was abandoning objectivity and subordinating the latest intelligence and facts on the ground to an imperious exercise of will. The Versailles meeting of 4 October provided a cold douche of reality when everyone present, including Brooke, stressed the priority of opening Antwerp. Then on 7 October Dempsey impressed on him that Second Army's problems, especially its inadequate strength, precluded an immediate new thrust. Gatwick was postponed, and on 9 October a reluctant Montgomery started to provide resources appropriate to the Canadian army's task of reducing the Breskens pocket, South Beveland, and Walcheren.

Montgomery had, for the most part, observed the principles of operational art and generalship during the Normandy campaign, with successful results. He generally continued to do so in September, far more consistently than Bradley or Eisenhower, but his manner was so egotistical as to be counterproductive. He pursued his aim of crossing the Rhine and flanking the Ruhr with single-minded intensity that took no account of the Supreme Commander's wider, alliance-driven requirement that Antwerp be opened quickly. At first he tried to talk Eisenhower into relegating the issue; when that failed, he simply paid hypocritical obeisance while ignoring his orders in practice. In so behaving, he showed a lack of loyalty that he would not have tolerated for a moment in his own subordinates; he also demonstrated a lack of foresight, broad operational-strategic perspective, and realism. His inability to shift his thinking from a narrow, purely military, operational-level focus to take in wider political and strategic concerns with a critical alliance dimension, added to his personal failings, rendered him unsuited to highest command.[55]

Increasingly as the 1944 campaigns developed, Montgomery demonstrated character failings that made him an abysmal multinational team player—egotism, excessive pride, a conviction that he was always right, an inability to consider others' points of view, and a total absence of tact. He dismissed as irrelevant Crerar's national concerns, exactly as he did Eisenhower's. He found it very difficult to deal with Bradley as an equal, so he made no effort to see him between 22 August and 3 September (even though, for most of that time, he was still ground forces commander). He not only deprecated Eisenhower's operational abilities but also showed scant respect to his superior, talking down to him, attempting to bully him, and refusing to meet him except on his own terms.[56] Even in his one brief meeting with Marshall, Montgomery demonstrated a lack of political awareness, even common sense, by belittling Eisenhower and his ideas. Moreover, he failed to learn. He never understood anything of significance outside the narrow field of the military-technical. He never grasped that the balance of power within the alliance had changed, and with it his ability to control decision making. He could not accept that others had ideas that might merit some attention, even if only to enable him more effectively to persuade them to his point of view. He would not listen, or at least heard only what he wanted to hear; thus, having been warned off the issue of command in the bluntest of terms in October, he returned to it again in December and would again be threatened with the sack. Montgomery was a principal cause and the focus of growing American hostility toward the British and the unraveling of the team so painstakingly built by Eisenhower. These personal defects and their consequences indicate that, however sound his operational ideas, Montgomery would have been a poor choice for land forces commander. His style, instinctively dogmatic and intolerant of dissent, would have resulted in political rows with destructive consequences for the alliance's unity of effort.

The Northwest European Theatre: General Eisenhower. Eisenhower proved to be a mediocre practitioner of operational art in the summer of 1944. This was hardly surprising, given that he had spent his military career as a staff officer, with a brief spell commanding a battalion and no combat experience at all before being catapulted into theatre command in 1942. He had studied military theory and history assiduously, but no amount of study can give a feel for battle or adequately prepare one for it—both essential for the practical problems of command. Nor was Leavenworth's interwar teaching a wholly reliable guide to fighting the Wehrmacht in 1944. Although it was certainly biased toward victory through attritional employment of superior firepower, it did not preclude operational maneuver. This was plainly what was required in the late summer of 1944, when an all but total enemy collapse afforded opportunities for the victors that were limited only by their logistic constraints—a situation never anticipated by the doctrine writers. Like all doctrine, Leavenworth's should have been considered a guide to action without being prescriptive, but over time, it became unthinking dogma.

The dominant Allied problem in post-Normandy operations was logistics. It was especially acute for the Americans. Unlike the British, they would be moving farther away from their source of supply, while their ally took ports in the course of the advance on Germany. Eisenhower understood this from the day he decided against an operational pause on the Seine. However, the answers he found were inadequate. He stressed from the time of the Cobra breakout that the Breton ports were urgently needed, but he did not press his commanders with sufficient force or even logic. Several times he reiterated his requirement for the reduction of Brest, the last time on 13 September. He wrote: "We never counted on [Brest] as much as we had from Quiberon Bay. . . . experience of the past proved that we were likely to be vastly disappointed in the usefulness of the Brittany ports. Not only did we expect them to be stubbornly defended but we were certain that they would be effectively destroyed once we captured them."[57] Yet on 3 September he accepted the abandonment of the Quiberon Bay project while persisting with Brest—only to accept on 14 September that Brest would not be utilized. Despite this decision, he allowed attacks to continue at great expense in casualties and ammunition until the port's fall five days later.

Of course, the progressive ditching of the Breton ports as the armies' lines of communication stretched beyond the breaking point made sense if alternatives were becoming available. The investment of Le Havre at the beginning of September was promising, but it would be over a month before it could be opened for even minimal discharges. Of vastly more importance was the seizure, on 4 September, of Antwerp with its facilities intact. Eisenhower had been warned in the clearest of terms that this windfall would be useless without the clearance of the Scheldt estuary. He repeated, several times, his injunction to Montgomery to make this a priority, but in such terms that the field marshal felt the need to do nothing more than issue vague reassurances while overtasking First Canadian Army. Moreover, Eisenhower critically weakened his demand by acknowledging the primacy of the Market Garden offensive. He had succumbed to victory disease, as his office memo of 5 September illustrates: "The defeat of the German armies is complete and the only thing now needed to realize the whole conception is speed."[58] By 15 September, he was writing to Montgomery about a rapid march on Berlin. It was not until 9 October, after the failure of the venture and following a warning by Ramsay that Canadian operations were being hamstrung by an ammunition shortage, that he returned to the Antwerp issue and addressed it in blunt terms in a telegram:

> I must repeat, we are now squarely up against the situation which we have anticipated for months; our intake into Continent will not support our battle. All operations will come to a standstill unless Antwerp is producing by middle of November. I must emphasize that I consider Antwerp of first importance of all our endeavors on entire front from Switzerland to Channel. I believe your personal attention is required in operation to clear entrance.[59]

Even that injunction did not convince Montgomery to shift his priority from Second Army operations to clear the west bank of the Meuse. It took another blistering rebuke in a letter of 13 October to force Montgomery to take Eisenhower seriously.[60]

By early September, the Supreme Commander knew that polite suggestions and reminders would be insufficient to deflect Montgomery from his chosen course. Only an unpolished, explicit order would suffice for an issue of such paramount importance as the opening of Antwerp. Eisenhower should have given such an order the moment he realized that bland assurances were not being matched by immediate action on the ground following his first, tactful directive of 5 September. Of course, he should have thought the problem through and offered troops—VIII Corps, which was now pointlessly besieging Brest, was the obvious choice—to help the overstretched 21 Army Group accomplish this vital task. It was too important and too urgent for anything but decisive action, and Eisenhower was the only man who could take it. Unfortunately, his thinking about Antwerp was neither clear nor consistent. During the critical period when the Germans were adjusting to the unexpected loss of the port and starting to organize their defense of the estuary, Eisenhower was apparently seduced into gambling on the Arnhem operation precipitating a German collapse that would make Antwerp unnecessary.[61] He apparently failed to understand that if the gamble did not pay off, critical time would be lost. Too late, he realized that the end of Market Garden would find Montgomery's command overextended and scattered, unable to make up for time lost in clearing the Scheldt. His belated provision of two American divisions to 21 Army Group was too little too late to prevent the full flowering of the logistic crisis that was paralyzing Bradley's forces.

In deciding on his theatre's operational formation and form of action, Eisenhower automatically followed the Leavenworth teaching and opted for an advance all along the front with only the airborne army as a reserve. The enemy would be kept under continuous pressure everywhere and ground down by superior firepower, with no opportunity to rest his formations, form a reserve to contest the initiative, or shift resources from one sector to another. Sooner or later he would crack somewhere, and this would enable the more mobile and flexible Americans, aided by air supremacy, to destroy him in pursuit. Normandy was seen as a vindication of this approach. Given the short frontage the Germans had to defend and the consequent density and depth of the defense, only relentless attrition could break their front, and this was finally achieved in Operation Cobra. There was, perhaps, a tendency to forget that Cobra's success was due in large measure to First Army's unusual concentration and deployment in depth for the attack. At any rate, none of the American armies would achieve similar concentration and depth in the autumn offensives, when there was a somewhat similar semistalemate.

In an advance against a withdrawing enemy, especially given superior mobility and armor and command of the air, there is much to be said for the broad-front concept. As the line of contact widens after the breakout, the enemy's ability to hold strongly everywhere diminishes; attacks can be mounted against weak spots, penetrations can be achieved and exploited, and further ground can be gained before the defense is restored. Then rapid regrouping can enable fresh blows on weakened sectors, and the process is repeated until the enemy's cohesion disintegrates. Once this happens, the advance becomes a pursuit as the enemy becomes a more or less helpless victim, reacting ever more belatedly and ineffectually to thrusts that can become bolder with impunity. Unless and until he can muster fresh forces to restore the situation, the size of this problem will become progressively more daunting; he may win the occasional tactical battle, but any elements that do so will be engulfed in a spreading operational catastrophe. In this way, the defeat of a corps may end in the disintegration of an army group.

One major argument adduced for the broad-front approach does not carry much weight in the circumstances of September 1944. The fear that halting Third Army would allow the enemy to reinforce against First Army or even mount a counteroffensive can be discounted. The Germans' divertible strength in Lorraine was meager and lacking mobility; they had to take seriously the possibility of Patton renewing his drive at any time; and the Dragoon forces advancing rapidly up the Rhône valley were a looming threat to southern Lorraine and Alsace.

However theoretically desirable, an effective offensive on a broad front requires the right conditions to be set. One of these conditions is the establishment of some operational reserves, at least at army level. Without them, it is usually difficult to exploit rapidly and turn tactical into operational success or to switch axes in good time to prevent the defense from solidifying. The American operational-level commanders generally neglected this precaution, and their offensives suffered in consequence, especially when they compounded the problem by persisting in unprofitable attacks such as Hodges's in the Hürtgen Forest and Patton's on Metz. Eisenhower did nothing to correct this. Another precondition is the creation of a logistic system that can sustain the forces involved to the planned depth of the operation. This did not exist as US forces began their exploitation over the Seine in August, aiming for objectives about 1,000 km (620 miles) from their source of supply; this was due to the unexpected way operations had developed and the design of the system—Eisenhower's fault in only a small way. The Supreme Commander had been worried about American logistic constraints as early as 24 August. Nevertheless, he was determined that both First and Third Armies should force the West Wall and cross the Rhine in a simultaneous advance. He knew that COMZ could maintain only ten to twelve divisions in the advance, even on reduced scales, and that this figure would decline even further. A general offensive would overstretch the enemy, but it would also inevitably overstretch his own forces; however, he persevered in the hope that the enemy would undergo political and/or military implosion before his own offensive culminated. It was a gamble, but one he believed worth taking. It was also a gamble that enabled him to avoid, or at least postpone, making a decision to halt a major formation and thus antagonize some influential players. Military logic—the importance of prioritizing the main effort and the greater effectiveness of fewer properly supported divisions in pursuit versus many inadequately supplied ones forced into an unpredictable stop-and-go pattern of activity—was lost to sight. An operational concept without sufficient means to implement it is a concept that should not be pursued.

It is clear that Eisenhower did not think through the implications of his directives, particularly for 12 Army Group, to the depth of his proposed operations. This was not the only example of his lack of operational-strategic foresight. He had consistently championed Operation Anvil/Dragoon in the teeth of British opposition. Yet he developed no concept for use of the forces coming up the Rhône corridor beyond tying down *Nineteenth Army* while the battle for Normandy was going on. When the newly designated 6 Army Group came under SHAEF control on 15 September, on Eisenhower's insistence, its forward troops had reached the Epinal-Belfort line, skirting the High Vosges mountains. Eisenhower had assigned it, in essence, two tasks: destroy enemy forces within boundaries (the linkup with Third Army had been too late to trap the retreating Germans), and cross the Rhine–West Wall from Strasbourg southward. On 15 September he speculated in a letter to Montgomery that Devers would execute a thrust eastward, aimed at the Augsburg-Munich area. This mission would involve not only forcing the Rhine and its fortifications but also pushing through 50 km (30 miles) of the all but impenetrable Black Forest to seize objectives almost 400 km (250 miles) distant and of negligible importance to the German war effort. Little thought went into finding a useful role for 6 Army Group, even though it had its own supply chain from the Mediterranean ports. Eisenhower's ideas never went beyond expressing a hope to Bradley that supply for Third Army's operations in Lorraine could be eased by Devers's logisticians and that his actions would support Patton's right; later in September he transferred XV Corps to Seventh Army to relieve COMZ of the burden of supplying it, thus shifting the army group boundary north. The Supreme Commander seems never to have considered continuing an offensive north on the Epinal-Saarbrücken axis (about 160 km [100 miles]) to envelop the enemy facing Patton, or a more promising deep turning movement Epinal-Strasbourg-Mainz (about 360 km [225 miles], skirting the High Vosges). Eisenhower may have thought the latter move unworthy of consideration, as it could not commence until October, by which time he hoped victory would be clinched further north.[62] He may have seen 6 Army Group as too marginal a force to contribute meaningfully to the campaign; it comprised five French, mostly colonial, divisions and only three American divisions, although more could and would be sent to it. He may have been influenced by his deep antipathy toward Devers. Whatever the excuses, he showed a lack of vision in his employment of a far from negligible asset when he confined it to Alsace, a strategic backwater.[63]

Eisenhower had an aim: to destroy the enemy west of the Rhine. But he neglected the harder part of strategic decision making—choosing what not to do. Nor did he explain how or where his aim was to be accomplished, confining himself to directions of advance and geographic objectives. There was no master plan other than a general desire to advance on all axes at the same time and somehow, somewhere destroy the German army. There was no single, developed concept under which both (later three) army groups worked synergistically to achieve an operationally significant result. In consequence, there was no meaningful prioritization of operations. Despite the centralization of command in his hands, operations became increasingly decentralized and fragmented as personalities, pride, politics, and doctrinal differences hampered their efficient development. This lacuna seemed to stem from a lack of foresight and flexibility in the operational sphere and a reluctance to make hard choices that might antagonize important people, in anticipation of problems to come. The result was a tendency toward opportunism and improvisation as the campaign progressed. Eisenhower was inclined to swither between courses of action, despite the advice of his clear-sighted chief of staff, Major General Bedell Smith. This led to an ever-changing emphasis in the stream of directives emanating from SHAEF and contradictory statements made to Marshall and to each of the army group commanders. Lack of consistency caused a dissipation of effort at a time when limited logistic resources demanded that objectives be limited as well, or at least that their achievement be sequenced in order of importance, with the lesser ones being tackled as and when resources allowed. As a result, there was no economy of effort in the secondary sector to achieve something decisive in the direction of the main effort, and the Allied offensive culminated short of achieving anything of critical importance anywhere.

In his role as commander of land forces, a mantle he had assumed under pressure from the top of the US military and political hierarchy, Eisenhower did not display great skill in applying the principles of operational art in the unusual circumstances of post-Normandy operations. The situation called for more foresight, judgment, decisiveness, and boldness in decision making than he could muster under the enormous pressure of events and responsibilities and a lack of time for reflection.[64] Eisenhower was also the theatre Supreme Commander, and in this role he was much more successful, a fact recognized by even his detractors. However, the very skills that made him effective in this position—political rather than military—were those that contributed significantly to his uninspired operational leadership.

Eisenhower's primary responsibility in his more important job was to keep the military side of the Anglo-American alliance together and working in harmony toward a common aim through a mutually agreed (or at least accepted) operational-strategic concept. He had been chosen for the top job because of his political skill as an alliance manager. This was a task beset by extraordinary difficulties. He had to satisfy the US government, Marshall, and the British. These elements were pulling in divergent strategic directions, and the British obstinately refused to recognize that they were now junior partners to an increasingly self-confident United States. Within his theatre, he had to keep together an Allied team that was increasingly sundered by doctrinal differences, mutual incomprehension, nationalistic prejudices, and consequent dislike and distrust. Virtually all the characters he had to deal with had strong opinions, wills, and self-belief; they were competitive with one another, and many of them had inflated egos. Most of them, both Americans and British, believed that they knew better than their boss and that Eisenhower was favoring or even kowtowing to their rivals. The job of Supreme Commander required more than a soldier who knew the purely military-technical aspects of soldiering; it needed a consummate politician who also understood operations.[65] Brooke's "main impression" of Eisenhower was that of "a swinger and no real director of thought, plans, energy or direction! Just a coordinator—a good mixer, a champion of inter-allied cooperation, and in those respects few can hold a candle to him. But is that enough? Or can we not find all qualities of a commander in one man? . . . I doubt it."[66] Brooke's answer to his own rhetorical question was correct, and no other country, much less an alliance, had found such a paragon—at least not in modern times. Later, when the strains of the campaign were beginning to tell, Brooke amplified the thought:

> There is no doubt that Ike is all out to do all he can to maintain the best of relations between British and Americans, but it is equally clear that Ike knows nothing about strategy and is quite unsuited to the post of Supreme Commander as far as running the strategy of the war is concerned! . . . With the Supreme Command set up as it is no wonder that Monty's real high ability is not always realized. Especially when "national" spectacles pervert the perspective of the strategic landscape.[67]

Unwittingly, of course, Brooke's last sentence revealed his bias. If someone disagreed with him and Montgomery, they were, by definition, wrong and revealed their inadequacies in doing so. To him, national viewpoints were valid only if they were British.

Talking to a war correspondent and historian after the war, Montgomery complained:

> The trouble was that Eisenhower did not know what he should do. He had no experience and no philosophy of battle by which to judge the rival plans. His method was to talk to everyone and then try to work out a compromise solution which would please everyone. He had no plan of his own. He was a sociable chap who liked talking, and he used to go from one HQ to another finding out what his various subordinates thought, instead of going to them and saying—here is the plan, you will do this, and so and so will do that. Eisenhower had conferences to collect ideas; I had conferences to issue orders.[68]

There is some foundation for these criticisms, but they also demonstrate how little Montgomery understood about the highest levels of command and how unsuited he was to fill them. Making one's allies feel valued and being prepared to compromise with them is part and parcel of alliance operations. The commander who ignores this elementary fact of coalition life not only will fail to secure their willing cooperation but also may unconsciously goad them into sabotaging his plans—as Montgomery had done with his high-handed treatment of Patton and Bradley in Sicily the year before.

From the start, Eisenhower knew he had to be much more a statesman than a straightforward issuer of arbitrary orders. His position was more akin to that of the chairman of an increasingly fractious board than a military autocrat. He wanted to—indeed, needed to—command through persuasion, consensus, and, when necessary to maintain harmony, through compromise. This was, he realized, the only way to keep the alliance working together:

> No written agreement for the establishment of an Allied Command can hold up against nationalistic considerations.... Every commander in the field possesses direct disciplinary power over all subordinates of his own nationality...; any disobedience or other offence is punishable.... But such authority and power cannot be given by any country to an individual of another nation. Only trust and confidence can establish the authority of an Allied commander-in-chief so firmly that he need never fear the absence of this legal power.[69]

If necessary, Eisenhower could compel obedience from unwilling American generals, as long as he was sure of Marshall's backing. But Montgomery was not just another army group commander. As the foremost British field commander and the principal champion of British views on operational-strategic issues, and given his intimate relations with the CIGS and the War Office and his massive popularity and prestige in the United Kingdom, he could not simply be ordered about. National considerations were as real a limit on Eisenhower's freedom of action as they had been for Montgomery when he contemplated getting rid of Crerar.

This role as coordinator, coaxer, and arbiter became increasingly difficult as national differences and personal rivalries and prejudices intensified at the top, to the detriment of military priorities. The temptation to challenge, selectively interpret, or simply ignore the wishes of the Supreme Commander grew with the feeling that the war was all but won and that glory (and the chance for promotion) had to be seized before it was too late and competitors hogged it all. Faced with these divisive tendencies, Eisenhower found that his style of command proved less and less effective. Careful qualifications, circumlocution, and tactful wording in directives were taken as signs of weakness, and their recipients searched for get-out phrases that would enable them to follow their own pet schemes in conscious (if unadmitted) disregard for their commander's intent. The more mutable and open to compromise and interpretation these directives were, the more they became the subject of debate and negotiation and the less force they carried. The problem was exacerbated by Eisenhower's tendency to equivocate and delay decisions in the hope of avoiding stark choices. Though sometimes an appropriate response, this was injurious at a time when speed and decisiveness were paramount. Of course, had the keenly anticipated German collapse actually happened, his methods would not have been questioned. In the event, the campaign lost its coherence as army groups and armies increasingly followed their own inclinations, to the detriment of both focus and synergy. In the end, the initiative was lost, and with it the opportunity to achieve an early end to the war.

Eisenhower's approach to the Supreme Command was correct in its essence, but he permitted his subordinates too much leeway and wound up losing considerable authority and control. Whether through his strong desire to be liked, his natural predisposition to compromise and avoid confrontation, his inexperience, or his sheer unfamiliarity with operational art, he failed to assert himself sufficiently in exercising command of the land forces. It was a slippery slope from liberty to license, and he allowed his senior commanders to slide too far down that slope before recognizing the error. The estimable Bedell Smith, watching the erosion of SHAEF's credibility, observed: "The trouble with Ike, instead of giving direct and clear orders, [he] dresses them up in polite language; and that is why our senior American commanders take advantage."[70] Montgomery, who needed to be kept on a much tighter rein, did likewise. When clear, unambiguous decisions had to be made and adhered to, even if unpopular in some quarters, Eisenhower delayed or equivocated. He need not have done so. He had the authority, underpinned by Marshall, to keep Bradley and Patton in line. On issues he deemed of fundamental importance, he could have gripped Montgomery and told him the period for discussion was over, and the time for implementation without dissent had come. On the occasions when he actually did so, Montgomery obeyed like the good, disciplined soldier he was. Of course, the longer Eisenhower let things slide, the more difficult it became to convince his subordinates that he was serious.

Eisenhower's main problems were linked. One was the lack of a well-thought-out plan to accomplish the aim: destruction of the enemy's forces. Absent this, the concept of operations became too generalized and, critically, mutable; without a clear idea of how the armies should act synergistically to achieve the desired end, it was difficult to see how each development in the campaign should be turned to the Allies' advantage. Foresight is difficult if the direction of travel is ill defined. Improvisation is necessary in the conduct of any operation, but it is unsatisfactory as the sole method. If actions are not set in context, there is danger of losing direction, fragmenting efforts, and reacting to rather than shaping events—the very problems that beset the Allies as September gave way to October. Eisenhower's difficulties were exacerbated by his lack of decisiveness. As Brooke observed in his diary, the strictly military requirements of Supreme Command are incompatible with the political. A politician, in most circumstances, finds that temporizing and compromise are prime virtues. When these are exercised in the context of command in fast-developing operations, they are likely to result in drift. Eisenhower saw his most important endeavor as keeping the alliance working synergistically toward the common end. The fact that it was not functioning harmoniously was not his fault, as he strove to preserve amity or, failing that, at least understanding.

Several factors combined to undermine Eisenhower's prospects of success. In taking on both Supreme Command and land command (in which he had no choice), he overextended himself. The multifarious tasks involved were all important to someone of consequence, even if they were sometimes tangential to victory. The enormous pressures allowed the Supreme Commander little time for the quiet reflection that is essential to judgment and creativity. For the critical period in September, he was semi-incommunicado. The base at Granville, which his HQ occupied for the first fortnight, was remote and poorly served by its communications; this was followed by the disruption of the weeklong move to Versailles. Eisenhower found it difficult to keep his finger on the pulse of operations, and his lack of practical command experience exacerbated the problem. This made it easier for his principal subordinates to deceive him about their implementation of his directives and their logistic states. Such behavior was symptomatic of the worst of his problems: the attitude of his army group commanders. Of his experience in Tunisia, Eisenhower wrote later:

It is easy to minimize the obstacles that always obstruct progress in developing efficient command mechanisms for large allied forces. Some are easy to recognize, such as those relating to differences in equipment, training and tactical doctrine, staff procedures and methods of organization. But these are overshadowed by national prides and prejudices. In modern war, with its great facilities for quickly informing populations of battlefield developments, every little difference is magnified . . . but success in allied ventures can be achieved if the chief figures in the government and in the field see the necessities of the situation and refuse to violate the basic principle of unity, either in public or in the confidence of the personal contacts with subordinates and staffs. Immediate and continuous loyalty to the concept of unity and to allied commanders is basic to victory.[71]

Neither Montgomery nor Bradley showed him much loyalty. They ignored the spirit of his directives, and occasionally the letter. They undermined his authority with their disparaging comments to their staffs and army commanders. Their mutual lack of understanding, born of personal and national rivalries, was inimical to cooperation. Eisenhower wanted a good working relationship with his subordinates, but however hard he worked for it, however much he sought compromises to achieve it, he could not overcome the corrosive and ultimately campaign-destructive animus between his principal lieutenants. Ultimately, his endless patience, tact, and compromise preserved only a veneer of united effort and a merely generalized sense of common purpose.

CONCLUSIONS

At the beginning of September the Allies enjoyed an enormous superiority in numbers, in mobility, and in the air. Morale had soared as the attrition of Normandy gave way to heady pursuit. Yet the remnants of the *Army of the West* were not yet finished off. Nowhere was the Rhine crossed, and on only a narrow sector at Arnhem was the river even reached by the time Eisenhower's Northern and Central Army Groups culminated. The West Wall was breached in only two places, each penetration being very restricted in both width and depth, and the Roer dams remained in enemy hands to blight later prospects of a smooth advance by First and Ninth Armies to even close on the Rhine. The Allies were forced to accept an operational pause. This inability in late summer to complete the destruction of *Army Group B*, the principal German grouping in the west, was primarily a failure of operational-level generalship. The Allies failed to turn two encirclements in Normandy into battles of annihilation, an accomplishment needed sooner rather than later, given the looming supply crisis. Although damage was certainly inflicted on the retreating Germans, especially in the Mons pocket, essential cadres escaped intact to form the kernel of rehabilitated formations—to immediate battle-winning effect, in the case of *II SS Panzer Corps* at Arnhem. The British army group, seeking conflicting objectives, failed to trap and destroy *Fifteenth Army*, open the port of Antwerp, and pursue the enemy without pause and to sufficient depth to prevent the recovery of the defense on favorable ground. The play of SHAEF's airborne card was botched and accordingly failed to restore momentum. The Americans wasted 20 percent of their strength in futile sieges in Brittany while the rest dissipated their offensive power in piecemeal attacks by advancing on a broad front on divergent axes against widely separated objectives, without prioritizing, concentrating, or ensuring adequate supply for any of their efforts. They fell short in all of them.

Both the British and the Americans blamed each other and logistic shortcomings for their lack of success. It is true that neither was able to keep its full combat power in action continuously, and shortages increasingly limited their capabilities until their advances petered out. But logistic problems were not some sort of nemesis, nor were they solely the fault of incompetent logisticians. These problems were entirely predictable and had been flagged well in advance, but they were ameliorated for some time by the drive and ingenuity of supply officers. They were the direct result of operational decisions, in particular the failure of those at the top to choose between different courses of action. It is the job of the operational-level commander to cut his coat according to his cloth, not to moan about there being insufficient cloth. Alike in their operational and logistic dispositions, the Supreme Commander and the army group commanders avoided hard choices. By trying to achieve all desirable ends at once, while at the same time avoiding risk, they squandered the fruits of the victory won in Normandy. Their actions were not sufficiently single-minded, consistent, coordinated, and bold to achieve a decision. The principal reason for this was the lack of a firm grip on operations from Eisenhower at the top, fatally combined with and partly caused by the narrow-minded, selfish disloyalty and willfulness of Montgomery and Bradley.

When the autumn campaign got under way, it was against an enemy that had recovered balance and some strength. There was no coherent operational-strategic master plan for that campaign, or even any meaningful guidance. It was a sorry affair of ill-coordinated, piecemeal operations seeking and achieving only tactical gains—an attritional struggle and a nadir of generalship. The German army was not destroyed; on the contrary, it recovered its strength and balance. It was able to resist these obstinately unsystematic

Allied efforts without a serious loss of ground and with absorbable, albeit heavy, casualties. Meanwhile, the Germans were able to re-create a significant reserve—twenty-eight new and rebuilt divisions, including eight panzer and panzer grenadier—for a counteroffensive. The decision to do so was made as early as mid-September: a thrust would be mounted through the Ardennes to take the port of Antwerp, cripple Allied logistic support, and deliver a fatal shock to the political unity and will of the alliance. When the blow was delivered in December, it cruelly exposed the futility of the Allied autumn campaign and the dangers of the resulting maldeployment.

Postscript

Compared with the Allies' preinvasion expectations, the summer campaign of 1944 was a great success. At his St. Paul's School briefing in May, Montgomery had posited that their armies would be up to the Loire and Seine by early September. Instead, they were 250 to 300 km (155 to 185 miles) further, on an arc from Antwerp to Commercy on the Meuse. But compared with the perhaps overblown hopes of post-Normandy, when there was a general expectation of at least crossing the Rhine, it ended in disappointment. As shown in chapter 7, mistakes and questionable judgments contributed to this letdown, as they do in every campaign, victorious and otherwise. But with the advantage of hindsight, it is clear that systemic problems were also partly responsible. Three of the more pernicious are highlighted below.

Several intelligence failures at critical moments helped give rise to faulty decisions. Most of these failures, as well as the decisions, were largely attributable to the commanders. The massive defeat inflicted on the Germans in the Falaise encirclement and subsequent pursuit led to an epidemic of "victory disease," characterized by operational commanders and their intelligencers egging one another on to stress encouraging signs of the enemy's imminent collapse and to downplay or even discount disagreeably contrary signs. Groupthink left no room for dispassionate analysis. For instance: Eisenhower saw too little danger in the operational formation of his armies (including the absence of a meaningful main effort and lack of reserves), their divergent axes, and their increasingly precarious supply position; Montgomery brushed aside the significance of Ultra revelations about the Germans' commitment to keeping the mouth of the Scheldt closed and various reports about the hardening of German defenses in southern Holland, including the presence of *II SS Panzer Corps* in the Arnhem area; Patton ignored his intelligence chief's warning that the enemy could and would put up a hard fight for Lorraine. In each case, decisions, or the absence thereof, contributed to operational failure. Plainly, the production and especially the consumption of intelligence were often much more subjective in practice than is prescribed in theory.

A considerable portion of the blame for failings in generalship must be laid at the door of doctrinal inadequacies. The conceptual boundaries of most Anglo-American generals of 1944 had been established in some cases by experience in the 1914–1918 war and in most cases by their respective interwar staff colleges and by the writings and mentoring of their formative years. Moreover, the British and US armies drew different, often incompatible lessons, from their historical experiences. The resulting ideas were not all well attuned to the demands the armies faced. When it came to fighting the Germans in 1944, most generals' thinking was firmly rooted in the experience of small wars and the linear-attritional campaigns of the First World War. The interwar armies had not fully grasped the implications of the revolution in military affairs that was taking place; they used new technologies to make incremental improvements to existing doctrine rather than experimenting with qualitatively new and different methods. They tended to regard the demands of operations at higher formation level as little more than those of tactics scaled up, rather than as qualitatively different and therefore requiring different solutions. Orders often failed to specify a main effort and never explained the operational idea behind them, the commander's intent; rather, they usually set terrain objectives and the phases by which they would be achieved. They afforded little room for subordinates' exercise of initiative to further the achievement of wider goals. Control was considered as important as command, and it had to be maintained even at the price of rapidity and agility in the advance. The emphasis was on seeking out and fighting battles and winning them by deploying superior firepower, rather than on using maneuver to place the enemy in an untenable position and thus make battle unnecessary. The aims of operations were generally limited. Accordingly, offensives were rarely organized in depth, with substantial forces held back from battle until they could be committed to conduct exploitation into the enemy's operational rear with the aim of precipitating a substantial and spreading collapse of his front. When penetrations were achieved, development of the operation was often conducted with cautious deliberation rather than an overriding concern for achieving the momentum that would progressively destabilize the defense and preempt its recovery by seizing depth defensive lines before they could be defended by reserves or redeployments.

Like all generalizations, those in the preceding paragraph had exceptions. Patton stands out as a champion of maneuver and speed as keys to victory, although even he could revert to linear thinking when an operation did not develop according to plan—as happened in Lorraine when Third Army was checked on the Moselle. Other, more pedestrian commanders could rise to the occasion. Bradley's Operation Cobra was a creative departure from standard American practice, and all the army and army group commanders adjusted well to the unfamiliar demands of pursuit when daring and speed were obviously necessary and seemed safe against an emasculated enemy. The post-Normandy pursuit was generally conducted with panache, but hardening resistance in late September resulted in reversions to conservative forms of operations, cautiously implemented; the attritional slog in the Hürtgen Forest is merely the most egregious example.

The inevitable problems inherent in prosecuting the campaign as an alliance helped ensure that the Allies' results fell short of expectations, given the sum of their resources. There was little meeting of minds at army group level, and American and British ideas and interests increasingly diverged. There was a resultant lack of synergy in their efforts as they pursued different aims, and tasks essential to Allied success (especially the opening of Antwerp) were neglected. Mutual misunderstandings and resentments grew, fanned by nationalistic politicians and newspapers. Of course, the Supreme Commander was there to resolve disagreements and to provide clear and firm direction in line with the directives he received from the CCS. His role was to preserve Allied unity and ensure the single-minded pursuit of his aim through the implementation of his campaign plan. Whatever the theory, however, there was no consistent theatre-wide main effort in practice, as Eisenhower's shifts and equivocations bear witness. Rather, there was a series of compromises and an increasingly uneasy pretense of unity of effort. Eisenhower did a sterling job of holding the alliance together; even his British critics gave him credit for this. But he failed in his other task. This was inevitable, as the two jobs were hardly compatible. One required a shrewd, politically sensitive, flexible statesman with an outgoing, charismatic, tolerant character. The other demanded a knowledgeable, experienced, military technician with a personality that could drive as well as coax difficult subordinates such as Bradley and, especially, Montgomery. As Brooke pointed out, such a paragon did not exist. Even if he had, it is unlikely that he could have surmounted the fact that approximately one-third of his force owed its ultimate loyalty to a government that did not always share his and his government's views on the situation and therefore on what needed to be done. National interests—indeed, national prejudices—would always complicate alliance endeavors and result in plans that were no better than the least objectionable compromise. These plans would almost always lead to outcomes that were disappointing to one or more of the alliance members.

Volume 2 examines the parallel Soviet campaign of the summer of 1944. The Red Army had its problems, but they did not include some of those affecting the Allies. The conceptual foundations of its operations were stronger. Its prewar doctrine took more cognizance of the accelerating revolution in military affairs, at least with regard to land warfare. This did not preserve it from near-fatal disasters in 1941–1942, but it did provide a sound base for the development of a doctrine well attuned to the demands of the times and one that could be implemented by cadres toughened and educated in the hardest of all schools of battle. The Red Army reaped a fine harvest from the doctrinal fruit of 1944. In doing so, it was unconstrained by allies. American and British concerns and wishes carried little weight in Moscow, and even less as the year wore on. Indeed, the main influence of the Western powers was to act as a spur to faster and deeper Soviet thrusts westward to seize as much of Europe as possible before the German collapse. For that matter, the Soviet government, and therefore its generals, did not have to adjust plans to satisfy an electorate nor worry about the casualty bill for operations (save in the sense of the expenditure of assets such as tanks or aircraft). The absence of the systemic problems that constrained the Allies allowed the Red Army to develop more radical operational ideas and to implement them with a daring and ruthlessness that were impossible for the armies of democratic states: how they did so is described in volume 2.

Notes

Introduction

1. For any reader unfamiliar with the concept of the staff ride, a brief explanation is in order. Starting in 1858, the Prussian Chief of the General Staff, von Moltke, used to conduct annual staff rides during which he took his principal subordinates, mostly members of the General Staff, on tours of areas that could be militarily significant in the event of war. These studies were used to train students in the making of military appreciations and decision making on the ground in a variety of hypothetical situations. Later, and in an increasing number of armies, staff rides were used to examine past operations to further the professional development of officers by expanding their understanding of military theory and its practical implementation. Specifically, the staff ride provided case studies: in the application of the principles of war; in operational art and tactics; in the relationship between technology and doctrine; in how terrain impacts plans and their execution; in leadership; in psychological factors, including unit cohesion; in how logistic considerations affect operations.

2. General George S. Patton Jr. wrote: "For a man to become a great soldier, it is necessary to be so conversant with all military possibilities that whenever an opportunity arises he has, at hand, without effort on his part, a parallel. To attain this end, I believe that it is necessary for a man to study [military history], permitting his mind to grow with his subject until he can grasp, without any effort, the most abstract question of the science of war because he is already permeated with its elements." Quoted in Carlo D'Este, *Patton: A Genius for War* (New York: HarperCollins, 1995), 94.

3. For a definition of these ideas, see "An Essential Guide to Soviet Terminology and Organizations" in volume 2.

4. Because the focus is on the ETO, there is no examination of the performance of 6 Army Group. General Devers's command did not come under Eisenhower's control until 15 September 1944, right at the end of the period covered by this study.

5. Brigadier General Shimon Naveh traces the development of American and British operational thinking in a seminal study titled *In Pursuit of Military Excellence—The Evolution of Operational Theory* (London: Frank Cass, 1997), 273–274. In it, he writes: "Comprising talented scholars like C Donnelly, P Vigor, CJ Dick and John Erickson, the British research group, concentrated in the Centre for Soviet Studies [sic] in the Royal Military Academy, Sandhurst, exercised great impact on the perception of Soviet operational theory held by the American school of reformers.

Being far ahead of their American colleagues in the study of Soviet deep operations, the British analysts managed to illuminate essential issues such as echeloning, operational breakthrough, simultaneous deep strike, momentum, deception and surprise. Moreover, aware of the conditions characterizing the Central European theater, they managed to translate the abstract principles of Deep Operations theory into operational scenarios understood by the military planner. The organizational form and the patterns of work that were developed by the British group later served their American counterparts as a model for both the establishment of the Soviet Army Study Office (SASO) in Fort Leavenworth, and the training of a talented generation of analysts who successfully researched Soviet operational theory." Of course, while lavishing praise on the Soviet Studies Research Centre at Sandhurst, Naveh should have mentioned the parallel pioneering work on the Red Army being carried out by Colonel David M. Glantz, one of the founding members of SASO, in 1986. Naveh shows how the exposition of the Soviet theory of operational art influenced the development of American and British doctrinal writing. Indeed, those who were soldiering in the late 1980s will remember how deployment patterns and schemes of maneuver and methods changed considerably.

6. A. P. Wavell, *Speaking Generally* (London: Macmillan, 1946).

7. George S. Patton Jr., *War as I Knew It* (Boston: Houghton Mifflin, 1975), 355. As with all generalizations, there were exceptions, such as Miles Dempsey, the commander of Second (British) Army.

Chapter 1. Immature Armies

1. This section is a somewhat bowdlerized summary of theory and concentrates on the nature of the offensive, for that was the Allies' primary mode of action in the summer-autumn campaign.

2. Quoted in David Glantz, *Soviet Military Operational Art: In Pursuit of Deep Battle* (London: Frank Cass, 1991), 23. Svechin explores in more detail the relationship among the three levels of war in his 1927 book *Strategiya* [Strategy] (Minneapolis: Eastview, 1992), 67–70. Svechin is generally credited with coining the term *operational art*.

3. Robert Leonhard, *The Art of Maneuver: Maneuver Warfare Theory and Air Land Battle* (New York: Presidio, 1994), expands on the key concepts of preemption, dislocation, and disruption in chapters 3 and 4.

4. On 1 July 1944 the Germans had 892,000 men in the west (less than half in Normandy) and 1,996,000 on the eastern front (excluding 60,000 in northern Norway and 974,000 Allied troops). David Glantz and Jonathan M. House, *When Titans Clashed: How the Red Army Stopped Hitler* (Lawrence: University Press of Kansas, 1995), 304. German casualties (killed, wounded, and missing) in the east prior to the invasion of Normandy totaled 4,120,232. In the months of June, July, and August, the Germans took 288,695 casualties in the west and 900,630 in the east. Niklas Zetter-

ling, *Normandy 1944: German Military Organization, Combat Power and Organizational Effectiveness* (Winnipeg, MB: J. J. Fedorowicz, 2000), 95.

5. The true opposite of maneuver is positional warfare, where each side tries to grind down the enemy through superior firepower.

6. The theory and practice of counterinsurgency are, of course, far removed from those of conventional warfare between states. Indeed, many of the difficulties and failures that have dogged American and British arms in the so-called war on terror, especially in Iraq after the defeat of Saddam's regular forces and in Afghanistan, stemmed from the misapplication of theory, weapons, and organizations designed for general war in wholly inappropriate circumstances.

7. These principles were first set out by the British Army in 1925 and are based on the writings of J. F. C. Fuller (though, not surprisingly, Clausewitz was there first). They have remained essentially unchanged; the version elaborated on here appeared in 1985 in *Army Field Manual*, vol. 1, pt. 1, *The Application of Force* (although the tenth principle is a recent formal addition). The US Army's list differs only in the wording. Other armies have produced similar lists with sometimes significant additions or differences. For instance, the Soviet principles included a unique demand for simultaneous action on the enemy to the entire depth of his deployment. V. Ye Savkin, *Osnovnyye Printsipi Operativnoye Isskustva i Taktiki* [The basic principles of operational art and tactics] (Moscow: Voyenizdat, 1974), 218.

8. For instance, Jim Storr, *The Human Face of War* (London: Continuum, 2009), 86, cites several authorities and the results of operational research. The psychological impact of surprise and how it can be a substitute for numbers is insightfully examined in "Holding up a Train," in *The Best of O. Henry* (London: Hodder and Stoughton, 1929), 667–681.

9. John A. Warden, *The Air Campaign: Planning for Combat* (Washington, DC: National Defense University Press, 1988), 13. Of course, he refers to interstate wars. In low-level conflicts, airpower exerts much less impact on the result and may even be counterproductive.

10. In the offensive, reserves should be used only to develop success, converting minor tactical achievements into bigger ones, and then converting tactical into operational success and operational success into campaign-changing success. In practice, reserves have too often been used to compensate for the deficiencies of a badly conceived or poorly executed plan.

11. Carl von Clausewitz, *On War*, trans. and ed. Michael Howard and Peter Paret (Princeton, NJ: Princeton University Press, 1976), 119. The term *chaos* might be more apt than *friction* as a descriptor.

12. Quoted in *Army Doctrine*, vol. 1, *Operations* (HQ Doctrine and Training, 1994), 3–10.

13. Clausewitz, *On War*, 104.

14. The lack of experience in their roles is often used to explain or excuse the deficiencies of some operational-level commanders during the campaign. This is a

fair point, but experience is not everything, and it is certainly not a substitute for the other criteria for good generalship, as evidenced by the many failed generals who owed their promotions largely to seniority or favoritism. As Frederick the Great pointed out: "A mule who has carried a pack for ten campaigns under Prince Eugene will not be a better tactician for it."

15. Sir Rupert Smith, *The Utility of Force: The Art of War in the Modern World* (London: Allen Lane, 2005), 64–65.

16. Some senior commanders are given wide latitude to hire and fire. Montgomery, for instance, was so favored, but even he was stuck with some subordinates he did not rate highly, most notably Lieutenant General H. D. G. Crerar, the commander of First Canadian Army. Nor did all his own selections prove up to the mark, such as Lieutenant General G. C. Bucknall of XXX Corps. And Montgomery was generally loath to admit error. Moreover, the talent pool was limited. As Lieutenant General Francis Tuker observed of the British Army: "Excellent staff officers emerged, men capable of the highest efficiency, exemplified by such projects as Overlord, but inevitably there came forth astonishingly few capable fighting commanders for a war of maneuver." *Approach to Battle, a Commentary: Eighth Army, November 1941 to May 1943* (London: Cassell, 1963), 145. General Sir Rupert Smith is forthright about responsibility lying squarely with the commander for the failure of subordinates who have been overtasked (whether the problem lies with the inadequacies of the executor or the weaknesses of his formation or unit). The commander must know his own forces intimately—the people, the structures, and their capabilities and limitations—and must tailor his demands and expectations accordingly.

17. Daniel J. Hughes, ed., *Moltke on the Art of War: Selected Writings* (New York: Presidio, 1993),186.

18. Smith, *Utility of Force*, 65.

19. Field Marshal Sir William Slim, quoted in *Application of Force*, 70. This source and Field Marshal Earl Wavell, *The Good Soldier* (London: Macmillan, 1948), pt. 1, among others, inform most of this section.

20. Smith, *Utility of Force*, 67.

21. The operational-level commander is less interested in *how* to defeat the enemy than *where* it should be done. As General George S. Patton Jr. points out in *War as I Knew It* (Boston: Houghton Mifflin, 1975), 358, this is revealed by a careful study of the operational features of terrain gleaned from road, rail, and river patterns on small-scale maps. (The senior commander who pores over large-scale maps is usually getting immersed in tactical detail and risks losing sight of the shape and significance of the woods whilst seeing all the trees.) On being asked how he always divined the intentions of the enemy so accurately, Napoleon I answered: "I did not know beforehand the mistakes the enemy would make that I would take advantage of; I simply studied my map." This revealed the possibilities open to the enemy as well as the constraints that bound him. Milan N. Vego, *Operational Warfare* (Newport, RI: Naval War College, 2000), 567.

22. Clausewitz, *On War*, 101.

23. Patton, *War as I Knew It*, 357.

24. Ibid., 354.

25. In his *Speaking Generally* (London: Macmillan, 1946), 77, General Sir A. P. Wavell gave sound advice: "When things look bad and one's difficulties appear great, the best tonic is to consider those of the enemy." A successful general devotes more time to thinking about what he can do to the enemy than what the enemy can do to him.

26. J. F. C. Fuller, *Generalship: Its Diseases and Their Cure* (Military Service Publishing Co., 1936), 78–80. Unfortunately, the British and Americans tended to view generalship and the conduct of operations as a science rather than an art. Thus, their teaching stressed adherence to formulas over creativity. When generals were able to give free rein to their imagination, it was despite the teaching they had received at staff college and elsewhere, not because of it.

27. Being aware of the fallibility of their subordinates, some of the most successful senior commanders adopted a policy of trust but verify. Thus, Montgomery set great store by his GHQ Liaison (Phantom) Regiment, which sent him unbiased reports about developments in lower formations, bypassing the normal chain of command. The system was copied by Patton, who used his 6 Cavalry Group in a similar role.

28. Clausewitz, *On War*, 87. This fact of life can be very galling to senior soldiers. As CIGS Brooke wrote to Montgomery on 13 August 1944: "Waging war may be difficult, but waging war under political control becomes at times almost impossible!!" Nigel Hamilton, *Monty, Master of the Battlefield 1942–1944* (London: Hamish Hamilton, 1983), 790.

29. The operational-level commander should, however, be his own principal intelligence officer. He has to achieve an abstract aim and, given his unique understanding of what he wants to achieve, has the deepest understanding of the questions he needs answered. Often these questions are of an unquantifiable nature related to a "feel" for the situation—not the sort of concrete details beloved by intelligence organizations as matters of fact and not conjecture. Thus, the commander specifies the essential elements of information, and his intelligence staff directs its resources to collect them, but he must be the ultimate interpreter of their import.

30. This pejorative term was used to describe those First World War commanders who remained remote from the battlefield, from their troops, and often from reality.

31. In the British and American systems the chief of staff has no direct command authority. In the Red Army he was a deputy commander with executive powers, and in the German army he was, for all intents and purposes, often a virtual co-commander.

32. Translation of a taped conversation with General Hermann Balck, 13 April 1979, performed under Contract No. DAAK40-78-C-0004, Battelle Columbus Laboratories, Columbus, Ohio, and kindly provided by Major General David T. Zabecki.

Balck was describing his Army Group G [sic] HQ but said that army HQs were about the same size.

33. His ability to prevent the often strained military relations between the Allies from breaking down and to preserve a degree of operational-strategic unity of purpose did not mean that Eisenhower accepted that political considerations should or even could be allowed to dominate military planning. He stoutly defended the quaint notion that politics and war did not mix—a curious position for such a keen student of Clausewitz.

34. It was not just arrogant, condescending British generals who counted Eisenhower's lack of operational experience as a failing. On 1 September 1944 Patton wrote in a letter: "Ike is all for caution since he has never been to the front and has no feel for actual fighting." Martin Blumenson, ed., *The Patton Papers* (Bridgewater, NJ: Da Capo Press, 1996), 537.

35. The total war establishment of 21 Army Group HQ, after a slight increase in November 1944, was 3,450 personnel, excluding various attachments such as signals and civil affairs and those providing for the HQ's defense and transportation. The HQ was divided into tactical, main, and rear (the latter did not include lines of communication). The centre of decision making was at "tac," which had approximately fifty officers, including Montgomery's liaison officers. Operational staff work was done at main HQ, and the logistic and administrative work was done at rear HQ.

36. In 21 Army Group most discussions, and the decisions and orders that followed from them, were oral; these were usually, though not invariably, confirmed in writing later. Because Montgomery's army and corps commanders were so thoroughly imbued with his interpretation of doctrine and trained in his methods, not to mention all too aware of the perils of nonconformity, it is often difficult to determine with any certainty where operational concepts and instructions really originated. For Montgomery's relationships with Dempsey and Crerar, see, for instance, Stephen A. Hart, *Montgomery and "Colossal Cracks": The 21st Army Group in Northwest Europe 1944–45* (Westport, CT: Praeger, 2000), chaps. 6 and 7, and numerous quotations from his staff scattered throughout their memoirs and diaries.

37. By contrast, 6 Army Group HQ contained only one-third the number of officers in Bradley's. This was because Devers insisted that it should follow theory and not duplicate the work being done at army level.

38. Dwight D. Eisenhower, *Crusade in Europe* (London: Heinemann, 1948), 129, develops the theme at some length.

39. Arthur Tedder, *With Prejudice* (Boston: Little, Brown, 1966), 552–571, contains an immoderate attack on Montgomery and the British Army.

40. Russell F. Weigley, *The American Way of War* (Bloomington: Indiana University Press, 1977), 140–145. The resilience of Lee's Army of Northern Virginia was graphically illustrated by the fact that it continued to fight after taking over 30 percent casualties in three days at Gettysburg in July 1863, enduring a campaign of unrelenting attrition from the Wilderness in May 1864 to Appomattox in April 1865. Of

course, Grant's army also took massive casualties—for instance, 29.6 percent in seven days in the Wilderness and at Spottsylvania. Thomas L. Livermore, *Numbers and Losses in the Civil War in America* (1900; reprint, Carlisle, PA: Kallman Publishers, 1996), table A.

41. Sources are in pretty close agreement on American losses but vary widely on Britain's. The figures cited here, from A. J. P. Taylor, *English History 1914–45, Oxford History of England* (Oxford: Oxford University Press, 1965), are generally accepted.

42. Quoted in Weigley, *American Way of War*, 221.

43. Allan R. Millett and Williamson Murray, *Military Effectiveness*, vol. 2, *The Second World War* (London: Allen and Unwin, 1988), 71–72.

44. Maurice Matloff, "The 90 Division Gamble," in *Command Decisions*, ed. Kent Roberts Greenfield (Washington, DC: Office of the Chief of Military History, 1971), 365–382.

45. Michael D. Doubler, *Closing with the Enemy* (Lawrence: University Press of Kansas, 1994), table on 236–237. The number excludes the two lightly equipped airborne divisions that were withdrawn from Normandy in mid-July and recommitted in mid-September in Holland.

46. At the outbreak of the Second World War, the US Army possessed nine regular and eighteen National Guard divisions; only three of the regular divisions even approached 50 percent strength. Millett and Murray, *Military Effectiveness*, 2:80. By July 1942 there were forty-five divisions, and by July 1943 there were eighty-eight. The eighty-ninth (and last) was formed by January 1944. In addition to the units organic to divisions, there were hundreds of independent artillery, tank, tank destroyer, engineer, and other units. And for every combat soldier there was another in the Services of Supply. All these units needed officers.

47. As Doubler, *Closing with the Enemy*, 301, points out, the cutting edge of the infantry division comprised the 5,211 officers and men in the twenty-seven rifle companies. That 36.5 percent of the division's manpower (not 68 percent, as the text states) took around 90 percent of the casualties (ibid., 240). It did not take much hard fighting to blunt that edge.

48. In the 337 days between D-Day and VE-Day, two infantry divisions saw more than 300 days of combat, ten saw more than 250 days, and seventeen saw more than 200. Ibid., 236.

49. Roland G. Ruppenthal, *United States Army in World War II, the European Theater of Operations: Logistical Support of the Armies*, vol. 1 (Washington, DC: Office of the Chief of Military History, 1953), 460.

50. Doubler, *Closing with the Enemy*, 246–248, explores the issue of the replacements' experiences at the hands of an unnecessarily indifferent system. Martin Van Creveld, *Fighting Power: German and US Army Performance, 1939–45* (Westport, CT: Greenwood Press, 1982), 76–79, excoriates the system. Both mention the improvements introduced, somewhat late in the day, by individual divisional commanders.

51. Doubler, *Closing with the Enemy*, 242.

52. *FM 100-5 Operations* sets forth the army's doctrine. The quotes here are from paragraphs 112 and 115 in the section titled "Doctrines of Combat," 1944 version. It is interesting to compare the May 1941 version, which guided the army in the Normandy campaign, with that issued in June 1944. An even more revealing comparison is with the German equivalent, the 1936 *Truppenführung*. See Bruce Condell and David T. Zabecki, eds., *On the German Art of War: Truppenfuhrung, German Army Manual for Unit Command in World War II* (London: Lynne Rienner, 2001), for a translation with commentary.

53. Doubler, *Closing with the Enemy*, 283–284, argues that for much of the time, the preconditions for operational maneuver were simply absent. This meant that the force with greatly superior firepower and mobility, with air supremacy, and possessing the initiative had to accept that the enemy could dictate the terms of engagement. Certainly tactically attritional combat was unavoidable, but it should have been conducted to enable operational maneuver.

54. An example is the V Corps battle of 9 June. The German 352 Infantry Division, much depleted by heavy fighting (it had only fourteen guns left), was holding about a 40 km (25 mile) frontage against 1 and 29 Infantry Divisions, with tanks and elements of the 2nd coming into action. The German left was smashed, and the right appeared to be in the air. Nevertheless, the 352nd was able to break clean and withdraw up to 20 km (12 miles) on foot, in good order, during the night and occupy a new defensive line on the Elle. See the account by the division's chief of staff in David C. Isby, *Fighting in Normandy: The German Army from D-Day to Villers Bocage* (London: Greenhill Books, 2001), 84–88. Gordon A. Harrison, *United States Army in World War II, the European Theater of Operations: Cross Channel Attack* (Washington, DC: Office of the Chief of Military History, 1951), 366–371, gives the US perspective, indicating that on 10 June, 1 and 2 Infantry Divisions merely followed up the withdrawal and then spent 11 June preparing a new attack. Over that two-day period, Harrison points out, the two US divisions were "facing a gaping hole in the German lines more than 10 miles broad." This allowed time for parts of the German 3 Parachute and 17 SS Panzer Grenadier Divisions to reinforce.

55. Even officers brought up on modern, "maneuverist" doctrine can still be swayed by the lure of the attritional approach. For instance, Peter Mansoor, *The GI Offensive in Europe: The Triumph of American Infantry Divisions* (Lawrence: University Press of Kansas, 1999), 3, says: "In World War II the most important aspect of tactical maneuver often was that it brought friendly units into a position where they could use fire support assets to destroy the enemy." In effect, he repeats the mantra that the enemy's physical destruction by fire is superior to the destruction of his cohesion and morale by maneuver (which then leads to his annihilation or surrender by placing him in a hopeless position). The ideal should be, through rapid maneuver, to preempt the enemy's establishment of a defense (which then has to be smashed

with firepower) or to dislocate his attack by delivering the first blow (which he is not prepared to parry).

56. Van Creveld, *Fighting Power*, goes into the doctrine, organization, personnel, and training of the US and German armies in some detail. Although his comparisons in favor of the latter are sometimes too extreme, and although he ignores some American improvements made during the course of the war, the work is enlightening. This criticism of American infantry does not extend to Airborne and Ranger units, both of which displayed considerable initiative and drive at junior levels. Of course, such units were allowed to select the best men available, to the detriment of the ordinary line infantry.

57. Russell A. Hart, *Clash of Arms: How the Allies Won in Normandy* (London: Lynne Rienner, 2001), 296, n. 38.

58. Patton quoted in John English, *On Infantry* (New York: Praeger, 1981), 133.

59. Kent Roberts Greenfield, *The Organization of Ground Combat Troops* (Washington, DC: Office of the Chief of Military History, 1947), 316.

60. *FM 100-5 Operations* (June 1944), 34–35.

61. Condell and Zabecki, *On the German Art of War*, 23.

62. Clausewitz, *On War*, 104.

63. *Auftragstaktik* is often translated as "control through directive," though more aptly it can be translated as "mission command." Subordinates are encouraged to exploit opportunities as they arise. The alternative system is *befehlstaktik*, or "control through detailed orders." In the latter, which typified American practice, especially in the early days, all units moved and fought according to a prescriptive higher plan. Under this approach, the key to victory is imposing the commander's will on the enemy, with irresistible momentum achieved through unified action.

64. The German command culture was deeply embedded, going back to at least the middle of the previous century. Thus Moltke, chief of the Prussian General Staff from 1857 to 1888, wrote in a midcentury essay: "Because of the diversity and rapid changes in the situation it is impossible to lay down binding rules. Only principles and general points of view can furnish a guide. Pre-arranged designs collapse and only a proper estimate of the situation can show the commander the correct way. The advantage of the situation will never be fully utilized if subordinate commanders wait for orders." In his 1869 "Instructions for Large Unit Commanders" he opined: "In general one does well to order no more than is absolutely necessary and to avoid planning beyond the situations one can foresee. These change very rapidly in war. Seldom will orders that anticipate far in advance and in detail succeed completely to execution. This shakes the confidence of the subordinate commander and gives a feeling of uncertainty when things develop differently from how the higher commander's order had presumed. Moreover, it must be pointed out that if one orders much then the important thing that needs to be carried out unconditionally will be carried out only incidentally or not at all because it is obscured by the mass of secondary things and those that are only valid under the circumstances. The higher the authority the

shorter and more general the orders will be. The next lower commanders will add what further precision appears necessary. The detail of the execution is left to [subordinate commanders]. Each thereby retains freedom of action and decision within his authority. . . . It is indispensable that the subordinate authorities recognize the objective of the one who gave the orders in order to strive for the goal when circumstances demand that they act otherwise than was ordered." Hughes, *Moltke on the Art of War,* 132, 184–185.

65. Michael J. Harwood, *Auftragstaktik: We Can't Get There from Here* (Leavenworth, KS: School of Advanced Military Studies, US Army Command and General Staff College, 1990); Condell and Zabecki, *On the German Art of War*; and Van Creveld, *Fighting Power*, all develop the theme of contrasting German and US styles in some depth. In practice, the differences became less marked over time. As the Americans grew in experience and confidence and as less successful commanders were weeded out, greater latitude was granted to junior leaders. As the German army declined in quality and overcontrol grew more common as a result of fear of failure and its consequences (which could be fatal), *befehlstaktik* increasingly supplanted *auftragstaktik*. Indeed, especially at the more senior levels, distrust and suspicions of treachery increasingly characterized the German army, particularly after the 20 July attempt on Hitler's life. As a result, reporting upward became steadily more unreliable (to the detriment of good decision making); slavish obedience to the letter of orders, no matter how ill informed or even irrational, became the rule; and back-covering (indeed, back-stabbing) became commonplace.

66. The learning experience and improvement are well described in several division histories. See, for instance, Joseph Balkoski, *Beyond the Beachhead: The 29th Infantry Division in Normandy* (Harrisburg, PA: Stackpole Books, 1989), and John Colby, *War from the Ground Up: The 90th Division in World War II* (Austin, TX: Nortex Press, 1991). The latter deals with an initially failing division that was turned around by a first-class new commander.

67. David French, *Raising Churchill's Army: The British Army and the War against Germany, 1919–1945* (Oxford: Oxford University Press, 2001), 58. The British officer cadet's tactical horizon was the handling of his platoon, while his German equivalent learned how to fight a battalion.

68. Ibid., 157–158.

69. Brian Bond, *British Military Policy between the Two World Wars* (Oxford: Clarendon Press, 1980), and Millett and Murray, *Military Effectiveness*, vol. 2, present a good picture of the interwar army.

70. French, *Raising Churchill's Army*, provides a very balanced and well-researched picture of the army's problems and development. Other useful contributions can be found in Millett and Murray, *Military Effectiveness*, vol. 2, and Hart, *Clash of Arms*.

71. As with the Americans, the manpower problem was most acute in the infantry. The War Office used the North African experience to predict the likely wastage

in Normandy. In the former, the infantry bore 48 percent of the total casualties; in the latter, 76 percent. English, *On Infantry*, 138. Moreover, the casualty rate was higher than predicted, so replacements were soon exhausted; this required the retraining of air defense gunners, RAF personnel, and others for the infantry role. Why 21 Army Group was not allowed to draw on the hundreds of thousands of troops in the United Kingdom for replacements, rather than disbanding units and whole formations, has never been satisfactorily explained.

72. The 1 Polish Armored Division was a uniquely difficult case, as Polish recruits were not available. Therefore, 856 Polish-speaking prisoners of war captured in Normandy were incorporated, but these men proved to be war-weary and disappointingly unenthusiastic; even with them, the division was 92 officers and 746 men below establishment by the beginning of October, and it was increasingly difficult to maintain the formation's combat effectiveness. However, the First Canadian Army did receive reinforcements; a British mountain division joined it in the autumn, and another Canadian corps of two divisions arrived from Italy in the spring of 1945. For a detailed treatment of the manpower issue, see Carlo D'Este, *Decision in Normandy* (London: Collins, 1983), 257–270.

73. It is certainly true that ideological fervor was lacking in the British Army. Attempts to stir up enthusiasm for an anti-Nazi crusade and to spread democracy were met with a cynicism stemming from the false propaganda and promises of the First World War. Most of the troops did not relish soldiering, but they recognized that the job had to be done; when they were well led, they could be relied on to do their duty—albeit with doggedness rather than heroics. There can be little doubt that British senior officers, whether consciously or unconsciously, sought scapegoats for their own failings—just as they had in the First World War, when they bemoaned the inadequacies of the TA, the Kitchener volunteers, and then the conscripts, on whom distance in time bestowed a retrospective glow.

74. See B. L. Montgomery, *Morale in Battle: Analysis* (British Army of the Rhine [BAOR], 1946).

75. The rates of desertion, absence without leave, and psychiatric casualties all increased significantly; the last rose to 20 percent of all casualties, and in Second Army, cases of "battle exhaustion" numbered 2,000 per week.

76. These issues are expanded on in Timothy Harrison Place, *Military Training in the British Army, 1940–1944: From Dunkirk to D-Day* (London: Frank Cass, 2000), and in R. A. M. S. Melvin's unpublished "German and Allied Doctrine in Normandy, 1944: A Comparative Perspective," which was produced to support a British Directorate-General Doctrine and Development staff ride in 2003. Of course, Montgomery had exercised a major influence on preparing the Home Army for operations in his eight months commanding the Southeastern Army before going to North Africa.

77. In his *The Canadian Army and the Normandy Campaign: A Study of Failure in High Command* (New York: Praeger, 1991), 117, John A. English quotes the Staff College teaching that "a brigade held up by enemy action could justifiably wait up to

three hours if it meant doubling the size of artillery support available. Lack of definitive information about an enemy's dispositions additionally made 'the provision of a barrage obligatory.'"

78. Military Training Pamphlet No. 23, *Operations*, pt. 9, 4. The 1942 version, pt. 1, 8–9, points out that the commander's "intention will usually best be expressed by a clear statement on the task which he proposes shall be performed by his whole command. By this means alone can subordinates be placed in a position where they can act intelligently and employ means at their disposal to further the interests of the higher commander's plan." It also stresses "initiative and readiness to take responsibility" (2–3).

79. It must be admitted that there were qualitative problems with the army's manpower. The navy and the air force had been more successful at attracting quality recruits before the war, and they were then given the pick of the conscript pool. Only a quarter of soldiers inducted in the second half of the war had received secondary education, and nearly 30 percent of them were of below-average intelligence. French, *Raising Churchill's Army*, 65. Then the army permitted the service arms to acquire the best-educated of their conscripts and compounded the problem for the teeth arms, especially the infantry, by forming many special forces such as the commandos, the Special Air Service, and the parachute troops. In all, nearly one-quarter of the infantry were so constituted, with much excellent line NCO material being wasted as private soldiers.

80. Field Marshal Lord Alanbrooke, *War Diaries 1939–45*, ed. Alex Danchev and D. Todman (London: Weidenfeld and Nicolson, 2001), 243. Perhaps rather dubiously, Brooke attributed this state of affairs to "the losses we sustained in the last war of all our best officers who should now be our senior commanders." The Germans, with much heavier casualties, managed to find an adequate supply for the Second World War.

81. French, *Raising Churchill's Army*, develops the theme of doctrine and command and control in his first two chapters.

82. Montgomery had formed such an armored exploitation force, X Corps, for the battle of El Alamein. He was disappointed in its performance and abandoned the concept as being beyond the competence of British armored formations.

83. L. F. Ellis, *Victory in the West*, vol. 1, *The Battle of Normandy* (London: HMSO, 1968), 536, 523.

84. TO&E and order of battle (ORBAT) details can be found in L. F. Ellis, *Victory in the West*, vol. 1, *The Battle of Normandy* (London: HMSO, 1962), appendix IV. In addition to the forces listed here, there were two commando and three infantry brigades (including one Belgian and one Dutch), an airborne division, and a division (not deployed as such) of special armor such as Crocodiles and Crabs.

85. The Americans, British, and Canadians never managed to emulate the Germans' ability, on the shortest notice, to put together an effective *kampfgruppe* (battle

group) of all arms, even from elements of different formations. The Allies lacked both the doctrine and the military-educational systems required.

86. English, *Canadian Army and Normandy Campaign*, is particularly insightful about the process of creating the CAO and the problems that persisted.

87. Hart, *Clash of Arms*, 171–175, delves into the manpower issue, and Terry Copp, *Fields of Fire: The Canadians in Normandy* (Toronto: Toronto University Press, 2003), 279, gives the day-by-day deficiencies in infantrymen.

Chapter 2. The Tipping Point

1. Dwight D. Eisenhower, *Crusade in Europe* (London: Heinemann, 1948), 247–248.

2. Eisenhower wanted Montgomery to command both First and Second Armies until such time as reinforcement of the theatre made it necessary to activate additional army and army group headquarters. Then, at a moment of his choosing, probably when the Allies reached the Seine, Eisenhower would assume land command as well as Supreme Command.

3. Montgomery's master plan is described more fully in Nigel Hamilton, *Monty, Master of the Battlefield 1942–1944* (London: Hamish Hamilton, 1983), chaps. 6 and 9, and Carlo D'Este, *Decision in Normandy* (London: Collins, 1983), chap. 6 (although the former puts a deceptive spin on the story, suggesting that every development in Overlord was both foreseen and planned). Both Hamilton and D'Este rightly point out that some senior officers at the time and some historians subsequently made far too much of the phase lines, which were speculative at best and not firm targets. Nevertheless, they are indicative of Montgomery's thinking, and they were regarded by some of his critics as indicators of success or otherwise.

4. The *bocage*, or hedgerow country, provided excellent defensive terrain, especially for an enemy that was well supplied with machine guns and mortars, as the Germans were. It is a close, intricate patchwork of irregularly shaped fields, typically about 200 by 400 m (220 by 440 yards) in area and bounded by 1 to 1.5 m (3 to 5 foot) high banks topped with dense hedges and trees. The hedgerows usually formed tank obstacles, and numerous villages, walled orchards, and stoutly built farms provided natural strongpoints. Roads and tracks were relatively few and far between and generally so narrow that only one-way traffic was possible. Off-route movement was difficult and slow, and navigation was problematic.

5. Brigadier General James M. Gavin, deputy commander of 82 Airborne Division, wrote candidly in his memoir of his first encounter with this problem: "The few days of fighting . . . had been surprisingly difficult. This was because of the hedgerows. Although there had been some talk in the UK before D-Day about the hedgerows, none of us had really appreciated how difficult they would turn out to be." James Gavin, *On to Berlin: Battle of an Airborne Commander* (London: Leo Cooper, 1979), 121.

6. Operation Fortitude continued to pin German formations to the Channel coast well into August. The protection of V-weapon launching sites was an added reason to keep the Pas de Calais strong, even as fear of a second landing weakened: Hitler hoped the assault on London would make the British government sue for peace. And whatever the outcome of field operations in France, the Channel port "fortresses" had to be denied to the Allies to slow down any logistic buildup for an assault on the heartland of the Reich.

7. The prospect of any further reinforcement from the eastern front ended abruptly on 23 June, when the Red Army began the Belorussian strategic offensive operation, the first of four that summer that would drive the enemy back up to 500 km (300 miles), across virtually the entire front from the Baltic to the Black Sea. The *Ostheer* was fighting for its life. From June to September, three out of every four Germans killed, seriously wounded, or captured would be lost in the east.

8. David French, *Raising Churchill's Army: The British Army and the War against Germany, 1919–1945* (Oxford: Oxford University Press, 2001), 147, points out that the average daily loss rate for the British in the Third Battle of Ypres (1917) was 2,324; for the Allies in Normandy it was 2,354.

9. After nearly seven weeks of fighting, the deepest penetrations were only about 50 km (30 miles) on a 130 km (80 mile) front. The Anglo-Canadian contingent had taken some 49,000 casualties, and the Americans about 73,000. These losses were almost completely replaced by the time of the breakout, and formations were almost all up to strength.

10. These were, in the west, the line (more or less) of the Lessay–Pérriers–St. Lô road and, in the Caen sector, the Verrieres and Bourguebus ridges.

11. The statistical data relied on in this section are based largely on Niklas Zetterling, *Normandy 1944: German Military Organization, Combat Power and Organizational Effectiveness* (Winnipeg, MB: J. J. Fedorowicz, 2000), chaps. 4 and 7, pt. 2, and appendix 4. This study is by far the most rigorous available in terms of both reliance on primary sources and methodology. Also used were H. F. Joslen, *Orders of Battle: Second World War 1939–1945* (reprint, London: HMSO, 1990), and Shelby S. Stanton, *Order of Battle US Army World War II* (New York: Presidio, 1984).

12. These are net figures, taking into account those evacuated as sick or wounded. Roland G. Ruppenthal, *United States Army in World War II, the European Theater of Operations: Logistical Support of the Armies*, vol. 1 (Washington, DC: Office of the Chief of Military History, 1953), 457–458.

13. Actually, most units used shrewd bartering and tricks to increase their holdings of favorite weapons such as the BAR, in some cases doubling their TO&E holdings.

14. The facts and figures in this section are taken primarily from Zetterling, *Normandy 1944*, chap. 6, appendices 5, 6, and 8, and John Buckley, *British Armour in the Normandy Campaign 1944* (London: Frank Cass, 2004), chaps. 5 and 6. There are minor differences between the two. Zetterling's appendix 6 underestimates Allied

tank destroyer numbers by 200, omitting corps-level antitank regiments and the SP element in infantry division antitank units. Nor does it include replacement AFVs in armored delivery units. The latter is very significant. For instance, in Operation Goodwood, three British armored divisions lost more than 400 tanks, yet a mere eight days later, they were back at virtually full strength for Operation Bluecoat.

15. The Sherman was known to British tank crews as the "Ronson," after the cigarette lighter that lit "first time, every time." To the Germans, it was known as the "Tommy Cooker."

16. As a rule, tanks were neither encouraged nor expected to fight enemy tanks. Their main armament was thus designed to maximize effects against nonarmored targets through HE engagements. The business of tank killing was entrusted to the purpose-built tank destroyers, lurking in ambush or stalking their prey. This concept might have had some validity against a Wehrmacht on the offensive, but it had none when the Allies were taking the battle to their enemy.

17. For instance, of the thirty Tigers left available to 101 SS Heavy Panzer Battalion on 1 July, five were destroyed by 11 August. But in any given week, one-quarter to one-third, and sometimes as many as two-thirds, could be found in workshops. T. L. Jentz, *Panzertruppen*, vol. 2 (Atglen, PA: Schiffer Military History, 1996), 184.

18. Eventually, both the British and the Americans fielded tanks capable of taking on German tanks on a more equal footing. The Americans deployed more than 1,000 M-36 tank destroyers from the summer of 1944 to year's end; though still lightly armored, this version of the M-10 at least mounted a 90mm gun that was almost as good as the 17-pounder. About 250 well-armored "Jumbo" variants of the Sherman, some mounting 76mm guns, were delivered in the late summer. The well-protected M-26 Pershing, with a 90mm gun, was issued in small quantities only from February 1945. The British continued to upgrade their M-10s and Shermans with the 17-pounder, but a new, capable tank did not appear until the Comet arrived in March 1945. Senior officers, both British and American (including Patton, a stout proponent of the tank), can be justly criticized for their complacency when it came to improving Allied tanks. Details of these and other developments can be found in Peter Chamberlain and Chris Ellis, *British and American Tanks of World War Two* (London: Arms and Armour, 1969).

19. The American and British infantry also possessed handheld antitank weapons—the bazooka and the PIAT, respectively. The latter was difficult and wildly inaccurate. Neither had the armor-defeating power of the German weapons, and many Allied units preferred to use captured *panzerfausts* rather than rely on their own weapons.

20. Zetterling, *Normandy 1944*, 152–157.

21. Light and mobile, with a high rate of fire, the 25-pounder was ideal for engaging targets in colonial warfare, but its shell was comparatively ineffective against well-dug-in infantry.

22. Figures extrapolated from Zetterling, *Normandy 1944*, 118–140; Joslen, *Or-*

ders of Battle, 463; L. F. Ellis, *Victory in the West*, vol. 1, *The Battle of Normandy* (London: HMSO, 1962), 523; and Stanton, *Order of Battle*, 394–424. These calculations do not include heavy antiaircraft units, which were used increasingly for ground fire as the enemy's air forces dwindled in importance; these units would, for instance, almost double the British nondivisional total.

23. Headquarters Second Army, comp., *An Account of the Operations of Second Army in Europe 1944–45* (reprint, MLRS, 2005), 82. The size of such concentrations was often devastating: "on several occasions, the fire of over 300 guns was concentrated on a single area." A. L. Pemberton, *The Development of Artillery Tactics and Equipment* (War Office, 1950), 222. It should be noted, however, that American control at the corps level was often too rigid, with nondivisional artillery failing to respond properly to divisions' needs and firing only on the orders of the corps' fire direction centre. J. B. A. Bailey, *Field Artillery and Firepower* (Annapolis, MD: Naval Institute Press, 2004), 324.

24. The ORS report on the countermortar problem can be found in Terry Copp, *Montgomery's Scientists: Operational Research in Northwest Europe* (Winnipeg, MB: Wilfred Laurier University, 2000), 431–440.

25. ORS Report No. 2 contained in Copp, *Montgomery's Scientists*, 395–406.

26. Buckley, *British Armour*, 107–109, 167–168. For a scathing indictment of British tank design, procurement, and performance in battle, see Peter Beale, *Death by Design: British Tank Development in the Second World War* (Stroud, UK: Sutton, 1998).

27. Williamson Murray and Allan R. Millett, *A War to Be Won* (Cambridge, MA: Harvard University Press, 2000), 463 (although it appears they were wrong to blame Patton for the unfortunate decision). The upgrading of the M-4's guns was an eminently practical improvement, as the Israelis demonstrated years later when they put 105mm guns into Shermans.

28. W. Victor Madej, *German War Economy: The Motorization Myth* (Game Publishing, 1984), 128–130.

29. Figures extrapolated from Zetterling, *Normandy 1944*, 213–396.

30. Russell A. Hart, "Feeding Mars: The Role of Logistics in the German Defeat in Normandy," *War in History* 3, 4 (November 1996): 425–427, expands on this theme.

31. Ruppenthal, *US Army in World War II*, 1:458; Ellis, *Victory in the West*, 1:536.

32. Steve R. Waddell, *United States Army Logistics: The Normandy Campaign 1944* (Westport, CT: Greenwood Press, 1994), 63–64, 85.

33. Hart, "Feeding Mars," 431–433. The situation on Panzer Group West's front, facing the British, was far from comfortable but not so dire. Seventh Army's plight was worse: it was further from the source of supply in Germany; it had to deal with the problem of the Loire barrier; and, owing to inadequate transport to haul supplies from dump to unit, it had been neglected in favor of the hitherto more threatened

eastern sector. Its collapse was due at least as much to logistics as to operational and tactical factors.

34. W. F. Craven and J. L. Cate, *The Army Air Forces in World War II*, vol. 2, *Europe—Torch to Pointblank* (Washington, DC: Office of Air Force History, 1949), 573.

35. W. A. Jacobs, untitled section in *Case Studies in Air Superiority*, ed. Benjamin Franklin Cooling (Washington, DC: Center for Air Force History, 1994), 275–276, 299.

36. W. F. Craven and J. L. Cate, *The Army Air Forces in World War II*, vol. 3, *Europe—Argument to VE-Day* (Washington, DC: Office of Air Force History, 1951), 139. The figures presumably include aircraft in Coastal Command and the Air Defense of Great Britain, both of which contributed to Operation Overlord both directly and indirectly. They exclude 15 Air Force, flying from bases in Italy, whose contribution to the strategic air offensive was considerable.

37. Air Historical Branch, *Rise and Fall of the German Air Force* (reprint, Poole, UK: Arms and Armour Press, 1987), 327–331.

38. In his 15 May presentation at St. Paul's School, Montgomery warned that although the Allies expected to have eighteen divisions ashore by 14 June, intelligence estimates suggested that the Germans could have as many as twenty-four divisions concentrated by then (including ten panzer). Hamilton, *Monty, Master of the Battlefield*, 586.

39. Arthur Tedder, *With Prejudice* (Boston: Little, Brown, 1966), 509.

40. E. K. G. Sixsmith, *Eisenhower as Military Commander* (London: Batsford, 1973), 128–131; Jacobs in Cooling, *Case Studies in Air Superiority*, 300–304. Spaatz apparently expected Operation Overlord to fail but did not want his lack of support to be blamed for its failure. He reportedly said: "This . . . invasion can't succeed and I don't want any part of the blame. After it fails, we can show them how we can win by bombing." Eduard Mark, *Aerial Interdiction in Three Wars* (Washington, DC: Center for Air Force History, 1994), 230.

41. The British government initially resisted the plan on the grounds that French civilian casualties would be unacceptably high. When experimental raids indicated an unexpectedly accurate bombing performance by British heavies, that opposition was lifted. In the event, instead of the feared 48,000 to 160,000 casualties (the latter figure derived from faulty calculations), there were only about 4,750 to 12,000 French casualties. Mark, *Aerial Interdiction*, 231–232; Lionel Lacey-Johnson, *Pointblank and Beyond* (Shrewsbury, UK: Airlife, 1991), 53–54.

42. Mark, *Aerial Interdiction*, 232–236.

43. Ibid., 251, n. 102. The figure for the Loire is misleading, as the Germans managed to get at least some traffic over the river at Tours on three days out of five.

44. Craven and Cate, *Army Air Forces in World War II*, 3:160.

45. See Zetterling, *Normandy 1944*, 45–47.

46. Craven and Cate, *Army Air Forces in World War II*, 3:219–225, go into more detail, as does Lacey-Johnson, *Pointblank and Beyond*, chap. 23.

47. Hart, "Feeding Mars."

48. Ibid.

49. Coningham (and Tedder) had worked closely and harmoniously with Montgomery in the desert war, but the latter's arrogance and vanity, evidenced by his hogging the credit for victory and barely acknowledging the air contribution, had soured relations. Personal hostilities between and within the services at the higher levels would bedevil cooperation in what had to be a joint ground-air campaign. (See, for instance, D'Este, *Decision in Normandy*, 218–223.)

50. W. A. Jacobs, untitled section in *Case Studies in the Development of Close Air Support*, ed. Benjamin Franklin Cooling (Washington, DC: Center for Air Force History, 1990), 261.

51. In the armored column cover system, a flight of four fighter-bombers was available at all times, thanks to a prearranged schedule. These planes supported each armored spearhead either by attacking targets designated by an air force officer, with the lead unit acting as a forward air controller, or by conducting armed reconnaissance ahead of the column if no obvious targets presented themselves. Armored column cover decentralized target assignment as well as attack control, and it required an entire wing to maintain support of each spearhead. It thus violated two cherished principles of the use of airpower. However, with the virtual demise of Luftwaffe opposition and an abundance of fighter-bombers, the downside was unimportant. The system had many advantages that helped maintain a high rate of advance: the armored division or combat command commander knew what support was available at all times, and he could be sure that urgent requests would be reacted to without delay. See Jacobs in Cooling, *Case Studies in Close Air Support*, 271, 281. Major General Hoyt S. Vandenberg, who took over command of Ninth Air Force in August, deprecated the use of fighter-bombers for tasks that were better left to the artillery: "Too much of . . . IX TAC was being employed within an area of 30–40 miles in advance of the Army's front line." Vandenberg war diary cited in Thomas Alexander Hughes, *Overlord: General Pete Quesada and the Triumph of Tactical Air Power in World War II* (New York: Free Press, 1995), 225.

52. Hughes, *Overlord*, 179.

53. Copp, *Montgomery's Scientists*, 173–176.

54. Ibid., 181–206, examines the impact of Allied airpower on the retreat in great detail.

55. Hughes, *Overlord*, 247–248.

56. Copp, *Montgomery's Scientists*, 71–106.

57. VII Corps' war diary noted on 25 July: "Neither bombing nor the artillery preparation prevented a great many of the German frontline infantry from continuing to fight the same dogged hedgerow to hedgerow defense they had carried on since the invasion." Cited in Russell F. Weigley, *Eisenhower's Lieutenants* (Bloomington: Indiana University Press, 1990), 162.

58. According to Zetterling, *Normandy 1944*, 43, 387–388, the thirty-one ser-

viceable tanks available on 23 July had shrunk to only twenty-seven by 1 August, despite both air and ground attack; in addition, the division was already chronically short of infantrymen. See P. Steinhardt, ed., *Panzer Lehr Division 1944–45* (Solihull, UK: Helion, 2008), 123–138, for the full story as related by Bayerlein. See Martin Blumenson, *United States Army in World War II, the European Theater of Operations: Breakout and Pursuit* (Washington, DC: Office of the Chief of Military History, 1959), 241–246, for a summary of Cobra's initial progress.

59. Eisenhower, *Crusade in Europe*, 297.

60. Cited in John Terraine, *A Time for Courage: The Royal Air Force in the European War 1939–45* (London: Macmillan, 1985), 656.

61. Letter quoted in Weigley, *Eisenhower's Lieutenants*, 381. The author points out that although Tedder was complaining only about British generals, the Americans were just as dependent. But the "bomber barons" were not totally unsympathetic to what they considered reasonable requests from the generals. On 14 September the CCS removed the "strategic direction" of their bombers from Eisenhower, making close air support a matter of request rather than command. They continued to help out when the situation demanded it.

62. Ian Gooderson, *Air Power at the Battlefront: Allied Close Air Support in Europe 1944–45* (London: Frank Cass, 1998), 155–156.

63. Albert Seaton, *The Fall of Fortress Europe 1943–1945* (London: Batsford, 1981), 108.

64. The most notorious German act of reprisal was perpetrated by elements of 2 SS Panzer Division. The division's move from Toulouse to Normandy was seriously delayed by SAS-vectored air attacks on its transporters and fuel and, to a minor extent, by guerrilla action. Venting their frustrations, SS troops killed 642 inhabitants of Oradour-sur-Glane and razed the village on 10 June. The incident illustrates why active resistance was not popular.

65. Mark Mazower, *Dark Continent* (London: Allen Lane, 1998), 192; Walter Laquer, *Guerilla* (London: Weidenfeld and Nicolson, 1977), 230. The communists were organizationally prepared and disciplined to operate in conditions of illegality, and this ensured that they played a leading role.

66. The Paris uprising was most unwelcome to the Supreme Commander, for it precluded his intention to bypass the city and burdened the Allies with the responsibility for feeding its citizens. The 4,000 tons a day required to do so utilized enough transport resources to supply seven reinforced divisions. Stephen E. Ambrose, *The Supreme Commander* (London: Cassell, 1971), 482.

67. There were also fifty-two Sussex teams, each with an officer and a radio operator, dedicated purely to intelligence gathering.

68. Julian Thompson, *War behind Enemy Lines* (London: Sidgwick and Jackson, 1998), 334–335, 433. T. B. H. Otway, *Airborne Forces* (London: Imperial War Museum, 1990), 239–259, a reprint of the 1951 official history, summarizes SAS operations.

69. Douglas Porch, *The French Secret Services* (London: Macmillan, 1995), chaps. 5 and 6, dissects the problems and shortcomings of the resistance and assesses its accomplishments.

70. In I. C. B. Dear and M. R. D. Foot, *The Oxford Companion to World War II* (Oxford: Oxford University Press, 1995), 946, Foot goes so far as to elevate this passive resistance over sabotage and air action as the main cause of unreliable rail movement.

71. Porch, *French Secret Services*, 227, quoting Julian Amery, "Of Resistance," *Nineteenth Century Magazine*, March 1949.

72. S. J. Lewis, *Jedburgh Team Operations in Support of the 12th Army Group, August 1944* (Leavenworth, KS: Combat Studies Institute, US Army Command and General Staff College, 1991), 4–16, 59–66, provides a useful summary of the concept and results produced by Jedburgh teams in support of 12 Army Group operations.

73. David M. Glantz, *Soviet Military Deception in the Second World War* (London: Frank Cass, 1989), 565. Allied intelligencers and commanders were not immune from similar cultural prejudices. In 1941–1942 both British and Americans suffered catastrophic defeats at the hands of the Japanese; these resulted at least partly from an underestimation of the enemy's capabilities.

74. Harold C. Deutsch, "Commanding Generals and the Uses of Intelligence," in *Leaders and Intelligence*, ed. Michael I. Handel (London: Frank Cass, 1989), 200.

75. This section is distilled from F. H. Hinsley et al., *British Intelligence in the Second World War*, vol. 3, pt. 2 (London: HMSO, 1988), chaps. 47 and 48, and David Bennett, *A Magnificent Disaster: The Failure of Market Garden, the Arnhem Operation September 1944* (Newbury, UK: Casemate, 2008), chaps. 3 and 4.

76. US War Department, Military Intelligence Division, *German Military Intelligence 1939–45* (University Publications of America, 1984), concentrates on the eastern front but contains excellent material on the organization, training, and capabilities of German intelligence. James A. Wood, *Army of the West: The Weekly Reports of German Army Group B from Normandy to the West Wall* (Mechanicsburg, PA: Stackpole Books, 2007), contains German intelligence appreciations, and Hinsley, *British Intelligence*, throws light on German misconceptions.

77. Alfred Price, *The Last Year of the Luftwaffe, May 1944 to May 1945* (London: Arms and Armour Press, 1993), 63–65.

78. The culminating point is the point at which a force no longer has the capacity to continue its form of operations. In the offensive, it occurs when continuing the attack is no longer possible and the force must either transition to the defense or at least suffer an operational pause; either eventuality gives the enemy breathing space to restore his defenses or even prepare a counteroffensive. In the defense, it is the point at which counteroffensive action is no longer possible and the initiative is, in consequence, irretrievably lost. The culminating point is dealt with at some length in Carl von Clausewitz, *On War*, trans. and ed. Michael Howard and Peter Paret (Princeton, NJ: Princeton University Press, 1976), 528, 566–573.

79. Carlo D'Este, *Eisenhower: Allied Supreme Commander* (London: Weidenfeld and Nicolson, 2003), 168.

Chapter 3. July: Breakthrough and Near Breakthrough

1. A further development increased the importance of breaking out of Normandy. In mid-June the Germans started the V-1 bombardment of London (and other cities). As the air forces proved incapable of ending these attacks, this created a political imperative to overrun the launch sites, mostly in the Pas de Calais, at the earliest possible moment.

2. The original LD for this breakout operation was supposed to be on the St. Lô–Coutances road, but Bradley had to settle for the more northerly road because the cost in men and time to attain even that less satisfactory LD had already proved exorbitant.

3. In this chapter and subsequently, where the various military units come into contact, German units are italicized to prevent confusion.

4. Martin Blumenson, ed., *The Patton Papers* (Bridgewater, NJ: Da Capo Press, 1996), 482.

5. Omar N. Bradley, *A Soldier's Story* (New York: Henry Holt, 1951), 266, 271–272.

6. Carlo D'Este, *Decision in Normandy* (London: Collins 1983), 333, quoting an interview with Dempsey in the Liddell Hart papers. To aid the American concentration for the breakthrough battle, Montgomery shifted the interarmy boundary to the west, relieving a US division in the Caumont area.

7. Russell F. Weigley, *Eisenhower's Lieutenants* (Bloomington: Indiana University Press, 1990), 137, argues: "Adversity . . . had pushed Bradley to contrive an excellent plan."

8. Although Cobra was tentatively scheduled to start on 18 July, the main effort VII Corps did not reach its LD on the road west from St. Lô until 20 July. And because each operation was critically dependent on a massive preliminary aerial bombardment, the start dates were determined by the weather (fair skies were needed over both the bombers' bases in the United Kingdom and the target area). The weather forced the postponement of Goodwood to 18 July and Cobra to 24 and then 25 July (the original start date of 18 July had to be pushed back because of the time required to take St. Lô). The unintended interval between the two operations was unfortunate. To continue to pin the enemy, the newly activated First Canadian Army mounted Operation Spring on 25 July, but this rapidly proved to be an expensive failure. On 27 July two panzer divisions moved west—fortunately, too late to prevent the breakthrough.

9. Niklas Zetterling, *Normandy 1944: German Military Organization, Combat Power and Organizational Effectiveness* (Winnipeg, MB: J. J. Fedorowicz, 2000); David C. Isby, ed., *Fighting the Breakout: The German Army in Normandy from Cobra*

to the Falaise Gap (London: Greenhill Books, 2004); and P. Steinhardt, ed., *Panzer Lehr Division 1944–45* (Solihull, UK: Helion, 2008), set out what is known about the organization and strength of the various battle groups.

10. Isby, *Fighting the Breakout*, 24.

11. As the surviving German records are incomplete, only approximate German strengths can be calculated from Zetterling, *Normandy 1944*, pt. 2. The force ratios given are therefore "guesstimates."

12. The two panzer divisions were limited by an acute fuel shortage, and 2 SS was lacking 40 percent of its transport anyway.

13. The *Seventh Army* situation estimate, deployment, and conduct of the defense are detailed by the army's former chief of staff and commander in Isby, *Fighting the Breakout*, 39–67.

14. Ibid., 32; James A. Wood, *Army of the West: The Weekly Reports of German Army Group B from Normandy to the West Wall* (Mechanicsburg, PA: Stackpole Books, 2007), 145.

15. More details of the plan, and different takes on it, can be found in Elbridge Colby, *The First Army in Europe 1943–45* (Nashville, TN: Battery Press, 1969), chap. 5; J. Lawton Collins, *Lightning Joe, an Autobiography* (Baton Rouge: Louisiana State University Press, 1979), chap. 12; Bradley, *Soldier's Story*, chap. 17; Martin Blumenson, *United States Army in World War II, the European Theater of Operations: Breakout and Pursuit* (Washington, DC: Office of the Chief of Military History, 1959), chaps. 10, 11; and James Jay Carafano, *After D-Day: Operation Cobra and the Normandy Breakout* (London: Lynne Rienner, 2000), chaps. 4, 5.

16. According to Bradley (*Soldier's Story*, 269): "Now we've got everything we own in the battle. There isn't a single division left in reserve." He saw nothing unusual in this, pointing out that he had gone through the Tunisian and Sicilian campaigns without even a regiment in reserve. Of course, the employment of reserves is one of the main ways a general can influence the course of a battle or an operation.

17. In addition to the forty-five battalions of field, medium, and heavy artillery, ten battalions of tank destroyers and heavy antiaircraft artillery were pressed into service in the indirect fire role. Though guns were plentiful, there were constraints on ammunition use; supplies of 81mm mortar, 8 inch howitzer, and 76mm armor-piercing rounds were well below target, and supplies of 105mm howitzer ammunition were slightly below target. These shortages were the result of profligate expenditure during the incessant broad-front attacks that characterized the early weeks of the campaign and resulted in the rationing of many types of ammunition from 15 July; both planning errors and distribution shortfalls contributed to the problem. Had Operation Cobra not resulted in a breakout, the ammunition problem would have become acute. Steve R. Waddell, *United States Army Logistics: The Normandy Campaign 1944* (Westport, CT: Greenwood Press, 1994), 84–90.

18. Both Patton's army and two corps HQs were ready for the activation of Third Army, which would soon be required, as First Army's span of command was already

stretched. Third Army took its place in the ORBAT on 1 August. Bradley, with Eisenhower's concurrence, resisted the earlier entry of Third Army (earnestly desired by Patton) because he wanted to complete the Cobra operation without the disruption of last-minute changes in command arrangements.

19. Shortly before the attack, Bradley told Collins: "Joe, if this thing goes as it should, we should be in Avranches in a week." Collins, *Lightning Joe*, 236.

20. Much more detailed accounts can be found in Carafano, *After D-Day*; Waddell, *United States Army Logistics*; Blumenson, *US Army in World War II*, chaps. 12–17; Martin Blumenson, *The Battle of the Generals* (New York: Quill, William Morrow, 1993), pt. 3; Colby, *First Army in Europe*, chaps. 5, 6A (which contains several errors, omissions, and dubious judgments); Collins, *Lightning Joe*, chap. 12; Weigley, *Eisenhower's Lieutenants*, 147–174; Bradley, *Soldier's Story*, chap. 17; Isby, *Fighting the Breakout*, chaps. 2, 3, 5; and F. H. Hinsley et al., *British Intelligence in the Second World War*, vol. 3, pt. 2 (London: HMSO, 1988), 225–246.

21. The casualties included General Lesley J. McNair, commander of the AGF and the phantom FUSAG that was threatening a second landing north of the Seine. He had come to observe the battle (proving that war is not a risk-free spectator sport). The episode illustrates the imperfect communications between the strategic air and ground forces and the soldiers' lack of understanding of the problems and limitations of strategic airpower in providing close air support. For a fuller, dispassionate analysis of the issue, including responsibility for the short-bombing, see Blumenson, *Battle of the Generals*, chap. 9; Carafano, *After D-Day*, 102–121; Carlo D'Este, *Eisenhower: Allied Supreme Commander* (London: Weidenfeld and Nicolson, 2003), 560–561.

22. Weigley, *Eisenhower's Lieutenants*, 154.

23. The Germans described this important attribute of generalship as *Fingerspitzengefühl*, "fingertip feel." It was sedulously fostered by the German army and owed much to its high level of professionalism to its stress on commanders going forward to get a personal and immediate sense of developments. Perhaps uncharitably, Carafano argues in *After D-Day* (193–194) that Collins had little option but to commit 1 Infantry Division early. Eddy's 9 Division had been overtasked and would not take Marigny anytime soon, so fresh troops were needed to restore momentum.

24. The Germans underestimated the attack by approximately 25 percent in infantry, 100 percent in armor, and 400 percent in artillery. This was a disastrous miscalculation of American capabilities, which in turn fed a mistaken idea of American intentions. Nor, thanks to the general weakness of *Seventh Army*, was the defense arrayed in the depth that had contributed so much to the failure of the preceding British Goodwood offensive.

25. The advance of 2 Armored Division was also aided by the fact that it was attacking down the *LXXXIV Corps* and *II Parachute Corps* boundary, for which *Panzer Lehr* was responsible.

26. Marshall, Chief of Staff of the Army, selected Corlett for a corps command in First Army because he had successfully commanded amphibious assaults in the

Pacific. Marshall anticipated that this expertise would prove valuable. He was wrong, but only because Corlett's experience was ignored as "bush league stuff" by Eisenhower and Bradley—a costly mistake born of narrow-minded parochialism.

27. Watson was then slow to reorganize and move on the new axis. Collins (perhaps looking for a scapegoat for the failure of the shallow encirclement) assessed that Watson was not suited to command an armored division; concurring, Bradley relieved him. Watson would later command 29 Infantry Division satisfactorily.

28. The airmen claimed 66 tanks, 204 vehicles, and 11 guns destroyed and another 56 tanks and 55 vehicles damaged by the combined actions of aircraft, artillery, and tanks. W. F. Craven and J. L. Cate, *The Army Air Forces in World War II*, vol. 3, *Europe—Argument to VE-Day* (Washington, DC: Office of Air Force History, 1951), 242. If the results of the ground attack at Mortain are any guide, most of the losses were inflicted by ground fire.

29. The exploitation of the gap sounds much easier and straightforward than it actually was. Funneling three armored and three infantry divisions through the narrow bottleneck in four days was a massive traffic control problem; in a ninety-six-hour period, 13,000 vehicles of all types crossed the Pontaubault bridge—one every thirty seconds. The air threat to these nose-to-tail columns was very worrisome, and the Luftwaffe made a concentrated effort to disrupt convoys and destroy bridges in the choke point (about 225 sorties in twenty-four hours); however, strong ground and fighter air defense (adequately warned by Ultra) rendered these attacks largely ineffective. A small scratch force tried to restrict the American bridgehead over the Sélune but was brushed aside.

30. This section is based primarily on Blumenson, *US Army in World War II*, 424–442, and D'Este, *Decision in Normandy*, 408–413. Isby, *Fighting the Breakout*, chaps. 6–8 were helpful on the German side. To provide Third Army with the same intimate air support enjoyed by First Army, XIX Tactical Air Command was created under Brigadier General Otto P. Weyland. He and Patton formed a close working relationship that was of great value to Third Army.

31. Destruction of the bridges by air interdiction was equated with the denial of crossings, although it was clear that ferrying operations were feeding reinforcements and supplies over the river.

32. Patton's demand for speed at the expense of security, ignoring open flanks and bypassing resistance, disturbed Middleton, the corps commander; it also concerned Bradley, who worried about a possible threat from the east. Both men were also exercised by the problem of controlling such far-reaching, high-speed maneuver; indeed, Patton maintained only an intermittent grip on operations spread over a large geographic area by using his 6 Cavalry Group in a fashion analogous to Montgomery's Phantom Regiment.

33. British accounts make too much of the German possession of the dominating heights, especially Mt. Pinçon. As a report on battle experience produced by 2 Panzer Division on 14 July pointed out, this high ground was less important because

the woods, orchards, and tree-topped hedgerows in *bocage* country limited visibility. More important was the holding of road junctions, as heavy weapons and vehicles could be moved only on roads. Ian Daglish, *Operation Bluecoat: Breakout from Normandy* (Barnsley, UK: Pen and Sword, 2009), 306.

34. The doctrinal norm for a full-strength infantry division, admittedly rarely achieved, was 6.5 to 10 km (4 to 6 miles).

35. This section and the next are based primarily on G. S. Jackson, *Operations of Eighth Corps: Account of Operations from Normandy to the River Rhine* (London: St. Clements Press, 1948), 115–145; H. G. Martin, *History of the 15 Scottish Division* (Edinburgh: William Blackwood and Sons, 1948); EWIP [Edgar W. I. Palamountain], *Taurus Pursuant: History of 11 Armoured Division* (British Army of the Rhine [BAOR], 1945); Daglish *Operation Bluecoat*; BAOR, *Battlefield Tour Guide: Operation Bluecoat* (BAOR, 1948); L. F. Ellis, *Victory in the West*, vol. 1, *The Battle of Normandy* (London: HMSO, 1962), 386–411; J. J. How, *Normandy: The British Breakout* (London: William Kimber, 1981); Wilhelm Tiecke, *In the Firestorm of the Last Years of the War* (Winnipeg, MB: J. J. Fedorowicz, 1999), 144–149; Michael Reynolds, *Sons of the Reich, II SS Panzer Corps: Normandy, Arnhem, Ardennes, Eastern Front* (Staplehurst, UK: Spellmount, 2002), 58–79; Hinsley et al., *British Intelligence in the Second World War*, 238–241.

36. The supply of replacement tanks was so abundant that the three armored divisions were more or less at full strength, despite losing more than 300 tanks destroyed or damaged a mere ten days earlier in Operation Goodwood.

37. Montgomery, in his *El Alamein to the River Sangro: Normandy to the Baltic* (London: Barrie and Jenkins, 1973), merely implies that Vire was always on 12 Army Group's side of the boundary, and most subsequent British accounts have accepted this. Nigel Hamilton, *Monty, Master of the Battlefield, 1942–1944* (London: Hamish Hamilton, 1983), 757, says Montgomery's communication with Brooke specified the axis of the attack as Caumont-Vire. Second Army's once secret official history states clearly that the initial objectives and boundaries were not projected forward of the line of contact (nor were they on First Army's or later 12 Army Group's situation maps). Headquarters Second Army, comp., *An Account of the Operations of Second Army in Europe 1944–45* (reprint, MLRS, 2005), 166. However, it states that on 31 July, 11 Armored was directed on Vire via either le Tourneur or Forêt l'Evêque, with Le Bény-Bocage as an intermediate objective (ibid., 168). Then on 1 August the division's stated objective was Flers to the southeast. G. P. B. Roberts, *From the Desert to the Baltic* (London: William Kimber, 1987), 191–192, is quite clear that Vire was his division's original objective until a change on 1 August. How, *Normandy*, 92, is adamant that there was a boundary change. To a considerable extent, the debate is pointless. If Vire was in the US sector, there was nothing to prevent Montgomery from suggesting a boundary shift to Bradley so that, for the benefit of all, 11 Armored could take the vital and defenseless town and threaten the rear of those Germans opposing the advance of First Army.

38. The *II SS Panzer Corps* order was a model of clarity and brevity, the essence of mission command orders: "II SS Panzer Corps with subordinated 9 and 10 SS Panzer Divisions is to clean up by counter-attack of 10 SS Panzer Division the enemy penetration at Coulvain and, with 21 Panzer Division and 9 SS Panzer Division close the gap between LXXIV Corps and the east wing of Seventh Army (II Parachute Corps). Contact with Seventh Army is to be established at Hill 205, directly west of Beny-Bocage." Quoted in Tiecke, *In the Firestorm*, 145. Thanks to a timely Ultra report, Montgomery and Dempsey were aware of this redeployment and the SS corps' mission. Hinsley et al., *British Intelligence in the Second World War*, 239.

39. Much was made, both then and subsequently, about the triumph of taking Mt. Pinçon in the face of determined opposition. Ultra made it clear that, in fact, the defense line between Thury Harcourt and Vire was being withdrawn on 5 August at the latest. Hinsley et al., *British Intelligence in the Second World War*, 240.

40. In fact, Cobra was mounted only just in time. By 1 August, five infantry divisions had been dispatched from *Fifteenth Army*; two were on their way from the Pas de Calais, one was crossing the Seine, one had just crossed, and one was already arriving in *Seventh Army*'s area. Another infantry division and *9 Panzer Division* had been released for Normandy from the south, with the infantry crossing the Loire at Angers.

41. Bradley was mistaken when he wrote in his memoir that, between the weather-driven postponement of Cobra on 21 July and the start of the operation: "Two panzer divisions left Monty at Caen and shifted over to our US front. . . . Five panzer divisions remained in front of Monty where we hoped he would contain them until after the attack." Bradley, *Soldier's Story*, 277. In fact, seven panzer divisions remained on the British sector until *2 Panzer* was released at midday on 27 July and then *116 Panzer* the next day—too late to prevent the breakthrough or save *LXXXIV Corps*' left wing.

42. Among the reasons for the failure of the Goodwood offensive a few days earlier were the failure to achieve surprise, a defense in depth unappreciated by British intelligence, and the ability of *Panzer Group West* to counterattack within hours with the better part of two panzer divisions. The contrast with *Seventh Army*'s situation is clear.

43. Unwittingly, Bradley adopted a very Soviet concept and scheme of maneuver, right down to the creation of inner and outer wings of encirclement.

44. Of course, Bradley had previously displayed poor judgment in not heeding the air commanders' warnings about both the practicalities of the air bombardment and the risks that accompanied it.

45. It is a pity that Collins did not remember his own aphorism: "I have always said that an order is but an aspiration, a hope that what has been directed will come true. The enemy has something to say about that." Collins, *Lightning Joe*, 243.

46. Branches are options built into the basic plan, and sequels are subsequent operations based on the possible outcomes of the current operation—victory, defeat, or stalemate.

47. Isby, *Fighting the Breakout*, 116.

48. Ibid., 52.

49. SOE and FFI activity, which was considerable in Brittany, helped prevent the Germans (short of time owing to the speedy American advance) from destroying important infrastructure elements such as the Morlaix trestle bridge.

50. American casualty figures reflected Hodges's choices. Between 2 and 7 August, 1 Infantry Division, used in the envelopment maneuver, lost 250 men; the other three divisions of VII Corps lost 1,750. Blumenson, *US Army in World War II*, 449.

51. The feat of getting into the minds of enemy commanders was made easier, in the case of army and army group commanders, by Ultra reports (e.g., regarding the state of *LXXXIV Corps* in late July). See Hinsley et al., *British Intelligence in the Second World War*, 232–234.

52. George S. Patton Jr., *War as I Knew It* (Boston: Houghton Mifflin, 1975), 358.

53. In fact, the stated aim of depriving the Germans of the essential hinge on which the defense could pivot is suspect. Capture of the Mt. Pinçon–Hill 361 ridge alone would have left the enemy in possession of the excellent defensive position comprising the river Souleuvre and the Le Bény-Bocage ridge on the south side.

54. Although Montgomery usually involved himself in the planning of army and sometimes even corps operations, it appears that the choice of axis for Bluecoat and the plan were Dempsey's alone. It is less clear what involvement the C-in-C had in the execution.

55. None of the thin works on XXX Corps or its component divisions contain a serious analysis of operations. With regard to Bluecoat (among other operations), they prefer to gloss over inadequacies in planning, execution, and command, using euphemisms to explain away shortcomings and dwelling instead on minor successes and individual examples of heroism. See, for instance, H. Essame, *43 (Wessex) Division at War 1944–45* (London: William Clowes, 1952).

56. Brigadier H. E. Pyman papers, quoted in D'Este, *Decision in Normandy*, 274. Montgomery had personally selected Bucknall to command XXX Corps, despite the severe doubts expressed by Brooke. His dismissal was in response to a request by Dempsey, who had tired of his persistent failure.

57. In describing the 4 km (2.5 mile) night infiltration by 11 Armored Division's infantry to capture St. Martin, the division historian (EWIP, *Taurus Pursuant*) wrote: "The smallest opposition would probably have sufficed to prevent such an advance . . . but not one rifle or machine gun had met the KSLI [King's Shropshire Light Infantry]." After the second successful infiltration through the Forêt l'Evêque, an officer remarked to Roberts that "two men and a boy could have held you up there"; the general quipped, "yes—but they did not have the boy." Jackson, *Operations of Eighth Corps*, 134. Both moves were regarded as highly unusual and daring. Yet the enemy's inability to oppose them was not simply lucky. The Germans were overstretched, surprised, and disorganized. It is little wonder that gaps and weak spots existed, especially off the main axis.

58. The situation was, in fact, somewhat similar to that which arose during Operation Epsom in late June, when both Dempsey and O'Connor had been "anxious to strengthen and widen" the corps penetration; they were concerned that "too deep and narrow an advance" by 11 Armored Division "would enable the Germans to cut off the Allied salient with counter-attacks from either flank." John Baynes, *The Forgotten Victor—General Sir Richard O'Connor* (London: Brassey's, 1989). Of course, the relative German and Allied strengths and operational situations had radically altered in the latter's favor in the intervening month, transforming what had once been proper caution into something approaching timidity.

59. Postwar interview with the commander of *Panzer Group West*, quoted in Reynolds, *Sons of the Reich*, 60.

60. It must be remembered that only *9 SS Panzer*, the Tiger battalion, and some minor units were available to fight VIII Corps at that time; *10 SS* and most of *21 Panzer Divisions*, as well as the remains of *326 Infantry*, were fully occupied with XXX Corps, which was at last beginning to advance.

61. Reynolds, *Sons of the Reich*, 63, 68–70.

62. By late July, the mission command of *auftragstaktik* was giving way to *befehlstaktik*—strict adherence to orders from the senior commander. In the wake of the 20 July attempt on Hitler's life, disobeying the Führer's orders could pose a serious threat to a general's health, let alone his career prospects. Overcontrol by a distant HQ that was ignorant of tactical and operational realities was swiftly leading *Army Group B* toward disaster.

63. German infantry divisions (with seven battalions to the British nine), less artillery and with little or no armor, routinely held frontages of 15 km (9 miles), and they could expect to be attacked because the enemy held the initiative (conversely, the Germans were in no condition to launch their own attack on XII Corps).

64. Montgomery, *El Alamein to the River Sangro*, 261.

Chapter 4. August: Incomplete Encirclements

1. Principal sources for this section are Martin Blumenson, *United States Army in World War II, the European Theater of Operations: Breakout and Pursuit* (Washington, DC: Office of the Chief of Military History, 1959), chap. 24; Elbridge Colby, *The First Army in Europe 1943–45* (Nashville, TN: Battery Press, 1969), chaps. 6A, 6B; Montgomery of Alamein, *El Alamein to the River Sangro: Normandy to the Baltic* (London: Barrie and Jenkins, 1973), chap. 9; Nigel Hamilton, *Monty, Master of the Battlefield 1942–1944* (London: Hamish Hamilton, 1983), pt. 6, chap. 14; David C. Isby, ed., *Fighting the Breakout: The German Army in Normandy from Cobra to the Falaise Gap* (London: Greenhill Books, 2004), chaps. 6–10; F. H. Hinsley et al., *British Intelligence in the Second World War*, vol. 3, pt. 2 (London: HMSO, 1988); Omar N. Bradley, *A Soldier's Story* (New York: Henry Holt, 1951), 298–303; Mark J. Reardon, *Victory at Mortain: Stopping Hitler's Panzer Counter-offensive* (Law-

rence: University Press of Kansas, 2002); Russell F. Weigley, *Eisenhower's Lieutenants* (Bloomington: Indiana University Press, 1990), 192–201; David W. Hogan, *A Command Post at War: First Army Headquarters in Europe 1943–45* (Honolulu, HI: University Press of the Pacific, 2000), 128–130.

2. The attack grouping comprised *2 SS* (into which the remains of *17 SS Panzer Grenadier* were folded), *116*, and *1 SS Panzer Divisions*, the last of which was delayed in transit; *12 SS* was left in the Caen sector; *21* and *9 SS* were holding the Bluecoat attackers; and the much-depleted *10 SS* was detached from *II SS Panzer Corps* on 7 August to reinforce *XLVII Panzer Corps*. Panzer Lehr was combat ineffective and had been withdrawn for refurbishment. At the time, *9 Panzer* was only just arriving and had to be committed against XV Corps' eastward drive. In all, *LVII Panzer Corps* mustered somewhere between 150 and an unlikely 240 AFVs for the operation (sources differ considerably on the subject, and record keeping was not a top German priority at this time). For comparison, on 1 August 3 Armored Division had 234 medium tanks, 2 Armored had 216, and 2 French Armored had 166; each infantry division had an attached tank (TO&E, 53 medium tanks) and tank destroyer battalion (TO&E, 36 tank destroyers).

3. At the end of July the Führer had actually accepted a proposal for a temporary restoration of the defense, followed by a phased withdrawal. He needed time to organize defense in depth, produce new "wonder weapons," and create new army formations (*volksgrenadier* divisions and panzer brigades). He would buy this time by restoring positional defense in Normandy for a while longer (the army could not conduct maneuver defense), then pull back while implementing a scorched-earth policy and holding port-fortresses until the last round to deny bases to the Allies (the formations so employed were not field-capable anyway). See the transcript of Hitler's often incoherent ramblings about the strategic situation and the treachery of the General Staff at his 31 July daily conference in Helmut Heiber and David M. Glantz, *Hitler and His Generals* (New York: Enigma Books, 2003), 464–468. Within a day he would change his mind and insist that victory in Normandy through a masterly counteroffensive was within his grasp.

4. Even if the Germans had temporarily cut the corridor, SHAEF was prepared to deliver 2,000 tons per day by air to resupply Third Army.

5. According to Patton's diary entry for 7 August: "We got a rumor last night from a secret source that several *panzer* divisions will attack west from . . . Mortain . . . on Avranches. Personally, I think it is a German bluff to cover a withdrawal, but I stopped the 80th, French 2 Armored and 35 [Divisions] in the vicinity of St. Hilaire just in case something might happen." Martin Blumenson, ed., *The Patton Papers* (Bridgewater, NJ: Da Capo Press, 1996), 503. A cynic might suggest that these divisions were merely passing at a fortuitous time and the entry was attributable to the fact that the attack went in during the very early hours of that day; either that or the "secret source" was Ultra.

6. Hamilton, *Monty, Master of the Battlefield*, 784.

7. Principal sources for this section are Blumenson, *US Army in World War II*, chaps. 25–27; Weigley, *Eisenhower's Lieutenants*, chap. 10; Colby, *First Army in Europe*, chaps. 6B, 6C; Bradley, *Soldier's Story*, chap. 18; Hogan, *Command Post at War*, chap. 5; Montgomery, *El Alamein to the River Sangro*, chap. 9; L. F. Ellis, *Victory in the West*, vol. 1, *The Battle of Normandy* (London: HMSO, 1962), chap. 19; Isby, *Fighting the Breakout*, chaps. 6–10; Samuel W. Mitcham, *Panzers in Normandy: General Hans Eberbach and the German Defence of France 1944* (Mechanicsburg, PA: Stackpole Books, 2009), chap. 4; Hinsley et al., *British Intelligence in the Second World War*, 250–268.

8. From 7 August until the end of the month, Ultra kept army and higher HQs well informed in a timely fashion about enemy capabilities and intentions. This may have emboldened Patton and ought to have done the same for Hodges and Bradley, but Haislip had only the comfort of cavalry reconnaissance to his east to mitigate the risks he was running.

9. Ready first, the inexperienced 80 Infantry Division actually started its advance that morning but, owing to faulty staff work, became hopelessly entangled with elements of Haislip's second-echelon 90 Division. By the time the mess was sorted out, new army missions were being worked out.

10. Blumenson, *Patton Papers*, 520.

11. William C. Sylvan and Francis G. Smith, *Normandy to Victory: The War Diary of General Courtney H. Hodges and the First US Army* (Lexington, KY: Association of the US Army, University Press of Kentucky, 2008), 94. VII Corps' advance took only a quarter of the time anticipated because the enemy still lacked the forces to oppose it effectively, despite the long time it took First Army to get around to exploiting the open flank.

12. This section is based primarily on John A. English, *The Canadian Army and the Normandy Campaign: A Study of Failure in High Command* (New York: Praeger, 1991), chap. 11; Brian A. Reid, *No Holding Back: Operation Totalize, Normandy, August 1944* (Toronto: Robin Brass Studio, 2005); Terry Copp, *Fields of Fire: The Canadians in Normandy* (Toronto: Toronto University Press, 2003), chaps. 8, 9; C. P. Stacey, *The Victory Campaign, Operations in North-West Europe, 1944–45: Official History of the Canadian Army in the Second World War*, vol. 3 (Ottawa: Queen's Printer and Controller of Stationery, 1966), chaps. 9, 10; Hubert Meyer, *History of the 12 SS Panzer Division Hitlerjugend* (Winnipeg, MB: J. J. Fedorowicz, 1994), sec. 5; Isby, *Fighting the Breakout*, chaps. 9, 11, 12.

13. Headquarters Second Army, comp., *An Account of the Operations of Second Army in Europe 1944–45* (reprint, MLRS, 2005), 178.

14. Michael Reynolds, *Sons of the Reich, I SS Panzer Corps: Normandy, Arnhem, Ardennes, Eastern Front* (Staplehurst, UK: Spellmount, 2002), 76, 82.

15. War Office records, quoted in Richard Lamb, *Montgomery in Europe, 1943–45—Success or Failure* (London: Buchan and Enright, 1983), 176.

16. It was not until 10 August, however, that the task of closing the trap in con-

junction with the Americans was made explicit to Crerar. Until then, he was under the impression that the southward attack would be followed by an eastward swing toward the Seine at Rouen, as per the original concept.

17. After the phase one attack, 51 Highland Division and 33 Armored Brigade reverted to the command of I British Corps and thereafter moved up on the Canadian corps' left, covering its flank.

18. The lack of progress by 4 Canadian Armored Brigade was explained when Brigadier Booth was found drunk, asleep in his tank. He was allowed to remain in command.

19. Paul Douglas Dickson, *A Thoroughly Canadian General: A Biography of General H. D. G. Crerar* (Toronto: Toronto University Press, 2007), 318–319.

20. Principal sources for this section and the next are Isby, *Fighting the Breakout*, chaps. 11–13; Hinsley et al., *British Intelligence in the Second World War*, 249–273; Mitcham, *Panzers in Normandy*, chap. 6; James A. Wood, *Army of the West: The Weekly Reports of German Army Group B from Normandy to the West Wall* (Mechanicsburg, PA: Stackpole Books, 2007), chap. 5; Weigley, *Eisenhower's Lieutenants*, chaps. 10, 12; Hogan, *Command Post at War*, chap. 5; Blumenson, *US Army in World War II*, chaps. 26–29; Colby, *First Army in Europe*, chaps. 6, 7; Forrest C. Pogue, *The United States Army in World War II, European Theater of Operations: The Supreme Command* (Washington, DC: Office of the Chief of Military History, 1989), chap. 13; Hamilton, *Monty, Master of the Battlefield*, pt. 6, chaps. 14, 15; Ellis, *Victory in the West*, chap. 20; Stacey, *Victory Campaign*, chaps. 10, 12; Martin Blumenson, *The Battle of the Generals* (New York: Quill, William Morrow, 1993), pts. 4, 5.

21. German tank strengths are from Niklas Zetterling, *Normandy 1944: German Military Organization, Combat Power and Organizational Effectiveness* (Winnipeg, MB: J. J. Fedorowicz, 2000); the number of runners in 116 Panzer for 11 August is unknown (eleven days later, there were eighteen), but the division was occupied with a counterpenetration mission at Argentan. How many US AFVs had been knocked out, broken down, or replaced in the brief time the divisions were in action is unknown, but the total establishment strength of the armored divisions and the two independent tank battalions and two tank destroyer battalions was 510 medium tanks and 72 SP tank destroyers.

22. The Führer would describe 15 August as the worst day of his life. Von Kluge had been absent from his HQ for twelve hours; he was actually pinned down by air attacks, his communications destroyed, as he tried to visit subordinates. Hitler suspected a treacherous attempt to surrender his army group. On the same day, American forces reached the Paris-Orléans gap, with nothing to stop them from advancing further, and an Allied army landed in the all-but-defenseless south of France. On 17 August Hitler replaced von Kluge with Field Marshal Walter Model, known as "Hitler's fireman" for his past rescue of doomed forces. He was an ardent Nazi, strong in a crisis (*krisenfest*), and therefore considered reliable. To the Führer's disappointment, Model endorsed von Kluge's assessment of the situation: "Roads are virtually impass-

able, tanks are repeatedly immobilized from lack of fuel, ammunition supplies are erratic, troops are hungry and exhausted and communications almost non-existent." With the unanimous support of his army commanders, he demanded a pullback to the Seine. Partly because he trusted Model, and partly because other developments invalidated a further defense of Normandy anyway, Hitler bowed to the inevitable.

23. Bradley later maintained that the Germans had largely escaped from the pocket by 14 August. This assertion directly contradicted the main reason he gave for halting at Argentan; in addition, reports from Ultra, tactical SIGINT, and air reconnaissance all indicated that, as 21 Army Group accepted, few fighting elements had been withdrawn. First Army's intelligence assessment concurred in this judgment. Admittedly, however, it was possible (though incorrect) to interpret senior German commanders' desire for a retreat to be a reflection of what was actually happening.

24. Terry Copp, *Montgomery's Scientists: Operational Research in Northwest Europe* (Winnipeg, MB: Wilfred Laurier University, 2000), 183–187. The destroyed vehicles included pre-August losses, but totals underestimated by up to 50 percent for AFVs and 30 percent for SSVs, as No. 2 ORS analysts did not explore all the secondary roads and tracks in their search for casualties. No attempt was made to assess the destruction of the vast amount of horse-drawn transport on which the Germans relied.

25. Bradley had suggested the Americans provide transport to move two British divisions around First Army to attack on the Dreux-Mantes axis toward Rouen (thus freeing his entire army group for a drive to the east). This idea was not adopted, as it would have involved much delay, no doubt aggravated by traffic and administrative chaos.

26. This section is based on Blumenson, *US Army in World War II*, 590–618; Colby, *First Army in Europe*, 86–89; Stephan T. Wishnevsky, *Courtney Hicks Hodges* (Jefferson, NC: McFarland, 2006), 122–123; Bradley, *Soldier's Story*, 310–328; Weigley, *Eisenhower's Lieutenants*, 249–252; Henry Maule, *Out of the Sand: The Epic Story of General Leclerc and the Fighting Free French* (London: Odhams, 1966), chaps. 9, 10; Carlo D'Este, *Eisenhower: Allied Supreme Commander* (London: Weidenfeld and Nicolson, 2003), 573–577.

27. Quoted in Blumenson, *Battle of the Generals*, 242.

28. RAF Bombing Analysis Unit Report No. 44. The Germans' success in extricating such large numbers is comparable, albeit on a greater scale, to their withdrawal of *XIV Panzer Corps* from Sicily over the Straits of Messina on 1–17 August the year before. There, they managed to get out 39,951 men and 14,772 wounded, 51 tanks, 9,789 vehicles, 163 guns, and 18,665 tons of ammunition and equipment. The four divisions thus saved provided the core of the defense of Italy.

29. Allied statistics are from Ellis, *Victory in the West*; German ones are from Zetterling, *Normandy 1944*, chaps. 4, 7. Exaggerated numbers continue to be turned out, even in recent works such as Anthony Beevor, *D-Day: The Battle for Normandy* (London: Viking [Penguin], 2009), 522.

30. Wood, *Army of the West*, 209. Model's 24 and 29 August reports to the Führer, cited in full, give his bleak assessment of Allied strengths and likely courses of action and German capabilities and options.

31. VIII Corps was placed in reserve and subsequently stripped of all but minimal transport to provide adequate mobility and logistic support for the rest of the army in the fast-moving, post-Normandy operations.

32. British formations had become adept at long and sometimes complicated moves by road, a not inconsiderable achievement. But movement is not synonymous with maneuver. The preplanned moving up of formations to fight a set-piece battle is very different from the ad hoc, improvised moves and short-notice changes in direction required in the rapidly changing situations of fluid battles developing over wide areas where there is no clearly defined front line.

33. The idea of creating APCs had been suggested by O'Connor, VIII Corps' commander, prior to Operation Goodwood. However, his army commander, Dempsey, displayed no enthusiasm for the concept.

34. Dickson, *Thoroughly Canadian General*, 305.

35. A limiting factor was the fact that 84 Group, designated to support First Canadian Army, was still flying most of its twenty-six squadrons (twenty-three of them fighters) out of bases in England, thanks to the ground forces' failure to capture enough airfield sites earlier in the campaign (causing much of Tedder's and Coningham's resentment of Montgomery). Moreover, the group HQ remained in England until 10 August. All Canadian requests for air support had to go through HQ 83 Group, which was colocated with HQ Second Army. However, below 2 Tactical Air Force (TAF) level, army-RAF relations were good, and the latter was willing to help despite the somewhat bureaucratic procedures laid down by 2 Tactical Air Force. Had Crerar or, better, Montgomery on his behalf pushed for priority, a major, sustained tactical air effort for Operation Totalize could have been laid on.

36. This is not to argue with the benefit of a hindsight that revealed the completeness of success that attended the first-echelon attack. If it had been followed by prompt, vigorous reconnaissance, the weakness of the German defense in the tactical depth would have been revealed. But such reconnaissance was prevented by the bomb line for phase two.

37. Students of Soviet military art will recognize the concept of the forward detachment, an essential component of deep battle. While main bodies were carrying out the breakthrough, smallish, highly mobile and maneuverable forward detachments would be inserted to push ahead to secure potential enemy defensive positions in depth or choke points before they could be defended. In this way, the initiative and momentum would be firmly retained. Of course, a forward detachment might become embroiled with enemy reserves and fail to reach its objective. Even so, it would contribute to operational tempo by providing aggressive reconnaissance and simultaneously preventing the enemy from meeting the main forces with an organized and balanced countermove.

38. *LXXXVI Corps* comprised the static, small, and ineffective *711 Infantry Division* on the coastal sector; the seriously weakened *346 Infantry Division* inland (although the flooded river Dives aided its defense); and the below-strength *272 Infantry Division*. Mobility was restricted, and armor strength was apparently limited to the seven assault guns available to *346 Division*.

39. Montgomery wrote scathingly that Crerar "seemed to have gained the idea that all you want is a good initial fire plan and then all the Germans run away!" He did not realize that "battles seldom go completely as planned." English, *Canadian Army and the Normandy Campaign*, 268.

40. Both quotations are from Kurt Meyer, *Grenadiers* (Winnipeg, MB: J. J. Fedorowicz, 1994), 159. It was rare for British and almost unheard of for Canadian or American division or corps commanders to be seen in the front line during intense combat. Apart from Patton, Allied army commanders did not go below formation-level HQs. This was perhaps the main reason they did not develop the sort of fingertip feel for the course of battle evidenced by the likes of Eberbach of *Fifth Panzer Army*, who conferred with *Panzer* Meyer within 5 km (3 miles) of a collapsing front at the moment of crisis on 8 August.

41. On 1 August the army's G2 wrote: "It is doubtful that the German forces in Normandy can continue for more than four to eight weeks as a military machine. . . . Surrender or a disastrous retreat will be the alternative for the German forces. In the next four to eight weeks the current situation may change with dramatic suddenness into a race to reach a chaotic Germany." Blumenson, *US Army in World War II*, 442. Colonel Dickson was correct in thinking a withdrawal to the Seine or beyond would be difficult and costly for an unmechanized army in the face of a more mobile enemy with command of the air, although forces from *Fifteenth Army* and elsewhere could prepare a stop line of sorts to check the pursuit. His prediction about time also proved to be largely correct, but mainly because the enemy made major, unforced, and unforeseeable mistakes.

42. Sylvan and Smith, *Normandy to Victory*, 78. In his diary entry for 23 July, Patton acerbically commented: "I am also nauseated by the fact that Hodges and Bradley state that all human virtue depends on knowing infantry tactics. I know that no general officer and practically no colonel needs to know any tactics. Tactics belong to battalion commanders. If generals knew less tactics, they would interfere less." Blumenson, *Patton Papers*, 486. Though intemperate, he showed a proper understanding of the need for operational-level thinking and decision making and for maneuver and tempo in the attack.

43. On 8 August Patton wrote to his wife: "I am the only one who realizes how little the enemy can do—he is finished." The next day he wrote: "If I were on my own, I would take bigger chances than I am now permitted to take." Blumenson, *Patton Papers*, 504–505. Patton's instinct, his "feel" for the operational situation, was better than Bradley's or Hodges's. Of course, his nature inclined him to think thus. In September, similar optimism was to prove unfounded.

44. Patton persisted in the belief that Montgomery sought glory and fame at his expense. This was a classic case of projection. Montgomery's judgments were driven by professional military and not personal considerations, and he was pleased with the rapid advances of Third Army. Patton misread Bradley's caution and occasionally prejudice for British interference.

45. Bradley also mandated a screening force to cover the Loire against sorties into the Americans' southern flank. Patton regarded this diversion of two formations "against a doubtful attack" as overly cautious, believing (rightly) that screening could be accomplished by XIX Tactical Air Command, cavalry, and the FFI. The enemy south of the river was weak and lacked both armor and mobility—in short, he was powerless.

46. Bradley, *Soldier's Story*, 307.

47. Patton's focus on destroying enemy forces would be frustrated again when his suggestion for another encirclement by Third Army north of Paris was ignored by Bradley.

48. He also had some difficulties inculcating his risk-taking philosophy into some of his corps commanders with an infantry background. For instance, Middleton (VIII Corps) was uncomfortable with the far-flung objectives he was assigned in Brittany, and Eddy (XII Corps) asked how worried he should be about his flanks when ordered, on 21 August, to seize bridgeheads over the Yonne, south of Paris (Patton replied that it depended on how nervous he was by nature).

49. Bradley, *Soldier's Story*, 283–284.

50. All that remained to *XXV Corps* was, as Ultra made clear, the very understrength 2 *Parachute Division* (less than 8,000 strong, immobile, and deficient in much equipment); 265, 266, and 343 *Infantry Divisions*, all of which had lost substantial (and its most combat-capable) elements in Normandy; and the small and ineffective remains of 77 *Infantry* and 91 *Airlanding Divisions*, both all but destroyed in Normandy before retreating into Brittany. Zetterling, *Normandy 1944*, divisional entries.

51. A year earlier in Sicily, Montgomery had persuaded 15 Army Group's commander, General Alexander, arbitrarily and without consultation, to change boundaries and reassign a crucial road to his Eighth Army. Patton and Bradley, the American commanders whose plans were thrown into disarray just as success was being realized, were understandably outraged; memory of the affront lingered.

52. Bradley, *Soldier's Story*, 305. According to Bradley, XV Corps had been stretched over 65 km (40 miles). But the distance from Falaise to the Forêt d'Ecouves obstacle was only about 30 km (18 miles), and XX Corps was not far to the south.

53. In his memoirs, Bradley sought to blame Montgomery's excessive caution and incompetence. Bradley, *Soldier's Story*, 304–305; Omar N. Bradley and Clay Blair, *A General's Life* (New York: Simon and Schuster, 1983), 298–301.

54. Bradley, *Soldier's Story*, 309. It was not uncommon for the aim of destruction to become subordinated to the lure of spectacular territorial gains. In May 1944, for

example, Lieutenant General Mark Clark failed to exploit his breakout from the Anzio bridgehead to cut off the retreat of German *Tenth Army*, despite the clear order and intent of his army group commander, who sought a battle of annihilation. Clark wanted the glory awaiting the general who became the first to enter Rome, and he changed his VI Corps' axis ninety degrees to seize it. See C. J. C. Molony et al., *The Mediterranean and the Middle East*, vol. 6, pt. 1 (London: HMSO, 1984), 287–290; Carlo D'Este, *Fatal Decision: Anzio and the Battle for Rome* (New York: HarperCollins, 1991), chap. 21.

55. Bradley, Hodges, and Patton all hoped to get through the West Wall before the Germans could refurbish and man the fortifications. But, as it soon became clear, hope is not a method.

56. Whatever the rationalizations in favor of Anvil/Dragoon, the fact is that Marshall (and Eisenhower) had settled on it as a means of emasculating the Italian campaign and concentrating overwhelming force in the main theatre, the traditional American way in war.

57. Quoted in Roland G. Ruppenthal, *United States Army in World War II, the European Theater of Operations: Logistical Support of the Armies*, vol. 2 (Washington, DC: Office of the Chief of Military History, 1959), 474.

58. Dwight D. Eisenhower, *Crusade in Europe* (London: Heinemann, 1948), 305.

59. Montgomery was not the only ally to try Eisenhower's patience. From his arrival in North Africa the year before, the French had been a source of constant difficulty and irritation. This came to a head (though not for the last time) on 20 August, when de Gaulle demanded that Leclerc's division be allowed to liberate Paris immediately in the name of the Free French cause. Although President Roosevelt was antipathetic to recognizing a de Gaulle government, Eisenhower showed a pragmatic acceptance of the need for Allied unity, a refusal to allow political considerations to endanger his campaign, and strength of character when he dealt with the Frenchman as de facto head of state. He backed the diversion of Leclerc and shortly afterward acceded to de Gaulle's request for an American show of strength to cow the strong communist elements in the capital.

60. Blumenson, *Battle of the Generals*, 258.

Chapter 5. September: Operational Ideas and Developments on the Ground

1. The material in this section and the next is based on Martin Blumenson, *United States Army in World War II, the European Theater of Operations: Breakout and Pursuit* (Washington, DC: Office of the Chief of Military History, 1959), chaps. 30–32; Charles B. MacDonald, *United States Army in World War II, European Theater of Operations: The Siegfried Line Campaign* (Washington, DC: Office of the Chief of Military History, 1961), chaps. 1, 2; Forrest C. Pogue, *The United States Army in World War II, European Theater of Operations: The Supreme Command* (Wash-

ington, DC: Office of the Chief of Military History, 1989), chaps. 14, 16; L. F. Ellis, *Victory in the West*, vol. 1, *The Battle of Normandy* (London: HMSO, 1962), chap. 21, and vol. 2, *The Defeat of Germany* (London: HMSO, 1968), chap. 1; Montgomery of Alamein, *Memoirs* (London: Collins, 1958,), chap. 15; Omar N. Bradley, *A Soldier's Story* (New York: Henry Holt, 1951), chaps. 19, 20; D. K. R. Crosswell, *The Chief of Staff: The Military Career of General Walter Bedell Smith* (Westport, CT: Greenwood Press, 1991), chap. 12. This description of the concepts and their evolution is a reduction to essentials and a simplification of a complex series of meetings, conferences, letters, and directives.

2. The airmen liked to have about 75 percent of their fighter-bomber fields within about 100 km (60 miles) of the front line to ensure a rapid reaction to requests for air support and a fast turnaround time for the aircraft involved.

3. The West Wall—or Siegfried Line, as the Allies persisted in calling it—was constructed in 1938–1939. It comprised antitank obstacles (artificial and natural) backed by more than 3,000 concrete pillboxes, observation posts, and shelters. At least in part because of highly effective German propaganda, the Allies considerably exaggerated its effectiveness as a defensive barrier. Four years of neglect following the German victory in 1940, exacerbated by stripping out everything (e.g., mines and barbed wire) that could be used to create the Atlantic Wall, had left the fortifications in disrepair. Moreover, the better armor protection of tanks had led to bigger antitank guns, so the positions could not accommodate the weapons of 1944 and were obsolete. Never intended to do anything more than delay the invader until strong mobile reserves could be assembled for a counterattack, the line required one infantry division every 10 km (6 miles) to hold it. In the late summer of 1944, there were neither the formations nor the reserves to defend it.

4. First Allied Airborne Army was commanded by Lieutenant General Lewis H. Brereton, an Air Corps officer of limited abilities. It comprised two British and three US airborne divisions (although 6 Division was not released from Normandy for refitting until early September), as well as a British air-landing division and a Polish parachute brigade.

5. How the figure of forty divisions was arrived at is unclear. Excluding the airborne army, the Anglo-Canadian contingent mustered fourteen armored and infantry divisions and eight independent armored brigades at the beginning of September; 12 Army Group totaled twenty-one divisions, with another one entering combat in September and five in October. Some forces would need to be left south of the Ardennes to cover Paris and the right flank of the great thrust, and the Brittany ports were still a SHAEF priority. And as Montgomery correctly argued all along, the simultaneous logistic support of every division was impossible.

6. Montgomery, *Memoirs*, 266–267.

7. Bradley, *Soldier's Story*, 321–322.

8. The nomenclature Northern, Central, and Southern for 21, 12, and 6 Army Groups, respectively, was adopted to avoid attaching national designations.

9. On 9 September Lieutenant General William Simpson's Ninth Army HQ took command of VIII Corps and the reduction of Brest, relieving Patton of the headache of commanding operations 850 km (525 miles) apart and freeing him to concentrate on the offensive to the east.

10. Nigel Hamilton, *Monty, Master of the Battlefield, 1942–1944* (London: Hamish Hamilton, 1983), 51.

11. The sole witness to the meeting, Tedder, the Deputy Supreme Commander (and no friend of Montgomery or his ideas), was quite clear on this. He believed the main result of the discussion was to ensure that the Ruhr thrust would get proper priority it deserved. Arthur Tedder, *With Prejudice* (Boston: Little, Brown, 1966), 591; Hamilton, *Monty, Master of the Battlefield*, 49.

12. Quoted in Ellis, *Victory in the West*, 2:25–26.

13. Ibid., 77.

14. Quoted in Montgomery, *Memoirs*, 280–281.

15. Ibid., 282. He added the complacent, self-congratulatory comment that Eisenhower had made the right decision exactly one month too late (harking back to his proposal of 23 August).

16. This section is based primarily on F. H. Hinsley et al., *British Intelligence in the Second World War*, vol. 3, pt. 2 (London: HMSO, 1988), chap. 51; David Bennett, *A Magnificent Disaster: The Failure of Market Garden, the Arnhem Operation September 1944* (Newbury, UK: Casemate, 2008), chap. 5; Canadian General Staff, *Report No. 77, German Operations from Falaise to the Ardennes (20 August–16 December 1944)* (1958; reprint, MLRS, 2005); James A. Wood, *Army of the West: The Weekly Reports of German Army Group B from Normandy to the West Wall* (Mechanicsburg, PA: Stackpole Books, 2007), chap. 6.

17. Hinsley et al., *British Intelligence in the Second World War*, 367–375.

18. There was a persistent failure to understand the extent to which the Allies' demand for "unconditional surrender" reinforced the Nazis' hold over Germany by denying another way out. Likewise, there was an overestimate of the likelihood of strategic bombing causing such a collapse of civilian and military morale that revolution rather than a coup could lead to regime change.

19. As both German and Allied commanders knew very well, no substantial forces could be redeployed from other fronts to restore the situation. In the east, from late June to August, the Wehrmacht suffered disasters of cumulatively much greater scale than Normandy and lost well over twice as many casualties. Two panzer grenadier divisions, however, were taken from Italy to check Patton's headlong advance to the very gates of the Reich. German sources succinctly summarized the force available in the west as of 5 September as follows: divisions capable of offensive action—thirteen infantry and three panzer or panzer grenadier, plus two panzer brigades; partially fit—twelve infantry; refitting—nine infantry and one panzer, plus two panzer brigades; not combat capable—fourteen infantry and seven panzer or panzer grenadier; refitting—nine infantry; dissolved—seven infantry.

20. The Allied description of German forces in the south as *Army Group G* was a misunderstanding and misnaming of the formation. It was, in fact, an *armeegruppe*—in Wehrmacht parlance, an undersized army. It was elevated to *heeresgruppe* (army group) status on 11 September, when *First* and *Fifth Panzer Armies* joined *Nineteenth Army* under its command.

21. At the beginning of September, German fighter strength in the west stood at no more than 420 aircraft and the bomber force at 175. All of them had declining combat value and were manned by aircrews with generally low skill levels and plummeting morale. The Luftwaffe was compelled to withdraw into Germany, suffering grievous losses in men and equipment as it did so. Given the dearth of servicing facilities and fuel, air operations were all but suspended. The Allied airborne assault in the Netherlands posed such a threat that almost the whole force defending the Reich was temporarily diverted to counter it, but even so, the Luftwaffe could manage no more than 250 sorties per day (and 100 bomber sorties were flown over two nights—the last appearance of the bomber force in the west). By the late summer of 1944, the Luftwaffe's contribution to the defense of the west was worth no more than a footnote. Air Historical Branch, *Rise and Fall of the German Air Force* (reprint, Poole, UK: Arms and Armour Press, 1987), 339–340.

22. The West Wall had been long forgotten by senior officers, and *First Army* had to ask its superior HQ where it was sited in the army's area; the reply suggested asking an officer in Kaiserslautern for the information.

23. The strength of the corps, most of it located just north and northeast of Arnhem, was relevant to Operation Market Garden and is worth detailing. It was very weak, each division being about 3,000 men strong: *9 SS Panzer Division* was preparing to move back to Germany for refitting and had handed over most of its heavy equipment to *10 SS Panzer*, retaining eleven weak alarm companies, its reconnaissance battalion with thirty-one light AFVs, and a panzer and an escort battalion each with a few AFVs. Its companion division mustered a similar-sized reconnaissance battalion, four understrength grenadier battalions, two artillery and one flak battalions, and sixteen Mk IV tanks and StuGs; one grenadier battalion and one artillery battalion were sent to Eindhoven to join the antitank battalion with twenty-one SP antitank and twelve 40mm towed guns. Michael Reynolds, *Sons of the Reich, II SS Panzer Corps: Normandy, Arnhem, Ardennes, Eastern Front* (Staplehurst, UK: Spellmount, 2002), chap. 12.

24. Wood, *Army of the West*, 214–216.

25. In its desperate search for forces to replace its horrendous losses and re-create a front, the Wehrmacht was forced into increasingly desperate expedients. Many units and formations consisted of a hodgepodge of companies and battalions of stragglers, replacements, convalescents, and semi-invalids; overage and noncombat troops; and other unpromising front-line personnel, thrown together in ad hoc groupings named after their commanders. For instance, *Division von Tettau*, which fought at Arnhem, had a small security regiment, two security battalions (one SS),

an SS NCO school, a Dutch SS-surveillance battalion, three battalions of naval and air force ground staff personnel, a parachute training and replacement battalion, an artillery battalion acting as infantry, a police company, and some light flak weapons. The defenders of Walcheren and part of the Albert Canal line were *70 Infantry* and *176 Training and Replacement* (later *Infantry*) *Divisions*, largely comprising the medically unfit grouped into units according to their complaint (e.g., eye, stomach ulcer, and ear battalions); *Division No. 462*, which defended Metz, comprised an officer candidate and an NCO school, a small rear-area security regiment, a couple of replacement battalions, and a few former Soviet guns towed by horses from a veterinary hospital.

26. The *volksgrenadier* divisions were mostly built around cadres of the shattered remnants of burned out infantry divisions. They were small (10,000 men) and abundantly equipped with automatic weapons but light on artillery, and they often lacked their proper complement of antitank weapons. They were organized around small cadres of hardened veteran soldiers, NCOs, and officers and then bulked out with anything the Replacement Army could get its hands on. Redundant personnel of the shrinking navy and air force, wounded soldiers from broken formations returning to duty from hospitals, older men who would have been considered too old or too unfit for the peacetime army, workers taken from hitherto reserved occupations, and teenagers were recruited into the ranks. The panzer brigades were usually based on the remains of panzer divisions. They comprised, in theory, one to two tank battalions, one to two infantry battalions, and companies of engineers, air defense, and assault guns. Most were very hastily thrown together with utterly inadequate unit or even subunit and individual training; they sometimes went into battle with tanks delivered straight from the factory to the assembly area.

27. Roland G. Ruppenthal, *United States Army in World War II, the European Theater of Operations: Logistical Support of the Armies*, vol. 1 (Washington, DC: Office of the Chief of Military History, 1953), 481–488.

28. Quoted in John A. Adams, *The Battle for Western Europe, Fall 1944* (Bloomington: Indiana University Press, 2010), 10.

29. The main sources for this section are MacDonald, *US Army in World War II*, chaps. 6–11; Ellis, *Victory in the West*, vol. 2, chaps. 1–4; C. P. Stacey, *The Victory Campaign, Operations in North-West Europe, 1944–45: Official History of the Canadian Army in the Second World War*, vol. 3 (Ottawa: Queen's Printer and Controller of Stationery, 1966), chaps. 12, 13; Headquarters Second Army, comp., *An Account of the Operations of Second Army in Europe 1944–45* (reprint, MLRS, 2005), chap. 4; Headquarters 21 Army Group, comp., *Administrative History of the Operations of 21 Army Group on the Continent of Europe, 6 June 1944–8 May 1945* (Germany: 21 Army Group, 1945), secs. 3, 4; P. B. Randel, *A Short History of 30 Corps, 1945* (reprint, MLRS, 2006), chaps. 2, 3; Terry Copp, *Cinderella Army, The Canadians in Northwest Europe, 1944–45* (Toronto: Toronto University Press, 2006), chaps. 1, 2; Brian Horrocks, *Corps Commander* (London: Sidgwick and Jackson, 1977), chaps.

5–7; T. B. H. Otway, *Airborne Forces* (1951; reprint, London: Imperial War Museum, 1990), chaps. 16, 20; Geoffrey Powell, *The Devil's Birthday, The Bridges to Arnhem 1944* (Barnsley, UK: Leo Cooper, 1984); Bennett, *Magnificent Disaster*, chaps. 4–14; William F. Buckingham, *Arnhem 1944* (Stroud, UK: Tempus, 2004), chaps. 6–20; G. S. Jackson, *Operations of Eighth Corps: Account of Operations from Normandy to the River Rhine* (London: St. Clements Press, 1948), chap. 5; Reynolds, *Sons of the Reich*, chaps. 11–19.

30. M-520 of 26 August, quoted in Blumenson, *US Army in World War II*, 671.

31. Along with much heavy and medium artillery, VIII Corps' HQ and three divisions were grounded, as most of its transport had been withdrawn to augment the logistic support of XII and XXX Corps.

32. Ellis, *Victory in the West*, 2:26–27.

33. Allied ground forces commanders had developed a mind-set that would not contemplate an attack on a fortified area without a massive preliminary aerial bombardment. Neither at Le Havre nor Boulogne, Calais nor Brest, the Metz forts nor the West Wall near Aachen did it produce material damage remotely commensurate with the effort involved or the soldiers' expectations. It did have some effect on enemy morale, however, especially against low-grade troops.

34. The Willems and Wilhelmina Canal at Zon and Veghel was approximately 25 to 30 m (30 to 35 yards) wide; the Maas-Waal Canal was almost 70 m (80 yards) wide. The Maas at Grave was 260 m (285 yards) wide, the Waal at Nijmegen was over 280 m (305 yards), and the Rhine at Arnhem about 100 m (110 yards) in summer.

35. Brereton was a commander of questionable competence, shuffled from command of Ninth Air Force to do a job he knew nothing about. Browning was a poor choice at the corps level: two-thirds of his command was American, and his US counterpart, Ridgway, had plenty of practical airborne experience, whereas Browning had none; besides, his HQ was a planning, administrative, and training organization, not a field HQ.

36. In the event, Urquhart, the commander of 1 Airborne Division, remained out of touch with his own HQ until his return on the morning of 19 September, after an absence of more than thirty-six hours. The inadequate airborne radios failed him, and he stayed far too long with the forward troops and became cut off by the Germans. (The rear link to the United Kingdom was pretty much the only radio communications the division had working, so such a request would have been possible.)

37. The Allies were lucky to take the road bridge intact, as Model had ordered that it be retained for possible countermoves. When the commander on the ground attempted to defy this order at the last minute, he discovered that the charges did not work, and it was too late to rectify the problem.

38. Up to the time the Nijmegen road bridge was taken, Guards casualties in the operation totaled 130. During the course of the entire operation, the whole of XXX Corps suffered 1,480 casualties, 82 Airborne lost 1,432, 101 Airborne lost 2,110, and 1 Airborne and the Polish brigade together lost 8,068.

39. Principal sources for this section are Elbridge Colby, *The First Army in Europe 1943–45* (Nashville, TN: Battery Press, 1969), chap. 7; John Nelson Rickard, *Patton at Bay: The Lorraine Campaign September to December 1944* (Westport, CT: Praeger, 1999), chaps. 4, 5; Blumenson, *US Army in World War II*, chaps. 30–32; Hugh M. Cole, *United States Army in World War II, the European Theater of Operations: The Lorraine Campaign* (Washington, DC: Office of the Chief of Military History, 1984), chaps. 1–5; MacDonald, *US Army in World War II*, chaps. 2–4; David W. Hogan, *A Command Post at War: First Army Headquarters in Europe 1943–45* (Honolulu, HI: University Press of the Pacific, 2000), chap. 5; Russell F. Weigley, *Eisenhower's Lieutenants* (Bloomington: Indiana University Press, 1990), chaps. 13, 14; J. Lawton Collins, *Lightning Joe, an Autobiography* (Baton Rouge: Louisiana State University Press, 1979), chap. 13; Adams, *Battle for Western Europe*, chaps. 5, 6.

40. Hodges quoted in Colby, *First Army in Europe*, 91.

41. Joachim Ludewig, *Rückzug: The German Retreat from France, 1944* (Lexington: University Press of Kentucky, 2012), 220.

42. Hogan, *Command Post at War*, chaps. 5, 6, gives a good picture of First Army's logistic position, including day-by-day inventories of critical items, and of Hodges's attitude toward the subject.

43. MacDonald, *US Army in World War II*, 62.

44. Hinsley et al., *British Intelligence in the Second World War*, 375.

45. At the resumption of the offensive, XII Corps could advance with only two divisions, as the third was guarding the extensive open flank to the south until it was released on 10 September. It was almost a week more before XV Corps' two divisions deployed on XII Corps' right flank.

46. The corps started into Brittany with two armored divisions, two infantry divisions, and a cavalry group. After being repulsed from Lorient and St. Nazaire but taking Nantes on 12 August, 4 Armored went east to join XII Corps. After failing to take Brest, 6 Armored remained in the peninsula in a static containment role until it was sent to screen the southern flank of Third Army on 12 September. Two infantry divisions reinforced VIII Corps from First Army (on 18 and 21 August) to enable it to reduce Brest. The corps was transferred to Ninth Army, shortly after its activation, on 10 September.

47. Steve R. Waddell, *United States Army Logistics: The Normandy Campaign 1944* (Westport, CT: Greenwood Press, 1994), 117.

48. Principal sources for this section are Ellis, *Victory in the West*, vol. 2, chaps. 4, 5; Pogue, *US Army in World War II*, chaps. 16, 17; MacDonald, *US Army in World War II*, chap. 11; Cole, *US Army in World War II*, chaps. 6, 7; Hogan, *Command Post at War*, chap. 6; Edward G. Miller, *A Dark and Bloody Ground: The Hürtgen Forest and the Roer River Dams 1944–45* (College Station: Texas A&M University Press, 1995), chaps. 3, 14.

49. Although failure to accept the reality of culmination is always counterproductive and can have very adverse consequences (as the Germans found at Moscow in

1941 and the Soviets discovered at Kharkov in 1942 and again in 1943), it is comparatively rare for senior commanders to have the insight and honesty to do so. Much more common is the reaction: "just one more effort and we shall triumph." Moltke justified the syndrome: "The decision of a battle begins when one side gives up the battle as lost. Many times battles have been won because the enemy believed himself beaten before the victor did.... In case of doubt one must therefore persist." Daniel J. Hughes, ed., *Moltke on the Art of War: Selected Writings* (New York: Presidio, 1993), 132. The concept of the culminating point is perhaps of more use to theoreticians and historians than to commanders at war.

50. On 9 October Eisenhower telegraphed him: "I must repeat, we are now squarely up against the situation which we have anticipated for months; our intake into Continent will not support our battle. All operations will come to a standstill unless Antwerp is producing by middle of November. I must emphasize that I consider Antwerp of first importance of all our endeavors on entire front from Switzerland to Channel. I believe your personal attention is required in operations designed to clear entrance." Quoted in Ellis, *Victory in the West*, 2:85.

51. Sixth Army Group had advanced about 650 km (400 miles) in scarcely a month since landing on the French Riviera on 15 August. It finally succumbed, as did the forces from Normandy, to a shortage of transport and fuel and culminated in October. Before it did so, however, it inflicted massive losses on *Army Group G*, including forces in the southwest of France. The Germans lost more than 143,000 men, mostly prisoners, but *Nineteenth Army* was not destroyed. Although it suffered grievously, it was able to form a coherent defense of the Vosges mountains and the Belfort gap at their southern end.

52. In late October Bradley had moved Ninth Army's area of responsibility to north of Aachen, arranging an exchange of formations between the First and Ninth. This was done so that if Eisenhower decided to put an American army under Montgomery's command, it would not be Hodges's army.

53. According to von Rundstedt's report to the OKW in mid-October, the *Army of the West* had lost about 150,000 men between 1 September and 15 October but had received 152,000 replacements (of course, most of them were poorly trained and of limited quality). In the same period, 86,000 men had been withdrawn for the refitting of formations and the activation of new ones. Thus the situation remained very precarious. He had to defend a front more than 1,000 km (620 miles) long with the equivalent strength of only twenty-seven infantry and six and a half panzer divisions, and he requested eight additional infantry divisions and one panzer division over and above those already promised. Danny S. Parker, *The Battle of the Bulge, the German View: Perspectives from Hitler's High Command* (London: Greenhill Books, 1999), 22–60.

54. November saw a great diminution of the supply crisis but a worsening of personnel shortages in certain critical areas, especially combat infantrymen. The flow of replacements had failed to keep up with losses, and US divisions were forced to fight

at reduced and diminishing strengths. Combat exhaustion rates rose, and combat effectiveness fell in many cases.

55. Ellis, *Victory in the West*, 2:166. Montgomery reprised his arguments for concentration on a main effort north of the Ardennes, with him in full command of it. Eisenhower rejected both his assessment and his remedy. Thus, the conceptual debate dragged on inconclusively until the German counteroffensive turned minds to other matters.

Chapter 6. Logistic Realities

1. This section is based primarily on Steve R. Waddell, *United States Army Logistics: The Normandy Campaign 1944* (Westport, CT: Greenwood Press, 1994), chaps. 5–7; Martin Van Creveld, *Supplying War: Logistics from Wallenstein to Patton* (New York: Cambridge University Press, 1977), chap. 7; Alan Gropman, ed., *The Big L: American Logistics in World War II* (Washington, DC: National Defense University, 1997), chap. 7; Roland G. Ruppenthal, *United States Army in World War II, the European Theater of Operations: Logistical Support of the Armies*, vol. 1 (Washington, DC: Office of the Chief of Military History, 1953), chaps. 11–14, and vol. 2 (Washington, DC: Office of the Chief of Military History, 1959), chaps. 1–6; Headquarters 21 Army Group, comp., *Administrative History of the Operations of 21 Army Group on the Continent of Europe, 6 June 1944–8 May 1945* (Germany: 21 Army Group, 1945), chap. 3; Headquarters Second Army, comp., *An Account of the Operations of Second Army in Europe 1944–45* (reprint, MLRS, 2005), 205–210, 276–282.

2. Of course, Allied concepts of scarcity would have been regarded as abundance by the Germans, who were facing a *materielschlacht* in which they could not compete.

3. Carlo D'Este, *Decision in Normandy* (London: Collins, 1983), 254–263; C. P. Stacey, *The Victory Campaign, Operations in North-West Europe, 1944–45: Official History of the Canadian Army in the Second World War*, vol. 3 (Ottawa: Queen's Printer and Controller of Stationery, 1966), 284–285, 630–633; Ruppenthal, *US Army in World War II*, vol. 1, chap. 11, and vol. 2, chap. 11.

4. A "day of supply" was the estimated average daily consumption of an item. For example, a day of supply of POL was the quantity needed to move every vehicle in an army 80 km (50 miles) in a day. A "unit of fire" was a quantity of ammunition used to measure stock levels in army depots and to establish a permitted level of expenditure; it represented a specified number of rounds per weapon (e.g., 125 rounds for a 105mm howitzer, 75 rounds for a 155mm, 50 rounds for an 8 inch).

5. Ruppenthal, *US Army in World War II*, 1:306–308. When giving tonnages in tables, Ruppenthal specifies that they are "long tons" (i.e., the British unit). In the text he merely refers to "tons." It is unclear whether he is consistent in his units of measurement. The Soviets used metric tonnes.

6. Principal sources for the section are Ruppenthal, *US Army in World War II*,

vol. 1, chap. 5; Waddell, *US Army Logistics*, chap. 1; Van Creveld, *Supplying War*, chap. 7; Gropman, *Big L*, 368–383.

7. Logistics remained a national responsibility throughout the war. The British, with a clear chain of command and unambiguous responsibilities and duties at each level, remained free of the problems that bedeviled US efforts.

8. The failure to provide adequate clothing for cold and wet conditions presumably had something to do with the doubling of the nonbattle casualty rate from October to November and December (from 28,364 to 56,261 and 56,695), exacerbating the infantry manpower problem. The soldiers had undergone the same privations in Italy the winter before. The American insistence on keeping formations almost continuously in the line inevitably led to a significant incidence of problems such as trench foot.

9. Ruppenthal, *US Army in World War II*, 1:445–450.

10. Such formation requirements are averages; in defense, about 20 percent less would generally suffice, and pursuit could require as little as half as much. Merely meeting daily requirements did not, however, allow for the accumulation of stocks (especially of ammunition) required for breakthrough operations. There seems to have been a disconnect between SHAEF's perception of needs and COMZ's, with the former reckoning on 650 tons per day per divisional slice and the latter 800. This might be due to differing definitions of what the slice comprised or the phase of operations considered.

11. Ruppenthal, *US Army in World War II*, 2:18, 1:464–467. The figures exclude the delivery of POL in bulk, as this does not normally enter into estimates of port discharge requirements or capacity; by the beginning of September, bulk fuel deliveries were expected to exceed 13,000 tons per day.

12. Memo quoted in Ruppenthal, *US Army in World War II*, 1:474.

13. Ibid., 470; Waddell, *US Army Logistics*, 117.

14. Ruppenthal, *US Army in World War II*, 2:52, 124; Waddell, *US Army Logistics*, 116.

15. Details are from Headquarters 21 Army Group, *Administrative History*, 34–36.

16. A standard SHAEF calculation held that a truck company could transport 200 tons 160 km (100 miles) in a day.

17. It was 140 km (90 miles) by road from Antwerp to Aachen and 310 km (190 miles) to Metz. The distances from Cherbourg were 710 km (440 miles) and 690 km (430 miles), respectively; from Brest they were 960 km (595 miles) and 910 km (565 miles).

18. Quoted in Peter Beale, *The Great Mistake: The Battle for Antwerp and the Bereland Peninsula, September 1944* (Stroud, UK: Sutton, 2004), 10–11. Much more detail on Antwerp and other ports can be found in Ruppenthal, *US Army in World War II*, vol. 2, chap. 4.

19. Principal sources for this section were Ruppenthal, *US Army in World War*

II, chaps. 13, 14; Waddell, *US Army Logistics*, chaps. 6, 7; Headquarters 21 Army Group, *Administrative History*, chap. 3; Headquarters Second Army, *Account of Operations*, chap. 3.

20. Red Ball convoys, with a peak flow rate of 400 vehicles per hour, would have made a perfect target for air interdiction. The project's success was thus dependent on Allied air supremacy.

21. In practice, COMZ favored First Army over Third Army, the former receiving 3,300 tons per day and the latter 2,500.

22. Detail on air transport is extracted mainly from Ruppenthal, *US Army in World War II*, vol. 1, chap. 14, and Waddell, *US Army Logistics*, chap 6. T. B. H. Otway, *Airborne Forces* (1952; reprint, London: Imperial War Museum, 1990), chap. 16, goes into the stillborn airborne operations for which the Airborne Army tried to keep its aircraft.

23. Principal sources for this section were Waddell, *US Army Logistics*, chaps. 5–7; Ruppenthal, *US Army in World War II*, vol. 1, chaps. 13, 14, and vol. 2, chaps. 1–9; David W. Hogan, *A Command Post at War: First Army Headquarters in Europe 1943–45* (Honolulu, HI: University Press of the Pacific, 2000), chaps. 5, 6; Kent Roberts Greenfield, ed., *Command Decisions* (Washington, DC: Office of the Chief of Military History, 1971), chap. 18.

24. On the basis of 550 tons per division slice and including Ninth Air Force needs.

25. The story of ammunition supply illustrates the unreliability of COMZ's controls, figures, and predictions. On 1 October COMZ presented 12 Army Group with figures indicating an improvement in supply, so the latter authorized heavier expenditure rates. However, First Army's ammunition officer pointed out that the amount of ammunition authorized simply did not exist in army depots and could not be obtained from COMZ. A full investigation in all three armies revealed that the shortage had actually reached critical proportions, with reserve stocks of some ammunition natures approaching exhaustion. The shortage was not, however, purely the fault of COMZ. Ammunition discharges had been a bottleneck, and there were plans to increase the number of Liberty ships unloading both in Cherbourg and over the beaches. SHAEF overrode that decision, giving priority in Cherbourg to the debarkation of fresh troops, and storms closed the beaches. Unloading fell to one-quarter of the planned level, but poor record keeping concealed the true situation.

26. Lieutenant General Leroy Lutes quoted in Hogan, *Command Post at War*, 165.

27. By contrast, Marseille (on which Third Army's supply hopes had originally hung) was 80 km (50 miles) further from Metz than Cherbourg was. It was better suited to supporting operations in Alsace than in Lorraine. By October, almost one-third of the supplies being landed in France were going through the south.

28. In addition to opening the way into Antwerp, the clearing of the Scheldt estuary made the inland port of Ghent usable, and it was opened on 19 December. It

was considered important insurance in case Antwerp were totally or partially denied to the Allies by V-1 bombardment.

29. Elbridge Colby, *The First Army in Europe 1943–45* (Nashville, TN: Battery Press, 1969), 98; Robert S. Allen, *Lucky Forward: Patton's Third US Army* (Vanguard Press, 1964), 99–100; Martin Blumenson, ed., *The Patton Papers* (Bridgewater, NJ: Da Capo Press, 1996), 531. Both officers were wrong, or at least overly simplistic (Allen went on to demonstrate an even more extraordinary level of both ignorance and partisanship), but the point is that these sentiments were frequently expressed and indeed encouraged by their commanding generals, as Patton's comment illustrates.

30. Ruppenthal, *US Army in World War II*, 2:10–11; Forrest C. Pogue, *The United States Army in World War II, European Theater of Operations: The Supreme Command* (Washington, DC: Office of the Chief of Military History, 1989), 254.

31. Headquarters Second Army, *Account of Operations*, 276.

32. Eindhoven was probably as far as rail communications could be pushed for some time, however. The Germans had destroyed the Maas bridge at Mook during Market Garden, and replacing it would be a task comparable to that facing the engineers working on the Seine rail bridge at Le Manoir.

33. L. F. Ellis, *Victory in the West*, vol. 2, *The Defeat of Germany* (London: HMSO, 1968), 133.

Chapter 7. Command, Operational Art, and Generalship

1. Montgomery of Alamein, *Memoirs* (London: Collins, 1958), 268–269.

2. Dwight D. Eisenhower, *Crusade in Europe* (London: Heinemann, 1948), 312.

3. By the end of August, there were twenty-three US and fourteen Anglo-Canadian divisions in the theatre, with another thirty or so American ones earmarked for the ETO. There would be no more British formations, although I Canadian Corps was transferred from Italy in 1945.

4. Montgomery pursued the issue with tactlessness, crassness, and downright stupidity when he complained about the Supreme Commander's lack of direction and grip to the latter's patron, Marshall, on 8 October. See Montgomery, *Memoirs*, 284.

5. Montgomery's argument and Eisenhower's reply are quoted in full in L. F. Ellis, *Victory in the West*, vol. 2, *The Defeat of Germany* (London: HMSO, 1968), 85–91.

6. For Montgomery, it was a matter of principle that, when meetings were necessary, the higher commander should go to the HQ of the lower, who could not afford time away from the battle. Though a sound bit of doctrine, it was simply counterproductive and self-defeating to demand that his boss play by his rules. Nor did the attitude endear him to Bradley and the other American commanders, who merely used his absence to push their own agendas with Eisenhower. It is worth noting that the only conference called by the Supreme Commander that Montgomery deigned to attend in person was that of 4 October, when the CIGS was going to be there too.

7. Interview with Brigadier General Betts, quoted in D. K. R. Croswell, *The Chief of Staff: The Military Career of General Walter Bedell Smith* (Westport, CT: Greenwood Press, 1991), 286.

8. Eisenhower was ETO as well as Allied commander. SHAEF's American section tended to act as theatre staff, encroaching on the responsibilities of Lee's HQ and creating problems of jurisdiction and coordination.

9. Between them, COMZ and its subordinate Seine Base Section HQs took over 296 hotels. The behavior of US administrative personnel in Paris, described as "little short of disgraceful," led to a strong protest from Eisenhower to Lee. Parisians made invidious comparisons with their previous occupiers. Roland G. Ruppenthal, *United States Army in World War II, the European Theater of Operations: Logistical Support of the Armies*, vol. 2 (Washington, DC: Office of the Chief of Military History, 1959), 32.

10. Simplistically, the system was supposed to work as follows: Base Sections received all manner of supplies coming into Normandy, sorted them into dumps, and inventoried them; the Advanced Section's responsibilities were loosely defined but boiled down to providing direct administrative support to the field armies up to their rear boundaries; COMZ oversaw and directed the activities of its subordinates and dealt with such matters as shipping, air supply, bulk POL storage and distribution, location of dumps, and the direction of administrative planning. This cursory look at arrangements of labyrinthine complexity is based on Steve R. Waddell, *United States Army Logistics: The Normandy Campaign 1944* (Westport, CT: Greenwood Press, 1994), chap. 5; Roland G. Ruppenthal, *United States Army in World War II, the European Theater of Operations: Logistical Support of the Armies*, vol. 1 (Washington, DC: Office of the Chief of Military History, 1953), chap. 11; Alan Gropman, ed., *The Big L: American Logistics in World War II* (Washington, DC: National Defense University, 1997), 368–371 (which contains a study of command relationships).

11. Eisenhower wrote to Marshall at the end of August: "I note little instances that seem to indicate that the Allies cannot hang so effectively in prosperity as they can in adversity." Nigel Hamilton, *Monty, Master of the Battlefield, 1942–1944* (London: Hamish Hamilton, 1983), 7. These instances would multiply and grow in significance until, by late December, there was a gulf of misunderstanding and dislike dividing the two armies.

12. David W. Hogan, *A Command Post at War: First Army Headquarters in Europe 1943–45* (Honolulu, HI: University Press of the Pacific, 2000), 142. It is of passing interest that Bradley deliberately and without consultation violated the army group boundary to execute the Tournai maneuver; presumably, he had conquered the scruples he had claimed as an inhibiting factor when explaining his refusal to close the Falaise pocket a fortnight earlier.

13. 12 Army Group administrative instruction, 27 August 1944, quoted in Martin Blumenson, *United States Army in World War II, the European Theater of Opera-*

tions: Breakout and Pursuit (Washington, DC: Office of the Chief of Military History, 1959), 677.

14. See Francis de Guingand's admittedly post hoc memoir, *Operation Victory* (London: Hodder and Stoughton, 1947), 411–413, which stresses the central importance of Antwerp.

15. It is a moot question with profound consequences whether Britain really would have been unable to supply such additional formations but, on the contrary, would have had to disband 59 Infantry Division in September and return 50 Division to England in November for want of replacements. At the beginning of 1944 there had been nine infantry divisions in the United Kingdom that were not designated for 21 Army Group but were used as training, draft-finding, and reserve formations. By early September, four of these had been broken up, but there were still three training and one holding division and two reserve divisions (55 and 61 Divisions) with "some degree of an operational role"; this number went up to three when 50 Division came home. Were so many reserve and training formations required in the autumn of 1944? After all, in late 1943 the government's planning assumption had been that Germany would be defeated by the end of 1944 and that the greatest striking power should be brought to bear in that year. John Ehrman, *Grand Strategy*, vol. 5 (London: HMSO, 1956), 45–46. For that matter, given that northwestern Europe was supposedly Britain's main effort, was it really true that no divisions could be spared from the Middle East and Italy until I Canadian Corps was transferred in January–February 1945 and then 5 Infantry Division in March? Churchill and Brooke's refusal to contemplate taking troops from the home base or the Mediterranean to reinforce Montgomery was a questionable strategic decision and a classic failure to follow the first principle of war—selection and maintenance of the aim. They failed in an important facet of strategy—choosing what not to do. Although northwestern Europe was theoretically the most important theatre, in practice, concern for the empire and the Middle East led to half measures. The Americans were right about Italy, and the British argument about tying down German forces does not really carry conviction; it was more like the Germans were tying down the Allies. After the latter missed the chance to destroy a substantial chunk of *Tenth Army* in early June 1944 and the enemy had withdrawn in good order to the Pisa-Rimini line, there was no strategic gain in the campaign that was commensurate with the expenditure. It was clear that 21 Army Group was below critical mass, unable to operate effectively as an army group; as a result, the British had to play second fiddle to the Americans in the decisive theatre and accordingly lost influence on the direction of strategy.

16. Eisenhower wrote: "Experience of the past proved that we were likely to be vastly disappointed in the usefulness of the Brittany ports. Not only did we expect them to be stubbornly defended but we were certain that they would be effectively destroyed once we had captured them. We did not expect this destruction to be so marked at Marseille because we knew that a large proportion of the defense force

had already been drawn north to meet our attacks. The capture should be so swift as to allow little time for demolition." Eisenhower, *Crusade in Europe*, 309–319. The Supreme Commander realized that the battle for Brest had become pointless and that the Mediterranean supply line had great promise; by 25 September, there was a working rail link as far as Lyon, and in October almost one-third of American supplies landing in France were going through Marseille.

17. If the threat to American sensitivities was adjudged to be high, one solution could have been to insert Ninth Army HQ over VIII Corps and thus have a US army directly under 21 Army Group, as would happen in December. This method had been used the year before, when Seventh Army had only a single corps under its command for the invasion of Sicily, but the expedient ensured equality of status between the British and American invading forces. It is worth noting, in the context of the vexed question of American formations coming under Allied command, that in October Eisenhower placed 104 Infantry and 7 Armored Divisions under the command of different British corps in a belated recognition of 21 Army Group's lack of combat power.

18. Jonathan Gawne, *Ghosts of the ETO: American Tactical Deception Units in the European Theatre, 1944–45* (Newbury, UK: Casemate, 2002), 109–119, gives details of this successful deception.

19. Military rationale and geography would suggest the desirability of redrawing the boundary between the Central and Southern Army Groups for such an autumn campaign. Ninth and First Armies would remain under 12 Army Group from the Ardennes northward, and Third Army would be reallocated to 6 Army Group. That would leave four armies focused on the main axis north of the Ardennes and three on the subsidiary axis in the south. Such an idea would never be considered, however, as logic often plays a minor role in decision making. Eisenhower disliked Devers and had a (mistakenly) low opinion of his abilities. He would do nothing to promote a rival at the expense of his favorite subordinate, Bradley.

20. Volume 2 explains and develops Red Army concepts of exploitation and pursuit. Those other champions of maneuver warfare, the Germans, acknowledged in practice the role of forward detachments, or *voransabteilungen*.

21. Even Patton publicly acknowledged the British achievement. At a news conference on 7 September he said: "The perfectly phenomenal advance of the 21 Army Group under Field Marshal Montgomery has just completely buggered the whole [German] show. I think that is a magnificent show, and as a result of that it would seem to me that the German plan of defense is completely dissipated. The advance of the Guards division and the other divisions up there has been something magnificent." Martin Blumenson, ed., *The Patton Papers* (Bridgewater, NJ: Da Capo Press, 1996), 539–540.

22. Dempsey noted in his war diary entry for 4 September: "The very rapid advance of the past few days has placed a big strain on administration. Starting tomorrow, 1,000 tons a day are being flown to Douai or Brussels for Second Army.

Even with this it will not be possible to operate at full strength with three corps until we have in operation a proper port between Havre and Antwerp." Quoted in Peter Rostron, *The Military Life and Times of General Sir Miles Dempsey: Montgomery's Army Commander* (Barnsley, UK: Pen and Sword, 2010), 131. All this was true, but it displayed too great an awareness of his own army's problems and too little of the enemy's. Pursuit has to be conducted with as much vigor as possible for as long as possible if the benefits of a fleeting advantage are to be harvested in full. It was the same safety-first approach that had prematurely ended a promising exploitation by 11 Armored Division during Operation Bluecoat.

23. There was a fundamental flaw in British operational methodology, stemming perhaps from a doctrinal lacuna. Advances were usually executed up to major obstacles, which were then presumably regarded as convenient places to consolidate gains. The Soviets and Germans both stressed immediate crossings if possible, on the basis that a bridgehead could often be seized cheaply and quickly from the line of march against a weak and unbalanced enemy, whereas a delay could necessitate a much larger force and more time for a deliberate forcing against a prepared defense, resulting in greater casualties.

24. Neither Horrocks nor Roberts was aware that the Albert Canal would pose a particularly difficult challenge once defended. They were perforce working off small-scale road maps that showed the city as a small circle and the canal as a thin blue line going through it. It was the job of the operational-level commanders to be aware of problems that could jeopardize the achievement of their objectives. In this case, Belgian liaison officers and intelligence could have provided the information required to inform decision making.

25. Quoted in Rostron, *Military Life and Times of Dempsey*, 133.

26. Eisenhower used the same principle to explain why Montgomery could not combine the roles of army group and land forces commander, an argument rejected by the latter. It appears that Montgomery regarded himself as so exceptional that he transcended his own principles.

27. As late as 20 September, army-level intelligence continued to suggest that the enemy would not put up a serious fight to hold the Antwerp approaches. Crerar would have been well advised to consider the precedents from Cherbourg through Brest to Le Havre and the Channel ports, not to mention the firm and repeated warnings from Ultra. This would have avoided the dangers inherent in mounting inadequately resourced attacks that then had to be rethought.

28. It should be noted that merely masking Calais was not an option. Naval advice was that Boulogne would be unusable as long as the German heavy batteries at Cap Gris Nez, near Calais, were able to command the approaches. At least the batteries would have to be captured.

29. For instance, Ellis, *Victory in the West*, 2:60, snidely comments that Crerar did "not seem to have recognized any great need for haste." And R. W. Thompson, *The Eighty-Five Days* (London: Hutchinson, 1957), 60, notes: "scarcely a thought

was given in the first three weeks of September to the urgent, complex and costly battle that must be planned and fought to gain this whole area. . . . On the Channel coast the Canadians were investing Boulogne and Calais as though there was all the time in the world, and without a trace of imagination."

30. It is said that the more imaginative Simonds suggested this approach but was turned down by Crerar. John A. English, *Patton's Peers: The Forgotten Allied Field Commanders of the Western Front 1944–45* (Mechanicsburg, PA: Stackpole Books, 2009), 31.

31. Harris needed much persuasion to commit Bomber Command, somewhat grudgingly, to attacks on the fortifications of Boulogne and Calais. Coningham, the commander of 2 TAF, was so dissatisfied with AVM L. O. Browne's enthusiastically cooperative relationship with Crerar and his army that he relieved him in November.

32. Crerar's difficulties, compounded by his method of command, are well explored in Paul Douglas Dickson, *A Thoroughly Canadian General: A Biography of General H. D. G. Crerar* (Toronto: Toronto University Press, 2007), chap. 20.

33. J. Lawton Collins, *Lightning Joe, an Autobiography* (Baton Rouge: Louisiana State University Press, 1979), 261.

34. Actually, Hodges was fortunate not to face a somewhat stronger defense even earlier. Hitler committed four of the five new panzer brigades sent to the western front to Lorraine for *Fifth Panzer Army's* doomed counterattack. Had a couple of brigades been deployed to defend the Aachen sector, First Army's lack of concentration and reserves would have resulted in an even more limited success.

35. Admittedly, the arbitrary cut in First Army's fuel allocation in early September undermined planning, and COMZ's temporary inability to deliver even the reduced allocation made calculations unreliable. The ammunition crisis that resulted in the reimposition of rationing on 2 October was unexpectedly severe, as COMZ did not warn the army about its inability to fulfill the requisition.

36. Both Hodges and Patton reflected different aspects of prewar Leavenworth teaching. It emphasized broad maneuver conducted by armies with a mission command approach to orders, as exemplified by Patton. But it also stressed the need for continuous fronts; concern for flanks; meticulous, detailed planning; and firepower-based methods of operation, as practiced by Hodges. British doctrine was similarly ambivalent. Both armies wished to have their cake and eat it and failed to even attempt to resolve the contradictions.

37. Patton actually resented being compelled by the more cautious Bradley to leave a guard covering the Loire flank, arguing that there was no real threat from the south. The Germans there were intent on getting home and lacked the mobility to pose any danger to American lines of communication. Together, the FFI and XIX Tactical Air Command (TAC) could maintain surveillance and give early warning of any burgeoning threat (and the latter could deal with it). Later, when he was forcing the Moselle and running into unexpectedly effective resistance, Patton asked for 6 Armored and 83 Infantry Divisions to be released from this task and Bradley told

him, "I can't take the risk." In Patton's view, this entailed the worse risk of his attack failing. Blumenson, *Patton Papers*, 545. On 16 September a German grouping south of the Loire that was 20,000 strong (though mostly not combat troops) was so worn down and demoralized by constant strikes by XIX TAC that it surrendered; General Elster, its commander, wished to surrender to the air commander who had compelled him to do so.

38. John Nelson Rickard, *Patton at Bay: The Lorraine Campaign September to December 1944* (Westport, CT: Praeger, 1999), 59.

39. For a keen student of military history, this was a surprising underestimate of the value of fortifications if properly used. They enable the defender to practice economy of force and increase the value of ill-trained, low-quality troops. Patton also grossly overestimated the impact of airpower on the Metz forts, ignoring the lessons of Cherbourg and his own VIII Corps operation to reduce Brest.

40. Patton had shown a similar disregard for the aim of the campaign in Sicily. There, he devoted much of his effort to overrunning the western half of the island, regardless of its irrelevance and to the detriment of the main purpose, which was destruction of the defending *XIV Panzer Corps*.

41. Ruppenthal, *US Army in World War II*, 1:306–307.

42. Omar N. Bradley, *A Soldier's Story* (New York: Henry Holt, 1951), 296–297.

43. Blumenson, *Patton Papers*, 532.

44. "Our primary terrain objective lay in the Ruhr . . . the industrial heart of Germany's war machine. . . . Without the Ruhr, Germany would be unable to support its armies in the field." Bradley, *Soldier's Story*, 338. He went on to argue that the best route to encircle the Ruhr from the south was not via Cologne but through Frankfurt and Kassel. Quite apart from the extra distance involved—no small consideration, given the logistic constraints—no one knowledgeable in German geography accepted his argument that the terrain on the longer route was easier than that on the direct route skirting the conurbation. Moreover, the latter advance would give the enemy less time to recover from his enormous losses in Normandy and organize a new defense.

45. On the primacy of the Ruhr, see Bradley, *Soldier's Story*, 322, 323, 338; on his retrospective belief in the Germans' will to resist (belied by all contemporary evidence), see ibid., 329. Bradley consistently misrepresents Montgomery's operational ideas and problems and goes through logical contortions in an attempt to justify his idea that the secondary axis should be of equal strength with equal logistic support. Bradley's memoirs are every bit as selective in what is remembered and in the use of evidence and hindsight, and as misleading and self-justificatory, as Montgomery's.

46. Bradley's choice of Verdun for 12 Army Group HQ, where he moved in mid-September, reflects his priorities. Verdun was behind Third Army and 200 km (125 miles) distant from First Army, over poor roads; most significantly, it was well beyond the reach of Montgomery's army group in north Belgium. In February 1945 Eisenhower, anxious for Bradley's HQ to be nearer Montgomery's in southern Holland to promote cooperation, required a move to Namur—which Bradley protested.

47. C. P. Stacey,*The Victory Campaign, Operations in North-West Europe, 1944–45: Official History of the Canadian Army in the Second World War*, vol. 3 (Ottawa: Queen's Printer and Controller of Stationery, 1966), 310, 358–360.

48. In his directive of 14 September, Montgomery actually promised massive air support; the movement of 49 Division from Le Havre to the Antwerp area, but only to relieve Second Army elements there; and an airborne assault. The last, of course, could not occur before the conclusion of the Arnhem operation, although the question proved academic when First Allied Airborne Army refused to undertake Operation Infatuate in view of the heavy flak and lack of suitable DZs in the area of the proposed landing.

49. Quite apart from other benefits, the opening of Antwerp would have drastically shortened the journey for supply columns and thus turnaround times. For instance, the Red Ball Express had an approximately 1,660 km (1,030 mile) round-trip from Cherbourg to Aachen, but the round-trip from Antwerp to Aachen was less than 300 km (185 miles).

50. Even his normally staunch supporter Brooke believed Montgomery was mistaken. The CIGS's diary entry for 5 October included this observation: "During the whole discussion one fact stood out clearly, that Antwerp must be captured with the least possible delay. I feel that Monty's strategy for once is at fault, instead of carrying out the advance on Arnhem he ought to have made certain of Antwerp in the first place. Ramsay brought this out well in discussion and criticized Monty freely. Ike nobly took all blame on himself as he had approved Monty's suggestion to operate on Arnhem." Field Marshal Lord Alanbrooke, *War Diaries 1939–45*, ed. Alex Danchev and D. Todman (London: Weidenfeld and Nicolson, 2001), 600.

51. By mid-September, Montgomery was becoming more modest in his aspirations, talking of establishing favorable conditions for an advance on Berlin rather than a continuous offensive. It was Eisenhower's directive of 15 September that maintained: "We shall soon . . . be in possession of the Ruhr, the Saar and the Frankfurt area. . . . We should concentrate all our energies and resources on a rapid thrust to Berlin . . . astride the axes Ruhr-Hannover-Berlin or Frankfurt-Leipzig-Berlin, or both." Quoted in full in Ellis, *Victory in the West*, 2:77.

52. Montgomery cannot be absolved of responsibility for some of these tactical failures. He was warned about the inadequacies of Browning's airborne plan by experienced and reliable members of his own staff but refused to use his influence to correct them, and he worked directly with Horrocks on the XXX Corps plan. Moreover, he seemed uncharacteristically reluctant to influence the conduct of Market Garden, even when it was clearly yielding disappointing results on both the main axis and the flanks; he did not visit Dempsey until 23 September, by which time the battle was effectively lost.

53. Montgomery of Alamein, *El Alamein to the River Sangro: Normandy to the Baltic* (London: Barrie and Jenkins, 1973), 324–325.

54. Ibid., 324; Montgomery, *Memoirs*, 294. Always reluctant to admit failure,

never mind mistakes in planning, Montgomery searched widely for scapegoats to relieve him of all blame and "remain[ed] Market Garden's unrepentant advocate." Montgomery, *Memoirs*, 298. Among those castigated for the defeat was SHAEF for failing to provide adequate logistic support. However, the Arnhem operation failed well before Second Army faced the difficulties that would have come in the wake of success.

55. Montgomery bitterly criticized Patton for his cavalier attitude toward orders—having recommended that very course of action to him during the Sicilian campaign: "George, let me give you some advice. If you get an order from army group that you don't like, why not ignore it. That's what I do." Quoted in Carlo D'Este, *Bitter Victory* (London: Collins, 1998), 108. Montgomery's strictly one-way approach to loyalty applied across the board. He accused Ramsay, the British C-in-C of Allied naval forces, of disloyalty for drawing Eisenhower's attention to his continued neglect of Antwerp.

56. Montgomery's own explanation for his nonappearance at Versailles on 22 September revealed that this was not just an operational matter: "I knew I was not popular at either supreme headquarters or with the American generals because of my arguments . . . ; I thought it best to keep away while the matter was being further agreed." Montgomery, *Memoirs*, 282. By permitting his emollient chief of staff to make his argument, Montgomery not only gave up an opportunity to personally influence his fellow senior commanders and avoid future misunderstandings but also demonstrated his personal disdain for them—a counterproductive approach. Of course, his dislike of conferences was typical of those who are used to being dictatorial and unchallenged.

57. Eisenhower, *Crusade in Europe*, 307–310.

58. Quoted in Crosswell, *Chief of Staff*, 258. As the author points out, this "was an amazing view given the immobilization of Bradley's forces for lack of supplies."

59. Quoted in Ellis, *Victory in the West*, 2:85.

60. The letter can be found in full in ibid., 88–91.

61. Eisenhower was pushed to decide in favor of Market Garden by his knowledge that Marshall and Arnold had made a considerable investment in US airborne forces and wished to see them employed in an operationally decisive role. The repeated cancellations of proposed operations raised the specter of the war being won without their commitment to battle. First Allied Airborne Army was like a coin burning a hole in SHAEF's pocket, and the pressure to spend it to achieve some spectacular coup de grâce was growing.

62. By mid-October, there were smoothly working rail communications as far north as Epinal carrying 12,000 tons per day; Marseille was handling about half as much tonnage as all the northern ports then operating. Ruppenthal, *US Army in World War II*, 2:156–158, 124.

63. Of course, Frenchmen, most significantly de Gaulle, could not be expected to see Alsace in this light. French First Army (so designated in late September) would

probably have to be devoted to the province's liberation for political-strategic reasons. Later, during the German winter counteroffensive, Eisenhower had to veto a sound military proposal to withdraw temporarily from Strasbourg. As ever, political exigencies trumped military logic. However, that does not mean that the rest of 6 Army Group, an appropriately reinforced Seventh Army, could not have been used to mount an offensive to free Lorraine and then continue northward as part of the autumn campaign.

64. Eisenhower would be a much more clear-sighted, decisive land forces commander when a surprise crisis blew up in mid-December with the German Ardennes counteroffensive.

65. The term "politician" is used here in the sense of one with a certain set of skills and ways of management, not in the sense of one who seeks to shape national policy. Like most Western soldiers of his generation, Eisenhower believed—naïvely, it now seems—that politics and war fighting did not mix. He would fight both Churchill and Roosevelt over the issue when they tried to interfere with supposedly purely military decisions.

66. Alanbrooke, *War Diaries*, 546, entry for 15 May 1944.

67. Ibid., 575, entry for 27 July 1944.

68. Nigel Hamilton, *Monty, the Field Marshal 1944–1945* (London: Guild Publishing, 1986), 54.

69. Eisenhower, *Crusade in Europe*, 33–34.

70. Quoted in Crosswell, *Chief of Staff*, 259. Of course, whatever his dedication to even-handedness in the pursuit of Allied unity, Eisenhower could not help being influenced by his temperament. He had a strong desire to be liked as well as respected, especially by his fellow American generals, and particularly by those he considered old friends, such as Bradley. He met frequently with senior US commanders, socialized with them, and was predisposed to cut them some slack. In contrast, Montgomery, with his alternating hectoring and condescending, often rude tone, was singularly uncongenial company that Eisenhower was happy to avoid; the field marshal's arrogant insistence that Eisenhower would have to visit him to gain an audience forfeited any chance of exerting an influence.

71. Eisenhower, *Crusade in Europe*, 174–175.

Selected Bibliography

Adams, John A. *The Battle for Western Europe, Fall 1944*. Bloomington: Indiana University Press, 2010.
Air Historical Branch. *Rise and Fall of the German Air Force*. Reprint, Poole, UK: Arms and Armour Press, 1987.
Alanbrooke, Field Marshal Lord. *War Diaries 1939–45*, ed. Alex Danchev and D. Todman. London: Weidenfeld and Nicolson, 2001.
Allen, Robert S. *Lucky Forward: Patton's Third US Army*. Vanguard Press, 1964.
Ambrose, Stephen E. *The Supreme Commander*. London: Cassell, 1971.
Army Field Manual, vol. 1, pt. 1, *The Application of Force*. British army doctrine publication, 1985.
Bailey, J. B. A. *Field Artillery and Firepower*. Annapolis, MD: Naval Institute Press, 2004.
BAOR [British Army of the Rhine]. *Battlefield Tour Guide: Operation Bluecoat*. BAOR, 1948.
———. *Battlefield Tour Guide: Operation Totalize*. BAOR, 1947.
Beale, Peter. *The Great Mistake: Battle for Antwerp and the Beveland Peninsula*. Stroud, UK: Sutton, 2004.
Beevor, Anthony. *D-Day: The Battle for Normandy*. London: Viking (Penguin), 2009.
Belcham, Maj. Gen. D. *All in the Day's March*. London: Collins, 1978.
Bennet, David. *A Magnificent Disaster: The Failure of Market Garden, the Arnhem Operation September 1944*. Newbury, UK: Casemate, 2008.
Bennett, Ralph. *Ultra in the West: The Normandy Campaign of 1944–45*. London: Hutchinson, 1979.
Blumenson, Martin. *The Battle of the Generals*. New York: Quill, William Morrow, 1993.
———. *United States Army in World War II, the European Theater of Operations: Breakout and Pursuit*. Washington, DC: Office of the Chief of Military History, 1959.
———, ed. *The Patton Papers*. Bridgewater, NJ: Da Capo Press, 1996.
Bond, Brian. *British Military Policy between the Two World Wars*. Oxford: Clarendon Press, 1980.
Bonn, Keith E. *When the Odds Were Even: The Vosges Mountains Campaign October 1944–January 1945*. New York: Presidio, 1994.
Bradley, Omar N. *A Soldier's Story*. New York: Henry Holt, 1951.

Bradley, Omar N., and Clay Blair. *A General's Life*. New York: Simon and Schuster, 1983.
Buckingham, William F. *Arnhem 1944*. Stroud, UK: Tempus, 2004.
Buckley, John. *British Armour in the Normandy Campaign 1944*. London: Frank Cass, 2004.
Burrin, Philippe. *France under the Germans*. New York: New Press, 1996.
Canadian General Staff. *Report No. 77, German Operations from Falaise to the Ardennes (20 August–16 December 1944)*. 1958. Reprint, MLRS, 2005.
Canadian Military Headquarters. *Report No. 188, Canadian Operations to Clear the Scheldt Estuary*. Reprint, MLRS, 2006.
Carafano, James Jay. *After D-Day: Operation Cobra and the Normandy Breakout*. London: Lynne Rienner, 2000.
Chalfont, Alun. *Montgomery of Alamein*. London: Weidenfeld and Nicolson, 1974.
Citino, Robert M. *Blitzkrieg to Desert Storm: The Evolution of Operational Warfare*. Lawrence: University Press of Kansas, 2004.
Clarke, Jeffrey, and Robert Smith. *United States Army in World War II, the European Theater of Operations: Riviera to the Rhine*. Washington, DC: Office of the Chief of Military History, 1993.
Clausewitz, Carl von. *On War*, trans. and ed. Michael Howard and Peter Paret. Princeton, NJ: Princeton University Press, 1976.
Colby, Elbridge. *The First Army in Europe 1943–45*. Nashville, TN: Battery Press, 1969.
Cole, Hugh M. *United States Army in World War II, the European Theater of Operations: The Lorraine Campaign*. Washington, DC: Office of the Chief of Military History, 1984.
Collins, J. Lawton. *Lightning Joe, an Autobiography*. Baton Rouge: Louisiana State University Press, 1979.
Condell, Bruce, and David T. Zabecki, eds. *On the German Art of War: Truppenfuhrung, German Army Manual for Unit Command in World War II*. London: Lynne Rienner, 2001.
Copp, Terry. *Cinderella Army: The Canadians in Northwest Europe, 1944–45*. Toronto: Toronto University Press, 2006.
———. *Fields of Fire: The Canadians in Normandy*. Toronto: Toronto University Press, 2003.
———. *Montgomery's Scientists: Operational Research in Northwest Europe*. Winnipeg, MB: Wilfred Laurier University, 2000.
Craven, W. F., and J. L. Cate. *The Army Air Forces in World War II*, vol. 2, *Europe—Torch to Pointblank*. Washington, DC: Office of Air Force History, 1949.
———. *The Army Air Forces in World War II*, vol. 3, *Europe—Argument to VE-Day*. Washington, DC: Office of Air Force History, 1951.
Crosswell, D. K. R. *The Chief of Staff: The Military Career of General Walter Bedell Smith*. Westport, CT: Greenwood Press, 1991.

Daglish, Ian. *Operation Bluecoat: Breakout from Normandy*. Barnsley, UK: Pen and Sword, 2009.

Dear, I. C. B., and M. R. D. Foot. *The Oxford Companion to World War II*. Oxford: Oxford University Press, 1995.

D'Este, Carlo. *Decision in Normandy*. London: Collins, 1983.

———. *Eisenhower: Allied Supreme Commander*. London: Weidenfeld and Nicolson, 2003.

———. *Patton: A Genius for War*. New York: HarperCollins, 1995.

Deutsch, Harold C. "Commanding Generals and the Uses of Intelligence." In *Leaders and Intelligence*, ed. Michael I. Handel. London: Frank Cass, 1989.

Dickson, Paul Douglas. *A Thoroughly Canadian General: A Biography of General H. D. G. Crerar*. Toronto: Toronto University Press, 2007.

Dixon, Norman. *On the Psychology of Military Incompetence*. London: Jonathan Cape, 1976.

Doubler, Michael D. *Closing with the Enemy*. Lawrence: University Press of Kansas, 1994.

Ehrman, John. *Grand Strategy*, vol. 5. London: HMSO, 1956.

Eisenhower, Dwight D. *Crusade in Europe*. London: Heinemann, 1948.

Ellis, John. *Brute Force: Allied Strategy and Tactics in the Second World War*. London: Andre Deutsch, 1990.

———. *The Sharp End of War: The Fighting Man in World War II*. London: David and Charles, 1980.

Ellis, L. F. *Victory in the West*, vol. 1, *The Battle of Normandy*. London: HMSO, 1962.

———. *Victory in the West*, vol. 2, *The Defeat of Germany*. London: HMSO, 1968.

English, John A. *The Canadian Army and the Normandy Campaign: A Study of Failure in High Command*. New York: Praeger, 1991.

———. *Patton's Peers: The Forgotten Allied Field Commanders of the Western Front 1944–45*. Mechanicsburg, PA: Stackpole Books, 2009.

Essame, H. *Patton, the Commander*. London: Purnell Book Services, 1974.

Foot, M. R. D. *SOE: The Special Operations Executive 1940–45*. London: Pimlico, 1999.

French, David. *Raising Churchill's Army: The British Army and the War against Germany, 1919–1945*. Oxford: Oxford University Press, 2001.

Fritz, Stephen G. *Frontsoldaten: The German Soldier in World War II*. Lexington: University Press of Kentucky, 1995.

Fuller, J. F. C. *Generalship: Its Diseases and Their Cure*. Military Service Publishing Co., 1936.

Gavin, James. *On to Berlin: Battle of an Airborne Commander*. London: Leo Cooper, 1979.

Gawne, Jonathan. *Ghosts of the ETO: American Tactical Deception Units in the European Theatre, 1944–45*. Newbury, UK: Casemate, 2002.

Gooderson, Ian. *Air Power at the Battlefront: Allied Close Air Support in Europe 1944–45*. London: Frank Cass, 1998.

Graham, Dominick. *The Price of Command: A Biography of General Guy Simonds*. Toronto: Stoddart, 1993.

Graham, Dominick, and Shelford Bidwell. *Coalitions, Politicians and Generals: Some Aspects of Command in Two World Wars*. London: Brassey's, 1993.

Greenfield, Kent Roberts. *The Organization of Ground Combat Troops*. Washington, DC: Office of the Chief of Military History, 1947.

———, ed. *Command Decisions*. Washington, DC: Office of the Chief of Military History, 1971.

Gropman, Alan, ed. *The Big L: American Logistics in World War II*. Washington, DC: National Defense University, 1997.

Guingand, Francis de. *Operation Victory*. London: Hodder and Stoughton, 1947.

Hallion, Richard P. *Strike from the Sky: The History of Battlefield Air Attack, 1911–45*. Shrewsbury, UK: Airlife Publishing, 1989.

Hamilton, Nigel. *Monty, the Field Marshal 1944–1945*. London: Guild Publishing, 1986.

———. *Monty, Master of the Battlefield 1942–1944*. London: Hamish Hamilton, 1983.

Handel, Michael I. *War Strategy and Intelligence*. London: Frank Cass, 1989.

Harrison, Gordon A. *United States Army in World War II, the European Theater of Operations: Cross Channel Attack*. Washington, DC: Office of the Chief of Military History, 1951.

Hart, Russell A. *Clash of Arms: How the Allies Won in Normandy*. London: Lynne Rienner, 2001.

———. "Feeding Mars: The Role of Logistics in the German Defeat in Normandy." *War in History* 3, 4 (November 1996).

Hart, Stephen A. *Montgomery and "Colossal Cracks": The 21st Army Group in Northwest Europe 1944–45*. Westport, CT: Praeger, 2000.

Harwood, Michael J. *Auftragstaktik: We Can't Get There from Here*. Leavenworth, KS: School of Advanced Military Studies, US Army Command and General Staff College, 1990.

Hastings, Max. *Overlord: D-Day and the Battle for Normandy*. London: Michael Joseph, 1984.

Haycock, D. J. *Eisenhower and the Art of Warfare: A Critical Reappraisal*. Jefferson, NC: McFarland, 2004.

Headquarters Second Army, comp. *An Account of the Operations of Second Army in Europe 1944–45*. Reprint, MLRS, 2005.

Headquarters 21 Army Group, comp. *Administrative History of the Operations of 21 Army Group on the Continent of Europe, 6 June 1944–8 May 1945*. Germany: 21 Army Group, 1945.

Selected Bibliography 427

Heefner, Wilson A. *Patton's Bulldog: The Life and Service of General Walton H. Walker*. Shippensburg, PA: White Mane Books, 2001.

Hinsley, F. H., et al. *British Intelligence in the Second World War*, vol. 3, pt. 2. London: HMSO, 1988.

Hogan, David W. *A Command Post at War: First Army Headquarters in Europe 1943–45*. Honolulu, HI: University Press of the Pacific, 2000.

Hooton, E. R. *Eagle in Flames: The Fall of the Luftwaffe*. London: Arms and Armour Press, 1997.

Horrocks, Brian. *Corps Commander*. London: Sidgwick and Jackson, 1977.

How, J. J. *Normandy: The British Breakout*. London: William Kimber, 1981.

Howard, Michael. *British Intelligence in the Second World War*, vol. 5, *Strategic Deception*. London: HMSO, 1990.

———. *Grand Strategy*, vol. 4. London: HMSO, 1972.

Hughes, Daniel J., ed. *Moltke on the Art of War: Selected Writings*. New York: Presidio, 1993.

Hughes, Thomas Alexander. *Overlord: General Pete Quesada and the Triumph of Tactical Air Power in World War II*. New York: Free Press, 1995.

Isby, David C., ed. *Fighting in Normandy: The German Army from D-Day to Villers Bocage*. London: Greenhill Books, 2001.

———. *Fighting the Breakout: The German Army in Normandy from Cobra to the Falaise Gap*. London: Greenhill Books, 2004.

Jackson, G. S. *Operations of Eighth Corps: Account of Operations from Normandy to the River Rhine*. London: St. Clements Press, 1948.

Jacobs, W. A. Untitled section in Benjamin Franklin Cooling, ed., *Case Studies in Air Superiority*. Washington, DC: Center for Air Force History, 1994.

———. Untitled section in Benjamin Franklin Cooling, ed., *Case Studies in the Development of Close Air Support*. Washington, DC: Center for Air Force History, 1990.

Joslen, H. F. *Orders of Battle: Second World War 1939–1945*. Reprint, London: HMSO, 1990.

Kay, John. *Obliquity: Why Our Goals Are Best Met Indirectly*. London: Profile Books, 2010.

Kemp, Anthony. *Metz: The Unknown Battle*. London: Frederick Warne, 1980.

Kershaw, Robert J. *It Never Snows in September: The German View of Market Garden and the Battle of Arnhem, September 1944*. Marlborough, UK: Crowood Press, 1990.

Koch, Oscar W., and Robert G. Hays. *G-2: Intelligence for Patton*. Philadelphia: Army Times Publishing, 1971.

Kohn, Richard H., and Joseph P. Harahan, eds. *Condensed Analysis of the Ninth Air Force in the European Theater of Operations*. Washington, DC: Office of Air Force History, 1984.

Lacey-Johnson, Lionel. *Pointblank and Beyond*. Shrewsbury, UK: Airlife, 1991.
Lamb, Richard. *Montgomery in Europe, 1943–45—Success or Failure*. London: Buchan and Enright, 1983.
Laquer, Walter. *Guerilla*. London: Weidenfeld and Nicolson, 1977.
Leonhard, Robert. *The Art of Maneuver: Maneuver Warfare Theory and Air Land Battle*. New York: Presidio, 1994.
Lewin, Ronald. *Montgomery as Military Commander*. London: Batsford, 1971.
Lewis S. J. *Jedburgh Team Operations in Support of the 12th Army Group, August 1944*. Leavenworth, KS: Combat Studies Institute, US Army Command and General Staff College, 1991.
Lind, William S. *Manoeuvre Warfare Handbook*. Boulder, CO: Westview Press, 1985.
Ludewig, Joachim. *Rückzug: The German Retreat from France, 1944*. Lexington: University Press of Kentucky, 2012.
MacDonald, Charles B. *United States Army in World War II, European Theater of Operations: The Siegfried Line Campaign*. Washington, DC: Office of the Chief of Military History, 1961.
Madej, W. Victor. *German War Economy: The Motorization Myth*. Game Publishing, 1984.
———. *Russo-German War*. Allentown, PA: Valor Publishing, 1987.
Mansoor, Peter. *The GI Offensive in Europe: The Triumph of American Infantry Divisions*. Lawrence: University Press of Kansas, 1999.
Mark, Eduard. *Aerial Interdiction in Three Wars*. Washington, DC: Center for Air Force History, 1994.
Martin, H. G. *History of the 15 Scottish Division*. Edinburgh: William Blackwood and Sons, 1948.
Mazower, Mark. *Dark Continent*. London: Allen Lane, 1998.
McFarland, Stephen L., and Wesley P. Newton. *To Command the Sky: The Battle for Air Superiority over Germany 1942–44*. Washington, DC: Smithsonian Institution, 1991.
Meyer, Hubert. *History of the 12 SS Panzer Division Hitlerjugend*. Winnipeg, MB: J. J. Fedorowicz, 1994.
Miller, Edward G. *A Dark and Bloody Ground: The Hürtgen Forest and the Roer River Dams 1944–45*. College Station: Texas A&M University Press, 1995.
Miller, Robert A. *August 1944: The Campaign for France*. New York: Presidio, 1988.
Millett, Allan R., and Williamson Murray. *Military Effectiveness*, vols. 2 and 3, *The Second World War*. London: Allen and Unwin, 1988.
Mitcham, Samuel W. *Panzers in Normandy: General Hans Eberbach and the German Defence of France 1944*. Mechanicsburg, PA: Stackpole Books, 2009.
———. *Retreat to the Reich: The German Defeat in France 1944*. Westport, CT: Praeger, 2000.
Montgomery of Alamein. *El Alamein to the River Sangro: Normandy to the Baltic*. London: Barrie and Jenkins, 1973.

———. *Memoirs*. London: Collins, 1958.
Moulton, J. L. *Battle for Antwerp: Liberation of the City and the Opening of the Scheldt 1944*. London: Ian Allan, 1978.
Murray, G. E. Patrick. *Eisenhower versus Montgomery: The Continuing Debate*. Westport, CT: Praeger, 1996.
Murray, Williamson. *Strategy for Defeat: The Luftwaffe 1933–45*. Maxwell Air Force Base, AL: Air University Press, 1983.
Murray, Williamson, and Allan R. Millett. *A War to Be Won*. Cambridge, MA: Harvard University Press, 2000.
Neilson, Keith, and Roy A. Prete. *Coalition Warfare: An Uneasy Accord*. Waterloo, ON: Wilfred Laurier University Press, 1983.
Nevenkin, Kamen. *Fire Brigades: The Panzer Divisions 143–45*. Winnipeg, MB: J. J. Fedorowicz, 2008.
Olsen, John Andreas, and Martin Van Creveld. *The Evolution of Operational Art*. Oxford: Oxford University Press, 2011.
Otway, T. B. H. *Airborne Forces*. 1951. Reprint, London: Imperial War Museum, 1990.
Parker, Danny S. *The Battle of the Bulge, the German View: Perspectives from Hitler's High Command*. London: Greenhill Books, 1999.
Parlour, A., and S. Parlour. *Phantom at War: The British Army's Secret Intelligence and Communications Regiment*. Bristol, UK: Cerberus, 2003.
Patton, George S., Jr. *War as I Knew It*. Boston: Houghton Mifflin, 1975.
Pemberton, A. L. *The Development of Artillery Tactics and Equipment*. War Office, 1950.
Perret, Geoffrey. *There's a War to Be Won: The United States Army in World War II*. New York: New York: Ballantine, 1991.
Place, Timothy Harrison. *Military Training in the British Army, 1940–1944: From Dunkirk to D-Day*. London: Frank Cass, 2000.
Pogue, Forrest C. *The United States Army in World War II, European Theater of Operations: The Supreme Command*. Washington, DC: Office of the Chief of Military History, 1989.
Porch, Douglas. *The French Secret Services*. London: Macmillan, 1995.
Powell, Geoffrey. *The Devil's Birthday: The Bridges to Arnhem 1944*. Barnsley, UK: Leo Cooper, 1984.
Price, Alfred. *The Last Year of the Luftwaffe, May 1944 to May 1945*. London: Arms and Armour Press, 1993.
Raus, Erhard. *Panzer Operations*, trans. Steven H. Newton. Bridgewater, NJ: Da Capo Press, 2003.
Reardon, Mark J. *Victory at Mortain: Stopping Hitler's Panzer Counter-offensive*. Lawrence: University Press of Kansas, 2002.
Reid, Brian A. *No Holding Back: Operation Totalize, Normandy, August 1944*. Toronto: Robin Brass Studio, 2005.

Reynolds, Michael. *Sons of the Reich, II SS Panzer Corps: Normandy, Arnhem, Ardennes, Eastern Front.* Staplehurst, UK: Spellmount, 2002.

———. *Steel Inferno: I SS Panzer Corps in Normandy.* Staplehurst, UK: Spellmount, 2002.

Rickard, John Nelson. *Patton at Bay: The Lorraine Campaign September to December 1944.* Westport, CT: Praeger, 1999.

Ricks, Thomas E. *The Generals— American Military Command from World War II to Today.* New York: Penguin Press, 2012.

Roberts, G. P. B. *From the Desert to the Baltic.* London: William Kimber, 1987.

Rostron, Peter. *The Military Life and Times of General Sir Miles Dempsey: Montgomery's Army Commander.* Barnsley, UK: Pen and Sword, 2010.

Royal Air Force. *Bombing Analysis Unit Report No. 44: The German Retreat across the Seine in August 1944.* Reprint, MLRS, 2010.

Ruppenthal, Roland G. *United States Army in World War II, the European Theater of Operations: Logistical Support of the Armies,* vols. 1 and 2. Washington, DC: Office of the Chief of Military History, 1953, 1959.

Sixsmith, E. K. G. *Eisenhower as Military Commander.* London: Batsford, 1973.

Smart, Nick. *Biographical Dictionary of British Generals of the Second World War.* Barnsley, UK: Pen and Sword, 2005.

Smith, Bradley F. *Sharing Secrets with Stalin: How the Allies Traded Intelligence 1941–1945.* Lawrence: University Press of Kansas, 1996.

Smith, Sir Rupert. *The Utility of Force: The Art of War in the Modern World.* London: Allen Lane, 2005.

Sokolov, S., ed. *Main Front: Soviet Leaders Look Back on World War II.* London: Brassey's, 1987.

Spires, David N. *Patton's Air Force: Forging a Legendary Air-Ground Team.* Washington, DC: Smithsonian Institution Press, 2002.

Stacey, C. P. *The Victory Campaign, Operations in North-West Europe, 1944–45: Official History of the Canadian Army in the Second World War,* vol. 3. Ottawa: Queen's Printer and Controller of Stationery, 1966.

Stanton, Shelby S. *Order of Battle US Army World War II.* New York: Presidio, 1984.

Steinhardt, P., ed. *Panzer Lehr Division 1944–45.* Solihull, UK: Helion, 2008.

Storr, Jim. *The Human Face of War.* London: Continuum, 2009.

Sylvan, William C., and Francis G. Smith. *Normandy to Victory: The War Diary of General Courtney H. Hodges and the First US Army.* Lexington, KY: Association of the US Army, University Press of Kentucky, 2008.

Tedder, Arthur. *With Prejudice.* Boston: Little, Brown, 1966.

Thompson, Julian. *War behind Enemy Lines.* London: Sidgwick and Jackson, 1998.

Thompson, R. W. *The Eighty-Five Days.* London: Hutchinson, 1957.

Tiecke, Wilhelm. *In the Firestorm of the Last Years of the War.* Winnipeg, MB: J. J. Fedorowicz, 1999.

Tugwell, Maurice. *Arnhem, a Case Study.* Tiptree, UK: Thornton Cox, 1975.

US Department of the Army. *German Defense Tactics against Russian Breakthroughs*. German Report Series, Pamphlet No. 20-233. Washington, DC, 1951.
———. *Operations of Encircled Forces*. German Report Series, Pamphlet No. 20-234. Washington, DC, 1952.
US War Department. *Report by the Supreme Commander to the Combined Chiefs of Staff on the Operations in Europe of the Allied Expeditionary Force 6 June 1944 to 8 May 1945*. Washington, DC: US Government Printing Office, 1945.
US War Department, Military Intelligence Division. *German Military Intelligence 1939–45*. University Publications of America, 1984.
Van Creveld, Martin. *Fighting Power: German and US Army Performance, 1939–45*. Westport, CT: Greenwood Press, 1982.
———. *Supplying War: Logistics from Wallenstein to Patton*. New York: Cambridge University Press, 1977.
Vego, Milan N. *Operational Warfare*. Newport, RI: Naval War College, 2000.
Waddell, Steve R. *United States Army Logistics: The Normandy Campaign 1944*. Westport, CT: Greenwood Press, 1994.
Warden, John A. *The Air Campaign: Planning for Combat*. Washington, DC: National Defense University Press, 1988.
Warlimont, Walter. *Inside Hitler's Headquarters 1939–45*. London: Weidenfeld and Nicolson, 1964.
Wavell, Field Marshal Earl. *The Good Soldier*. London: Macmillan, 1948.
Weigley, Russell F. *The American Way of War*. Bloomington: Indiana University Press, 1977.
———. *Eisenhower's Lieutenants*. Bloomington: Indiana University Press, 1990.
Wilt, Alan F. *The French Riviera Campaign of August 1944*. Carbondale: Southern Illinois University Press, 1981.
Winton, Harold R., and David R. Mets. *The Challenge of Change: Military Institutions and New Realities, 1918–1941*. Lincoln: University of Nebraska Press, 2000.
Wishnevsky, Stephan T. *Courtney Hicks Hodges*. Jefferson, NC: McFarland, 2006.
Wood, James A. *Army of the West: The Weekly Reports of German Army Group B from Normandy to the West Wall*. Mechanicsburg, PA: Stackpole Books, 2007.
Zabecki, David T., ed. *Chief of Staff*. Annapolis, MD: Naval Institute Press, 2008.
Zetterling, Niklas. *Normandy 1944: German Military Organization, Combat Power and Organizational Effectiveness*. Winnipeg, MB: J. J. Fedorowicz, 2000.

Index

1 Airborne Corps, 103
1 Airborne Division, 248, 320, 407n36, 407n38
    Market Garden and, 249–250, 251, 253–254, 255, 256
First Allied Airborne Army, 222, 227, 232, 250, 289, 320, 403n4, 420n48, 421n61
I Armored Corps, Patton and, 41
First Army, 32, 37, 38, 40, 41, 53, 78, 132, 133, 134, 166, 178, 181, 184, 185, 202, 206–207, 209, 211, 228, 232, 238, 257, 262, 266, 271, 276, 305, 333, 340, 352, 379n2, 389n25, 390n30
    VIII Corps and, 207
    21 Army Group and, 311
    advance of, 115–116, 150, 161, 164, 165, 183, 229, 332
    ammunition for, 412n25
    Argentan and, 204
    Bluecoat and, 135, 145
    Bonn and, 341
    casualties for, 119, 198
    Coblenz and, 341
    Cobra and, 85, 121, 123, 124, 127, 128, 146, 156
    Cologne and, 318, 341
    communication with, 235
    encirclement and, 161, 164
    Falaise and, 175, 198
    fuel for, 259, 263, 293, 418n35
    intelligence and, 177
    leadership of, 193–196, 326–332
    Lille-Brussels road and, 259
    logistics and, 272, 408n42
    Mayenne and, 207
    Mortain and, 161
    Normandy and, 72, 112
    operational grouping of, 122
    Osnabrück and, 344
    Overlord and, 70
    plan of, 121–123, 331
    priority for, 309
    reinforcements for, 313
    resistance to, 258, 328
    Rhine and, 247, 346, 347, 352, 359
    Ruhr and, 233, 339
    Saar and, 226
    Second Army and, 186
    Seine and, 147, 327, 332
    span of command of, 388–389n18
    supplying, 228, 229, 230, 259, 286, 289, 290, 291, 294–295, 312, 412n21
    support for, 95, 339–340
    Trun-Chambois and, 195
    Venlo-Wesel axis and, 347
    West Wall and, 352
First Army, 167, 180, 237, 405n22
    Lorraine and, 264
    resistance by, 183
I British Corps, 168, 190, 191, 192, 397n17
    Falaise and, 170
First Canadian Army, 39, 66, 78, 112, 157, 159, 164, 174, 184, 192, 203, 204, 246, 247, 280, 344, 346, 370n16, 377n72, 387n8, 399n35

433

First Canadian Army, *continued*
  Second Army and, 321
  advance of, 312–313
  Antwerp and, 257
  Bluecoat and, 135
  Channel ports and, 257, 346
  Dieppe and, 244
  encirclement and, 113, 161
  Falaise and, 168, 175
  leadership of, 321–326
  Le Havre and, 244
  maintenance for, 245
  Operation Totalize and, 160–161
  overtasking of, 323–324
  reinforcement of, 168, 205
  secondary tasks for, 313
  Trun-Chambois and, 195
I Canadian Corps, 39, 65, 413n3, 415n15
  Dieppe and, 247
  Le Havre and, 245
I Corps, 191, 203, 204, 247, 257
  Boulogne and, 323–324
  Seine and, 175
  support for Second Army, 269
  trucks of, 288
First French Army, 105, 421n63
  Alsace/Lorraine and, 314
1 Infantry Division, 122, 128, 130, 148, 150, 165, 263, 374n54, 389n23, 393n50
  Aachen and, 262
  advance of, 166
  Cobra and, 124, 127
  Mayenne and, 194, 207
  supplying, 286
First Panzer Army, 405n20
First Parachute Army, 238, 241, 254, 347
1 Parachute Brigade, Arnhem and, 253
1 Polish Armored Division, 175, 377n72
I SS Panzer Corps, 145, 173, 180, 191, 192, 207
  Falaise and, 169

I SS Panzer Division, 170, 395n2
  Falaise and, 176
  redeployment of, 189
First US Army Group (FUSAG), 72, 108, 109, 111, 112, 389n21
2 Armored Division, 41, 120, 122, 124, 149, 160, 389n25
  Cobra and, 128, 129, 146
Second Army, 159, 164, 165, 178, 187, 202, 207, 238–239, 269, 288, 322, 326, 327, 340, 379n2, 391n37, 399n35, 416n22
  First Army and, 186
  First Canadian Army and, 321
  administrative position of, 296
  advance of, 161, 228, 244, 245, 345
  Albert Canal and, 239
  Antwerp and, 339
  Arnhem and, 248
  Bluecoat and, 112, 135, 137–139, 140, 152, 156, 167, 194
  Cobra and, 116, 203
  combat power of, 346
  communications and, 347
  Dempsey and, 39, 71
  Falaise and, 168, 172, 174, 175
  Goodwood and, 112
  Krefeld and, 348
  Market Garden and, 248
  Meuse and, 350–351
  Nijmegen and, 235
  operational art of, 184, 185, 247
  as operational backwater, 204
  Osnabrück and, 344
  Panzer Group West and, 72
  reserves and, 138–139
  Rhine and, 346
  Ruhr and, 226, 256–257
  Seine and, 241
  support for, 95, 248, 257, 297, 313, 323
  West Wall and, 230

Second British Army, 32, 132, 134, 317, 368n7
  Arnhem and, 318
  Cobra and, 118
  detaches division to Canadian Army, 204
  divisions of, 311
  Elbeuf and, 195
  leadership of, 184–187, 316–321
  Overlord and, 70
2 Canadian Armored Brigade, 170, 174
II Canadian Corps, 66, 168–169, 189, 190, 192, 244, 321, 323
  Antwerp and, 324
  Falaise pocket and, 166
  Leopold Canal and, 247
  logistic support for, 245
  Normandy and, 187
2 Canadian Infantry Division, 172, 174, 191, 323
  Dieppe and, 245
  Dunkirk and, 247
  Falaise and, 170, 173
  replacements for, 321
II Corps, 38, 41
2 French Armored Division, 160, 164, 166, 182, 229, 395n2, 395n5
2 Infantry Division, 39, 65, 374n54
II Parachute Corps, 120, 127, 389n25
  Cobra and, 128
  withdrawal of, 154
2 Parachute Division, 401n50
II SS Panzer Corps, 92, 109, 112, 143, 151, 156, 173, 177, 180, 217, 345, 392n38, 395n2
  Arnhem and, 239, 360, 362
  Bluecoat and, 155, 167
  Cobra and, 185
  counterattack by, 154, 176
  Market Garden and, 250
  Normandy and, 72, 101
2 SS Panzer Division, 94, 119, 120, 127, 129, 130, 176, 385n64, 388n12, 390n33, 392n41, 395n2
  Bluecoat and, 137
  Falaise and, 176
  redeploying, 148
2 Tactical Air Force, 90, 94, 96, 160, 174, 252, 399n35, 418n31
3 Armored Division, 120, 122, 123, 124, 150, 160, 165, 395n2
  Bluecoat and, 153
  Cobra and, 127, 128
  Marigny and, 148
  Mayenne and, 194, 207
  Stolberg corridor and, 262
  tanks of, 291
Third Army, 38, 46, 95, 112, 118, 120, 121, 133, 160, 166, 167, 178, 181, 207, 209, 210, 226, 228, 232, 237, 238, 258, 260, 262, 263, 264, 327, 328, 329, 390n30, 401n44, 401n47
  activation of, 388n18
  advance of, 147, 161, 164, 198, 211, 229, 309, 313, 339
  ammunition for, 268
  Beauvais and, 210
  Brittany and, 72, 134, 158, 206
  casualties in, 198
  Cobra and, 206, 282
  Cotentin Peninsula and, 200
  counterattacking, 266
  defense by, 294
  Falaise and, 165, 180
  Frankfurt and, 309
  fuel for, 287, 293
  halting of, 227, 313, 314, 333, 334
  Karlsruhe and, 341
  leadership of, 196–200, 332–337
  logistic support for, 234, 265
  Lorraine and, 313, 353
  Mainz and, 341
  Mannheim and, 311, 341
  Meuse and, 294

Third Army, *continued*
  Moselle and, 363
  Normandy and, 123
  ORBAT and, 389n18
  performance of, 336
  reinforcing of, 132, 229
  resistance movements and, 103, 104
  Rhine and, 267, 295, 334, 352
  Saar and, 233, 339
  supplying, 229, 235, 270, 286, 287, 289, 291, 312, 343, 395n4, 412n21, 412n27
  suspension of offensive, 313
  Verdun-Metz axis and, 327
  West Wall and, 352
3 Canadian Infantry Division, 176, 191, 247
  Falaise and, 170
  Laison and, 174
III Corps, 314
III Flak Corps, 78, 109
3 Infantry Division, 142, 143, 144, 155, 157
3 Panzer Grenadier Division, Lorraine and, 238
3 Parachute Division, 92, 119, 143, 144, 145
  Bluecoat and, 156
4 Armored Brigade, 144, 153, 155, 397n18
4 Armored Division, 175, 190, 208, 408n46
  Brittany and, 197
  Cobra and, 130
  exploitation by, 46
  Nancy and, 266
  replacing, 165
  West Wall and, 266
4 Canadian Armored Division, Falaise and, 170, 173, 174, 175
4 Cavalry Group, 329
4 Independent Armored Brigade, 143
4 Infantry Division, 122, 160, 165, 182, 194
  Cobra and, 128

5 Armored Division, 133, 164, 199
  advance of, 180–181
  disembarkation of, 73
V Corps, 122, 165, 181, 195, 208, 257, 260, 270, 327, 330, 374n54
  Ardennes and, 259, 329
  Argentan and, 166
  Meuse and, 331
  Roer and, 271
  Vire and, 194
5 Infantry Division, 265, 415n15
Fifth Panzer Army, 113, 114, 160, 187, 237, 240, 266, 334, 335, 400n40, 405n20, 418n34
  attack by, 210
  Bluecoat and, 145
  disaster for, 178, 182–184, 204, 209, 239, 322, 337
  encirclement of, 161
  logistic situation of, 93
  Lorraine and, 238
  strength of, 180
6 Armored Division, 132, 165, 208, 229, 266, 334, 418n37
  advance of, 267
  Brittany and, 199
  Cobra and, 130
  Metz and, 313
  as reserve, 335
  transfer of, 339
6 Army Group, 270, 281, 353–354, 367n4, 403n8, 409n51, 416n19, 422n63
  Alsace/Lorraine and, 235, 314
  officers in, 372n37
  Rhine and, 226
  SHAEF and, 353
  supplying of, 224, 295
6 Cavalry Group, 326, 371n27, 390n32
VI Corps, Rome and, 402n54
6 Guards Tank Brigade, 138, 153
  Bluecoat and, 142, 155, 168

Sixth Panzer Army, 271, 272, 330, 331, 342
7 Armored Division, 164, 175, 244, 266, 269, 318, 339, 416n17
   Bluecoat and, 138, 140, 142, 152
   Ghent and, 245, 344
   reinforcement by, 168
   removal of, 265
   West Wall and, 334
   withdrawal of, 168
Seventh Army, 41, 126, 237, 334, 416n17, 422n63
   XV Corps and, 353
   advance of, 229, 313
   Alsace/Lorraine and, 314
   Besançon and, 236
   Dijon and, 303
   Rhône valley and, 266
Seventh Army, 123, 132, 147, 187, 193, 259, 382n33, 388n13, 392n38, 392n40, 392n42
   ammunition shortage of, 85
   annihilation of, 114, 178, 182–184, 209, 238, 337
   attacking, 109, 154
   Bluecoat and, 145
   Cherbourg and, 72
   Cobra and, 109–110, 128, 146
   combat formations of, 119, 120–121
   countermoves by, 148
   deterioration of, 94, 112, 114, 130, 145, 239
   disaster for, 322
   encirclement of, 134, 161
   Falaise and, 176
   logistics for, 164, 197, 198
   Mons pocket and, 326
   Normandy and, 112
   ORBAT of, 121
   Panzer Group West and, 143, 144
   strength of, 98, 180, 389n23
   supplies for, 93, 94
   transport for, 84
   withdrawal of, 113, 151, 184, 245, 317
VII Corps, 98, 130, 133, 134, 157, 158, 160, 165, 181, 195, 199, 326, 327, 329, 384n57, 387n8
   XV Corps and, 166
   LVII Panzer Corps and, 194
   Aachen and, 259, 260, 270
   advance of, 208
   Cobra and, 122, 124, 127, 128, 146
   Coutances and, 148
   Hürtgen Forest and, 271
   Liège and, 263
   Mortain and, 161
   strength of, 126
   supplies for, 262
   support for, 194
   West Wall and, 328
Eighth Air Force, 90, 98, 133, 188, 319
   close air support and, 97
   Cobra and, 123
8 Armored Brigade, Bluecoat and, 138, 140
Eighth Army, 36, 58, 59, 401n51
VIII British Corps, 143, 156, 184, 234, 248, 270, 288, 394n60, 399n33, 407n31
   Bluecoat and, 138, 139, 140, 142, 151, 152, 153, 154, 155
   casualties in, 144
   Grouse and, 157, 185
   Maas and, 269
   Market Garden and, 249
   support by, 295
   Vire and, 205
VIII US Corps, 122, 127, 130, 132, 133, 149, 165, 199, 257, 258, 267, 288, 332, 404n9, 407n31, 408n46
   First Army and, 207
   advance of, 150, 195
   Ardennes and, 270
   Brest and, 351

438   Index

VIII US Corps, *continued*
  Brittany and, 226
  Cobra and, 128, 146
  failure of, 147
  reinforcement of, 209, 312
  Sélune and, 158
  supplying, 338
  transfers involving, 314, 339
Ninth Air Force, 9, 90, 99, 133, 268, 384n51, 403n35
  casualties for, 338
  Cobra and, 123, 129, 130
  interdiction by, 127, 312
  supplying, 412n24
  support for, 278
Ninth Army, 258, 270, 404n9, 408n46, 416n17, 416n19
  area of, 409n52
  redeployment of, 234
  truck companies of, 288
9 Infantry Division, 124, 165, 194
  Cobra and, 148
  Marigny and, 389n23
  Stolberg corridor and, 262
9 SS Panzer Division, 126, 144, 154–155, 217, 392n38, 392n40, 394n60, 395n2
  Aachen and, 238
  Arnhem and, 239
  Le Bény-Bocage ridge and, 143
  refitting for, 405n23
IX Tactical Air Command, 95, 96, 97, 98, 123, 130, 160, 199, 384n51
IX Troop Carrier Command, 289
Tenth Army, 402n54, 415n15
X Corps, 40, 378n82
10 SS Panzer Division, 143, 144, 217, 392n38, 394n60, 395n2, 405n23
  Arnhem and, 239
  Falaise and, 176
  Market Garden and, 251
  withdrawal of, 144, 168, 185

11 Armored Division, 104, 138, 144, 317–318, 320
  advance of, 394n58
  Antwerp and, 245
  Bluecoat and, 139, 142, 156–157, 417n22
  casualties in, 143
  Caumont and, 143
  Orne and, 185
  reinforcements for, 318
  rest/maintenance for, 168
  St. Martin and, 153, 393n57
  superiority of, 154–155
12 Army Group, 37, 38, 41, 157, 232, 257–260, 262–268, 270, 276, 294, 298, 303, 345, 386n72, 391n37, 403n8, 412n25
  advance of, 180
  Ardennes and, 226
  Cobra/Falaise pocket and, 158–161, 164–167
  command of, 336
  divisions of, 403n5
  establishment of, 34, 132, 200
  fuel from, 263
  leadership of, 206–211, 337–342
  moving, 347
  operations of, 261 (map)
  role of, 233
  Ruhr and, 226
  Saar and, 340
  supplying, 224, 228, 279, 288, 289, 291, 293, 310
  transfer to, 313, 353
XII British Corps, 132, 175, 185, 191, 244, 248, 318, 323, 324
  Antwerp and, 246, 247
  attack on, 394n63
  Bluecoat and, 140, 144
  Falaise and, 156, 167, 170, 174
  Ghent and, 245, 344
  Market Garden and, 249, 323

Index 439

Orne and, 138
support by, 246, 317
support for, 204
12 SS Panzer Division, 144, 145, 169–170, 172
casualties for, 187
counterattack by, 173
XII US Corps, 178, 209, 258, 267, 332, 401n48, 408n46
advance of, 197–198, 199
Commercy and, 263
Darmstadt and, 266
logistic support for, 407n31
Moselle and, 46, 266
Nancy and, 334, 335
Orléans and, 167
POL for, 265
Seine and, 208
supplying, 294
Troyes and, 263
12 Volksgrenadier Division, 238, 240, 262, 327
XIII Corps, 39
XIV Panzer Corp, 398n28, 419n40
Fifteenth Air Force, 90, 383n36
Fifteenth Army, 71, 120, 159, 172, 193, 237, 280, 322, 392n40, 400n41
Albert Canal and, 239
attack on, 240
combat power of, 244
destruction of, 360
divisions from, 126
Fortress Southern Holland and, 248
invasion and, 72
Market Garden and, 255, 347
reinforcements from, 182
resistance by, 183
strength of, 180
trapping, 246, 317, 319–320
withdrawal of, 244, 245, 317, 318, 324, 344, 345
15 Army Group, 401n51

XV Corps, 132, 133, 167, 176, 178, 180, 181, 194, 195, 209, 258, 264, 267, 270, 334, 335, 401n52, 408n45
VII Corps and, 166
advance of, 150, 161, 164, 165, 186, 197, 199, 395n2
Argentan and, 203, 207
Dreux and, 166
encirclement and, 164
Falaise and, 177, 197, 207
halting of, 199
Le Mans and, 160, 161, 196
Mannheim and, 266
Mantes and, 178, 206
Mayenne and, 159, 206
Moselle and, 334
Seine and, 208
subordination of, 332
support by, 266
transfer of, 313, 314, 353
15 Infantry Division, 145
Bluecoat and, 138, 139, 140, 142, 152, 155
withdrawal of, 168
15 Panzer Grenadier Division, 238, 267
17 SS Panzer Grenadier Division, 94, 119, 127, 238, 395n2
Nineteenth Army, 237, 238, 239, 353, 405n20, 409n51
XIX Corps, 122, 130, 165, 195, 209, 246, 257, 260, 262, 269, 271, 327, 328, 331, 339
Aachen and, 265, 270, 329
advance of, 181, 186, 343
Albert Canal and, 259
Cobra and, 128
Dreux and, 178
reinforcements from, 229
Tournai and, 305, 326
Vire and, 194
XIX Tactical Air Command (TAC), 104, 390n30, 401n45, 418–419n37

440   Index

XX Corps, 132, 159, 160, 164, 166, 178, 209, 258, 401n52
  advance of, 197–198, 199, 265
  Falaise and, 180
  Frankfurt and, 266
  Metz and, 333, 335
  Meuse and, 263
  POL for, 265
  reinforcements for, 197
  Seine and, 208, 263
  supplying, 294
21 Army Group, 58, 63, 94, 112, 132, 157, 164, 211, 227, 234, 269, 305, 309, 321, 326, 339, 340, 351, 372nn35–36, 398n23, 403n8
  First Army and, 311
  administrative appreciation of, 310
  advance of, 178, 243–251, 253–257
  Antwerp and, 317
  attack by, 203
  Bluecoat and, 135, 167–170, 172–176
  Caen-Falaise axis and, 159–160
  encirclement and, 161
  Falaise pocket and, 167–170, 172–176
  firepower issues and, 82
  leadership of, 201–206
  logistics and, 248
  Market Garden and, 270
  Pas de Calais and, 244
  replacements for, 377n71
  Ruhr and, 226, 233, 246, 346
  shortages for, 274
  strength of, 203
  supplying, 224, 266, 281, 288, 289, 297
  support for, 227, 235, 295
21 Panzer Division, 154, 240, 392n38, 394n60
  Bluecoat and, 137, 140, 142, 153
  counterattack by, 153
  reinforcing, 143
23 Special Troops, Metz and, 313
XXV Corps, 132, 401n48

29 Guards Armored Brigade, Bluecoat and, 168
29 Infantry Division, 374n54, 390n27
XXX Corps, 144, 156, 195, 244, 245, 256, 344, 345, 370n16, 393n56, 394n60
  advance of, 246, 319
  Antwerp and, 317
  Beeringen and, 263
  Bluecoat and, 138, 139, 140, 151, 152, 393n55
  Caen and, 143
  casualties in, 407n38
  Market Garden and, 248–249, 250, 254
  performance of, 184
  Scheldt estuary and, 248
  support for, 246, 407n31
30 Infantry Division, 124, 128, 160
31 Tank Brigade, 156
33 Armored Brigade, 170, 191, 397n17
34 Tank Brigade, 156
35 Infantry Division, 160, 164, 208, 395n5
38 Group (RAF), 289
43 Infantry Division, 143
  Arnhem and, 246
  Bluecoat and, 138, 139, 140, 152
  Grave bridge and, 255
  Market Garden and, 256
46 Group (RAF), 289
XLVII Panzer Corps, 96, 130, 134, 144, 159, 193, 240, 395n2
  Bluecoat and, 146
  Cobra and, 127
  sorties against, 160
  withdrawal of, 195
49 Division, 420n48
50 Infantry Division, 318, 415n15
  Bluecoat and, 138, 152
51 Highland Division, 170, 190, 191, 397n17
52 British Division, 257
55 Division, 415n15
56 Infantry Brigade, Bluecoat and, 138

LVII Panzer Corps, 194, 240, 395n2
LVIII Panzer Corps, 240
59 Infantry Division, 168, 185, 255, 415n15
61 Division, 415n15
70 Infantry Division, Albert Canal and, 406n25
LXXIV Corps, 143, 392n38
    Bluecoat and, 137, 140
77 Infantry Division, 92, 401n50
79 Armored Division, 78, 133
79 Infantry Division, 158, 181, 206, 328
LXXX Corps, 167
80 Infantry Division, 164, 166, 199, 395n5, 396n9
LXXXI Corps, 134, 164
82 Airborne Division, 379n5
    casualties in, 407n38
    Grave and, 248
    Market Garden and, 253, 255
    Nijmegen and, 248
83 Group (RAF), 95, 251, 399, 399n35
83 Infantry Division, 266, 339, 418n37
LXXXIV Corps, 94, 120, 127, 130, 149, 389n25, 392n41, 393n51
    Cobra and, 126
    escape of, 129
84 Group (RAF), 95, 399n35
85 Infantry Division, 172, 173
LXXXVI Corps, 180, 190, 191, 192, 204, 400n38
89 Infantry Division, 169, 172, 173, 188
90 Infantry Division, 166, 176, 396n9
91 Airlanding Division, 401n50
101 Airborne Division, 248, 407n38
    Market Garden and, 253–254
101 SS Heavy Panzer Battalion, tanks of, 381n17
102 SS Heavy Tank Battalion, 143, 173
104 Infantry Division, 257, 339, 416n17
116 Panzer Division, 120, 127, 130, 164, 392n41, 395n2, 397n21
    Bluecoat and, 137

176 Infantry Division, Albert Canal and, 406n25
185 Infantry Brigade, 157
265 Infantry Division, 401n50
266 Infantry Division, 401n50
271 Infantry Division, 175
272 Infantry Division, 400n38
276 Infantry Division, Bluecoat and, 137, 140
326 Infantry Division, 153, 156, 394n60
    Bluecoat and, 140
    reinforcing, 143
343 Infantry Division, 401n50
346 Infantry Division, 400n38
352 Infantry Division, 374n54
353 Infantry Division, 127
462 Infantry Division, 265, 406n25
708 Infantry Division, 134
711 Infantry Division, 400n38

Aachen, 220, 226, 240, 265, 292, 311, 313, 326, 346, 347, 411n17, 418n34, 420n49
    advance on, 238, 260, 262, 270, 306, 328, 329
    bombardment of, 407n33
    capture of, 271, 327, 330
Aa River, 248
Adair, Sir Alan, 320
Advanced Section (COMZ), 276, 285, 414n10
AEAF. *See* Allied Expeditionary Air Forces
AFVs, 76, 78, 79, 94, 96, 130, 381n14, 395n2, 397n21, 398n24
    Allied, 77
    German, 77
    losses of, 98
AGF. *See* Army Ground Forces
AGRAs. *See* Army Groups, Royal Artillery
Aircraft industry, offensive against, 87–88

Aircrews, 100
  casualties among, 87, 88, 89
Air Defense (Great Britain), 251, 383n36
Air interdiction, 71, 90–94, 114, 120, 390n31, 405n21, 412n20
  impact of, 92, 94, 95, 98, 100
  limits of, 101
Airpower, 13, 91, 136, 146, 384n54, 386n70
  conclusions about, 100–101
  control of, 21
  impact of, 4, 94
  land campaigns and, 87–101
  tactical, 53, 88, 97
Air preparation for ground attack, 99
Air superiority, 19, 48, 68, 79, 95, 351
  air supremacy and, 87–90
  establishing, 89, 100
Air support, 62, 64, 134, 139, 346, 403n2
  tactical, 148
Air supremacy, 95, 109, 156, 351, 374n53, 412n20
  air superiority and, 87–90
Albert Canal, 220, 238, 239, 246, 259, 262, 332, 406n25, 417n24
  advance on, 317, 318
  bridgehead over, 244
Alençon, 157, 159, 161, 164, 165, 176, 284, 285
  advance on, 168, 194
Alexander, General, 301, 401n51
Allied Airborne Army, 250
Allied Expeditionary Air Forces (AEAF), 90, 91, 108, 178, 182, 219
Allied Expeditionary Force (AEF), 68, 101, 114, 187, 219, 220, 224, 228
  chain of command of, 33–43
Allied Naval Expeditionary Forces (ANEF), 219
Allied Rapid Reaction Corps (NATO), 1
Alsace, 220, 226, 313, 352, 354, 412n27, 421n63

advance on, 235, 314
defending, 238
Ammunition, 272, 297, 307, 342, 412n25
  dumps, 90, 91, 109
  shortages of, 9, 33, 85, 94, 149, 273, 274, 276, 290, 388n17, 398n22
  supply of, 52, 81, 93, 268, 277, 290, 292, 294
  types of, 60, 79, 85, 94, 274
Amsterdam, 220
  advance on, 239, 247
Antiaircraft guns, 79, 172–173, 388n17
  antitank role for, 78
Antitank battalions, 49, 77, 137, 381n14
Antitank guns, 63, 78, 140, 183, 189, 381n19, 403n3, 405n23
  German, 76, 83
  SP, 77, 80, 172
Antwerp, 226, 230, 238, 244, 280, 298, 309, 323, 346, 361, 362, 364
  advance on, 228, 259, 311, 318, 324
  capture of, 224, 226, 227, 232, 234, 245, 247, 310, 312, 317, 320, 322, 343, 344, 350
  clearing of approaches, 229, 313–314, 322, 346, 417n27
  importance of, 108, 235, 239, 257, 269, 272, 409n50, 415n14, 420n50, 421n55
  opening of, 41, 269, 282, 292, 310, 322, 324, 339, 343, 347, 348, 351, 360
  pipelines from, 284
  port of, 220, 222, 229, 246, 247, 257, 312
  supply through, 224, 281, 292, 293, 296
APCs. See Armored personnel carriers
Arado 23, photoreconnaissance by, 110
Ardennes, 102, 224, 226, 227, 230, 257, 259, 270, 271, 294, 308, 311, 312, 313, 327, 329, 331, 338, 361
  counteroffensive through, 272, 422n64

described, 222
offensive in, 214, 217
Argentan, 70, 165, 166, 176, 195, 197, 207, 208, 209, 283, 397n21
  advance on, 164, 168, 199, 203
Armor, 76–78, 155, 223
Armored divisions, 45, 46, 49, 53, 147, 149, 170
Armored personnel carriers (APCs), 169, 174, 187, 191, 399n33
Army Ground Forces (AGF), 44, 82, 389n21
Army Group B, 84, 93, 109, 111, 113, 116, 130, 173, 176, 187, 198, 238, 240
  Bluecoat and, 145
  combat effectiveness and, 237
  decline of, 109, 204–205
  defeat of, 134, 394n62
  Normandy and, 217
  Oosterbeek and, 239
  reinforcements and, 121
  report of, 112
  Rhine and, 359
  subordinate commanders and, 300
  withdrawal of, 177
Army Group G, 104, 237, 372n32, 405n20, 409n51
Army Group of the Centre, 227, 229
Army Group of the North, 227, 229
Army Group of the South, 227
Army Groups, Royal Artillery (AGRAs), 63, 65, 66, 73, 79, 138, 170, 173, 188
Army of the West, 111
  cohesion of, 217
  combat effectiveness of, 237
  losses of, 359, 409n53
Army Y, 177
Arnhem, 239, 247, 248, 263, 318, 319, 328, 346, 351, 405n23, 405n25, 407n34
  advance on, 251, 323, 344
  bridge at, 246, 251, 253, 254, 255, 347

  crossing Rhine at, 230, 297, 313
  failure at, 256–257, 348, 421n54
  reinforcing, 345
Arnold, Henry H., Market Garden and, 250, 421n61
Artillery, 53, 79–81, 90, 136
  Allied, 79, 81
  antiaircraft, 79, 81, 172–173, 388n17
  command of, 79–80
  German, 79, 80, 81, 83
  overestimation of, 49–50
  SP, 49, 120, 123, 140
  support, 49
Atlantic Wall, 220, 238, 264, 403n3
Auftragstaktik, 52, 375n63, 376n65, 394n62
Avranches, 110, 119, 134, 150, 159, 160, 178, 193, 395n5
  advance on, 176, 389n19
  counteroffensive toward, 177, 202

Balance, 5, 19, 28, 349
  need for, 20
  psychological/physical, 52
  recovering, 360
BARs. *See* Browning automatic rifles
Base Section (COMZ), 276, 414nn9–10
Battle of Britain, air superiority and, 87
Bayerlein, Lieutenant General, 98
Bayeux, supply through, 289
Beauvais, 180, 199, 209, 210, 211, 283
Beeringen, 246, 263, 345
BEF. *See* British Expeditionary Force
Befehlstaktik, 375n63, 376n65, 394n62
Berlin, 226, 228, 230
  advance on, 233, 234, 308, 337
BG *Krause*, 189
BG *Olboeter*, 144, 173, 174, 189
BG *Waldmüller*, 172, 173
BG *Weiss*, 143, 144
BG *Wünsche*, 172, 173, 174
  retreat of, 191–192

Bismarck, Otto von, 215
Blaskowitz, Colonel General, 104
Bocage, 118, 119, 124, 127, 134, 136, 142, 150, 152, 164, 216
   close air support in, 96
   fighting through, 50, 53, 60, 61, 273
Boer War, 74
Bomber Command, 90, 188, 418n31
   close air support and, 97
Bonn, 257, 270, 295, 341
   advance on, 234, 247, 313
   bridgehead at, 340
Booth, Brigadier, 190, 397n18
Boulogne, 239, 245, 281, 297, 312, 417–418nn28–29
   advance on, 240, 311
   bombardment of, 407n33, 418n31
   capture of, 247, 269, 322, 323–324
   PLUTO and, 284
   supply through, 310, 313, 323, 343
Bradley, Omar N., 175, 180, 192, 195, 196–197, 216, 227, 244, 257, 270, 272, 289, 326, 329, 334, 335, 364, 372n37, 387nn6–7, 388n16, 389n18, 391n37, 392n41, 392nn43–44
   Third Army and, 198
   XV Corps and, 199, 207, 401n52
   Bonn and, 234
   Brest and, 268, 338, 341
   Brittany and, 158, 206
   close air support and, 94
   Cobra and, 112, 116, 120, 121–122, 123, 124, 128, 146, 147, 150, 206, 363
   Collins and, 389n19
   Cologne and, 234
   command issues and, 38, 184, 299, 301, 306
   COMZ and, 276
   Corlett and, 390n26
   criticism of, 208–209, 341
   Dempsey and, 186, 204
   Eisenhower and, 38, 161, 200, 202, 214, 215, 228, 235, 301, 336, 337, 341, 343, 347, 359
   Falaise and, 165
   frontal attacks and, 198
   fuel and, 293
   Gerow and, 166
   Hodges and, 39, 40, 116, 132, 328, 339
   intelligence and, 107
   Leavenworth and, 341
   logistics and, 296
   Market Garden and, 351
   Metz-Saar-Frankfurt axis and, 264, 309
   Montgomery and, 37, 38, 150, 161, 178, 201, 202, 204, 205, 206, 209, 211, 226, 232, 305, 311, 339, 340–341, 343, 344, 348, 356, 401n51, 401n53, 419n45
   Mortain and, 199
   Normandy and, 72, 215
   operational art/generalship of, 8, 206–211, 337–342
   Overlord and, 70, 210
   Paris-Orléans gap and, 167
   Patton and, 41, 158–159, 196, 197, 199, 208, 229, 232, 263, 266, 295, 311, 314, 333, 338–339, 341, 357, 390n32, 400n42, 401n45, 418n37
   Rhine and, 342
   Ruhr and, 337, 340
   Saar and, 308, 309
   security and, 133
   southern axis and, 309
   supplies for, 342
   tactical solutions and, 217
   Verdun and, 419n46
   views of, 1
   working relations with, 95
Breda, advance on, 247
Brereton, Lewis H., 250, 289, 319, 403n4, 403n35

Breskens pocket, 239, 247, 312, 325, 326, 348
Brest, 50, 132, 208, 224, 229, 232, 267, 270, 341
  battle for, 165, 268, 295, 407n33, 416n16
  capture of, 114, 234, 279, 338
  port of, 258
  reduction of, 312, 342, 350, 404n9
  supply through, 278, 279, 281, 338
Breton ports, 213, 242, 279, 281, 309, 339, 350
  capture of, 114, 276, 289
  supply through, 278
  urgent need for, 349
British Army, 1, 17, 370n16, 372n39, 377n73
  approach to war of, 54–64, 369n7
  command and control and, 61
  deep operations and, 315
  in 1944, 43–66
British Directorate-General Doctrine and Development, 377n76
British Expeditionary Force (BEF), 57, 59
British Joint Intelligence Committee, 236
Brittany, 70, 72, 92, 103, 115, 118, 120, 123, 128, 130, 132, 134, 197, 201, 207, 209, 210, 213, 229, 240, 242, 258, 266, 267, 268, 275, 290, 312, 332, 335
  breakout into, 147, 150, 199, 206
  clearing, 70, 146, 158
  importance of, 208, 279
  retreat from, 401n50
  sieges in, 360
Brittany ports, 121, 201, 203, 242, 268, 350, 403n5, 415–416n16
  capture of, 146
  supply through, 279, 292, 338
Broadhurst, Harry, 95, 189

Brooke, Sir Alan, 36, 57, 62, 212, 213, 214, 216, 235, 302, 322, 358, 364, 378n80, 391n37
  Antwerp and, 269, 348
  Bluecoat and, 135, 139
  Montgomery and, 355, 371n28, 420n50
Brooks, Edward H., 128, 129, 149
Brown, L. O., 94–95, 418n31
Browning, Frederick "Boy," 250, 254, 255, 407n35
  airborne plan of, 320, 420n52
  Market Garden and, 248, 253
Browning automatic rifles (BARs), 75, 81, 380n13
Bruges-Ghent Canal, 245
Brussels, 244, 246, 257, 283, 303, 416n22
  advance on, 259
  capture of, 245, 317
  supply through, 289, 296
Bucknall, C. Gerald, 138, 152, 256, 370n16

C-47 (air transport), 289
Cab rank system, 95, 97, 189
Caen, 5, 42, 127, 130, 136, 138, 139, 143, 145, 151, 155, 156, 159, 202, 207
  battle for, 215, 307
  capture of, 39, 71, 72, 115, 134
  defense of, 135
Caen-Falaise axis, 70, 109, 112, 113, 157, 161, 168, 174
  offensive on, 159–160
Calais, 239, 244, 245, 324, 417–418nn28–29
  advance on, 240, 247, 311
  bombardment of, 407n33, 418n31
  capture of, 247, 269, 322
  opening of, 323
  supply through, 281, 310, 313, 343
Camberley Staff College, 307
Canadian Army, 43–66
  approach to war of, 64–66

446   Index

Canadian Army Overseas (CAO), 65, 379n86
Canadian Expeditionary Force, 39
Canadian National Defense, 321
Cap Gris Nez, 324, 417n28
Cassino, close air support at, 97
Casualties, 24, 33, 47, 74, 118, 144, 149, 168, 361, 373n47, 377n71, 417n23
  aircrew, 87, 88, 89
  Allied, 54, 66, 76, 98, 183, 268, 274, 380n9
  civilian, 383n41
  German, 80, 82, 92, 183, 267, 368n4
  heavy, 50–51, 67, 378n80
  intelligence about, 108
  minimizing, 59, 66, 98, 275, 332
  psychological, 47, 377n75
  rates, 72, 377n71, 411n8
  resistance movements and, 103
  sensitivity to, 315, 321
Caumont, 118, 121, 129, 135–136, 137, 139, 143, 159, 161, 387n6
CCA. *See* Combat Command A
CCB. *See* Combat Command B
CCS. *See* Combined Chiefs of Staff
Central Army Group, 294, 339, 403n8, 416n19
  advance of, 232, 359
  tasks for, 337
Channel ports, 203, 222, 226, 244, 247, 268, 280, 322, 323, 343, 346, 380n6, 417n27
  capture of, 227, 293, 309, 310, 344
  clearing, 99, 224, 226, 310
  supply through, 296
Charteris, Brigadier, 105
Chartres, 159, 178, 181, 197, 201, 284, 285
  capture of, 167
  railheads at, 283
  supply through, 286
Cherbourg, 38, 50, 70, 202, 206, 222, 223, 282, 284, 296, 338
  advance on, 71
  bombardment of, 419n39
  capture of, 72, 115, 134, 215, 279, 280
  supply through, 224, 279, 281, 283, 292, 338
Chief of Imperial General Staff (CIGS), 36, 39, 135, 177, 182, 214, 356, 413n6, 420n50
Chief of Staff of the Army, 34
Chief of the Air Staff, 99
Churchill, Winston S., 72, 212, 213, 415n15, 422n65
Churchill tanks, 77, 78, 79, 82
CIGS. *See* Chief of Imperial General Staff
Civil War, US, 43, 44, 215
Clark, Mark, 402n54
Clausewitz, Carl von, 18, 20, 52, 107, 114, 346, 369n7, 372n33
  fog of war and, 15
  generals and, 24
  on war, 26, 30
Close air support, 48, 50, 86, 128, 155, 157, 160, 189, 251, 272, 389n21
  air supremacy and, 89
  firepower and, 90
  impact of, 94–100
  interdiction and, 244
  reliance on, 123, 223, 251, 254, 267, 329, 385n61
Coasters, 273, 279, 280, 281, 283, 287
Coblenz, 257, 258, 260, 264, 327, 341
Collins, J. Lawton, 148, 195, 260, 262, 389n23, 390n27, 392n45
  Bradley and, 389n19
  Cobra and, 122, 124, 126, 128, 129, 147
  encirclement and, 146
  Falaise and, 166
  Hodges and, 326, 328
  Hürtgen Forest and, 330
  Roer and, 271
  Stolberg corridor and, 328

Cologne, 219, 220, 222, 257, 269, 270, 271, 295, 311, 318, 327, 328, 330, 341, 347
  advance on, 234, 247, 313, 342, 419n44
  bridgehead at, 340
Combat Command A (CCA), 45, 128, 129, 130, 150
Combat Command B (CCB), 45, 122, 129, 149, 160
Combat Command R, 45, 149
Combined-arms approach, 14, 49, 54, 66
Combined Chiefs of Staff (CCS), 35, 67, 68, 87, 219, 227, 229, 306, 322, 364, 385n61
Command, 5, 8, 86, 342
  challenges of, 22–43, 299–305
  high, 21, 30, 41–42
  leadership and, 24–25
  operational, 23, 33
  responsibility of, 27
  tactical, 22, 23
Command and control, 5, 8, 13, 14, 85–86, 341
  British, 61
  disruption of, 98
  doctrine and, 378n81
Commanders
  army group, 35, 36
  chiefs of staff and, 31
  corps, 316, 317
  described, 24–30
  divisional, 62, 192–193
  freedom of action for, 48
  lack of awareness of, 217–218
  operational-level, 7, 12, 14, 15, 24, 50, 315, 316, 360, 369n14, 371n29
  press and, 42
  senior, 62, 67
  staffs and, 31, 33–34
  subordinate, 26, 27, 31, 32, 300, 376n64
  tactical, 15, 321
  trust between, 53

Communications, 18, 19, 20, 31, 68, 81, 88, 101, 102, 106, 107, 148, 285, 288, 311, 346
  development of, 41, 62
  disrupting, 62, 98, 104, 338, 398n22
Communications zone (COMZ), 47, 84, 275, 284, 285, 298, 352, 411n10, 412n25
  criticism of, 293
  liaison by, 277
  pressure on, 274, 282
  relieving, 353
  sections of, 276
  SHAEF and, 285, 303, 304
  successes for, 287–288
  supplying by, 228, 229, 263, 286, 287, 291–292, 293, 295, 412n21, 418n35
  War Department and, 303
Concentration, 18, 19, 48, 112, 116, 123, 156, 185, 196, 197, 270, 271, 307, 325–333, 341–342, 346, 351
Conceptual divide, 224, 226–230, 232–236
Coningham, Arthur, 94, 251, 399n35, 418n31
  desert war and, 384n49
Connor, Fox, 114
Cooperation, 14, 20–21, 33, 54, 201, 214, 217, 305, 311, 340, 356, 359
  ground-air, 49, 107, 174
  tank-infantry, 49, 60, 64, 86, 142, 152, 154, 173, 190
Corlett, Charles H., 262, 263, 326, 331
  Cobra and, 128
  corps command for, 389n26
  experience of, 390n26
  Roer and, 271
Cotentin Peninsula, 115, 118, 120, 128, 200
Coutances, 118, 119, 120, 122, 123, 124, 126, 127, 128, 146
  encirclement at, 148

Crerar, H. D. G. (Harry), 161, 173, 174, 175, 178, 257, 323, 348, 370n16, 372n36, 397n16, 399n35, 417n27, 417n29
- Boulogne and, 269
- Bruges and, 244
- Calais and, 244, 269
- career of, 39
- Channel ports and, 247
- commanders and, 192–193
- creativity and, 184
- criticism of, 321, 322, 326
- Dempsey and, 204
- divisions under command, 203–204
- Falaise and, 168
- health problems of, 325, 326
- Hodges and, 195
- Le Havre and, 245
- Montgomery and, 40, 191, 192, 205, 321–322, 324, 325, 343, 344, 357, 400n39
- operational art/generalship of, 187–193
- Operation Totalize and, 189
- Simonds and, 189, 190, 191, 192
- supply shortage for, 248
- tactical solutions and, 217
- working relations with L. O. Brown, 95

Cromwell tanks, 76, 77, 82

Culminating point, 5, 114, 155, 243, 256, 269, 328, 386, 409

D-Day, 39, 46, 53, 57, 83, 183, 319, 373n48, 379n5
- objectives of, 71

Deception, 10, 12, 13, 18, 19, 68, 70–71, 336, 368, 416n18
- operational-level, 9, 313
- Operation Fortitude, 89, 92, 100, 111, 145
- resources for, 53
- Soviet, 106

Decision making, 7, 17, 28, 186, 316, 349
- operational-level, 9, 110, 360
- strategic, 3, 9, 354
- tactical, 52

Deep battle, forward detachment and, 399n37

Deep Operations theory, 315, 368n5

de Gaulle, Charles, 101, 182
- Alsace and, 421n63
- resistance movements and, 102
- Roosevelt and, 402n59

de Guingand, Francis, 227, 234, 302, 415n14

Dempsey, Miles, 71, 161, 175, 178, 203, 208, 210, 258, 305, 322, 325, 348, 368n7, 387n6
- Albert Canal and, 332
- Antwerp and, 246, 317
- Bluecoat and, 135, 138, 151, 152, 154, 156, 393n54
- Bradley and, 186, 204
- Cobra and, 116
- corps commanders and, 153
- creativity and, 184
- Crerar and, 204
- criticism of, 318, 321
- Eindhoven and, 297, 347
- Market Garden and, 250, 251, 254, 256, 320
- Montgomery and, 37, 39, 187, 192, 201, 204, 205, 372n36, 392n38
- O'Connor and, 184
- operational art/generalship of, 184–187, 316–321
- Operation Overlord and, 70
- plan by, 320
- publicity and, 42
- Ruhr and, 244, 269, 319
- tactical solutions and, 217
- Tournai and, 259
- working relations with Broadhurst, 95

Devers, Jacob L., 270, 353, 354, 367n4
  Dijon and, 300
  Eisenhower and, 416n19
  progress of, 342
  theory and, 372n37
Dick, C. J., 367n5
Dieppe, 65, 245, 247, 288, 321
  capture of, 244, 245
  opening of, 280, 281, 283
  supply through, 297, 310, 343
Dijon, 229, 303, 313
Dives, 166, 169, 175, 177, 181, 182
Division von Tettau, 405n25
Doctrine, 10, 11–17, 20, 22, 23, 59, 63, 86, 306, 307
  American, 113
  British, 55
  command and control and, 378n81
  differences in, 35, 156, 354, 355
  effective common, 15–16
  experiments in, 63
  German, 52
  inadequacies in, 34, 42, 67, 73, 362
  interpretation of, 58, 372n36
  tactical, 47–48, 153, 359
"Doctrine of Combat" (manual), 47–48
Domfront, 70, 93, 157, 161, 165, 194
Donnelly, C., 367n5
Dreux, 159, 165, 166, 178, 197, 199, 283, 285
Dunkirk, 36, 64, 65, 111, 216, 239, 245
  advance on, 240, 323
  capture of, demanded, 322
  masking of, 247, 323
  supply through, 343
Düren, 271, 330
Düsseldorf, 38, 270, 271, 347
Dyle, crossing, 245

Eberbach, General, 160, 173, 176, 188
  on Allies/Seine, 217
  on British pause, 154

Eddy, Manton S., 334, 401n48
  Marigny and, 389n23
  Orléans and, 167
  Patton and, 266, 267, 336
  POL for, 265
  reinforcements for, 335
  support for, 266
Eifel, 260, 327, 328, 330–331
Eindhoven, 239, 253, 254, 283, 284, 347, 348, 413n32
  advance on, 255, 297
Eisenhower, Dwight D., 201, 242, 266, 276, 277, 298, 309, 334, 335, 364, 367n4, 385n61, 389n18
  airpower and, 91, 99
  Antwerp and, 269, 351, 409n50, 421n55
  Anvil/Dragoon and, 353, 402n56
  Bluecoat and, 135, 139
  Bradley and, 38, 161, 200, 202, 214, 215, 228, 235, 301, 336, 337, 341, 343, 347, 413n6
  Brest and, 268, 338, 416n16
  Brittany and, 158, 213, 279, 415–416n16
  CCS and, 229
  commanders and, 35, 42
  command issues and, 8, 213, 214–217, 226–227, 299–302, 304, 306, 310, 314
  culminating point and, 114
  fuel resources and, 263
  Hodges and, 228, 327, 329
  leadership of, 68, 355, 357, 358
  logistics and, 294, 296, 352
  Market Garden and, 256, 259, 347, 350, 351, 421n61
  Marshall and, 212, 242, 243, 299, 320, 355, 356, 414n11
  Montgomery and, 35, 36, 37, 99, 147, 202, 213, 214, 215, 224, 227, 228, 229, 230, 233, 234, 272, 282, 299,

Eisenhower, Dwight D., *continued*
    300, 301, 302, 303, 310–311, 319,
    339, 347, 348, 349, 351, 356, 357,
    358, 360, 379n2, 402n59, 409n52
  operational art/generalship of,
    211–216, 308, 349–359, 362, 364
  Paris and, 181–182, 385n66
  Patton and, 41, 199–200, 228, 263,
    372n34
  political imperative of, 311–312
  resistance efforts and, 104
  Rhine and, 318, 354
  Ruhr and, 312, 345
  Scheldt estuary and, 239
  Seine and, 349
  supplies and, 289, 313
  Tunisian campaign and, 358–359
  Versailles conference and, 235, 267
  views of, 2
El Alamein, 36, 57, 378n82
Elbeuf, 178, 181, 183, 195, 206
Encirclement, 113, 134, 146, 148, 149,
    164, 166, 185, 186, 359
  deep, 176–178, 180–184
  Falaise, 176–178, 180–184
  short, 158–161
Erickson, John, 367n5
Escaut Canal, 246, 249, 317
Eugene, Prince, 370n14
Eure, 92, 164, 166, 181, 186
European theatre of operations (ETO),
    4, 9, 34, 35, 46, 47, 274, 276, 300,
    367n4, 413n3
Experimental Mechanized Force, 55

Falaise, 42, 70, 136, 145, 159, 161, 170,
    172, 173, 174, 177, 401n52
  advance on, 156, 157, 167, 191, 197,
    202, 207
  capture of, 164–165, 166, 175, 203
Falaise-Argentan-Alençon road, 161, 166,
    178, 194

Falaise pocket, 96, 158–161, 164–167,
    167–170, 172–176
  closing of, 178, 182, 204, 362
  creation of, 161, 162 (map), 163 (map)
  encirclement and, 176–178, 180–184
  southern jaw of, 161, 164–167
FFI. *See* Forces Françaises de l'Intérieur
Field Service Regulations, 4, 17, 58, 61
Firefly tanks, 77, 82
Firepower, 6, 7, 50, 53, 79, 82
  close air support and, 86, 90
  deficiency in, 81
  mobility and, 13, 14, 85
  superior, 22, 59–60, 307, 326, 363,
    369n5, 374n53
First World War, 4, 12, 16, 17, 40, 42, 58,
    61, 65, 67, 72, 85, 105
  British casualties in, 54, 55
  Montgomery and, 59
  United States and, 43, 44
Flers, 142, 144, 154, 159, 161, 167
flexibility, 5, 20, 307
  imagination and, 28–29
FM 100-5 Operations, 4, 45, 51, 52, 53,
    315
Fontainebleau, bridgehead at, 167
Foot, M. R. D., 386n70
Force
  concentration of, 18, 48, 307
  correlation of, 73–81
  ratios, 74, 307
  structures, 10
Forces Françaises de l'Intérieur (FFI),
    101, 104, 105, 181, 182, 199, 268,
    312, 338, 393n49, 401n45, 418n37
Forêt de Cinglais, 137
Forêt de Grimbosq, 156
Forêt de St. Sever, 128
Forêt l'Evêque, 136, 138, 139, 142, 153,
    391n37, 393n57
Fortress Southern Holland, 240, 247, 248,
    325

Forward Echelon Communications Zone, 304
Forward Section (COMZ), 276
Fougères, 121, 133, 150, 160, 196
Frankfurt, 229, 233, 296, 335, 337, 420n51
   advance on, 226, 264, 266, 295, 419n44
   importance of, 308, 309
Frederick the Great, 370n14
Fuel, 259, 297, 342, 418n35
   availability of, 33
   aviation, 100
   delivery of, 278, 287, 411n11
   depots, 91, 93
   shortages of, 83, 84, 93, 94, 100, 108, 149, 249, 263, 293, 398n22
Fuller, J. F. C., 369n7
FUSAG. *See* First US Army Group
Gavin, James M., 379n5
Generalship, 3, 6, 8, 116, 145–157, 315–359, 364, 370n14, 389n23
   army group, 200–216, 337–359
   army level, 184–200
   château, 31
   concepts of, 306–315, 348
   creativity/originality and, 29
   failings of, 43, 362–363
   operational-level, 359
   responsibility of, 33
   science/art and, 371n26
   successful, 371n25
   theatre level, 200–216, 337–359
General Strike (1926), 55–56
Gerow, Major General, 166, 182, 260, 326, 331
Ghent, 245, 259, 284, 412n28
Glantz, David M., 368n5
Göring, Hermann, 241
Gothic Line, 236
Graham, Major General, 304
Grant, Ulysses S., 43, 45, 373n40
Granville, 72, 303, 358

Grave, 247, 248, 253, 407n34
   bridge at, 251, 255
Grimbosq, 167
   bridgehead at, 172, 174, 191
Guards Armored Division, 138, 142, 143, 144, 154, 157, 246, 248, 254, 317, 320
   advance of, 416n21
   Bluecoat and, 140, 155
   Brussels and, 245
   Market Garden and, 256
Guderian, Heinz, on logistics/armored warfare, 306
Guerrilla warfare, 102, 103, 295

Haig, Field Marshall, 55, 59, 64, 105
Haislip, Wade H., 132, 133, 176, 207, 208, 334
   advance of, 197
   encirclement and, 164
   Falaise and, 165
   Patton and, 196
   reconnaissance for, 396n8
Harris, Sir Arthur, 90, 418n31
Hausser, Paul, 120, 121, 126, 129, 133–134
High Command West, 183
Hill 309, 138, 139, 142, 155
Hill 361, 136, 138, 143, 155
Hitler, Adolf, 92, 112–113, 121, 126, 145, 151, 176, 207, 238, 267, 334, 337
   assassination attempt on, 236, 376n65, 394n62
   Avranches corridor and, 159
   counteroffensive and, 177, 266
   decision making and, 110
   Fortress Southern Holland and, 240
   Normandy and, 111
   Paris and, 181–182
   Scheldt estuary and, 239
   space/time/forces and, 314
   strategic concepts and, 12
   V-weapons and, 380n6
   von Kluge and, 160

Hodges, Courtney H., 33, 38, 161, 175, 178, 181, 182, 199, 232, 233, 257, 258, 259, 262, 313, 324, 393n50, 396n8, 400n43
  Aachen and, 270
  Argentan and, 166
  Bradley and, 39, 40, 116, 132, 328, 339
  career of, 40
  Cobra and, 150
  Collins and, 326, 328
  creativity and, 184
  Crerar and, 195
  Eisenhower and, 228, 327, 329
  Falaise pocket and, 198
  fuel shortage for, 293
  Gerow and, 260
  Hürtgen Forest and, 352
  Leavenworth and, 341
  Leclerc and, 195
  logistics and, 328, 400n42, 408n42
  Montgomery and, 235, 311, 328
  operational art/generalship of, 193–196, 326–332
  Patton and, 211, 291, 336, 340, 400n42, 418n36
  Rhine and, 234, 270
  Ruhr and, 345
  support for, 294, 295
  tactics and, 196, 217
  working relations with, 95
Horrocks, Sir Brian, 246, 255, 256, 317, 318, 417n24
  command of, 254
  plan by, 320, 420n52
Huebner, Clarence R., 127, 129, 130, 148, 149
Hürtgen Forest, 260, 262, 271, 328, 330, 331, 347, 352, 364
  attacks into, 332
  impact of, 272

Ideology, 10, 17, 102, 106
Indian Army, 56

Infantry divisions, 44–45, 46, 53, 272
  casualties in, 51
  frontage of, 85, 175, 394n63, 374n54, 403n3
  full-strength, 391n34
  replacements for, 47
  transportation for, 84
"Instructions for Large Unit Commanders" (von Moltke), 375n64
Intelligence, 5, 29, 31, 32, 236, 362
  Allied, 106–108, 108–110, 236–241, 386n73
  failures, 362
  German, 110–113, 386n76
  limited, 312
  Normandy and, 108–110, 110–113
  operational-level, 105–113
  SHAEF, 236, 239
  signals, 106, 110, 111, 177, 193, 398n23
  tactical, 108, 110
  Ultra-derived, 107, 108, 128, 239
  See also Ultra

Jedburgh teams, 103, 104, 105, 386n72
Joint Chiefs of Staff, 343

Kampfgruppen, 167, 378–379n85
Karlsruhe, 258, 264, 341
King, Mackenzie, 64, 65
King's Shropshire Light Infantry (KSLI), 393n56
Koch, Oscar, 332
KV-1 tanks, 82

Laison, 169, 173, 174, 175, 188, 190, 191
Laize, 169, 174, 191
La Manoir, bridge at, 283
Lancaster bombers, close air support and, 97
Land Forces Command, leadership of, 201–206

Landing ships tank (LSTs), 281
Leadership, 17, 23, 27, 50, 68, 357, 358
  command and, 24–25
  operational, 355
  responsibility and, 51
League of Nations, 54
Leavenworth Command and Staff College, 215, 306, 341, 349, 351, 368n5, 418n36
Le Bény-Bocage ridge, 135, 142, 143, 151, 153, 154, 155, 201, 391n37, 393n53
Leclerc, Phillipe, 164, 166, 182, 195, 402n59
Lee, J. C. H., 216, 276, 277, 286, 303, 304, 414nn8–9
Lee, Robert E., 372n40
Le Havre, 92, 112, 158, 268, 309, 338, 339, 350, 417n22, 417n27, 420n48
  advance on, 240
  bombardment of, 407n33
  capture of, 244, 245, 279, 288, 322, 323
  opening of, 280, 323
  pipelines from, 284
  port of, 229
  supply through, 224, 281, 287, 343
Leigh-Mallory, Trafford, 99, 182
  Operation Pointblank and, 91
  time constraints and, 124
  Transportation Plan and, 90
Le Mans, 133, 159, 160, 164, 187, 198, 207, 283
  advance on, 196, 197, 199
Leopold Canal, 247
Liberty ships, capacity of, 280
Liddell Hart, Basil, 387n6
Liège, 238, 283, 286, 288
  supply through, 286
Lincoln, Abraham, 43
Logistics, 8, 13, 14, 31, 37, 70, 93, 115, 224, 243, 270, 282, 304, 308, 311, 314, 328, 336, 338
  Allied, 83–85, 178, 310
  armored warfare and, 306
  business of, 273–278
  constraints of, 26, 327
  deterioration of, 7
  problems in, 5–6, 7, 10, 26, 35, 113, 210, 223, 243, 274, 276–278, 284, 289–293, 294–298, 315, 316, 327, 349, 360, 361
  responsibility for, 33, 411n7
Loire, 70, 92, 93, 132, 134, 158, 159, 164, 165, 201, 202, 210, 276, 362, 382n33, 383n43
  crossing, 392n40
  guarding, 418n37
  lodgment up to, 275
Lorient, 132, 267, 268, 408n46
  capture of, 279
  masking of, 312
  supply through, 278, 338
Lorraine, 220, 238, 264, 267, 313, 314, 334, 335, 352, 353, 362, 363
Luftwaffe, 95, 107, 180, 237, 241, 253, 297, 290n29, 405n21
  absence of, 295
  demise of, 88, 89, 91, 110, 384n51
  maximum effort by, 160
  offensive against, 87–88
  problems for, 99, 100
  reinforcements for, 109
Lutes, Leroy, 512n26

M-4s. *See* Sherman tanks
M-10 tank destroyers, 77, 381n18
M-18 tank destroyers, 77
M-26 Pershing tanks, 82, 273
M-36 tank destroyers, 82, 381n18
M516 directive, 159, 161, 168, 202, 206
M518 directive, 161, 204
Maas, 220, 253, 262, 269
  crossing of, 247, 248, 319
Maastricht, 238, 244, 257, 259, 260, 347
Maas-Wall Canal, 403n34

454 Index

Machine guns, 74, 75, 81, 82, 140, 169, 379n4
Maginot Line, 264
Mainz, 226, 263, 266, 341, 353
Maneuver, 44, 45, 114, 274, 275, 363, 369n5
  desirability of, 218
  importance of, 48, 58–59, 63, 86, 307
  limiting of, 100
  movement and, 399n32
  operational, 2, 5, 10, 12, 13, 14, 16, 41, 126, 148, 184, 196, 198, 209–210, 326, 349, 363
  tactical, 15
Mannheim, 223, 226, 266, 341
  advance on, 311
Manpower, 46, 307, 378n79
  infantry, 411n8
  intelligence about, 108
Mantes-Gassicourt, 159, 167, 180, 197, 198, 206, 209, 242
  bridgehead at, 181
Manual for Commanders of Large Units, 44
Marigny, 122, 124, 130, 148–149, 389n23
  bypassing, 127
  capture of, 148
Mark IV tanks, 77, 137, 405n23
Marne, 216, 263
Marseille, 212, 232, 412n27, 415n16, 421n62
  supply through, 224, 270, 416n16
Marshaling yards, 91, 94, 282–283
Marshall, George C., 34, 38, 40, 277, 349, 357, 390n26
  alliance management and, 35
  Anvil/Dragoon and, 402n56
  command issues and, 301
  divisions and, 46
  Eisenhower and, 212, 242, 243, 299, 320, 355, 356, 414n11
  Market Garden and, 250, 421n61
  Montgomery and, 72

Mayenne, 133, 134, 150, 157, 159, 165, 199, 206, 207, 208, 285
Mayenne-Domfront-Flers axis, 165
McNair, Leslie J., 44, 47, 82, 389n21
Mediterranean theatre, 9, 34, 301
Meindl, General, 120
Melun, 181, 286
  advance on, 198
  bridgehead at, 167
Metz, 50, 222, 227, 232, 238, 263, 264, 266, 267, 268, 270, 286, 288, 292, 306, 309, 327, 333, 335, 336, 352, 407n33, 419n39
Meuse, 220, 222, 235, 257, 259, 263, 331, 350, 362
  advance on, 104
  crossing, 332
  pause at, 334–335
Meyer, Kurt, 172, 173, 188, 192
Middleton, Troy H., 122, 267, 390n32, 401n48
  Cobra and, 128–129
  St. Malo and, 268
Military Review, 44
Military theory, 1, 4, 349, 367n1, 369n6
  development of, 16–17
Military Training Pamphlet No. 23 (*Operations*), 4, 61
Mobility, 7, 10, 62, 83–85, 146, 148, 342, 400n38
  firepower and, 13, 14, 85
  high level of, 20, 223
  lacking, 86, 93, 352
  superior, 150, 155, 307, 312, 351, 359, 374n53
Model, Walter, 238, 397–398n22, 407n37
  subordinate commanders and, 300
Mons pocket, 259, 305, 326, 327, 363
Montgomery, Bernard L., 57, 63, 182, 186, 193, 208, 216, 244, 270, 304, 353, 370n16, 371n27
  Antwerp and, 269, 318, 320, 343

Ardennes and, 227, 410n55
Arnhem and, 256–257, 347
Berlin and, 226, 234, 420n51
Bluecoat and, 135, 139, 142, 145, 393n54
Bradley and, 37, 38, 150, 161, 178, 200, 201, 202, 204, 205, 206, 209, 211, 226, 232, 305, 311, 339, 340–341, 343, 344, 348, 356, 401n51, 401n53, 419n45
Brittany and, 206, 213, 279
Brooke and, 355, 371n28, 420n50
Browning and, 320
Caen and, 215, 392n41
Calais and, 322
career of, 36–37
Channel ports and, 227, 309, 310, 323
Churchill and, 72
CIGS and, 177
Cobra and, 116, 146
commanders and, 58, 62, 153, 301
command issues and, 38, 184, 212, 299, 300, 301, 316
Coningham and, 94, 399n35
Crerar and, 37, 40, 191, 192, 205, 321–322, 324, 325, 343, 344, 357, 372n36, 400n39
criticism of, 37, 42, 72–73, 150, 205–206, 301, 305, 401n44
Dempsey and, 37, 39, 187, 192, 201, 204, 205, 372n36, 392n38
directives of, 159, 161, 168, 174, 202, 206
doctrine of, 59, 63
Eisenhower and, 35, 36, 37, 99, 147, 202, 213, 214, 215, 224, 227, 228, 229, 230, 233, 234, 272, 282, 299, 300, 301, 302, 303, 305, 310–311, 319, 339, 347, 348, 349, 351, 356, 357, 358, 359, 360, 379n2, 402n59, 409n52
Falaise and, 157, 166, 174, 204
force concentration and, 307

fuel for, 293
FUSAG and, 112
Hodges and, 235, 311, 328
intelligence and, 107, 362
inter-army group boundary by, 243–244
invasion and, 71, 72
logistics and, 296, 297, 298, 403n5, 419n45
maneuver, scheme of, 132–133
Market Garden and, 217, 230, 234, 249, 250, 251, 256, 316, 321, 322, 345, 347, 351, 421n54
Marshall and, 72
master plan of, 68, 379n3
Meuse and, 350
Normandy and, 41, 66, 71, 205
operational art/generalship of, 200, 201–206, 321–326, 342–349
operational concepts of, 58, 116, 308, 309–310, 346
Patton and, 196, 197, 198, 206, 207, 210, 305, 356, 401n44, 401n51, 421n55
Phantom Regiment of, 326, 439n32
Rhine and, 246, 269, 271–272, 348
Ruhr and, 246, 296, 297, 312, 322
Scheldt estuary and, 239
set-piece battles and, 62–63
SHAEF and, 219
Simonds and, 193
subordinates and, 370n16, 372nn35–36
Tedder and, 42, 72, 399n35
Tournai and, 259
Trun and, 175
views of, 1
von Kluge and, 109
von Rundstedt and, 109
Morale, 15, 19, 26, 65, 82, 135, 236, 374n55
air interdictions and, 98
boosting, 103, 359

456   Index

Morale, *continued*
  civilian, 87, 115
  collapse of, 317, 404n18
  lowering of, 27, 104
  maintenance of, 17–18
  military, 115, 332
Mortain, 96, 118, 119, 121, 133, 134, 151, 194, 199, 202, 203, 207
  counterattack from, 110, 112–113, 145, 154, 158–161, 169, 193, 213
Mortars, 75, 80, 81, 272, 379n4
Moselle, 222, 258, 264, 267, 363, 418n37
  advance on, 46, 335
  crossing, 232, 265, 266, 332, 333, 334
  halting at, 313
Mt. Pinçon, 136, 151, 154, 390n33, 392n39
  capture of, 144
mulberry harbors, 115, 278, 280
Mulhouse, capture of, 236
Münster, 246, 297, 343

N158 Caen-Falaise road, 170, 173, 175, 189, 191
Namur, 257, 259, 327, 419n46
Nancy, 222, 264, 266, 335
  fall of, 334
Nantes, 92, 268, 408n46
Napoleon I, 54, 370n21
National Defense Act (1920), 44
National Guard, 44, 373n46
NATO, 1, 10
Naveh, Shimon, 367–368n5
Nebelwerfers, 76, 80–81
Neerpelt, 246
  advance on, 297
  bridgehead at, 248, 254, 317, 319, 320, 345
Nijmegen, 235, 247, 248, 318, 328, 347, 407n34, 407n38
  advance on, 251
  bridge at, 234, 251, 253, 255, 257, 269

Non-Permanent Active Militia (NPAM), 39, 64–65
Normandy, 6, 9, 13, 32, 35, 36, 37, 38, 39, 48, 49, 58, 64, 70, 71, 134, 145, 147, 159, 187, 199, 208, 210, 212, 213, 214, 215, 223, 237, 250, 258, 267, 268, 275
  airpower and, 89
  armor in, 76–78
  attrition in, 5, 359
  battle for, 4, 62, 63, 65, 201, 353, 359
  breakout from, 112–113, 123, 132, 161, 387n1
  casualties in, 74, 183, 368n4, 380n8
  close air support in, 97
  Cobra and, 117 (map), 118
  divisions in, 73, 74
  end of campaign, 180, 237
  envelopments in, 145–146, 159, 161, 177, 182, 197–199, 201–202, 204–207, 213, 217
  intelligence in, 108–110, 110–113
  reinforcing, 72, 83, 100, 101, 115
  success in, 7, 74, 242, 243
  supply through, 285, 286, 292, 338
  tactical deficiencies during, 60
  terrain conditions in, 59, 86
  victory in, 299, 308, 315, 337, 360
Normandy Base Section, 287
Northern Army Group, 232, 359, 394, 403n8
Northwest European theatre, 211–216
"Notes on Command in Western Europe" (Eisenhower), 302
Numbers, 22
  superior, 17, 307, 326, 359

Oberbefehlshaber West, 183
Oberkommando der Wehrmacht (OKW), 71, 72, 110, 111, 126, 237, 239, 267
O'Connor, Richard, 143, 394n58, 399n33
  Bluecoat and, 138, 142, 154
  Dempsey and, 184

Offensives, 341
  conducting, 306
  described, 18
  momentum for, 19–20
  strategic, 2, 3, 383n36
Oil Plan, 91, 99
Oil production, natural/synthetic, 91, 99, 100, 222–223
OKW. *See* Oberkommando der Wehmacht
On War (Clausewitz), 114
Operational art, 3–6, 9, 11–17, 54, 145–157, 367–368nn1–2
  army group, 200–216, 337–359
  army level, 184–200, 315–337
  concept of, 16, 21, 306–315, 348, 369n7
  described, 12, 14
  tactics and, 14, 28
  theatre level, 200–216, 337–359
Operational concepts, 10, 11, 12, 23, 35, 36, 306–315, 367n5
  broad versus narrow front, 224, 225 (map)
  rival, 219–220, 222–224, 226–230, 232–236
Operational level, 1, 7, 12, 15, 22, 23, 341, 348
Operational Research Section (ORS), 76, 382n24, 398n23
Operational-strategic plans, 1, 36, 68, 306, 309, 312, 314, 315, 347, 355
Operational success, 150, 156, 224, 316, 369n10
  tactical success and, 148
Operation Anvil/Dragoon, 226, 290, 314, 352, 353, 402n56
  launching, 212–213
Operation Atlantic, 118
Operation Bluecoat, 100, 110, 112, 134–140, 167–170, 172–176, 184, 187, 188, 256, 381n14, 393nn54–55, 395n2, 417n22
  background of, 134–135
  close air support in, 97
  end of, 140, 144, 157
  execution of, 139–140, 142–145
  German defense in, 137
  map of, 141
  operational art/generalship in, 151–157
  reserves for, 138–139
  start of, 145, 155
  terrain in, 135–136
Operation Charnwood, 97
Operation Cobra, 5, 48, 54, 66, 78, 86, 109–110, 111, 112, 118–124, 135, 137, 158–161, 164–167, 203, 213, 242, 284, 349, 363, 385n48, 387n8, 389n18
  aim of, 121, 147
  air plan for, 93–94, 123
  background of, 115–116, 118
  bomber force and, 99
  breakthrough and, 98, 156, 185, 388n17
  close air support in, 97
  development of, 124, 206
  divisions for, 46
  end of, 131 (map)
  execution of, 123–124, 126–130
  German defense for, 119–121
  Normandy and, 117 (map), 118
  operational art/generalship in, 145–151
  operations following, 132–134
  routes for, 118–119
  start of, 85, 113, 116, 307
  success of, 136, 147–148, 156, 351
  supplying, 273, 282, 290
  surprise attack in, 307
  terrain of, 118
Operation Comet, 82, 248, 318–319, 345
Operation Crossbow, 91
Operation Fortitude, 68, 70–71, 100, 108, 111, 145, 380n6
Operation Garden, 249, 256
Operation Gatwick, 348

Operation Goodwood, 39, 118, 142, 153, 184, 188, 205, 213, 347, 381n14, 387n8, 389n23, 391n36, 392n42, 399n33
  axis/timing of, 112
  close air support in, 97
  lessons from, 135, 139
  tactical failure of, 99, 169
Operation Grouse, 157, 167, 185
Operation Infatuate, 420n48
Operation Lucky Strike, 158, 201
Operation Market, 253–254, 289, 345
Operation Market Garden, 217, 230, 234, 263, 270, 281, 321, 345, 347, 350, 351, 405n23, 413n32, 420n52, 421n54, 421n61
  aim of, 248
  Antwerp and, 108
  axis of, 239
  control over, 316
  defense against, 317
  end of, 256
  execution of, 248–249, 319, 320
  failure of, 297, 347
  logistic priorities for, 265
  map of, 252
  near success of, 250–251, 254, 344
  start of, 348
  supplying, 288, 289, 296, 322
  transportation for, 288
Operation Overlord, 88, 115, 121, 132, 198, 212, 306, 370n16, 379n3, 383n36, 383n40
  aim of, 210
  air interdiction and, 90–94
  breakout phase of, 73
  Brittany and, 213
  end of, 241
  lodgment, 70, 72, 101, 201
  map of, 69
  Operation Pointblank and, 87
  plan for, 68, 206, 242
  replacements and, 47
  success of, 279
  territorial gains and, 202
Operation Pointblank, 87, 91
Operations, 352
  conducting, 10, 11, 12, 22
  land-air, 23
  maneuver-dominated, 15
  mobile, 148
  prioritization of, 354
  tactics and, 30
Operation Spring, 135, 169, 187, 387n8
Operation Totalize, 100, 113, 151, 160–161, 166, 168, 175, 185, 187, 189, 203
  ammunition for, 60
  close air support in, 97
  development of, 172
  end of, 174
  errors during, 98
  map of, 171
  operational thinking and, 192
  tactical air effort for, 399n35
Operation Tractable, 166, 172, 187, 191
  Canadian operational thinking and, 192
  close air support and, 97
  described, 175
  errors during, 98
  map of, 171
  orders for, 174
Order of battle (ORBAT), 106, 110, 121, 378n84, 389n18
Orléans, 92, 178, 180, 197, 208, 332
  capture of, 167
Orne, 136, 138, 167, 168, 174, 177, 185, 202, 207
ORS. *See* Operational Research Section
Osnabrück, 297, 343, 344
  advance on, 246
OSS. *See* US Office of Strategic Services
Ostend, 281, 284, 311
  supply through, 310

P-47 Thunderbolt, close air support and, 95
Panzer companies, abandonment of, 94
Panzer divisions, 84, 119, 180, 267, 272
Panzerfausts, 77, 78, 140, 381n19
Panzer grenadier divisions, 78, 84, 267
Panzer Group Eberbach, Falaise and, 176
Panzer Group West, 109, 116, 126, 142, 154, 382n33, 392n42, 394n59
   Second Army and, 72
   Seventh Army and, 143, 144
   Bluecoat and, 137, 145
Panzer Lehr Division, 98, 119, 122, 123, 129, 389n25, 395n2
   Cobra and, 126
Panzer Meyer, 400n40
Panzers, 76, 77, 82, 144, 383n38, 388n12
Panzerschreck, 77, 140
Paris, 91, 121, 159, 164, 167, 180, 229, 303
   advance on, 181–182, 201, 210
   bridges in, 284
   liberation of, 182, 241, 385n66, 402n59
   marshaling yards at, 283
   supplies for, 284, 286
Paris-Orléans gap, 93, 118, 158, 159, 166, 178
   advance on, 397n22
Pas de Calais, 71, 111, 244, 380n6, 387n1, 392n40
   airpower and, 89
   capture of, 244
   deception involving, 68
   defenses at, 70
   ports of, 343
Patton, George S., Jr., 6, 38, 72, 116, 121, 123, 160, 164, 195, 216, 226, 233, 238, 258, 270, 326, 328, 352, 353, 382n27, 395n5, 396n8
   advance of, 166, 198, 199, 404n19
   Beauvais and, 209, 211
   Bradley and, 41, 158–159, 196, 197, 199, 208, 229, 232, 263, 266, 295, 311, 314, 333, 338–339, 341, 357, 390n32, 400n42, 401n45, 418n37
   Brittany and, 70, 147
   career of, 40–41
   Cobra and, 130, 132, 150, 389n18
   commanders and, 8, 27, 51, 263
   Eddy and, 266, 267, 336
   Eisenhower and, 41, 199–200, 228, 263, 372n34
   Falaise and, 165, 166, 199
   fuel for, 293
   FUSAG and, 111
   on great soldiers, 367n2
   Haislip and, 196
   Hodges and, 211, 291, 336, 340, 400n42, 418n36
   intelligence and, 362
   Le Mans and, 133
   logistics and, 265, 296
   Lorraine and, 313, 335
   maneuver/speed and, 363
   Metz and, 264, 333, 334, 352, 419n39
   Meuse and, 334–335
   Montgomery and, 196, 197, 198, 206, 207, 210, 305, 356, 401n44, 401n51, 416n21, 421n55
   Moselle and, 230, 232, 265, 313, 332
   Normandy and, 315
   operational art/generalship of, 196–200, 332–337
   on planning, 150–151
   resistance movements and, 104
   Ruhr and, 337
   Seine and, 332
   Sélune and, 158
   Sicily and, 315, 419n40, 421n55
   speed/security and, 390n32
   supplying, 229, 294, 295
   working relations with, 95
Permanent Active Militia (PAM), 64–65
Perriers ridge, 142, 143, 144, 154, 157
Pershing, John J., 34

Petrol, oil, and lubricants (POL), 109, 120, 263, 265, 266, 278, 281, 284, 297, 328, 410n4, 411n11, 414n10
  delivering, 282, 289
  shortage of, 259, 260, 292, 332
  supply of, 93, 259, 290, 294
  transporting, 288, 293
  See also Fuel
Phantom Regiment, 37, 62, 207, 301, 326, 371n27, 390n32, 439n32
"Phony War," 57
Pipelines, 275, 277, 282, 287, 290, 291, 346
  impact of, 284, 285
PLUTO, 284
POL. *See* Petrol, oil, and lubricants
Polish Armored Division, 166, 323
Politics, 10, 11, 30, 35, 311–312, 422n65
Pontaubault, 118, 130, 150, 390n29
Power, combat, 4, 5, 28, 47, 60, 70, 71, 85, 100, 111, 113, 116, 130, 146, 148, 149, 177, 180, 184, 204, 217, 241, 244, 342, 346
Principles of war, 17–22
Professionalism, 103, 305, 389n23
  judgment and, 26–27
Propaganda, 17, 101, 103, 377n73, 403n3
Prussian General Staff, 375n64
  staff ride and, 367n1

Quesada, Elwood R., 95, 97, 98
Quesnay woods, 173, 174, 191
Quiberon Bay, 132, 224, 267, 268, 350
  capture of, 279
  supply through, 278, 292, 338

Radar, 81, 88
Radios, 85, 98, 106
RAF. *See* Royal Air Force
Railroads, 84, 91, 283, 285
  disruption of, 92
  rehabilitation of, 284, 346
  sabotage against, 93, 104
  supply delivery and, 288, 290, 291
Ramcke, 338
Ramsay, Admiral, 246, 281–282, 350, 420n50, 421n55
Rear maintenance area (RMA), 280, 281, 282, 283, 288, 296, 297, 310
Reconnaissance, 399n37
  air, 80, 88, 89, 90, 110, 120, 127, 177, 193, 258
  armed, 133, 384n51
  problems with, 265
Red Army, 1, 23, 53, 56, 105, 236, 313
  buildup of, 106
  civil war and, 16
  doctrinal basis for, 10
  fighting by, 3, 46, 106, 380n7, 416n20
  German war production and, 89
  land combat power and, 100
  operational art and, 4, 9, 10
  problems for, 364–365
  strength of, 13
Red Ball Express, 285, 286, 288, 291, 295, 412n20, 420n49
  effectiveness of, 290
  transportation by, 287
Red Lion Express, 287, 289, 297
Reichswehr, 56, 61
Reims, 226, 258, 266
  supply through, 287
Reinforcement Army, 241
Replacement Army, 347, 406n26
Replacements, 47, 274, 275, 321, 377n71
Resistance, 10, 126, 260
  communist, 102
  operations by, 101–105
Rhine, 180, 220, 222, 223, 228, 230, 254, 256, 264, 294, 298, 354
  advance on, 6, 99, 216, 219, 226, 232, 234, 235, 240, 255, 257, 258, 260, 263, 265, 266, 267, 269, 270, 271, 272, 290, 295, 311, 313, 318, 319,

327, 328, 330, 332, 342, 344, 346, 347, 348, 352, 359
  bridgeheads over, 3, 7, 232, 247, 269, 312
  crossing, 226, 230, 233, 234, 246, 247, 248, 297, 313, 334, 347, 348, 353, 362
  defending, 340, 343
  possible axes to, 221 (map), 222
Rhino hedge cutter, 53, 119, 123, 128, 136
Rhône, 180, 229, 306, 313, 353
Rhône valley, 213, 238
  advance up, 237, 266
Ridgway, Matthew, 407n35
Ritchie, Neil, 138, 316
Riviera, 212, 213, 238, 409n51
  advance from, 308
  landings on, 201
RMA. *See* rear maintenance area
Roberts, Major General, 154, 317–318, 320, 393n57, 417n24
  Bluecoat and, 142, 155
Roer, advance on, 271, 329, 330
Roer River dams, 271, 330, 331
Roosevelt, Franklin D., 212, 299, 402n59, 422n65
Rotterdam, 220, 224, 229, 246
  advance on, 239
  capture of, 232, 282, 344
Rouen, 158, 159, 178, 183, 191, 209, 397n16
  advance on, 398n25
  capture of, 279
  pipelines from, 284
Royal Air Force (RAF), 55, 289, 324, 325, 377n71
  air superiority and, 87
  air support from, 64, 94
  Market Garden and, 251
Royal Army Service Corps, 84
Royal Military Academy, Sandhurst, 56, 367–368n5

Royal Navy, 55, 64
Ruhr industrial region, 70, 227, 230, 269, 346, 404n11, 420n51
  advance on, 222, 226, 228, 229, 234, 235, 238, 244, 256–257, 310, 339, 343, 345, 347
  capture of, 229, 232, 233, 337, 340
  defending, 220, 319
  encircling, 296, 311, 347, 419n44
  flanking, 230, 319, 348
  importance of, 219, 306, 308, 312, 337, 419n45

Saar, 220, 222, 226, 227, 228, 229, 233, 238, 258, 264, 337, 340, 420n51
  advance on, 232, 311, 339
  crossing, 333
  importance of, 308
Saarbrücken, 222, 266, 295, 334
Saône, 180, 229, 313
SAS. *See* Special Air Service
Scheldt estuary, 246, 269, 298, 322, 325, 344, 348, 362, 412n28
  advance on, 108, 248
  blocking, 282
  clearing, 99, 247, 318, 323, 324, 343, 350, 351
  importance of, 239
  opening of, 312, 314
Schlieffen plan, 226, 342
Sée River, 118, 130, 133, 134, 150
Seine, 67, 70, 72, 74, 91, 93, 96, 108, 111, 121, 132, 164, 165, 167, 196, 197, 201, 207, 217, 241, 263, 267, 276, 285, 286
  advance on, 147, 159, 175, 178, 179 (map), 181, 185, 186, 198, 204, 205, 206, 208, 210, 214, 216, 290, 317, 397n16
  bridgehead over, 180, 209, 228
  bridges over, 92, 283
  crossing, 182, 223, 242, 275, 281

Seine, *continued*
    pause on, 349
    ports, 158, 242
    rail break at, 283
    withdrawal to, 202
Seine Base Section HQ, 414n9
Sélune, 118, 130, 133, 134, 276, 390n29
    advance on, 150
    crossing of, 158
Services of Supply, 50
SF. *See* Special Forces
SHAEF. *See* Supreme Headquarters, Allied Expeditionary Force
Sherman, William Tecumseh, 43
Sherman tanks, 76, 77, 78, 82, 272, 381n15, 381n18, 382n27
Shortages, 50, 277
    ammunition, 9, 85, 94, 149, 273, 274, 276, 290, 388n17, 398n22
    fuel, 83, 84, 93, 94, 100, 108, 149, 263, 293, 398n22
    personnel, 409–410n54
    POL, 259, 260, 292, 332
    spare part, 93, 291
Sicily, 211, 315, 388n16, 401n51, 419n40
    invasion of, 416n17
    withdrawal from, 398n28
Siegfried Line, 229, 243, 403n3
    breaching, 99, 337, 338
Signals intelligence (SIGINT), 106, 110, 111, 177, 193, 398n23
Simonds, G. G., 168–169, 205, 323, 324, 418n30
    Breskens pocket and, 326
    Crerar and, 189, 190, 191, 192, 321
    division commanders and, 192–193
    Falaise and, 173, 174
    Fortress Southern Holland and, 325
    Montgomery and, 193
    Operation Totalize and, 187, 188, 189
    Walcheren and, 326
Simpson, William, 404n9

Smith, Sir Rupert, subordinates and, 370n16
Smith, Walter Bedell, 212, 354, 357
SOE. *See* Special Operations Executive
Soft-skinned vehicles (SSVs), 94, 96, 119, 398n24
Somme, 72, 111, 112, 182, 242, 245, 317
Souleuvre, 136, 139, 142, 153, 393n53
South Beveland peninsula, 239, 245, 246, 248, 257, 324, 348
Southern Army Group, 232, 403n8, 416n19
Soviet Army Study Office (SASO), 368n5
Spaatz, Carl A., Oil Plan and, 91
Special Air Service (SAS), 103, 104, 105, 378n79
Special Forces (SF), 103–104, 105
Special Operations Executive (SOE), 101, 103, 393n49
SSVs. *See* Soft-skinned vehicles
Staff, 30–32
    commanders and, 33–34
    procedures/differences in, 359
    work of, 31, 32
Staff rides, conducting, 367n1
Stalin, Joseph, Tehran conference and, 212
Stalingrad, 216
Stereotypes, 2, 28, 52, 106
St. Gilles, 122, 124, 128, 130
Stimson, secretary of war, command issues and, 299
St. Lô, 71, 118, 128, 285, 387n8
    capture of, 72, 93
    communications hub, 115
    marshaling yards at, 282–283
    supply through, 286
St. Lô-Lessay road, 115, 118, 119, 121, 124, 149, 380n10
St. Malo, 132, 224, 267
    supply through, 279, 338
St. Martin-des-Besaces, 136, 142, 153, 393n57

St. Nazaire, 132, 267, 268, 408n46
Stolberg corridor, 262, 271, 329, 330, 347
Straits of Messina, 398n28
Strasbourg, 236, 270, 353
Strategiya (Svechin), 368n2
Strategy, 2, 3, 11–17, 35, 201, 306, 337
    ambitions of, 23
    formation of, 22
Subordinates, 25, 27, 32, 300, 372nn35–36, 376n64
    commanders and, 26, 32
    overcontrol of, 53
    responsibility of, 370n16
Supply, 68, 149, 306, 308
    air, 289, 295, 297, 346
    approach to, 277–278
    backlog of, 290
    buildup of, 7, 279
    crisis, 409–410n54
    delivering, 278–282, 288
    shortage of, 81–83, 259, 260
Supply lines, maintaining, 7, 310
Supreme Allied Commander, 8, 34
Supreme Headquarters, Allied Expeditionary Force (SHAEF), 6–7, 42, 72, 101, 103, 114, 123, 200, 212, 226, 227, 229, 235, 241, 242, 267, 268, 276, 282, 283, 293, 309, 310, 312, 338, 343, 354, 360, 395n4, 411n10, 411n16, 412n25
    Berlin and, 219
    communications and, 311
    COMZ and, 285, 303, 304
    contingency plans of, 158
    credibility of, 357
    directions from, 35
    Frankfurt and, 335
    Granville and, 303
    intelligence and, 236, 239
    logistics and, 7, 296, 336
    Lucky Strike and, 201
    operational concept of, 223–224, 302
    Paris and, 181
    post-Normandy operations and, 219
    preinvasion appreciation by, 219–220, 222–223, 248, 306, 337
    statistics from, 292
Svechin, A. A., 11, 368n2

T-34 tanks, 82
Table of organization and equipment (TO&E), 44, 119, 120, 378n84, 380n13, 395n2
Tactical success, 150, 369n10
    operational success and, 148
Tactics, 3, 11–17, 23, 25, 49, 52, 53, 54, 60, 136, 196, 241, 315, 352, 400n42
    operational art and, 9, 12, 14, 15, 21, 28, 30
Tank battalions, US, 45, 49
Tank Corps, US, 34
Tank destroyers, 45, 73, 74, 76, 77, 208, 388n17, 395n2, 397n21
Tanks, 61, 208, 381nn15–16
    British, 76, 77, 78, 79, 82, 136
    correlation of forces, 73, 74
    development of, 13
    German, 76, 77, 82, 135, 137, 143, 144, 172, 381n17, 383n38, 388n12, 394n60, 405n23
    operable condition for, 291, 292
    replacement, 391n36
    Soviet, 82
    US, 76, 77, 78, 82, 272, 273, 381n15, 382n27
Technology, 10, 17, 12, 74, 85, 341
Tedder, Arthur, 385n61, 404n11
    desert war and, 384n49
    Goodwood and, 99
    Montgomery and, 42, 72, 399n35
    Pointblank and, 91
    Transportation Plan and, 90
Tehran conference, 212
Territorial Army (TA), 56

Tessy-sur-Vire, 119, 122, 128, 130, 135, 195
Third Battle of Ypres, 72, 380n8
Tiger tanks, 76, 77, 82, 135, 137, 143, 172, 381n17, 394n60
"Time on target" (TOT), 80
TO&E. *See* Table of organization and equipment
Tournai, 244, 257, 259, 262, 326
  airborne drop at, 245
  maneuver, 305, 414n12
Training, 3, 15, 22, 47
  American, 113
  deficiencies in, 73
  differences in, 359
  education and, 23
  theoretical, 53
Transportation, 7, 63, 85, 296, 308, 372n35
  air, 412n22
  capacity of, 291–292
  communications and, 288
  development of, 13, 293
  motorized, 84, 280, 284–285
  problems with, 99, 282–289
  tank, 297
Transportation Corps, 285
Transportation Plan, 90, 91, 99
Trenchard, lord, Operation Goodwood and, 99
Trident conference (1943), 87
Troop Carrier Command, 289
Troyes, 98, 180, 226, 263
Trucks, 285, 288
  losses of, 83, 93
  shortage of, 79, 289–290
Trun, 166, 175, 176, 204, 208
Tuker, Francis, on British Army, 370n16
Tunisian campaign, 36, 216, 358–359, 388n16
Typhoon, close air support and, 95

Ultra, 9, 120, 127, 150, 154, 177, 178, 189, 193, 199, 237, 264, 322, 390n29, 392nn38–39
  intelligence from, 106, 107, 108, 109, 110, 128, 239
  See also Intelligence
United Nations, 219
US Air Corps, 50
US Army
  approach to war of, 43–54
  command and control and, 61
  deep operations and, 315
  in 1944, 43–66
US Army Air Force (USAAF), close air support and, 94
US Marine Corps, 50
US Navy, 50
US Office of Strategic Services (OSS), 101, 103, 104
US Strategic Air Forces (USSTAF), 90
Utrecht, advance on, 247

V-1 launch sites, capture of, 227, 244, 293
V-2 launch sites, 246
Vandenberg, Hoyt S., 384n51
Venlo, 239, 319, 347, 348
Verdun, 104, 283, 303, 327, 332, 419n46
  bridgehead at, 263
Versailles, 286, 303, 348, 358, 421n56
Versailles conference, 235, 267, 340, 344
"victory disease," 243, 362
Victory Program, 46
Vire, 72, 136, 139, 142, 143, 145, 146, 150, 151, 156, 159, 205, 391n32, 391n37
  advance on, 119, 194
  capture of, 154
  defense at, 153
  importance of, 135
Vire River, 118, 119, 120, 121, 122, 128, 130, 133
Vire-Vassy road, 142, 144, 151

Volksgrenadier divisions, 241, 264, 395n3, 406n26
Von Choltitz, Dietrich, 126, 127, 129, 149
Von Kluge, Günther, 116, 120, 121, 126, 127, 129, 130, 133–134, 159, 173, 176, 187, 397n22
    Hitler and, 160
    Montgomery and, 109
    subordinate commanders and, 300
    withdrawal and, 160
Von Manteuffel, Hasso, 266, 267
Von Moltke, Helmut, 20, 25, 100, 147, 367n1, 375n64, 409n49
Von Rundstedt, Gerd, 109, 238, 239, 240, 241, 409n53
Von Zangen, 318
Vosges, 102, 353, 409n51
V-weapons, 104, 112, 226, 230, 347, 380n6, 387n1, 413n28

Waal, 220, 249, 251, 253, 255, 407n34
    crossing, 247–248
Walcheren, 239, 240, 246, 248, 326, 344, 348, 406n25
Waldmüller, SS Major, 172
Walker, Walton H., 166, 197, 266
    Metz and, 265, 333, 335
    POL for, 265
War Department, 212, 273–274, 276
    COMZ and, 303
    logistics and, 274, 291
    statistics for, 292
    trucks and, 285
War fighting, concepts of, 11–22
War Office, 58, 276, 297, 356–357
    casualties and, 274
    manpower problem and, 376–377n71
Waterloo, 54, 85

Watson, Leroy H., 127–129, 149, 390n27
Wavell, Sir A. P., on successful generals, 371n25
Wehrmacht, 4, 13, 14, 23, 56, 79, 83, 86, 105, 186, 220, 222
    deception against, 106
    decline of, 6, 183, 376n65
    demoralization of, 317
    pressure against, 99
    production for, 89
    resilience of, 216, 243, 319
    victories for, 45
Wellington, Duke of, Waterloo and, 85
Wesel, 219, 257, 269, 313, 347
    advance on, 319
West Wall, 220, 222, 236, 240, 242, 260, 263, 267, 329, 331, 332, 353, 359
    advance on, 262, 266, 270, 328, 334, 347, 352
    bombardment of, 407n33
    breaching, 99, 265, 327, 337
    capture of, 311
    defending, 238, 244, 264
    discounted by Patton, 333
    outflanking, 230
Weyland, Otto P., 95, 96, 390n30
White Ball Express, transportation by, 287
Wilhelmina Canal, 248, 255, 407n34
Willems Canal, 248, 407n34
Worthington Force, 173, 188, 190

XX Committee, 111

Y Service, 108, 109, 110

Zetterling, Niklas, 380–381n14
Zon bridge, 253, 255, 256, 407n34
Zuider Zee, 247, 248, 249–250, 311

South Huntington   DEC 07 2016